HUMAN HERITAGE
A WORLD HISTORY

MIRIAM GREENBLATT
F. KENNETH COX
STANLEY S. SEABERG

MERRILL PUBLISHING CO.
Columbus, Ohio

AUTHORS

Miriam Greenblatt is a free-lance writer, editor, and educational consultant. During the past 20 years she has contributed to more than 30 elementary, junior high, and high school social studies texts, workbooks, testing programs, and teacher's guides. A graduate of Hunter College of the City of New York and the University of Chicago and a former teacher, Greenblatt is a member of the National Council for Social Studies, the Illinois Council for Social Studies, and the Asia Society. She is also treasurer of the American Historical Association's Committee on History in the Classroom. Greenblatt is listed in *Who's Who of American Women* for 1985-86.

F. Kenneth Cox is a teacher of Ancient History in the Bethel Park School District of Bethel Park, Pennsylvania, where he has taught for more than 15 years. A graduate of Clarion State College and West Virginia University, Cox has taught special classes for the gifted and has been instrumental in the development of a seventh grade social studies curriculum and a Minimal Skills Competency Test.

Stanley S. Seaberg is a teacher of social studies and humanities at Henry M. Gunn Senior High School in Palo Alto, California, where he has taught since 1966. Seaberg was the recipient of a General Electric Fellow in Economics, Claremont Graduate School, 1962; John Hay Fellow, Yale University, 1963–1964; NDEA Fellow, University of Washington, 1966, and San Francisco State, 1968; and a Fulbright grant, 1972. He has authored several social studies texts and has been a consultant for the California State Framework for the Social Studies.

ISBN 0-675-01860-9

Published by
MERRILL PUBLISHING CO.
Columbus, Ohio

PREFACE

*Not to know what happened before one was born
is to remain a child.*

CICERO

Cicero, the Roman orator who spoke the words you have just read, lived many years before the birth of Christ. But his words are just as true today as they were then. What happened before you were born is history, just as what happens today is history.

Lives of individuals living today are influenced by events that took place long before they were born and by beliefs and actions of previous generations. What might communication be like today if the Phoenicians had not refined and spread the alphabet? How might populations be spread around the world today if Queen Isabella had not given Columbus the funds and ships he needed to make his voyages?

Questions of a different type also come to mind. Why does Great Britain have a royal family, while the United States does not? Why do Western Europeans speak a variety of languages? Possible answers to these questions can be found in *Human Heritage,* which explores the past and discusses it in an easy-to-read style complemented by colorful maps, charts, and illustrations.

Each of the 13 units opens with a two-page time chart and closes with a two-page review. The time chart highlights the important events of the time period covered in the unit. The review summarizes the main points of the unit and provides exercises that focus on those points and develop social studies skills. Overview questions alert you to the unit theme. One-page unit introductions give you a broad picture of the topics covered. Two-page Cultural Close-Ups that focus on a person, culture, or event allow you an in-depth look at history in the making.

The text's 40 chapters are divided into sections and subsections, each of which is followed by a question or group of questions. Unfamiliar terms are boldfaced and are defined. Many are redefined in the glossary, which also offers a pronunciation key. A review section at the end of each chapter provides a summary of main points and exercises designed to review, clarify, and reinforce understanding.

Human Heritage uses art, photographs, and the written word to acquaint you with both the distant and not-so-distant past. An ancient Greek named Dionysus once said "History is philosophy teaching by examples." *Human Heritage* records many of those examples.

CONTENTS

CULTURAL CLOSE-UPS

CHARTS, DIAGRAMS, AND ILLUSTRATIONS

MAPS

REVIEWERS

M. A. Cancella
Chairperson, Social Studies Department
Scotch Plains-Fanwood High School
Scotch Plains, New Jersey

Dr. Owen H. Case
Social Studies Coordinator
Springfield R-12 Schools
Springfield, Missouri

Phillip Mattingly
Secondary Social Studies Supervisor
Dayton Public Schools
Dayton, Ohio

Dr. Savannah C. Jones
Social Studies Program Specialist
Birmingham City Schools
Birmingham, Alabama

Karla McComb
Social Studies Curriculum Consultant
Clark County School District
Las Vegas, Nevada

STAFF

Project Editor: Brenda Smith;   *Editors:* Tom Photos, Priscilla Ross;   *Production Editor:* Kimberly Munsie;   *Designer-Illustrator:* William Walker;   *Project Artist:* Catherine Bookwalter White;   *Artist:* Scott Sommers;   *Photo Editors:* Lindsay Gerard, Kristy Ellwood;   *Cartographer:* June Barnes, Intergraphics of Tucson, Arizona;   *Illustrators:* Jim Jackson, Dick Kranz

COVER PHOTOS

(left to rt.; top to bot.) Smithsonian Institution (1) 78-8736; (2) 78-8733; (3) 78-8723; (4) 78-8727; (5) Eugene Gilliom; (6) Smithsonian Institution 78-8759; (7) Freer Gallery; (8) Hirshhorn Gallery; (9) Smithsonian Institution; (10) ARAMCO; (11) Courtesy of British Museum; (12) Vladimir Bibic; (13) Reproduced from the collection of the Library of Congress; (14) NASA.

PHOTO CREDITS

PROLOGUE

The world is not the same today as it was when Wilbur and Orville Wright flew their first airplane at Kitty Hawk. Nations have won their independence, rulers and heroes have come and gone, wars have been won and lost, and scientists and inventors have brought twentieth-century people into the Space Age. But what led to life as people know it today? From where and from whom did such people as Fleming and Drew get their inspirations? This way of life so taken for granted by people today did not just come about overnight. It is a result of the past — of many, many years of history. This text provides views of that history.

SCIENCE AND TECHNOLOGY IN THE TWENTIETH CENTURY

Date	Event	Date	Event
1903	first successful airplane flight made by Wright Brothers	1969	first lunar landing made by Neil Armstrong and Edwin Aldrin, Jr.
1905	theory of relativity advanced by Albert Einstein	1977	first manned flight of new space transportation system made by U.S. space shuttle Enterprise
1926	television successfully demonstrated by John Baird	1979	U.S. surgeons use microsurgery to perform first successful reattachment of major limb to body
1926	first liquid-fuel rocket successfully launched by Robert Goddard	1982	first implantation of a permanent artificial heart in a human
1928	first antibiotic drug, penicillin, discovered by Sir Alexander Fleming		
1940	use of blood plasma for transfusions introduced by Dr. Charles Drew		
1942	first nuclear chain reaction produced by Enrico Fermi		
1944	first automatic digital computer completed at Harvard University		
1957	first artificial earth satellite, Sputnik I, launched by Russia		

UNIT 1

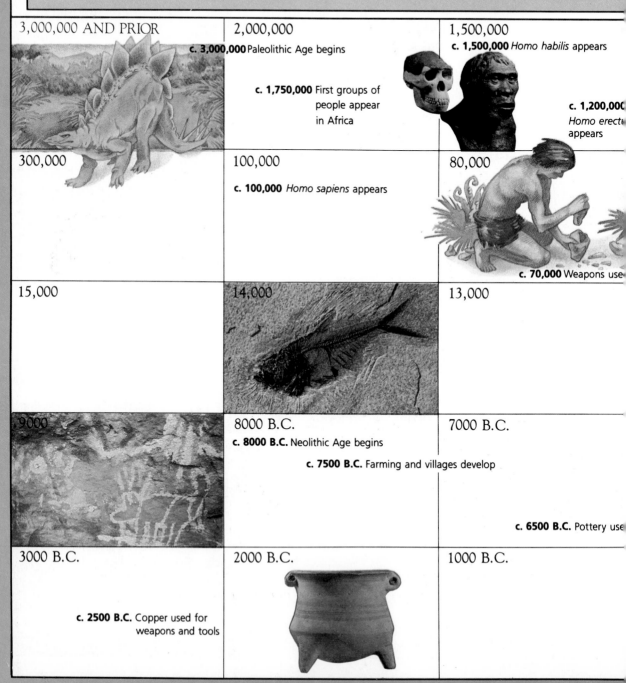

3,000,000 AND PRIOR	2,000,000	1,500,000
	c. 3,000,000 Paleolithic Age begins **c. 1,750,000** First groups of people appear in Africa	**c. 1,500,000** *Homo habilis* appears **c. 1,200,000** *Homo erect* appears
300,000	100,000 **c. 100,000** *Homo sapiens* appears	80,000 **c. 70,000** Weapons use
15,000	14,000	13,000
9000	8000 B.C. **c. 8000 B.C.** Neolithic Age begins **c. 7500 B.C.** Farming and villages develop	7000 B.C. **c. 6500 B.C.** Pottery use
3000 B.C. **c. 2500 B.C.** Copper used for weapons and tools	2000 B.C.	1000 B.C.

PREHISTORIC TIMES

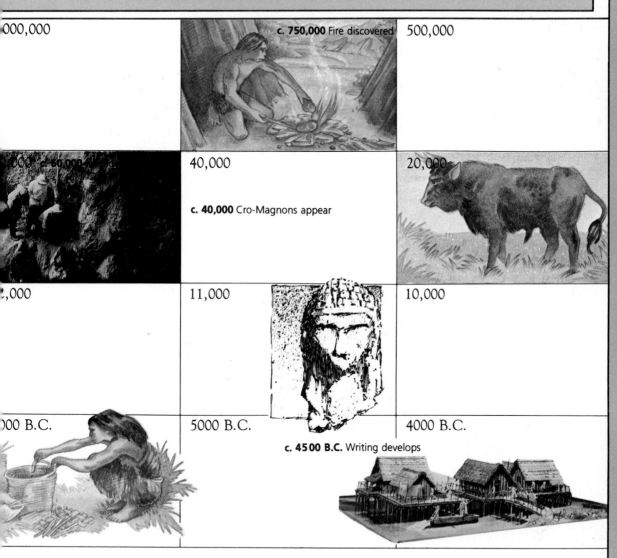

000,000 | c. **750,000** Fire discovered | 500,000

000 c. 60,000 | 40,000 | 20,000

c. **40,000** Cro-Magnons appear

2,000 | 11,000 | 10,000

000 B.C. | 5000 B.C. | 4000 B.C.

c. **4500 B.C.** Writing develops

1. HOW IS HISTORY DETERMINED?
2. HOW DID PEOPLE LIVE DURING PREHISTORIC TIMES?

Most experts believe that there have been people on earth for more than 1,750,000 years. During most of those years, there was no written history because people did not develop the skill of writing until about 5,000 years ago. The period of time beginning with the appearance of people on earth and ending with the first written records of history is called the **prehistoric period**. After that time, people began to advance culturally and to live in cities. This was the beginning of **civilization**.

Before the rise of cities, people went through several stages of development. At first, they wandered from place to place in search of food. Experts call this period the **hunting-and-food-gathering period**. During this period, people made several important discoveries. These discoveries included tools, language, fire, clothing, art, and religion.

About 10,000 years ago, people invented farming and became food producers instead of hunters and food-gatherers. Once they began to farm, they settled in one place and built villages. There, they developed such skills as making pottery, weaving cloth, and working metals. They also developed more formal ideas about government and religion.

Almost all of what is known about the prehistoric period has been learned in the last few hundred years. Each year, scientists discover something new about the distant past. Each discovery that the scientists make brings them closer to piecing together the mystery of how civilization was formed.

CHAPTER 1

CLUES TO THE PAST

G**eologists**, or scientists who study the earth, say that the earth is more than 4 billion years old. **Archaeologists**, or scientists who study ancient peoples and civilizations, say that there have been people on earth for more than 1,750,000 years. But people did not learn to write until about 5,000 years ago. How then has so much been learned about the people who lived on this earth in the far distant past?

LEGENDS

Every group of people on earth has **legends**, or folktales, that explain the past. The Chinese, for example, have a legend about the beginnings of China. It says that the universe was a huge egg. When the egg split open, the upper half became the sky, and the lower half became the earth. Out of the split egg came P'an Ku, the first man. Each day for 18,000 years, P'an Ku grew taller, the sky grew higher, and the earth grew thicker. Then, P'an Ku died. His head split and became the sun and the moon. His blood filled the rivers and the seas. His hair became the forests and the meadows. His perspiration became the rain. His breath became the wind and his voice the thunder. His fleas became the ancestors of the Chinese.

The Africans have a legend about why the sun shines more brightly than the moon. It says that God created the Moon and then the Sun. The Moon was bigger and brighter than the Sun. The Sun became jealous and attacked the Moon. They fought and wrestled until the Sun begged for mercy. Then, they wrestled again. This time, the Sun threw the Moon into the mud.

Dirt splashed all over the Moon, and it was no longer as bright as before. To stop the fighting, God stepped in. He told the Sun that from then on it would be brighter and shine during the day for kings and workers. He told the Moon that from then on it would only shine at night for thieves and witches.

Like the Chinese and the Africans, the Rumanians have their own legends. One is about the creation of mountains and valleys. It says that when God finished making the heavens He measured them with a little ball of thread. Then, He started to create the earth to fit under them. A mole came along and offered to help. So, God let the mole hold the ball of thread while He created the earth.

While God was weaving and shaping the earth, the mole let out the thread little by little. God was too busy to notice that at times the mole let out more thread than it should have. When God was finished, He was amazed to find that the earth was too big to fit under the heavens.

The mole, seeing what it had done, was afraid. So, it ran off and buried itself in the earth. God sent the bee to find the mole and ask it what should be done. When the bee found the mole, it would not answer the question.

The bee hid in a flower, hoping the mole would think it was alone and start talking to itself. The mole thought out loud, saying that it would squeeze the earth so that the mountains would stick up, the valleys would sink down, and the earth would be smaller. Upon hearing this, the bee buzzed off. The mole heard the buzzing and became angry. It put a curse on the bee, saying, "Henceforth, feed on yourself."

The bee told God what the mole had said. God squeezed the flat earth so the mountains rose up, the valleys sank down, and the earth fit under the heavens. God then made the mole's curse a blessing. Since then, the bee makes its own honey. The mole lives underground and is afraid to come out.

The Chinese, African, and Rumanian legends are all concerned with creation and the heavens. This is not true of all legends. Many are about the deeds of godlike men and women or strange and wonderful lands.

Many of these legends were later written down. Some of them came to be thought of as historical fact. In time, archaeologists and **anthropologists**, or scientists who study the origin and development of humans, became curious about how much of certain legends was fiction and how much was fact. That curiosity led them to search out the truth of some of the legends.

1. According to archaeologists, how long have there been people on earth?
2. How have legends helped the study of history?

ARCHAEOLOGY

Archaeology began about 500 years ago. At that time, many people found they could dig up old marble statues and ornaments made by the ancient Greeks and Romans and sell them for a great deal of money. People began to study these **artifacts**, or things made by early people. They found they could learn from them about the ways of life of people who had lived long ago. Artifacts do not have to be works of art. They can be any item

ARCHAEOLOGICAL SITES

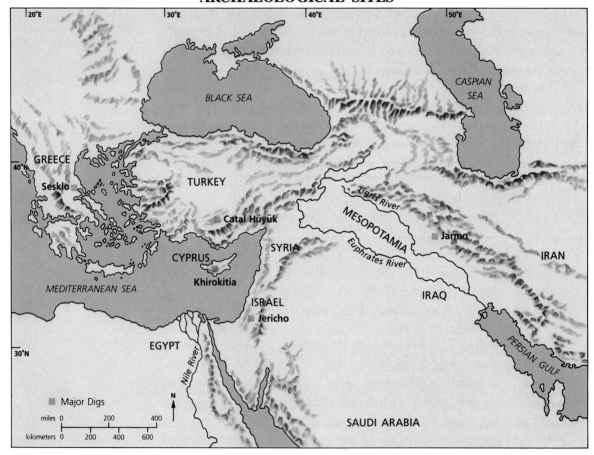

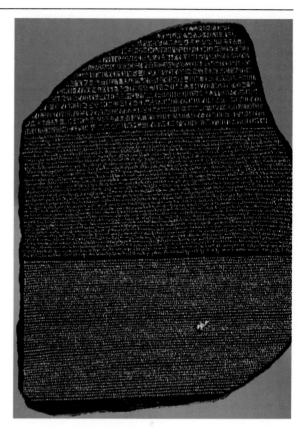

EGYPTIAN ARTIFACTS

Archaeologists have uncovered many artifacts in Egypt. This spearhead (left), from about 15,000 B.C., is one of the oldest objects found in the region. The Rosetta Stone (right), from around 200 B.C., is one of the most famous archaeological finds. On it is carved a decree issued by Egyptian priests to honor a leader.

What kinds of objects can be considered artifacts?

made by people rather than by nature. The earliest artifacts were pieces of hard rock that had been chipped into the form of cutting or digging tools or weapons such as arrowheads.

Around 1700, some Italian farmers discovered they were living on top of an ancient Roman city named Herculaneum that had been buried for more than 1,000 years. In 1719, archaeologists began to uncover the ancient city. After more than 50 years, they uncovered not only Herculaneum, but another Roman city called Pompeii. The archaeologists found that the cities had, among other things, fine houses, theaters, streets, and temples. More important, from what they unearthed they learned exactly how ancient Romans lived.

The discovery of the two Roman cities was followed in 1799 by what some people consider one of the greatest of all archaeological discoveries. This was the finding in Egypt of the Rosetta Stone, a slab of stone on which was carved ancient Egyptian picture-writing and its Greek translation. Although scholars knew the Greek language well, they had not been able to **decipher**, or decode, the ancient Egyptian language. The Rosetta Stone gave them the key to the meaning of Egyptian picture-writing. Now, they could learn much more about the history of Egypt and its people.

A great many archaeological finds have been uncovered since the discovery of the Rosetta Stone. Between 1850 and 1950, archaeologists uncovered five lost civilizations in different parts of the world. During approximately the same time period, they also unearthed prehistoric artifacts from every part of Europe. Since then, archaeologists have discovered several ancient Indian and Chinese civilizations. These were just the beginning. Finds are still being made today in every part of the world.

1.   What do archaeologists learn from artifacts?

2.   Why is the discovery of the Rosetta Stone considered so important?

TELLS AND KITCHEN MIDDEN   In Iraq, in the valley of the Tigris and Euphrates rivers, when ancient mud houses collapsed, other houses were built on top of them. Over thousands of years they formed **tells**, or great mounds that rise high above ground level. Some of the tells have 20 or more levels, each representing a time period of at least 100 years. From these tells, archaeologists have dug tools, pottery, and other household items.

Prehistoric Pitcher

Archaeologists call the remains of ancient households **kitchen midden**. They first began to study kitchen midden in Denmark in 1848. Since then, they have been able to learn a great deal from the kitchen midden. Their location, size, and depth allow scientists to estimate the size of the **population**, or number of people, at the time. The utensils tell how advanced the people were. Often, the archaeologists find bones or animal remains that tell them about climate, seasons, tools, hunting patterns, and eating habits.

Over thousands of years, whole cities of past civilizations were covered over with mud, dust, and rubbish. This packed down into hard soil or clay or hardened into stone. New civilizations came along, and new buildings were constructed on top of the old ones. Archaeologists **excavated**, or dug deep into the earth, to find the remains of these lost civilizations. Once they were unearthed, the finds still had to be dated.

1. What caused tells to form?
2. Of what value to archaeologists are kitchen midden?
3. Why do archaeologists excavate?

DATING ARCHAEOLOGICAL REMAINS   In 1832, C. J. Thomsen, a Danish archaeologist, divided the stages of historic progress into three **ages**, or periods, based on the materials used

---

ARCHAEOLOGICAL SITES

Archaeological research is a major method for learning about ancient civilizations. This archaeological excavation (left) is one at the Valley of the Queens, near Luxor, Egypt. The archaeologist shown (right) is making careful notes about the numbers, types, and locations of the artifacts he has found.

What do bones and animal remains tell archaeologists about a people?

---

for tools and weapons. They were the Stone Age, the Bronze Age, and the Iron Age. Later, scientists divided the Stone Age into three periods—old, middle, and new. Then, they discovered that the ages appeared at different times in different parts of the world.

Still later, archaeologists discovered that the kinds of materials used in tools were not as important as the changes in the ways early people got their food. So, they began to consider the ages in terms of food production and the development of cities.

To determine the date of an archaeological site, scientists first used trees. Each year, trees form a new growth ring. By counting the number of rings in a cross-section taken from the tree trunk, scientists could determine age. They took the core and matched its pattern with those of trees whose age they knew. In this way, they could carry dating back as far as 3,000 years.

Then, in 1946, an American chemist named Willard Frank Libby discovered that all living matter contains a radioactive element called carbon-14. He developed a method for determining age by measuring the amount of carbon-14 in objects. In 1960, Libby won the Nobel Prize in chemistry for his work with carbon-14. Because of Libby's efforts, scientists now can tell almost exactly how old an object is as far back as 30,000 years. This means that they can fix reasonably exact dates for ancient civilizations. They also can identify and compare distant civilizations within set time periods. The result has been more careful and exact conclusions about human history.

1. Into what three ages did Thomsen divide the stages of historic progress?
2. In what terms did later scientists consider the ages?
3. How did archaeologists determine the date of archaeological sites before carbon-14 was developed?
4. What did Willard Libby contribute to the study of history?

THE CHALLENGE OF MODERN HISTORY

The major challenge for historians in the past was the lack of information. Historians today face a different problem—too much information. Historians using computers can collect and file in seconds more **data**, or information organized for analysis, than their ancestors could in a lifetime. Some people call this the "Information Revolution."

Wooden Ax

Modern historians must know how to select the information they need from a huge amount of published facts. This need for selection has led them to become **specialists**, or people devoted to one branch of study or research. Most concentrate on a smaller time period than they did in the past. For example, a historian may be an expert in fifteenth-century military life or in the religion of one specific country.

Archaeologists, for example, have to do more than just excavate a site. They need to interpret and record what they have uncovered. They will want to preserve whatever they find, and at times they will have to restore certain objects. This means help from many different specialists, including historians, anthropologists, geologists, chemists, linguists, architects, engineers, and photographers. By working together, these people can increase human knowledge about the past.

1. What was the major challenge for historians in the past?
2. What is the major challenge for historians today? In what ways do they work to meet this challenge?

CHAPTER 1 REVIEW

SUMMARY

1. Most experts believe that people have been on earth for more than 1,750,000 years.

2. People developed the skill of writing only about 5,000 years ago.

3. One way experts have learned about how people lived before writing developed is through legends.

4. Every group of people on earth has legends that explain its past.

5. Artifacts are another way by which experts have learned how people lived in prehistoric times.

6. Archaeologists have unearthed several lost civilizations in different parts of the world.

7. After archaeologists unearth remains of former civilizations, they must date their finds.

8. At first, scientists used trees to determine the dates of archaeological sites.

9. Since 1946, scientists have used the carbon-14 method of dating, which was developed by Willard Libby.

10. In the past, historians lacked information, but today so much information is available that many historians have to specialize.

11. Historians work with archaeologists, anthropologists, and many other scientists to increase human knowledge about the past.

BUILDING VOCABULARY

1. *Identify the following:*
   P'an-Ku   Pompeii   Rosetta Stone   Willard Libby
   Herculaneum

2. *Define the following:*

geologists	population	tells	ages
archaeologists	artifacts	kitchen midden	data
anthropologists	decipher	excavated	specialists
legends			

REVIEWING THE FACTS

1. When did people develop writing?
2. With what are legends concerned?
3. How did archaeology begin?
4. Why are excavations important?
5. What do archaeologists do with the artifacts they unearth?
6. In what ways is carbon-14 a better dating tool than trees?
7. What is the "Information Revolution"? What caused it to develop?
8. Why have so many historians become specialists?

DISCUSSING IMPORTANT IDEAS

1. What legends do you know? Do you think they are fact or fiction? What makes you think so?
2. Why is it important to date archaeological sites as exactly as possible?
3. How do ideas about the past change as more knowledge becomes available?
4. What might people of the future learn about life today by examining a telephone directory?

USING MAPS

Study the map on page 8, and answer the following questions:
1. What is the main subject of the map?
2. How many major digs are shown?
3. Where are the digs located?
4. Which dig is on an island?

CHAPTER 2

PREHISTORIC PEOPLE

Prehistoric time can be divided into the Paleolithic and Neolithic Ages. Sometimes, the Paleolithic Age is called the Old Stone Age, while the Neolithic Age is called the New Stone Age. Once, experts believed that the major difference between the two ages was the way in which people worked with stone. During the Paleolithic Age, they shaped stone by chipping. During the Neolithic Age, they shaped stone by grinding. Today, most experts believe that the major difference centers around the way in which people got food.

THE PALEOLITHIC AGE

During the Paleolithic Age, people got food by hunting and gathering. Many important dicoveries were made as a result of people's activities as hunters and food gatherers. These discoveries made life easier for Paleolithic people.

HUNTING AND FOOD GATHERING   In hunting-and-food-gathering societies, people lived in small **bands**, or groups of about 20 members. The members of a band usually followed the decisions of two or three leaders. These leaders were probably the oldest or strongest men in the band. However, everyone had a chance to speak before decisions were made.

Few of the band members were more than 30 years old. More than half of the children born into a band died from illnesses or were killed by animals before their first birthday. Band members cared for those who became injured or sick. Because the people in a band lived and worked together and shared food, they felt very close to one another.

Each band gathered food within an area known as its **home territory**, which might cover 10 square miles, or 16 square kilometers. There were campsites at various places throughout this area. Early people did not live in houses or in caves. Caves were too cold and damp to live in except during emergencies. People camped out in the open. They protected themselves from the wind by digging pits in the ground or piling up brush to build windbreaks. The band stayed at a campsite until it used up the available food supply. Then, it moved to another campsite.

Band members divided the responsibilities for getting food. Women and children gathered most of the food. They gathered nuts, berries, and turtle eggs. They also dug roots from the ground. The men caught fish using their bare hands. They also hunted small animals with sticks and stones. Occasionally, they were able to kill a larger animal that was too old or too badly hurt to run away. A good kill meant that the band would have enough food for several days.

1. How were early people organized?
2. Where did early people usually live?

MAKING TOOLS   Life for hunters and gatherers became easier when they learned to make tools. At first, the only tools

EARLY TOOLS

For more than 2 million years, prehistoric people lived by hunting animals and gathering plants. They used tools made of wood and stone. The wooden tools have decayed. But, archaeologists have found many stone tools.

For what purposes did prehistoric people use stone tools?

people had were sticks and stones that they found on the ground. After a while, however, they learned to shape stones to make them more useful.

The earliest well-shaped tool was the **fist-hatchet**, or hand-ax. One end had a cutting edge, and the other was shaped to fit a person's hand. The fist-hatchet was an all-purpose tool. People used it to scrape animal skins, cut down trees, and chop up plants. Later, people developed special tools for many different purposes.

1. What were the first tools?
2. What was the earliest well-shaped tool?

DEVELOPING LANGUAGE   In addition to learning to make tools, early people developed language. Before they learned to talk, they simply made sounds. Each sound meant something different. A yell, for example, meant that a person was angry.

Early people also pointed at objects and tugged at elbows or shoulders to express meaning. They probably used hand signals for such important things as water, food, animals, and weapons.

Gradually, people developed language. Experts think this came about when people began to hunt large animals after the invention of spears and bows and arrows. Since the people had to hunt large animals in a group, they needed to be able to give one another clear instructions. Sounds and hand signals were not enough.

1. How did early people communicate with one another before they learned to talk?
2. Why do experts think people developed language?

DISCOVERING FIRE People also learned to make fire during the Paleolithic Age. At first, the only fires they knew about were in nature, such as those started when lightning struck a tree. Eventually, people learned to make fire themselves by rubbing sticks or striking stones together.

Once people learned to make fire, they could cook their food instead of eating it raw. They discovered cooked food was easier to chew and digest. So, they spent less time eating and had more time to do other things.

Fire had other uses. By about 750,000 years ago, people were using fire to keep warm. They also used it as a weapon. They threw burning sticks of wood at animals to drive them away. By about 80,000 years ago, people were using fire to harden the points of their wooden weapons. The fire-hardened points were strong enough to go through the skin of large animals, such as the horse, leopard, and rhinoceros. So, hunters were able to get more food.

1. How did early people know about fire?
2. How did early people make fire?

MAKING CLOTHING After hunters began killing large animals, they learned to make clothing. They found that animal skins could be used to protect their bodies and to provide warmth. At first, they just wrapped the skins around themselves. Later, they learned how to fasten skins together. They used a sharp stone or bone to punch holes in the skins. Then, they drew **thongs**, or long, thin strips of animal skin, through the holes to

Cutting Tool

GROUP LIFE

Experts believe that most early people lived in groups made up of several families. Here a group of hunters uses stones to sharpen tools. Two men carry a large animal killed in a hunt, as a few women tend fires near their tents.

How was fire useful to early people?

join one skin to another. Before long, they had fashioned the first needle—probably from bone.

Clothing affected where people lived. Before they had clothing, most people stayed in areas that were warm and dry. Once they had clothing to protect them from the weather, people began to move into areas that were cooler and wetter.

1.   What did early people use for clothing?
2.   How did early people fasten their clothing together?

THE ICE AGES   The Ice Ages also affected where people lived. Four times during the last 500,000 years, great ice sheets called **glaciers** have spread out from the North and South Poles. These ice sheets covered much of the earth. They brought freezing weather that drove people and animals away.

ICE AGES

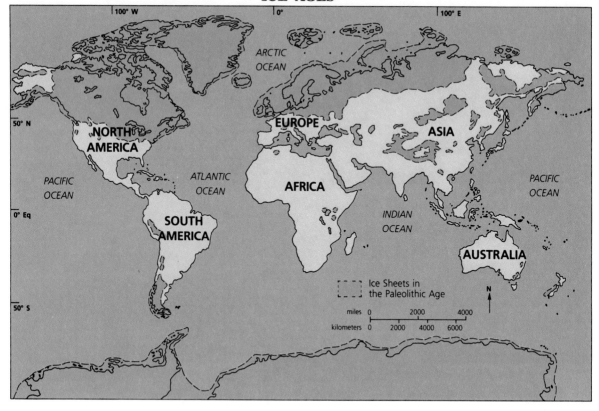

The glaciers also changed the earth's surface, grinding hills into plains, creating lakes, and forcing rivers into new channels. Each time, however, the ice sheets retreated, and the weather became milder. People then moved back into the areas once covered by glaciers.

1. How often have glaciers covered parts of the earth?
2. What changes in the earth's surface did the movement of glaciers cause?

THE PEOPLE　　The first people were about four and a half feet, or about 1.4 meters, tall. They had large jaws and teeth, and their noses were somewhat flat. They also had low foreheads, and their hair started just above their eyebrows. They probably had dark skin and thick patches of hair on their bodies. It is likely that the first people lived in Africa and Southeast Asia where the weather was warm all year. Over time, people spread out into other areas.

The first people on earth were *Homo habilis*, or "man with ability." Next came *Homo erectus*, or "man who walks upright." Then, about 100,000 years ago, came *Homo sapiens*, or "man who thinks."

There are two kinds of *Homo sapiens*. The first is the Neanderthal, named after the Neander River in West Germany where remains were first discovered in 1857. Since then, experts have found other Neanderthal remains throughout Europe and in parts of Asia and Africa.

Neanderthals were very good hunters. They hunted small game and fished, but they also hunted large animals, such as bison and elephants. They used **pitfalls** to catch large animals. A pitfall was a large hole in the ground that was covered with branches, leaves, and dirt. As an animal ran across this hole, it crashed through the covering and fell into the pit. The people then speared the animal until it was dead.

The second kind of *Homo sapiens* is the Cro-Magnon, named after the rock shelter in France where remains were first discovered in 1868. Cro-Magnons appeared about 40,000 years ago and lived in North Africa, Asia, and Europe.

PREHISTORIC PEOPLE

These models show the facial features of a Neanderthal (left) and a Cro-Magnon (right).

What were the first people on earth like?

Cro-Magnons were very good toolmakers. They were the first to make **flake tools**. These were tools made from thin strips of stone chipped off larger stones. Cro-Magnons also made needles and fishing hooks from bone, antler, and ivory, which were more workable than stone. They invented weapons such as the bow and arrow and the **spear thrower**, or a device that throws spears farther than the arm can.

Cro-Magnons were artists as well as toolmakers. They carved statues out of ivory and bone or molded them out of clay. Their major art form, however, was cave paintings. These paintings were done in bright reds, browns, yellows, and blacks. They showed hunters and such animals as bison, reindeer, and **mammoths**, or hairy elephants.

CAVE PAINTING
Prehistoric artists painted scenes of animals and people on the walls of caves. Experts believe the artists either rubbed the paint onto the rock, or blew it onto the surface through a hollow bone.
Why did prehistoric artists make cave paintings?

Many anthropologists think these paintings had religious significance. Cro-Magnons believed that everything was alive and filled with spirits. They thought that creating an animal in paint gave them a kind of magic power over that animal's spirit. They felt that this power would help them find the animal and kill it in the hunt.

Evidence indicates that Paleolithic people also believed in life after death. Archaeologists have found a number of skeletons buried in caves. Near the skeletons were tools and weapons. Also, remains of herbs used for healing were found in the graves of early people.

1. What hunting techniques did the Neanderthals use?
2. What was the major art form of the Cro-Magnons?
3. What was the religious significance of Cro-Magnon cave paintings?

THE NEOLITHIC AGE

With the start of the Neolithic Age around 8000 B.C., people began to get most of their food from farming. The results of the change from hunting and food gathering to food producing were great. For this reason, experts have called the beginning of farming the Neolithic Revolution. Although the change to an agricultural way of life was a revolution, it did not take place quickly.

FOOD PRODUCING Two important discoveries changed people from food gatherers to food producers. One was learning to grow food. Experts believe that people in the Middle East first discovered that seed from wild grains, such as wheat and barley, could be planted and harvested. This probably came about when a woman gathering food noticed that new shoots had grown from spilled grain.

The other discovery that changed people from food gatherers to food producers was learning to herd animals. This probably came about when hunters built fences to enclose herds of wild animals chased into a ravine. The hunters generally killed one animal at a time according to their needs. Gradually, the rest of the animals became **domesticated**, or tamed, and the hunters became herders. The herd provided a more stable source of

food. In time, Neolithic people began to breed animals for certain qualities. They bred fatter pigs and more timid cattle.

1. Where do experts believe people first learned to plant seeds?
2. How did early people learn to farm?
3. What happened to wild animals when they were enclosed?

EARLY VILLAGES Once people began to produce food, it became possible for them to settle in one place. They built permanent shelters and formed villages in places that had good soil and a water supply. These villages generally had about 150 to 200 people.

The earliest known villages in the world have been found in the Middle East. The oldest of these is Jericho in Israel, which archaeologists believe dates back to 8000 B.C. Another early village is Catal Hüyük in southern Turkey. People lived there from about 6500 to 5700 B.C.

The houses of Catal Hüyük were made of sun-dried mud-brick. They had flat roofs of reeds supported by a **post-and-lintel**,

or a horizontal length of wood or stone placed across two upright posts. The post-and-lintel was important to architecture because it allowed builders to support weight above an open space.

As protection against attack, the houses had no doors. People went in and out by a ladder through a hole in the roof. The houses were crowded together on the side of a hill. Here and there among the houses were open courtyards, which contained large ovens used to bake bread. Beyond the houses were vegetable gardens, apple orchards, and grain fields. Farther out were pastures where sheep and cattle grazed.

The increased food supply in the Neolithic Age resulted in increased population. There was more food available, and people lived longer. Experts think there were about 5 million people in the world when the Neolithic Revolution began. In 4,000 years, the population had grown to 90 million.

1. How large were Neolithic villages?
2. Why was the post-and-lintel important to architecture?
3. How much did population increase during the first 4,000 years of the Neolithic Revolution?

SPECIALIZATION   Another result of the increased food supply was the coming of **specialization**. This was the development of occupations. With more food available, fewer people were needed to produce it. People began to take up jobs that had nothing to do with food. They became potters, weavers, and metal workers and exchanged the products they made for grain, fruit, and meat. This was the beginning of trade.

Specialization was aided by a number of developments. One was that people learned to make pottery by baking clay. They used pottery to prepare, serve, and store food. The invention of pottery enabled them to add such things as soups and stews to their diet.

In addition, people learned to weave cloth. They took wool from sheep and spun it into thread. They wove the thread into

HAMMERED NECKLACE

In ancient times, people used simple tools and the skill of their own hands to produce jewelry of great beauty. Necklaces, like the one below, were formed by beating hot metal into thin sheets, and cutting it into shapes with flint knives. What other crafts were practiced by early people?

cloth on the loom, which was invented during the Neolithic Age. They dyed the cloth bright colors and used it for clothing.

People also learned to work metals. They picked up lead, copper, and gold from the ground and hammered these metals to make jewelry and other items. After a while, they learned how to shape metal into weapons. However, since metals found on the ground were scarce, people continued to work mostly in stone, bone, and wood.

1. How did people who specialized get food?
2. How did the invention of pottery affect people's diets?

Metal Worker

GOVERNMENT   Another development of Neolithic times was village government, which was more complex than government in earlier times. The main reason that village government was more complex was land ownership. People's lives depended on the use of a given piece of land. Because of the growing importance of land, people began to think about protecting what they had. They took steps to set boundaries and pass land on to their children. But disputes often arose over land ownership. They needed a leader to help settle disputes.

To keep order in Neolithic villages, a single chief was chosen. Besides settling disputes, the chief planned and directed village activities. The chief was helped by a small group of people who spent all their time doing government work.

1. What was often the subject of disputes in Neolithic villages?
2. Who settled disputes in Neolithic villages?

RELIGION   Experts believe that the chiefs of most villages were priests as well as rulers. Chiefs handled certain religious duties for the whole village. They offered prayers for things people needed, such as healthy animals, fertile soil, and water for crops.

At first, Neolithic people prayed to the forces of nature, such as thunder, the sun, the moon, and the sea. After a time, they created gods and goddesses to represent these forces. The most important was the Earth Mother, the goddess of fertility. Many of the houses in early villages had **shrines**, or altars, on which stood a stone statue of this goddess.

1. What two roles did village chiefs play?
2. What goddess was most important to Neolithic villagers?

CHAPTER 2 REVIEW

SUMMARY

1. Prehistoric time can be divided into the Paleolithic and Neolithic Ages.

2. During the Paleolithic Age, people lived in small hunting-and-food-gathering bands that moved from place to place in search of food.

3. Over time, people learned to make tools, developed language, discovered how to make fire, and began making clothing.

4. The movement of glaciers caused people to move and changed the surface of the earth.

5. There are two types of *Homo sapiens*. One is the Neanderthal, and the other is the Cro-Magnon.

6. Religion played a part in the lives of Paleolithic people.

7. During the Neolithic Age, people got most of their food from farming.

8. The shift from food gathering to food producing brought so many changes in the way people lived that experts have called the beginning of farming the Neolithic Revolution.

9. Food production made it possible for people to settle in one place and develop villages.

10. The increased food supply in the Neolithic Age resulted in increased population and specialization.

11. Neolithic villagers learned to make pottery, invented the loom, and began to work metals.

12. Neolithic villagers developed new ideas about land, government, and religion.

BUILDING VOCABULARY

1. *Identify the following:*

Neolithic Age	*Homo erectus*	Cro-Magnon	Catal Hüyük
Paleolithic Age	*Homo sapiens*	Neolithic Revolution	Earth Mother
Homo habilis	Neanderthal	Jericho	

2. *Define the following:*

bands	glaciers	spear thrower	post-and-lintel
home territory	pitfalls	mammoths	specialization
fist-hatchet	flake tools	domesticated	shrines
thongs			

REVIEWING THE FACTS

1. What do most experts today believe was the main difference between the Paleolithic and Neolithic Ages?

2. Why did more than one half of the children born into a band fail to reach their first birthday?

3. Why did prehistoric bands move from one place to another?
4. How did early men and women divide up the work of getting food?
5. How did the discovery of fire affect people's lives?
6. What difference did clothing make in the way people lived?
7. How did the Ice Ages affect where people lived?
8. Why do experts think that Paleolithic people believed in life after death?
9. Why did the development of farming result in the establishment of villages?
10. Why did the increased food supply result in increased population?
11. Why did people in the Neolithic Age begin to take up occupations?
12. Why did people in the Neolithic Age develop government?

DISCUSSING IMPORTANT IDEAS

1. Do you think the development of language is important? Explain.
2. Do you think the development of farming should be called a revolution? Give reasons for your opinion.
3. Do you think you would have enjoyed living in Catal Hüyük? Give reasons for your opinion.
4. How would you have organized village activities if you were a village chief?

USING MAPS

Study the map on page 20, and answer the following questions:

1. In which continents did ice sheets cover a large area?
2. In which continents did ice sheets cover a fairly small area?
3. Along what lines of latitude were ice sheets common?
4. Which continent was completely covered by ice sheets?

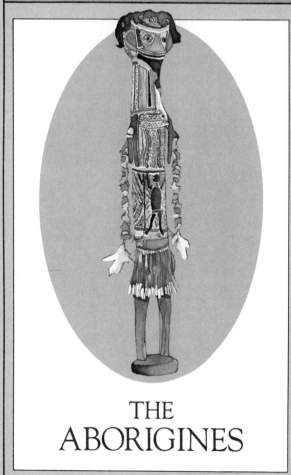

THE
ABORIGINES

The aborigines lived in groups all over Australia. They used tools and weapons of wood and stone. Those who lived along the coasts fished for food. Those who lived in the desert areas hunted animals and gathered wild foods. Men hunted large animals like the kangaroo or an ostrich-like bird called an **emu**. Women and children gathered seeds, berries, and roots and trapped small animals.

Myths, or legends, were important to the aborigines and were passed from the old to the young. The myths told where the first aborigines came from, how the land was formed, and how people should act. They taught the difference between right and wrong. They kept the aborigines united and also helped to keep peace and order.

When British settlers came, they arrived in large numbers. Soon, they out-

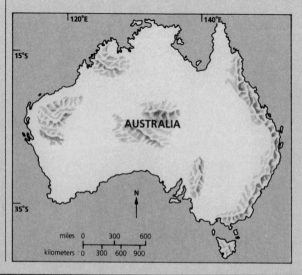

The first people to live in Australia are called aborigines, which means "first inhabitants." Archaeologists have discovered sites that indicate that the aborigines have lived in Australia for at least 20,000 years. Before British settlers arrived in 1788, the aborigines had little or no contact with other areas of the world. Since the arrival of the British, their life has been greatly changed.

numbered the aborigines. The settlers took the aborigines' land. Without their land, the aborigines could not live as they had in the past. Although few British settlers went to desert areas, ranchers and traders set up outposts there. Aborigines came to the outposts to trade. Some stayed on and took jobs, mostly as ranch helpers. Church missionaries set up posts to teach them Christianity.

Around 1930, the Australian government decided to try to bring aborigines into mainstream society. But the values of the aborigines were different from those of most other Australians. Many aborigines could not understand the need for money. They did not place any importance on owning things. As their groups were broken up, they felt helpless.

Since the 1960's, the government has set land aside for the aborigines and has tried to let them decide their own way of life. However, much of the land is too poor to support many people. The aborigines want to keep their old beliefs. But it is almost certain that the more contact they have with other Australians, the more they will have to change.

1. How did the aborigines live before British settlers came to Australia?

2. Why were myths important to the Australian aborigines?

3. How did the arrival of the British affect the aborigines?

4. What has been the government's policy toward the aborigines since 1960?

UNIT 1 REVIEW

SUMMARY

1. Much of what is known about prehistoric times comes from legends and artifacts.

2. In the Paleolithic Age, people lived in small bands that moved from one campsite to another and got food by hunting, fishing, and gathering.

3. During the Paleolithic Age, people discovered how to use fire, developed a spoken language, and made tools and clothing.

4. Civilization began in the Neolithic Age, when people learned how to grow food and herd animals and then began building permanent shelters and settling down in one place.

5. During the Neolithic Age, people learned how to make pottery, weave cloth, and work metals. They also developed new ideas about government and religion.

REVIEWING THE MAIN IDEAS

1. Discuss the ways in which scientists have been piecing together the mystery of how civilization was formed.

2. Explain why and how daily life gradually became easier for people in the Paleolithic Age.

3. Explain why prehistoric people had to learn to farm before the growth of villages was possible.

4. Explain how farming and living in villages changed daily tasks, government, and religion.

DEVELOPING SKILLS

Reading a history textbook is one of the most common ways in which people learn about the past. But in order to get the most out of reading, there are certain skills a person must have. One skill is being able to identify the main idea of a paragraph.

Sometimes the main idea is stated in the first sentence of the paragraph. This sentence is called a **topic sentence** because it contains the main **topic**, or idea, of the paragraph. Sometimes the main idea is stated in the last sentence of the paragraph. This sentence is called a **summary sentence** because it **summarizes**, or sums up, what the paragraph is about. Sometimes the main idea is not stated directly. Then the paragraph contains information about the main idea, but the reader must decide what the idea actually is.

This exercise is designed to provide practice in identifying the main idea of a paragraph. Listed are references to paragraphs in the textbook. Below each are three possible main ideas. Reread each paragraph, and then choose the correct main idea.

1. Chapter 1: second paragraph under "Archaeology" on page 9.

a. The city of Herculaneum had been buried for more than 1,000 years.

b. Archaeologists uncovered Pompeii after they uncovered Herculaneum.

c. Uncovering Herculaneum and Pompeii helped archaeologists learn exactly how ancient Romans lived.

2. Chapter 2: first paragraph under "Developing Language" on page 17.

a. In addition to learning to make tools, early people developed language.

b. Before people knew how to talk, they used sounds to express meaning.

c. A yell meant a person was angry.

3. Chapter 2: first paragraph under "Specialization" on page 26.

a. Another result of the increased food supply was specialization.

b. With more food available, fewer people were needed to produce it.

c. People became potters, weavers, and metal workers.

SUGGESTED UNIT PROJECTS

1. Working in groups of four or five, without speaking, act out a story about tracking down and killing an animal.

2. Draw a picture showing one of the earliest uses of fire.

3. Make a chart comparing life in the Paleolithic Age with life in the Neolithic Age. Be sure to include information about how people obtained food, where people lived, what kind of government people had, and what inventions people made.

4. In 1971, a hunting-and-food-gathering people called the Tasaday were discovered on an island in the Philippines. Research the Tasaday and prepare a report on them.

SUGGESTED READING

Batterberry, Michael and Ariane Ruskin. *Primitive Art.* New York: McGraw-Hill, 1973. An illustrated account of the art of prehistoric people.

Collier, James Lincoln. *The Making of Man: The Story of Our Ancient Ancestors.* New York: Scholastic Book Services, 1974. A description of the way of life of prehistoric people.

Millstead, Thomas. *Cave of the Moving Shadows.* New York: Dial Press, 1979. Tells the story of a 12-year-old Cro-Magnon boy who must choose between his training as a magician and his wish to be a hunter.

Simak, Clifford. *Prehistoric Man.* New York: St. Martin's Press, Inc., 1971. Traces the development of tools, fire, permanent shelter, religion, art, and farming.

Steele, William O. *The Magic Amulet.* New York: Harcourt Brace Jovanovich, 1979. Tells the story of a young wounded hunter left behind by his band who must find a new band to join in order to survive.

UNIT 2

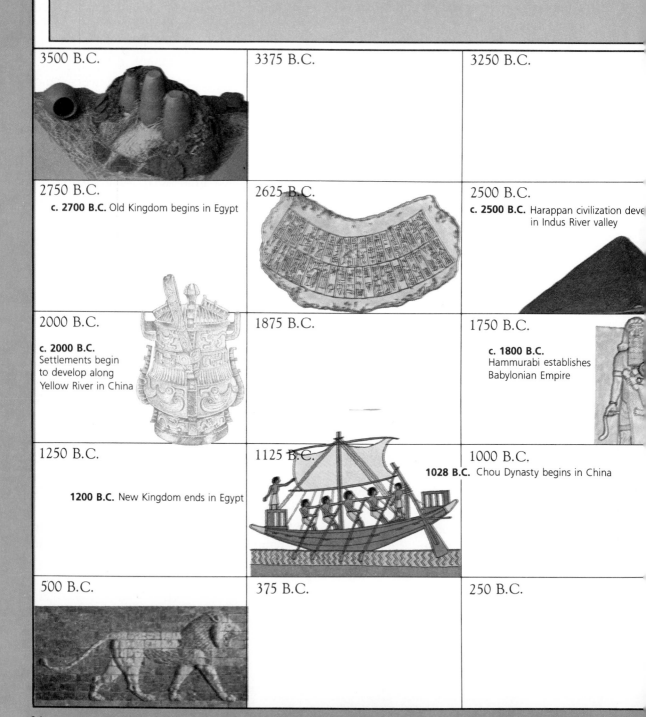

3500 B.C.	3375 B.C.	3250 B.C.
2750 B.C. **c. 2700 B.C.** Old Kingdom begins in Egypt	**2625 B.C.**	**2500 B.C.** **c. 2500 B.C.** Harappan civilization deve in Indus River valley
2000 B.C. **c. 2000 B.C.** Settlements begin to develop along Yellow River in China	**1875 B.C.**	**1750 B.C.** **c. 1800 B.C.** Hammurabi establishes Babylonian Empire
1250 B.C. **1200 B.C.** New Kingdom ends in Egypt	**1125 B.C.**	**1000 B.C.** **1028 B.C.** Chou Dynasty begins in China
500 B.C.	**375 B.C.**	**250 B.C.**

THE RIVER VALLEY CIVILIZATIONS

3000 B.C.

3000 B.C. Ur is a major Sumerian city

2875 B.C.

...B.C.

c. 2300 B.C.
Sargon I creates world's first empire

2250 B.C.

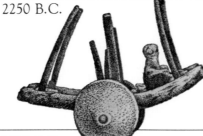

2125 B.C.

2060 B.C.
Middle Kingdom begins in Egypt

...B.C.

1600 B.C. New Kingdom begins in Egypt

1500 B.C.

1523 B.C. Shang Dynasty begins in China

1500 B.C. Mohenjo-daro and Harappa begin to decline

c. 1480 B.C. Thutmose III expands Egyptian control into Syria and Palestine

1375 B.C.

c. 1370 B.C. Amenhotep IV becomes pharaoh of Egypt

...B.C.

750 B.C.

672 B.C. Assyrians conquer Egypt

625 B.C.

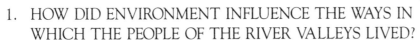

1. HOW DID ENVIRONMENT INFLUENCE THE WAYS IN WHICH THE PEOPLE OF THE RIVER VALLEYS LIVED?
2. IN WHAT WAYS WERE THE RIVER VALLEY CIVILIZATIONS ALIKE? IN WHAT WAYS WERE THEY DIFFERENT?

Around 4000 B.C., civilizations began to develop. Two of these, Mesopotamia and Egypt, were in an area now called the Middle East. A third, the Indus River valley, was in Pakistan and India. A fourth, the Yellow River valley, was in China. Each civilization developed separately. Yet, all started as villages along the banks of a river.

The people of these civilizations depended on the rivers for food. The rivers flooded and left behind rich soil good for raising crops. The people learned to control the floodwaters and to store the water to use on their fields in the dry season. This took much planning. People had to learn to work together. They became more organized. They set up governments to make laws so they would know what was expected of them. The population grew. The people began to build cities.

In each civilization, farmers were able to produce more food than was needed. In time, fewer farmers were needed to produce food. Thus, many people became free to do other things. Certain kinds of work came to be considered more important. Some people had more land or lived better. People were no longer equal.

People could not produce everything they wanted. So, they began to trade their **surplus**, or extra, products for the goods they did not have. As trade grew, there was a need for records. This led to writing.

Trade and conquest helped spread customs and ideas. Soon, ideas and customs of one civilization were being borrowed and changed by others.

CHAPTER 3
MESOPOTAMIA

The Tigris and Euphrates are twin rivers that begin in the mountains of eastern Turkey. They flow more than 1,000 miles, or 1,600 kilometers, southeast across a great plain. Then, the waters join and empty into the Persian Gulf. Today, the land between the two rivers is called Iraq. In ancient times, it was called Mesopotamia, "the land between the rivers." Around 5000 B.C., the people who lived in this area began to move south in search of more farmland. The land in the southeast was rich and fertile. It also had fish and waterfowl that could be used for food.

THE RISE OF SUMER

The people who settled in southern Mesopotamia around 3500 B.C. were called Sumerians. Their area of Mesopotamia was called Sumer. The Sumerians were a short, stocky, black-haired people. Sumerian civilization is the earliest known on earth. For the first time, a people began to control their physical environment.

The Sumerians knew they had to control the twin rivers. The rivers flooded each spring. When the waters went down, natural **levees**, or raised areas of earth, remained behind. The Sumerians built these even higher and used them to keep back the floodwaters. When the land was dry, they poked holes in the levees. The river water that ran through the holes watered the fields where they had planted crops. The main crop of the Sumerians was barley. Other crops included wheat, sesame, and flax. The Sumerians also grew fruit trees, date palms, and many kinds of vegetables.

The water that flowed through the holes in the levees made channels in the soil. Eventually, the Sumerians enlarged the channels until they became canals. They used the canals to **irrigate**, or water, their crops. They also built rafts so they could travel up and down the canals.

There was no building stone and little timber in Sumer. The Sumerians had to find other materials to use for their houses and public buildings. They mixed mud from the river with crushed reeds to make bricks. They left the bricks out in the sun to bake. They used the bricks to build their cities. One of the great cities of Sumer was Ur. The Sumerians were the first city-builders in this area of the world.

1. Who were the Sumerians?
2. How did they control the twin rivers?
3. What was their main building material?

CITY-STATES   Each Sumerian city was considered a state in itself, with its own god and government. Each **city-state** was made up of the city plus the farmland around it. Each city was surrounded by a wall of sun-dried brick. The wall had bronze gates that were opened during the day and closed at night to keep out lions and bandits.

Sumerian Figurine

Narrow, winding streets led from the gates to the center of the city. Near the center were the houses of the upper class—priests and merchants. These houses were two stories high with wooden balconies. The balconies overlooked courtyards around which the living quarters were built. The courtyards provided light and air for rooms. Outside walls were windowless to keep out the hot sun and the smells of the streets.

Behind the houses of the rich were houses of the middle class—government officials, shopkeepers, and craftspeople. These houses also were built around open courtyards. But they were only one story high. Farther out were the houses of the lower class—farmers, sailors, unskilled workers, and people who made their living by fishing.

The Sumerians were very proud of their cities. Often, one city-state would go to war with another city-state. They fought

---

SUMERIAN LIFE

This well-preserved limestone and shell mosaic from the city of Ur shows scenes of Sumerian life about 2600 B.C. In the upper row, a king and his court are entertained by musicians. The second and third rows show servants bringing animals and war prizes to the banquet.

How were Sumerian cities protected?

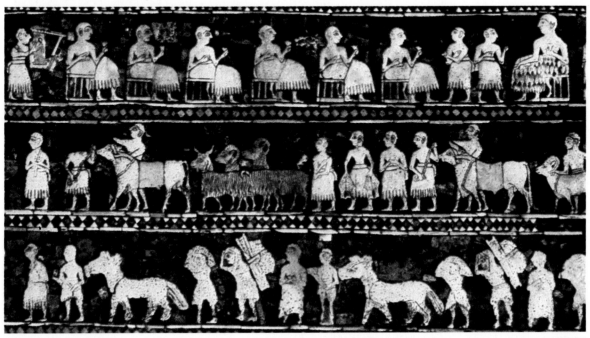

over boundary lines. They also fought to prove which city-state was stronger.

1. What were some physical features of a city-state?
2. What were Sumer's social classes? Who belonged to each?

RELIGIOUS AND FAMILY LIFE   At the center of each Sumerian city was a temple, called a **ziggurat.** The word "ziggurat" means "mountain of god" or "hill of heaven." The ziggurat was made up of a series of square terraces. Each terrace was smaller than the one below it. Great stairways led to the top of the ziggurat, which was the home of the city's chief god. Only priests could enter the home of the god.

Around the ziggurat were courts. The courts and the temple were the center of Sumerian life. Craftspeople worked there. Children went to school there. Farmers, craftspeople, and traders stored their goods there. The poor were fed there. All great events were celebrated in this area.

ZIGGURAT

Ziggurats were the first major structures built by the Sumerians. Many workers helped in the building of a ziggurat. This picture shows a ziggurat in Iraq. Where were ziggurats located in a Sumerian city-state?

The Sumerians believed that all the forces of nature, such as wind, rain, and flood, were alive. Because they could not control these forces, the Sumerians viewed them as gods. In all, there were more than 3,000 gods.

The Sumerians believed that at first there were only male gods. Then, female gods appeared. The male gods found they had to work very hard to please the female gods. The male gods decided that they needed servants to do the work for them. So, from the mud of the river, they made humans who would be their servants. The Sumerians believed that they were on earth only to serve the gods. If the gods were unhappy with them, their crops would not grow, and they would not live a happy life. Therefore, the goal of each Sumerian was to please the gods.

Only priests, however, could know the will of the gods. This made Sumerian priests very powerful. For example, all the land was owned by the city's god. But the priests controlled and administered the land in the god's name. The priests also ran the schools.

Cuneiform Clay Cones

The schools in Sumer were only for the sons of the rich. Poorer boys worked in the fields or learned a trade. The schools were called **edubbas**, or tablet houses, because their main purpose was to teach students how to write. Classes were held in rooms off the temple courtyards. Students sat in rows on brick benches. They wrote with wedge-shaped instruments on clay tablets about the size of a postcard. Sumerian writing was called **cuneiform**. It was made up of hundreds of word signs.

When a student graduated from school, he became a **scribe**, or writer. He worked for the temple, the palace, the government, or the army. Some scribes went to work for a merchant or set up their own business as public writers.

Although only Sumerian males went to school, females did have rights. They could buy and sell property. They could run businesses. They were allowed to own and sell slaves.

Although a woman could handle her husband's affairs when he was away, the husband was the head of the household. He could divorce his wife by saying, "You're not my wife." If he needed money, he had the right to sell or rent his wife and children as slaves for up to three years. He also arranged the marriages of his children.

Children were expected to support their parents when their parents became too old to support themselves. Children were also expected to obey any older family member, including brothers or sisters. All family members were expected to obey the gods and the priests.

1. What served as the center of Sumerian life?
2. Why did the Sumerians believe they should please the gods?
3. What was school like in Sumer?
4. What rights did Sumerian women have?

Gilgamesh

PRIESTS AND KINGS   At first, Sumerian priests were also kings of city-states. One of the most famous **priest-kings** was Gilgamesh of Uruk. Tales told about Gilgamesh made him seem more like a god than a person. One tale written about 1700 B.C. is the oldest known story in the world.

In the story, Gilgamesh and his friend Enkidu travel the world performing great acts of courage. When Enkidu dies, Gilgamesh searches for a way to live forever. He learns that only the gods can live forever and that all people must die someday. He also learns that people can and should take pride in what they do. Part of the Gilgamesh story tells of a great flood that covered the entire world. The account of the flood is very much like the biblical story of Noah and the ark.

The Sumerian priest-king received advice from an **assembly**. The assembly was made up of free men. When war broke out with another city-state, the assembly would choose one of its members to serve as the military leader until the war was over. As time went on, these military leaders stayed in charge even after peace had returned. They gained more and more power. By about 3000 B.C., they replaced the priests as permanent kings. At the same time, kingship became **hereditary**, or passed down from father to son.

1. What did Gilgamesh do?
2. How did Sumerians who were not priests become kings?

LATER MESOPOTAMIAN CIVILIZATIONS

About 2400 B.C., the power of Sumer started to fade. New civilizations began to develop in Mesopotamia as conquerors moved in from nearby areas.

SARGON I   Sargon I was a ruler from an area in northern Mesopotamia known as Akkad. About 2300 B.C., he moved his armies south and began to conquer the city-states of Sumer one by one. He united the conquered city-states with Akkad and became known as king of Sumer and Akkad. Thus, Sargon I created the world's first **empire**, or group of states under one ruler. He extended this empire to include all of Mesopotamia.

Under Sargon I, Akkadian became the language of the people. Sumerian was used only for religious purposes. The Akkadians, however, worshipped the Sumerian gods. They also wrote their language in Sumerian cuneiform. Sargon I ruled his empire for more than 50 years. Shortly after his death, the empire fell.

1. Where did Sargon I come from?
2. What happened to Sumer under Sargon I's rule?

HAMMURABI OF BABYLON　　Following the death of Sargon I, the separate city-states again rose to power. Then, about 1800 B.C., a new group of people called Amorites entered the Tigris-Euphrates Valley and built cities of their own. One of these cities was Babylon. The king of Babylon, Hammurabi, conquered Akkad and Sumer. He became the ruler of a great new empire.

MESOPOTAMIA

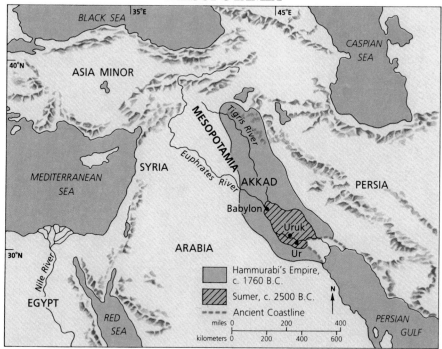

The people of Babylon took as their own much of the culture of the people they had conquered. For example, the Babylonians took over the language of the city-states. They worshipped the same Sumerian gods that the Akkadians had worshipped, but they gave the gods Babylonian names.

Hammurabi was a great conqueror. He extended his rule to the Mediterranean Sea. As a ruler, he carried out many **reforms**, or improvements. He improved the irrigation system by building and repairing canals. He reformed religion by raising the god of Babylon above all other gods. The people began to worship this god as well as their own local god. By worshipping a common god, they became more united. Hammurabi also reorganized the tax system and began a government housing program.

The reform for which Hammurabi became most famous, however, was his code of law. Each city-state had had its own code. Hammurabi took what he felt were the best laws from each code. He put these together and then issued one code by which

---

CODE OF HAMMURABI

The code of Hammurabi defended the rights of the individual. Here a Babylonian citizen pleads for justice before Hammurabi and his court.
Why was the code of Hammurabi important?

---

the entire empire was to live. Hammurabi wanted to make sure that his code was carried out fairly and justly. To do this, he appointed royal judges. Judges who were not honest and witnesses who did not tell the truth were punished.

Hammurabi's code covered almost everything in daily life. A person was believed innocent until proven guilty. Once proven guilty, a person was punished. The punishments ranged from fines to death. There were no prison sentences. Members of the upper class usually were punished more severely than members of the middle or lower classes.

During Hammurabi's rule, Babylon became an important trade center. The Babylonians brought their goods to city markets by carrying them overland on the backs of donkeys or by floating them down the twin rivers on rafts. People from faraway parts of the world came to trade. Some experts think they came from as far away as India and China. These traders paid gold and silver for the grain and cloth the Babylonians produced.

Hammurabi ruled for more than 40 years. The time he reigned is known as the Golden Age of Babylon.

1. What happened to Sumerian culture under Hammurabi's rule?
2. What were some reforms Hammurabi made?

CONTRIBUTIONS OF MESOPOTAMIA

From the beginnings of Sumer until the death of Hammurabi, the influence of Mesopotamia on other civilizations was felt in many ways. The inventions, customs, and ideas of the Sumerian and Babylonian cultures were copied and, in some cases, improved upon by other peoples. Some are still in use today in a slightly different form.

The Sumerians developed the earliest known civilization in the world. For this reason, Mesopotamia has been called "the cradle of civilization." The oldest written records known are Sumerian. The Sumerians were the first people to write down their laws. Sumerian cuneiform became the model for the writing of other civilizations.

The Sumerians also invented many things that helped to improve their well-being. They invented the wheel, which helped them to transport people and goods. They invented the plow, which enabled farmers to grow more food with less effort.

Water Clock

And they invented the sailboat, which replaced muscle power with wind power.

By mapping the night sky, the people of Mesopotamia developed a 12-month calendar based on the cycles of the moon. The calendar marked the times for religious festivals. It also told farmers when to plant their crops.

From Mesopotamia also came contributions in the field of mathematics. The people developed a number system based on 60. From that system came the 60-minute hour, the 60-second minute, and the 360-degree circle. The people of Mesopotamia also used a clock that was operated by controlled drops of water.

1. Why was Mesopotamia called "the cradle of civilization?"
2. What did the people of Mesopotamia contribute to other cultures?

CHAPTER 3 REVIEW

SUMMARY

1. Civilization began in an area known as Mesopotamia, located between the Tigris and Euphrates rivers.

2. Sumer was the first known civilization in the world.

3. The chief occupation of the Sumerians was farming.

4. The Sumerians developed an irrigation system for growing crops.

5. Sumerian civilization consisted of a series of city-states, the most important of which was Ur.

6. Life in each Sumerian city-state centered around the temple and its courts.

7. The Sumerians believed that all forces of nature were alive and were gods.

8. Each Sumerian city-state had its own chief god and government.

9. Eventually, kingship developed in Sumer, becoming permanent and hereditary abut 3000 B.C.

10. The oldest known story in the world was written about a Sumerian priest-king called Gilgamesh.

11. Sargon I of Akkad created the world's first empire by conquering the Sumerians in 2300 B.C.

12. About 1800 B.C., Hammurabi conquered Akkad and Sumer and established the Babylonian Empire.

13. Hammurabi unified the Babylonian Empire by setting up a single code of law and by raising the god of Babylon above all others.

14. Hammurabi's rule, which lasted over 40 years, was known as the Golden Age of Babylon.

15. Major contributions of the Mesopotamian civilizations to later civilizations include a model for writing, the wheel, the plow, the sailboat, and a number system based on 60.

BUILDING VOCABULARY

1. *Identify the following:*

Tigris and Euphrates	Ur	Sargon I	Babylon
Mesopotamia	Gilgamesh	Akkad	Hammurabi
Sumer			

2. *Define the following:*

levees	ziggurat	scribe	hereditary
irrigate	edubbas	priest-kings	empire
city-state	cuneiform	assembly	reforms

REVIEWING THE FACTS

1. Where did civilization first begin?
2. Why did the Sumerians build levees?
3. Why were sun-dried bricks the main building material of the Sumerians?
4. What was a Sumerian city like?
5. Why were the ziggurat and its courts important to the Sumerians?
6. Who went to school in Sumer?
7. What was expected of children in Sumer?
8. What did Gilgamesh learn about life?
9. What did Sargon I accomplish?
10. How did Hammurabi unite the Babylonian Empire?

DISCUSSING IMPORTANT IDEAS

1. Why were the twin rivers important to Sumerians?
2. What role did religion play in Sumerian life?
3. How important was education in Sumer? What kinds of work did educated Sumerians do?
4. What personal qualities does the story of Gilgamesh teach? Do you think these qualities are important? Explain.
5. Why did Hammurabi believe it was important to have a single code of law for the Babylonian Empire? Do you agree? Why or why not?

USING MAPS

Study the map on page 43, and answer the following questions:

1. What lands surround Mesopotamia?
2. Which was larger in area—Sumer or Hammurabi's empire?
3. Does the Tigris lie to the east or the west of the Euphrates?
4. Is Babylon or Ur farther east?

EBLA

Not long ago, archaeologists working in northwest Syria uncovered the ruins of an ancient city. By studying and translating some of the clay tablets they found in the ruins, they learned of a great civilization called Ebla.

Ebla existed between 2700 B.C. and 2200 B.C. The archaeologists discovered that Ebla had been as great a power in the ancient Near East as Egypt or Mesopotamia. Ebla was an important trading center. It grew wealthy through trade agreements with neighboring states. Ebla's wealth helped it become a large and powerful city-state.

Approximately 30,000 people lived inside the walls that surrounded Ebla. Another 230,000 people lived in the suburbs and in the nearby city-states that Ebla controlled. These city-states paid **tribute**, or taxes, to Ebla in grain and livestock.

The people of Ebla were called Eblaites. They were closely related to the Phoenicians, a people from the plains north of Mesopotamia, and to the Hebrews, a people from the deserts south of Mesopotamia. The Eblaites spoke a language much like ancient Hebrew. Most earned their living by making metal and wood products, textiles, and pottery.

People entered and left Ebla through four gates, each of which was dedicated to a different god. Streets led from the gates to the center of the city where the temples and the king's palace stood. The walls of the palace were 50 feet, or about 15 meters, high. Inside was a large **archive**, or place to store records. There,

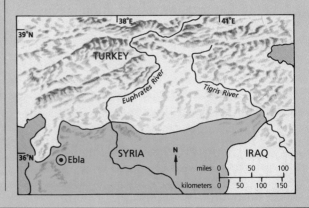

more than 15,000 clay tablets were kept on wooden shelves. A great stairway with steps inlaid with shell led to the audience court of the palace. There, the king met with people who wanted his help.

The kings of Ebla were elected by the people for seven years. They were responsible for the welfare of widows, orphans, and the poor. The kings had to account to the people. A king who did not do his duty could be removed.

The king had close to 12,000 government officials helping him. Most of the kings could not read or write. As a result, scribes carried out the royal decrees and handled the daily activities of the government. They wrote peace agreements, kept trading records, and described events. They also collected prayers and hymns. The scribes kept their records on clay tablets, which they covered on both sides with Sumerian cuneiform.

The kings of Ebla were powerful and prosperous until about 2400 B.C. Then, they went to war with Sargon I of Akkad over the Euphrates River. Whoever controlled the river gained the trade in metals from Asia Minor and in wood from Syrian forests near the Mediterranean. Around 2300 B.C., Sargon I defeated the Eblaites.

Later, Sargon I's grandson Naram-Sin captured and burned Ebla. Although the city rose again, it did not survive for long. In 2000 B.C., it was destroyed by the Amorites, who rebuilt it and introduced a new culture. After 1800 B.C., however, the city once again declined. Within 200 years, it had disappeared.

1. How did archaeologists find out about Ebla?
2. How was Ebla ruled?
3. What led to the fall of Ebla?

CHAPTER 4
EGYPT

A people called Egyptians settled in the Nile River valley of northeast Africa. They probably borrowed from the Sumerians the idea of farming, seeds for wheat and barley, and the idea of writing. The Egyptian civilization lasted longer than those of Mesopotamia. While the city-states of Mesopotamia fought among themselves, Egypt became a rich, powerful, and united nation. The Egyptians built a civilization that lasted for more than 2,000 years.

THE NILE

The Nile River flows north 4,000 miles, or 6,400 kilometers, from the mountains of central Africa to the Mediterranean Sea. The last 600 miles, or 960 kilometers, is in Egypt. There, the river cuts a narrow, green valley through the desert. Shortly before the Nile reaches the sea, it branches to form a fan-shaped area of fertile land called a **delta**. Most ancient Egyptians lived in this delta area. For a long time, they were protected from foreign invasions by the desert, the sea, and waterfalls called **cataracts**.

The Egyptians had an advantage over the people of the other river valley civilizations. They knew that every year, about the middle of July, the Nile would overflow its banks. By November, the floodwaters would go down. But the waters left behind large amounts of rich soil good for growing crops.

NILE RIVER

Over thousands of years, the flooding of the Nile River has left rich soil all along its banks. The Nile River valley is only 3 percent of Egypt's land, yet most Egyptians live and work in this area.

Why was the Nile River important to the early Egyptians?

Shadoof

The Egyptians learned to control the flood waters. To do this, they built a system of dams and ditches to drain the extra water from the land. They also dug out **basins**, or bowl-shaped holes. They used these to hold and store the extra water. A machine called a **shadoof** lifted the water from the river to the basins. To bring the water to the fields during the dry season, the Egyptians dug irrigation canals.

While cattle and goats grazed nearby, the Egyptians raised flax, wheat, barley, and grapes along the banks of the river. Poor Egyptians ate mostly bread, vegetables, and fish. Rich Egyptians also ate meat.

1. Where did the Egyptians live?
2. What advantage did they have over the people of other river valley civilizations?
3. How did the Egyptians control the Nile River?

THE OLD KINGDOM

At first, Egypt consisted of two **kingdoms,** or states having kings as rulers. One was Upper Egypt. It lay in the south in the river valley. The other was Lower Egypt. It lay in the north in the delta.

Around 3100 B.C., Narmer, a king of Upper Egypt, led his armies from the valley north into the delta. He conquered Lower Egypt and married one of its princesses. Narmer united the two kingdoms. He wore a double crown, the high white one of the south plus the shallow red one of the north. Narmer had many titles. He was called "Lord of Upper and Lower Egypt," "Wearer of Both Crowns," and "Lord of the Two Lands." Narmer set up a new capital at Memphis, a city on the border between Upper and Lower Egypt.

Around 2700 B.C., a period known as the Old Kingdom started in Egypt. It lasted for about 650 years. During the Old Kingdom, Egyptian cities became centers of religion and government. There lived kings, priests, government officials, and craftspeople who worked for the temples or the government.

Most Egyptians, however, did not live in the cities. They lived on large estates along the banks of the Nile. The rich Egyptians who owned the estates lived in wood and brick houses with beautiful gardens and pools. The walls were decorated with

EGYPTIAN LIFE

A lot of knowledge about everyday life in ancient Egypt comes from wall paintings and objects found in tombs. The wall painting above shows men and children harvesting wheat. It also illustrates clothing and hair styles of ancient Egyptians. How did the lives of the rich differ from those of the poor in Egypt?

brightly colored paintings that showed scenes of daily life. The household included the owner's family, servants, and craftspeople. The craftspeople were hired to build boats, weave linen, and make tools and pottery.

Most Egyptians were farmers who lived in villages on the estates. At first, their houses were made of reeds and mud. Later, they were made of sun-baked mud-brick. The houses usually had only one room and a roof made of palm leaves. They were built on high ground so that they would be safe from the yearly flood. The farmers worked in the fields and the vineyards and took care of the cattle. During the dry season, they built monuments, dug ditches, and repaired roads.

1. What did Narmer do?
2. In what kinds of homes did rich Egyptians live during the Old Kingdom?
3. Why did Egyptian farmers build houses on high ground?

THE PHARAOH   The Egyptians believed that the strength and unity of their nation came from having a strong ruler. At first, Egyptian rulers were called kings. Later, they were called **pharaoh**, meaning "great house." To the Egyptians, the pharaoh was a ruler, a priest, and a god. The pharaoh was the center of Egyptian life and ruled on earth the way the other gods ruled in heaven.

The pharaoh owned all the land in Egypt. However, the pharaoh gave gifts of land to rich Egyptians and priests. To make sure that the land produced well, the pharaoh saw to it that dams and irrigation canals were built and repaired. The pharaoh also ordered the building of brick **granaries**, or storage buildings for grain. The granaries were used to store the grain from good harvests so that the people would not starve in times of bad harvests.

The pharaoh also chose all the government officials. The officials made certain that taxes were collected and building permits were issued. Trade with foreign lands was in the pharaoh's hands. The word of a pharaoh was law.

The Egyptians believed that what happened to Egypt depended on the pharaoh's actions. As chief priest, the pharaoh

performed certain rituals. For example, the pharaoh made the first break in the irrigation dikes each year to open the land to the water. When the water went down, the pharaoh drove a sacred bull around the capital city. The Egyptians believed that this ritual would make the soil fertile. Then, they could grow good crops. The pharaoh was the first to cut the ripe grain. The Egyptians believed this ritual would guarantee a good harvest.

Pharaohs were treated with great respect. Whenever they appeared in public, the people played special music on flutes and cymbals. They also bowed and "smelled the earth," or touched their heads to the ground.

1. What did the pharaoh do?
2. How did the people show their respect for the pharaoh?

THE PYRAMIDS Another way the people of the Old Kingdom showed their feeling for the pharaohs was by building them great tombs called **pyramids**. Because the sun sank in the west, these "Houses of Eternity" were built on the west bank of the Nile. They were designed to protect the pharaohs' bodies from floods, wild animals, and robbers after they died. The Egyptians

believed that the pharaohs would be happy after death if they had their personal belongings. Therefore, they placed the pharaohs' clothing, weapons, furniture, and jewelry in the pyramids.

The Egyptians tried to protect the pharaoh's body because they believed that the soul could not survive without the body. It was important for a pharaoh's soul to live after death. In that way, the pharaoh would continue to take care of Egypt.

It took a great number of people and a lot of work to build the pyramids. Farmers worked on them during the three summer months that their fields were flooded. They used copper tools to cut huge granite and limestone bricks from quarries across the Nile Valley or in Upper Egypt. The blocks were tied with ropes on wooden sleds, pulled to the Nile, placed on barges filled with sand, and floated across the river. Another group of workers then unloaded the stone blocks and pulled them to the place where the pyramids were being built. Huge mud and brick ramps were built alongside each pyramid. The workers dragged the blocks up the ramps to each new layer of the pyramid. They built 80 pyramids in this way.

1. Why were the pyramids built?
2. Who built the pyramids? How were they built?

Cat Mummy

RELIGIOUS BELIEFS   The Egyptians believed in many gods. Most Egyptian gods had the bodies of humans and the heads of animals. Two of the most important gods were the river god Hapi and the sun god Re. They were important because the Egyptians depended on the river and the sun. The river brought them water and fertile soil. The sun helped their crops to grow.

Another important god was Osiris, the god of the harvest and of eternal life. According to Egyptian legend, Osiris was an early pharaoh who gave his people laws and taught them farming. He and his wife Isis ruled over the dead. The Egyptians believed that the souls of the dead went to the underworld. There, they were weighed on a scale. If a person had led a good life and knew certain magic spells, the scales balanced. Then, Osiris would grant the person life after death. To learn the correct magic spells, the Egyptians studied a special book called the *Book of the Dead*.

The Egyptians also used a process called **embalming** to preserve the bodies of the dead. At first, they used the process to

THE GODDESS ISIS

Each Egyptian village had its own gods and goddesses. Some were worshipped throughout the land. Isis was one of the most popular goddesses. Here she stretches out her winged arms as a sign of her motherly care.

How did Egyptians regard their gods and goddesses?

preserve the body of the pharaoh. Later, the custom of embalming became more widespread. To embalm a body, the Egyptians placed it in a wooden box and covered it with a chemical called natron. Natron dried up the water in the body, causing the body to shrink. After the shrunken body had dried, it was wrapped with long strips of linen. The wrapped body was known as a **mummy**. The mummy of a poor person was usually buried in a cave or in the sand. The mummy of a rich person was placed inside a special case or coffin, on which an artist had painted the person's portrait. The coffin was then placed in a tomb.

1. Who were some Egyptian gods? What did they do?
2. What did the Egyptians believe happened to a person after death?
3. How did the Egyptians preserve a person's body after death?

THE MIDDLE KINGDOM

Around 2300 B.C., government officials, jealous of the pharaoh's power, took control of Egypt. Almost 200 years of confusion followed. Finally, a new line of pharaohs took over and again brought unity. Out of this unity came a new period called the Middle Kingdom.

The main difference between the Middle Kingdom and the Old Kingdom was that the pharaoh had less power. After death, pharaohs were no longer buried in pyramids. Instead, they were buried in tombs cut into cliffs. Another difference was that the Egyptians began to trade with countries beyond the Nile Valley.

Egyptian Pharaoh

The Middle Kingdom lasted over 300 years. It came to an end in 1750 B.C. when Egypt was invaded by the Hyksos, a people from western Asia. The Hyksos crossed the desert in horse-drawn chariots and used weapons made of bronze and iron. The Egyptians had always fought on foot with weapons made of copper and stone. They were not used to the Hyksos' weapons or style of fighting and were defeated.

The Hyksos ruled Egypt for about 150 years. They copied some Egyptian customs and tried to get the support of the Egyptian people. But the Egyptians hated them and worked to gain their freedom. Around 1600 B.C., an Egyptian prince named Ahmose, using Hyksos weapons and style of fighting, led an uprising and drove the Hyksos out of Egypt.

1. How did the Middle Kingdom come about?
2. Who were the Hyksos? How did they defeat the Egyptians?
3. What ended Hyksos rule?

THE NEW KINGDOM

Ahmose founded another line of pharaohs and began the period known as the New Kingdom. During this time, Egypt changed in many ways. It became richer, and its cities grew larger.

During the New Kingdom, most pharaohs were interested mainly in war and conquest. They were no longer content to remain within the Nile Valley but marched their armies into lands to the east. It was during this period that the Egyptian Empire was established. One warrior-pharaoh, Thutmose III, with an army of 20,000 archers, spear throwers, and charioteers, expanded Egyptian control into Syria and Palestine.

One of the few pharaohs who was not interested in conquest was Hatshepsut, Thutmose III's stepmother. Her main interests were trade and the building of temples. During her rule,

ANCIENT EGYPT

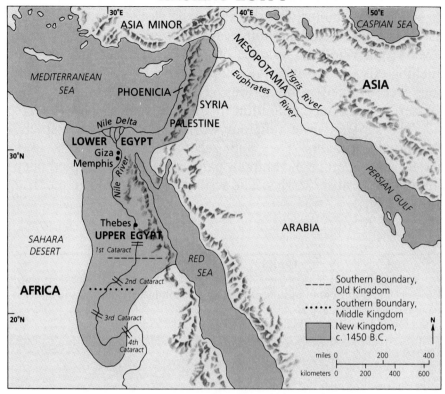

Egyptian traders sailed along the coast of east Africa and brought new wealth into Egypt.

1. What were some of the changes that took place in Egypt during the New Kingdom?
2. How was Hatshepsut different from the other pharaohs of the New Kingdom?

RELIGION The Egyptians of the New Kingdom began to worship a new god. As the god of the city of Thebes, his name had been Amen. When Thebes became the capital of Egypt, the Egyptians combined the god Amen with their sun god Re. They called the new god Amen-Re. He became the most powerful god of all, and people built many temples in his honor. These temples were built, in part, by slaves who had been captured by the warring pharaohs.

The temples were more than houses of worship. They were industrial centers, treasuries, and schools. As industrial centers, they provided work for the sculptors and craftspeople who carved statues, built furniture, and made clothes for the priests. As treasuries, their warehouses overflowed with copper, gold jewelry, glass bottles, bundles of grain, dried fish, and sweet-smelling oils. As schools, the temples were places where young boys were trained to be scribes. The right to be a scribe was passed on from one generation to another.

The scribes wrote religious works, which included spells, charms, and prayers. They kept records of the pharaohs' laws and lists of the grain and animals paid as taxes. They copied fairy tales and adventure stories. The scribes also wrote down medical prescriptions.

TEMPLE AT KOM OMBO

Warring pharaohs of the New Kingdom built large temples to honor their gods. The stone block in front of this temple shows Egyptian hieroglyphs. This temple has many statues and monuments.

Who provided the labor to build temples?

HIEROGLYPHS
Ancient Egyptians viewed hieroglyphs as gifts from the gods. The pictures were first used as a way of keeping records. Later, they represented the sounds of spoken language. Here, hieroglyphs are painted on a coffin lid.
How did hieroglyphs differ from cuneiform?

There were several kinds of Egyptian writing. One was the **hieroglyphic system**, or a writing system based on pictures. The Egyptians carved and painted **hieroglyphs**, or picture symbols, on their monuments. However, the scribes needed an easier form of writing to keep records. So, they developed two other kinds of writing in which hieroglyphs were rounded off and connected.

1. For what purposes were Amen-Re's temples used?
2. What did scribes do?

DECLINE OF EGYPT   Over time, the priests of Amen-Re gained much power and wealth. They owned one third of Egypt's land and began to influence government decisions. As time passed, the pharaoh's power declined.

Then, about 1370 B.C., a new pharaoh named Amenhotep IV came to the throne. He did not like the priests. He did not agree with them on what was good for the country. He wanted Egyptians to look to the pharaoh for both religious and political

Ramses II

leadership. Amenhotep IV closed the temples of Amen-Re and fired all the temple workers. He set up his own religion and god, Aton. He changed his name to Akhnaton, which means "Spirit of Aton." But only his family and close advisors accepted the new religion. After Amenhotep IV's death, the priests forced the new pharaoh to return to the older religion.

Little by little, Egypt lost its power. Several things helped to make Egypt weak. One was the struggle between the priests and the pharaohs. Another was the pharaohs' attempts to keep neighboring countries under Egyptian control. Too much energy and money were spent on war. Then, too, other peoples of the eastern Mediterranean were beginning to use iron weapons. Since Egypt had no iron ore, a great deal of money was spent to bring in small amounts to make weapons.

By 1150 B.C., Egypt's empire was gone. Over the next several **centuries**, or periods of 100 years, Egyptian civilization continued to decline until Egypt was conquered by a people called the Assyrians in 672 B.C.

1. What did Amenhotep IV do?
2. Why did Egypt become weak?

Contributions of the Egyptians

The Egyptians made many contributions to other civilizations. One was a type of paper called **papyrus**. It was made from a reed also called papyrus. To make paper, the Egyptians cut the stems of the reed into thin strips that were pressed together to make a sheet. Then, they pasted the sheets together to make a roll. Some rolls were as long as 100 feet, or 30 meters. In order to write on papyrus, the Egyptians invented ink. The dry climate of Egypt preserved some writings so well that they can still be read today.

Papyrus had other uses. It was made into baskets and sandals. It was tied in bundles to make columns for houses. Even rafts and riverboats were made of papyrus.

The Egyptians were excellent mathematicians. They used a number system based on ten. They also used fractions and whole numbers. They used geometry to **survey**, or measure, land. When floodwaters washed away the boundary markers that separated one field from the next, the Egyptians surveyed the fields to see where one began and the other ended.

The Egyptians knew the Nile flooded about the same time every year. They used this knowledge to develop a calendar. The calendar contained three seasons of 120 days each, plus five special feast days for the gods.

The Egyptians also made contributions in the field of medicine. As dentists, eye doctors, veterinarians, and surgeons, Egyptian doctors were the first medical specialists. The Egyptians were the first to use splints, bandages, and compresses. They were experts at sewing up cuts and at setting and splinting broken bones. They treated less serious problems, too, such as

MEDICAL PRACTICE IN ANCIENT EGYPT

An Egyptian doctor gives medicine to a patient. The doctor's assistant holds a scroll listing directions for treating the illness. Egyptian skill in medicine was highly valued in the Mediterranean area for 2,500 years.

What kind of medical help did Egyptian doctors give their patients?

indigestion and baldness. For indigestion, they used castor oil. For baldness, they used a mixture of dog toes, dates, and a donkey hoof.

1. How did the Egyptians make papyrus?

2. What mathematical contributions did the Egyptians make to other civilizations?

3. What medical contributions did the Egyptians make to other civilizations?

CHAPTER 4 REVIEW

SUMMARY

1. Egyptian civilization began in the Nile River valley over 5,000 years ago.

2. About 3100 B.C., Narmer united Upper and Lower Egypt.

3. The Old Kingdom began around 2700 B.C. and lasted for about 650 years.

4. The kings of Egypt became known as pharaohs and were viewed by the Egyptians as rulers, priests, and gods.

5. During the Old Kingdom, pyramids were built as tombs for the pharaohs.

6. The Egyptians worshipped many gods.

7. The Egyptians placed great importance on life after death and created a process to preserve bodies as mummies.

8. The Middle Kingdom began about 2100 B.C. and lasted until the Hyksos' invasion of Egypt in 1750 B.C.

9. The New Kingdom began after Ahmose, an Egyptian prince, drove the Hyksos out of Egypt around 1600 B.C.

10. During the New Kingdom, most of the pharaohs were interested mainly in war and conquest.

11. During the New Kingdom, the priests of Amen-Re became very powerful.

12. The pharaoh Amenhotep IV, or Akhnaton, tried to establish a new religion in Egypt around 1370 B.C. but did not succeed.

13. Toward the end of the New Kingdom, Egypt began to decline.

14. The Egyptians made several contributions to later civilizations, including surveying, certain medical treatments, and a kind of paper called papyrus.

BUILDING VOCABULARY

1. *Identify the following:*

Egypt	Re	Middle Kingdom	Thutmose III
Nile	Hapi	Hyksos	Hatshepsut
Old Kingdom	Osiris	Ahmose	Amen-Re
Narmer	*Book of the Dead*	New Kingdom	Amenhotep IV

2. *Define the following:*

delta	kingdoms	embalming	centuries
cataracts	pharaoh	mummy	papyrus
basins	granaries	hieroglyphic system	survey
shadoof	pyramids	hieroglyphs	

REVIEWING THE FACTS

1. What did the Egyptians borrow from the Sumerians?

2. What did the Nile give to the Egyptian people?

3. What did Egyptian farmers do when they were not working in the fields?

4. Why did the Egyptians show such great respect for the pharaoh?

5. How did the Middle Kingdom differ from the Old Kingdom?

6. What role did the Hyksos play in the development of Egyptian civilization?

7. How did the New Kingdom differ from the Middle Kingdom?

8. What kinds of writing did the Egyptians have, and for what were they used?

9. Why did Akhnaton oppose the priests of Amen-Re?

10. How did the Egyptians use the papyrus reed?

DISCUSSING IMPORTANT IDEAS

1. Why do you think some experts call Egypt "the gift of the Nile"? Do you think that is a good name? Explain.

2. What role did religion play in Egypt during the Old Kingdom? During the New Kingdom?

3. Why were scribes important to Egyptian government?

4. How did the government of Egypt resemble that of Babylon? In what ways was it different?

5. Do you think Akhnaton was wise to oppose the priests of Amen-Re? Give reasons for your opinion.

6. Would you have liked living in ancient Egypt? Why or why not?

USING MAPS

Study the map on page 59, and answer the following questions:

1. What is the time period of the map of ancient Egypt?

2. How many kingdoms are shown?

3. During which kingdom did ancient Egypt occupy the largest area?

4. Which river is longer—the Nile or the Euphrates? How can you tell?

5. Which city—Memphis or Thebes—is farther south? How can you tell?

6. How far is Memphis from Thebes?

CHAPTER 5
EASTERN RIVER VALLEYS

In 3500 B.C., civilization began in Sumer. Some 400 years later, it began in Egypt. Several hundred years after that, river valley civilizations began to appear in the East. By 2500 B.C., cities started to develop in the Indus River valley of South Asia. By 1500 B.C., they were being established in the Yellow River valley of China.

The people of these eastern civilizations were more isolated than the people of Mesopotamia or Egypt. They were cut off from other parts of the world by high mountains, broad deserts, and large bodies of water. As a result, they became **self-sufficient**, or able to take care of all of their needs. Compared to the Sumerians and the Egyptians, they did little trading with other groups of people.

Less is known about life in the eastern civilizations than is known about Sumerian or Egyptian life. Very few remains have been found of the ancient eastern civilizations. Much of what is known about them comes from legend. Until more records are found, the early life of these eastern peoples will remain, in part, a mystery.

The Indus River Valley

The Indus River flows through the countries known today as Pakistan and India. About 2500 B.C., a group of people called Harappans settled in the valley of the Indus. Although others had lived there before, the Harappans were the first to create a civilization. Harappan civilization extended about 1,000 miles, or 1,600 kilometers, from the foothills of the Himalayas to the Indian Ocean. This area was more than twice the size of either Mesopotamia or Egypt.

The lives of the people were shaped by the Indus River. The river fertilized the land and made its soil rich. But when the river flooded, it swept away everything in its path. The people had to control the Indus in order to settle near it. To do this, they built dikes and dams. They cleared the land for farming. They built irrigation systems to bring the water to their dry land. They grew crops of barley, wheat, peas, melons, and dates. They also fished in the river.

The Harappans were the earliest known people to grow cotton. They spun the cotton, wove it into cloth, and dyed it bright colors. They produced cotton cloth hundreds of years before anyone else.

Kiln

The river influenced the way the Harappans built their cities. To protect the cities from floods, the Harappans built them on raised mounds. They used the soft river mud to make bricks, which they baked in the sun. Then, they went one step further. They **fired**, or baked, some bricks in **kilns**, or ovens. They used these kiln-dried bricks as a covering over the mud bricks. These fired bricks were stronger and lasted much longer than the sun-dried ones. The Harappans used the fired bricks for their houses and public buildings.

1. Who were the Harappans?
2. In what ways did the Indus River influence the Harappans?
3. How did the Harappans make bricks?

HARAPPA AND MOHENJO-DARO   Harappan civilization centered around two major cities, Harappa and Mohenjo-daro. These cities were about 400 miles, or 640 kilometers, apart. Many experts believe they were twin capitals.

Harappa and Mohenjo-daro are the oldest examples yet found of **planned communities**, or cities built to a definite plan. Both cities contained hundreds of small buildings. Some of the buildings served as homes, while others served as shops. The buildings were laid out on a planned street **grid**, or uniform network. The streets crossed each other at almost perfect right angles. The buildings that lined the streets were arranged in blocks of about the same size.

EARLY INDIA

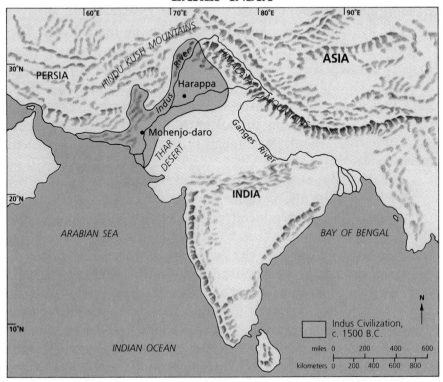

THE GREAT BATH AT MOHENJO-DARO
The people of Mohenjo-daro may have washed themselves at the Great Bath. To make the Bath watertight, they used cement, tar, and four layers of brick. What was the purpose of the Great Bath?

Most of the buildings were two stories high and were built around a courtyard. The courtyard opened into several rooms. The outer walls of the buildings had no windows, and the walls fronted on narrow lanes in such a way as to break the force of the wind. Almost every building had its own well, a bathroom, and drains. The drains carried waste away from the houses and emptied it into drain holes lined with brick. These drains were cleaned often. This sanitation system helped protect the health of the Harappan people.

The most important buildings of Harappa and Mohenjo-daro were built high above the houses and shops so as to be safe from neighboring peoples and floods. In each city, a **citadel**, or fortress, stood on a mound at least 40 feet, or 12 meters, high. It was surrounded by a thick brick wall. Inside the citadel at Mohenjo-daro was a huge watertight tank called the "Great Bath." Some experts believe it was used for religious ceremonies or baths. Next to the Great Bath stood a huge granary. Traders from other regions who stopped at Mohenjo-daro probably left their goods there.

Harappa also contained a series of huge granaries. The floor of each granary was supported on low walls. In the walls were air holes that allowed the air to move around in the granary. This kept the grain dry and prevented it from spoiling. Nearby were circular brick platforms. Each had a scooped out area in the center where grain could be pounded. The platforms were placed so that workers pounding grain could be watched over from the citadel.

1. In what ways were Harappa and Mohenjo-daro alike?
2. What were some of the outstanding features of Harappa and Mohenjo-daro?

DECLINE OF THE HARAPPANS   No one knows for certain how Harappan civilization came to an end. One reason may have been that the people used up their **natural resources**, or materials supplied by nature. For example, farmers may have tried to raise more and more crops on the same plots. This would have robbed the soil of chemicals needed to make it fertile enough to produce well. Without good harvests, there would not have been enough food to feed everyone, especially if the Harappan population was increasing.

Another reason may have been that the Harappans cut down too many trees to fuel their ovens. Without tree cover, the floods became heavier and forced the people to leave their cities and farming villages and move on. It is known that parts of Mohenjo-daro had to be rebuilt several times because of floods. At first, the city was rebuilt carefully. But as time went on, the new buildings were not made as well, and the older ones were patched up. Then, too, the people may just have gotten tired of rebuilding and decided to move somewhere else.

A third reason may have been that the Indus Valley was invaded. The Harappans could not defend themselves, and all were killed. Unburied skeletons of groups of men, women, and children were found in the streets of the ruins of Mohenjo-daro. Every skeleton showed some kind of injury.

All that is certain is Harappan civilization began to change about 1500 B.C. Homes were no longer built as well. Pottery was no longer made as carefully. By 1200 B.C., a group of people called Aryans had taken over the Indus Valley, and Harappan civilization ceased to be.

1. In what two ways did the Harappans apparently misuse their natural resources?
2. What evidence is there that the Harappan civilization came to an end because the Indus Valley was invaded?

EVIDENCE OF A LOST CIVILIZATION   Very little is known about the Harappan people and their civilization. As yet, no one has been able to read Harappan writing. There is no record of the civilization's political history. No royal tombs have been discovered. All that is known about Harappan religion is that the people had more than one god and most were female.

Much of what is known comes from the ruins of Harappa and Mohenjo-daro. There, scientists have found jewelry made of gold and a blue stone called lapis lazuli as well as weapons of stone, copper, and bronze. Scientists have also found clay models of animals, rattles, dice, and toy carts with movable wheels. The carts are very much like those many farmers of Pakistan and India use today to transport goods.

One of the most important finds was a series of tiny seals made of soapstone. An animal and a line of writing were carved

---

HARAPPAN SEAL

This Harappan seal is 1 inch, or 2.5 centimeters, square. It shows a bull facing an incense burner. In eastern civilizations, the bull was a symbol of strength. The seal also shows Harappan writing.

What is unusual about Harappan writing?

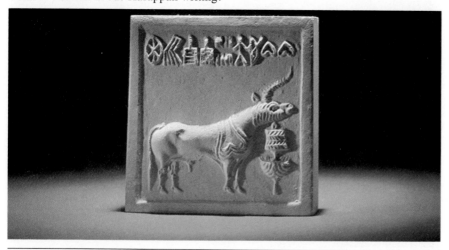

---

on each seal. Most of the seals had a small hole in them and could be worn as necklaces or bracelets. The seals may have stated the names, titles, or trades of a person, family, or business. Experts believe the seals were used to stamp the wet clay that sealed packages of goods. Some Harappan seals have been found as far away as Sumer.

    1.   Why is so little known about the Harappans?
    2.   What examples of Harappan civilization have experts found?

THE YELLOW RIVER VALLEY

About 2000 B.C., or 500 years after the Harappans settled in the Indus River valley, a civilization developed in the Yellow River valley of northern China. There are no records of its beginnings, and no remains have been found. For this reason, much of what happened comes from legend.

According to Chinese legend, a man-god named Yü the Great drove out the serpents and dragons that lived along the Yellow River. He drained the land so that people could live there

---

THE WISE MAN FU HSI

The Chinese used legends of man-gods to explain the beginnings of their civilization. One legend was about Yü. Another was about Fu Hsi. In this drawing, Fu Hsi points to eight geometric designs used to tell the future. He discovered them by studying the marks on the back of a turtle.

Why do modern historians study legends?

---

and grow crops. He also made the rivers flow to the east. Yü founded a kingdom called Hsia and united most of northern China under his rule.

Many experts believe that the early settlers of China chose the Yellow River valley for their home because it was fertile. The river flooded every year, bringing rich soil with it. But since the flood could also wipe out everything in its path, the Chinese call the river "the great sorrow."

The valley was cut off from other civilizations. The people who lived there developed their way of life without borrowing from other civilizations. By 1800 B.C., there were villages and farms all along the river. The people farmed the land and used the river for travel and some trade. They made clay ovens, cupboards, benches, and pottery. They built small round clay houses with thatched roofs.

CITIES OF THE SHANG   The first records of Chinese civilization come from a **dynasty**, or ruling family, called Shang. The Shang came to power in 1523 B.C. They built the first Chinese cities. Most were designed in the same way. At the center stood a palace and a temple. Public buildings and the homes of high government officials were built around the palace. Within an outer district were workshops, burial grounds, and the homes of the workers.

Most of the Shang people, however, did not live in the city. The city was the home of the rich, the learned, and the skilled. The poorer people lived in the countryside. They were farmers, who grew such grains as millet, wheat, and rice. They also raised cattle, sheep, and chickens. The farmers produced the silk used to make the clothes of the very rich.

Shang Dagger

1. Who were the Shang?
2. What were Shang cities like? Who lived in them?
3. Where and how did the poorer Shang people live?

SPIRITS, ANCESTORS, AND KINGS   The Shang worshipped **spirits**, or supernatural beings, which they believed lived in the mountains, rivers, and seas. The people believed they had to please the spirits. If the spirits became angry or unhappy, the people might suffer a poor harvest or lose a battle.

The Shang believed that **ancestors**, or those from whom one is descended, also influenced people's fortunes. So, they offered

SHANG CHINA

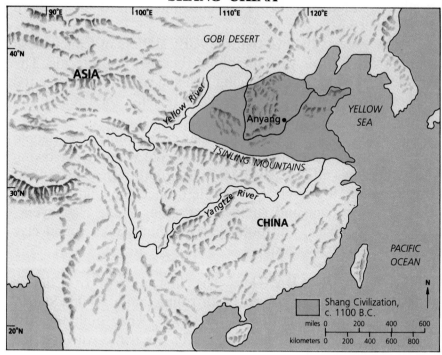

their ancestors food, wine, and special prayers. They hoped that their ancestors would help them in time of need and bring them good fortune. Because of this respect for ancestors, family ties were very important to the Shang. They had rules about how family members should act toward one another. The young were taught to obey their parents and to respect older people. Wives were trained to obey their husbands.

The Shang believed that their kings received their power from the spirits of nature and their wisdom from their ancestors. For this reason, religion and government were closely linked. An important duty of the king was to contact the nature spirits to make sure that they provided enough water for farming.

Kings also asked the advice of their ancestors before making important decisions. They had messages scratched on a flat, polished piece of bone. The bone had a hole drilled in it. A hot bar was put in the hole. The heat from the bar produced a pattern of cracks on the bone. The cracks were believed to be the ancestors' replies to a king's question. A special interpreter gave the king the meaning of the ancestors' replies. These bones are known as **oracle bones**. The writing on them is the oldest known form of Chinese writing.

Under the kings was a large class of **nobles**, or people of high rank in a kingdom. They spent much of their time hunting for pleasure and as preparation for war. The nobles often fought with each other about land. They united only when they had to fight other people who refused to accept Shang rule.

The nobles rode into battle in horse-drawn bronze chariots. They wore bronze helmets and armor made of buffalo or rhinoceros hide. They were skilled in the use of the bow and arrow. Their arrows had sharp points of bone or bronze. Soldiers marched on foot behind the nobles' chariots. These soldiers usually were poor peasants whom the nobles had forced to leave their farms and join the army.

1. How did the Shang people feel about the nature spirits? About their ancestors?
2. What was the role of Shang kings?
3. How did the nobles spend much of their time?

SHANG ELEPHANT

This richly decorated bronze elephant is 9 inches, or 22.5 centimeters, in height. It is an example of the high quality of Shang art. The Shang made bronzes of real and imaginary animals.
For what other purposes did the Shang use items of bronze?

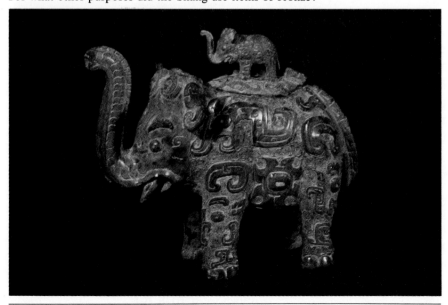

DECLINE OF THE SHANG   There was a large gap between the rich and the poor during the rule of the Shang. The rich lived in cities in wooden houses. They owned bronze weapons and ornaments, and wore linen, wool, fur, and silk clothes. The poor lived in the countryside and worked with wooden or stone tools. Their houses were thatched or mud huts or caves scooped out of the ground. Neither group felt any loyalty toward the other.

Many experts believe that this gap between rich and poor weakened the Shang civilization. In 1028 B.C., a people known as the Chou invaded the Shang kingdom. The Shang nobles and peasants were not united enough to resist the invaders. Shang civilization came to an end.

The Shang left behind a great gift to the world in their works of bronze. These include sculptures, cups, vases, fancy vessels, and other items used for religious purposes. Art experts consider these objects the finest works of bronze ever made.

Shang Vessel

1. What may have been one reason for the decline of the Shang civilization?
2. What did the Shang give to the world?

CHAPTER 5 REVIEW

SUMMARY

1. Eastern river valley civilizations began to develop in the Indus River valley about 2500 B.C. and in the Yellow River valley about 2000 B.C.

2. The first known people to establish a civilization in the Indus River valley were the Harappans.

3. Like other river valley peoples, the Harappans learned to control the river.

4. The Harappans are believed to have been the first people to produce cotton cloth, to bake bricks in ovens, and to construct sanitation systems.

5. The Harappan cities of Harappa and Mohenjo-daro are the oldest known planned communities.

6. No one knows for certain how Harappan civilization came to an end, but about 1200 B.C., Aryans moved into and took over the Indus River valley.

7. The earliest dynasty in China, the Hsia, probably started about 2000 B.C.

8. The first recorded Chinese dynasty, the Shang, came to power in 1523 B.C.

9. The Shang believed that their lives were influenced by spirits and ancestors.

10. The oldest known form of Chinese writing is found on Shang oracle bones.

11. The Shang produced many fine works of art made from bronze.

12. Shang civilization ended with the Chou invasion in 1028 B.C.

BUILDING VOCABULARY

1. *Identify the following:*
Indus River	Harappa	Aryans	Shang
Yellow River	Mohenjo-daro	Yü the Great	Chou
Harappans	Great Bath	Hsia	

2. *Define the following:*
self-sufficient	planned communities	natural resources	ancestors
fired	grid	dynasty	oracle bones
kilns	citadel	spirits	nobles

REVIEWING THE FACTS

1. How did the Harappans protect their cities from floods?

2. Why were oven-fired bricks more useful than sun-baked ones?

3. Why were Harappa and Mohenjo-daro healthy places in which to live?

4. Who took over the Indus River valley from the Harappans?

5. What evidence suggests the possibility of trade between Harappa and Sumer?

6. What is the Chinese legend of Yü the Great?

7. Why do the Chinese call the Yellow River "the great sorrow"?

8. Why were family ties important to the Shang people?

9. Why did the Shang kings use oracle bones?

10. Why was the gap between rich and poor a disadvantage to the Shang?

DISCUSSING IMPORTANT IDEAS

1. Why is so little known about the early life of people in the Indus River and Yellow River valleys?

2. Why did the peoples of eastern river valleys develop their ways of life without borrowing from other civilizations?

3. What do you think may happen to a civilization if it uses up its natural resources? Why?

4. What may happen to a civilization if different classes are not loyal to each other?

USING MAPS

Compare the maps on pages 68 and 74, and answer the following questions:

1. Which civilization—Harappan or Shang —is farther east? Farther south? How can you tell?

2. Which river—the Indus or the Yellow— is longer?

3. Which civilization—Harrapan or Shang —appears to lie in a more mountainous region?

4. Which civilization—Harappan or Shang —has a longer coastline?

UNIT 2 REVIEW

SUMMARY

1. Around 4000 B.C., civilization began developing along river banks in different parts of the world.
2. People learned how to control the rivers, depended mostly on farming for a living, built cities, and developed writing.
3. Each of the four earliest civilizations developed separately.
4. Each of the earliest civilizations contributed many things to later civilizations, including the wheel, the plow, surveying, sanitation, and medical treatments.

REVIEWING THE MAIN IDEAS

1. For each of the four civilizations in the unit, explain how the environment influenced the way the people lived.
2. Explain in what ways the four civilizations described in the unit were alike and in what ways they were different. Include the following:
   a. how the people earned their living
   b. how the people controlled the river
   c. materials used for building
   d. form of government
   e. religious beliefs
   f. importance of trade
   g. ways of traveling
   h. influence of other civilizations
   i. contributions to other civilizations
   j. reasons why the civilization ended

DEVELOPING SKILLS

In studying history, it is important to be able to read maps. A person can learn many things about a civilization from maps. They tell where a civilization is located and what natural features are found there. They tell where people built their cities. They tell about the distances between places and in what direction one place is from another.

Some maps tell other things, too. They tell whether the land is flat or hilly. They tell whether there is enough rainfall for farming or if the land is a desert where few crops will grow. They tell something about the climate —whether it is mostly hot or cold or has four seasons in the year. They tell about the natural resources.

Without maps, it would be hard to know as much about how people lived in the past.

This exercise is designed to give you practice in reading a map. Look at the map of the river valley civilizations on page 79, and answer the following questions.

1. On what continent were three of the four river valley civilizations located?
2. Into what body of water does the Nile River flow?
3. What two river valley civilizations could be reached directly by ships sailing on the Indian Ocean?
4. In what general direction does the Yellow River flow?

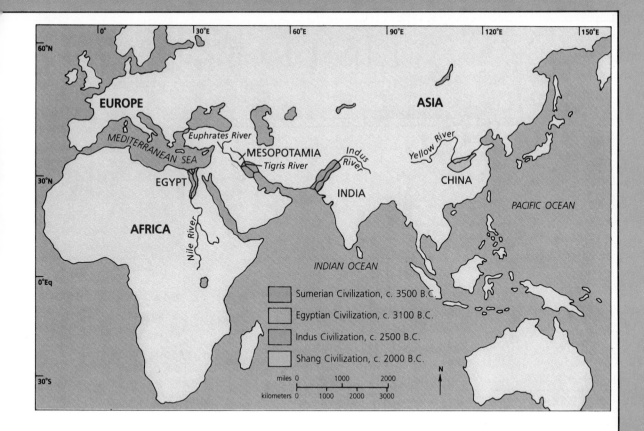

SUGGESTED UNIT PROJECTS

1. Write a letter that an Egyptian farmer working on a pyramid might send home.

2. Make a tablet out of clay, and put a line of cuneiform writing on it.

3. Prepare an advertisement for a Sumerian school. Include the courses offered and the jobs graduates can fill.

4. Describe the sights a Harappan farmer in Mohenjo-daro would find impressive.

5. Take the role of a Shang ruler, and have three classmates take the roles of a noble, a farmer, and a married woman. Discuss the similarities and differences in the way each person views life.

SUGGESTED READING

Hodges, Elizabeth Jamison. *A Song for Gilgamesh.* New York: Atheneum Publishers, 1971. Weaves the story of a Sumerian potter with Gilgamesh's journey to the Land of the Living.

Macauley, David. *Pyramid.* Boston: Houghton Mifflin Company, 1975. An illustrated account of the building of a pyramid combined with many facts about Egyptian culture.

Westwood, Jennifer. *Gilgamesh, and Other Babylonian Tales.* New York: Coward, McCann & Geoghegan, 1970. A retelling of ancient tales that captures the style and flavor of the originals.

UNIT 3

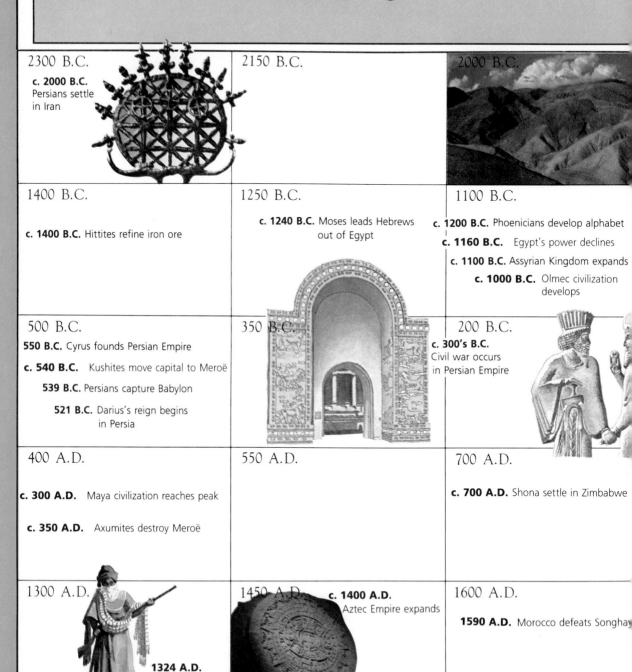

2300 B.C.

c. 2000 B.C. Persians settle in Iran

2150 B.C.

2000 B.C.

1400 B.C.

c. 1400 B.C. Hittites refine iron ore

1250 B.C.

c. 1240 B.C. Moses leads Hebrews out of Egypt

1100 B.C.

c. 1200 B.C. Phoenicians develop alphabet

c. 1160 B.C. Egypt's power declines

c. 1100 B.C. Assyrian Kingdom expands

c. 1000 B.C. Olmec civilization develops

500 B.C.

550 B.C. Cyrus founds Persian Empire

c. 540 B.C. Kushites move capital to Meroë

539 B.C. Persians capture Babylon

521 B.C. Darius's reign begins in Persia

350 B.C.

200 B.C.

c. 300's B.C. Civil war occurs in Persian Empire

400 A.D.

c. 300 A.D. Maya civilization reaches peak

c. 350 A.D. Axumites destroy Meroë

550 A.D.

700 A.D.

c. 700 A.D. Shona settle in Zimbabwe

1300 A.D.

1324 A.D. Mansa Musa begins pilgrimage

1450 A.D.

c. 1400 A.D. Aztec Empire expands

c. 1500 A.D. Inca and Aztec Empires destroyed

1600 A.D.

1590 A.D. Morocco defeats Songhay

IDEAS AND ARMIES

1850 B.C.	1700 B.C.	1550 B.C.
c. 1900 B.C. Abraham leads Hebrews into Canaan **c. 1830 B.C.** Phoenicians settle in northern Canaan **c. 1800 B.C.** Hebrews migrate to Egypt		

950 B.C.	800 B.C.	650 B.C.
c. 969 B.C. Phoenician trade increases **922 B.C.** Hebrews establish two kingdoms **800 B.C.** Assyrians conquer Mesopotamia		**612 B.C.** Ninevah falls to Chaldeans **c. 600 B.C.** Medes defeat Persians

50 B.C.	100 A.D.	250 A.D.

850 A.D.	1000 A.D.	1150 A.D.
 **c. 900 A.D.** Maya civilization disappears	 **1042 A.D.** Arabs defeat Ghanaians	**c. 1240 A.D.** Mali becomes power

1. WHAT WERE THE IMPORTANT CULTURAL AND RELIGIOUS CONTRIBUTIONS OF THE PHOENICIANS AND HEBREWS?
2. HOW DID THE RISE OF EMPIRES AFFECT THE ANCIENT PEOPLES OF THE MIDDLE EAST? OF AFRICA? OF THE AMERICAS?

From 1200 to 900 B.C., the Middle East went through a time of confusion. Egypt and Mesopotamia had lost much of their power and wealth. Many peoples were on the move. Bad harvests or the need for grazing land forced them to find new places to live.

As time passed, the wanderers founded permanent settlements and began to develop civilizations. The Phoenicians and Hebrews set up small kingdoms and learned to live in peace. They developed new ideas, like the alphabet and the belief in one god and in social justice, and became interested in trade. At first, trade took place among neighboring peoples. Then, seafarers began to trade with kingdoms far away. Not only were goods exchanged, but ideas as well. The Assyrians, Chaldeans, and Persians formed powerful empires that were interested in war as well as in trade and ideas.

Powerful empires also formed in Africa south of the Sahara Desert. However, the empires of Kush, Axum, Ghana, Mali, Songhay, Zimbabwe, and Kilwa were interested mostly in trade. Some traded salt and gold across the Sahara. Others served as middlemen between Africa and the Far East.

About 25,000 years ago, people began to migrate into the Americas from Asia across a land bridge that has since disappeared. After a time, these peoples developed farming, invented pottery and weaving, and developed civilizations. Some, like the Olmecs and the Maya, were interested in trade and religion. Others, like the Aztecs and the Inca, were interested in war.

CHAPTER 6
PHOENICIANS AND HEBREWS

At the eastern end of the Mediterranean Sea lies a piece of land shared today by Lebanon and Israel. In ancient times, it was the bridge that connected Egypt and Mesopotamia, and it was known as Canaan. Soldiers, shepherds, and merchants who passed through Canaan carried new ideas and goods between Egypt and Mesopotamia.

Two groups—the Phoenicians and the Hebrews—settled in Canaan and formed small kingdoms. The Phoenicians and the Hebrews were interested in trade and in learning. Through these peaceful activities, they made important contributions to later civilizations.

The Phoenicians

The Phoenicians lived in the northern part of Canaan. Most of what is known about them comes from the Bible, the writings of other ancient peoples, and the ruins of their cities and ships.

Two different groups formed the Phoenician people. One was the Canaanites, who came from the desert south and east of Canaan. The Canaanites were herders who wandered from pasture to pasture. The second group was the Aegeans, who came from the eastern Mediterranean near Greece. The Aegeans were traders and shipbuilders.

1. From what three sources do we get our knowledge about the Phoenicians?
2. Who were the Phoenicians? From where did they come?

THE GROWTH OF TRADE   By 1200 B.C., the Phoenicians had built cities and towns along a narrow strip of land between the mountains and the sea. Though the land was fertile, there was not enough to grow food for all the people. Therefore, many Phoenicians turned to the sea to make a living.

The mountains that overlooked Phoenicia were covered with cedar forests. The forests provided timber that the Phoenicians used to build strong, fast ships. The Phoenicians also provided timber to the people of other lands. They started out as coastal traders. In time, they became widely traveled merchant shippers who controlled the trade of the Mediterranean. They exchanged cedar logs, cloth, glass trinkets, and perfume for gold and other metals. Many Phoenician ships were traveling workshops. Sailors who were craftspeople carried their tools with them and worked on board the ships.

Phoenician sailors and explorers plotted their courses by the sun and the stars. They traveled to places where no one else dared to go. They brought the culture of the Middle East to unexplored areas of the western Mediterranean. Some experts believe that the Phoenicians actually sailed around the west coast of Africa to India. They may even have sailed across the Atlantic Ocean to the Americas 2,000 years before Columbus.

From their business dealings, the Phoenicians learned the value of making agreements. They used the same idea to keep peace with their larger, more powerful neighbors. They signed peace **treaties**, or agreements between states or countries. Under

PHOENICIAN TRADE
From the beginning of their history, the Phoenicians were sea-going traders. The forests of Phoenicia provided timber for strong, fast ships. Phoenician ships carried timber as well as trinkets and crafts.
Why was Phoenician trade important to the Mediterranean area?

the treaties, the Phoenicians promised to supply free shipments of goods. In exchange, the other countries agreed to guarantee Phoenician independence.

1. Why did the Phoenicians turn to trade to make a living?
2. Where did the Phoenicians trade?
3. How did the Phoenicians keep peace with their powerful neighbors?

THE CITIES OF PHOENICIA   Phoenicia never became a united country. Mountains separated one group of Phoenicians from another. The only contact was through narrow mountain passes or by sea. As a result, Phoenicia remained a collection of independent city-states. The largest of these were Tyre, Byblos, Beirut, and Sidon.

Though the people of all the city-states spoke the same language and practiced the same religion, they did not always get along. The search for more profit from trade led to jealousy and quarrels. Phoenicians called themselves by the name of their city-state. Only outsiders called them Phoenicians.

At first, each city-state was ruled by a king who also served as high priest. In time, rich merchant families forced the kings to share their power with councils of merchants. Soon, the councils were telling the kings what to do.

Most Phoenician cities had stone walls around them for protection. Behind the walls stood the family-owned shops of merchants and craftspeople. Shopkeepers displayed and sold their goods outside the shops. Since timber was plentiful, many Phoenicians were excellent carpenters and cabinetmakers. They also excelled at metalwork, a skill learned from the Egyptians and Mesopotamians.

Phoenician cities were very crowded. The streets were narrow, and the buildings were close together. Most buildings were made of stone or brick and had high, narrow doors,

---

PHOENICIAN CRAFTS

Many Phoenicians learned the craft skills of other lands and became artisans. The products of their workshops were known for their high quality. Vases (left) held water, oil, and wine. Colorful glass beads (right) were exchanged in trade for such metals as gold.

What kinds of crafts were made by the Phoenicians?

windows, columns, and tiled roofs. Some of the houses had roof gardens.

Outside the walls of the city stood the port. It was the center of activity. Ships docked to load and unload goods. Phoenician merchants kept records of shipments of papyrus, gold, and linen from Egypt, pottery from Mesopotamia, and copper and hides from Cyprus. The goods were stored in great warehouses until they went to market in Phoenicia or were shipped overseas.

The cities were important cloth-dyeing centers. The Phoenicians made an expensive purple dye that was in great demand. In fact, the name "Phoenician" means "the purple people." According to legend, a Phoenician god named Melqart was walking along the seashore with his girlfriend Tyrus and a dog. When the dog picked up a shellfish called a murex and bit into it, the dog's mouth turned purple. Tyrus liked the color so much that she said she would not marry Melqart unless he gave her a gown of that color. Melqart gave her the gown and started the dye-making trade in Phoenicia.

1. Why did Phoenicia remain a collection of city-states rather than become a united nation?
2. What were some of the features of a Phoenician city-state?
3. What is the legend of Melqart and Tyrus?

GODS AND GODDESSES   The Phoenicians believed in many gods who were closely linked to nature. Since they thought the gods met humans only on hills and under trees, they worshipped only in these places at first. Later, they built temples. Each temple contained a **foyer**, or lobby; a main hall; and a **holy of holies** where the image or sacred stone of a god was kept. Priests offered sacrifices of wine, perfume, animals, and humans at a nearby stone altar. Only priests could offer the sacrifices that strengthened the power of the gods and kept them friendly toward the people.

The Phoenicians believed in a life after death. At first, they buried their dead in clay urns. Later, under Egyptian influence, they embalmed bodies, wrapped them in linen, and placed them in stone coffins in hillside cemeteries.

1. How did the Phoenicians view their gods?
2. Where did the Phoenicians worship before they built temples? Why did they worship there?
3. What were some features of Phoenician temples?

CARTHAGE   Some Phoenician sailors and traders set up trading posts along the coast of North Africa. Other Phoenicians built **colonies**, or permanent settlements, in these areas. The settlements soon turned into cities.

The most famous of these cities was Carthage, founded in 814 B.C. in present-day Tunisia. Legend states that the city was founded by a Phoenician princess named Dido. Dido was the ruler of the city of Tyre. Her brother thought that he should rule. So, he killed Dido's husband and overthrew Dido. She fled to North Africa where she and her followers built Carthage.

Carthage soon became a Mediterranean power. It was a great trading city. Ships from Carthage may have traveled to the British Isles in search of tin, a metal highly valued by merchants.

1. Why did Phoenicians develop colonies along the coast of North Africa?
2. What did Dido do?
3. Why was Carthage important?

THE ALPHABET   Through trade, Phoenicians spread ideas as well as goods. Their most important gift was the idea of an

---

ALPHABETS

This chart shows how different alphabets developed from the Phoenician alphabet. The characters of the alphabets closely resemble each other. On whose system of writing did the Phoenicians base their alphabet?

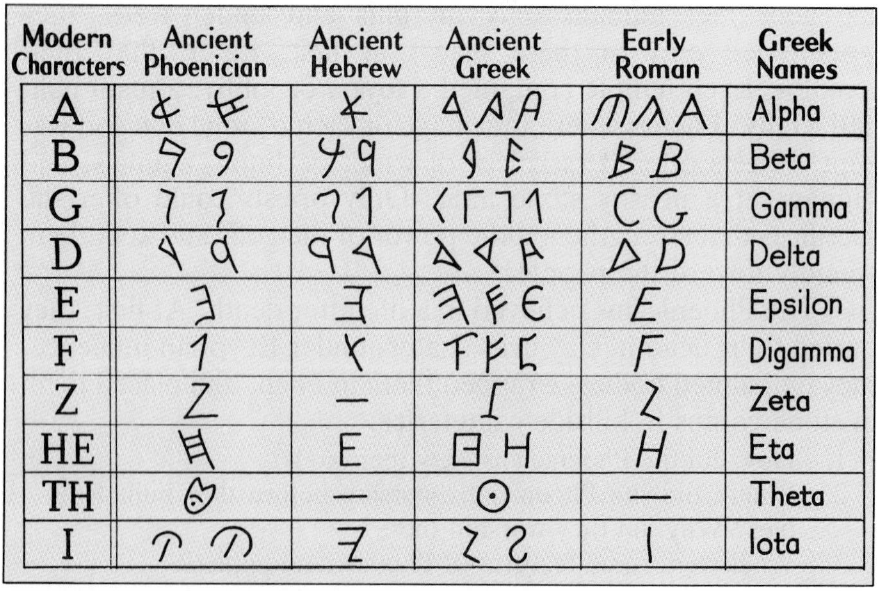

Modern Characters	Ancient Phoenician	Ancient Hebrew	Ancient Greek	Early Roman	Greek Names
A	⚹ ⚹	✳	⊿ Λ A	ጠ Λ A	Alpha
B	⁊ 9	⅋ ٩	໑ Ɛ	Ƀ B	Beta
G	⁊ ⁊	⁊⁊	⟨ Γ ⟩⟩	C G	Gamma
D	◁ ٩	٩ ◁	⊿ ⟨ ρ	⊿ D	Delta
E	ⴹ	ⴹ	ⴹ Ϝ Ɛ	E	Epsilon
F	⁊	Y	Ϝ Ϝ ⌐	F	Digamma
Z	Z	—	Ɩ	Z	Zeta
HE	⊟	E	⊟ H	H	Eta
TH	⊘	—	☉	—	Theta
I	↑ ⟨ᐢ	Ⴭ	⟨ ⟨	⟨	Iota

alphabet, or a series of symbols that stand for sounds. They did not invent the alphabet. They did, however, pass it on to other cultures.

At first, the Phoenicians used a system of picture writing. However, it was difficult to keep trade records this way. So, the Phoenicians looked for an easier writing system. They borrowed a simple version of Egyptian hieroglyphs from the people of the Canaanite towns that lay to the south. By the time the Canaanite system of writing reached Phoenicia, it had become an alphabet.

The Canaanite system of writing had 22 symbols, or letters, from which any number of words could be formed. Since it was easy to use, the Canaanite system provided the writing system Phoenician traders needed for keeping records.

The Phoenicians made the Canaanite alphabet their own. They carried it to Europe where the Greeks borrowed it and made a few changes. Later, the Romans borrowed it from the Greeks. Most western alphabets, including the English, are based on the Roman alphabet.

1. Who created the alphabet?
2. Why were the Phoenicians interested in the alphabet?

THE HEBREWS

Like the Phoenicians, the Hebrews were a small group among the peoples of the ancient Middle East. Yet, because of their religion, they have had a great influence on the world. Their religion still exists today. It is called Judaism.

The early Hebrews were traveling merchants. Leading long trains of donkeys loaded with goods, they walked from one trading post to the next. This habit of walking gave them their name. As they walked, their leather sandals and their donkeys' hooves kicked up dust that settled on them. Other people began to call them *Abiru*, or "dusty ones." Later, Abiru became "Hebrew."

The Hebrews followed a route that started from the city of Ur on the Euphrates River. There, Hebrew craftspeople made goods from gold, copper, and ivory. Hebrew merchants then stuffed the goods into bags, loaded them on donkeys, and started up the valley of the Tigris and Euphrates. At Harran, a city near the Turkish mountains, they exchanged the goods for silver. Sometimes, the merchants continued west and then south along

Hebrew Ivory Box

the Mediterranean coast to trade with Egyptian, Phoenician, and Cretan merchants.

1. Who were the Hebrews? How did they get their name?
2. Where did the Hebrews trade? What did they trade?

THE GOD OF ABRAHAM The story of the Hebrews and their god is written in the Bible. It states that Yahweh, or God, made an agreement with Abraham, the leader of the Hebrews. Abraham and his followers were to leave Ur and go to Canaan. There, they were to worship and obey Yahweh as the one true god. In exchange, Yahweh promised that they and their descendants could always live in Canaan.

During ancient times, most people believed in many gods. The gods behaved like humans, but were more powerful. The Hebrews, however, believed that Yahweh was different from humans. He did not get hungry or thirsty, marry, or have

PHOENICIA AND THE HEBREW KINGDOMS

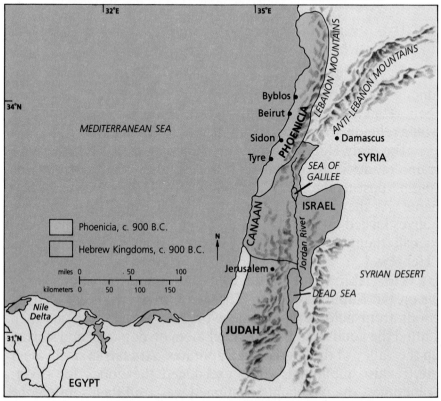

ABRAHAM

Abraham taught the Hebrews to worship and obey Yahweh as the one true god. In this seventeenth-century painting, Abraham greets a friendly ruler who welcomes him to Canaan.

What did the Hebrews do for a living in Canaan?

children. Although Yahweh was powerful and could do whatever He wanted, He did only what was just and right.

Abraham led the Hebrews to Canaan around 1900 B.C. In Canaan, instead of trading, they raised flocks of sheep and grew wheat, figs, and olives. They stayed in Canaan for about 100 years. While there, the Hebrews organized themselves into 12 tribes. Then, a drought came, and they went to Egypt where they could get food.

1. Who was the leader of the Hebrews?
2. What agreement did God make with Abraham?
3. Why did the Hebrews leave their homes in Canaan? Where did they go?

MOSES AND THE TEN COMMANDMENTS   About 600 years after the Hebrews settled in Egypt, they were forced into

MOSES AT MOUNT SINAI

At Mount Sinai, God gave Moses the Ten Commandments on two stone tablets. This fifteenth-century European painting shows Moses receiving the Commandments and bringing them to the Hebrews. He throws down the tablets in anger when he sees the people worshipping a golden calf.

Why did Moses protest the worship of the golden calf?

slavery. Years later, Moses, the Hebrew leader at the time, appeared before the pharaoh of Egypt. Moses told the pharaoh that Yahweh wanted the pharaoh to end Hebrew slavery and let the Hebrews leave Egypt. The pharaoh at first refused but later agreed. Moses then led the Hebrews out of Egypt. The pharaoh once again changed his mind, and he led his army in pursuit. But the Hebrews crossed the Red Sea and escaped into the Sinai Desert. They believed that Yahweh helped them in their **exodus**, or escape.

Life in the desert was hard, but Moses told the Hebrews not to give up. Moses led them to Mount Sinai. There, he climbed to the top of the mountain to receive a message from God. Yahweh told Moses that He would protect the Hebrews and lead them back to Canaan. In return, the Hebrews were to make a

covenant, or agreement, with Him. They were to promise to remain true to Him and obey certain laws, the most important of which became known as the Ten Commandments.

The Ten Commandments stated that the Hebrews were to give their loyalty only to Yahweh. They were not to worship other gods or idols. The Ten Commandments also taught that it was wrong to lie, steal, or kill, and that people should honor their parents and respect other people's property.

The Hebrews believed that God was just and that they too should be just. They did not try to influence the way God behaved by performing ceremonies or offering gifts. Instead, they used laws to try to influence the way people behaved. Their laws affected not only individuals but the whole community. The Hebrews believed in **social justice.** Everyone—male or female, rich or poor, neighbor or stranger—had a right to be treated fairly.

1. What did Moses do for the Hebrews?
2. What are the Ten Commandments?
3. What did the Hebrews believe? How did they try to influence the way people behaved?

THE PROMISED LAND   Moses died shortly before the Hebrews reached Canaan. The Hebrews were afraid that without a strong leader they would not be able to enter Canaan. The people who already lived there had built many walled cities on hilltops. Soldiers in lookout towers guarded the cities against enemy attack. But Joshua, a new leader, brought the Hebrews safely into the promised land.

Joshua

Once they had settled in Canaan, the Hebrews became farmers and shepherds. They copied the Canaanites' tools and borrowed their alphabet. Canaan was rocky and dry. There was little water. So, during the two months of the rainy season, the farmers collected and stored water in **cisterns**, or small caves or underground basins. During the dry season, they used what they had stored to irrigate their crops of olives, flax, barley, wheat, and grapes.

Most of the Hebrews lived in one-room houses. The room was divided in two, with one section slightly higher than the other. During the day, the Hebrews cooked and did other household chores in the lower level. At night, donkeys and goats bedded down there, while the family slept in the upper level.

HARVEST IN ANCIENT ISRAEL

Hebrew writers called Canaan "a land flowing with milk and honey." This area, however, had a dry climate and little water. The Hebrews had to work hard to farm the land. Here Hebrew farmers and their workers gather in the harvest. Why was Canaan known as the Promised Land?

The walls of the houses were made of mud-brick or stone plastered with mud and whitewashed. The floors were made of beaten clay. Wooden beams supported a flat, thatched roof that was covered with clay.

1. What did the Hebrews do after they settled in Canaan?
2. In what kind of houses did most Hebrews live?

KINGS   After Joshua died, the 12 Hebrew tribes split apart. Each tribe had its own leader, called a **judge**. The judges settled disputes and led troops into battle.

In time, the Hebrews decided they needed a king to unite them. A warrior-farmer named Saul became their first king. He ruled well for several years. Toward the end of his reign, however, he lost the people's support. When Saul died in battle, David became the new king.

David reunited the Hebrews and defeated the Canaanites. He captured a Canaanite fortress and established on the site Jerusalem, the capital of the Hebrew kingdom. A fine musician, David wrote many of the **psalms**, or songs, found in the Bible.

After David died, his son Solomon became king. Through trade and treaties with other lands, Solomon brought peace and made the Hebrew kingdom more powerful. He obtained timber from Phoenicia to build a huge temple in Jerusalem. Solomon's wealth and wisdom became known all through the Middle East.

Many Hebrews, however, were not happy with Solomon. They resented the harshness of his rule. They did not like paying high taxes or working on his building projects. After Solomon died, the Hebrews in the northern part of the country set up their own separate kingdom, called Israel. The southern kingdom, which was ruled from Jerusalem, became known as Judah. For nearly 200 years, the two kingdoms fought each other off and on. Gradually, Israel and Judah became weak enough for others to conquer.

David Playing Harp

1. What happened to the Hebrews after Joshua died?
2. Why did the Hebrews want a king? Who was their first king?
3. What did David do for the Hebrews? What did Solomon do?
4. Into what two kingdoms did the Hebrew nation split following Solomon's death?

THE PROPHETS　　**Prophets**, or persons claiming to have messages from God, appeared in the Hebrew kingdoms. They came from the cities and the villages. They were teachers, farmers, and shepherds. The prophets criticized the way the Hebrews were living. The rich were mistreating the poor, and government officials were accepting bribes. The prophets reminded the Hebrews of their duty to God and to one another. They warned the Hebrews that Yahweh would punish them if they did not return to His ways.

Some of the prophets added a new meaning to the laws of Moses. They taught that the idea of social justice was for everyone. They explained that Yahweh was not just the god of the Hebrews but the god of all peoples.

The people refused to listen to the prophets' warnings. Then, it was too late. Powerful neighbors took over the Hebrew kingdoms. After 722 B.C., the Israelites, the people of the northern kingdom, disappeared. Though the people of Judah survived, most of them were forced to move to Babylon in 586 B.C.

While in Babylon, the people of Judah, who were then known as Jews, made changes in their religion. Having lost the great temple at Jerusalem, they had to find some other way to worship God. They began meeting in small groups on the **sabbath**, or day of rest, to pray and to talk about their religion and their history. From these meetings came the idea of a **synagogue**, or a community of Jews who gather together to practice their religion. The Jews wrote down their laws, sayings,

HEBREW PROPHETS

Name	Teachings
Elijah c. 850 B.C.	Everyone should behave in a moral way.
Amos c. 755 B.C.	Prayers and sacrifices do not make up for bad deeds. Behaving justly is much more important than ritual.
Hosea 745–730 B.C.	God is a god of love and compassion who loves His people the way a father loves his children. God suffers when people turn from Him and do not follow His commandments.
Isaiah of Jerusalem 740–701 B.C.	People can have peace and prosperity only if they carry out God's will. The future depends on how justly one behaves in the present.
Micah 714–700 B.C.	Both rich and poor have to obey God's laws. It is important to "do justly, love mercy, and walk humbly with thy God."
Jeremiah 626–587 B.C.	Suffering is the result of wickedness. God will make a new covenant with the Jews in the future.
Ezekiel 593–571 B.C.	People are responsible for their own behavior.
Isaiah of Babylon c. 545 B.C.	God is the god of all people. God will free Israel and lead it back to the promised land.

DEAD SEA SCROLLS

The Dead Sea Scrolls are ancient writings that were found in caves near the Dead Sea. Experts believe that most of the manuscripts were written during the period from about 100 B.C. to about 70 A.D. by a Jewish religious sect.
What did the Jews write about in their scrolls?

and stories of the past on **scrolls**, or long rolls of parchment. The study of these sacred writings led the Jews to value learning. Their **rabbis**, or teachers, became important leaders.

The Jews spent 70 years in Babylon before they were allowed to return to their homeland. Not all of them wanted to go. Those who did return rebuilt Jerusalem and the temple. Under a scribe named Ezra, they wrote down the laws of Moses in five books called the **Torah**, or the Law. Other writings were added later to make the Old Testament of the Bible.

1. Who were the prophets? What did they tell the Hebrew people?
2. What happened to the Hebrews who did not heed the prophets' warnings?
3. What changes did the Jews make in their religion while they were in Babylon?

MAJOR CONTRIBUTIONS   The Hebrews were the first people to believe in one god. At first, they believed that God was concerned only about them. They expected other people to worship many gods. Later, some of the prophets claimed that God cared about all peoples and all nations.

The Hebrews were the first to believe in a just god. As a result, they believed that individuals and society should likewise be just. Their laws were designed to teach people to treat one another fairly.

1. What major new ideas did the Hebrews contribute to later civilizations?
2. What did Hebrews believe was the purpose of laws?

CHAPTER 6 REVIEW

SUMMARY

1. Phoenician civilization began to develop about 1830 B.C.
2. Since Phoenicia's farmland was limited, many Phoenicians turned to the sea to make a living.
3. Phoenicia became well known for its cedar and an expensive purple dye.
4. The Phoenicians had many gods.
5. One of the most important Phoenician contributions to later civilizations is the alphabet, which they borrowed about 1200 B.C. and passed along.
6. The Phoenicians established many colonies along the North African coast, the most important of which was Carthage, founded in 814 B.C.
7. Around 1900 B.C., Abraham led the Hebrews from the city of Ur into the land of Canaan.
8. According to the Bible, God made an agreement with Abraham whereby the Hebrews could always live in Canaan if they would worship Him alone as the one true god.
9. After a drought hit Canaan around 1800 B.C., the Hebrews moved to Egypt.
10. About 1200 B.C., the Hebrews, who had been enslaved by the Egyptians, escaped and under Moses' leadership, made a new covenant with God, promising to obey the Ten Commandments and other laws.
11. The Hebrews settled once again in Canaan and after a while chose a king to rule over them.
12. In 922 B.C., the Hebrew kingdom split into the kingdoms of Israel and Judah, both of which were eventually conquered by powerful neighbors.
13. The Hebrews' major contribution to later civilizations was the belief in one just god rather than many gods.

BUILDING VOCABULARY

1. *Identify the following:*

Canaan	Judaism	Ten Commandments	Solomon
Tyre	Abiru	Joshua	Israel
Melqart	Yahweh	Saul	Judah
Tyrus	Abraham	David	Ezra
Carthage	Moses	Jerusalem	Torah
Dido			

2. *Define the following:*

treaties	alphabet	cisterns	sabbath
foyer	exodus	judge	synagogue
holy of holies	covenant	psalms	scrolls
colonies	social justice	prophets	rabbis

REVIEWING THE FACTS

1. Why were the Phoenicians successful long-distance sailors?
2. What two things did the Phoenicians get from their business dealings?
3. Why were many Phoenicians good carpenters and cabinetmakers?
4. Why were the Phoenicians called "the purple people"?
5. What did the Phoenicians learn from the Egyptians?
6. Why did God promise the land of Canaan to the Hebrews?
7. Why did the Hebrews believe in social justice?
8. Why were many Hebrews unhappy with King Solomon?
9. Why did the Jews make changes in their religion while they were in Babylon?
10. What led the Jews to place a high value on learning?

DISCUSSING IMPORTANT IDEAS

1. How can people who have very limited natural resources still manage to earn a living?
2. Why were language and religion by themselves not enough to unify the Phoenician people?
3. Why is the alphabet a major contribution to civilization?
4. How does the idea that God is just affect the way in which people behave?
5. Explain the meaning of the phrase, "do justly, love mercy, and walk humbly with thy God."
6. Do you think it is all right for people to make changes in their religious beliefs and practices? Why or why not?

USING MAPS

Study the map on page 90, and answer the following questions:

1. What four kingdoms are shown in color?
2. Which kingdom is farthest south?
3. Which kingdoms are inland and which border the Mediterranean Sea?
4. How far north is the city of Tyre from the city of Jerusalem?
5. Which Phoenician city is directly west of Damascus?
6. Between what bodies of water does the Jordan River lie?
7. Which kingdom appears to be most mountainous? How can you tell?

HINDUISM

The caste system divided people into four main groups. The highest caste was made up of priests and teachers. Next came rulers and warriors; then merchants; **artisans,** or skilled workers; and unskilled workers.

Lowest of all people were the **outcasts**, or those who existed outside the caste system. They were also called **untouchables**. The untouchables had to work at the dirtiest jobs, such as handling dead animals and sweeping the streets. Because they worked with dirt and blood, they were thought to be impure. They were forbidden to touch caste members.

The caste system included strict rules about every part of daily life. Each per-

Hinduism is the major religion of India. It developed over thousands of years from the beliefs and practices of many different peoples.

Hinduism teaches that each person is born into a **caste**, or social group. The idea of caste began about 1500 B.C. At that time, a dark-skinned people from northern India, the Dravidians, were conquered by the Aryans. The Aryans set up a caste system that limited contact between themselves and the Dravidians.

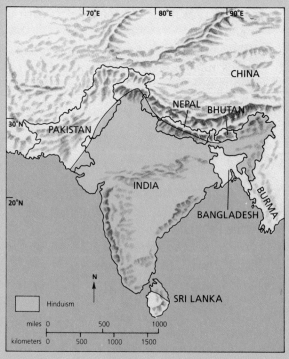

son's job was determined by his or her caste. Members of one caste could not marry, eat with, or work with members of another caste.

Hindus were willing to follow the rules of caste because of their belief in **reincarnation**, or rebirth of the soul into a new body. They believed that each person would be reborn again and again until that person reached spiritual perfection. The Hindus thought that a person's caste was a reward or punishment for the way he or she lived in a past life. Those who led a good, dutiful life might be reborn into a higher caste. Those who lived a bad life might be reborn into a lower caste, or even into the body of an animal.

The Hindus worshipped many gods. The three main gods were Brahma, the Creator; Vishnu, the Preserver; and Shiva, the Destroyer. Together, the three gods could be thought of as one god, called Brahman.

The Hindus made beautiful statues of their gods to worship at home and in temples. Brahma is shown with four heads to represent his great wisdom and the four quarters of the earth. Shiva is often shown as Lord of the Dance or with his wife Uma and his divine bull Nandi. Vishnu is usually seen as the hero of Indian **epics**, or heroic poems.

1. How did the caste system begin?
2. How did the caste system influence the daily life of Hindus?
3. How did the belief in reincarnation support the caste system?

CHAPTER 7
MILITARY EMPIRES

While the Phoenicians and Hebrews were developing their civilizations, empires rose and fell in Mesopotamia. These empires were created by the Assyrians, Chaldeans, and Persians. None of these peoples was content to stay where its civilization began. They raised powerful armies and expanded into neighboring lands. They developed new ways of ruling and increased trade. Thus, they spread their ideas and customs.

THE ASSYRIANS

About 1,000 years after Hammurabi ruled, a people called the Assyrians rose to power in Mesopotamia. Their country,

Assyria, lay in the upper part of the Tigris River valley. The Assyrians spoke the same language and used the same writing system as the Babylonians.

The Assyrians were warriors. Experts believe their liking for war was influenced by geography. Assyria's rolling hills and rain-watered valleys did not provide protection against invaders. Assyrian shepherds and farmers had to learn to fight to survive. In time, fighting became a way of life.

The Assyrians built up a powerful army. By 1100 B.C., they had defeated their neighboring enemies. By 800 B.C., they were strong enough to take over cities, trading routes, and fortresses throughout Mesopotamia.

1. Where did the Assyrians live?
2. How did geography influence the Assyrian way of life?

THE ASSYRIAN ARMY The Assyrian army was well-organized. It was divided into **infantries**, or groups of foot soldiers, armed with shields, helmets, spears, and daggers. The army also had units of charioteers, cavalry, and archers.

At first, the Assyrians fought only during the summer months when they did not have to be concerned about planting or harvesting crops. Later, as they took over more land,

---

ASSYRIAN WARFARE
Assyrian kings often celebrated their victories by decorating palaces and temples with scenes of warfare. This ancient painting shows enemy soldiers being killed. How was the Assyrian Army organized?

soldiering became a year-round job. When the Assyrians needed more soldiers, they hired them from other places or forced the people they had conquered to serve.

Assyrian power was due partly to Assyrian weapons. The weapons, which were made of iron, were harder and stronger than weapons made of copper or tin. Iron had been used in the Middle East for many centuries. But until about 1400 B.C., it was too soft to be made into weapons. Then, a people called Hittites developed the process of **smelting**. They heated the iron ore, hammered out its impurities, and rapidly cooled it. This made the iron stronger and harder. The Assyrians borrowed the skill of smelting from the Hittites.

The Assyrians were cruel warriors. For several hundred years, their armies spread death and destruction throughout the Middle East. They were especially skilled in attacking cities. They tunneled under the walls or climbed over them on ladders. They used beams mounted on movable platforms to ram holes through city gates. Once they captured a city, they set fire to its buildings and carried away its citizens and goods.

Anyone who resisted Assyrian rule was punished. Those who did not resist had to pay heavy taxes. The Assyrians also found a way to conquer people without fighting. They spread stories of their cruelty. People got scared and surrendered.

1. What were the strengths of the Assyrian army?
2. Why were the Assyrians feared?

KINGS AND GOVERNMENT   Assyria's kings were strong leaders. They had to be to rule an empire that extended from the Persian Gulf in the East to the Nile Valley in the West. Assyrian kings spent much of their time fighting battles and punishing enemies. But they were also involved in such peaceful activities as building cities and palaces. A great Assyrian king, Ashurbanipal, created one of the world's first libraries. It contained 25,000 tablets of hymns, stories, and biographies.

The Assyrian kings had to control many peoples spread over a large area. To do this, they divided the empire into provinces. They then chose officials to govern the provinces. The officials collected taxes and made certain the king's laws were obeyed.

The provinces were linked by a system of roads. Although only the roads near major cities were paved, all were level enough for carts and chariots to travel on. Over the roads moved

Assyrian Official

the trade of the empire. Government soldiers were posted at stations to protect traders from bandits. Messengers on government business used the stations to rest and change horses.

In time, the empire became too large to govern. After Ashurbanipal died, various conquered peoples worked to end Assyrian rule. One group was the Chaldeans. In 612 B.C., they captured Nineveh, the Assyrian capital. The Assyrian Empire crumbled shortly after.

1. What was the role of the Assyrian kings?
2. Why were roads important to the Assyrians?
3. Why did the Assyrian Empire fall?

THE CHALDEANS

Like the Assyrians, the Chaldeans were warriors who conquered many different peoples. Under their king Nebuchadnezzar, they extended their empire's boundaries as far west as

THE ASSYRIAN AND CHALDEAN EMPIRES

Assyrian Empire, c. 665 B.C.

Chaldean Empire, c. 570 B.C.

Syria and Palestine. The Chaldeans called themselves Babylonians. They built a new capital at Babylon in which nearly 1 million people lived.

Babylon was the world's richest city up to that time. It had its own police force and postal system. The huge brick walls that encircled the city were so wide that two chariots could pass on the road on top of them. Archers guarded the approaches to the city from towers built into the walls.

In the center of the city stood palaces and temples. A huge ziggurat reached more than 300 feet, or over 90 meters, into the sky. Its gold roof could be seen for miles when the sun shone.

The richness of the ziggurat was equaled by that of the king's palace. The palace had "hanging gardens." The gardens consisted of a series of terraces planted with large trees and masses of flowering vines and shrubs, all of which seemed to hang in mid-air. Nebuchadnezzar built the gardens for his wife.

BABYLON'S HANGING GARDENS
The city of Babylon had beautiful walls, buildings, and parks. Its "hanging gardens" were known as one of the Seven Wonders of the Ancient World.
What do the "hanging gardens" reveal about life in Babylon?

To please the people, Nebuchadnezzar built a special street near the palace. It was paved with limestone and marble and lined by walls of blue glazed tile. Each spring, thousands of pilgrims crowded into Babylon to watch the gold statue of the god Marduk being wheeled along the street. The people believed that the procession would make their crops grow and help keep peace in the empire.

Babylonian Queen

Outside the center of Babylon were houses and marketplaces. There, craftspeople made pottery, cloth, and baskets, which they sold to passing **caravans**, or groups of traveling merchants. Traders came to the marketplace from as far away as India and Egypt. Trade helped make Babylon rich.

In addition to being a trade center, Babylon was also a center of science. Chaldean astronomers believed that changes in the heavens revealed the plans of the gods. So, they studied the stars, the planets, and the moon. They recorded what they learned. Once they understood the movement of heavenly bodies, they made maps that showed the position of the planets and the phases of the moon. They developed one of the first sundials, and they were the first to have a seven-day week.

Babylon was the center of a great civilization for many years. But as time passed, the Chaldeans began to lose their power. They found it hard to control the peoples they had conquered. Some years, crops were poor and trade was slow. Then, in 539 B.C., Persians from the mountains to the northeast captured Babylon. Mesopotamia became just another part of the Persian Empire.

1. What were some of the features of Babylon?
2. Why was Babylon such an important city?
3. What led to the fall of the Chaldeans?

THE PERSIANS

Originally, the Persians were part of the people known as the Aryans, who were cattle herders from the grasslands of central Asia. About 2000 B.C., however, the Persians began to separate from other Aryans. The Persians may have been searching for new pastures for their cattle. More likely, they were drawn farther west by reports of the rich civilizations in Mesopotamia and Egypt. They finally settled on a high plain between the Persian Gulf and the Caspian Sea, where they established Persia. Today, this region is called Iran, or "the land of the Aryans." Modern Persians are Iranians.

The Persians lived peacefully in the highlands for over 1,000 years. They divided most of the country into large farms owned by nobles. The nobles spent most of their time riding horses and practicing archery. Their farms were worked by laborers.

There was little water on the hot plain. Farmers depended on streams that came down from the mountains. The farmers dug underground tunnels from the springs to the fields. The tunnels kept the water from evaporating in the hot sun. With the water, the farmers were able to grow wheat and barley and to pasture flocks of sheep.

1. Where did the Persians come from? Where did they settle?
2. How did Persian farmers water the land?

ARMY AND EMPIRE   About 600 B.C., the Persians were conquered by the Medes, a neighboring people. But the Medes were soon overthrown by the Persians under King Cyrus. Cyrus then organized an army to conquer new territory. The army grew until it numbered in the hundreds of thousands. Its officers were Persians, while its soldiers were either Persians or conquered peoples.

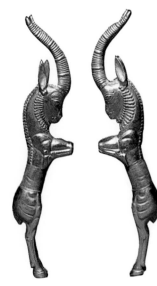

Persian Metalwork

The best fighters in the Persian army were the Immortals. They earned this name because their number never fell below 10,000. When an Immortal became sick, was wounded, or died, another soldier took his place. The Immortals had the honor of leading the army into battle.

Within a short time, the Persians ruled an empire that stretched from Egypt to India. The Persians were mild rulers who allowed their subjects to keep their own language, religion, and laws. The Persians believed that loyalty could be won more easily with fairness than with fear or force. They wanted their subjects to pay taxes and to produce goods for trade. They felt these things would not be done if those under their rule were treated badly.

One of the strongest Persian kings was Darius. He wanted a monument to honor his military victories. So, he brought craftspeople from many lands to build a grand palace-fortress-treasury in the capital city of Persepolis. Buildings with many columns were constructed on giant stone terraces. In the gateways, workers carved figures that were half human and half

DECREE OF CYRUS

Cyrus was a wise and generous ruler who treated conquered peoples kindly. So that the people would know his wishes, Cyrus had his decrees carved on stone and sent throughout the Persian Empire.

How far did the Persian Empire extend at the time of Cyrus?

beast. Persepolis became the most magnificent city in the empire.

The king did not govern the empire alone. There were many officials to carry out his orders. They all spoke Aramaic, the language used by Middle Eastern merchants.

The king chose a governor, a secretary, and a general for each of the 20 **satrapies**, or provinces, of the empire. In each province, the three officials collected taxes of gold, silver, sheep, horses, wheat, and spices and sent them to the royal treasury in Persepolis. The officials also settled local quarrels and protected the people against bandits. Each reported separately to the king. This forced them to be honest. If one official was keeping taxes or behaving badly, the others were sure to tell. The king would then remove the dishonest official from office.

Another group of officials was the inspectors. Called "The Eyes and Ears of the King," they traveled all over the empire. They decided if people could afford to pay their taxes. They also checked on rumors of possible rebellion. The inspectors never warned any provincial official they were coming. This made officials careful about doing a good job.

The last group of officials was the judges. They made sure that the king's laws were carried out properly.

1. How did the Immortals earn their name?
2. How did the Persians treat the peoples they conquered?

FAMILY LIFE   Persians lived in houses with pointed roofs and porches that faced the sun. Poor families had one-room houses. Noble families had houses with one set of rooms for men and another for women and children.

Persian families were large. Fathers ruled their families in much the same way the king ruled the empire. A father's word was law. Poor children worked with their parents. The children of nobles were cared for by their mothers until they were five years old. Then, they were raised by slaves. Often, they did not see their fathers until they reached adulthood. Boys were trained to ride horses, to draw a bow, and to speak the truth. Girls were trained to run households and raise children.

Rich women lived very sheltered lives. They spent most of their time at home apart from the men. If they had to leave the house, they stepped into a closed **litter**, or a carriage without wheels that was carried by servants. Poor women had more freedom, but they had to work hard.

Persian Tomb

1. What was life like in Persian families?
2. What were Persian boys taught? What were Persian girls taught?

RELIGION   At first, the Persians worshipped many gods. About 570 B.C., a religious leader named Zoroaster told the Persians about two gods. One god, Ahura Mazda, was wise and truthful. He created all good things in the world. The other god, Ahriman, made all evil things in the world. Ahura Mazda and Ahriman were at war with each other all of the time.

Zoroaster said that human beings had to decide which god they would support. Zoroaster then listed the good and bad deeds a person had performed. Good deeds were keeping one's word, giving to the poor, working the land, obeying the king, and treating others well. Bad deeds included being lazy, proud, or greedy. Zoroaster could tell from the list which god a person had chosen. He believed that in the end Ahura Mazda would defeat Ahriman. People who supported Ahura Mazda would enjoy happiness after death. Those who supported Ahriman would be punished.

1. According to Zoroaster, how did a good person behave? What was such a person's reward?
2. According to Zoroaster, how did a bad person behave? What happened to such a person?

TRADE   The Persians thought they should be warriors, farmers, or shepherds. They refused to become traders. They believed that trade forced people to lie, cheat, and be greedy. They did, however, encourage trade among all of the peoples they conquered.

The Persians improved and expanded the system of roads begun by the Assyrians. One road, the Royal Road, ran more than 1,600 miles, or over 2,500 kilometers. A journey that took

THE PERSIAN EMPIRE

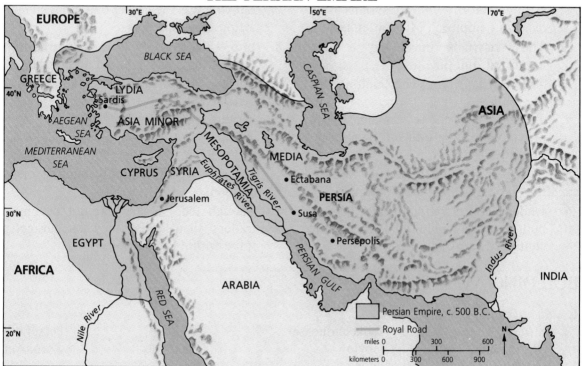

three months before the Royal Road was built took only 15 days after it was built. The Persians also opened a caravan route to China. Silk was first brought to the West along this route.

The Persians spread the idea of using coins for money. The first known coins had been made in Lydia, a tiny kingdom in Asia Minor bordering on the Aegean Sea. After conquering Lydia, the Persian king decided to use gold coins in his empire. This helped to increase trade. It also changed the nature of trade. Merchants who had sold only costly goods began to sell everyday, cheaper things as well. They sold chickens, dried fish, furniture, clothing, and pots and pans. Since people could get more goods, they began to live better than they had before.

1. What was the Persian attitude toward trade?
2. In what ways did the Persians contribute to the growth of trade within their empire?

CHAPTER 7 REVIEW

SUMMARY

1. Around 800 B.C., the Assyrians established an empire in Mesopotamia.
2. The Assyrians developed a well-organized, full-time army.
3. The Assyrians borrowed smelting from the Hittites.
4. The Assyrian Empire was divided into provinces that were linked by a system of roads.
5. In 612 B.C., the Chaldeans captured the Assyrian capital of Nineveh.
6. Under Nebuchadnezzar, the Chaldeans built a new capital at Babylon that contained many wonders.
7. Babylon was the center of a great civilization for many years.
8. In 539 B.C., Babylon was captured by the Persians, who created an empire.
9. The Persians divided their empire into provinces and governed it well through various groups of officials.
10. About 570 B.C., Zoroaster taught a new religion in which the forces of good and evil were constantly fighting one another.
11. Though the Persians did not become traders themselves, they encouraged trade within their empire.

BUILDING VOCABULARY

1. *Identify the following:*

Hittites	Nebuchadnezzar	Cyrus	Persepolis
Ashurbanipal	Babylon	Immortals	Zoroaster
Nineveh	Medes	Darius	Lydia

2. *Define the following:*

infantries   caravans   satrapies   litter
smelting

REVIEWING THE FACTS

1. What do experts believe influenced the Assyrians to become warriors?
2. What did the Assyrians learn from the Hittites?
3. How were the Assyrians able to conquer people without fighting?
4. What did Ashurbanipal do?
5. Why did the Babylonians wheel a statue of Marduk through the streets?
6. Who were "The Eyes and Ears of the King" and what did they do?
7. What good deeds were Persians expected to perform?
8. Why did the Persians refuse to become traders?
9. What did the Persians get from China?
10. What did the Persians learn from the Lydians?

DISCUSSING IMPORTANT IDEAS

1. What things helped the Assyrians to conquer their neighbors?
2. Why is a good system of transportation important?
3. Would you have enjoyed living in Babylon? Why or why not?
4. How did Zoroaster explain the existence of good and evil in the world?
5. Do you think the Persians were good rulers? Why or why not?
6. Would you support the Persian attitude toward trade? Why or why not?

USING MAPS

Compare the maps on pages 105 and 111, and answer the following questions:

1. What is the oldest empire shown?
2. In which empire was Nineveh?
3. Of the empires shown, which was the largest? How can you tell?
4. Which of the empires extended the farthest west?
5. About how far was it from Sardis to Susa along the Royal Road?

CHAPTER 8
AFRICA AND THE AMERICAS

Some civilizations developed in the Middle East. Others developed in Africa south of the Sahara Desert and in the Americas. Like the Middle Eastern civilizations, those of sub-Saharan Africa and the Americas were of two kinds. One kind was interested in trade and ideas. The other was interested in war.

ANCIENT AFRICAN KINGDOMS

Other civilizations besides Egypt flourished in ancient Africa. Less is known about them than about Egypt. However, archaeologists have discovered enough remains to be able to tell what African civilizations were like.

KUSH   The first of these civilizations was Kush. It lay south of Egypt on the Nile River in present-day Sudan. Its history began about 2000 B.C. At that time, the Kushites were **nomadic**, or wandering, cattle herders. They grazed long-horned cattle on the **savannah**, or grassy plain.

During the New Kingdom, Egyptian armies conquered Kush. Kush remained part of Egypt for almost 500 years. Over time, the Kushites learned many things from the Egyptians. They learned to worship the god Amen-Re. They learned how to work copper and bronze. And they adapted Egyptian hieroglyphs to their own language.

About 1160 B.C., Egypt's power began to decline. In time, the Kushites won back their independence. They set up a capital at Napata. From Napata, they sent caravans into Egypt. These caravans carried gold, ivory, a black wood called **ebony**, and other things to trade.

Ebony Art

About 750 B.C., the Kushite king Kashta set out to conquer Egypt. He led his cavalry into Egypt and took some territory. His son Piankhy completed the conquest and founded a dynasty that ruled Egypt for 70 years. However, during the seventh century B.C., the Assyrians invaded Egypt. Armed with iron weapons, they drove the Kushites back up the Nile.

Despite their losses, the Kushites gained something from the Assyrians. They learned the secret of iron-smelting. Soon, Kushite farmers, using iron hoes, could grow large amounts of grain. Kushite blacksmiths could fashion iron knives and spears, which they exchanged for cotton textiles and other goods from India, Arabia, and China. Kush became a great trading nation.

Around 540 B.C., the Kushites moved their capital to Meroë. The city was on the Nile, which provided an avenue for trade and transportation. Nearby were large deposits of iron ore and trees to fuel smelting furnaces. Meroë also lay in the center of good grazing land. Because the area received enough rain, its farms and pastures were not limited to the banks of the river.

KUSHITE PYRAMIDS
The Kushites copied many elements of Egyptian art, language, and religion. The pyramids near the cities of Meroë and Napata are imitations of Egyptian pyramids. The Kushite pyramids are smaller, however, and have more steeply sloped sides. What happened to the city of Meroë?

In Meroë, there was a huge temple dedicated to Amen-Re, with a long avenue of stone rams leading to its entrance. Sandstone palaces and houses of red brick filled the city. Both palaces and houses had a number of rooms around an open courtyard. The walls of the buildings were tiled in blue and yellow or covered with paintings. Small pyramids stood in the royal cemetery. And the smelting furnaces poured forth huge columns of smoke. Around the furnaces lay heaps of shiny black **slag**, or waste.

Kush remained a great trading country for some 600 years. Then, it began to decline. As it declined, another kingdom rose to take its place. This was Axum in present-day Ethiopia. About 350 A.D., Axumite armies burned Meroë to the ground.

1. What did the Kushites learn from the Egyptians?
2. Why did the Kushites choose Meroë as their capital?

AXUM   Like Kush, Axum was a trading country. Through ports on the Red Sea, Axumite merchants served as middlemen for nations on the Mediterranean and in the Far East. They imported silks, spices, and elephants from India. They exported gold, ivory, and slaves from Africa. Arabs who took part in this trade crossed the Red Sea and settled beside local farmers and herders. Jewish and Greek merchants also settled in Axum.

It was most likely the Greeks who brought Christianity to Axum. King Ezana, whose armies had destroyed Meroë, converted to Christianity in 324 A.D. This heritage was passed down to the present day.

The Axumites achieved much. They developed a writing system. They learned to farm on **terraces**, or raised pieces of land. They minted gold coins and built stone monuments 60 feet, or 18.3 meters, tall.

Over time, Axum's power as a trading country began to decline. This was because other kingdoms began to interfere with Axum's trade. After Arab armies swept across North Africa in the seventh century A.D., the Axumites retreated toward the interior of their country. There, they lived in isolation for more than 1,000 years.

1. For what two things is Ezana famous?
2. What were some achievements of the Axumites?

THE MIDDLE KINGDOMS OF AFRICA

In West Africa, several large trading kingdoms flourished after 400 A.D. Their rise was aided by the knowledge of iron-smelting. This was most likely brought to West Africa by refugees from Kush. The strength of these kingdoms was maintained by the trade in gold and salt.

GHANA   The first of these kingdoms was Ghana. According to legend, Ghana was founded about 200 A.D. Around 350 A.D., the Ghanians learned how to smelt iron. With iron swords and lances, Ghanian warriors expanded the boundaries of their country. They also established control over West Africa's major trade routes.

Along the trade routes, goods were carried by caravans of camels or donkeys. The most important goods were salt and gold. Caravans carried salt south from Taghaza in present-day

Algeria. They returned north with gold from Wangara, an area southwest of Ghana.

Ghanian merchants and Wangara gold miners used a trading technique called **"silent barter."** Ghanian merchants would travel to a trading site along a river in Wangara. They would place salt and other goods on the ground and beat drums to signal the gold miners. Then, they would withdraw. Next, the gold miners would appear, look at the goods, and leave some gold. Then, they would withdraw. If the Ghanians thought they had received enough gold, they would take it and leave. If not, they would withdraw and wait for the miners to leave more gold. When the exchange was over, the Ghanians traded the gold to merchants from North Africa. Often, the gold was shipped to Europe and Asia for sale.

Only gold dust could be used in trade. **Nuggets**, or pieces of gold, became the property of the king, who controlled the economy. According to legend, one nugget was so heavy that it served as a hitching post for the king's horses.

In 1042 A.D., Arabs from North Africa started a war against Ghana. They destroyed the capital and made the Ghanaians pay them tribute. Ghana managed to regain its independence but was not strong enough to survive.

Gold Nugget

1. What were the two most important goods in West African trade?
2. What became of Ghana?

MALI   By 1240 A.D., Ghana was a part of Mali, the second large trading kingdom in West Africa. The king of Mali, whose army had conquered Ghana, was Sundiata Keita, or "Hungering Lion."

Sundiata Keita did several things to make his kingdom strong. He reestablished the salt-gold trade, which the Arabs had disrupted. He organized a permanent army. He divided the kingdom into provinces, each headed by a general. The generals were supposed to keep the peace and see that there was enough food for the people. To cement relations with different groups in the kingdom, he moved his capital from place to place.

Sundiata Keita wanted to impress the people with his power. So, when he appeared in public, trumpeters announced his arrival. He sat on an ebony throne under an arch made from large elephant tusks. He never spoke directly to the people. Instead, requests were answered by servants standing at the foot of the stairs leading to the throne.

One of the most famous kings of Mali was Mansa Musa I, or King Moses I. One reason Mansa Musa was famous was because of a **pilgrimage**, or religious journey, he made to Arabia in 1324–25. It took more than 14 months to cover the 3,000 miles, or 4,800 kilometers. Some 12,000 servants traveled with the king. Each carried a four-pound, or 1.8-kilogram, gold bar. Mansa Musa gave many of these bars to poor people he met along the way. As a result of this trip, news of Mansa Musa and Mali reached as far as Europe.

In Arabia, Mansa Musa met a Spanish architect whom he brought back to Mali. There, the architect built a university in the trading city of Timbuktu. It became a great center of learning and had students from Europe, Asia, and Africa.

TIMBUKTU

From the 1200's to the 1500's, Timbuktu was one of the richest commercial cities of Africa and a center of Muslim learning. Goods from North Africa were exchanged there for products from South and West Africa.

Who was responsible for making Timbuktu a center of learning?

After 25 years, Mansa Musa's reign ended. The rulers who followed him were weak. Within 100 years after his death, Mali lost its land to others.

1. How did Sundiata Keita make Mali strong?
2. What were some results of Mansa Musa's pilgrimage to Arabia?

SONGHAY   The kingdom that replaced Mali as the most powerful in West Africa was Songhay. By the late 1400's, it controlled almost all the lands that had been part of Mali. Songhay also conquered other lands and became the largest of the three trading kingdoms.

Songhay was more organized than the other kingdoms. The ruler divided it into provinces and appointed a governor for each. He also appointed judges and tax collectors. Everyone used the same weights and measures and followed the same legal system.

Only members of the ruling Songhay could become political leaders or join the cavalry. Other groups were given special jobs. One group took care of army horses, while another served at the royal court. Most slaves, who were usually prisoners of war, worked as farmers.

Despite its power, Songhay lasted only 100 years. In 1590 A.D., the ruler of Morocco sent an army across the Sahara to seize Songhay's gold mines. Although only one half of the Moroccan soldiers survived the trip, they had guns. They easily defeated Songhay's soldiers, who were armed with only swords and spears.

1. In what ways was Songhay organized?
2. What brought about Songhay's downfall?

EAST AFRICAN CIVILIZATIONS

The growth of trading kingdoms in West Africa was matched by the rise of trading kingdoms and city-states in East Africa. Goods moved from the interior of East Africa to coastal markets, which, in time, became large city-states. Each of these had its own ruler and government.

THE KINGDOM OF ZIMBABWE   One of the best-known trading kingdoms was Zimbabwe. The people of Zimbabwe

African Dress

speak a language known as Bantu. Their ancestors, the Shona, once lived in present-day Nigeria. About 100 A.D., a population explosion took place. Since the land could not support the increased number of people, many began to leave their home-land to look for new homes.

The Shona settled in Zimbabwe about 700 A.D. There, they built towns with stone houses. The stones were cut in such a way that they fitted together without mortar. The capital, in addition to houses, had a fort and a temple. The fort stood on top of a hill. In times of danger, the people would seek safety inside the fort. The temple was surrounded by a huge wall over 30 feet, or 9.1 meters, high and 14 feet, or 4.3 meters, thick. Besides the temple, the enclosed area contained the houses of the chief and his officials.

Zimbabwe Ruins

The Shona viewed their chief as a god-king. They approached him by crawling on their stomachs. Officials imitated him. If he coughed, they coughed. When he ate, they ate. The chief kept his throne as long as he was in good health. When he grew old, however, he was expected to take poison. Then, a younger man could become chief, and Zimbabwe would remain strong.

One reason Zimbabwe remained strong was trade. The Shona people were part of a great trading network. They traded gold, copper, and ivory from inland Africa to cities along the continent's east coast. From these cities, trade was carried on with the East.

1. Why did the Shona leave their homeland in present-day Nigeria?
2. How did the Shona view their chief?

KILWA One of the most important trading city-states was Kilwa. From Kilwa, merchants sailed across the Indian Ocean to trade in Arabia, Persia, India, and China. Besides trading themselves, the people of Kilwa also collected heavy taxes from traders of other countries. They used their wealth to extend their power over neighboring city-states. They also used it to dress in fine cotton and silk and to fill their four-story houses with vases and hangings from the East.

A culture known as Swahili developed in Kilwa and other East African city-states. Many Arab traders had settled in the

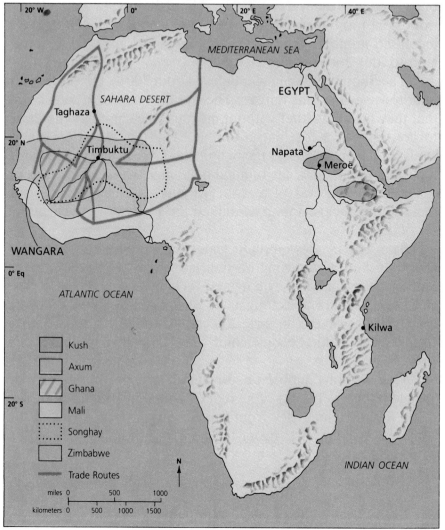

Map legend:
- Kush
- Axum
- Ghana
- Mali
- Songhay
- Zimbabwe
- Trade Routes

coastal cities. For this reason, the Swahili culture is a blend of Arabic and native African cultures. The Swahili language is a combination of Bantu and Arabic.

1. With what countries did the merchants of Kilwa trade?
2. How did the people of Kilwa use their wealth?

PATH TO THE AMERICAS

Until about 25,000 years ago, there were no people in the Americas. Then, hunting-and-food-gathering bands began to cross into the Americas from Asia over a land bridge. This land bridge was formed during the last ice age. At that time, large amounts of ocean water were frozen into huge glaciers, and sea levels dropped. Today, this bridge is covered by the waters of the Bering Strait.

The bands came in search of food, following grass-grazing animals that had crossed earlier. The bands lived off their kill and also gathered wild plants. Gradually, they spread out over the Americas. Experts believe that people reached the southern tip of South America by about 9000 B.C.

About 7000 B.C., the last ice age ended. The climate became hotter and drier, and in many areas deserts took the place of grasslands. Large game almost disappeared. So, people had to find other ways of getting food.

By 6000 B.C., people in the Tehuacán Valley south of present-day Mexico City had developed farming. By 3000 B.C., there were thousands of small farming villages throughout the Americas. The most important crop was **maize**, or corn.

Between 3000 B.C. and 1000 B.C., people developed such skills as weaving and pottery making. They domesticated peanuts, tomatoes, and potatoes. In a few areas, they developed irrigation systems that helped support a growing population.

1. How did hunting-and-food-gathering bands from Asia reach America?
2. How long did it take people to spread out over the Americas?
3. What was the most important crop grown by people in the Americas?

MESOAMERICA

As the number of people grew, societies became more complex. People began to build cities. Several great civilizations rose in Mesoamerica, or Middle America. Some developed before 900 A.D. and others later. The earlier civilizations were peaceful and had rulers who were interested in learning. People were bound together by religious loyalty and by trade. The later civilizations were warlike. Religion was marked by human sacrifice. Government was based on fear.

Olmec Art

THE OLMECS   One of the earliest civilizations in Mesoamerica was that of the Olmecs. It developed around 1000 B.C.

About 900 years later, it disappeared mysteriously. The Olmecs had great influence on other peoples of the area. For this reason, theirs is called the "mother culture" of Mesoamerica. Some things that carried over into other civilizations were planned cities, hieroglyphic writing, and a calendar.

The Olmecs lived along the southern coast of the Gulf of Mexico. Part of the year, the people farmed. The rest of the time they built stone cities, which were chiefly religious centers. The cities stood on top of huge hills. They had temples; sacred pools; and houses for priests, artists, and architects. The people lived in nearby villages. They visited the cities on festival and market days, bringing food to the priests and offering corn and jade to the gods.

The major god of the Olmecs was the jaguar. It most likely stood for the forces of nature, especially rain. Rain was important for crops. The Olmecs used the jaguar symbol everywhere. They painted their pottery with spots and claws. They carved jaguar masks on their axes and altars. They even gave jaguar-like features to many of their human sculptures.

1. How did the Olmecs spend most of their time?
2. When did the Olmecs visit their cities?

THE MAYAS   Another great civilization, that of the Mayas, began in Mesoamerica about 500 B.C. It reached its peak between 300 and 900 A.D. The Mayas lived in present-day southeastern Mexico, Belize, and Guatemala.

Like the Olmecs, the Mayas lived in farming villages surrounding religious cities. Mayan cities had temples and houses for priests and nobles. They also had a sacred ball court. In this court, players would use hips and elbows to thrust a hard rubber ball through a vertical stone hoop 20 feet, or 6.1 meters, above the ground. The Mayas played the game for religious reasons. The rubber ball stood for the sun, and the game represented the struggle between life and death.

The Mayas were great traders. Their cities, linked by raised roads paved with white cement, had busy marketplaces. Canoes large enough to hold 40 people handled trade along the Atlantic and Pacific coasts. Coastal trade was mostly in luxuries, such as copper bells from central Mexico, gold dishes from Panama, and pearls from Venezuela. Their local trade was mainly in food and slaves.

Maya Pyramid

Slaves were generally criminals. The Mayas had no jails. They punished people by selling them into slavery. Slaves ground corn, paddled canoes, and carried goods over the roads. The Mayas used people to carry goods because they had neither draft animals nor carts.

The Mayas, however, had many accomplishments. They adapted their own hieroglyphs from the Olmecs. Mayan mathematicians developed the idea of zero and a counting system based on 20. Mayan astronomers were able to tell ahead of time when eclipses of the sun and moon would take place. They developed a calendar based on that of the Olmecs. And they discovered that the year was about 365 days long. The Mayas also made cotton cloth and paper.

About 900 A.D., most of the Mayas abandoned their cities and disappeared. No one knows why. A plague may have broken

---

MAYAN MURAL

Mayan artists decorated walls with brightly colored murals. These murals often featured battles and religious festivals. In this Mayan mural, warriors in animal headpieces return from a raiding party with their frightened captives.
Where was the Mayan Empire located?

out. Perhaps the soil could no longer produce enough food. War may have interfered with trade.

1. What were some accomplishments of the Mayas?
2. What became of the Mayan civilization?

THE AZTECS   Later, a third great civilization, that of the Aztecs, rose in Mesoamerica. About 1200 A.D., the Aztecs began moving south into the fertile central valley of Mexico. Through military conquest, they expanded their empire to include all of central Mexico. By 1400 A.D., the Aztec Empire had 5 million people.

MONTEZUMA II

Montezuma II was the most famous ruler of the Aztecs. This Spanish painting (left) shows Montezuma in his palace with his council of advisors. Montezuma at first welcomed Spanish explorers to his capital (right). Later, his kingdom was defeated by the Spaniards.

Why were Montezuma's warriors unable to defend their empire?

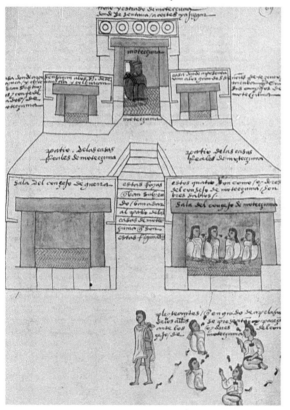 

The Aztecs made the people they conquered pay tribute. This was in the form of corn, clothing, rubber, and wood. It is believed that each year 2 million cotton cloaks alone were sent to the capital, Tenochtitlán.

Tenochtitlán was built on an island in Lake Texcoco. **Causeways**, or paved roads, connected the island to the mainland. The city had pyramid-temples, palaces, gardens, zoos, schools, and markets. About 300,000 people lived there. Some dressed in feathered capes and cloaks of many colors. Women wore flowers and feathers in their hair.

To feed the people, the Aztecs had to create more farmland. They filled in parts of the lake and dug drainage canals. They planted crops in earth-filled reed baskets anchored in the lake. The Aztecs also built **aqueducts**, or water conductors, to bring fresh water to the city's reservoirs from springs on the mainland. Canoes delivered drinking water from the reservoirs to people's houses.

The Aztecs were a warlike people. Most young men were expected to go to war. Warriors fought with swords and bows and arrows made of hard wood and volcanic matter. They wore armor made of quilted cotton.

War and religion were closely connected. The people worshipped two major gods. One was the rain god that stood for the peaceful life of farming. The other was the sun god that stood for war and expanding empire. The Aztecs believed that the sun god needed human sacrifices. They felt that if they did not make such sacrifices, the sun would not rise in the morning. The victims were generally prisoners of war. This was one reason the Aztecs made war on other peoples.

The Aztec Empire reached its height under Montezuma II in the early 1500's. During his reign, however, Spaniards, who had guns and horses, attacked the Aztecs. The Spaniards easily defeated the Aztecs, and they lost their empire.

1. What were some features of Tenochtitlán?
2. What was one reason the Aztecs made war?
3. How did the Aztec Empire come to an end?

THE INCAS OF SOUTH AMERICA

About the same time the Aztecs moved south into central Mexico, the Incas moved out from Peru. They established an

EARLY AMERICAN EMPIRES

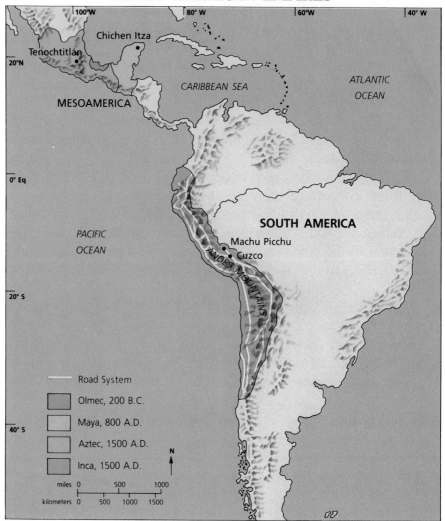

empire that stretched along the west coast of South America for about 2,500 miles, or 4,000 kilometers. By the 1500's, there were 12 million people in the Inca Empire.

HISTORY The Incas started out as farmers and shepherds. They built villages on the rocky slopes of the Andes Mountains. In the fertile valley below, they grew corn, potatoes, and other crops. On pastures above, they grazed alpacas and llamas, both of which are related to the camel. Alpacas gave the Incas thick, silky wool. Llamas gave them meat and served as pack animals.

In 1438, the Inca ruler Pachacuti conquered several neighboring peoples and founded the Inca Empire. Pachacuti used several techniques to hold the empire together. He ordered the different peoples to worship the Inca sun god in addition to their own gods. He made the Inca language of Quechua the official language. He moved people who had been living under Inca rule into newly conquered lands. These settlers helped spread Inca culture and watched for signs of rebellion.

Pachacuti also had a huge system of stone-paved roads built. Fiber suspension bridges crossed canyons and rivers. Way stations were set up on the roads with food, weapons, and other supplies needed by the Inca army. Only soldiers and government officials were allowed to use the roads.

1. How did the Incas use alpacas? Llamas?
2. How did Pachacuti hold the Inca Empire together?

THE INCA WAY OF LIFE   A ruler, known as the Inca, determined the way of life. Land belonged to the ruler and not to the people who worked it. Villagers who farmed the land paid taxes to the empire in two ways. They paid through their labor. This involved not only farming the land, but building roads and mining gold. They also paid taxes in kind. For example, they turned over part of their harvest to the ruler. Some of this food was stored in warehouses to be distributed among the people in case of famine.

Inca Poncho

The Inca had to keep track of people and goods. Because there was no written language, special accountants used **quipus**, or counting devices, to do this. Quipus were made up of knotted strings of different colors. Each color represented a different item. The knots in each string stood for tens, hundreds, and so on. Spaces between the knots stood for zero.

The wealth of the Inca Empire was shown in the way the ruler lived. His palace was the size of a town. There were hundreds of rooms and thousands of servants. Rugs covered both the floors and walls. The Inca's bodyguard wore gold armor. The poles of the litter in which he was carried were covered with gold. A desire for this wealth was part of the reason Spaniards destroyed the Inca Empire in the early 1500's.

1. In what two ways did the Incas pay their taxes?
2. How did the Inca keep track of people and goods?

CHAPTER 8 REVIEW

SUMMARY

1. For about 500 years, Kush was ruled by Egypt. Later, a Kushite dynasty ruled Egypt.

2. The Kushites learned the secret of iron-smelting from the Assyrians and developed a trading empire.

3. The Axumites destroyed Kush and then developed a trading empire themselves.

4. Ghana, Mali, and Songhay developed trading empires in West Africa based on the shipment of gold and salt.

5. Mansa Musa I of Mali made a famous pilgrimage to Arabia and established a university at Timbuktu.

6. Bantu-speaking Shona set up a trading kingdom at Zimbabwe.

7. Kilwa and other coastal cities handled trade between Africa and the East.

8. About 25,000 years ago, people began to cross from Asia to the Americas over a land bridge.

9. People in the Americas domesticated corn, potatoes, and other crops; developed weaving and pottery making; and built cities.

10. The Olmecs developed planned cities, hieroglyphic writing, and a calendar, and passed them on to other civilizations.

11. The Mayas were great traders, mathematicians, and astronomers.

12. The Aztecs built a capital at Tenochtitlán from which they ruled central Mexico.

13. The Incas controlled their empire through a common religion, a common language, and a system of roads.

BUILDING VOCABULARY

1. *Identify the following:*

Napata	Ezana	Timbuktu	Tehuacán
Kashta	Wangara	Bantu	Tenochtitlán
Piankhy	Sundiata Keita	Shona	Pachacuti
Meroë	Mansa Musa I	Swahili	Quechua

2. *Define the following:*

nomadic	slag	nuggets	causeways
savannah	terraces	pilgrimage	aqueducts
ebony	"silent barter"	maize	quipus

REVIEWING THE FACTS

1. Why did the Axumites live in isolation for more than 1,000 years?

2. How did Ghana get control over West Africa's trade routes?

3. Why did Mansa Musa's pilgrimage gain fame for Mali?
4. Why did the kingdom of Zimbabwe remain strong?
5. How did the last ice age affect the settlement of the Americas?
6. What was the main difference between the Mesoamerican civilizations that developed before 900 A.D. and those that developed later?
7. What was the relationship between Olmec religion and Olmec art?
8. What was the role of slaves in Mayan society?
9. How did the Aztecs treat the people they conquered?
10. Who determined the Inca way of life?

DISCUSSING IMPORTANT IDEAS

1. Do you think African civilization would have grown so rapidly if the Kushites had not learned the secret of iron-smelting? Explain.
2. Why was trade important to the growth of African civilization?
3. Which Mesoamerican civilization appeals to you most? Explain the reasons for your answer.
4. What contributions did early American civilizations make to present-day life in the United States?

USING MAPS

Study the maps on pages 122 and 128, and answer the following questions:
1. Which kingdom was larger, Mali or Ghana?
2. What kingdoms developed along the Nile River?
3. What is located about 20° north latitude and 98° west longitude?
4. Which American empires were located in Mesoamerica?

UNIT 3 REVIEW

SUMMARY

1. From 1200 to 500 B.C., new civilizations rose and fell in the Middle East.

2. The Phoenicians and Hebrews were interested in trade and learning.

3. The major contribution of the Phoenicians was the alphabet.

4. The Hebrews contributed the belief in one god and the idea of social justice to later civilizations.

5. The Assyrians, Chaldeans, and Persians were empire builders who developed new methods of war and government.

6. From 2000 B.C. to 1500 A.D., new civilizations rose and fell in sub-Saharan Africa and the Americas.

7. The African kingdoms of Kush, Axum, Ghana, Mali, Songhay, Zimbabwe, and Kilwa were interested in trade.

8. The Olmec civilization is called the "mother culture" of Mesoamerica because of its many important influences on later civilizations.

9. The Olmecs and the Mayas were peaceful people who were interested in trade and learning.

10. One of the major contributions of the Mayas was the concept of zero.

11. The Aztecs and the Incas were empire builders who developed new methods of government.

REVIEWING THE MAIN IDEAS

1. Compare the ways of life and accomplishments of groups in the Middle East and in the Americas.

2. How would your life be different if the Phoenicians had never existed? If the Hebrews had never existed?

3. Explain how empires such as those of the Songhay and the Incas were able to rule a variety of peoples.

4. Explain what influence trade had on the spread of ideas in the Middle East, in Africa, and in the Americas.

DEVELOPING SKILLS

An important element of history is time. It is not possible to study history without understanding time relationships. Historians, as well as students, must concern themselves with **chronology**, or the order or sequence in which events occur.

Often, one event is a cause of a later event or a result of an earlier one. Knowing the order in which events have occurred allows historians to arrive at conclusions.

History textbooks present chronology in various ways. Facts or events often are presented in a visual form to make them easier to remember and understand. For example, look at the time chart on pages 80 and 81. It shows the important events discussed in this unit in the order in which they occurred. There is a time chart at the beginning of each unit of the book. Each time chart provides a chronology of the important events in the unit.

Mastering chronology is an important social studies skill. This exercise is designed to provide practice in ordering events. Listed below are a number of events. Arrange them in proper order. Then, on a separate sheet of paper, draw a bar 8 inches, or 20 centimeters, long. Each 2 inches, or 5 centimeters, represents about 500 years. Label the events which follow in their proper order in relation to the four time spans on the bar. You have just created a time line.

a. Moses receives the Ten Commandments.

b. The Phoenicians build cities in Canaan.

c. The Shona settle in Zimbabwe

d. The Assyrians take over Mesopotamian cities, trading routes, and fortresses.

e. The Phoenicians found Carthage.

f. The Spaniards defeat the Aztecs

g. Cyrus expands the Persian Empire.

h. Abraham leads the Hebrews to Canaan.

i. Nebuchadnezzar builds a new capital at Babylon.

j. The Jews begin 70 years of exile in Babylon.

k. The Hittites develop smelting.

SUGGESTED UNIT PROJECTS

1. Form two teams for a debate. One will tell why the Hebrews at the time of Moses should be allowed to leave Egypt. The other will give reasons why they should not be allowed to leave.

2. Prepare an editorial that might have appeared in a local Mesopotamian newspaper around 800 B.C., urging the people to surrender to the Assyrians. Include the benefits the Assyrians can offer.

3. Write a report that one of "The Eyes and Ears of the King" might have sent to the Persian ruler.

4. Write an article that might have appeared in an Egyptian newspaper describing the visit of Mansa Musa I.

SUGGESTED READING

Asimov, Isaac. *The Land of Canaan*. Boston: Houghton Mifflin Company, 1971. An account of the Hebrews, Phoenicians, Assyrians, Babylonians, and others who lived and fought over Canaan beginning in Neolithic times.

Brooks, Lester. *Great Civilizations of Ancient Africa*. New York: Four Winds Press, 1971. A discussion of the black civilizations that once flourished in Ghana, Mali, and Songhay and the economic and political ties between black Africa and ancient Egypt.

Collins, Robert. *The Medes and Persians: Conquerors and Diplomats*. New York: McGraw-Hill, 1975. An account of the daily lives, beliefs, and government of the ancient Persians.

Gerez, Toni, comp. *2-rabbit, 7-wind*. New York: Viking Press, 1971. Aztec poems.

Glubok, Shirley. *Digging In Assyria*. New York: Macmillan, 1970. An adaptation of archaeologist Sir Henry Layard's account of his excavation of Nineveh.

Synge, Ursula. *The People and the Promise*. New York: S. G. Phillips, 1974. The exodus of the Hebrews from Egypt as viewed through the eyes of Leah as she experiences it from childhood to old age.

UNIT 4

2800 B.C.	2650 B.C.	2545 B.C.
c. 2800 B.C. Minoan civilization begins		
2125 B.C.	2020 B.C.	1915 B.C.
	c. 2000 B.C. Minoans control Mediterranean trade Myceneans move into Balkan Peninsula	
1495 B.C.	1390 B.C.	1285 B.C.
	c. 1400 B.C. Myceneans capture Crete	
865 B.C.	760 B.C.	655 B.C.
	776 B.C. First Olympic games c. 750 B.C. Homer writes *Iliad* and *Odyssey*	c. 580 B.C. Philosophy and science begin
235 B.C.	130 B.C.	25 B.C.
	197 B.C. Romans defeat Greeks	

THE GREEKS

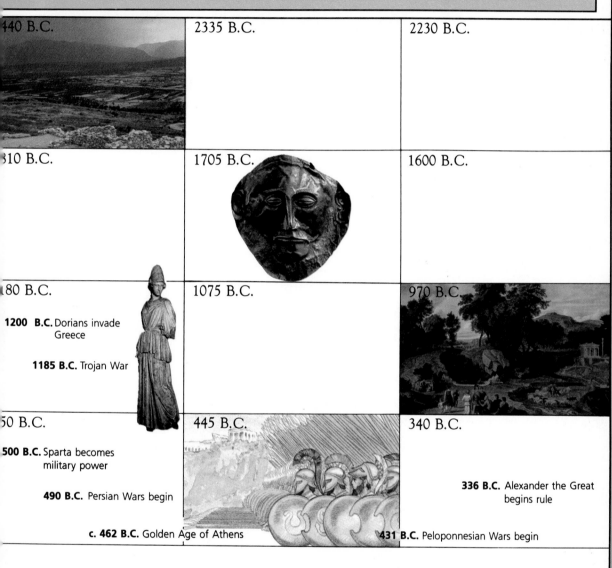

2440 B.C.	2335 B.C.	2230 B.C.
1810 B.C.	**1705 B.C.**	**1600 B.C.**
1180 B.C. **1200 B.C.** Dorians invade Greece **1185 B.C.** Trojan War	**1075 B.C.**	**970 B.C.**
550 B.C. **500 B.C.** Sparta becomes military power **490 B.C.** Persian Wars begin **c. 462 B.C.** Golden Age of Athens	**445 B.C.**	**340 B.C.** **336 B.C.** Alexander the Great begins rule **431 B.C.** Peloponnesian Wars begin

1. HOW DID GREEK CULTURE DEVELOP?
2. WHAT DID THE GREEKS CONTRIBUTE TO WESTERN CIVILIZATION?

Western civilization owes a great debt to the Greeks. Much of what has been accomplished since ancient times is based on Greek thought and culture. Greek civilization lasted about 500 years. The center of Greek culture was the city-state of Athens.

The list of Greek contributions is long. The following are just a few. In politics, the Greeks gave the western world rule by the people and the first democratic constitution. They also provided the first study of written government.

In science and philosophy, the Greeks contributed new ways of thinking. They placed great importance on the ability to learn and reason. The Greeks learned that the world is ruled by natural laws.

In the arts, the Greeks contributed the play. They also created new styles of architecture and magnificent sculpture. From the Greeks came the Olympic Games and athletic competition in such events as wrestling, boxing, discus throwing, and running.

The most important Greek contribution, however, cannot be seen or touched. It is a belief. The Greeks were the first to believe in the freedom and worth of the individual. They did not view people as the instruments of powerful gods. Instead, they saw people as intelligent beings who were capable of great achievements. The Greeks believed that they could best please the gods by developing their political and physical powers to the fullest. Thus, they gave people a sense of achievement and self-respect that has endured to the present.

CHAPTER 9
THE BEGINNINGS

Greek civilization developed out of a combination of two earlier civilizations, Minoan and Mycenean. The Minoans, who were also known as Cretans, were a seafaring people. Their civilization rose around 2800 B.C. on Crete, an island in the Mediterranean Sea.

THE MINOANS

At first, the people of Crete grew wheat, barley, grapes, and olives. When the olive groves and vineyards produced more than they needed, the Minoans traded the surplus for goods they could not produce.

Since there were many forests on Crete, the Minoans learned to work with wood and became good carpenters. They also learned to work with metal. They used their metalworking and carpentry skills to build ships and began to earn a living from trade instead of farming.

When pirates threatened them, the Minoans changed the design of their ships. They made the ships slimmer, with two or three masts instead of one. Thus, the ships could go faster. The Minoans also put a deck over the heads of rowers to protect them. And they placed a large wooden beam in the **prow**, or front part of the ship. The beam was used to smash a hole in enemy ships and sink them.

Over time, the Minoans succeeded in driving off the pirates. By about 2000 B.C., Crete was the world's first important seafaring civilization. Minoan merchant ships traveled far to trade pottery, leather and bronze armor, and metal jewelry.

1. How did the Minoans earn a living?
2. Why did the Minoans change the design of their ships?
3. What were the Minoans' new ships like?

THE PEOPLE   The Minoans were a small people with bronzed skin and long dark hair. The men wore striped loincloths, long robes embroidered with flowers, or trousers that bagged at the knees. The women wore full skirts and short-sleeved jackets that laced in front. The Minoans were proud of their small waists and wore tight belts to show them off. They also wore jewelry, such as gold and silver earrings, necklaces, bracelets, and rings.

The men farmed and fished. They raised cattle, long-horned sheep, and goats. They also served in the navy and the royal guard. The women performed household duties, attended sporting events, and went hunting in chariots.

The people of Crete loved sports. They built what was probably the world's first arena. It stood in the open air. Stone steps formed grandstands where about 500 people could sit and watch the action. The king and the royal party had their own special box seats.

Boxing matches were held in the arena. Another favorite sport held there was **bull leaping**, a form of bullfighting. A young man and woman "fought" the bull together. The man would

Minoan Man

BULL LEAPING

This painting from the palace of Knossos shows Minoans bull leaping. In the center, a man leaps over the bull's back. Another man puts his arms around the bull's horns so that it will lift its head and toss him. The woman behind the bull prepares to catch the leapers.

What was the purpose of bull leaping?

grab the bull's horns. As the bull raised its head to toss him, the man would do a somersault, landing on his feet on the bull's back. He would then do a back flip. Standing behind the bull, the woman would catch her partner as he landed. Many experts believe bull leaping was a religious ceremony as well as a sport.

1. How did the Minoans dress?
2. What were Minoan interests?

CITIES AND PALACES　　The Minoans built many cities, which were different from those of other ancient civilizations in two ways. At the heart of each Minoan city stood a palace rather than a temple. Also, Minoan cities did not have walls around them. Instead, the people depended for protection on the sea and on their navy.

One of the largest cities of Crete was Knossos. It covered about 28 acres, or 11.2 hectares. About one fifth was taken up by a five-story palace that served as a government building, temple, factory, and warehouse. Its walls were built of stone and sun-dried brick framed with wooden beams. The Minoans plastered the inside walls and decorated them with brightly colored paintings called **frescoes**. The palace had bathrooms, complete with bathtubs and flush toilets. It also had hot and cold running water and portable fireboxes to heat the rooms.

The palace had several entrances. Passageways and rooms twisted and turned in all directions to form a **labyrinth**, or maze. Because labyrinth means "double ax," the palace was called the "House of the Double Ax." The palace was also called by that name because throughout it were pictures, carvings, and bronze models of a double ax.

Sea captains, merchants, and shipbuilders lived in houses around the palace. Beyond their houses stood those of the artisans who did not live and work in the palace. They made beautiful cups and vases and designed delicate jewelry.

Clay Figurine

The houses were built side by side around courtyards. Most were two stories high. The lower walls were made of stone, the upper walls of sun-dried brick. Some houses were painted bright colors. On the inside walls were painted scenes of daily life. Each house also had its own well and drains.

Many early Minoan houses had no entrance from the street. To go in or out, a person lowered a ladder over the side of the house. Later, wooden doors and windows made of oiled and tinted **parchment**, or thin animal skin, were added.

1. What made the cities of Crete different from those of other ancient civilizations?
2. What was the "House of the Double Ax"?
3. What were some features of Minoan houses?

RULERS AND RELIGION   The kings of Crete were priest-kings. They made the laws and represented the gods on earth. They would climb to the top of Mount Juktas to look for a sign from heaven that would tell them the will of the gods. Then, the kings would tell their people what the gods wanted them to do.

The Minoans had many gods. The main one was the Great Goddess, Mother Earth. She made plants grow and brought children into the world. To honor her, the Minoans built shrines. The shrines were built in palaces, on housetops, on hilltops, and in caves. The people believed that the hilltops led to heaven, and the caves led to the underworld.

Sacred horns made of clay and covered with stucco rested against the back wall of each shrine. A hole between the horns held a bronze double ax. Around the horns were clay models of animals. The people left offerings of human hair, fruit, flowers, jewels, and gold at the shrines.

MINOAN RELIGION

This fresco shows a Minoan religious ceremony. As a musician plays the harp, two women and a man carry offerings to a shrine. Two pillars (left) support double axes with birds sitting on them. These objects stood for the power of the Great Goddess. What was Minoan religion like?

The Minoans believed that certain things were sacred. The lily was their sacred flower. The king wore a plumed crown of lilies and a lily necklace. The double ax was sacred. It stood for the power of Mother Earth and the authority of the king. The dove was sacred because it flew to the heavens. Snakes were sacred and were kept in most houses. They were thought to be spirits of the underworld who would protect the house.

1. What was the role of the Cretan king?
2. Why was Mother Earth an important goddess?
3. What things did the people of Crete consider sacred?

THE FALL OF THE MINOANS   No one is certain why Minoan civilization came to an end. Legend explains it with the story of Theseus and the Minotaur. A young Greek prince named Theseus was brought to Knossos. He was to be sacrificed to the Minotaur, a huge monster the king kept in the palace labyrinth. The Minotaur had the body of a man and the head of a bull and lived on human flesh.

Theseus was put into the labyrinth. When he met the Minotaur, he did not try to run away. He fought the monster with a magical sword and killed it. When the Minotaur died, the power of the Minoans died too. And Theseus became the ruler of Crete.

All that experts know for certain is that about 1400 B.C. control of the sea and of Crete passed to the Myceneans.

Minotaur

1. How does legend explain the fall of Minoan civilization?
2. What do experts know for certain about the fall of Minoan civilization?

THE MYCENEANS

The Myceneans came from the grasslands of southern Russia. Around 2000 B.C., they made their way west into Europe and then south through the Balkan **Peninsula**, or piece of land that extends into the water. Finally, they settled in the lowlands of mainland Greece.

The Myceneans did not build cities like the Sumerians or the Egyptians. Instead, their kings built fortress-palaces on hilltops. In times of danger or attack, the people in the villages outside the palace walls took shelter within the palace. The main feature of the palace was the **megaron**, or a square room with a hearth in

THE EARLY AEGEAN WORLD

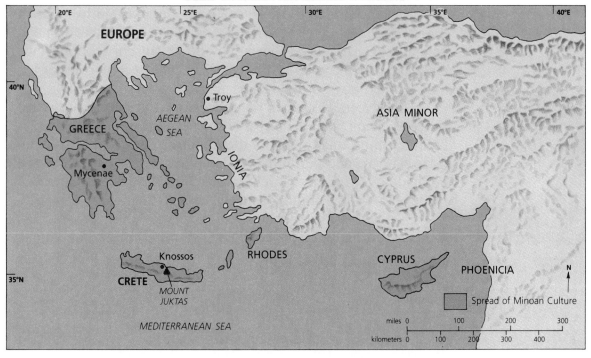

its center. The hearth was surrounded by four pillars that supported the roof. The king held council meetings and entertained in the megaron. Meals were cooked and eaten there.

The land was divided into estates that were farmed either by slaves or by **tenants**, people who live on and work another person's property. The landowners gave the king horses, chariots, weapons, wheat, livestock, honey, and hides in exchange for protection. Tenants supplied many of these items.

Although they kept large herds of cattle, the Myceneans relied on hunting to provide more meat. They hunted rabbit, deer, boar, wild bulls, and game birds. Women rode with the men in chariots during the hunt. When the hunters were after big game, they used greyhounds. The game was captured with nets or killed with spears, slings, or bows and arrows.

1. From where did the Myceneans come? Where did they finally settle?
2. What did the Myceneans build instead of cities?
3. What did the Myceneans give their kings? What did the Myceneans receive in return?
4. Why did the Myceneans hunt? How did they hunt?

TRADERS AND PIRATES   Shortly after the Myceneans settled in the lowlands of Greece, they were visited by Minoan traders from Crete. The Myceneans began to imitate Minoan gold and bronze work. They adapted Cretan script to their own language. They copied Minoan fashions. Most important of all, they learned how to build ships and how to navigate.

The Myceneans began to grow olives. They made presses to squeeze the oil from the olives. They used the oil for cooking, as fuel for lamps, and to rub on their bodies. They sold plain oil in large clay jars and perfumed oil in painted vases. The sale of the oil made the Myceneans rich. It also led to the establishment of Mycenean trading stations and settlements on nearby islands.

Despite their success in trade, the Myceneans were warriors at heart. In battle, they wore fancy bronze armor, used small

---

MYCENEAN SEASCAPE

The Myceneans were great seafarers, who controlled Mediterranean trade for 200 years. This view shows a harbor of one of the Greek islands in the Aegean Sea. In this area, the Myceneans built many settlements.

How did geography affect the growth of Mycenean civilization?

metal shields, and fought with spears and swords. At first, they fought one another. After they learned about shipbuilding and navigation, they outfitted pirate fleets and began to raid nearby lands. By about 1400 B.C., they had replaced the Minoans as the main power of the Aegean world.

The Myceneans remained strong for nearly 300 years. Then, a people called the Dorians conquered them. Thousands of Myceneans fled the Greek mainland and settled in the Aegean islands and on the western shore of Asia Minor. These settlements later became known as Ionia.

Mycenean Gold Cup

1. In what ways were the Myceneans influenced by Minoan culture?
2. How did the Myceneans become rich and powerful?
3. What happened to the Myceneans around 1100 B.C.?

THE TROJAN WAR   The Myceneans are famous for their attack on Troy, a major trading city of Asia Minor. The Trojans controlled the trade routes to the Black Sea. They made money by taxing the ships that carried grain and gold from southern Russia to Greece.

Several hundred years after the Myceneans attacked Troy, a blind Greek poet named Homer wrote about the event in an epic poem called the *Iliad.* Homer also wrote a poem called the *Odyssey,* which tells about the wanderings of Odysseus, a Mycenean hero of the Trojan War. Homer drew his material for the two poems from songs and legends that had been handed down by word of mouth. He then added his own descriptions of everyday life.

According to Homer's account in the *Iliad,* the Trojan War was fought over a woman. The king of Troy had a son named Paris, who fell in love with Helen, the wife of a Mycenean king. When Paris took Helen to Troy, her husband became angry. He formed an army and sailed after them. But the walls of Troy were so tall, thick, and strong that the Myceneans could not get into the city. They had to camp on the plain outside the walls of the city.

After years of fighting, the Myceneans still had not taken Troy. Then, Odysseus suggested a way they could capture the city. He had the Myceneans build a huge, hollow wooden horse. The best soldiers hid inside the horse, while the rest boarded their ships and sailed away.

THE TROJAN HORSE

The first Greek myths came from the Myceneans. Later, the poet Homer gathered these legends and used them to write his works. This painting shows the Trojan horse from Homer's epic poem, the *Iliad*.
What historical event does Homer's *Iliad* describe?

The Trojans saw the ships leave and thought they had won the war. They did not know that the Mycenean ships would return after dark. The Trojans tied ropes to the wooden horse and pulled it into the city as a victory prize. When the Trojans fell asleep, the Mycenean soldiers hidden inside the horse came out. They opened the city gates and let in the rest of the Mycenean army. The Myceneans killed the king of Troy and burned the city. Then, with Helen, they returned to their homes.

1. Why was the city of Troy important?
2. How does the *Iliad* describe the Trojan War?

A "DARK AGE" The Dorians conquered the Myceneans about 1100 B.C. Their iron swords were not as well made as the Mycenean bronze swords. Nevertheless, the Dorian swords were stronger.

The Dorians were not interested in furthering civilization. As a result, the Aegean world entered a "Dark Age" that lasted for more than 300 years.

The "Dark Age" was a time of wandering and killing. Overseas trade stopped. The people of the Aegean forgot how to write and keep records. The skills of fresco painting and working with ivory and gold disappeared. The Dorian invasion cut the Aegean region off from the Middle East. The people had to create a new civilization on their own.

The people started over. Once again, herding and farming became the main ways of life. Local leaders ruled small areas. These leaders called themselves kings, but they were little more than chiefs. At first, the borders of the areas they ruled kept changing. But in time, the borders became fixed, and each area became an independent community. The people of these communities began calling themselves Hellenes, or Greeks.

Dorian Sword

1. What happened in the Aegean world during the "Dark Age"?
2. How did the people of the Aegean world begin to create a new civilization?

CHAPTER 9 REVIEW

SUMMARY

1. Minoan civilization began to develop on the Mediterranean island of Crete around 2800 B.C.

2. At first, the Minoans were farmers, but eventually, most turned to trade to earn a living.

3. Minoans were very fond of sports, especially bull leaping.

4. Since the Minoans depended on the sea and their ships for protection, their cities were not walled.

5. Minoans worshipped many gods, the most important of which was Mother Earth.

6. About 1400 B.C., control of the Mediterranean passed to the Myceneans, who came to Greece from southern Russia.

7. Instead of cities, the Myceneans built fortress-palaces on hilltops.

8. The Myceneans learned many things from the Minoans, including a writing script and the skills of shipbuilding and navigation.

9. The Myceneans fought a lengthy war against Troy.

10. The Trojan War and its results are described in two epic poems, the *Iliad* and the *Odyssey,* written by the blind Greek poet Homer.

11. About 1100 B.C., the Myceneans were conquered by the Dorians.

12. During the 300 years in which the Dorians were in power, the people of the Aegean area lost many skills and had to create a new civilization.

BUILDING VOCABULARY

1. *Identify the following:*

Minoan	Mother Earth	Asia Minor	*Iliad*
Mycenean	Theseus	Ionia	*Odyssey*
Crete	Minotaur	Troy	Hellenes
House of the Double Ax	Dorians	Homer	

2. *Define the following:*

prow	frescoes	parchment	megaron
bull leaping	labyrinth	peninsula	tenants

REVIEWING THE FACTS

1. What civilizations combined to form Greek civilization?
2. How were the Minoans able to gain control of the Mediterranean Sea?
3. How do experts view bull leaping?
4. Why did Minoan cities have no walls around them?
5. What were some features of the palace at Knossos?
6. How did the Minoans honor Mother Earth?
7. What is the legend of Theseus and the Minotaur?
8. What uses did the Myceneans have for olive oil?
9. What is the legend of the Trojan Horse?
10. Why did the people of Greece have to create a new civilization?

DISCUSSING IMPORTANT IDEAS

1. Did the Minoans use their natural resources wisely? Explain.
2. What effect did being an island civilization have on the Minoans?
3. What role did religion play in Minoan life?
4. What type of person do you think Odysseus was? Explain.
5. Compare and contrast the ways of life of the Minoans and the Myceneans. In which civilization would you have preferred to live? Why?

USING MAPS

Study the map on page 143, and answer the following questions:

1. Where was the Minoan city of Knossos located?
2. What does the triangle symbol on the island of Crete represent?
3. What body of water separates Greece from Asia Minor?
4. To what areas of the world did Minoan culture spread?

CHAPTER 10

THE CITY-STATES

The Hellenes of different communities shared a common language and many customs and beliefs. But they did not have much contact with one another. Their communities were separated by mountains and the sea. Thus, no single community controlled the others. Rather, each controlled its own affairs. Nevertheless, a sense of unity began to develop among the people within each community. So, by 750 B.C., the basic guidelines for Greek civilization were formed.

THE POLIS

Greek Woman

The **polis**, or city-state, was the geographic and political center of Greek life. At first, each polis consisted of farming villages, fields, and orchards grouped around a fortified hill called an **acropolis**. Atop the acropolis stood the temple of the local god. At the foot was the **agora**, an open area used as a marketplace. Gradually, artisans, traders, and members of the upper class settled near the agora. By 700 B.C., this inner section of the polis had become a city. Together with the villages and farmland around it, it formed a city-state.

Each city-state had its own government and laws. The average city-state contained between 5,000 and 10,000 citizens. Workers born outside Greece, as well as women, children, and slaves, were not citizens. Citizens had certain rights that others did not have. They could vote, own property, hold public office, and speak for themselves in court. In return, they were expected to take part in government and to defend their polis in time of war or conflict.

For Greek citizens in ancient times, civic and personal honor were one and the same. The polis gave them a sense of belonging. They felt they had some say in what happened to them. They put the good of the polis above everything else.

Two of the greatest Greek city-states were Sparta and Athens. Sparta had the strongest army in Greece, while Athens had the strongest navy. Yet, each developed differently with a different kind of government and a different way of life.

1. What was the polis? How did it develop?
2. Who were the citizens of the Greek city-states? What rights did they have? What duties did they have?
3. What were the two greatest Greek city-states?

SPARTA

Sparta was in the southcentral region of Greece in an area known as the Peloponnesus. By 500 B.C., it had become the greatest military power in Greece.

At first, Sparta was ruled by a king. About 800 B.C., the **aristocrats**, or nobles, took over the government. From that time on, Sparta had two kings who ruled jointly. Although they kept the title of king, they had little power. Their only tasks were to lead the army and conduct religious services.

Only aristocrats could be Spartan citizens. All citizens over the age of 20 were members of the Assembly, which passed laws and decided questions of war and peace. Each year, it chose five overseers to manage public affairs and guide the education of young Spartans. The Council of Elders assisted the overseers. The Council was made up of men over 60 who were chosen for life. It suggested laws to the Assembly and served as a supreme court.

1. Where was Sparta?
2. What was the role of Spartan kings after 700 B.C.?
3. How was the government of Sparta organized?

ARISTOCRATS, HELOTS, AND PERIOECI   The Spartans had little interest in farming. The land was worked by **helots**, or slaves owned by the city-state. The helots had to turn over one half of their crops to the aristocrats who owned the land but lived in the center of the polis.

The Spartans were not interested in industry or trade either. They left those to the **perioeci**, or merchants and artisans who lived in the villages. The perioeci were neither slaves nor citizens. The helots and perioeci worked, while the aristocrats trained for the army and war.

By about 750 B.C., there were 20 times as many helots and perioeci as there were aristocrats. The aristocrats were faced with a decision. They could make life better for their workers by letting them share in the government. Or they could keep things the way they were. To do that meant keeping the workers down by force. Since the aristocrats were afraid that any change would destroy their way of life, they decided to keep things the way they were.

Greek Roof Ornament

1. What did the helots contribute to Sparta?
2. What did the perioeci contribute to Sparta?
3. Why did the aristocrats decide against letting workers share in the government?

THE SPARTAN WAY OF LIFE   Spartans tried to become the strongest people in Greece. Newborn babies were examined to see if they were healthy. If they were, they were allowed to live. If they were not, they were left on a hillside to die.

When Spartan boys turned seven, they were sent to live in military camps. There, they were trained in groups under teenage leaders. They learned to read, write, and use weapons. The boys received only small amounts of food. They had to go barefoot and were given only one cloak to wear. They walked in silence, with their eyes to the ground, and spoke only when necessary. They slept outdoors without a cover. Every ten days they were lined up and examined to make sure they were not getting fat.

Spartan men were expected to marry at age 20. But they could not have a household of their own. They had to live and eat in military barracks, where they shared expenses with other soldiers. They could retire from the army at age 60.

Spartan women had more freedom than the women of other Greek city-states. In the other city-states, women spent most of their time at home performing household duties. They did not go out without a chaperone. Then, they only went to visit other

THE SPARTAN WAY OF LIFE

Spartan men spent most of their time serving in the army. In the illustration, a group of young warriors performs exercises on a Spartan racecourse. Why was the army so important in Sparta?

women or attend religious festivals. They never spoke to men on the street or entertained their husbands' friends.

Spartan women mixed freely with their husbands' friends. They wrestled, boxed, and raced with men. Spartan women had to be healthy so they could produce healthy male warriors. When Spartan women sent their men into battle, they told the men to come home with their shields or on them. If the men brought their shields with them, it meant they had won the battle. Dead warriors were carried home on their shields.

The Spartans believed new ideas would weaken their way of life. So, they tried to prevent change. When the people of other Greek city-states began to use coins as money, Spartans continued to use iron rods. Other city-states developed literature and sculpture. Spartans spent their time and energy only on the arts of war. Other city-states developed industry and trade and improved their standard of living. Sparta remained a poor farming society that depended on the labor of slaves.

Greek Boxer

From its beginnings until its downfall in 371 B.C., Sparta had only one goal—to be militarily strong.

1. What was life like for a Spartan male?
2. How was the life-style of Spartan women different from that of most other Greek women?
3. How was Sparta different from other Greek city-states?

ATHENS

Like all other Greek city-states, Athens started out as a monarchy. However, about 750 B.C., some Athenian nobles, merchants, and manufacturers took over the government. After a time, fights broke out between them and the farmers and artisans over land ownership and debt. Since the upper-class Athenians did not want the fights to turn into a revolution, they agreed to make reforms. To do this, they had to reorganize the government.

The first attempt to reorganize the government was made by Draco, a noble. But Draco failed in his efforts. So, in 594 B.C., a rich merchant named Solon was chosen to undertake the task.

Solon developed a **constitution**, or a set of principles and rules for governing a community, that broke the political power of the rich. Solon set a limit on how much land a person could own and gave all landowners the right to vote in the Assembly.

THE ATHENIAN WAY OF LIFE
The people of Athens gathered in the agora to trade and to discuss important issues. Here a public speaker (center) addresses the crowd from the speaker's box. Many Athenians enjoyed taking part in debates.
How did life in Athens differ from life in Sparta?

The Assembly was given the power to pass laws. Solon cancelled all debts. He freed the people who had been forced into slavery because of debt. He also did away with the law that had allowed this. He offered citizenship to artisans who were not Athenians, and he ordered every father to teach his son a trade.

Under Solon, more Athenians began to take part in government. Trade also increased. Still, people were not happy. The rich thought Solon had gone too far, while the poor thought he had not gone far enough.

Around 560 B.C., the government was taken over by another Athenian named Peisistratus. Peisistratus was supported by the lower classes. He divided the large estates among the landless farmers. He decreed that a person no longer had to own land to be a citizen. He also encouraged sculpture and other arts.

1. Why did Athenian aristocrats agree to reform the government after 750 B.C.?
2. What were some of the reforms Solon made?
3. What changes did Peisistratus make?

A DEMOCRATIC CONSTITUTION   When Peisistratus died, his sons took over as leaders of the Athenian government. Not long after, their government was overthrown by the Spartans, who defeated the Athenians in a battle.

In 508 B.C., the Spartans were themselves overthrown by a noble named Cleisthenes. A year later, Cleisthenes put into effect the world's first generally democratic constitution. It gave to Athenians such rights as freedom of speech and equality before the law. The political reforms made by Cleisthenes lasted until the fall of Greece almost 200 years later.

Cleisthenes opened the Assembly to all males over the age of 20. Each year, the Assembly elected ten generals to run the army and navy and to serve as chief **magistrates**, or judges. One of the generals was named commander-in-chief.

The Council of Five Hundred handled the daily business of Athens. Members were chosen each year by lot. The names of 500 citizens were drawn from a large pot. Since no one could serve on the Council for more than two terms, every citizen had a chance to be a Council member.

Under Cleisthenes, citizens were required to educate their sons. Since there were no public schools, boys had a tutor or attended a private school. Starting at age seven, they studied writing, mathematics, and music. They also practiced sports and memorized the works of Homer and other noted Greek poets.

Homer

When they turned 18, Athenian males became citizens. They went to the temple of the god Zeus and took an oath of citizenship in front of their family and friends. In the oath, they promised to help make Athens a better place in which to live. They also promised to be honorable in battle, preserve the constitution, and respect their religion.

1. What changes did Cleisthenes make in the laws of Athens?
2. What did Athenian boys do at school?
3. What did Athenians promise when they took their oath of citizenship?

THE PERSIAN WARS   About the time Athens was going through government changes, the Persians ruled the largest and most powerful empire in the western world. In 520 B.C., the Persians conquered Ionia—the Greek city-states in Asia Minor and on the Aegean islands. About 20 years later, the Ionians revolted and asked the city-states on the Greek mainland for help. Athens and another polis sent a few warships. After five years of fighting, the Persians put down the revolt. But Darius, the Persian king, was not satisfied. He wanted to punish the mainland Greeks for helping the Ionians.

In 490 B.C., Darius sent a fleet of 600 ships and a well-equipped army to Greece. The Persians landed on the plain of Marathon about 24 miles, or 38.4 kilometers, north of Athens. After several days, the Persians decided to sail directly to Athens and attack it by sea. They began loading their ships. The cavalry, the strongest unit of the Persian army, boarded first. As soon as the cavalry was aboard, Greek soldiers ran down in close order from the hills around Marathon. The remaining Persians were not prepared to meet this kind of attack and were defeated. Winning the Battle of Marathon gave the Greeks a great sense of confidence.

Shortly after the Battle of Marathon, rich silver mines were found near Athens. The Athenians spent their new wealth on warships called **triremes**. Soon, Athens had the largest navy in Greece. The Athenians planned to be prepared if the Persians returned.

The Persians did return. In 480 B.C., Darius's son Xerxes sent 250,000 soldiers across the Aegean. Within a few weeks, the Persians conquered northern Greece. In order to stop them, 20 Greek city-states banded together. The Spartans led the army, while the Athenians led the navy.

First, 7,000 Greek soldiers headed for the narrow pass of Thermopylae, about 100 miles, or 160 kilometers, from Athens. There, they held off the Persian army for three days. This gave the Athenians time to flee to the island of Salamis. Meanwhile, all but 300 Spartans withdrew from Thermopylae. The Persians then killed the 300 Spartans and marched on Athens. Finding the city deserted, they set it on fire.

Then, the Greeks tricked the Persian fleet into sailing into the **strait**, or narrow strip of water, between Athens and Salamis. Since the strait was too narrow for all the Persian ships to enter at once, the Greeks could take them on a few at a time. Also, once the Persian ships were in the strait, their large size made them difficult to handle. With their lighter, faster ships, the Greeks defeated the Persian fleet.

Following the defeat, Xerxes returned to Asia. However, he left some troops behind. In 479 B.C., they were defeated by the

Marathon Runner

BATTLE OF SALAMIS

The Greek fleet, led by the Athenians, defeated the Persian Navy in the Bay of Salamis (left). The Greeks won because of their knowledge of ships and of the sea. The urn (right) shows Greek soldiers in battle.

How did the victory at Salamis affect the outcome of the Persian Wars?

Greeks in the Battle of Plataea. A few days later, Greek ships destroyed what was left of the Persian navy. The Persian Wars were over.

1. What started the Persian Wars?
2. What happened at the Battle of Marathon?
3. How did the Greeks stop Xerxes in 480 B.C.?
4. How did the Persian Wars finally come to an end?

THE DELIAN LEAGUE AND THE ATHENIAN EMPIRE

The Persians had been driven from Greece, but they still ruled Ionia. So, the Athenians suggested that the Greek city-states form a **defensive league**, or protective group. Since the league had its headquarters on the island of Delos, it was called the Delian League. Sparta was one of the few Greek city-states that did not join the League.

Once a city-state became a League member, it could not withdraw unless all the other members agreed. The League had a common navy. Its ships were built and crewed by Athenians, but the other city-states paid the costs.

The League worked well for a while. But as time passed, Athens gained more and more power. Other city-states had to ask Athens for permission to sail or to trade. Criminal cases were brought to Athens for trial. Athenian coins replaced other Greek money. Athenian soldiers interfered in the politics of other Greek city-states. In short, the Delian League had turned into the Athenian Empire.

The main leader of Athens at the time was a general named Pericles. Pericles was known as the "first citizen" of Athens. He had a vision of Athens as the most beautiful and perfect city of the period. Therefore, he rebuilt the palaces and temples on the acropolis. It took 11 years to build the Parthenon, the temple of the goddess Athena. Much of this building was done with money that belonged to the Delian League.

Pericles also built the Long Walls. They were two parallel, fortified walls with tile roofs that connected Athens with its seaport of Piraeus some five miles, or eight kilometers, away. Having the Long Walls meant Athens could get supplies even in wartime.

Pericles led the Athenians for almost 30 years. During this period, art, philosophy, and literature reached new heights. Many people who came to Athens from other city-states settled there and became citizens.

Pericles

1. Why was the Delian League formed?
2. Why did League members begin to resent Athens?
3. What did Pericles do?

DECLINE OF ATHENS   The more powerful Athens became, the more resentful other Greek city-states grew. Anti-Athenian feelings soon spread throughout Greece. When Athenians attacked one of Sparta's allies, a group of city-states led by Sparta declared war on Athens. The war, which was called the Peloponnesian War, lasted almost 30 years. It ended in 404 B.C. when

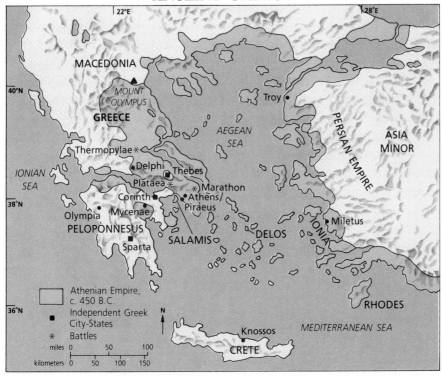

Athens surrendered to Sparta. The Athenians lost their fleet, their power, and their confidence.

Between the war and a plague that struck during the war, Athens also lost more than one quarter of its population. Since much of its land was ruined, thousands of young Athenian men left home and became soldiers in the Persian army.

When the Spartans took control of Athens in 404 B.C., they chose 30 Athenian men to rule Athens. Not long after, the Athenians successfully revolted and once more set up a democracy. But Athens was never again as powerful as it had been before the Peloponnesian War.

1. Why did Sparta declare war on Athens?
2. What happened to Athens as a result of the Peloponnesian War?

DECLINE OF THE CITY-STATES

After the Peloponnesian War, most Greeks began to lose their sense of community. The war had lasted a long time and

Philip II

had cost a great deal of money. People were discouraged. They began to lose interest in what was good for their city-state. Instead, they became more interested in making money and having a good time. Soon, bitterness developed between the upper and lower classes within each polis.

After the war, Sparta ruled Greece. But the Spartans were harsh rulers who angered other Greeks. In 371 B.C., a group of city-states led by Thebes overthrew Spartan rule. The rule of Thebes, however, was no better than that of Sparta. It weakened the city-states even more. The Greeks were no longer strong or united enough to fight off an invader. In 338 B.C., Philip II of Macedonia conquered Greece.

1. How did the Peloponnesian War help destroy the unity of each Greek city-state?
2. What were some other reasons for the decline of the Greek city-states?
3. Who conquered Greece in 338 B.C.?

CHAPTER 10 REVIEW

SUMMARY

1. The geographic and political center of Greek life was the polis, or city-state, which developed around 700 B.C.

2. The two greatest Greek city-states were Sparta and Athens.

3. Since Sparta's main goal was to be militarily strong, much time and energy were spent training its citizens for war.

4. Spartan women had more freedom than the women of other Greek city-states.

5. Since they believed new ideas would weaken their way of life, Spartans tried to prevent change.

6. Between 750 and 507 B.C., Athens went through a series of government reorganizations and reforms that changed the rules of Greek citizenship.

7. In 507 B.C., Cleisthenes put into effect the world's first generally democratic constitution.

8. Between 490 and 479 B.C., the Greek city-states fought several wars with the Persian Empire.

9. After the defeat of the Persians, Athens became, under Pericles, Greece's leading polis.

10. Sparta defeated Athens in the Peloponnesian War, which was fought between 431 and 404 B.C.

11. As a result of the Peloponnesian War, Greek city-states lost their sense of community.

12. Greece was conquered by Philip II of Macedonia in 338 B.C.

BUILDING VOCABULARY

1. *Identify the following:*

   Sparta   Cleisthenes   Thermopylae   Pericles
   Athens   Marathon   Salamis   Long Walls
   Solon   Xerxes   Delian League   Peloponnesian War

2. *Define the following:*

   polis   aristocrats   constitution   strait
   acropolis   helots   magistrates   defensive league
   agora   perioeci   triremes

REVIEWING THE FACTS

1. Why did Greek communities have little contact with one another?
2. About how many citizens did the average polis contain?
3. What did the citizens of a polis consider most important?
4. What was the main goal of Sparta's aristocrats?
5. Why was it important for Spartan women to be healthy?
6. Why did Sparta remain a poor farming society?
7. How did the Athenians choose members of the Council of Five Hundred?
8. Why was the Battle of Marathon important for the Greeks?
9. How did the Athenians use the silver they found in mines near Athens?
10. How did the Delian League become the Athenian Empire?

DISCUSSING IMPORTANT IDEAS

1. Do you think the Athenian nobles were wise to reform their government?
2. Do you approve of the Athenian method of choosing members of the Council of Five Hundred by lot? Why or why not?
3. Do you think Pericles deserved the title of "first citizen" of Athens? Why or why not?
4. What may happen to a community as a result of a long war?

USING MAPS

Study the map on page 159, and answer the following questions:

1. In what area of Greece was Sparta?
2. Approximately how far was Athens from Sparta?
3. What battles are shown?
4. Which battle was fought farthest north?
5. Where is Ionia located?
6. What bodies of water bordered the Athenian Empire in 450 B.C.?

CHAPTER 11
CULTURAL CONTRIBUTIONS

The Greeks made many contributions to western civilization in the arts and sciences. Much of what they contributed came about because of their attitude toward their gods. They saw their gods as the source of all power.

The Greeks felt they could honor their gods by imitating them. This meant trying to be the best they could in everything they did. The greater the skill the Greeks showed in thinking, athletic games, or the arts, the more the gods were honored. The result was "the Golden Age" of Greek culture, also known as "the Classical Age of Greece."

RELIGIOUS BELIEFS AND PRACTICES

Although most Greeks held similar religious beliefs, there was no single Greek religion. Each city-state worshiped its own gods. Officials within each polis took charge of feasts and sacrifices. Heads of families could pray and offer sacrifices to the gods in their own households.

Greek priests often served as **oracles**, or persons who could communicate with the gods. Greeks went to the oracles for advice, which was given in the form of a **prophecy**, or a statement of what might happen in the future. Often, the prophecy could be interpreted in more than one way. The person

---

THE DELPHIC ORACLE

The most popular oracle was a priestess in the city of Delphi. Kings and common people came to seek her advice on many questions. She answered them in strange messages that priests alone could interpret.

Why were oracles important in ancient Greece?

---

seeking advice had to decide what the prophecy of the oracles really meant.

1. What religious practices did the Greek city-states have in common?
2. What did oracles do?

GODS AND GODDESSES OF MOUNT OLYMPUS   During the Golden Age, Greeks worshipped the gods of Mount Olym-

OLYMPIAN GODS AND GODDESSES

Name	Realm
Zeus	ruler of Mount Olympus, king of the gods, god of the weather
Aphrodite	goddess of love and beauty
Apollo	god of the sun; patron of truth, archery, music, medicine, and prophecy
Ares	god of war
Artemis	goddess of the moon; mighty huntress and "rainer of arrows;" guardian of cities, young animals, and women; twin sister of Apollo
Athena	goddess of wisdom; city god of Athens; patron of household crafts; protectress in war of those who worshipped her; daughter of Zeus
Demeter	goddess of crops, giver of grain and fruit
Dionysus	god of fertility, of joyous life and hospitality, and of wild things
Hephaestus	god of fire and artisans; maker of Pandora, the first mortal woman; husband of Aphrodite
Hera	protectress of marriage, children, and the home; wife of Zeus
Hermes	god of orators, writers, and commerce; protector of thieves, and mischief-makers; guardian of wayfarers; messenger to mortals; son of Zeus
Poseidon	god of the sea and earthquakes, giver of horses to mortals

pus. There were 12 major gods and goddesses. Each of them had specific roles to perform.

Most ancient peoples feared their gods. They believed that people were only instruments put on earth to obey and serve the gods. The Greeks were the first people to feel differently. They placed importance on the worth of the individual. Because they believed in their own value, the Greeks had a great deal of self-respect and approached their gods with dignity.

Zeus

The Greeks built temples to honor their gods. Each temple contained a statue of a god. In front of the statue was an altar. Because the Greeks considered the temple to be the god's home, they did not enter it. They worshipped outside at the entrance as a sign of respect.

Another way the Greeks honored their gods was with different kinds of festivals. Each festival reflected the power of the god in whose honor it was given. Out of the festivals came two important contributions to western culture—the Olympic Games and the theater.

1. Why did most ancient peoples fear their gods?
2. How did the Greeks honor their gods and goddesses?

THE OLYMPIC GAMES   Every four years, in the middle of summer, a festival was held in Olympia to honor Zeus. Olympia was not really a town. It was a group of temples and arenas built in fields. A 40-foot, or 12-meter, gold and ivory statue of Zeus stood in one of the temples.

The festival was known as the Olympic Games and was the most important sporting event in Greece. While the games were going on, the Greeks would stop fighting any war in which they were involved. When the Spartans refused to call a truce during the Peloponnesian War to compete in the games, they had to pay a fine.

Athletes came from all over Greece and from the Greek colonies in Africa, Italy, and Asia Minor to take part in the games. Individuals, rather than teams, competed. Only male athletes were allowed to take part. Women were not even allowed to watch. Each athlete had to swear on the sacred boar of Zeus that he would observe the rules of the games. Those who broke the rules were fined.

The Olympics consisted of many events. One of the most exciting was the chariot race, which was held in the Hippodrome, an oval track surrounded by grandstands. The chariots had small wheels and were open in the back. At first, the chariots were pulled by four horses. In later Olympics, only two horses were used. About 40 chariots started the race, but only a few could finish the 9 miles, or 14.4 kilometers. The owner of the winning chariot received a crown made from olive leaves.

Another major event was boxing. Boxers did not use their fists. They wrapped their hands with ox-hide thongs and slapped one another with the flat of the hand. There were no set rounds

---

OLYMPIC GAMES

The modern Olympic Games are based on the original Olympics held in ancient Greece. Today's Olympic athletes come from many countries and compete in a variety of sports. One sport practiced in both the ancient and modern Olympic Games is the discus throw.

Why did the ancient Greeks hold the Olympic Games?

or points. A match between two boxers went on until one raised a finger in the air as a sign of defeat.

Another fighting event was the **pancratium**. It was a combination of boxing and wrestling in which no holds were barred between the two fighters. The only thing a fighter could not do was bite or gouge an opponent's eyes.

The winner of the **pentathlon** was considered the best all-round athlete. The pentathlon itself was five events in one. Athletes who took part had to run, do the long jump, throw the discus, hurl the javelin, and wrestle. Like winners of other events, the pentathlon winner was crowned with an olive-leaf wreath.

Olympic winners were considered heroes. Poets wrote about them. City-states held parades for them. Some city-states even gave them free meals for a year.

Between the various events at the games, poets recited their verses. Herodotus, the "Father of History," first read his account of the Persian War at the Olympics. Greek historians even dated events by **Olympiads,** or the four-year periods between the games. The first recorded date in Greek history is 776 B.C., the date of the first Olympic Games.

1. Who took part in the Olympics?
2. What were three events in the Olympics?
3. How were Olympic winners treated?

THE THEATER   The theater grew out of festivals given in honor of the god Dionysus. About 600 B.C., the Ionians began telling stories about Dionysus at festivals. A chorus chanted and danced each story to the music of a flute. At certain points, the chorus fell silent. The chorus leader then delivered a **soliloquy**, or talk in which personal thoughts and feelings are expressed to the audience.

Comedy and Tragedy Masks

In time, the chorus became shorter and the soliloquies longer. Stories were then told about other gods and heroes. About the time of the Peloponnesian War, a Greek poet named Aeschylus added an additional character to each story. Instead of singing or telling the story, it was acted out. Thus, Aeschylus created what came to be known as a play.

The first Greek plays were **tragedies**, or stories about suffering. All dealt with the past and with the relationship between people and gods. Not all of them had unhappy endings. However, all did point out that though people suffered, most individuals managed to carry on despite suffering.

Three of the greatest writers of tragedy were Aeschylus, Sophocles, and Euripides. All three lived in Athens during its Golden Age. Aeschylus wrote about power and its effect on people. Sophocles showed that people suffered because of their sins and mistakes and that suffering could make someone a better person. Euripides tried to show that people suffered because they did bad things. One of his plays dealt with people who broke the laws of their city-states rather than break those of the gods.

Soon after the development of tragedy, a second type of play came into being. It was **comedy**, or a play with humor. Unlike tragedies, Greek comedies dealt with the present. Early comedies poked fun at individual politicians and other polis leaders, who often were in the audience. Later comedies did away with the chorus. They also changed from poking fun at an individual politician to poking fun at a certain type of person, such as a son who wastes money or a slave who plots against a master. One of the greatest writers of Greek comedy was Aristophanes. He found something humorous about everyone.

Greek plays were performed only at community festivals. Performances began at sunrise and went on all day. Tragedies were presented in the morning and comedies in the afternoon. All performers were men. Women were allowed to watch the plays but could not act in them.

Each actor wore a huge canvas and plaster mask that showed the sex, age, and mood of the character. The mouth of the mask was shaped like a funnel. This helped carry the sound of the actor's voice to the entire audience. Actors also wore heavy padding under their robes and boots with thick soles. This made them seem larger than they really were.

The plays were given in open-air theaters. Some theaters were large enough to hold all of the people in the community. Anyone who could not afford to buy a ticket was admitted free. The audience sat on rows of stone seats and benches set on the slope of a hill. The seats were arranged in a semicircle around a stage that was level with the ground.

The Greeks considered support of the theater to be a public responsibility. An official of each polis chose the plays to be

Euripides

GREEK OPEN-AIR THEATER

The Greeks performed many plays in open-air theaters. The stage was in the center, and the seats were built in raised rows around it.
At what occasions were Greek plays performed?

performed. The official then assigned each play to a wealthy citizen to stage. A panel of citizens judged the plays at each festival, and the author of the winning play was awarded an ivy crown.

1. How did the Greek theater start? How did it change over the years?
2. In what ways were tragedies and comedies different from one another?
3. How did the Greeks feel about the theater?

SCIENCE

Among the things on which the Greeks placed great importance was **intellect**, or the ability to learn and reason. The Greeks thought intellect should be used to its fullest. So, they asked questions about the scheme of things and studied the laws of nature. They came to love wisdom. To the Greeks, studying the laws of nature and loving wisdom were the same thing. They called it *philosophia*. Today, the people who search for such knowledge and wisdom are known as scientists and **philosophers**, or people who think about the meaning of life. Much of what they know is based on the studies and theories of the Greeks.

1. What attitude did the Greeks have toward intellect?
2. Why did the Greeks study the laws of nature?

SOCRATES   In 399 B.C., a trial was held in Athens. The person on trial was Socrates, a 70-year-old Athenian philosopher who was interested in the thinking process. Socrates gave up private business so he could spend his time searching for truth. He believed people could discover truth if they knew how to think.

In his search for truth, Socrates walked all over Athens trying to teach people how to think. He did this by asking questions. Each question was designed to make a person arrive

---

DEATH OF SOCRATES

Socrates faced death with self-control and dignity. In this eighteenth-century painting, he is surrounded by his sorrowing friends as he prepares to drink hemlock poison.

What influence did Socrates have on the Greeks?

---

step-by-step at a final conclusion, or truth. This form of questioning is known as the **Socratic method**.

All Athenians did not react in the same way to Socrates' teachings. Some were pleased that they had learned how to examine their own beliefs and to think things out. Others saw Socrates' ideas as dangerous. They did not like self-examination, particularly when it pointed out their own mistakes. In time, they considered Socrates a threat to Athens. Finally, they accused him of denying the gods, corrupting the young, and trying to overthrow the government.

Socrates was tried before a jury of some 500 citizens. He defended himself by speaking about truth and goodness. In his speech, he said, "Wealth does not bring goodness. But goodness brings wealth and every blessing, both to the citizen and to the polis." He also said he would not change his beliefs even to save his life.

The jury found Socrates guilty and sentenced him to death. The sentence was carried out by making Socrates drink poisonous hemlock juice. Later, the Athenians were sorry for having executed Socrates and put up a bronze statue in his honor.

1. What did Socrates try to teach? How did he do this?
2. How did the Athenians react to Socrates' teachings?
3. Why was Socrates tried?

Plato

PLATO Socrates left no writings. All that is known about him comes from one of his pupils, an Athenian aristocrat named Plato. Plato recorded the speeches Socrates made at his trial and just before his death.

Plato was 30 years old when Socrates died. Until then, Plato had wanted to become a politician. But in 399 B.C., he changed his mind. He left Greece, and for the next 12 years traveled in Egypt and Italy. When he returned home, he set up a school outside Athens in the sacred grove of the hero Academus. The school, where Plato hoped to train government leaders, became known as the Academy. Plato taught at the Academy for almost 40 years. The Academy itself lasted for almost 900 years after Plato's death.

Plato's beliefs were contrary to the ideas that had made Athens great. Plato believed in order. He thought that political liberty was disorder and did not approve of it. He thought only the wise and the good should rule.

GREEK PHILOSOPHERS
The ideas of Greek thinkers influenced the development of western civilization. In this sixteenth-century European painting, Plato and Aristotle discuss the meaning of human achievement with their pupils.
What were the interests of the Greek philosophers?

Plato set down his ideas about an ideal state in a book called *The Republic.* It is the first book ever written on **political science**, or the study of government. In it, Plato examined different types of government and explained how to avoid political mistakes.

Like Socrates, Plato believed in truth. He thought it could be found only after a long, hard search. He showed how difficult it is to discover truth in a work called *The Dialogues. The Dialogues* consists of a series of discussions in which different people talk about such things as truth and loyalty. Socrates is the leading speaker in many discussions. Through these discussions, Plato brings out the self-questioning that goes on within a person troubled by basic issues.

1. Why did Plato set up the Academy?
2. What were some of Plato's beliefs?

ARISTOTLE   One of Plato's brightest pupils was Aristotle. Aristotle came to the Academy when he was 17 years old and stayed for 20 years. Before he died in 322 B.C., he founded his own school in Athens and wrote more than 200 books.

Aristotle was known as "the master of them that know." He believed in using one's senses to discover the laws that govern the physical world. He was the first to **classify**, or group together, plants and animals that resemble each other. His system of classification, with few changes, is still used today. Over the centuries, it has helped scientists to handle a great amount of information in an orderly way.

Aristotle made another contribution to modern science when he added to the ideas of an earlier Greek scientist named Thales of Miletus. Thales developed the first two steps of what is known today as the **scientific method**. First, Thales collected information. Then, based on what he observed, he formed a **hypothesis**, or possible explanation. Aristotle provided the third step of the scientific method when he tested the hypothesis to see if it was correct.

Another important contribution Aristotle made was in **logic**, or the science of reasoning. He developed the **syllogism**, which consists of three related statements. The third statement is a conclusion based on the information given in the first two statements. For example:

Aristotle

Athenians are Greeks.
Socrates is an Athenian.
Therefore, Socrates is Greek.

1. How did Aristotle's classification system help scientists?
2. What other contributions to science did Aristotle make?

DISCOVERIES AND INVENTIONS   Greek scientists were not looking for ways to make life easier or better. They were trying to increase their store of knowledge. They had none of the equipment scientists have today, such as telescopes, microscopes, or scales that weigh small amounts. Still, they managed to make important discoveries.

Their curiosity about nature led Greek scientists to discover that natural events are not the result of the behavior of gods. They also learned that the world is governed by natural laws that humans can discover and understand.

GREEK SCIENTISTS

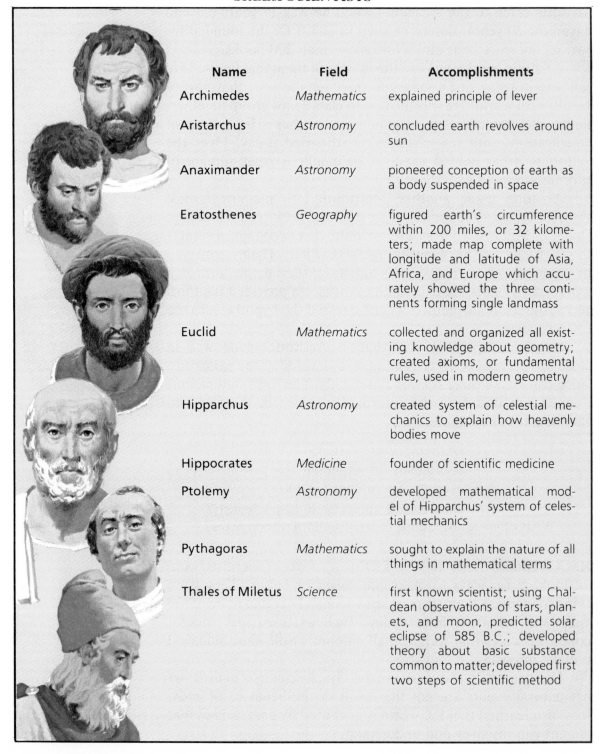

Name	Field	Accomplishments
Archimedes	*Mathematics*	explained principle of lever
Aristarchus	*Astronomy*	concluded earth revolves around sun
Anaximander	*Astronomy*	pioneered conception of earth as a body suspended in space
Eratosthenes	*Geography*	figured earth's circumference within 200 miles, or 32 kilometers; made map complete with longitude and latitude of Asia, Africa, and Europe which accurately showed the three continents forming single landmass
Euclid	*Mathematics*	collected and organized all existing knowledge about geometry; created axioms, or fundamental rules, used in modern geometry
Hipparchus	*Astronomy*	created system of celestial mechanics to explain how heavenly bodies move
Hippocrates	*Medicine*	founder of scientific medicine
Ptolemy	*Astronomy*	developed mathematical model of Hipparchus' system of celestial mechanics
Pythagoras	*Mathematics*	sought to explain the nature of all things in mathematical terms
Thales of Miletus	*Science*	first known scientist; using Chaldean observations of stars, planets, and moon, predicted solar eclipse of 585 B.C.; developed theory about basic substance common to matter; developed first two steps of scientific method

There were many Greek scientists. The first was Thales of Miletus, who came from Ionia. Thales not only developed the first two steps of the scientific method, but he also predicted correctly an eclipse of the sun in 585 B.C. The contributions made by Thales and other Greek scientists were important to the later development of scientific thought.

Greek scientists also contributed to the field of medicine. The "Father of Scientific Medicine" was Hippocrates, who was considered the perfect physician. He traveled all over Greece diagnosing illnesses and curing sick people. Hippocrates believed diseases came from natural causes. At the time, most other doctors thought diseases were caused by evil spirits entering the body.

Hippocrates drew up a list of rules about how doctors should use their skills only to help their patients. His rules are known as the **Hippocratic oath**. It binds doctors to honor their teachers, do their best for the sick, never give poisons, and keep the secrets of their patients. Doctors all over the world still promise to honor Hippocrates' oath.

1. What two major discoveries did Greek scientists make?
2. Who were three important Greek scientists? Why were they important?
3. What did Hippocrates do?

CHAPTER 11 REVIEW

SUMMARY

1. Ancient Greeks believed individuals should honor their gods by doing the best they could in everything they did and said.

2. During the "Golden Age," the Greeks made many contributions in thinking, athletics, and the arts.

3. The Olympic Games, which were held every four years in honor of Zeus, were the most important sporting event in Greece.

4. The play developed out of a festival in honor of Dionysus.

5. Socrates was an Athenian philosopher who developed a form of questioning known as the Socratic method.

6. The Socratic method used questions to help a person arrive at a conclusion.

7. Socrates was tried and sentenced to death in 399 B.C. because many people considered his teachings to be a threat to Athens.

8. Plato, who was one of Socrates' pupils, founded a school and wrote the first book on political science.

9. Aristotle developed a system of classification and provided the third step in the scientific method.

10. Greek scientists learned that the world is governed by natural laws that humans can discover and understand.

11. Hippocrates believed diseases came from natural causes rather than from evil spirits.

BUILDING VOCABULARY

1. *Identify the following:*

Golden Age	Herodotus	Euripides	*The Republic*
Mount Olympus	Dionysus	Aristophanes	Aristotle
Zeus	Aeschylus	Socrates	Thales of Miletus
Olympic Games	Sophocles	Plato	Hippocrates

2. *Define the following:*

oracles	soliloquy	philosophers	hypothesis
prophecy	tragedies	Socratic method	logic
pancratium	comedy	political science	syllogism
pentathlon	intellect	classify	Hippocratic oath
Olympiads	*philosophia*	scientific method	

REVIEWING THE FACTS

1. How did the Greeks believe they could best honor their gods?
2. Why did the Greeks worship outside their temples?
3. What effect did the Olympic Games have on Greek warfare?
4. What role did women play in the Olympic Games?
5. What relationship was there between historians and the Olympic Games?
6. What did Greek actors wear on the stage to help their audience hear and see them better?
7. How did the Greeks view intellect?
8. How do people know what Socrates taught?
9. What are the three steps in the scientific method?
10. In what were Greek scientists the most interested?

DISCUSSING IMPORTANT IDEAS

1. How important was religion in ancient Greek civilization? Explain.
2. How did the Olympic Games honor the gods?
3. Do you think that support of the theater should be a public responsibility?
4. Would you like being taught by the Socratic method? Why or why not?
5. Do you think the Athenians were right to put Socrates on trial? Why or why not?
6. Why is the scientific method important to modern science?

CHAPTER 12

THE HELLENISTIC PERIOD

Affter the Greek city-states lost their independence, many changes took place. The new rulers of Greece built empires and increased trade. At the same time, they spread Greek culture and customs. Before long, Greek ideas and achievements were influencing people from Gibraltar to India.

The Greek language came to be spoken by many people. Greek architecture was copied for new buildings. Children studied Greek literature in schools. People used Greek furniture in their homes. Greek plays became a popular form of entertainment. Business people adopted Greek methods of banking. Greek influence could be found in almost every part of daily life.

The period in which all of this took place has come to be called the "Hellenistic Age."

Philip II of Macedonia

By 338 B.C., Greece had a new ruler, Philip II of Macedonia. Macedonia was a small, mountainous country north of Greece. Most Macedonians were farmers who tended the land. They cared little for the Greeks and had fought against them in the Persian Wars. Macedonian kings, however, were of Greek descent and admired Greek culture.

Philip became the ruler of Macedonia in 359 B.C. During his youth, he was held hostage for three years in Thebes. In those years, he learned to love Greek culture. At the same time, however, he learned to hate the weaknesses of the Greek form of government.

Soldier

Philip believed it was his destiny to unify the Greek city-states and spread Greek culture. As soon as he became ruler of Macedonia, he sought to fulfill that destiny. It took him a little over 20 years.

Philip went about reaching his goal in many ways. For example, until his time, the Macedonian army consisted of volunteers who fought only in summer. Philip turned this part-time volunteer army into a year-round, well-organized, professional one.

Philip developed a special infantry formation called a **phalanx** to be used in battle. Foot soldiers formed a solid body some 16 rows deep. Those in each line stayed so close together that their shields overlapped. This gave them added protection. The phalanx charged as a group, which meant it had more striking power than its enemies.

Philip also armed the soldiers with spears that were 14 feet, or over 4 meters, long. This was twice as long as ordinary spears. In addition, he added soldiers skilled in the use of slingshots and bows and arrows. These soldiers could fight in hilly areas where the phalanx was unable to go.

Philip flattered local Greek officials and gave them gold. He found ways to cause disagreements among Greek city-states. Then, when city-states were weak from fighting each other, his army invaded and conquered them.

Philip made treaties with Greek leaders only to break them when the Greeks relaxed their guard. He saw marriage as a way of forming political **alliances**, or partnerships. He married six or seven times for this reason.

Demosthenes, an Athenian **orator**, or public speaker, tried to warn the Greeks that Philip was dangerous. But most would not listen. They were unhappy with their local governments and tired of the bickering that constantly went on. They thought Philip might bring efficiency and discipline.

When Philip led his troops into central Greece in 338 B.C., Thebes and Athens raised a small army to stop the invasion. But the Greek army was not strong enough and was defeated. Having gained control of Greece, Philip began preparing for a campaign against the Persians. But in 336 B.C., in the middle of his preparations, Philip was killed. His son Alexander took over.

1. What did Philip II believe his destiny to be?
2. How did Philip II go about fulfilling his destiny?
3. Why was Philip II able to conquer the Greek city-states?

DEMOSTHENES

Demosthenes worked for the freedom of the Greek city-states. He was known for his ability as a public speaker. It is said he trained himself by shouting above the roar of the ocean waves with his mouth full of pebbles.

What did Demosthenes tell the Greeks about Philip of Macedonia?

ALEXANDER THE GREAT

Alexander took over Philip's throne at the age of 20. He had been a commander in the army since he was 16. One of the first things he did upon becoming a commander was to cut his shoulder-length hair. At the same time, he ordered his soldiers to shave their beards. This, he said, would prevent enemy soldiers from grabbing them in close combat.

Alexander was physically strong and good-looking. He had a lot of energy and a quick mind. Aristotle tutored him for three years in such subjects as literature, political science, geography, and biology. Because of this, Alexander included philosophers and scientists in his army. The philosophers advised him on political matters. The scientists collected plant and animal specimens from newly conquered lands. The specimens were sent back to Aristotle so he could examine them.

Alexander was a great general who feared nothing. He crushed the Persian Empire and then marched as far east as Pakistan. He would have gone farther, but his troops refused. In the course of his conquests, Alexander covered more than 22,000 miles, or over 35,000 kilometers, from the Nile to the Indus rivers. Through all that territory, he never lost a battle.

1. What kind of person was Alexander?
2. What conquests did Alexander make?

Greek-Egyptian Sphinx

ALEXANDER'S EMPIRE   Alexander had a vision of a worldwide state in which all people would live together in peace. He wanted to bring unity and justice to his empire.

Alexander believed there was only one way to achieve his goal. That was to unite Macedonians, Greeks, and Persians. He began by taking Persian soldiers into his army. Next, he married a Persian woman and had 80 of his leading army officers marry Persian women, too. Then, he began to dress in the Persian fashion and to follow some Persian customs.

One custom was for rulers to claim they were gods. So, Alexander claimed he was a god and insisted that people treat him that way. The Macedonians and Greeks, however, refused to do so. The Greeks also objected to equal treatment for the Persians. They looked down on all people who did not speak Greek or follow Greek customs. They called such people *barbaroi*, from which the word "barbarians" comes.

THE EMPIRE OF ALEXANDER THE GREAT

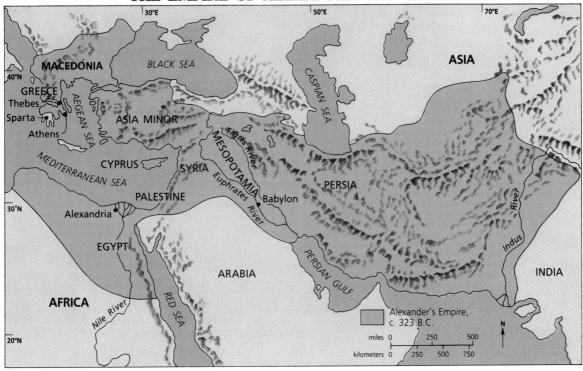

As a result of such feelings, Alexander's attempt to achieve unity among his people was not successful.

1. What was Alexander's goal?
2. How did Alexander treat his Persian subjects? How did the Greeks and Macedonians feel about this?

ALEXANDRIA Alexander ruled for 13 years. During that time, he founded about 70 cities, 16 of which were named Alexandria after him. He encouraged Greeks and Macedonians to settle in the new cities, which were scattered all over the empire.

The most famous Alexandria was in Egypt. Within 70 years after its founding, it had become a great center of trade and learning. Greeks from all over the eastern Mediterranean came there. They wanted to take advantage of its economic opportunities and be a part of its intellectual and social life.

Alexandria had two great harbors. They were protected by **breakwaters**, or barriers that break the force of waves. A lighthouse 400 feet, or about 121.9 meters, tall dominated the

LIGHTHOUSE OF ALEXANDRIA

The lighthouse of Alexandria was one of the Seven Wonders of the Ancient World. A fire on top provided light to guide the ships into port.
What was life like in Alexandria?

scene. Overlooking the main harbor was a palace containing a museum and a library staffed by famous philosophers and scientists. The library had the greatest collection of books of ancient times. There, Euclid wrote his book on geometry. There, Eratosthenes reasoned that a ship could reach India by sailing west from Spain.

1. How did the physical features of Alexandria, Egypt, help the city's trade?
2. What was the city's main cultural feature?

END OF THE EMPIRE

In 323 B.C., when Alexander was in Babylon, he caught a fever and died. He was 33 years old. His body was wrapped in gold and placed in a glass coffin in the Royal Tombs of Alexandria, Egypt. After his death, Alexander became a romantic legend. More than 80 versions of his life have been written in more than 20 languages.

After Alexander's death, fights broke out over who was to rule the empire. The areas Alexander had conquered in India returned to their original rulers. Three of Alexander's generals divided the rest of the empire among themselves. Antigonus became king of Macedonia. Ptolemy established the dynasty of the Ptolemies in Egypt. Seleucus formed the Seleucid Empire in Persia. Athens and Sparta again became independent city-states. Most other Greek city-states banded together into one of two leagues. But neither league had much power or importance.

Greek cultural influence, however, became stronger than ever after Alexander's death. The rulers who took Alexander's place adopted Greek as their language and used Alexander's titles. They even stamped his picture on their coins.

Trade grew. From Africa and Asia came spices, ivory, incense, pearls, and rare woods. From Syria and Egypt came glass, metals, and linen. From Greece came olive oil, wine, and pottery. From Sicily and Egypt came wheat.

HELLENISTIC ART

Hellenistic artists showed action and feeling in their works. The portrait of a Greek-Egyptian (left) and the statue of the goddess of victory (right) reflect these qualities.

What aspects of life were influenced by the spread of Greek culture?

The cities that had been a part of Alexander's empire now existed mainly for trade. They grew along with trade. They kept Greek culture alive. City officials made their law, language, calendar, and coins Greek. Teachers brought Greek customs and ideas into the schools. Merchants and bankers used Greek methods to run their businesses.

Greek Coins

The Greek city-states, however, were never the same again. Although they kept their political independence, they could not regain the power of the past. In time, economic conditions worsened. Great **factories**, or places where goods are manufactured, had been built in the new Hellenistic cities. Greek manufacturers now found they could not compete with these factories. As a result, more and more young Greeks left their homes to earn a living in other countries. Population in the Greek city-states fell. There were not enough people to work the land, and many farms once again became wilderness. In 197 B.C., when Roman armies came, the Greeks were too few and too weak to resist.

1. What happened to Alexander's empire after he died?
2. How did Greek influence continue to grow and spread after Alexander's death?
3. What happened in Greece during the Hellenistic Age?

CHAPTER 12 REVIEW

SUMMARY

1. Philip II, ruler of Macedonia, believed it was his destiny to unify the Greek city-states and spread Greek culture.

2. Philip II conquered Greece in 338 B.C.

3. When Philip II died in 336 B.C., his son Alexander took over the throne.

4. Alexander was a great general who never lost a battle and whose conquests stretched from the Nile to the Indus rivers.

5. Alexander tried without success to achieve unity among the Macedonians, Greeks, and Persians within his empire.

6. The most famous city founded by Alexander was Alexandria, Egypt, which contained a large library.

7. After Alexander died in 323 B.C., his empire was broken up.

8. After Alexander's death, Greek cultural influence became stronger than ever.

9. Although the Greek city-states again became independent following Alexander's death, economic conditions in Greece grew worse.

10. The Greeks were conquered by the Romans in 197 B.C.

BUILDING VOCABULARY

1. *Identify the following:*

Hellenistic Age	Demosthenes	Alexandria	Ptolemy
Philip II	Alexander	Antigonus	Seleucus
Macedonia			

2. *Define the following:*

phalanx	orator	*barbaroi*	breakwaters
alliances			factories

REVIEWING THE FACTS

1. How did Philip II learn to love Greek culture?
2. What changes did Philip II make in his army?
3. How did Philip II view marriage?
4. Why did Demosthenes try to prove that Philip II was dangerous?
5. Why did Alexander order his soldiers to shave their beards?
6. What did Alexander learn from his tutor Aristotle?
7. How did Alexander help Aristotle?
8. Why was Alexander unable to achieve unity among his people?
9. Why did many Greeks go to Alexandria, Egypt?
10. Why were the Greeks unable to resist the Romans?

DISCUSSING IMPORTANT IDEAS

1. What changes did Philip II bring about in warfare?
2. Would you have listened to Demosthenes? Why or why not?
3. Was Alexander wise in trying to achieve unity among his people? Explain.
4. What do you think was Alexander's main accomplishment?
5. Do you think Alexander deserved to be called "the Great"? Why or why not?
6. Can cultural influence spread without conquest? Explain.

USING MAPS

Study the map on page 181, and answer the following questions:

1. About how far did Alexander's empire extend east to west? North to south?
2. What sea is located 40° north and 50° east?
3. What city is located approximately 30° north latitude and 29° east longitude?
4. Which Greek city-state was not part of Alexander's empire?

CONFUCIUS

Confucius was a Chinese teacher and **scholar**, or student of knowledge, who was born in 551 B.C. His Chinese name was K'ung Fu-tzu, but Europeans call him Confucius. Confucius developed a philosophy about how people should act and treat each other. It shaped Chinese society for over 2,000 years.

Confucius was born to an upper-class family that had no money. He was a bright student who studied endlessly. He wanted to be a politician, but he was not successful. As a teacher, however, he was deeply respected.

During Confucius' lifetime, China had many problems. Powerful leaders fought each other for control of the land. Poor farmers worked hard. But they received little reward and were forced to pay heavy taxes.

Confucius thought that if people were taught to behave correctly, it would help to end China's troubles. He said that there were Five Relationships that were most important—ruler and ruled, father and son, husband and wife, older brother and younger brother, and friend and friend. He believed each person owed respect to those above him or her. For instance, sons owed respect and honor to their fathers. Those above were bound to set a good example for those below.

Confucius hoped to reform the government of China. Most rulers of the

time governed by military force. Confucius advised rulers to govern instead by being wise because the people would obey a wise ruler. He believed that "If one leads the people by goodness, the people will feel their duty and correct themselves."

Most government officials at the time were members of the upper class. They received their jobs because of family connections rather than their ability. Confucius believed that only officials with education and ability should be appointed to government jobs.

Beginning around 200 B.C., Confucius' teachings were used in **civil service tests**, or tests for government jobs. At first, only members of the upper class were allowed to take the tests. Later, the system grew to include other classes.

Confucius' teachings were very demanding. To follow them, people had to live ideal lives. For this reason, not everyone wanted to accept the teachings. Still, Confucius had many students who later became government officials. Within time, Confucius' ideas became the basis of both Chinese society and government.

1. What was life like in China during Confucius' early years?
2. What did Confucius believe would help solve China's problems?
3. Who did Confucius believe should have government jobs?

UNIT 4 REVIEW

SUMMARY

1. Greek civilization developed out of the Minoan and Mycenean civilizations.

2. The polis was the geographic and political center of Greek life.

3. The Greeks developed government by the people and the first generally democratic constitution and made major contributions in the arts and sciences.

4. Even after the decline of the city-states, Greek influence spread through military conquests and trade.

5. One of the most important Greek contributions to later civilizations was a belief in the worth of the individual.

6. Greek thought and culture is one basis of modern western civilization.

REVIEWING THE MAIN IDEAS

1. Explain what parts of the Minoan culture and the Mycenean culture were carried over to the Greek city-states.

2. Compare the reasons for the decline of the Athenian Empire to the reasons for the decline of Greece after the Peloponnesian Wars.

3. What ideas did the Greeks contribute to western civilization? What institutions did they contribute?

DEVELOPING SKILLS

In learning about history, it is important to be able to tell the difference between fact and opinion. It is a fact, for example, that Christopher Columbus sailed westward from Europe in 1492 A.D. and discovered the New World. But whether or not he was a great explorer is a matter of opinion.

Some people feel Columbus was a great explorer. He persuaded his sailors to continue sailing in spite of unknown dangers. Also, his voyage led the way for large numbers of Europeans to come to the New World. If Columbus had not made his voyage, history probably would have been very different.

Other people, however, feel Columbus was not a great explorer. They point out that when Columbus landed in the New World, he thought he had reached Asia. They ask how Columbus could be great if he did not even know where he was.

Opinions depend on both facts and **values**, or what a person considers important. To think clearly, a person has to be able to tell the difference between fact and opinion.

This exercise is designed to give you practice in this skill. Read each of the following statements, and then tell whether it is fact or opinion.

1. Greek civilization developed out of a combination of two earlier civilizations, Minoan and Mycenean.

2. The Minoans contributed more important things to Greek civilization than the Myceneans did.

3. The Minoans depended on their ships for protection from attack.

4. The Myceneans depended on fortresses for protection from attack.

5. Mycenean communities generally were better protected than Minoan communities were.

6. The polis was the geographic and political center of Greek life.

7. The Athenians developed the world's first generally democratic constitution, which gave them certain rights.

8. Athens was a better place than Sparta.

9. If Athens had not lost the Peloponnesian War, Philip II of Macedonia would not have been able to conquer Greece.

10. One contribution the Greeks made to western civilization was the theater.

11. The most important contribution the Greeks made to western civilization was the idea of democracy.

12. Alexandria, Egypt, was the most famous city founded by Alexander the Great.

SUGGESTED UNIT PROJECTS

1. Make a clay or papier-mâché model of the Trojan horse.

2. Make a chart with one column headed Athens and another headed Sparta. Under each, list the following:
   a. form of government
   b. religious beliefs
   c. type of education
   d. main occupations
   e. role of women
   f. contributions to Greek culture

3. Compare the Athenian oath of allegiance with the oath of allegiance to the United States.

4. Write a speech that Demosthenes might have given about Philip II of Macedonia.

5. Write seven newspaper headings about events in the life of Alexander the Great.

SUGGESTED READING

Cottrell, Leonard. *The Mystery of Minoan Civilization*. New York and Cleveland: World Publishing Company, 1971. An acount of Minoan civilization.

Edmonds, I. G. *The Mysteries of Troy*. New York: Thomas Nelson, Inc., 1977. A discussion of the history, literature, legends, archaeology, and art of ancient Troy.

Evslin, Bernard. *Greeks Bearing Gifts: The Epics of Achilles and Ulysses*. New York: Four Winds Press, 1976. A retelling of the *Iliad* and the *Odyssey*.

Fagg, Christopher. *Ancient Greece*. New York: Warwick Press, 1978. A discussion of the civilization of the ancient Greeks and how they developed a democratic way of life.

Serraillier, Ian. *Heracles the Strong*. New York: Henry Z. Walck, Inc., 1970. A retelling of the legend of Heracles.

Van Duyn, Janet. *The Greeks: Their Legacy*. New York: McGraw-Hill, 1972. A description of the contributions the Greeks made to western civilization.

Walsh, Jill Paton. *Children of the Fox*. New York: Farrar, Straus & Giroux, Inc., 1977. Three stories set during the Persian Wars.

UNIT 5

1200 B.C.	1125 B.C.	1050 B.C.
1200 B.C. Latins settle on Palatine Hill		

650 B.C.	575 B.C.	400 B.C.
600 B.C. Etruscans rule central Italian Peninsula	**509 B.C.** Romans set up republic **450 B.C.** Twelve Bronze Tablets become basis of Roman law	

100 B.C.	25 B.C.	100 A.D.
81 B.C. Lucius Sulla becomes dictator of Rome	**c. 30 A.D.** Jesus is crucified **46 B.C.** Julius Caesar appointed dictator of Rome **27 B.C.** Octavian takes title of Augustus *Pax Romana* begins	

400 A.D.	575 A.D. **600 A.D.** Archbishop of Rome takes title of Pope	650 A.D.
410 A.D. Alaric conquers Rome **476 A.D.** Roman Empire ends in West **529 A.D.** Benedictine Rule		

1050 A.D.	1125 A.D.	1200 A.D.
1054 A.D. Latin and Greek Churches separate		

THE
ROMANS

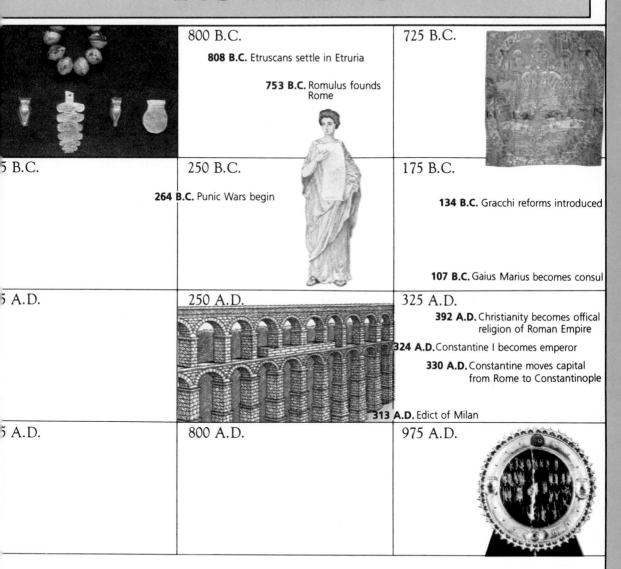

800 B.C.	725 B.C.
808 B.C. Etruscans settle in Etruria **753 B.C.** Romulus founds Rome	

5 B.C.	250 B.C.	175 B.C.
	264 B.C. Punic Wars begin	**134 B.C.** Gracchi reforms introduced **107 B.C.** Gaius Marius becomes consul

5 A.D.	250 A.D.	325 A.D.
		392 A.D. Christianity becomes offical religion of Roman Empire **324 A.D.** Constantine I becomes emperor **330 A.D.** Constantine moves capital from Rome to Constantinople **313 A.D.** Edict of Milan

5 A.D.	800 A.D.	975 A.D.

1. WHAT WAS ROMAN CIVILIZATION LIKE?
2. HOW DID THE ROMANS INFLUENCE THE GROWTH AND DEVELOPMENT OF WESTERN CULTURE?

Rome began as a small settlement on a hill in central Italy. Before its fall hundreds of years later, it ruled most of the western world. At its peak, the Roman Empire had a population of nearly 100 million. The Roman Empire was made up of many different groups of people, including Egyptians, Spaniards, Syrians, Greeks, and Jews.

The Romans left a great legacy to western civilization. Rome itself became a model for many European cities. Roman architecture was copied in the United States and elsewhere. Some works of Roman literature are still treasured today. Many English, Spanish, French, and Italian words come from Latin, the language of the Romans. The English word "justice," for example, comes from the Latin word *jus*, meaning "law."

A famous Roman named Cicero once wrote, "What sort of thing is the civil law? It is of a sort that cannot be bent by influence or broken by power or spoiled by money." The Roman system of law was developed on the basis of the same justice for all. This idea helped shape the legal tradition of the western world.

After a slow start, Christianity grew and ripened in Rome. It helped to shape the Roman Empire, just as the Empire helped to shape the Church. The archbishop of Rome became the head of the Roman Catholic Church.

The memory of Rome's greatness inspired western leaders for many centuries. The Roman heritage is a major ingredient of western civilization as it is known today.

CHAPTER 13

THE BEGINNINGS

Italy is a boot-shaped peninsula that extends south from Europe into the Mediterranean Sea. On the west coast of the peninsula is the mouth of the Tiber River. Fifteen miles, or 24 kilometers, upstream, the river is shallow. There stands a group of seven hills. On the hill known as the Palatine, a settlement was founded that came to be known as Rome.

FOUNDING OF ROME

Romans have a legend about the founding of their city. After the fall of Troy, the gods ordered a Trojan prince called Aeneas to lead his people to a promised land in the West. When Aeneas' group reached Italy, they joined forces with a people known as the Latins.

About 800 B.C., a Latin princess gave birth to twin sons fathered by the god Mars. The princess had taken an oath never to have children. Because she broke her word, she was punished. Her sons, Romulus and Remus, were taken from her and left to die on the bank of the flooding Tiber.

Romulus and Remus were found by a she-wolf, which fed and cared for them. One day a shepherd killed the she-wolf and discovered the babies. He took them to his home. There, the shepherd and his wife raised them as their sons.

THE TRIUMPH OF ROMULUS

After defeating Remus in battle, Romulus gained the support of the people of Rome. Under his rule, Rome expanded until it became the most important city in the Tiber region. After his death, Romulus was worshipped as a Roman god.
What is the legend of Romulus and Remus?

When the boys grew older, they decided to build a city on the Tiber. Romulus traced the city's boundaries with his plow. But the brothers could not agree on which one should rule the city. They decided to let the gods choose between them.

Each brother climbed to the top of a different hill to watch for a sign from the gods. When 12 vultures flew over the Palatine, the brothers took it to be the sign they sought. Since Romulus stood atop the Palatine, he claimed to be king. He and Remus then fought, and Remus was killed. Romulus became king of the city, which he named Rome.

Romulus and Remus

Over the years, many experts have tried to discover the truth about the founding of Rome. All they have learned is that around 1200 B.C. groups of people with iron weapons began invading the lands around the Mediterranean. One group invaded Egypt and brought down the New Kingdom. Another group, the Dorians, moved into the Balkan Peninsula. A third group settled on the Palatine. This group, the Latins, was the one to which the Romans belonged.

The area where the Latins settled had a pleasant climate and fertile soil. Nearby were dense forests that supplied the Latins with timber. The Latins built gravel roads to bring salt and other items from the coast.

By 776 B.C., the settlement on the Palatine had become a village of about 1,000 people. Most of the people were farmers who lived in wooden huts and worked the land. Their main crops were wheat and barley.

1. According to legend, how was Rome founded?
2. From where did the Latins come? Where did they settle? How did they live?

THE ETRUSCANS

Around 800 B.C., a people called the Etruscans settled in Etruria, the rolling hill country north of the Latin village on the Palatine. The Etruscans wrote in an alphabet borrowed from the Greeks. They spoke a language different from any other in the ancient world. To this day, no one knows for certain from where they came.

The Etruscans dug tunnels and built dams to drain their marshy fields. High on hilltops, they built a number of cities, each surrounded by a thick wall. From these hilltop cities, they

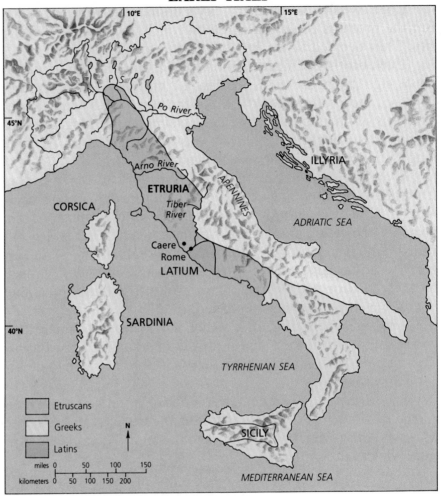

EARLY ITALY

could see all the surrounding land, including the plains over which enemies might attack.

The Etruscans were Italy's first highly civilized people. They were known as "people of the sea." As pirates, they were feared and envied throughout the Mediterranean. As traders, they were admired and respected.

Etruscan farmers used mostly iron tools to grow barley, millet, wheat, grapes, and other fruits. They raised pigs, goats, sheep, ducks, chickens, and cattle. They used the cattle for food and to pull plows and wagons. They made different kinds of cheese from ewe's milk.

Etruscan miners dug copper, lead, iron, and tin. Etruscan metalworkers and sculptors turned these metals into weapons, utensils, and jewelry. Etruscan merchants exchanged both metals and finished goods for luxury items of gold, silver, and ivory from Syria, Cyprus, Greece, and other eastern Mediterranean countries.

The Etruscans had a strong army, which marched into battle to the sound of bronze trumpets. The soldiers learned much about weapons and battle techniques from the Greeks. Their infantry formed a phalanx much like the one used by the Greeks. The Etruscans had one "weapon" no one else had—their shoes. They wore heavy leather shoes which laced firmly around the ankle. This gave them better footing than their enemies on rough or hilly ground.

Over time, the Etruscan cities grew in size and power. The Etruscans became rich. By 600 B.C., they dominated all of northern Italy, including the Latin village on the Palatine.

1. From where did the Etruscans come? Where did they settle?
2. How did the Etruscans earn their living?
3. What were some features of the Etruscan army?

DAILY LIFE   The Etruscans enjoyed bright colors, luxury, and a good time. They amused themselves by gambling with ivory dice or by playing games similar to chess and backgammon. Frequently, they attended or took part in such sports as wrestling, running, boxing, and horse racing.

Most of all, the Etruscans loved music and dancing. Sounds from a double flute or a stringed lyre accompanied most of their activities. Much of their dancing was linked to religion. The dances were intended to gain favor from the gods.

Both Etruscan men and women danced. Dancing was just one of the freedoms enjoyed by Etruscan women. Unlike Greek or Latin women, Etruscan women were encouraged to take part in public celebrations. It was not unusual for an Etruscan woman to be seen eating and drinking with her husband. Etruscan women also could own property.

The Etruscans had a strong sense of **social order**, or the way groups of people are classed. At first, there were no great class differences among them. Only acrobats and slaves, who were captives of war, were thought to be inferior. In later years, however, the people were divided into three classes. The upper

Etruscan Woman

ETRUSCAN COUPLE

The Etruscans were known for their love of food, music, and sports. This tomb sculpture shows an Etruscan noble and his wife. The Etruscans rested on couches while eating or listening to music.

What were the homes of wealthy Etruscans like?

class consisted of a small group of wealthy landowners, nobles, and priests. The middle class was made up of farmers and city workers. The lower class was slaves.

A few wealthy families owned most of the land. They also owned most of the slaves who tended the land and did other work. The rich lived in rectangular, one-story homes made of sun-dried brick on a frame of heavy timbers. A pitched roof covered with clay tiles extended beyond the house to protect the bricks and timber from rain. Most homes also had broad, walled courtyards open to the sky. A roofed hall led from the courtyard to three rooms that were lined up side-by-side across the width of the house. During the day, the center room was usually used to conduct business. At night, it was the scene of banquets and other entertainments enjoyed by wealthy Etruscans. Stone-lined drains led from each house into the main drains that ran along the pebble-paved streets.

1. What did Etruscans do for entertainment?
2. What was the role of Etruscan women?
3. How was Etruscan society divided?
4. What were some features of the homes of wealthy Etruscans?

RELIGIOUS BELIEFS   The Etruscans had many gods, most of whom were modeled after those of the Greeks. At first, the Etruscans worshipped their gods outdoors on platforms of stone or earth. Later, they built temples of wood, mud-brick, and clay on stone foundations. The temples had peaked, tiled roofs adorned with sculptures.

The Etruscans believed that the universe was divided into provinces. Each province was ruled by different gods. Humans lived in the center of the universe, facing south toward the gods of nature and earth. To the right lay the West, which was ruled by the gods of death and of the underworld. To the left lay the East, which was ruled by the gods of the heavens. The Etruscans believed that the West and the right were unlucky, while the East and the left were lucky. Thus, they planned their cities and built their temples to face the East and the left.

The Etruscans also believed that humans were powerless before the gods. More than anything else, Etruscans wanted to please the gods. But first they had to discover what the gods willed. They did this through a priestly group of aristocrats called **soothsayers**.

The soothsayers read certain **omens**, or signs. One group of soothsayers read omens in the livers of sacrificed animals. The parts of the liver corresponded to the provinces ruled by different gods. Another group of soothsayers interpreted the will of the gods by studying the direction and sounds of thunder and lightning and the flight of birds.

1. How did the Etruscans worship their gods?
2. What was the Etruscan view of the universe?
3. What did soothsayers do?
4. Why did the Etruscans consult soothsayers?

Etruscan Horse

THE TOMBS OF GOLD When an Etruscan noble died, a great banquet was held. At the banquet, two of the noble's slaves fought one another to the death. The spirit of the slave who lost accompanied the noble's spirit to the underworld.

The dead were buried in underground tombs called **catacombs**. Much of what is known about Etruscan life comes from such tombs, whose inside walls were brightly painted with scenes of daily life. The tombs contained chairs and beds. The bodies of the dead rested on the beds.

Etruscans believed that life after death lasted longer and was more important than life on earth. So, they carved their tombs out of natural rock, a material that would last for a long time. They filled the tombs with works of art and treasures of gold, silver, bronze, and ivory. Because of this, the Etruscan tombs are known as "tombs of gold."

Outside of each Etruscan city was a **necropolis**, or cemetery, made up of acres of these tombs. The necropolis outside the city of Caere is one of the largest Etruscan cemeteries. There, great

ETRUSCAN TOMB CHAMBER

The Etruscans looked forward to life after death and built many underground tombs. They believed the souls of the dead lived on in these chambers. To keep the departed soul happy, the Etruscans covered the walls of the tomb with colorful paintings.
What was Etruscan religion like?

mounds of earth are piled in the shape of a dome on top of foundations. Some of the mounds measure 100 feet, or about 30 meters, across. The foundations, which cover the tombs, are built on a grid of wide boulevards, each opening onto small plazas.

1. How did the Etruscans view life after death?
2. What were Etruscan tombs like?

CONTRIBUTIONS TO ROMAN CIVILIZATION

In 616 B.C., Lucius Tarquinius became the first Etruscan ruler of Rome. No one is certain whether Tarquinius took the throne from the Latin king by force or by cleverness. Nevertheless, his dynasty ruled Rome for more than 100 years.

The Etruscans were more culturally advanced than the Latins. They made many contributions to Roman civilization. For example, the Etruscans taught the Latins how to use the arch in building bridges. They laid the foundations of Rome's first sewer system. They drained the swamp at the foot of the Palatine. This later became the place where the Roman Forum, an area much like the Greek Agora, was built. The Forum housed a palace, government buildings, and law courts.

The Etruscans borrowed the Greek alphabet and made some changes in it. The Romans, in turn, borrowed the alphabet from them.

The Romans also borrowed some Etruscan customs and symbols of authority. The slave fights held at Etruscan funerals were the model for **gladiatorial games** with which the Romans amused themselves. The gladiatorial games were fights between armed men, between men and animals, between women and dwarfs, and between animals.

The **triumph**, or the parade-like welcome given a Roman hero returning from battle, was an Etruscan custom before it became a Roman one. Also borrowed from the Etruscans was the **fasces**, or a bundle of rods bound around a central ax. It became the symbol of a Roman ruler's power to flog or execute.

The Etruscans also introduced the Romans to soothsayers and to gods with human forms. They built the first temple on Capitoline hill. The Capitoline later became the religious and political heart of Rome. Today, it is the center of Rome's **municipal**, or city, government.

Etruscan Gold Clasp

The Romans founded their cities according to a ritual borrowed from the Etruscans. Soothsayers read omens that told where the city's boundaries should be. A furrow was dug to mark the boundaries. The plow used to dig the furrow had a bronze blade and was pulled by a white bull and cow yoked together. Workers then dug a trench at the center of the city. After each of the city's founders had tossed a handful of dirt into the trench, the priests took over. The priests laid out the main street and determined the principal cross street. The place where the two streets met was marked by a stone.

The Etruscans believed that the stone covered a shaft leading to the underworld. Three times a year, an Etruscan priest lifted the stone to allow the souls of the dead to return to earth. The Romans believed the place where the two streets met was the **mundus**, or the meeting point for the worlds of the living and the dead.

The Etruscans were not the first to develop or use many of the ideas and practices the Romans borrowed from them. They were, however, the people who brought these ideas to the notice of the Romans. Thus, they played an important role in the development of Roman civilization.

1. What were some of the contributions the Etruscans made to Roman civilization?
2. How did the Etruscans and the Romans found their cities?

CHAPTER 13 REVIEW

SUMMARY

1. Rome was founded about 800 B.C. as a small settlement on the Palatine.
2. Rome's first settlers were Latins who invaded the Mediterranean region.
3. The main occupation of the Latins was farming.
4. North of the Latins lived the Etruscans, who conquered Rome in 616 B.C.
5. The Etruscans were noted throughout the Mediterranean world as traders and pirates.
6. The Etruscans enjoyed living and had a strong sense of social order.
7. The Etruscans worshipped many gods and used soothsayers to learn what the gods wanted.
8. The Etruscans placed importance on life after death and built elaborate tombs.
9. The Etruscans taught the Romans many things, including the use of the arch in building, an alphabet, and a ritual for establishing cities.

BUILDING VOCABULARY

1. *Identify the following:*
   Tiber River   Aeneas   Romulus and Remus   Lucius Tarquinius
   Palatine   Latins   Etruscans

2. *Define the following:*
   social order   catacombs   gladiatorial games   fasces
   soothsayers   necropolis   triumph   municipal
   omens   mundus

REVIEWING THE FACTS

1. Why did Romulus fight with his brother Remus?

2. How did the kind of shoes the Etruscans wore help them in battle?

3. Who were the first highly civilized people of the Italian Peninsula?

4. What group of people owned most of the land in Etruria?

5. Why did Etruscan temples face the East and the left?

6. What was the purpose of the slave fights held at Etruscan funerals?

7. How have experts learned much of what they know about Etruscan life?

8. Who was the first Etruscan ruler of Rome?

9. What Etruscan custom did the Romans borrow to welcome home heroes?

10. How did the Etruscans and the Romans decide the boundaries of a city?

DISCUSSING IMPORTANT IDEAS

1. What part did religion play in Etruscan life? How did Etruscan religious ideas differ from those of the Greeks?

2. Do you think the Etruscans used their natural resources wisely? Explain.

3. Why were the Etruscans able to conquer northern Italy?

4. Compare the role of women in Etruria with their role in Greek civilization.

5. Do you think the Etruscan conquest of Rome was a good thing for the Romans? Why or why not?

6. Do you think you would have enjoyed living in Etruria? Why or why not?

USING MAPS

Study the map on page 196, and answer the following questions:

1. Where did the Etruscans settle in Italy?

2. What is the northernmost river shown on the map?

3. Into what body of water does the northernmost river flow?

4. What is the approximate latitude and longitude of Rome?

5. On what river is Rome located?

6. What mountains follow the northern border of Italy?

CHAPTER 14

THE ROMAN REPUBLIC

In 509 B.C., Roman farmer-soldiers overthrew Tarquin the Proud, their Etruscan king. They abolished the monarchy and set up a **republic**, or a form of government in which the people choose their rulers.

Roman society was divided into two classes, **patricians** and **plebians**. Patricians were members of the oldest and wealthiest families. Plebians were poorer people, such as farmers and artisans.

Patricians made up about 10 percent of the population. They had the real say in the government because they were the only people allowed to perform the religious rituals required to hold public office.

Plebians were citizens. They paid taxes and served in the army. But they could not marry patricians or serve in the government. If they fell into debt, they could be sold as slaves.

THE GOVERNMENT

At the head of the Roman Republic were two **consuls** who were elected each year. The consuls were administrators and military leaders. Each could **veto**, or say no to, the actions of the other. Both had to agree before any policy could be made.

ROMAN GOVERNMENT OFFICIALS

Consuls and senators played an important part in the government of Rome. They came from Rome's wealthiest and most powerful families. Senators (left) enter a hall in the forum for a meeting. A consul (right) issues a decree.
What duties did consuls and senators perform in the Roman Republic?

Next in importance to the consuls was the Senate. It was made up of 300 men called senators who were chosen for life. The Senate handled the daily problems of government. It advised the consuls. It debated foreign policy, proposed laws, and approved public contracts for building roads and temples.

The government also included judges, assemblies, and **tribunes**, or officials who protected the rights of the plebians. All Roman citizens belonged to assemblies, which could declare war or agree to peace terms. The office of tribune was not added to the government until 494 B.C. From then on, 10 tribunes were elected each year.

Until about 450 B.C., Roman laws were not written down. Patricians told plebians what the laws were. The plebians, however, did not trust the patricians and resented having them explain the laws. So, about 450 B.C., Roman laws were carved on 12 bronze tablets known as the Twelve Tables. The tablets were placed in the Forum so that everyone might see them and know their rights and duties. The laws dealt mainly with such things as wills, property rights, court actions, and the behavior of citizens in public. The laws carved on the Twelve Tables became the foundation for all future Roman law.

The election of tribunes and writing down of laws were the first steps to a more democratic government. Later, more plebian demands were met, which made the government even more democratic. By about 250 B.C., no one could be sold into slavery for debt. In addition, plebians were permitted to marry patricians and to hold public office.

1. What was the role of the consuls in the government of the Roman Republic?
2. What was the role of the Senate?
3. What were some of the changes made in Rome's government and laws by around 250 B.C.?

ROMAN EXPANSION

Once the Romans had established a republic, they set out to protect it. They were afraid that the Etruscans would try to regain control of Rome. To prevent this, the Romans crossed the Tiber River and conquered several Etruscan cities. Roman territory now bordered that of other Italian people. To protect their new boundaries, the Romans either conquered their neighbors or made alliances with them. By 290 B.C., Rome was the leading power in central Italy. By 275 B.C., it ruled the entire peninsula. Two centuries later, Rome ruled most of the Mediterranean region.

The Romans were able to expand their territory because they had a strong army that was organized into **legions**. Each legion contained some 5,000 soldiers called **legionaries** and was divided into groups of 60 to 120 soldiers.

The legion had several advantages over the phalanx. It was smaller and could move faster. Soldiers in a phalanx fought as a group and attacked only from one direction. Each legionary depended on his own fighting ability. The groups within a legion could split off from the main body and attack from the sides and the rear as well as the front.

Legionaries were well trained. They spent hours practicing with their double-edged iron swords. They went on long marches every day. Before going to sleep, they had to build complete

---

ROMAN LEGION

The legions provided the military strength that made Rome great. They conquered new territories and guarded the frontiers. Here, a Roman legion led by its general celebrates a military triumph.

What advantages did the legion have over the phalanx?

Roman Bronze Lamp

fortified camps, even when the legion would stay in the area only one night. They built roads out of lava blocks so troops and supplies could move forward more rapidly.

The Romans were mild rulers. At first, they did not tax the people they conquered. They let the conquered people keep their own governments and manage their own affairs. Some were even allowed to become Roman citizens. In return, the conquered were expected to serve in the Roman army and to support Rome's foreign policy. As a result, many enemies of Rome became loyal Roman allies.

1. Why did the Romans conquer Etruscan cities?
2. How did the Romans protect their new boundaries?
3. What were some features of the Roman legion?
4. What kind of rulers were the Romans?

THE PUNIC WARS

By 264 B.C., the Romans had conquered some Greek city-states in southern Italy. This brought them into contact with the Phoenician city of Carthage. Carthage controlled all of North Africa, most of what is now Spain, and some islands off the coast of Italy. It also ruled the western half of Sicily, a large island at the toe of the Italian "boot." The Romans felt threatened by the Carthaginians. They also wanted the granaries that were on Sicily.

Legionary

1. What territory did Carthage control?
2. Why did Rome decide to fight Carthage?

THE FIRST PUNIC WAR   In 264 B.C., the Romans and Carthaginians clashed. A war broke out that lasted for 23 years. It was the first of three wars that came to be known as the Punic Wars.

The military strength of Carthage lay in its navy. Rome had no navy. The Romans built their first fleet to fight the Carthaginians. They modeled their ships after a Carthaginian warship they found abandoned on a beach. The Romans made one improvement on the Carthaginian model. They added a **corvus**, or type of movable bridge, to the prow. The Romans knew they could not outsail the Carthaginians, but they believed they could outfight them. The corvus allowed soldiers to board an enemy ship and fight hand-to-hand on its decks. In a sense, it changed a sea war into a land war.

The Romans lost many ships and men in storms during the First Punic War. Yet, in the end, they defeated the Carthaginians. In 241 B.C., the Carthaginians agreed to make peace and leave Sicily.

1. What was the military strength of the Carthaginians? Of the Romans?
2. Who won the First Punic War?

HANNIBAL AND THE SECOND PUNIC WAR   In 218 B.C., the Carthaginians, led by General Hannibal Barca, attacked the Romans by land from the north. Hannibal and his troops surprised the Romans by crossing the Alps into Italy. They came by way of Spain through southern Gaul, or present-day France. They brought elephants with them across the mountains to help break through the Roman lines. Hannibal's attack was the start of the Second Punic War.

Hannibal

Hannibal's army fought its way to the very gates of Rome, winning victory after victory. But when it got to the city, it did not have the heavy equipment needed to batter down the city's walls. It was short on supplies and soldiers and could not get more because the Roman navy controlled the sea.

Unable to capture Rome, Hannibal and his troops roamed the countryside of southern Italy for 15 years. They raided and burned towns and villages and destroyed crops. Then, the Romans attacked Carthage, and Hannibal was called home to defend it. Hannibal lost his first battle—and the war—at a town south of Carthage. The power of Carthage was broken.

In 201 B.C., Carthage agreed to pay Rome a huge sum of money and to give up all its territories, including Spain. The Spanish resources of copper, gold, lead, and iron now belonged to the Romans.

1. What role did Hannibal play in the Second Punic War?
2. What did the Romans gain from the Second Punic War?

THE THIRD PUNIC WAR   Following the Second Punic War, there was peace for about 50 years. Then, Carthage began to show signs of regaining power. To prevent this, the Romans attacked in 149 B.C. Within three years, they won the Third Punic War. They burned Carthage and plowed salt in its fields so that nothing would grow. They killed the Carthaginians or sold them into slavery.

THE CAPTURE OF CARTHAGE
Rome won the Third Punic War because it had better resources and more soldiers than Carthage. This painting shows Roman armies destroying the city.
How did Rome's treatment of its conquered peoples change as a result of the Punic Wars?

That same year, 146 B.C., the Greek city-state of Corinth and some of its allies refused to obey a Roman order. The Romans attacked Corinth and burned it to the ground. The Romans already controlled Macedonia and Syria. Now, they added Greece to the areas under their rule. Rome had become the leading power of the Mediterranean region.

1. What led to the Third Punic War?
2. What happened to Carthage and its people at the end of the Third Punic War?
3. How did Rome become the leading power of the Mediterranean region?

EFFECTS OF CONQUEST

The conquests and the wealth that came with them changed the Roman economy and government. Among the changes was the coming of slavery, a movement from farms to the cities, and the decline of the Roman government.

AGRICULTURAL CHANGES   Most Romans had been small farmers who believed in hard work and service to Rome. They had few luxuries. As Roman conquests grew, this began to change. The small farms disappeared and were replaced by huge estates called **latifundias**.

Instead of growing wheat, the main Roman food staple, latifundias produced cash crops for market. Most latifundias were sheep and cattle ranches. Some contained olive groves and vineyards. Thus, the Romans began to import wheat from conquered areas, especially Sicily and North Africa.

A major reason for the change in Roman agriculture was Hannibal's invasion. While his troops were in Italy, they lived off the land. To prevent them from getting enough food, Roman farmers burned their fields and crops. By the time the Second Punic War was over, the land was ruined. Most Roman farmers did not have the money to fix up their farms or restore the land. Only patricians and rich business people had that kind of money. They bought the small farms and combined them to make latifundias. The owners of the latifundias did not need the farmers to work the land because they had slaves to do it instead.

Thus, slavery was another major reason for the change in Roman life. When Rome first began expanding, the Romans did not make slaves of the people they conquered. By 146 B.C., that was no longer true. The Romans were impressed by the wealth of Greece, Syria, and Carthage. They liked the way people in those areas lived and decided to imitate them. Since those areas had widespread slavery, the Romans sent thousands of prisoners to Rome as slaves. Most lived and worked on latifundias.

Roman Farmer

1.   How did latifundias start?
2.   How was Roman agriculture influenced by Hannibal?
3.   How was Roman agriculture influenced by slavery?

FROM FARM TO CITY   The small farmers who had sold their land had little choice. They could stay and work the land for

ROMAN APARTMENTS

Wealthy Romans built brick and stone apartments. They decorated the floors with mosaics and the walls with paintings. These apartment dwellers owned only a few pieces of furniture, most of which were simple in design.

What were living conditions like for poor Romans during the Republic?

the new owners or move to the city. Almost all the small farmers moved to Rome.

There, the farmers crowded into wooden apartment buildings six or more stories high. Living conditions were terrible. The aqueducts that brought water to the city were not connected to the apartment buildings. Neither were the sewers that carried away the wastes. The buildings often caught fire or collapsed. Such diseases as typhus were common.

Most farmers could not earn a living in the city. Except for construction, Rome had almost no industry. Most businesses were staffed by Greek slaves, who were better educated and had more skills than Roman farmers. About the only way farmers could get money was by selling their votes to politicians. They sold to the highest bidder.

1. Why did Roman farmers move to the city?
2. What conditions did farmers face in Rome?

DECLINE OF THE ROMAN REPUBLIC   As Rome expanded beyond Italy, the Romans began to demand taxes, as well as slaves, from the provinces and cities they conquered. Tax **contracts**, or legal agreements, were sold to people called **publicans**. The publicans paid Rome in advance for the contracts. Then, they collected taxes from the conquered people. The amount of taxes collected was supposed to be no more than 10 percent above the price paid for the contract. Most publicans, however, tried to make as much profit as they could.

By about 135 B.C., Rome was in serious difficulty. Farmers had lost their land and, as a result, their economic and political independence. Merchants had become poorer because wealthy Romans could get luxury items elsewhere. Craftspeople had lost business because wealthy Romans preferred goods from Greece and Syria. Government officials were too busy getting rich to worry about solving the republic's problems.

The gap between rich and poor grew greater. The poor hated the rich for what the rich had done to them. The rich hated and feared the poor. Rome was no longer politically stable.

1. What was the job of a publican?
2. What was life like in Rome during the decline of the republic?

ATTEMPTS TO SAVE THE REPUBLIC

Over the next 100 years, many different popular leaders tried to improve conditions in Rome. Some were reformers, while others were generals.

THE REFORMERS   Tiberius Sempronius Gracchus was the first reformer. He thought forcing small farmers off their land had created Rome's problems.

When he became a tribune in 134 B.C., Tiberius Gracchus suggested limiting the amount of land a person could own. He wanted to divide up public lands and give them to the poor. Another tribune vetoed his suggestion. Tiberius Gracchus then convinced the assembly to ignore the veto, to get rid of that tribune, and to put his suggestion into effect.

Then, Tiberius Gracchus ignored the law and ran for a second term as tribune. The Senate organized a riot and had him and hundreds of his followers killed.

Tiberius Gracchus

In 124 B.C., Tiberius Gracchus's younger brother Gaius Sempronius Gracchus was elected tribune. He thought moving the poor from the city back to the countryside was the answer to Rome's problems.

Gaius revised and extended the reforms of his brother. He also suggested that the government take over the sale of wheat and sell it to the poor below market price. This suggestion became law. Soon, wheat was being given away rather than sold. Nearly one out of every three Romans was receiving free wheat. Meanwhile, the Senate began to feel threatened by some of Gaius's suggestions and in 121 B.C. had him killed.

1. What reforms did Tiberius Gracchus make? Why was he killed?
2. What reforms did Gaius Gracchus make? Who had him killed?

Gaius Marius

THE GENERALS   After the reformers came the generals. In 107 B.C., Gaius Marius, a military hero, became consul. The son of a day laborer, Marius was the first lower-class Roman to be elected to such a high office. He was supported by many ex-soldiers who felt the rich and the government had taken advantage of them. Many had been farmers who had lost their farms when they left to serve in the army.

Marius thought he could solve Rome's problems by creating a professional army. Until this time, only property owners could become legionaries. Marius opened the army to everyone. He convinced the poor to join by offering them pay, land, pensions, and booty. Marius's plan helped Rome by providing jobs for many out-of-work Romans. At the same time, it hurt the Roman Republic. Instead of giving loyalty to the government, the soldiers gave it to the general who hired and paid them.

Marius was opposed by another general, Lucius Cornelius Sulla. Sulla had been given a military command that Marius wanted. Marius tried to get the assembly to take the command away from Sulla and give it to him. An angry Sulla marched his army on Rome and seized the city. It was the first time a Roman commander had led his troops against the capital.

Civil war, or war between groups within a country, broke out. When it was over, Sulla made himself **dictator**, or absolute ruler, of Rome. Sulla believed the way to solve Rome's problems was by increasing the power of the Senate rather than that of the army. So, he doubled the Senate's size. He gave the senators more duties and weakened the power of the tribunes. At the same time, he stopped generals from holding the same army command for more than one year at a time.

1. How did Gaius Marius try to solve Rome's problems?
2. What did Marius do to anger Lucius Sulla?
3. What reforms did Sulla make?

JULIUS CAESAR When Sulla retired in 79 B.C., a new group of generals fought for control of Rome. Two of them—Gnaeus Pompeius, known as Pompey, and Julius Caesar—had different ideas about how Rome should be ruled.

Pompey was supported by Marcus Tullius Cicero. Cicero was an orator, politician, and philosopher, who once served as consul. Cicero believed strongly in a republic that was ruled by

THE EXPANSION OF THE ROMAN REPUBLIC

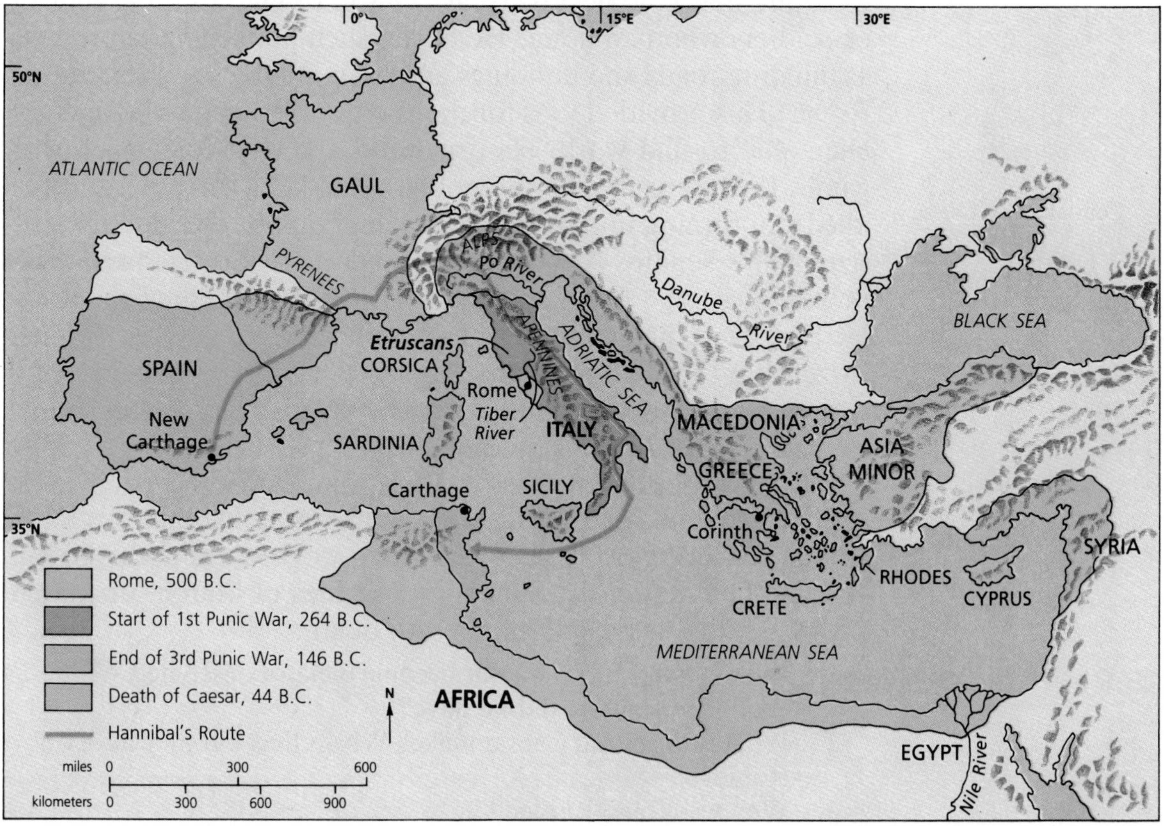
0°
15°E
30°E
50°N
35°N
ATLANTIC OCEAN
GAUL
PYRENEES
SPAIN
New Carthage
ALPS
Po River
APENNINES
ADRIATIC SEA
Etruscans
CORSICA
SARDINIA
Rome
Tiber River
ITALY
SICILY
Carthage
Danube River
BLACK SEA
MACEDONIA
GREECE
ASIA MINOR
Corinth
RHODES
CRETE
CYPRUS
SYRIA
MEDITERRANEAN SEA
AFRICA
EGYPT
Nile River
N
Rome, 500 B.C.
Start of 1st Punic War, 264 B.C.
End of 3rd Punic War, 146 B.C.
Death of Caesar, 44 B.C.
Hannibal's Route
miles 0 300 600
kilometers 0 300 600 900

aristocratic senators. He continued to oppose Caesar up to the time of Caesar's death.

In the struggle for power, Caesar finally gained control after Pompey was murdered in 48 B.C. Caesar was a well-educated politician who had become a soldier. He had both military strength and strong family alliances to back him. He also had the economic support of Marcus Licinius Crassus, the richest man in Rome.

In 58 B.C., Caesar was appointed governor of a Roman province. There, he built up a large, strong army that was loyal to him. Within seven years, he conquered what is now northern France and Belgium and invaded Britain. The Senate began to fear he was growing too strong. So, in 50 B.C., it ordered Caesar to disband his legions and return to Rome. Instead, Caesar entered Rome at the head of his troops. By 46 B.C., he was dictator of Rome.

Caesar brought about many reforms. He helped solve the land problem by redistributing state lands in Italy and by founding new colonies overseas. This gave land to thousands of ex-soldiers who had none. He began such public works projects as building roads and buildings and draining the marshes around Rome. This provided jobs for thousands of Romans who had not been able to find work. He organized and paid for gladiatorial games that were free to the public. This kept the poor and the idle from turning into unhappy and angry mobs. He doubled the size of the Senate. Although this made individual senators less powerful, it gave business people a chance to become senators. He restricted the activities of the publicans. He granted Roman citizenship to Greeks, Spaniards, and Gauls. And he adopted a new calendar based on the Egyptian calendar. Called the Julian calendar, it is still in use today.

Caesar did a great deal for Rome and its people. Still, some Romans were afraid that Caesar planned to make himself king. About 60 men, most of them senators, worked out a plan to kill him. As he entered the Senate on the Ides of March, or March 15, 44 B.C., Caesar was stabbed to death.

Coin of Julius Caesar

1. What helped Julius Caesar become dictator of Rome? Whose economic support did he have?
2. What reforms did Caesar make? What effect did they have on Rome?
3. Why was Caesar killed?

END OF THE REPUBLIC   Angered by Caesar's death, the Roman people turned against those who had killed him. Political power passed to a **triumvirate**, or a group of three persons with equal power. Marcus Antonius, or Mark Antony, Caesar's closest follower and a popular general, took command of Rome's territories in the East. Octavian, Caesar's grand-nephew and adopted son, took charge of the West. Marcus Aemilius Lepidus, one of Caesar's top officers, took over the rule of Africa. All three shared control of the Italian homeland.

Octavian

For a while, the triumvirate worked. Then, fights broke out among the three leaders. When the fighting ended in 31 B.C., Octavian had won. Within four years, he became absolute head of the Roman Empire.

1. How was political power divided after Caesar's death?
2. What finally happened to the triumvirate?

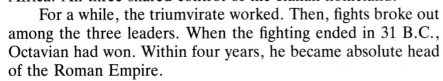

CHAPTER 14 REVIEW

SUMMARY

1. In 509 B.C., the Romans overthrew the Etruscans and established a republic.

2. About 450 B.C., the Romans wrote down for the first time the laws that were to be the foundation for all future Roman law.

3. Rome gradually enlarged its boundaries until by 275 B.C. it ruled all of Italy.

4. Roman military power was based on a well-trained and well-organized army that was divided into legions.

5. Between 264 and 146 B.C., Rome and Carthage fought three wars known as the Punic Wars.

6. As a result of its conquests, Rome's small farms were replaced by large estates, and most farmers had to leave the land and move to the city.

7. By 135 B.C., Rome was facing serious political and economic problems.

8. The Gracchi brothers tried to improve conditions in Rome by giving land to the poor and by providing free wheat for the hungry.

9. Gaius Marius tried to solve Rome's problems by giving power to the army.

10. Lucius Cornelius Sulla tried to solve Rome's problems by giving more power to the Senate.

11. In 46 B.C., Julius Caesar became dictator of Rome and brought about many reforms.

12. In 44 B.C., a group of Romans, who were afraid that Caesar was planning to make himself king, killed him.

13. After Caesar's death, political power was divided among Mark Antony, Octavian, and Marcus Lepidus.

14. In 31 B.C., Octavian became the sole ruler of Rome.

BUILDING VOCABULARY

1. *Identify the following:*

Senate	Punic Wars	Gaius Gracchus	Julius Caesar
Twelve Tables	Hannibal Barca	Gaius Marius	Mark Antony
Carthage	Tiberius Gracchus	Lucius Cornelius Sulla	Octavian

2. *Define the following:*

republic	veto	corvus	civil war
patricians	tribunes	latifundias	dictator
plebians	legions	contracts	triumvirate
consuls	legionaries	publicans	

REVIEWING THE FACTS

1. What changes were made in Rome's government as a result of demands by plebians?
2. Why was the Roman legion so effective in battle?
3. At first, how did the Romans treat the people they conquered?
4. Why did Rome fight the Punic Wars?
5. How were the Romans able to overcome the Carthaginian navy?
6. What effect did latifundias have on Rome's small farmers?
7. Why were most farmers who moved to Rome unable to earn a living?
8. What effect did Marius's reforms have on the loyalty of legionaries?
9. Why did the Senate order Julius Caesar to disband his legions?
10. Who won the struggle for political power after Caesar's death?

DISCUSSING IMPORTANT IDEAS

1. Do you think the Romans were wise to start making slaves of the people they conquered? Why or why not?
2. Do you think the Romans were wise to start taxing the people they conquered? Why or why not?
3. If you had lived in Rome after 135 B.C., what would you have done to try to solve its problems?
4. If you have lived in Rome when Caesar was killed, how would you have felt about his murder? Explain.

USING MAPS

Study the map on page 215, and answer the following questions:

1. When did the Roman Republic reach its greatest expansion?
2. How far north did the Republic reach? How far east?
3. During what period did Rome spread mostly into North Africa?
4. During what period did the Roman Republic spread into Spain?

CHAPTER 15
THE ROMAN EMPIRE

In 27 B.C., Octavian announced to the Senate that he had restored the republic. When he offered to resign, the Senate gave him various offices. They named him *princeps*, "first citizen," and *Pater Patriae*, "Father of the Country." He took for himself the title of Augustus, or "revered one." That is what historians usually call him. Octavian thus became the first **emperor**, or absolute ruler, of the Roman Empire.

THE RULE OF AUGUSTUS

Augustus was a clever politician. He held the offices of consul, tribune, high priest, and senator all at the same time. But he refused to be crowned emperor. Augustus knew most Romans would not accept one-person rule unless it was within the

Caesar Augustus

framework of a republic. So, he restored the republic in form but not in practice.

Augustus kept the assemblies and officials of the republic and was careful to make senators feel respected. He talked of tradition and the need to bring back "old Roman virtues." He made the official religion important once again.

At the same time, Augustus strengthened his authority in two ways. First, he had every soldier swear allegiance to him personally. This gave him control of the armies. Second, he built up his imperial household to take charge of the daily business of government. He chose people because of their talent rather than their birth. This gave slaves and **freedmen**, or former slaves, a chance to be part of the government.

Augustus wanted boundaries that would be easy to defend. So, he rounded out the empire to natural frontiers—the Rhine and Danube rivers in the north, the Atlantic Ocean in the west, and the Sahara Desert in the south. To keep these boundaries safe from invaders, he stationed legions there.

Augustus was not interested in conquering new territory for Rome. Instead, he concentrated on governing the existing empire. He gave provincial governors long terms of office so they could gain experience in their jobs. He paid them large salaries so they would not feel the need to overtax the people or keep public money for themselves. To make sure that people did not pay too little or too much tax, Augustus ordered that a **census**, or population count, be taken from time to time throughout the empire.

Augustus also made Rome more beautiful. He built marble buildings, many of which were temples and shrines. He wrote strict laws to govern people's behavior in public. He protected the city and the people by creating a fire brigade and a police force. He encouraged learning and reading by building Rome's first library.

Augustus ruled for 41 years. During that time, he brought peace and a new sense of patriotism and pride to the people. He made Roman citizenship available to people in the provinces. Most important, however, Augustus reorganized the government of Rome so that it ran well for over 200 years.

1. How did Augustus make the people think Rome was still a republic? Why did he want them to think this?
2. How did Augustus strengthen his authority?

The Pax Romana

The peace that Augustus brought to Rome was called the *Pax Romana*. It lasted for 200 years. Revolts and other internal problems were not unknown during this period. Overall, however, the empire and its people prospered. Cities did not need walls for protection. Legionaries served for 20 years without having to fight a battle. Civilization spread, and cultures mixed.

TRADE   With peace came increased trade. The same coins were used throughout the empire. There were no **tariffs**, or taxes placed on goods brought into the country. Goods and money moved freely along the trade routes. The Mediterranean was

THE EXPANSION OF THE ROMAN EMPIRE

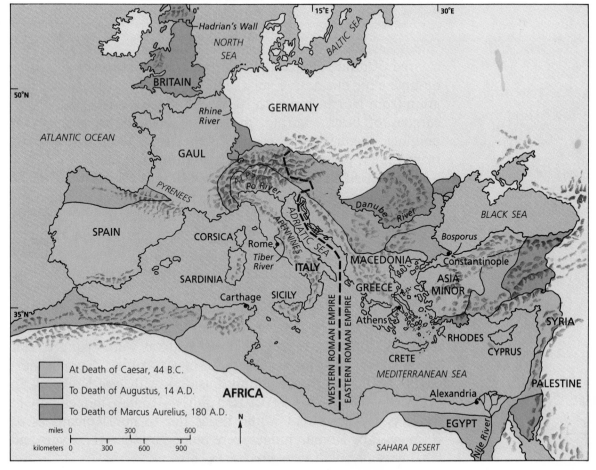

At Death of Caesar, 44 B.C.

To Death of Augustus, 14 A.D.

To Death of Marcus Aurelius, 180 A.D.

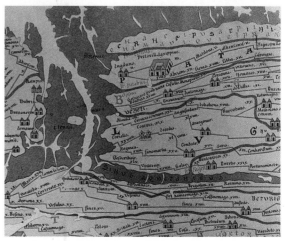

ROMAN TRADE

Roman ships (left) carried goods and money throughout the Roman Empire. The Roman map (right) shows trade routes around Britain, Spain, and Gaul. What did increased trade mean to the Romans?

cleared of pirates, making it safe for trade and travel. Shipping became a big business. Every summer, hundreds of ships carried grain from North Africa to Italy. Other ships were loaded with cargoes of brick, marble, granite, and wood to be used for building. Luxury items, such as amber from the north and silk from China, passed overland across Roman roads.

Increased trade meant increased business for Romans. The city hummed. Shopkeepers grew richer. Wine and oil were the main items bought by other countries. Italy became a manufacturing center for making pottery, bronze, and woolen cloth.

1. Why was the Pax Romana important?
2. What happened to trade during the Pax Romana?

LAW During the Pax Romana, Roman law went through major changes. Because conditions were different, the laws originally set down on the 12 bronze tablets were changed. For example, when Rome conquered a new territory, Roman merchants found themselves doing business with non-Romans. In order that both sides be treated fairly, Roman judges had to develop new laws that would be as fair to non-Romans as to Romans. The Roman judges were helped by special lawyers and legal writers called *juris prudentes*.

After a while, the judges and their assistants developed certain legal principles that were fair to everyone. A law was considered just because it was reasonable, not because the government had the power to enforce it. Everyone was considered equal before the law. A person was innocent until proven guilty. The accuser, rather than the person accused, had to prove his or her case.

By about the year 125 A.D., Roman law was **standardized**. This meant that all legal procedures were the same throughout the empire. This helped Rome govern a large area successfully. In later years, Roman legal principles formed the basis for the laws of most western nations and of the Christian Church.

1. What happened to law during the Pax Romana?
2. What were some of the legal principles that developed during the Pax Romana?

DAILY LIFE

In the early years of the empire, about 1 million people lived in Rome. Rome suffered from many of the same problems cities do today. There was too little housing and too much traffic. The air was polluted. There was crime in the streets. The cost of living was high. Many Romans could not find jobs. Romans had to pay taxes on almost everything—slaves, estates, roads, crops.

The rich of Rome lived in a *domus*, or house, with marble walls, colored mosaic floors, and windows made of small panes of glass. A furnace heated the rooms, and pipes brought water even to the upper floors.

Most Romans, however, were not rich. They lived in small, smelly rooms in apartment houses six or more stories high called **islands**. Each island covered an entire block. At one time, there were 26 blocks of islands for every private house in Rome. The ground floor of most islands was given over to shops, which opened onto the street from large arched doorways.

Roman Couple

Rents were high in Rome. They varied according to the apartment floor—the higher up the apartment, the lower the rent. July 1 was **eviction day**, or the day anyone who had not paid the rent was forced to move out.

1. What was living in Rome like during the early years of the empire?
2. Who lived in a domus?
3. What were the homes of most Romans like?

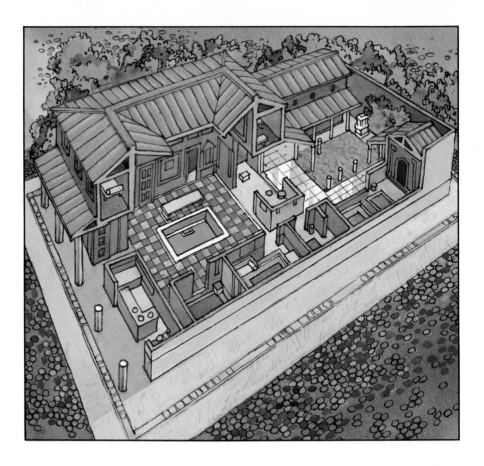

THE FAMILY   In Rome, the family was all-important. The father was the head of the household. His word was law. He arranged the children's marriages to improve the family's social position or to increase its wealth. Cousins were expected to help one another politically.

Until they were 12 years old, most Roman boys and girls went to school together. Then, the sons of poor families went to work, while the sons of rich families began their formal education. The government usually paid the salaries of the school staff. Each school taught a different subject.

The sons of the wealthy studied reading, grammar, writing, music, geometry, commercial arithmetic, and shorthand. When they were 15, they entered a school of **rhetoric**, or speech and writing, to prepare for a political career. Some went to schools in Athens or Alexandria for philosophy or medicine.

Girls received a different kind of education. When they reached 12, their formal education stopped. Instead of going to school, the daughters of the wealthy were given private lessons at home. As a result, many Roman women were as well or better informed than Roman men. Some women worked in or owned small shops. Wealthy women had slaves to do their domestic chores for them. This left them free to study the arts, literature, and fashions, or to ride chariots in the countryside for a day's **pig-sticking**, a type of hunt.

1. How did Romans feel about the family?
2. What kind of schooling did Roman children have?

AT LEISURE At home, the Romans amused themselves by gambling with dice. They socialized at public bathhouses. The bathhouses provided more than baths. Some included gymnasiums, sports stadiums, and libraries. At a bathhouse, Romans could take warm, cold, or steam baths. They could watch or play games. They also could listen to lectures, see musical performances, exercise, or just sit and gossip.

The Romans had no team sports to watch. Instead, they flocked to see free public games, which often ran from dawn to

---

ROMAN GLADIATOR

On festival days, 50,000 Romans jammed the Colosseum to watch the gladiatorial games. The public games also included circuses and chariot races.
What did it cost to attend the public games?

---

dusk. Under the empire, the games were staged by the government. Under the republic, they had usually been staged by politicians who were looking for votes. The games included circuses, chariot races, and gladiatorial games. The most exciting chariot races were held at the Circus Maximus, an oval arena that could seat more than 250,000 people. Every year in September a festival called *Ludi Romani* took place in the Circus.

The people who fought animals and one another in arenas were called **gladiators**. Most were slaves, prisoners of war, criminals, or poor people. They were trained by contractors who hired them out. A few gladiators were upper-class Romans who wanted excitement and public attention.

A ROMAN BANQUET MENU

APPETIZERS AND SOUPS
Snails Fed on Milk
Fried Bulbs
Grilled Truffles in Sausage Skin
Minced Sea-Crayfish-Tail Balls
Barley Soup with Dried Vegetables Topped with
Cabbage Leaves
Puree of Lettuce-Leaves with Onions

MAIN COURSES
Boiled Electric Ray with Hot Raisins
Boiled Crane with Turnips
Smoked Pig's Stomach Stuffed with Brains, Pine
Kernels, and Peppercorns
Roast Hare in White Sauce
Leg of Boar
Roast Flamingo with Jericho Dates, Dried Onion,
Honey, and Wine
Wood-Pigeon Baked in Oil-Flour Pastry

DESSERTS
Sweet Fricassee of Pumpkin
Egg Sponge with Milk in Honey
Stew of Apricots

The night before they were to fight, gladiators would appear at a banquet. There, they could be looked over by fans and gamblers who wanted to bet on the outcome of contests. When gladiators entered the arena on the day of the games, they would walk past the emperor's box saying, "Hail Emperor, those who are about to die salute you."

Many gladiators did die. Those whose fighting pleased the crowd became popular idols. A few won their freedom. Those who did not give a good performance had their throats cut.

Gladiator and Animal

All kinds of animals were used in the public games. Some animals pulled chariots or performed tricks. Most, however, fought one another or gladiators. Sometimes, as many as 5,000 wild animals were killed in a single day. In some cases, such as that of the Mesopotamian lion and the North African elephant, whole species were wiped out.

1. What did the Romans do for entertainment?
2. Where were public games?
3. What was the role of the gladiator?

FALL OF THE EMPIRE

The Pax Romana ended after approximately 200 years. From then on, conditions within the Roman Empire grew steadily worse. By 476 A.D., there was no empire left. Instead, much of western Europe was a patchwork of Germanic kingdoms. The eastern portion of the empire, however, lasted about 1,000 years longer as part of the Byzantine Empire.

There are many reasons why the Roman Empire fell. Three reasons stand out. The first was political. Neither Augustus nor the emperors who followed him had a formal rule about who was to inherit the throne upon an emperor's death. Sometimes, the title was inherited by a son. But usually an emperor's son was too spoiled to be a good ruler. Sometimes, an emperor adopted an heir to the throne, choosing the most able and hardest working individual he knew. Between 96 and 180 A.D., all emperors were adopted. The system worked well until 180 A.D.

Emperor Marcus Aurelius was kind, intelligent, and devoted to duty. His son was just the opposite. He became emperor when Marcus Aurelius died in 180 A.D. But he was so cruel and unpopular that in 192 A.D. he was strangled by the Praetorian Guard, the soldiers on duty at the palace. After

Emperor	Reign	Accomplishments
Augustus	27 B.C.–14 A.D.	first emperor of Roman Empire
		reorganized government of Rome; brought peace to Rome
Tiberius	14 A.D.–37 A.D.	reformed taxes and improved financial state of government
Caligula	37 A.D.–41 A.D.	repaired roads and began construction of two aqueducts
Claudius	41 A.D.–54 A.D.	conquered most of England
		extended citizenship to many people outside Rome
		set up ministries to handle government administration
Nero	54 A.D.–68 A.D.	rebuilt Rome after the fire of 64 A.D. and gave it a city plan
Flavian Emperors Vespasian Titus Domitian	69 A.D.–96 A.D.	brought people from the provinces into the Senate
		secured frontier regions
		brought Rome new prosperity
		built the Coliseum
Five Good Emperors Nerva Trajan Hadrian Antoninus Pius Marcus Aurelius	96 A.D.–180 A.D.	built aqueducts, bridges, and harbors
		extended citizenship to more provinces
		cut dishonesty in business and government

killing the emperor, the Praetorian Guard sold the throne to the highest bidder. This set a dreadful example. For nearly 100 years, legion fought legion to put the emperor of its choice on the throne. By 284 A.D., Rome had had 37 different emperors. Most were murdered by the army or the Praetorian Guard.

This political problem helped to create the second and third major reasons for Rome's downfall. The second reason was economic. To stay in office, an emperor had to keep the soldiers who supported him happy. He did this by giving them high wages. This meant more and more money was needed for the army payroll. So, the people had to pay higher taxes.

In addition to higher taxes, Romans began to suffer from **inflation**, or a period of ever-increasing prices. Since there were no new conquests, gold was no longer coming into Rome. Yet, much gold was going out to pay for luxury items. This meant there was less to use in coins. As the amount of gold used in coins decreased, money began to lose its value. Prices went up. Many people stopped using money. Instead, they began to barter to get what they needed.

The third major reason why Rome fell centered on foreign enemies. While Romans argued and fought with each other over politics and money, they left Rome's frontiers open to attack. Gradually, Germanic hunters and herders from northern and central Europe began to raid Greece and Gaul. Trade and farming in those areas declined. Cities once again began to surround themselves with walls for protection.

1. How did the lack of a formal rule of inheritance affect the throne of Rome?
2. Why did Rome begin to suffer from inflation?

DIOCLETIAN AND CONSTANTINE I   Two emperors, Diocletian and Constantine I, made strong attempts to save the Roman Empire from collapse.

Constantine I

Diocletian, who was the son of a freedman, ruled from 284 to 305 A.D. He made many changes as emperor. He fortified the frontiers to prevent invasion. He reorganized the state and provincial governments to make them function better. He set maximum prices for wages and goods throughout the empire to stop prices from rising. He ordered workers to stay in the same jobs until they died to make sure goods were produced. He made city officials personally responsible for the taxes their communities had to pay.

One of the most important changes Diocletian made concerned the position of the emperor. Diocletian established the official policy of **rule by divine right**. This meant that the emperor's powers and right to rule came not from the people but from the gods.

Diocletian realized that the Roman Empire covered too much territory for one person to rule well. So, he divided it in two. He allowed someone else to govern the western provinces, while he kept control of the richer eastern provinces.

In 312 A.D., Constantine I became emperor. He ruled until 337 A.D. Constantine took even firmer control of the empire than Diocletian. To keep people from leaving their jobs when things got bad, he issued several orders. Sons of workers had to follow their fathers' trades. Sons of farmers had to stay and work the same land their fathers worked. Sons of ex-soldiers had to serve in the army.

To escape government pressure and control, wealthy land-owners moved to their **villas**, or country estates. Most estates were like small, independent cities or kingdoms. Each produced enough food and goods to supply the needs of everyone who lived on it.

Despite the changes made by Diocletian and Constantine, the Roman Empire continued to decline in the west. In 330 A.D., Constantine moved his capital from a dying Rome east to the newly built city of Constantinople in present-day Turkey.

1. What did Diocletian do to try to save the Roman Empire?
2. What did Constantine I do to save the Roman Empire?
3. How did the wealthy landowners react to Constantine's orders?

ATTILA THE HUN

Attila was a king of the Huns, a Mongoloid tribe that invaded the Roman Empire during the 400's A.D. Here Pope Leo I persuades Attila to spare Rome. When did Rome fall to the Germanic invaders?

END OF THE EMPIRE   Both Diocletian and Constantine I worked hard to save the Roman Empire. However, neither emperor succeeded in the end.

Diocletian

German raids increased, especially in western Europe. There, the Germans crossed the Danube River in order to escape from the Huns, nomadic herders who had wandered west from Outer Mongolia in Asia. In 378 A.D., a Germanic group defeated Roman legions at the Battle of Adrianople.

By around 400 A.D, Rome had grown quite weak. In the winter of 406 A.D., the Rhine River froze. Groups of Germans crossed the frozen river and entered Gaul. The Romans could not force them back across the border.

In 410 A.D., the Germanic chief Alaric and his soldiers invaded Rome. They burned records and looted the treasury. The Roman Senate told the people, "You can no longer rely on Rome for finance or direction. You are on your own."

1.   Why did German raids on the empire increase?
2.   How did the Germanic invaders gain control of the empire?

CHAPTER 15 REVIEW

SUMMARY

1.   Octavian, better known as Augustus, became the first emperor of the Roman Empire in 27 B.C.

2.   Augustus reorganized the Roman government so well that a period of peace known as the Pax Romana existed for over 200 years.

3.   Trade increased within the empire during the Pax Romana.

4.   During the Pax Romana, Roman law went through many changes until it was standardized about 125 A.D.

5.   During the Pax Romana, about 1 million people lived in Rome, which suffered from such problems as overcrowding, fires, and unemployment.

6.   Most Romans were not wealthy and lived in apartment houses that were called islands.

7.   The Roman government staged free public games to entertain the people.

8.   The major reasons for the fall of the Roman Empire were the lack of a formal rule about who was to inherit the throne, inflation, and attacks by Germanic invaders.

9.   Two emperors, Diocletian and Constantine I, tried to save the Roman Empire from collapse, but neither succeeded in the end.

10.   In 410 A.D., Rome itself fell to Germanic invaders.

BUILDING VOCABULARY

1. *Identify the following:*
   Augustus   Marcus Aurelius   Diocletian   Adrianople
   Pax Romana   Praetorian Guard   Constantine I   Alaric
   Circus Maximus

2. *Define the following:*
   emperor   *juris prudentes*   eviction day   inflation
   freedmen   standardized   rhetoric   rule by divine right
   census   *domus*   pig-sticking   villas
   tariffs   islands   gladiators

REVIEWING THE FACTS

1. Why did Augustus give provincial governors long terms of office?
2. How did Augustus make life in Rome safer for its people?
3. How did increased trade during the Pax Romana affect Rome and the Romans?
4. Why did the Romans change the laws set down on the 12 bronze tablets?
5. What was the importance of standardizing Roman law?
6. What did Rome's public bathhouses provide besides baths?
7. What happened to some species of animals as a result of the public games?
8. What did the Praetorian Guard have to do with the fall of the Roman Empire?
9. Why did Diocletian divide the Roman Empire in two?
10. What were the major reasons for the final fall of Rome?

DISCUSSING IMPORTANT IDEAS

1. Do you think Augustus was a good ruler? Why or why not?
2. Why are the principles of Roman law that developed during the Pax Romana important?
3. Do you think you would have enjoyed living in Rome during the Pax Romana? Explain.
4. What happens to a government if there is no rule for passing on its power?

USING MAPS

Study the map on page 221, and answer the following questions:

1. Into what areas did the Roman Empire expand between the deaths of Augustus and Marcus Aurelius?
2. What is located at about 54° north latitude and 0° longitude?
3. What is located at about 35° north latitude and 8° east longitude?
4. What is the approximate longitude of the division between the western and eastern halves of the Roman Empire?

CHRISTIANITY

Just as the Romans influenced the people they conquered, the conquered people influenced the Romans. Among
those who were to have a major influence were the Christians.
Their religion, Christianity, started in Palestine among the Jews.
Like other religions from the Middle East, Christianity was ulti-
mately brought to Rome.

At first, most Romans ignored or ridiculed Christianity.
Some emperors treated Christians cruelly. By 400 A.D., however, attitudes had changed. Christianity had become the official
religion of the Roman Empire.

THE BEGINNINGS

Christianity is based on the life and teachings of Jesus, who lived in Palestine during the reign of Augustus. After Jesus died, his teachings were spread by his followers. Christianity survived the fall of Rome and grew to be one of the major influences on western civilization.

THE LIFE OF JESUS   Jesus, born a Jew in the town of Bethlehem, grew up in Nazareth. There, he received a Jewish education in the local synagogue. He studied the **scriptures**, or sacred writings, and learned prayers in the Hebrew language. Later, he went to work as a carpenter.

When he was about 30 years old, Jesus began to travel throughout Palestine preaching to the people. Men and women came in large numbers from all over the country to see and hear him. Jesus taught that God created all humans and loved them the way a father loved his children. Therefore, people should behave like God's children and love God and one another. Jesus particularly extended God's love to people who had sinned. He told the people that if they were truly sorry and placed their trust in God, they would be forgiven.

Jesus spoke in the everyday language of the people. He presented his teachings in **parables**, or stories, about persons and things that were familiar to his listeners. In this way, they could better understand the religious principles that he was trying to teach them.

In 30 A.D., after about three years of preaching, Jesus and 12 of his **disciples**, or followers, went to Jerusalem to celebrate Passover, the holiday that marks the exodus of the Jews from Egypt. At the time, there was much unrest in the city. Many Roman officials believed all Jews were guilty of treason because they refused to worship statues of the Roman emperor. The Jews were tired of the high taxes they had to pay and of the pressure put on them by the Romans. They hoped and waited for a **messiah**, or someone who would save them.

When Jesus arrived in Jerusalem, many Jews greeted him as the messiah. This worried other Jews and Romans alike. Jesus was convicted of treason under Roman law and was **crucified**, or executed on a cross, outside of Jerusalem. Usually, only lower-class criminals were executed in this way.

Jesus' Disciples

JESUS AND DISCIPLES

Jesus chose 12 disciples to travel with him throughout Palestine. In this thirteenth-century painting, Jesus calls the fishermen-brothers Peter and Andrew to leave their trade and to follow him.

Why were people willing to follow Jesus?

Jesus' disciples were greatly saddened by the loss of their leader. Then, they heard that Jesus had risen from the dead. Following the **resurrection**, or rising from the dead, Jesus reportedly remained on earth for 40 days before going directly to heaven. This convinced his disciples that Jesus was the Son of God who had become man. The disciples felt that because Jesus had suffered death and had risen to life, he could forgive the sins of humanity. They thought that anyone who believed in Jesus and lived by his teachings would know eternal life after death. From then on, the disciples called him Christ, after the Greek word *Christos*, meaning "messiah."

1. What did Jesus teach? How did he die?
2. How did Jesus' disciples view him after his death?

PAUL   The disciples were among the first people to become Christians. After Jesus died, they tried to spread his **gospel**, or teachings, among the Jews in Palestine. They had little success, however. Most Palestinian Jews wanted a political messiah instead of a religious one. The disciples were more successful when they began to preach to Jews who lived outside Palestine. Soon, small groups of believers were meeting near the synagogues of Antioch, Corinth, Rome, and other trading cities of the Mediterranean region.

Meanwhile, a Jew named Paul decided to preach Christianity to **gentiles**, or non-Jews, as well as to Jews. At one time, Paul had been a strict follower of Judaism. He had **persecuted**, or mistreated, Christians since he thought Christianity was a threat to Judaism. However, after reportedly hearing Christ's voice and being blinded by a bright light, Paul became a Christian. He then began to preach Christianity throughout the Roman world.

In each city where Paul preached, new Christian communities formed. Paul wrote letters to guide and advise the members. In his letters, he stated that gentiles who became Christians did not have to follow Jewish rituals and laws. All they needed was to have faith in Jesus. This appealed to many people.

Christianity began to grow from the belief of a few into a world religion. Paul was the first Christian **missionary**, or person who spreads religious beliefs to non-believers. After Paul's death, other Christian missionaries continued his work.

1. Who were the first Christians? How was their message received in Palestine? How was it received in other places?
2. What change did Paul make in the Christian message?

Paul

CHRISTIANITY AND ROME

The Roman Empire helped Christianity spread. The Pax Romana allowed missionaries to travel all over the empire in safety. The Roman system of roads helped them go from one place to the next quickly. As most of the people spoke either Latin or Greek, the missionaries could talk with them directly.

POLITICAL CONDITIONS   Political conditions did not favor the spread of Christianity, however. Although all people in the Roman Empire were allowed to worship freely, Romans expected everyone to honor the emperor as a god. The Chris-

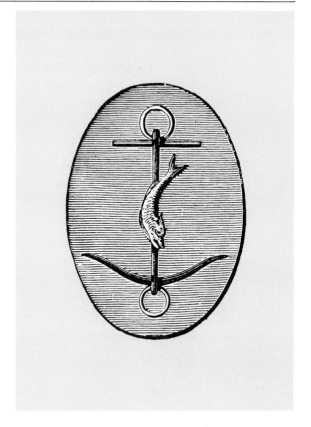

EARLY CHRISTIANITY

Many Christians died during the years of Roman persecution. Christian widows and their children (left) pay their respects at a tomb. The anchor and fish (right) are Christian symbols found on many early Christian tombs.

Why were the Christians persecuted?

tians, like the Jews, refused to do this. They claimed that only God could be worshipped. This greatly annoyed the Romans.

The Romans also did not like some other Christian attitudes. For example, Christians did not want to serve in the army or hold public office. They often criticized Roman festivals and games. They taught that all people would be equal in heaven if they followed Jesus' teachings.

Thus, the Romans blamed and punished the Christians for all kinds of disasters, such as plagues and famines. In 64 A.D., they accused the Christians of starting a fire that burned down much of Rome. Christianity was then made illegal, and many Christians were killed. Some officials ignored the law that made

Christianity illegal, but Christians still had a difficult time in most areas of the empire. In Rome, they were forbidden to use regular burial places. They had to bury their dead in crowded catacombs.

1. What helped Christianity spread?
2. Why did most Romans dislike Christianity?
3. How did Roman dislike affect the Christians?

THE SPREAD OF CHRISTIANITY   In spite of the difficulties, however, Christianity continued to spread. At first, the

THE SPREAD OF CHRISTIANITY

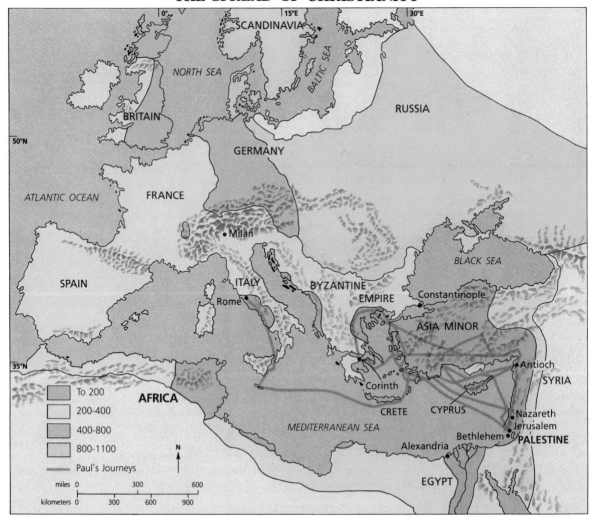

To 200
200-400
400-800
800-1100
Paul's Journeys

rich were not interested in it. They did not want anything to do with a religion whose founder had died by crucifixion. Christianity was of more interest to the poor workers and slaves in the cities. They led very hard lives. A religion that promised a happier life after death attracted them.

Over time, Christianity began to draw people from all classes. After 250 A.D., Romans grew tired of war and feared the collapse of the empire. They began to admire the certainty and courage of the Christian missionaries. They wanted the love, kindness, and security that Christianity offered. At the same time, many Christians became less opposed to the empire. Christian writers began to claim that it was possible to be both a good Christian and a good Roman.

Silver Cup

1. What groups of people were first attracted to Christianity? Why were they attracted?
2. What factors brought about a change in attitudes between Romans and Christians?

CONSTANTINE I AND THEODOSIUS   In 312 A.D., Christianity gained the support of Constantine I, who was a general at the time. Legend says that as he was about to go into battle, Constantine saw a flaming cross in the sky. Written beneath the cross were the Latin words *In hoc signo vinces,* "In this sign thou shalt conquer." Constantine won the battle and with it the throne of the Roman Empire. He believed that God had helped him, so he ordered his soldiers to paint crosses on their shields.

The following year, the Edict of Milan was issued. It granted religious freedom to all and made Christianity legal. Constantine I did a great deal to encourage the growth of Christianity. He had churches built in Rome and Jerusalem. He allowed the use of government money to support Christian schools. He permitted church leaders to enter government service and excused them from paying taxes.

The emperor who followed Constantine I continued pro-Christian policies. In 392 A.D., the emperor Theodosius made Christianity the official religion of the Roman Empire and outlawed all other religions.

Christian Inscription

1. Why did Constantine I support Christianity?
2. How did relations between Christians and the Roman government change during Constantine I's reign?
3. What did Theodosius do to help Christianity?

THE CHURCH

Early Christians thought the end of the world was near. At the time, they believed Jesus would return to set up God's kingdom on earth. While they were waiting for this to happen, they lived together in small groups called **churches**. They shared whatever goods they had and took turns conducting worship services in homes and outdoors. Each group managed its own affairs. **Apostles**, or those followers Jesus chose to preach his gospel, visited the various groups. The apostles taught and gave advice on problems. They also provided a sense of unity.

1. What did early Christians believe?
2. What did the apostles do?

The Apostle Matthew

CHURCH STRUCTURE   After the apostles died, Christians realized that Jesus was not going to return to earth as quickly as they had expected. So, they looked for ways to hold their churches together. They began to develop a church organization. Since they lived in the Roman Empire, they borrowed its structure of government.

By 300 A.D., each local church was called a **parish** and had a fulltime leader known as a **priest**. Several parishes were grouped together into larger units. Each unit was called a **diocese**, a term that originally meant a Roman military district. A **bishop** headed each Christian diocese. The most important bishops were called **archbishops**. They governed churches in the larger cities of the empire. The five leading archbishops were called **patriarchs**.

As time went on, the archbishop of Rome began to claim authority over the other archbishops. By 600 A.D., he was called **Pope,** a Latin word meaning "father." Latin-speaking Christians regarded him as the head of all of the churches. Greek-speaking Christians, however, would not accept his authority over their churches. They turned instead to the archbishop of Constantinople. In 1054 A.D., the Latin and Greek churches split. The Latin churches as a group became known as the Roman Catholic Church. The Greek churches became known as the Eastern Orthodox Church.

1. Why did Christians develop a church organization?
2. How was the church organized?
3. Why did the Latin and the Greek churches split?

EARLY CHURCH ORGANIZATION

Patriarchs

Patriarchs were archbishops with the highest standing. They headed churches founded by apostles.

Archbishops

Archbishops were bishops of large cities. They governed an area of several dioceses.

Bishops

Bishops headed a group of parishes called a diocese. They preached, performed important church rituals, collected offerings for the poor, and appointed priests.

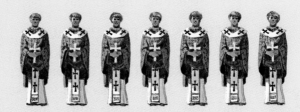

Priests

Priests headed the local Christian community, or parish. They advised bishops, preached, led worship services, and carried out missionary work.

Deacons

Deacons assisted bishops and priests in church worship, cared for the poor, and looked after finances.

THE NEW TESTAMENT   At the same time that Christians were developing a church organization, they were deciding what writings to include in the New Testament, or Christian scriptures. Jesus had left no written records. However, after the crucifixion, others wrote about his life and teachings.

Toward the end of the fourth century A.D., four of these accounts were accepted as part of the New Testament. The accounts were believed to have been written by Matthew, Mark, Luke, and John, four of Jesus' early followers. A number of letters written by Paul and other disciples were also accepted as sacred writings.

At about the same time, bishops met in councils to discuss questions about Christian thinking. The decisions they reached at these councils came to be accepted as official **doctrine**, or teachings. The points of view the councils did not accept were considered **heresy**, or false doctrines.

1. What writings make up the New Testament?
2. What did the councils of bishops do?

Jerome

FATHERS OF THE CHURCH   Between 100 and 500 A.D., various scholars wrote works that greatly influenced later Christian thinkers. These scholars were known as "Fathers of the Church." Jerome was one such scholar. He translated the Old and New Testaments into Latin. His work, called the *Vulgate,* became the official Latin bible used by the Roman Catholic Church.

Augustine was another important leader of Christian thought. His most famous work was *City of God.* In it, he defended Christianity against those who claimed that Rome would not have fallen to Germanic invaders if it had not accepted Christianity. Augustine argued that Rome's fall was a punishment for having become rich and corrupt and for having persecuted Christians. He explained that Rome would have fallen sooner or later because the only eternal city is the city of God.

1. Who were the "Fathers of the Church"?
2. What did Jerome contribute to Christian thought?
3. What argument did Augustine make in the *City of God*?

MONASTERIES   In the early years of Christianity, thousands of Christians often left the cities to live and pray alone in the desert. Such people were called **hermits**. In Egypt and Syria especially, thousands of hermits lived apart from other people. They believed that being a hermit would help them grow closer to Christ.

A hermit was protected from the temptation of daily life. But at the same time, the hermit was not doing anything to improve society. Near the end of the fourth century A.D., a bishop named Basil suggested a different way of life. He said that dedicated Christians should form religious communities near cities. In this way, they would be protected from the evils of the world. At the same time, they could help others by performing good deeds and by setting an example of Christian living. Many Christians took Basil's advice.

The Christian men who did as Basil suggested were called **monks**. Their communities were known as **monasteries**. The Christian women who did the same were called **nuns**. They lived in quarters of their own called **convents**. Basil drew up a list of rules for these communities. This list, which is known as the Basilian Rule, became the model for Eastern Orthodox religious life.

In the West, another rule called the Benedictine Rule was followed. It was created in Italy about 529 A.D. by Benedict. The monks who followed Benedict's rule promised to give up all their possessions before entering the monastery. They agreed to wear simple clothes and eat only certain foods. They could not marry. They had to obey without question the orders of the **abbot**, or leader of the monastery. They had to attend services seven times during the day and once at midnight. In addition, they were expected to work six or seven hours a day in the fields surrounding the monastery. When they grew older, the monks did clerical work or worked as carpenters and weavers. In this way, they spent their entire lives serving Christ.

By 800 A.D., monks were playing an important role in spreading Christianity throughout Europe. By taking care of old Roman and Greek writings, they helped western civilization survive.

1. What type of life did hermits lead? Why did they live this way?
2. What did Basil suggest? Why did he suggest this?
3. What were some of the rules by which Benedict expected monks to live?

Monastery Bell Tower

Monk

CHAPTER 16 REVIEW

SUMMARY

1. Jesus was born a Jew in the town of Bethlehem in Palestine.
2. Jesus grew up in Nazareth, where he received a Jewish education, and then went to work as a carpenter.
3. When he was 30, Jesus began to preach about God and His love for all humans.
4. In 33 A.D., Jesus was convicted of treason and was crucified.
5. Following his resurrection, Jesus became known as Christ, which means "messiah."
6. Paul preached Christianity to non-Jews, as well as to Jews, and thus helped make Christianity a world religion.
7. In 313 A.D., Constantine I issued the Edict of Milan making Christianity legal in the Roman Empire.
8. In 392 A.D., Theodosius made Christianity the official religion of the Roman Empire.
9. Christians developed a church organization based on the structure of government of the Roman Empire.
10. By 600 A.D., the archbishop of Rome was called Pope and was regarded by Latin-speaking Christians as head of the Church.
11. In 1054 A.D., Greek-speaking Christians split from the Latin churches.
12. Between 100 and 500 A.D., scholars, such as Jerome and Augustine, wrote works that greatly influenced later Christian thinkers.
13. A bishop named Basil suggested that dedicated Christians become monks and nuns rather than hermits so they could help others by performing good deeds and by setting an example of Christian living.
14. Western monks lived according to rules drawn up by Benedict about 529 A.D.

BUILDING VOCABULARY

1. *Identify the following:*

Jesus	Constantine I	Eastern Orthodox Church	*City of God*
Bethlehem	Edict of Milan	Jerome	Basil
Nazareth	Theodosius	*Vulgate*	Benedict
Paul	Roman Catholic Church	Augustine	

2. *Define the following:*

scriptures	gentiles	priest	heresy
parables	persecuted	diocese	hermits
disciples	missionary	bishop	monks
messiah	churches	archbishops	monasteries
crucified	apostles	patriarchs	nuns
resurrection	parish	Pope	convents
gospel		doctrine	abbot

REVIEWING THE FACTS

1. Where did Christianity start?
2. What sort of early education did Jesus receive?
3. Why did Jesus teach in parables?
4. Why were the Jews hoping and waiting for a messiah?
5. What is the legend associated with Constantine I?
6. What did the Edict of Milan do?
7. After 1054 A.D., what name was given to the Latin churches as a group?
8. After 1054 A.D., what name was given to the Greek churches as a group?
9. What kinds of work did monks do?
10. How did monks help western civilization survive?

DISCUSSING IMPORTANT IDEAS

1. Do you think that teaching in parables is effective? Why or why not?
2. How did the Roman Empire help Christianity spread?
3. Do you believe in religious freedom, like Constantine I, or in an official religion, like Theodosius? Why?
4. How would you have organized the early Christian Church?
5. Do you think anything could have been done to prevent the split between the Latin and Greek churches? Explain.
6. Would you have become a monk or nun in 600 A.D.? Why or why not?

USING MAPS

Study the map on page 238, and answer the following questions:

1. During what time period did Christianity spread to Antioch?
2. During what time period did Christianity spread the most?
3. Into what areas did Christianity spread between 400 and 800 A.D.?
4. Into what areas did Christianity spread between 800 and 1100 A.D.?
5. In what area did Paul make most of his journeys?
6. To what cities did Paul travel during his journeys as a missionary?

BUDDHISM

Siddhartha Gautama was born in the foothills of the Himalayas about 563 B.C. He was born a Hindu, but he grew up to found a new religion called Buddhism. This much of his life is known to be true. The rest is legend. Yet, the story has an important place in Buddhism.

Siddhartha Gautama was the son of a rich noble who wanted to protect his son from human sorrow. The boy grew up shielded from sights that were not pleasant. As a young married man, Gautama lived in luxury. His palaces were surrounded by parks filled with strange birds and rare fish. He was followed wherever he went by servants.

When Gautama was about 30 years old, he made three trips outside his palace grounds. On these trips he met two men, one very old and one quite sick. He also saw a dead man. For the first time, Gautama learned about aging, sickness, and death. He was troubled that humans had to suffer these many tragedies.

On a fourth trip, Gautama met a holy man. This man had nothing but a bowl for begging and a single yellow garment. Yet, he looked very happy. Gautama realized that there was more to happiness than possessions. He decided to leave his wife and newborn son and to seek truth and wisdom.

For several years, Gautama lived as a wandering monk. He starved himself and read the holy books of Hinduism. Still, he could not find an answer to freedom from life's suffering.

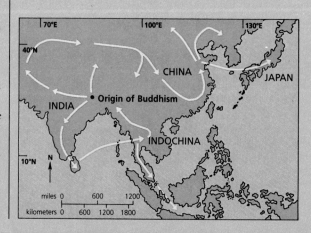

Finally, Gautama decided to find life's answers through his own thinking. One day, he wandered into a village and sat under a tree. He decided to **meditate**, or think, until he gained **enlightenment**, or understanding. Several hours later, enlightenment came.

Gautama learned that people could find freedom from suffering in **nirvana**, or a state of complete happiness and peace. He believed that suffering was caused by human desires. Therefore, by not desiring anything and by living correctly, a person would find peace.

Others learned of Gautama's experience and began to call him Buddha, which means "Enlightened One." His teachings became a new religion that is called Buddhism.

One of India's most famous kings, Asoka, was influenced by Buddha's teachings. Asoka ruled India about 260 B.C. He followed Buddha's teachings and became **tolerant**, or respectful, of all living things. Asoka also sent Buddhist teachers to other lands. In later years, Buddhism became one of the major religions of Asia.

1. What kind of life did Siddhartha Gautama lead in his youth?
2. What led Gautama to change his way of life?
3. What did Buddha teach? How did his teachings influence others?

UNIT 5 REVIEW

SUMMARY

1. The Etruscans contributed many ideas and customs to Roman civilization.
2. In 509 B.C., the Romans abolished the monarchy and in its place established a republic.
3. Through conquests and alliances, the Romans expanded their territory until eventually they ruled most of the western world.
4. War and conquest changed Roman life and gradually led to the decline of the republic.
5. Augustus, the first Roman emperor, brought to Rome the period of peace and prosperity known as the Pax Romana, during which trade increased, laws were standardized, and Christianity spread.
6. Christianity became the official religion of the Roman Empire and a major influence on western civilization.
7. Political and economic problems that weakened the Roman Empire and made it possible for foreign invaders to defeat Roman armies led to the fall of Rome.

REVIEWING THE MAIN IDEAS

1. Explain how the daily life of Romans during the Pax Romana showed the influence of the Etruscans.
2. Explain in what ways the Romans were affected by the religion and the economic life of the different people they conquered over the years.
3. Compare the government of the Roman Republic with the government of the Greek city-states.
4. Explain why the Roman Republic was unable to survive.
5. Describe Rome's three most important contributions to western culture.

DEVELOPING SKILLS

One skill that is needed in order to think clearly is the ability to relate cause and effect. Sometimes, one event causes another event. Other times, one event follows another in time, but there is no cause-and-effect relationship between the two. That is, the first event does not cause the second event.

This exercise is designed to give you practice in deciding if one event is the cause of another event. Below are five pairs of events. For each pair, tell whether or not the first event was a cause of the second.

1. a. Roman legions conquered what is now the nation of France.
   b. Many French words come from Latin, the language of the Romans.
2. a. Hannibal Barca and his troops roamed the countryside of southern Italy for 15 years.
   b. The Romans began using prisoners of war as slaves.
3. a. Gaius Marius was elected consul of Rome.

b. Julius Caesar became dictator of Rome.

4. a. Augustus reorganized the government of Rome.

b. The Pax Romana lasted for 200 years.

5. a. A Jew named Paul decided to preach Christianity to gentiles as well as to Jews.

b. Christianity began to spread gradually throughout all the regions of the Roman Empire.

SUGGESTED UNIT PROJECTS

1. Find out which words in the preamble to the Constitution of the United States come from Latin.

2. Working in a group, put out a newspaper, complete with headlines, articles, advertisements, and classified ads, that covers events in the Roman Republic or Empire.

3. Prepare a report on the Roman water system. Tell where the water came from, how aqueducts carried it across the valleys, and how it was distributed in the cities.

4. Bring in pictures of buildings or other structures in the United States that resemble those in ancient Rome.

SUGGESTED READING

Cunliffe, Barry. *Rome and the Barbarians*. New York: Henry Z. Walck, Inc. 1975. A description of what archaeologists have learned about the Roman legions and the Gauls, Britons, and Germans against whom they fought.

Dillion, Ellis. *Rome Under the Emperors*. New York: Thomas Nelson, Inc., 1974. A description of the daily life of the families of a senator, a rich businessman, a farmer, and a flower-and-fruit seller in Imperial Rome.

Fagg, Christopher. *Ancient Rome*. New York: Warwick Press, 1978. A description of the civilization of the Romans.

Honness, Elizabeth. *The Etruscans: An Unsolved Mystery*. Philadelphia and New York: J.B. Lippincott Company, 1972. A description of Etruscan civilization.

Liversidge, Joan. *Everyday Life in the Roman Empire*. New York: G.P. Putnams' Sons, 1976. A description of the influence of Rome on the life of people in different parts of the Roman Empire.

Macnamara, Ellen. *Everyday Life of the Etruscans*. New York: G.P. Putnams' Sons, 1973. A description of Etruscan art and artifacts discovered in Etruria.

Stearns, Monroe. *Julius Caesar: Master of Men*. New York: Franklin Watts, Inc., 1971. An account of the life and times of Julius Caesar.

UNIT 6

375	400	425
378 Battle of Adrianople		
	410 Goths attack Rome Angles, Saxons, and Jutes enter Britain	

525	550	575
		597 Christia missiona arrive in Britain

675	700	725
	711 Arab Muslims conquer Spain	**732** Battle of Tours

825	850	875
	843 Treaty of Verdun	871 Alfred becomes king of Wessex

975	1000	1025
	c. 1000 Vikings explore north Atlantic	

THE EARLY MIDDLE AGES

0	475	500
455 Vandals sack Rome	**c. 476** Roman Empire ends in West **481** Clovis becomes king of Franks	

00	625	650

50	775	800
		800 Charlemagne crowned emperor

00	925	950
911 Normans settle in Normandy		

1. WHY IS THE MIDDLE AGES AN IMPORTANT PERIOD IN HISTORY?
2. HOW DID THE EVENTS IN THE MIDDLE AGES INFLUENCE THE GROWTH OF WESTERN EUROPE?

The period from the fall of the Roman Empire to the beginning of modern times is called the Middle Ages. It lasted from about 500 to about 1500. Historians have looked at the Middle Ages in several different ways.

Some historians see the Middle Ages as a time of darkness. They base their judgment on the fact that during much of the period there was little learning in Europe. Except for religious leaders and some townspeople, few individuals could read or write. Trade and city life declined throughout Europe. Most people lived in the country and knew little about life beyond their villages. There was no central government to keep the peace. Political and military power was mostly in the hands of local nobles.

Other historians consider the Middle Ages as the beginning of present-day western civilization. They point out that western ideas of society, trade, and government began to develop in this period. It was also the time when students and teachers were forming the first universities and when modern European languages were evolving.

For others, the Middle Ages is the "Age of Faith"— that is, the period in which the Catholic Church shaped people's lives. Churches and monasteries were built in every part of Europe. People were willing to serve in armies to fight for the Church.

Most historians agree that the Middle Ages was a time in which western Europe created a new civilization. It was based on Greco-Roman culture, Christian faith, and Germanic practices.

CHAPTER 17
THE GERMANS

During the first 400 years after the birth of Christ, a tall, fair-haired people, the Germans, left the forests and marshes of northern Europe. Looking for a warmer climate and new grazing land for their cattle, they slowly moved south toward the Roman Empire. They were also attracted to Rome by its wealth and culture. The Germans hoped to live peacefully within the borders of the Roman Empire.

At first, the Romans did not want to let the Germans enter their territory. They considered the Germans their enemies. But by about 300, the Romans realized they were not strong enough to keep the Germans out. So, they began to let Germans cross the border in small groups.

Many Germans moved into the Danube River valley. They settled there, became farmers, and gradually adopted Roman ways. They traded with Roman merchants and joined the Roman army. Some Germans became Christians.

VILLAGE LIFE

Although the Germans took part in Roman life, they also kept much of their own culture. They lived in villages surrounded by farmlands and pastures. Most homes were long thatched-roof huts with an open space around them. The family lived in one end of the hut and divided the other end into animal stalls. The body heat of the animals helped to warm the hut during the cold winters. Wooden tables and benches placed along the walls of the hut were the only furniture. A few wealthier villagers added wall hangings or carpets.

The villagers made their living herding cattle, which provided food and clothing. They also traded cattle for Roman glass vessels, table articles, and jewelry. The Germans farmed as well. They grew barley, rye, wheat, beans, and peas. Most farm work was done by women, children, and slaves. They drew water from wooden wells and stored food in pits lined with basketwork. When the women were not working in the fields or cooking, they spun wool and wove cloth on upright looms.

German dress was simple. Women wore long skirts made of different yarns or one-piece sack-like dresses that extended from the shoulders to the feet. Sometimes, they wore scarves or shawls tied with a bone pin. Men wore short woolen tunics and close-fitting trousers. They covered the tunics with cloaks fastened on the right shoulder with a brooch.

The Germans believed in **hospitality**, or welcoming guests and strangers warmly. It was against the law to turn away anyone who came to the door. Invited guests and strangers alike were fed and entertained. Feasting, drinking, and dancing were favorite German pastimes. The men also enjoyed gambling with dice. Sometimes, they took part in such organized sports as boxing and wrestling. In winter, they skated on ice using skates made of flat bone.

The Germans spoke a language that later became modern German. At first, the people could not read or write because their language had no alphabet. However, some learned to

German Helmet

GERMAN VILLAGE
The Germans built their villages just within the borders of the Roman Empire. They lived in family groups that included grandparents, aunts, uncles, and cousins. What was German village life like?

speak and write Latin. Gradually, they began to use Roman letters to write their own language.

1. Where did the Germans live? How did they earn their living?
2. What did the Germans do for entertainment?
3. How was the German language influenced by the Romans?

WARRIORS German men were warriors. They spent most of their time fighting, hunting, or making weapons. They began training for war when they were young boys. When a male reached manhood, he was brought before a special gathering held in a sacred grove under a full moon. He received a shield and a spear, which he had to carry with him at all times. The loss of the shield and spear meant the loss of honor.

The Germans were divided into **clans**, or groups based on family ties. At first, the Germans gave their greatest loyalty to

GERMAN WARRIORS

Some German families claimed descent from the gods, had wealth, and supplied leaders in time of war. A German warrior and his family (left) are dressed in their finest clothing. A warrior band and its chieftain (right) celebrate a victory over the Romans.

How did German warriors dress for battle?

their clan. But after a while, they developed a strong feeling of loyalty toward a military leader called a **chieftain**. A warrior had to be a good fighter to be a chieftain. In the beginning, the chieftain was elected by a band of warriors. Later, the office of chieftain became hereditary.

Chieftains provided warriors with leadership, weapons, and a chance for wealth and adventure. They also settled disputes among warriors. In some cases, the chieftains gave warriors food and shelter. In return, warriors gave their chieftains total loyalty. Warriors took an oath to defend and protect their chieftains. Individual warriors even gave chieftains credit for brave deeds the warriors themselves performed. In battle, chieftains fought for victory, and warriors fought for their chieftains.

Chieftains and their bands did not have fixed plans of fighting. Each warrior band was small. It usually fought on its own, apart from other bands. The bands made surprise raids against their enemies. Warriors on foot and on horseback would charge wildly, yelling in loud voices to frighten their foes. They fought with daggers, short swords, and heavy axes made of metal and stone. They carried light wooden shields and wore suits of leather. A successful attack provided warriors with human captives, cattle, and other treasures.

The Germans' love of battle was closely linked to their religion. They had many gods who liked to fight and to hunt. The chief god, Woden, was the god of war, learning, poetry, and magic. Another god of war was Woden's son Thor, who was also the god of thunder. The Germans believed that the sound of thunder came from Thor's chariot wheels.

The Germans admired bravery. Like the Spartans, they expected their warriors to win in battle or to die fighting. The only German shields left on the battlefield were those of dead warriors. The Germans believed that goddesses carried the spirits of warriors who died in battle into the afterlife. There, in Valhalla, the warriors would feast and fight forever.

1. What kind of training did a German boy receive?
2. How were chieftains chosen?
3. How did the Germans fight?
4. What were some features of the German religion?

THE LAW   The Romans believed that law came from the emperor. The Germans believed it came from the people. German rulers could not change the law unless the people approved.

The Germans based their laws on the customs of their ancestors. Instead of writing down the laws, the Germans memorized them and passed them from parent to child.

Reckless fighting, usually caused by too much drinking, created a problem in the German villages. The Germans wanted to keep such fights from becoming **blood feuds**, or quarrels in which the families of original fighters seek revenge. Blood feuds could go on for generations. To stop such violence, the Germans set up courts. Judges listened to each side's argument and tried to find a settlement that would bring peace to the community.

The Germans determined who was guilty or innocent in different ways. One way was by oath-taking. People accused of crimes would declare their innocence by oath. Then, they would present statements from **oath-helpers**, or people who swore that the accused was telling the truth. The Germans believed that

German Shield

anyone who did not tell the truth when taking an oath would be punished by the gods.

People accused of crimes could not always find oath-helpers to prove their innocence. In such cases, guilt or innocence was decided by **ordeal**. Persons accused of a crime had to walk barefoot over red-hot coals or place an arm into boiling water. The burns of the innocent were supposed to heal within three days. There was also an ordeal by water. A person was bound hand and foot and thrown into a lake or river. The Germans viewed water as a symbol of purity. They believed the water would accept anyone who was pure and reject anyone who was not pure. If the person sank to the bottom, it was a sign of innocence. If the person floated, it was a sign of guilt.

The Germans did not always require a person who was judged guilty to be punished physically. The courts could impose fines called *wergeld*. The exact amount of the wergeld varied. For example, an injury to a chieftain called for a larger payment than one to an ordinary person. The payment for killing a teenage girl was greater than one for killing a woman too old to have children. Although the courts could impose fines, they did not have the power to collect them. They had to rely on public opinion to force a guilty person to pay the fine.

The German legal system kept the peace, but it did not treat all people fairly. A person's wealth and importance, instead of the crime, determined the penalty. Still, the Germans believed that laws came from the people rather than the ruler. And no ruler could change the laws without the people's approval.

1. What led the Germans to set up courts?
2. How did the Germans determine guilt or innocence?
3. What were some strengths of German law? What were some weaknesses?

German Chieftain

THE GOTHS AND THE VANDALS

The Goths were a Germanic people who lived in the Balkan Peninsula of Europe. They were divided into two groups called Ostrogoths, or East Goths, and Visigoths, or West Goths.

In the late 300's, both groups of Goths were attacked by the Huns. The Huns swept into Europe from central Asia under a leader named Attila, or "Little Daddy." Attila and the Huns conquered the East Goths. The West Goths were afraid that

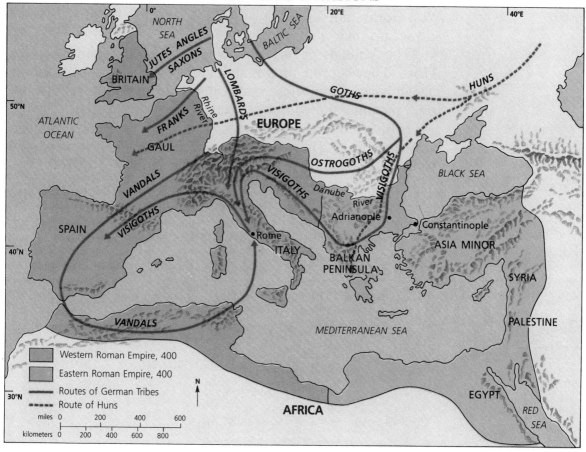

they, too, would be conquered. So, they asked the Roman emperor for protection. The emperor allowed them to settle just inside the frontier of the Roman Empire. In return, they had to give up their weapons and promise to be loyal to Rome.

Before long, trouble broke out between the West Goths and Roman officials. The Romans were supposed to supply the West Goths with food and clothing. Instead, the West Goths had to buy food at very high prices. The Romans kidnapped many young West Goths and sold them as slaves.

Finally, the West Goths rebelled against the Romans and defeated them at the Battle of Adrianople in 378. But the West Goths did not stop there. In 410, led by the chieftain Alaric, they captured and robbed Rome.

After the capture of Rome, the West Goths continued on to Gaul. Then, they moved into Spain, which was occupied by the

Romans and another Germanic group called the Vandals. The West Goths ended Roman rule in Spain, drove out the Vandals, and set up their own kingdom.

The Vandals in turn crossed the Mediterranean to North Africa. They became pirates and raided cities along the Mediterranean coast. From these raids came the English word "**vandalism**," meaning the willful destruction of property.

In 455, led by their king, Gaiseric, the Vandals attacked and burned Rome. They did, however, spare the lives of the Romans. Afterwards, the Vandals returned to North Africa.

1. What happened to the East Goths? What effect did this have on the West Goths?
2. Why did the West Goths come to dislike Roman officials? What did they do to show their dislike?

THE GERMANIC KINGDOMS

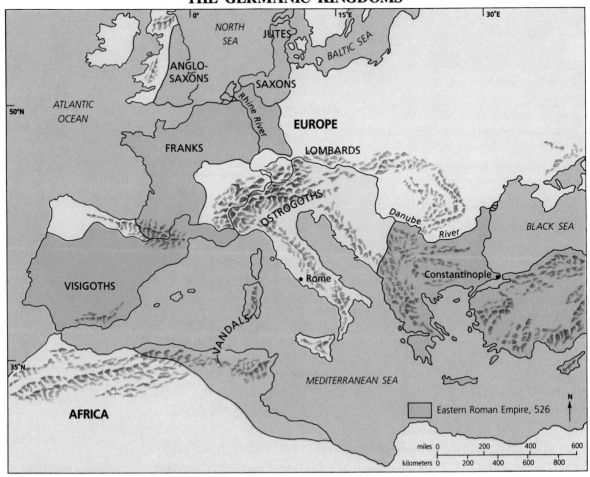

Eastern Roman Empire, 526

THE END OF THE ROMAN EMPIRE

As a result of Germanic invasions, the Roman Empire in the West began to fall apart. Generals fought each other for control of Rome and Italy. Many of these generals were Germans who, when victorious, usually chose Roman citizens to serve as emperor. These emperors had little power of their own.

In 476, a general named Odoacer took control of the government. He did not bother to appoint an emperor. Instead, he ruled the western part of the empire for almost 15 years. After his death, a group of East Goths invaded Italy and set up a kingdom under their leader, Theodoric.

By 550, the Roman Empire in the West had faded away. In its place were six major and a great many minor Germanic kingdoms. Although Roman rule was no more, many Roman beliefs and practices remained to shape later civilization.

Theodoric

1. What happened to the office of emperor after the invasions?
2. What replaced the Roman Empire in the West?

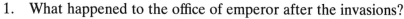

CHAPTER 17 REVIEW

SUMMARY

1. About 300, groups of Germans began settling in the Roman Empire.

2. German men were warriors, while German women did the farm work.

3. German warriors were organized into bands headed by chieftains, to whom the warriors gave complete loyalty.

4. The Germans' love of battle was closely linked to their religion.

5. The Germans determined a person's guilt or innocence through oath-taking or ordeal.

6. German courts often imposed fines rather than physical punishment.

7. The penalty for a crime depended on a person's wealth or importance.

8. The Germans believed that law came from the people and that a ruler could not change the law without the people's approval.

9. In 378, the West Goths defeated the Romans at the Battle of Adrianople.

10. In 410, the West Goths captured and robbed Rome before setting up their own kingdom in Spain.

11. The Vandals, who had lived in Spain, moved to North Africa and began to raid cities along the Mediterranean coast.

12. By 550, the Roman Empire in the West had been replaced by six major and a great many minor Germanic kingdoms.

BUILDING VOCABULARY

1. *Identify the following:*

Woden	Goths	Alaric	Odoacer
Thor	Huns	Vandals	Theodoric
Valhalla	Attila	Gaiseric	

2. *Define the following:*

hospitality	chieftains	oath-helpers	*wergeld*
clans	blood feuds	ordeal	vandalism

REVIEWING THE FACTS

1. Why did the Germans begin to move south toward the Roman Empire?
2. Why did the Romans start allowing Germans to cross the borders of the Roman Empire?
3. Who did the farm work in German villages?
4. What did the loss of his shield and spear mean to a German warrior?
5. What did a German chieftain do for the members of his band?
6. How did warriors show their loyalty to their chieftain?
7. What did the Germans believe the afterlife would be like?
8. According to the Germans, where did law come from?
9. Why did the Germans use an ordeal by water?
10. Why did the West Goths want to enter the Roman Empire? What did they do after capturing Rome?

DISCUSSING IMPORTANT IDEAS

1. What parts of Roman culture did the Germans adopt? What parts of their own culture did they keep?
2. What role did religion play in German life?
3. Do you think you would have liked living in a German village? Why or why not?
4. Do you believe that the penalty for a crime should depend on a person's wealth or importance? If not, on what do you think it should depend? Explain.
5. What do you think might have happened if Roman officials had treated the West Goths fairly? Explain.

USING MAPS

Study the maps on pages 259 and 260, and answer the following questions:

1. From what area of Europe did the Germans move?
2. Which Germanic group appears to have moved the farthest?
3. Which groups of Germans formed the Germanic kingdoms in 526?
4. Which group of Germans settled in Italy?

CHAPTER 18

THE FRANKS

The decline of the Roman Empire led to disorder everywhere in western Europe. Many of the Germanic invaders were too weak to govern well. As a result, towns and villages fell into ruin. Roads and bridges were not repaired. Robbers roamed the countryside, making it unsafe for travelers. Trading and business slowed down, and there were shortages of food and other goods. People were no longer interested in learning, and many books and works of art were damaged or lost.

This period of hardship is called the Early Middle Ages. Some historians have also called it the Dark Ages. It lasted from about 500 to 1000.

Clovis

CLOVIS

During this period, a Germanic people called the Franks became very important. They began to build a new civilization, one that later developed into modern France and Germany. The Franks lived along the Rhine River in the area now known as western Germany. They were more successful in governing than other Germans. One reason for this was that the area in which they lived was close to their homeland, and they felt fairly secure. Also, unlike the Goths and Vandals, the Franks did more than just fight and rule. They became farmers.

At first, the Franks were divided into separate groups without a common ruler. In 481, one of the groups chose a king named Clovis. Although Clovis was cruel and greedy, he was a good general and an able king. And he eventually brought all of the Franks under one rule. Part of Clovis' kingdom later became the nation of France, which took its name from the Franks.

Clovis was the first Germanic king to accept the Catholic religion. The following story is told about how this happened. Clovis was not happy with the Frankish gods. Even though he prayed to them faithfully, they failed to help him win battles. His Christian wife suggested that he pray to God. Clovis agreed to do so, saying that if he defeated the enemy, he would become a Christian. The Franks won their next battle. Clovis and some 3,000 of his soldiers, still in full battle dress, immediately **converted**, or changed religion, to Christianity. It was not long before all the Franks followed their king's example.

When Clovis became a Christian, he gained the support of the Romans in his kingdom. They had lived in Gaul before the Franks arrived, and most of them already were Christians. Before long, the Franks began speaking a form of Latin that later became the modern French language. Now, all the people of Clovis' kingdom practiced the same religion and spoke the same language. This helped them feel more united.

The Church taught that God gave the king the right to rule. Therefore, in order to govern, a king had to have the blessing of the Church. Clovis had that blessing. The Pope and other church officials gave him their support. Priests served in Clovis' government and won for it the respect of the people. In return for this help, Clovis was expected to protect the Church against any non-believers.

Clovis extended his rule over what is now France and western Germany and set up his capital in Paris. He admired the Roman Empire and tried to copy its ways. He wore the purple robes of the Roman emperors and used purple ink for his royal decrees. He made Latin the official language of the court and of his kingdom.

1. Why were the Franks more successful at governing than other Germanic peoples?
2. Why did Clovis become a Christian?
3. In what ways did Clovis copy the Roman emperors?

CHARLES THE HAMMER

The Frankish kings who followed Clovis were weak rulers. Instead of keeping the kingdom united, they divided it among their sons. The sons often fought over their shares of land. They spent so much time and energy fighting that they lost much of their power to local nobles.

It was not long before the Franks began to accept the leadership of a government official known as the "Mayor of the Palace." The Mayor was a noble and the most important official in the king's household. As the kings grew weaker, the Mayors took over many of their duties. In time, they were conducting wars, giving out land, and settling disputes. Of all the Mayors, the most powerful was Charles Martel. He wanted to reunite all the Frankish nobles under his rule. Before long, he had gained the support of the Church.

Charles Martel became known as "The Hammer" because of his strength in battle. In 732, he led the Franks in the Battle of Tours, one of the most important battles in European history. The Franks defeated an army of Arabs who had conquered Spain in 711. The Arabs were Muslims, or followers of a religion known as Islam. They hoped to spread Islam everywhere.

When Charles Martel died, his son Pepin became Mayor of the Palace. With the help of the Pope and most of the Frankish nobles, Pepin removed the king and started a new dynasty. Pepin was the first Frankish king to be **anointed**, or blessed with holy oil, by the Pope. In return for the Church's support, Pepin helped the Pope when he was threatened by a group of Germans known as the Lombards. Pepin led an army into Italy, defeated the Lombards, and gave the land they held in central Italy to the

Frankish Pendant

BATTLE OF TOURS

Charles Martel (center) leads his army against the Muslims at the Battle of Tours. The Frankish victory halted the Muslim advance into western Europe. It also helped the Frankish rulers to build a strong kingdom.

Why was Charles Martel known as "The Hammer"?

Pope. This gift made the Pope the political ruler of much of the Italian Peninsula.

1. What was the role of the Mayor of the Palace?
2. What did Charles Martel want to do?
3. Why was the Battle of Tours important?
4. How did Pepin help the Pope?

CHARLEMAGNE

When Pepin died in 768, his kingdom was divided between his two sons. His son Carloman died within a few years. His other son Charles then became king of the Franks. He is best known by his French name Charlemagne, which means "Charles the Great."

Charlemagne wanted to bring all of western Europe under his rule. He also wanted all the Germanic peoples to become Christians. To achieve these goals, he waged a series of wars.

First, Charlemagne defeated the Lombards, who had tried to take their land back from the Pope. Next, he turned his attention to a Germanic people called the Saxons. For years, the Saxons had been raiding towns and monasteries inside the Frankish border. Charlemagne killed many of the Saxon leaders and sent thousands of Saxons to Frankish territory. Then, he moved his own people onto Saxon lands in what is now northern Germany. Eventually, the Saxons accepted Christianity.

Charlemagne also led his armies in several campaigns across the Pyrenees Mountains to fight the Muslims in Spain. A mountain people known as the Basques did not want the Frankish armies to cross their territory. When Charlemagne was returning home from one of his Spanish campaigns, Basque warriors attacked the rear guard of his army in a narrow mountain pass. The rear guard was led by Roland, a fine warrior and a close friend of Charlemagne. Since Roland had far fewer soldiers than the Basques, he lost the battle. The fight between Roland and the Basques was remembered, told, and retold throughout Europe. Over time, the event became legend and was written down in French as a poem called *The Song of Roland.*

Frankish Warrior

By 800, Charlemagne had created a large empire that included most of the Germanic peoples who had settled in Europe since the early 400's. Charlemagne also fought against non-Germanic peoples in northern and eastern Europe. These people managed to keep their freedom, but they agreed to respect Charlemagne's power and not fight against his army.

1. Why did Charlemagne go to Italy?
2. How did Saxon lands become part of Charlemagne's empire?

A CHRISTIAN EMPIRE   Charlemagne became the most powerful leader in western Europe. The people considered him as important as any Roman emperor. Charlemagne wanted to keep close ties between the Church and the government. Church officials kept records and helped Charlemagne run the country.

CROWNING OF CHARLEMAGNE
Many western Europeans wanted to bring back the glory of ancient Rome. In 800, Charlemagne became emperor of a new Christian Roman Empire. Here Charlemagne is crowned "Emperor of the Romans" by the Pope. The new emperor is surrounded by members of his royal court.
What goal did Charlemagne and the Pope have in common?

Charlemagne appointed the bishops and regarded any act against the Church as a sign of disloyalty to him.

Both Charlemagne and the Pope wanted a new Christian Roman Empire in western Europe. Charlemagne's conquests had brought him closer to their goal. On Christmas day in 800, Charlemagne was worshipping in St. Peter's Church in Rome. When the religious ceremony was over, the Pope placed a crown on Charlemagne's head. He then declared that Charlemagne was the new Roman emperor. Although Charlemagne accepted the title, he was not pleased that the Pope had crowned him. Crowning by the Pope made it seem as if the emperor's right to rule came from the Pope rather than directly from God.

Charlemagne was a wise and just ruler who issued a variety of laws. To make sure they were obeyed, he set up law courts throughout the empire. He chose officials called **counts** to run the courts. The counts took care of local problems, stopped feuds, protected the poor and the weak, and raised armies for Charlemagne.

Charlemagne often had trouble keeping the counts under his control because of poor transportation and communication. So, he sent special royal messengers throughout the land to check on them. The messengers reported to Charlemagne how well the counts were doing their jobs. Once a year, Charlemagne called the counts and warriors together. They expressed grievances and discussed new laws for the empire. The final decision on what new laws were acceptable was made by Charlemagne. In this way, he could keep better control.

Charlemagne ruled his empire from Aachen, known today as Aix-la-Chapelle. He did not always stay in the capital. He traveled throughout the empire accompanied by his advisors and servants. The royal party would stop and rest at different palaces or homes. Wherever the king and his officials went, they were given food and entertained by the people. Such royal visits insured the loyalty of local officials and people to the imperial government.

1. What sort of relationship did Charlemagne want between the Church and the government?
2. Why did Charlemagne object to the Pope crowning him emperor?
3. What were some duties of the counts?
4. How did Charlemagne keep control of his empire?

EDUCATION   Most of the people in Charlemagne's empire could neither read nor write. But Charlemagne appreciated learning. Unlike earlier Frankish rulers, he believed in education and was proud of the fact that he was able to speak both Latin and Greek.

Charlemagne wanted his people to be educated. He worked hard to push back the darkness that had followed the decline of the Roman Empire. He encouraged churches and monasteries to found schools. He had a scholar named Alcuin start a school in one of the palaces to train the children of government officials to serve in the Church or in the royal household. The children studied religion, Latin, music, literature, and arithmetic.

Scholars came from all over Europe to teach in Charlemagne's school. One of their tasks was to copy manuscripts. This

Students

CHARLEMAGNE'S SCHOOL

Charlemagne often visited his palace school, which was attended by children of the court. Directed by the monk Alcuin, the school also provided a place where scholars could gather to share their knowledge and to inspire one another. Why was Charlemagne interested in learning?

led to the development of a new form of writing. The Roman writing the scholars used contained only capital letters. These took up a lot of space on a page. So, the scholars began to write with small letters instead of capital ones. The new letters not only took up less space, but were also easier to read. They became the model for the small letters used today.

Under Charlemagne, the arts began to flower again. Painters, sculptors, and metalworkers developed their talents. They built and decorated palaces and churches in the old Roman style of a group of buildings around a large courtyard. Artists covered palace and church walls with scenes depicting stories from the Bible. They made book covers and ornamental weapons, and they decorated the manuscripts copied by scholars.

1. How did Charlemagne feel about learning? What did he do to encourage it?

2. What led to the creation of a new form of writing? How was it different from Roman writing?

ESTATE LIFE   **Lords**, or nobles who were the descendants of Frankish warriors and Roman landowners, were the most powerful people in Charlemagne's empire. Most of their wealth came from goods grown or made on their estates. As there was little trade in Charlemagne's empire, each estate took care of its own needs. Craftspeople who lived on the estates made weapons, cooking vessels, and jewelry. Shoemakers, carpenters, and blacksmiths lived and worked on the estates, too.

The nobles lived in stone farmhouses on their estates. Wooden **stockades**, or fences, often surrounded the houses. Each farmhouse had a banquet hall, sleeping quarters, cellars, stables, storage places, and a small chapel.

Farmers lived in simple wooden houses in small villages on the estates. They worked in the fields, vineyards, orchards, and forests that surrounded their villages. The fields were owned by the nobles, but the farmers worked them three days a week. The rest of the time they worked small plots of land the nobles had given them as their own.

The farmers divided the land into three sections. They did not use one section at all. On the other two sections, they used heavy metal plows suitable for the hard but fertile soil. In the autumn, they planted wheat or rye in one section. In the spring, they planted oats or barley in the other section. Each year, the farmers **rotated**, or changed by turns, the type of crops they grew in each section. This helped to make better use of the soil because each section got a rest every three years.

In addition to working the land, the farmers had to give the nobles food and animals. They had to perform many services for the nobles, too. The men repaired buildings on the estates, cut down trees, carried loads, gathered fruits, and served in the army. The women worked as hard as the men. They looked after the children and the small animals, wove cloth, and sewed clothing copied from earlier Roman styles. The farmers gradually did more for the nobles and less for themselves. They were becoming **serfs**, or poor people bound to the land.

Neither the nobles nor the farmers had much time to learn to read or write or to think about religion. Both groups accepted Christianity, but the new religion had little effect on their daily lives. Both the rich and the poor, however, sang, danced, and feasted on religious holidays. They listened to traveling musicians called **minstrels**. The minstrels wandered from place to place singing the praises of Charlemagne and his empire and entertaining the people.

1. Who were the most powerful people in Charlemagne's empire? Why were they so powerful?
2. What were some of the main features of estates?
3. How did most of the farmers live? In what ways did they serve the nobles?

THE COLLAPSE OF THE EMPIRE   The glory of the empire did not last long after Charlemagne's death in 814. The empire needed a strong and able ruler. Charlemagne's heirs were neither. The many counts and nobles became increasingly independent. They cared more about their own estates than about the good of the empire. They refused to obey Louis the Pious, Charlemagne's son and heir.

THE FRANKISH EMPIRE

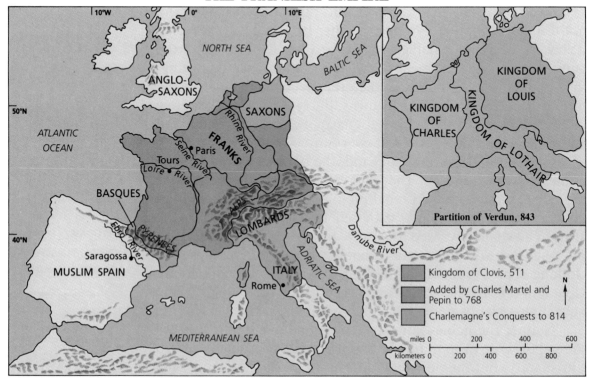

Louis unknowingly weakened the empire further when he divided it among his three sons. After he died, they began fighting among themselves over their shares. Lothair, Louis' oldest son, had received the title of emperor. His younger brothers Charles and Louis were jealous of Lothair's position.

In 843, the brothers agreed to a new and different division of the empire. Under the Treaty of Verdun, Lothair kept the title of emperor, but he ruled only a narrow strip of the land that stretched from the North Sea to the Italian Peninsula. Louis received the area to the east. Called the East Frankish Kingdom, it later became the nation of Germany. Charles received the area to the west. Called the West Frankish Kingdom, it later became the nation of France.

The brothers were weak rulers who allowed the counts and nobles to have most of the power. Once again, a united western Europe was divided into smaller territories.

Lothair

1. What happened to Charlemagne's empire after he died? Why did this happen?
2. What were the terms of the Treaty of Verdun?

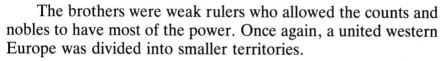

CHAPTER 18 REVIEW

SUMMARY

1. During the late 400's, the Franks began to build a new civilization that was to develop into the modern countries of France and Germany.

2. Clovis united the Franks and set up a capital in Paris.

3. Clovis was the first Germanic king to accept the Catholic religion.

4. The Frankish kings who followed Clovis were weak rulers, so power gradually came into the hands of an official known as the "Mayor of the Palace."

5. In 732, a Mayor called Charles Martel defeated a Muslim army in the Battle of Tours, thus keeping western Europe Christian.

6. Charles Martel's son Pepin, who started a new dynasty, was the first Frankish king to be anointed by the Pope.

7. Pepin's son Charlemagne brought all of western Europe under his rule.

8. In 800, the Pope crowned Charlemagne the new Roman emperor.

9. Charlemagne was very interested in learning and encouraging the founding of schools throughout his empire.

10. Louis the Pious divided the Frankish Empire among his three sons.

BUILDING VOCABULARY

1. *Identify the following:*

Early Middle Ages	Charles Martel	Pepin	Roland
Franks	Arabs	Charlemagne	*The Song of Roland*
Clovis	Muslims	Saxons	Louis the Pious
Mayor of the Palace	Battle of Tours	Basques	Treaty of Verdun

2. *Define the following:*

converted	counts	stockades	serfs
anointed	lords	rotated	minstrels

REVIEWING THE FACTS

1. What happened in western Europe after the decline of the Roman Empire?
2. What helped the people of Clovis' empire feel united?
3. Why did the Mayor of the Palace become important?
4. How did Charles Martel gain the nickname "The Hammer?"
5. What were Charlemagne's main goals when he became king of the Franks?
6. How was Charlemagne helped by the Church officials?
7. What purpose did Charlemagne's travels throughout the empire serve?
8. Under Charlemagne what happened to the arts?
9. What did farmers do to make the best use of the land?
10. How were the nations of France and Germany formed?

DISCUSSING IMPORTANT IDEAS

1. What do you think might have happened to western Europe if the Franks had lost the Battle of Tours?
2. Do you think Charlemagne was wise to travel all over his empire? Explain.
3. Do you think Charlemagne deserved his title of "the Great?" Explain.
4. What do you think Louis the Pious might have done instead of dividing the Frankish Empire among his three sons?

USING MAPS

Study the map on page 272, and answer the following questions:

1. Under which leader did the Frankish Empire begin?
2. Into what areas did Charlemagne extend the Frankish Empire?
3. Which city is farther east—Paris or Tours?
4. Who got control of the western section of the Frankish Empire in 843?

CHAPTER 19
IRISH AND ANGLO-SAXONS

Off the west coast of Europe lies a group of islands that never became part of Charlemagne's empire. Known today as the British Isles, they consist of Britain, Ireland, and many smaller islands.

Roman legions led by Julius Caesar invaded Britain in 55 B.C. The Romans eventually conquered much of the island and ruled it for almost 400 years. They built cities, country estates, bridges, and roads. They introduced the rose and the beech tree. Missionaries taught Christianity and helped spread Roman culture.

Although the Romans brought peace and prosperity, they could not control the entire island. In the northern part of Britain, in the area known today as Scotland, lived peoples called the Picts and the Scots. They resisted Roman rule and attacked Roman settlements in the south. To keep them out, Roman soldiers built great walls with forts and towers.

The Romans also had difficulties in the area that they did rule. They could not win over a conquered people called the Celts. Most Celts lived in their own villages, apart from the Roman cities. They grew wheat in small fields and raised animals in pastures they shared with one another. They were not interested in or influenced by Roman culture.

Roman rule in Britain began to crumble during the fourth century A.D. This was because Roman soldiers were called home to defend the empire's borders against invasions by the Germans and the Huns. After the last legions left in 410 A.D., the island was gradually overrun by groups from nothern Germany and Denmark called Angles, Saxons, and Jutes. All three were seafaring peoples who traveled across the North Sea to Britain in long, open boats. They were strong warriors and controlled most of the island by the seventh century A.D.

The Angles, Saxons, and Jutes united to become the Anglo-Saxons. They built settlements, farmed the land, and set up several small kingdoms. The southern part of Britain soon became known as Angleland, or England. The people became known as the English.

CELTIC IRELAND

After the Anglo-Saxons chased the Celts from Britain, Ireland became the major center of Celtic culture. Ireland had no cities. The people were divided into clans that lived in small villages. Most of them farmed and raised cattle. The more cattle a person owned, the wealthier that person was considered to be.

Irish Bowl

The Irish were a seafaring people, too. They made boats called **coracles** by stretching cow hides over a wooden frame. Some coracles were large enough to hold as many as 30 people. The boats handled well at sea and were used for travel, trade, and fishing.

The Irish were able to remain free of Germanic attacks because their island was located farther out in the Atlantic

Ocean than Britain. The peace and safety of Ireland attracted scholars, artists, merchants, and monks from many parts of Europe.

Irish scholars and artists were strongly influenced by Christianity. The Irish Church was founded by Saint Patrick. Born in Britain in the 400's, Saint Patrick was kidnapped when a teenager and taken to Ireland by Irish pirates. He escaped to Europe, where he studied to be a priest. After becoming a bishop, he returned to Ireland to win the people to Christianity. He preached throughout the island and set up many churches for the new believers.

Ireland lost contact with Rome during the Germanic invasions of the Roman Empire. Since it was no longer possible to

---

IRISH MONASTERY

Irish Christian monks established monasteries throughout the British Isles and Europe. Many of their stone living quarters, like the ones below, still stand today along the rocky coast of western Ireland.
What attracted monks to Ireland?

Irish Cross

rely on the Pope for leadership, the Irish Church turned to its abbots. Many of them were related to the heads of the various clans. Each clan sponsored its own monastery.

The monasteries became centers of Irish life even though many were in faraway places on rocky coasts or steep hills. A monastery usually consisted of a group of huts surrounded by a protective wooden stockade. Later, some monasteries were built of stone. Because of poor transportation and communication, church organization was weak. So, each monastery controlled its own affairs. Irish monks soon began to follow practices different from those of the Roman Church. They wore their hair in a different style and celebrated Easter on a different day. The rituals they performed were not the same as those in Rome.

Irish monasteries set down few rules. A monk was free to move from one monastery to another. While many monks chose to be hermits, others set up schools to teach Christianity. Still others became missionaries and did a lot of traveling. They sailed the North Atlantic and the Irish Sea seeking new converts and looking for islands on which to build new monasteries.

One of the most famous traveling monks was Saint Columba. He established a monastery on Iona, an island off the west coast of Scotland. From his base on Iona, he did missionary work among the non-Christian Celts along the coast.

Monks from Iona went to northern England to preach to the Anglo-Saxons. Other Irish monks went to northern Europe, where they built monasteries and churches. Many Irish scholars became part of Charlemagne's palace school. They helped spread Christianity and learning throughout his empire.

1. How did the Irish earn a living?
2. How did Saint Patrick influence Christianity in Ireland?
3. How did the Germanic invasion affect the Irish Church?
4. What did Saint Columba do to further Christianity?

Pope Gregory I

ANGLO-SAXONS AND CHRISTIANITY

Ireland was Christian, but the Anglo-Saxon kingdoms of Britain were not. They followed the Germanic religions. Then, Pope Gregory I decided to convert the Anglo-Saxons to Christianity. Legend states that he saw some Anglo-Saxon boys waiting in the marketplace of Rome to be sold as slaves. Gregory admired their light skin, handsome faces, and yellow hair and asked what their homeland was. When he learned that the boys were Angles, he said they had the faces of angels and should be Christians.

In 597 A.D., Pope Gregory sent a mission of 41 monks to England under the leadership of the monk Augustine. The missionaries landed in the small kingdom of Kent in southern England. Kent's queen, Bertha, was already a Christian, but its king, Ethelbert, was not. At first, Ethelbert was very suspicious of Augustine and the other monks. He even insisted on meeting with them only in the open air where their "magic" could not hurt him. But within a year, Ethelbert became a Christian. He allowed Augustine to build a church in the town of Canterbury and to teach the people about Christianity. The Anglo-Saxons

---

AUGUSTINE

Augustine brought Christianity to the Anglo-Saxons. Augustine preached before the king of Kent and persuaded him to become a Christian. Soon, all England accepted Christianity.

Who sent Augustine to England to preach Christianity?

---

were quick to accept the new religion, and by 700 A.D., all England was Christian. The Pope was head of their church.

Many monasteries were built in England. As in Ireland, they became centers of religion and culture. With the help of the monks, the Irish, Roman, and German cultures blended together to form a new culture.

One of the monks, Bede, was a great scholar. He wrote the first history of the English people. He also introduced the English to the Christian practice of dating events from the year of Jesus' birth.

Even though they accepted Christianity, the Anglo-Saxons kept much of their old culture. They told and retold old legends about brave warriors fighting monsters and dragons. One such legend was about a warrior named Beowulf. In the eighth century A.D., it was written down as an epic poem called *Beowulf*. It became known as the most important work of Anglo-Saxon literature.

1. According to legend, why did Pope Gregory I decide to convert the Anglo-Saxons to Christianity?
2. How did Augustine help spread Christianity?
3. What did Bede contribute to English culture?

King Alfred

ALFRED About 835 A.D., bands of Danes began raiding the coast of England. Before long, they were making permanent settlements in conquered areas. The English kingdoms decided to resist the invaders. They chose as their leader Alfred, King of Wessex. Alfred later became known as Alfred the Great, one of England's best-loved monarchs.

Alfred knew the Anglo-Saxons were not yet strong enough to drive out the Danes. To gain time to build a stronger army, he paid the Danes a sum of money each year to leave England alone. When he felt his army was strong enough, he refused to make any more payments. The Danes invaded the country and defeated the Anglo-Saxons. The next year, Alfred once again gathered his army and met the Danes in battle. This time, Alfred and his soldiers defeated the Danes.

Alfred continued to strengthen his army. He built the first English fighting ships and constructed fortresses at regular intervals throughout the country. The entire country rallied behind him. He was no longer just the king of Wessex but the king of all England.

Alfred never became strong enough to drive the Danes completely from England. So, he signed a treaty with them. It recognized the right of the Danes to rule the northeast part of the country, an area that became known as the Danelaw. In return, the Danes promised to stay within the Danelaw and not try to conquer more English territory. In later years, the English took control of the Danelaw and made it part of their kingdom.

The Danes had destroyed part of the English city of London. Alfred had it rebuilt, and before long, it was the country's leading city. To gain the continued loyalty and obedience of the people, Alfred issued new laws based on old Anglo-Saxon customs. The customs protected the weak against the strong and stressed honesty in making agreements.

Alfred was well-educated. He wanted the English people to be well-educated, too. Like Charlemagne, Alfred started a

ENGLAND AND THE DANELAW

school in one of his palaces to train nobles' sons for government positions. At that time, books were usually written in Latin, a language that most church and government officials did not know. Alfred's scholars translated the books into English. So that the people would become familiar with their history, Alfred had the monks begin a record of English history starting with the time of the Romans.

1. How did Alfred defeat the Danes?
2. What did Alfred do to unite the country?
3. What did Alfred do to improve learning among the people?

THE GOVERNMENT   The king was the most important person in Anglo-Saxon England. A council of lords usually elected kings from among members of the royal family. After 700 A.D., the Church usually crowned the new rulers. The king directed the central government, which was made up of royal servants and advisors. They handled the king's personal needs and carried out his wishes.

English Sheriff

The central government, however, was too weak to govern the entire country. So, the king set up a system of local government. England was divided into districts called **shires**. Each shire was run by a sheriff who was a local noble appointed by the king. The sheriff collected money owed to the king, enforced the law, called out soldiers when necessary, and kept the king informed about local affairs.

It was the custom for the king and his household to move from place to place instead of remaining in a capital city. Whatever area the royal household was in was considered to be under the **king's peace**, or royal protection. Fighting and other lawless acts were forbidden. Anyone who committed a crime was punished under the king's laws rather than local laws. In time, the king's peace spread to all areas of the kingdom, whether the king was there or not. Thus, everyone could benefit from the king's laws and protection.

Nobles and church officials gave the king advice on how to run the country. They could not, however, order a king to act against his will. A council of nobles and church leaders, known as the **witan**, or "wisemen," met with the king to discuss problems. It approved laws drawn up by the king and his household and acted as a court of law.

1. What were the duties of a sheriff?

2. How did the king's peace help unite the country?
3. Who helped the king run the country?

THE PEOPLE   An Anglo-Saxon became a noble by birth or as a reward for special service to the king. Nobles had to attend the witan, keep the peace in local areas, and serve the king in war. Noblemen wore pants and knee-length tunics covered by a silk or fur cloak. Noblewomen wore tunics and long cloaks held in place on each shoulder by a brooch.

The king rewarded many nobles with gifts of gold, silver, horses, and weapons. He also gave them estates all over the country. As a result, nobles spent a great deal of time moving from one place to another with their families and servants. A noble's house always had a large hall where family meals were served and guests were entertained. Its walls were covered by **tapestries**, or woven hangings. The only furniture was tables and benches. The bedrooms of the nobles and their families were next to the hall or in a separate building.

Most English people were not nobles. They were peasants who lived in small villages on or near a noble's estate. They

---

A NOBLE'S ESTATE

Nobles were the most powerful people in Anglo-Saxon England. In the illustration, a noble and his family give out food to hungry peasants on their estate. What were the duties of a noble?

---

helped each other farm the land by sharing their tools and oxen. Each year, the land was redivided, and each peasant received different strips. This practice ensured that each peasant would be treated equally. The peasants produced little more than they needed and did not send much to market.

Peasants lived in one-room wood and plaster huts. Both the family and the animals shared the same room. An open fireside, which provided protection during the cold winter, stood in the center. The smoke from the fire escaped from the hut through a hole in the thatched straw roof.

Peasants led a hard life, constantly facing famine, disease, and enemy attack. Some of them sought the protection of a nearby noble. The noble often took control of the peasants' land in return. Other peasants rented land from the noble to produce more food. The peasants continued to work the land plus pay the nobles with food from the fields. Many nobles also had the peasants work several days a week in the fields of the estates.

1. What was the life of a noble like?
2. What was the life of a peasant like?

CHAPTER 19 REVIEW

SUMMARY

1. Roman legions led by Julius Caesar invaded Britain in 55 B.C.

2. The Romans ruled most of Britain for about 400 years, but they were unable to win over the conquered Celts.

3. In 410 A.D., Britain was overrun by peoples from northern Germany and Denmark, who eventually united to become the Anglo-Saxons.

4. After the Anglo-Saxons drove the Celts from Britain, Ireland became the major center of Celtic culture.

5. The Irish Church was founded in the fifth century A.D. by Saint Patrick.

6. The monasteries became centers of Irish life.

7. Irish monks gradually began to follow practices different from those of the Roman Church.

8. In 597 A.D., Pope Gregory sent a mission of monks led by Augustine to England, and by 700 A.D., the entire island had become Christian.

9. Around 835 A.D., bands of Danes began raiding England.

10. The Anglo-Saxons united behind Alfred the Great to keep the Danes from spreading their control.

11. Alfred was interested in learning and did much to educate his people, including having books translated from Latin into English.

BUILDING VOCABULARY

1. *Identify the following:*
Britain	Anglo-Saxons	Augustine	*Beowulf*
Ireland	Saint Patrick	Ethelbert	Alfred the Great
Picts	Saint Columba	Canterbury	Danelaw
Celts	Gregory I	Bede	London

2. *Define the following:*
coracles	king's peace	witan	tapestries
shires			

REVIEWING THE FACTS

1. Who led Roman legions into Britain?
2. Why did the Romans have difficulty ruling Britain?
3. Why did Roman rule in Britain crumble during the fourth century A.D.?
4. What happened to Britain when the Roman legions left?
5. Why did Ireland become the major center of Celtic culture?
6. Why did the Irish Church turn to its abbots for leadership?
7. What were some differences between Irish monks and Roman monks?
8. What was the most important work of Anglo-Saxon literature?
9. Why did the king divide England into shires?
10. What were the duties of the witan?

DISCUSSING IMPORTANT IDEAS

1. What effect did the Roman conquest have on the development of England?
2. Do you think it is important to be familiar with history? Why or why not?
3. Why did Ireland attract people from other parts of Europe?
4. Do you think Alfred deserves to be called "the Great"? Explain.
5. Do you think it was a good idea for a king to move from place to place instead of remaining in a capital city? Why or why not?

USING MAPS

Study the map on page 281, and answer the following questions:

1. In what part of England is the kingdom of Wessex?
2. What two groups of people settled in the northernmost section of the island of England?
3. In what area of England did the Danes settle?
4. What is the distance across the narrowest part of the English Channel? The Irish Sea?

CHAPTER 20
THE VIKINGS

During the 900's, Charlemagne's empire and Anglo-Saxon England were attacked by a new group of invaders known as Norsemen, or Vikings. They came from the far northern part of Europe now called Scandinavia. The tall, fair-skinned Vikings became known as brutal fighters and robbers. They spread fear and destruction throughout western Europe for several hundred years. At the same time, however, they opened up new trade routes and brought shipping skills to other Europeans.

The Vikings captured parts of Britain and France. They ruled cities in Russia and set up colonies on islands in the North Atlantic. They even paid a brief visit to North America. Those who went abroad married the people they conquered. They also accepted a new religion and customs. Others stayed in Scandinavia and set up the kingdoms of Norway, Sweden, and Denmark.

THE LAND

The Viking homeland of Scandinavia was an area of forests and long, rugged coastlines. The southern part, known as Jutland, or Denmark, had many natural harbors and was well suited for farming. It had large plains where the Vikings grew grains and pastured their cattle, sheep, and pigs.

The rest of Scandinavia was not as well suited to farming. Winters were long and cold, summers short and mild, and the soil rocky. The coastline, however, had many **fjords**, or bays. So, the people turned to the sea to making a living.

1. Where was Jutland? What was it suited for?
2. How did people in the rest of Scandinavia make a living?

SHIPS AND TRADE   The Vikings built ships with timber from the dense forests. The ships were large and well suited for long voyages. The bodies were long and narrow. The sides, where a single row of 16 oars was placed, were usually decorated with black or yellow shields. The tall bows were carved in the shape of a dragon's head. This was supposed to frighten both enemies and the evil spirits of the ocean. The strongly sewn sails were square and often striped red and yellow. The ships bore names like "Snake of the Sea," "Raven of the Wind," and "Lion of the Waves."

An awning in the forepart of the ship protected the sailors from bad weather. They slept in leather sleeping bags and carried bronze pots in which to cook their meals. Whenever possible, they cooked their meals ashore to avoid the danger of a fire on board ship.

The Vikings plotted their courses by the positions of the sun and stars. They sailed far out into the North Sea and the Atlantic Ocean in search of good fishing areas and trade. They did most of their traveling and trading in the spring after their fields were sown, or in the fall after their crops were harvested. They spent the long winters repairing their boats and weapons.

Dragon Carving

VIKING TRADE
Viking towns and villages were centers of trade. This Viking wall hanging shows traders carrying goods to market.
How was trade carried out in Viking towns and villages?

The Vikings were as successful in trade as the Phoenicians. Viking traders carried furs, hides, fish, and slaves to western Europe and the Mediterranean. They returned from these areas with silk, wine, wheat, and silver.

1. What were some features of Viking ships?
2. Where did the Vikings sail?
3. When did the Vikings sail?

TOWNS, VILLAGES, AND JARLS   Trade led to the growth of market towns in Scandinavia. These towns usually had two main streets that ran along the water's edge. Buyers and sellers set up booths and displayed their wares along the streets. The towns were protected on their land side by mounds of earth surrounded by wooden walls with towers.

Most Vikings lived in villages scattered throughout the country. Their houses were made of logs or boards. The roofs, which were made of sod-covered wood, slanted deeply to shed the heavy winter snows. Carvings of dragons decorated gables at either end. In front of each house was a small porch supported by carved pillars.

Distance and the cold winters isolated the people of one village from those of another. As a result, there was no central government. The people were divided into groups ruled by military chieftains called *jarls*. Jarls either inherited their position or were elected to it. They saw to it that their group's laws were obeyed. Sometimes, a jarl became strong enough to take over and unite neighboring territories. When a jarl had enough territory under his rule, he was recognized as a king.

1. What were some features of Viking towns?
2. What kind of government did the Vikings have?

DAILY LIFE

Family life was important to the Vikings. Most households contained 20 to 30 members, including parents, grandparents, married children, and grandchildren. Families often fought bloody feuds to maintain their honor. The payment of fines later put an end to such feuds.

THE PEOPLE   Viking men were warriors called *berserkers*. They believed in a life of action and valued deeds that called for strength and courage. They fought to gain wealth, honor, and fame. They believed that a liking for war brought special honors from the gods.

To call their warriors to battle, the Vikings lit bonfires on the tops of mountains. Those who saw a fire would light a new one to spread the message. The warriors fought with battle axes, swords, and spears. Metal helmets decorated with animal figures protected their heads. Shirts made of iron rings and covered by a large cloth protected their bodies. The warriors preferred to die by their own hand rather than give their enemies the satisfaction of capturing or killing them.

A Viking groom bought his wife from her family on their wedding day. If he was not pleased with her, he could sell her. Yet, the position of Viking women was quite high. They took

VIKING CELEBRATION

Viking men enjoyed celebrating special events. Here trader-warriors raise their drinking horns to toast the discovery of new territory.

What were the weapons and clothes of Viking warriors like?

complete charge of the home. They could attend public meetings and talk with men other than their husbands. They could own property and get a divorce. Many Viking women grew herbs that were used as medicine. Most of the women encouraged their men to fight.

Both men and women liked fine clothes. The men usually dressed in trousers and woolen shirts covered by knee-length tunics. Broad leather belts held the clothing in place. Sheepskin hoods and caps kept their heads warm. For special events, the men wore red cloaks with brooches and carried decorated swords and daggers. The women also wore tunics held in place by a belt. They covered their heads with woolen or linen caps and wore large brooches, pins, and bracelets. Both men and women wore their hair long, and the men took great pride in their mustaches and beards. Calling a Viking man "beardless" was an insult that could be wiped out only by death.

The Vikings had no schools. Parents taught daughters such household skills as spinning, weaving, and sewing. They taught sons to use the bow and arrow and to be good fighters. The boys also memorized tales of heroic warriors and gods and competed in games that tested their strength and endurance.

1. In what did berserkers believe? How did they dress?
2. How did Vikings call their warriors to battle?
3. What kind of education did Viking children receive?

RELIGION The Vikings worshipped many gods that at first were closely related to Germanic gods. In time, they changed the names and activities of their gods to suit the harsh life of Scandinavia. The Vikings believed that the gods were responsible for the weather and for the growth of crops. Since the gods

---

VIKING CRAFTS

Vikings made metal tools and household articles as well as ships and weapons. This bowl was once used at Viking feasts.

What do Viking crafts show about the way Vikings lived?

---

liked to hunt, fish, and play tricks on one another, the Vikings viewed them as extra-powerful human beings.

The Vikings bargained with their gods to get what they wanted. Priests offered sacrifices of crops and animals on behalf of the whole community. Most Vikings also had small shrines in their homes where they could pray or offer sacrifices.

The Vikings were proud of their gods and told stories of their great deeds. These stories later became written poems called *eddas*. The Vikings also composed **sagas**, or epic stories. At first, skilled storytellers used to recite sagas at special banquets. One such saga took 12 days to recite. After 1100, the Vikings wrote down their sagas. With the coming of Christianity, the people lost interest in these tales. Many were forgotten or were forbidden by the Church. Only the people of Iceland passed on the old tales.

At first, the Vikings spoke a language similar to that of the Germans. In time, the one language developed into four—

NORSE GODS

Name	Realm
Odin (or Wotan)	king of the gods; sky god; god of war and wisdom; *Wotan's day became Wednesday.*
Baldur	god of light, joy, and spring
Bragi	god of poetry and stories
Freya	goddess of love and beauty
Freyr	god of rain, sunshine, and the harvest
Frigga	goddess of earth, marriages, and motherly love; Odin's wife; *Frigga's day became Friday.*
Hel (or Hela)	goddess of the dead
Idun	goddess of youth
Loki	god of fire; the mischief-maker
Niord	god of the wind
Thor	god of thunder, lightning, and the tides; *Thor's day became Thursday.*
Tyr	god of legal contracts and of truth; *Tyr's day became Tuesday.*

Danish, Norwegian, Swedish, and Icelandic. They were written with letters called *runes*, which few people except the priests could understand or use. The Vikings used the runes as magic charms. They wrote the runes in metal and carved them in bone in the hope that they would bring good luck. When the Vikings accepted Christianity, they began to write their language with Roman letters.

Rune Stone

1. How did the Vikings view their gods?
2. How did the coming of Christianity influence the development of Viking languages?

RAIDS AND ADVENTURES

Scandinavia's population kept increasing. By the end of the 800's, many Viking villages were overcrowded, and there was not enough food for everyone. Since there was no central government, the kings constantly fought one another and made life difficult for their enemies. Before long, many Viking warriors began to seek their fortunes elsewhere.

FROM RUSSIA TO NORTH AMERICA   Groups of warriors attacked merchant ships on the open seas. Danish Vikings began raiding the coasts of France, England, and Spain. Swedish Vikings crossed the Baltic Sea and traveled down the rivers toward Russia. They founded settlements and began to trade. They established a water route from the Baltic to the Black Sea and on to the wealthy city of Byzantium. This water route came to be known as the Varangian Route. In 862, a Swedish chieftain named Rurik founded a Viking state that became the basis of the Russian monarchy. Norwegian Vikings established trading towns in Ireland, explored the North Atlantic, and founded a colony on the island of Iceland.

Led by an adventurer named Eric the Red, the Norwegian Vikings began to move even farther west. In 986, they founded a colony on the island of Greenland. Then, Eric's son, Leif Ericson, sailed across the Atlantic Ocean and landed on the northeast coast of North America. He and his followers named the spot where they landed Vinland because of the wild grapes they found growing there. Today, the area is called Newfoundland. The Vikings did not set up a colony in Vinland because it was so far away from home and the winters were so cold.

Leif Ericson

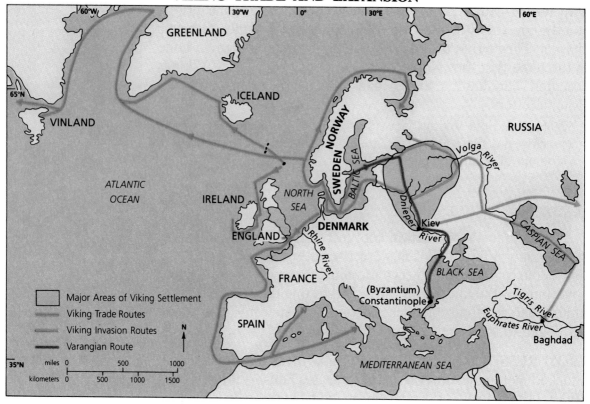

Most Viking adventurers, however, went to western and southern Europe in search of food and valuables. They disguised their ships to look like wooded islands by covering them with tree branches. Then, they traveled far up the rivers to make surprise attacks. They stole goods, destroyed homes, burned churches, and killed or sold as slaves any people they captured. All Europe feared the Vikings and the people prayed, "From the fury of the Norsemen, Good Lord, deliver us!"

1. Why did many Vikings leave Scandinavia?
2. What discovery did Eric the Red make?
3. What discovery did Leif Ericson make?
4. Why did Europeans fear the Vikings?

THE DANES   Some of the Danish Vikings settled in the areas they raided. One group of Danes invaded England and set up settlements there. In 954, an heir of Alfred the Great forced them to leave the Danelaw. In 978, Ethelred, nicknamed the Unready, became king of England. The Danes saw their chance and began raiding England again. At first, Ethelred was able to buy them off with silver. But in 1017, a Danish king called Knut, or Canute, took over the country and made it part of his North Sea Empire. Canute was a powerful but just ruler. He converted to Christianity and brought peace and prosperity to England. Soon after his death in 1035, however, Danish control of England came to an end. Some Danes left England. Those who remained became a part of the English people and culture.

VIKING SHIPS

The Vikings were among the best shipbuilders of their time. At sea, the Vikings depended on the wind and large sails for power. On a river, rowers powered the ship. Why were the bows of Viking ships carved in the shape of a dragon's head?

Viking Warrior

Another group of Danes tried to take the city of Paris in France, but the French managed to fight them off. In 885, the Danes tried again. The people of Paris held them off for ten months. Finally, the French king paid the Danes in gold to abandon their attack.

Led by a warrior named Rollo, the Danes then began settling in large numbers along the French coast opposite England. In 911, the French king signed a treaty with Rollo. He gave the Danes the land on which they had settled. In return, the Danes became Christians and promised to be loyal to the French king. The region in which the Danes settled became known first as the Norselaw and then as Normandy. The people became known as Normans.

1. What happened to the Danes who settled in England?
2. What happened to the Danes who settled in France?

CHAPTER 20 REVIEW

SUMMARY

1. The Vikings lived in northern Europe in an area now called Scandinavia.

2. The Vikings were excellent warriors, sailors, and navigators who earned their living mainly by fishing and by trading with other European regions.

3. The Vikings lived in villages that were basically isolated from one another.

4. The Vikings worshipped many gods and often told stories about their great deeds.

5. At first, the Vikings spoke one language, but over time, it developed into four separate languages.

6. When the Vikings accepted Christianity, they stopped writing their languages in runes and began to write with Roman letters.

7. By the 800's, Scandinavia was overpopulated, and many Viking warriors began to seek their fortunes in other places.

8. In 862, a Swedish Viking named Rurik established a settlement, and that settlement later developed into the Russian nation.

9. In 986, Norwegian Vikings founded a colony on Greenland, and several years later sailed as far west as the northeast coast of North America.

10. In 1017, a Danish king named Canute conquered England, but after his death, Danish control of England came to an end.

11 Other Danish Vikings, after besieging Paris, settled along the French coast in an area known as the Norselaw.

BUILDING VOCABULARY

1. *Identify the following:*

Vikings	Iceland	Eric the Red	Canute
Scandinavia	Varangian Route	Leif Ericson	Rollo
Jutland	Rurik	Vinland	Normandy

2. *Define the following:*

fjords	*berserkers*	*eddas*	sagas
jarls			*runes*

REVIEWING THE FACTS

1. Why did many Vikings turn to the sea to make a living?

2. How did the Vikings plot their courses?

3. How were Viking houses protected against the winter?

4. Why was there no central government in Scandinavia?

5. How did a jarl become a king?

6. What was the role of Viking women?

7. About what did the Vikings tell stories?

8. How did the Vikings use runes?

9. What effect did the Vikings have on Russia?

10. Why didn't the Vikings set up a colony in North America?

DISCUSSING IMPORTANT IDEAS

1. Did the Vikings make good use of their natural resources? Explain.

2. What was the role of women in Viking life?

3. Do you think you would have liked being a Viking? Why or why not?

4. What do you think might have happened in Scandinavia if many Viking warriors had not left during the 800's?

5. What effect did the Vikings have on the development of Europe during the Early Middle Ages?

USING MAPS

Study the map on page 294, and answer the following questions:

1. Where was the largest area of Viking settlement?

2. What cities were invaded by Vikings?

3. Where did the Varangian Route run?

4. On what body of water is the area of Vinland located?

5. How far south did the Vikings sail? How far west?

THE HAN AND THE T'ANG

By the tenth century A.D., eight dynasties had ruled China. They were the Hsia, Shang, Chou, Ch'in, Han, Six Dynasties, Sui, and T'ang. Each contributed something different to China's development. The Ch'in, for example, was the first dynasty to unite the Chinese people. From the Ch'in came the name China.

The Han Dynasty followed the Ch'in in 206 B.C. During Han rule, the public granaries were well stocked, and the gov-ernment treasuries were full. The arts flowered, and learning and literature flourished. But the Han's greatest contribution to China was a stable form of government that lasted into modern times. It was made up of four main parts—a single ruler; **bureaucrats**, or officials; a system of laws; and an official **ideology**, or philosophy.

The single ruler was the emperor. He made laws, took charge of the bureaucrats, and interpreted the ideology. The bureaucrats were responsible for the proper conduct of China's affairs. There were thousands of bureaucrats organized into six ministries and nine ranks. Each rank wore special clothes and caps with a different color badge. All received their posts on the basis of ability.

The system of laws was strict. There were heavy penalties for those who did not obey the laws. The ideology was Confucianism. All Chinese agreed on the

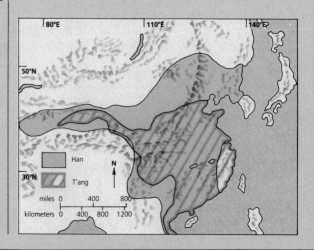

importance of Confucian values. They united the Han and made them strong.

More than 350 years passed before another dynasty, the T'ang, came to power. In the nearly 300 years they ruled, the T'ang enlarged China's borders.

The T'ang's greatest contribution, however, was cultural. T'ang artisans were the first to add the mineral feldspar to clay to produce porcelain. The graceful upward curves of the roof edges of Chinese buildings were first seen in T'ang cities. Court **calligraphers**, or artists who write characters, made texts using fine paper tinted in lemon or sulphur yellow or slate blue. They rolled the paper on ivory or sandalwood cylinders tipped with jade, amber, or rock crystal knobs. T'ang artists were the first to use bright colors in their paintings.

1. What did the Han Dynasty contribute to China?
2. What did the T'ang Dynasty contribute to China?

UNIT 6 REVIEW

SUMMARY

1. The invasions by Germanic peoples from northern Europe helped bring about the fall of the Roman Empire. They also led to the establishment of a number of German kingdoms.

2. The period that began the fall of the Roman Empire and ended with the beginning of modern times is known as the Middle Ages.

3. During the Early Middle Ages, the Christian religion continued to spread, and the Church gained widespread power and influence.

4. The Franks set up a German kingdom that became France and Germany.

5. After Roman rule ended in the British Isles, present-day England was taken over by Angles, Saxons, and Jutes. Present-day Ireland became the home of the Celts. Present-day Scotland remained in the hands of Picts and Scots.

6. The Vikings established the kingdoms of Denmark, Norway, and Sweden and captured parts of England and France. They founded colonies in Russia and Greenland and visited North America.

REVIEWING THE MAIN IDEAS

1. Explain in what ways the Church influenced Charlemagne's empire, England, Ireland, and Scandinavia.

2. Compare the German attitude toward law with that of the Roman attitude toward law.

DEVELOPING SKILLS

Collecting data is part of being a historian. But unless data are analyzed, they do not help historians learn more.

One important step in analyzing data is arranging them in order of **significance**, or importance. A person examining several bits of information has to be able to put the most important information first and the least important information last.

This exercise is designed to help you arrange data in order of significance. Read each group of data. Then rank each in order from the most to the least important.

1. The Germans were good fighters because
a. they admired bravery.
b. they began training for war when they were young boys.
c. they were tall and fair-haired.

2. The Frankish civilization developed into the Western Europe of today because
a. the Franks became farmers as well as fighters.
b. the Frankish ruler Charlemagne created a large empire that included most of the Germanic peoples who had settled in Europe since the fifth century A.D.
c. the Pope crowned Charlemagne in the year 800 A.D.

3. Ireland became the major center of Celtic culture because
a. the island attracted a great many scholars and artists from Europe.
b. the Anglo-Saxons chased the Celts from Britain.
c. there were many monasteries in all parts of Ireland.

4. The Vikings were successful traders because
a. most of their homeland was not suited for farming.
b. their ships were large and well-designed for long voyages.
c. they did most of their trading in the spring and fall.

SUGGESTED UNIT PROJECTS

1. Compare the school that was held at the court of Charlemagne with the school you attend.
2. Find out what modern nations are located within the boundaries of Charlemagne's empire.
3. On an outline map of the world, show the routes taken by Danish, Swedish, and Norwegian Vikings during the ninth, tenth, and early eleventh centuries A.D.
4. Working in groups of five, make a chart with five columns, headed Germans, Franks, Irish, Anglo-Saxons, and Vikings. Each person in the group should fill in information about a different people. Make sure to include information about where people lived, how most people earned a living, and what people considered important. Then, as a group, compare and contrast the five peoples.

SUGGESTED READING

Carter, Samuel. *Vikings Bold: Their Voyages and Adventures.* New York: Crowell Company, 1972. Traces the history, way of life, trading voyages, and conquests of the Vikings.

Gibson, Michael. *The Vikings.* New York: G. P. Putnams' Sons, 1972. A description based on sagas and other sources of the Vikings as farmers, artisans, traders, storytellers, and warriors.

Knox, Robert. *Ancient China.* New York: Warwick Press, 1979. A history of China from 1500 B.C. to 907 A.D.

Koenig, Alma Johnson. *Gudrun.* New York: Lothrop, Lee & Shepard, 1979. The story of the granddaughter of an Irish king who falls in love with the king of Zealand.

Lester, G.A. *The Anglo-Saxons.* Chester Springs, Pa.: Dufour Editions, 1976. A description of how Anglo-Saxon society was organized and how the people lived, played, worked, worshipped, and fought.

Manton, Jo and Robert Gittings. *The Flying Horses.* New York: Holt, Rinehart and Winston, 1977. A collection of 27 Chinese stories, many of them dating from the Han and T'ang periods.

Munro, Eleanor S. *Through the Vermilion Gates.* New York: Pantheon, 1971. An account of the events and cultural achievements of China's T'ang Dynasty.

Treece, Henry. *The Invaders.* New York: Crowell, 1972. Three stories of England's invaders.

UNIT 7

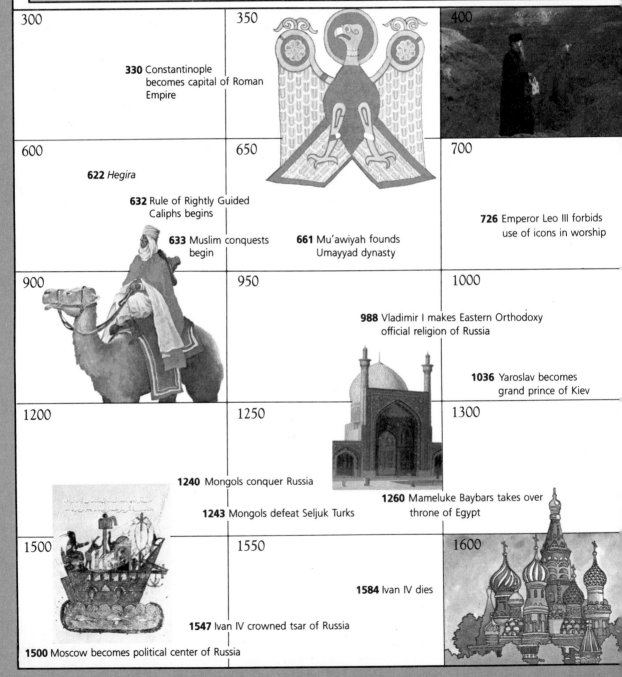

300	350	400
330 Constantinople becomes capital of Roman Empire		
600	650	700
622 *Hegira*		
632 Rule of Rightly Guided Caliphs begins		**726** Emperor Leo III forbids use of icons in worship
633 Muslim conquests begin	**661** Mu'awiyah founds Umayyad dynasty	
900	950	1000
	988 Vladimir I makes Eastern Orthodoxy official religion of Russia	
		1036 Yaroslav becomes grand prince of Kiev
1200	1250	1300
1240 Mongols conquer Russia		**1260** Mameluke Baybars takes over throne of Egypt
1243 Mongols defeat Seljuk Turks		
1500	1550	1600
	1584 Ivan IV dies	
1547 Ivan IV crowned tsar of Russia		
1500 Moscow becomes political center of Russia		

FLOWERING
OF THE EAST

50

500

c. 500 First Slavic settlements develop
in eastern Russia

527 Justinian I becomes emperor
of Byzantine Empire

550

571 Mohammed born in Mecca

50

60 Abassids become new rulers of Arab Empire

762 Baghdad becomes capital
of Arab Empire

800

850

843 Icons used again
in worship

862 Rurik becomes prince
of Novgorod

050

1055 Seljuk Turks capture Baghdad

1100

1150

350

1378 Prince Dmitry of
Moscow defeats Mongols

1400

1450

1453 Ottoman Turks capture
Constantinople

1462 Ivan III becomes prince of
Moscow

1. HOW DID RELIGION INFLUENCE THE GROWTH AND
   DEVELOPMENT OF THE MIDDLE EAST AND EASTERN
   EUROPE?
2. IN WHAT WAYS DID THE BYZANTINES, ARABS, AND
   RUSSIANS INFLUENCE WESTERN EUROPE?

From 500 to 1500, there was a flowering of civilization in what is today Eastern Europe and the Middle East. Two peoples, the Byzantines and the Arabs, built large empires. A third people, the Russians, developed a civilization modeled on that of the Byzantines. Until 1200, the Byzantine and Arab civilizations were more advanced than those of western Europe.

After the fall of Rome in 476, the Byzantines inherited the authority of the Roman emperors and ruled in the eastern half of the Roman Empire. There, they preserved classical learning and grew wealthy through trade. Christianity was important to Byzantine life.

The Russians lived to the north of the Byzantine Empire. At the heart of Russian life was the Orthodox Church. Most rulers of Russia were strong leaders who claimed complete control over both the government and the people. They also fought to unite Russia and to extend its boundaries.

The Arabs were traders and warriors from the deserts of the Middle East who were united by a religion called Islam. The desire to spread Islam led Arab armies to conquer lands in Asia, North Africa, and Spain. Arab scholars and scientists studied the classical writings of the West and made many important discoveries. Later, this knowledge led to a new interest in learning.

Other Asiatic peoples besides the Arabs made Islam their religion. When the Arab Empire broke apart, they built new Islamic empires in Asia and North Africa. As a result, Islamic culture continued to develop.

CHAPTER 21

THE BYZANTINE EMPIRE

The emperor Constantine moved the capital of the Roman Empire from Rome to Constantinople about 330. About 100 years later, the Roman Empire in the West fell. The Roman Empire in the East survived and prospered. It became known as the Byzantine Empire. Its people were called Byzantines.

The empire in the East survived for several reasons. One reason was the unity and loyalty of the people. Most were Christians. Their religion united them and taught them to obey and be loyal to their emperor. Another reason was that Constantinople was a mighty fortress that needed few soldiers to defend it. This freed more soldiers to protect other cities and provinces. Still another reason was the empire's wealth, gained through industry, trade, and taxes. There was enough money to support a large army and many officials and to pay invaders to move farther west.

The Byzantines developed a civilization based on a blend of Greek, Roman, and Christian ideas. They were eager to spread this civilization to neighboring peoples. In this, they were successful. Their ideas and practices later shaped the development of Russia and other Eastern European nations.

CONSTANTINOPLE

When Constantine first chose the old Greek city of Byzantium as the site for his new capital, he was well aware of its advantages. The Roman Empire depended on trade, and the great centers of trade lay to the east. Byzantium was on the waterway between the Black and Aegean seas. Its harbor offered a safe haven for fishing boats, merchant ships, and warships. The city sat at the crossroads of the trading routes between Europe and Asia. Its location gave it control of the sea trade between Russia and the Mediterranean area. One of the most important east-west land routes passed through the city, too.

The location also favored the city's defense. The sea protected it on three sides, and a huge wall protected it on the fourth side. Invaders would have a hard time trying to take the new capital, which was renamed Constantinople.

It took more than six years to build Constantinople. Constantine modeled it after Rome. The city stood on seven hills. Government buildings and palaces were designed in the Roman style. Streets were narrow and apartment houses crowded. Constantinople even had an oval area much like the Circus Maximus where races and other events were held.

Emperor at Races

The city's political and social life was patterned on that of Rome, too. The emperor operated under Roman laws and ruled with the help of highly trained officials, who took charge of building roads, bridges, wells, and caravan shelters. The army followed Roman military customs. The poor people received free bread and enjoyed circuses and chariot races put on by the government. The wealthier people lived in town or on large farming estates. Constantine convinced many wealthy Romans to move to Constantinople by offering to build them homes and palaces like the ones they had in Rome.

CONSTANTINOPLE

Constantinople was located at the crossroads of the trading routes between Europe and Asia. The city was protected by its harbor and tall stone walls. Why was Constantinople called the "new Rome"?

There was, however, one important difference between Constantinople and Rome. From the beginning, Constantinople was a Christian city. It had been dedicated to God by Constantine, who viewed the city as the center of a great Christian empire. Instead of temples, Constantinople had Christian churches. Constantine saw to it that they were the most magnificent buildings in the city. Government and church leaders gathered **relics**, or valued holy objects from the past, from all over the Christian world and placed them in public monuments, palaces, and churches. The bodies of saints rested in richly decorated shrines. Thousands of people came to the shrines seeking cures for their ills.

The city's Christian character could be seen in its attitude toward the needy. The Byzantines believed each Christian was responsible for the well-being of other Christians. Wealthy Byzantines formed organizations to care for the poor, aged, and blind. Even members of the emperor's household took great pride in founding and supporting good causes.

About 600,000 people lived in Constantinople during Constantine's rule. There were Greeks, Turks, Italians, Slavs, Persians, Armenians, and Jews. They spoke Greek among themselves but used Latin, the official language, for government business. Most people became Christians, and all called themselves Romans. Byzantine nobles and rulers continued to boast of their ties to Rome for the next 1,100 years.

1. Why did Constantine choose Byzantium as the site for the empire's new capital?
2. What were some features of Constantinople?
3. In what ways was Constantinople like Rome? In what ways was it different?
4. How did the Byzantines regard themselves?

JUSTINIAN I

After Constantine died, his sons ruled the empire. They were followed first by a general named Julian and then by a series of other emperors. Finally, in 527, a Macedonian named Justinian came to the throne. He was a strong and wise ruler who came to be considered the greatest of the Byzantine emperors.

Justinian had served in the army and was a good commander. He was well trained in law, music, theology, and architecture. He chose the people who served him for their ability rather than their wealth or social position.

As emperor, Justinian controlled the army and navy, made the laws, headed the Church and government, and was supreme judge. He could declare war or make peace. The Church taught that the emperor's acts were inspired by God. Therefore, what Justinian did could not be questioned. Those who came into contact with him were expected to bow down before him and kiss his feet and hands.

Byzantine Coins

1. What type of person was Justinian?
2. What powers did Justinian have as emperor?

THEODORA   Justinian's wife, the Empress Theodora, often helped him. Theodora's family had been poor, and she had worked as an actress before meeting Justinian. The people of the

JUSTINIAN AND THEODORA
  Justinian and Theodora ruled the Byzantine Empire in the early 500's. In this mosaic, they are dressed in ceremonial robes.
How did the Church support the acts of Justinian?

empire had a low opinion of actresses. There was even a law forbidding marriages between them and high government officials. But Justinian wanted to marry Theodora. After he became emperor, he abolished the law and made Theodora his empress.

At first, Theodora only entertained guests and attended palace ceremonies. Gradually, she began to take an interest in politics. Soon, she was helping Justinian fill government and church offices. Then, she convinced Justinian to allow women more rights. For the first time, a wife could own land equal in value to her **dowry**, or the wealth she brought with her when she married. A widow could raise and support her young children without government interference.

In 532, Theodora made her most important contribution. A group of senators had organized a revolt to protest high taxes.

They were able to gain much support from the people. The poor were angry because they were receiving less free food and entertainment than before. The wealthy were angry because, for the first time, they had to pay taxes. The leaders of the revolt were prepared to crown a new emperor. Justinian's advisors urged him to leave the city. Theodora, however, urged him to stay and fight. Justinian and his supporters took Theodora's advice. They stayed in Constantinople, trapped those revolting, killed 30,000 of them, and crushed the uprising. As a result, Justinian kept control of the government and became a stronger ruler.

1. How did Theodora help Justinian rule the empire?
2. What was Theodora's most important contribution to the empire?

LAW AND PUBLIC WORKS   Justinian worked to improve the laws of the empire. He was very interested in the law and spent much time reading laws made by other emperors. He decided that the old system of laws was too complicated and disorganized. He appointed a group of ten men headed by a legal scholar named Tribonian to work out a simpler and better system.

Tribonian and the others collected and organized the existing laws. They did away with those that were no longer needed. They arranged in order those that remained and rewrote them. Within six years, they had created a legal code that represented the law of the land.

This code came to be known as Justinian's Code. It is considered one of his greatest achievements. It provided a summary of Roman legal thinking and gave future generations insight into the basic ideas of Roman law. The code has had a great influence on the legal systems of almost every western country.

Justinian was as interested in public works as he was in law. He was almost always busy with some building program. He built churches, bridges, monasteries, forums, and a system of forts connected by a vast network of roads. When an earthquake destroyed the city of Antioch, he had the entire city rebuilt.

One of Justinian's greatest accomplishments was the church called Hagia Sophia, "Holy Wisdom." Nearly 10,000 workers, watched over by 200 supervisors, labored in shifts to build the

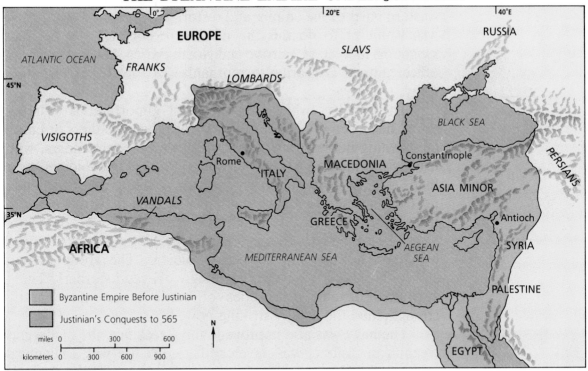

church according to Justinian's instructions. The church had a gold altar and walls of polished marble. Gold and silver ornaments, woven textiles, and colorful **mosaics**, or pictures made up of many bits of colored glass or stone, were everywhere. Figures of Justinian and Theodora were among the angels and saints that lined the walls.

Most impressive was the huge dome with its many windows that rose high over the central part of the church. It was the first time such a huge circular dome had been set atop a rectangular opening. During the day, sunlight poured through the many windows. At night, thousands of oil lamps turned the building into a beacon that could be seen for miles.

Hagia Sophia was later called St. Sophia. For more than 900 years, it served as the religious center of the Byzantine Empire. It still stands today.

1. How did Justinian feel about the old system of Roman laws? What did he do about it?
2. What were some of the features of Hagia Sophia?

CONQUEST　　Justinian wanted to reunite the eastern and western parts of the empire and restore the glory and power that was Rome's. To do this, he needed to conquer the German kingdoms in western Europe and North Africa. He appointed an officer named Belisarius to reorganize and lead the Byzantine army.

The cavalry, which was the most important part of the army, had been divided into groups of private soldiers hired by landowning nobles. Each group had its own commanders, who usually did not cooperate with one another. Foot soldiers, who made up the largest part of the army, were called up when needed and then sent back to their homes. As a result, they felt little loyalty towards their officers.

When Belisarius took command, he set up a basic group of loyal and heavily armed cavalry soldiers. The group was so strong that the other soldiers willingly obeyed its orders. Then, Belisarius developed a series of battle moves that greatly strengthened the army's striking power.

The navy was also improved, and **Greek fire**, the first secret weapon in history, was developed. Greek fire was a chemical mixture that ignited when it came into contact with water. It burned the skin and was not easily put out. The Byzantines guarded their secret so carefully that its exact formula is still unknown.

Eastern Orthodox Patriarch

With these improvements, the Byzantines extended their control in the Mediterranean and won back much of Italy and North Africa. They defeated the Persians, who had again risen to power, and insured the security of the empire's eastern borders. But most of the western provinces Justinian regained were lost again within a generation or so after his death.

1. What was Justinian's goal?
2. What did Justinian do to accomplish his goal? How successful was he?

THE EASTERN ORTHODOX CHURCH

Church and government were closely linked in the Byzantine Empire. Christianity was the official religion; everyone was required to be a Christian. The emperor represented Christ on earth. Thus, he was not only the head of the government but of the Church.

At the head of the Church in Constantinople was the Patriarch, who was appointed by the emperor. Under the Patriarch were church officials called **metropolitans** and archbishops. They took charge of large cities and important provincial centers. Under them were the bishops and local priests. Most of the priests were married. All of the higher officials, however, came from monasteries and were unmarried.

The monasteries played an important role in the empire. They helped the poor, provided hospitals, and ran schools for needy children. They sent missionaries to neighboring lands to help keep the peace. The missionaries translated portions of the

---

BYZANTINE ICON

The Eastern Orthodox Church was the center of Byzantine life. Byzantines often paid respect to icons in their homes and churches. This mosaic shows Christ and a saint giving a blessing.

Why did Byzantines argue over the use of icons?

Bible into several different eastern European languages. They believed that more people would become Christians if the Bible and church rituals were presented to them in their own language. The missionaries also gave one group of eastern Europeans called Slavs a new alphabet based on the Greek alphabet. It was called the Cyrillic alphabet in honor of Saint Cyril, the Byzantine Empire's leading missionary.

Religious beliefs and practices were very important to the Byzantines. They often argued about such matters. An argument that divided the empire for more than 100 years centered around the use of **icons**, or religious images, in worship.

Many Byzantines paid respect to icons. They also kept statues of saints in their homes and covered the walls of their churches with religious paintings and mosaics. Monasteries owned icons believed to work miracles. Some Byzantines, however, demanded an end to the use of icons. They considered devotion to them a form of idol worship, forbidden by God.

In 726, Emperor Leo III forbade the use of icons in religious worship. He had two reasons for issuing the order. He himself did not approve of images. Beyond that, however, he wanted to keep church officials who favored them from gaining too much political power. The emperor and church leaders argued over the use of icons for many years. Most people sided with the priests, bishops, and monks and refused to give up their icons. In 843, the emperor recognized that the cause was lost and once again permitted their use.

The feud over icons damaged the empire's relations with western Europe. Because so few people in the West could read, western bishops and priests used images to explain Christian teachings to the people. When Leo decided to do away with icons, the Pope at Rome called a council of bishops. The council declared that the emperor and his supporters were no longer members of the Church.

An argument also developed between the Pope and the Patriarch of Constantinople. The Patriarch had refused to recognize the Pope as head of the Church. The Pope began to press the Patriarch to accept his authority. When the Patriarch continued to refuse, the Pope broke his ties with the Byzantine emperor and turned to the Frankish kings for military protection. When the Pope crowned Charlemagne "Emperor of the

Romans" in 800, the Byzantines were furious. They believed that the title belonged only to their emperors. These disputes helped pave the way for the final split between Western and Eastern Christianity in 1054.

1. What role did Christianity play in the Byzantine Empire?
2. How was the Church organized?
3. Why did Leo III forbid the use of icons? How did the Byzantines react to Leo's order?
4. What caused the dispute between the Pope of Rome and the Patriarch of Constantinople?

DECLINE OF THE EMPIRE

The Byzantine Empire lasted for about 1,000 years. Its capital was the largest, richest, and most beautiful city in Europe. Its people were among the most educated and creative of the period. They preserved Greek culture and Roman political techniques for future generations. The empire also spread

---

BYZANTINE HOME

Byzantine nobles lived in richly decorated homes. In this sitting room, a noblewoman prepares to receive guests.

What contributions did the Byzantines make to later generations?

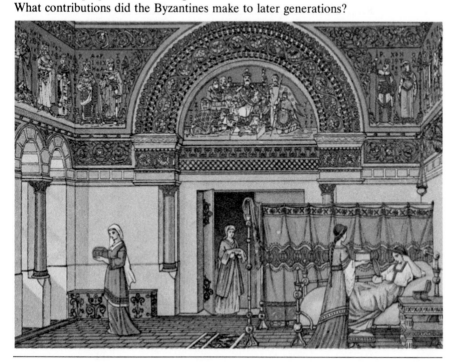

Christianity to eastern peoples. It did much to help the growth of trade. It gave the world new techniques in the fine arts.

In spite of all these achievements, internal problems and outside forces weakened the empire and led to its downfall. Early Byzantine emperors had relied on the small farmers to make up the army. In return for their services, the emperors gave them land and protected them from the wealthy landlords.

By the 1100's, the empire's borders were secure, and not as many soldiers were needed. The emperor decided to cut military costs by changing the policy toward the farmers. Without the emperor's support, the farmers could not stop aristocrats from taking over their property. Once they had lost their land, the farmers found little reason to remain loyal to the empire.

At the same time, the empire began to have problems with trade. When the Vikings conquered Byzantine lands in southern Italy in 1080, they threatened to attack Constantinople. The Byzantines no longer had enough soldiers to fight them off. So, they turned for help to the Italian city-state of Venice.

The Venetians defeated the Vikings. In return, the Byzantine emperor gave them the right to do business tax-free in all of the cities of the empire. Venetian ships and merchants soon

THE END OF THE BYZANTINE EMPIRE

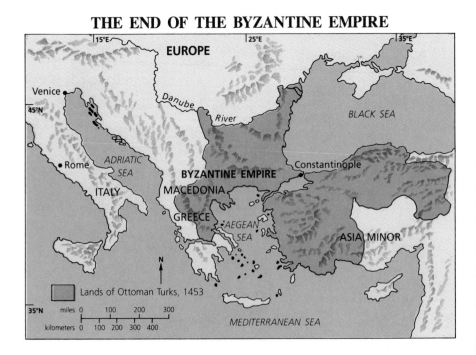

controlled most of the empire's trade. This meant a great loss of income for the Byzantines.

Meanwhile, Christians from the West and Muslims from the East attacked the empire. It lost Asia Minor to the invaders. The empire had depended on Asia Minor for food and materials as well as soldiers for the army. This loss greatly weakened the empire. One by one, the invaders took over more lands. Before long, the Byzantine empire was reduced to a small area around Constantinople.

The population dropped to less than 100,000. Docks and marketplaces stood empty. Even the emperors were poor. When Turkish armies with guns and gunpowder attacked Constantinople in 1453, they found it easy to conquer the Byzantines.

1. What internal problems helped bring about the decline of the Byzantine Empire?
2. What outside forces contributed to the empire's downfall?

CHAPTER 21 REVIEW

SUMMARY

1. About 330, the Emperor Constantine moved the capital of the Roman Empire from Rome to Constantinople, the site of the old Greek city of Byzantium.

2. Constantinople's buildings and political and social life were patterned on those of Rome.

3. Constantinople was a Christian city, filled with churches and shrines, and its people were extremely charitable.

4. After the Roman Empire in the West fell during the 400's, the Roman Empire in the East became known as the Byzantine Empire.

5. In 527, Justinian became emperor of the Byzantine Empire.

6. One of Justinian's many achievements was a code of law that influenced the legal systems of western countries.

7. Another of Justinian's achievements was Hagia Sophia, which served as the religious center of the Byzantine Empire for more than 900 years.

8. Under Justinian, a general named Belisarius reorganized the Byzantine army and expanded the boundaries of the empire.

9. Byzantine missionaries developed the Cyrillic alphabet.

10. Between 726 and 843, the Byzantine emperor and Orthodox Church leaders argued over the use of icons.

11. Relations between the Pope and the Patriarch of Constantinople were weakened by the argument over icons and by the Pope's crowning of Charlemagne.

12. In 1054, the Eastern Orthodox Church and the Roman Catholic Church split.

BUILDING VOCABULARY

1. *Identify the following:*
Constantinople	Justinian	Hagia Sophia	Saint Cyril
Byzantine Empire	Theodora	Belisarius	Leo III
Byzantium	Justinian's Code	Cyrillic	

2. *Define the following:*
relics	mosaics	Greek fire	metropolitans
dowry			icons

REVIEWING THE FACTS

1. Why did the Roman Empire in the East survive?

2. Why was Constantinople a great trading center?

3. How did Constantinople's appearance reflect its Christian character?

4. How did Christianity affect the way Byzantines took care of poor, aged, and blind persons?

5. On what basis did Justinian choose the people who served him?

6. How did Theodora help the role of women in the Byzantine Empire?

7. Why is Justinian's Code important in the world today?

8. Why did Byzantine emperors change the law and again permit the use of icons?

9. Why did Byzantine farmers gradually lose their loyalty to the emperor?

10. Who conquered the Byzantine Empire in 1453?

DISCUSSING IMPORTANT IDEAS

1. Why were church and government closely linked in the Byzantine Empire?

2. Do you agree with Justinian that ability is more important than wealth or social position when choosing government officials? Why or why not?

3. Do you think images are a good way of teaching people who do not know how to read? Explain.

4. Do you think the Byzantine emperors were wise to ask Venice for help against the Vikings? Why or why not?

USING MAPS

Study the maps on pages 312 and 316, and answer the following questions:

1. What areas did the Byzantine Empire include before Justinian?

2. Into what areas did the Byzantine Empire spread under Justinian?

3. What peoples lived in the areas surrounding the Byzantine Empire?

4. What areas did the Ottoman Turks control in 1453?

CHAPTER 22
THE SPREAD OF ISLAM

Between the northeast coast of Africa and central Asia lies the Arabian Peninsula. The people who live there are known as Arabs. At one time, most were Bedouins. They were herders who roamed the desert in search of grass and water for their camels, goats, and sheep. They lived in tents woven from camel or goat hair.

Bedouin warriors raided other peoples and fought one another over pastures and springs. They valued their camels and swords above all else. They enjoyed poetry and music. They believed in many gods. They worshipped stones, trees, and pieces of wood that they believed were the homes of spirits with supernatural powers.

In the 600's, a new religion called Islam appeared in the mountainous area of western Arabia known as the Hejaz. Within 100 years, an Arab empire based on Islamic beliefs had developed. It came to dominate an area larger than that of the Roman Empire.

Islam

The word Islam means "the act of **submitting**, or giving oneself over, to God." The followers of Islam are called Muslims, which means "believers." The Islamic religion was founded by an Arab merchant named Mohammed. He came to be known as the prophet of Allah, or God.

Islam shook the foundations of Byzantium and Persia, the two most powerful civilizations of the time. It made Arabic the common language of more than 90 million people. It came to shape a way of life for one out of every seven persons on earth.

MECCA   By the middle of the 500's, three major towns had developed in the Hejaz. They were Yathrib, Taif, and Mecca. Of the three, Mecca was the largest and the richest.

Mecca was supported by trade and religion. Traders stopped there for food and water on their way north to Constantinople. Arab **pilgrims**, or travelers to a religious shrine, came there to worship. Arabia's holiest shrine, the *ka'bah*, stood in the center of Mecca. It was a low cube-shaped building surrounded by 360 idols. A black stone was imbedded in one of its walls. The people believed the stone had fallen from paradise. Nearby was the *zemzen*, or holy well.

According to legend, the original ka'bah had stood in heaven. When Adam was forced to leave the Garden of Eden, he built a structure on earth exactly like the one in heaven. Nearby, Ishmael, the legendary founder of the Arabs, kicked open a well. Mecca grew up around the ka'bah and the well.

1. Why was Mecca an important Arabian town?
2. What legend was told about the ka'bah? About the zemzen?

MOHAMMED   In 571, a child named Mohammed was born to a poor widow in Mecca. When Mohammed was six years old, his mother died, and he went to live with an uncle. He began working as a camel driver when he reached his teens. At the age of 25, he married a rich 40-year-old widow named Khadijah.

In time, Mohammed was very successful in the caravan business. Then, he became troubled by the drinking, gambling, and corruption in Mecca. He began spending a lot of time alone in a cave on a hillside outside the city. There, he thought and **fasted**, or went without food or drink. He decided that the people of Mecca had been led into evil by their belief in false gods. He concluded that there was only one God, Allah, the same god as the God of the Jews and Christians.

In 610, Mohammed had a **revelation**, or vision. When he was asleep in the cave, an angel appeared and ordered him to read some writing. He awoke frightened and fled to the top of a mountain. There, he heard the voice of the angel Gabriel telling him to preach about God. Mohammed told Khadijah what had happened. She went to see a holy man. He said that the heavenly

---

MOHAMMED

Mohammed spent his early life in the Arabian city of Mecca. He was troubled by the drinking, gambling, and corruption there. After long periods of thinking and fasting, he blamed the evil of the Meccans on their belief in false gods. In whom did Mohammed believe?

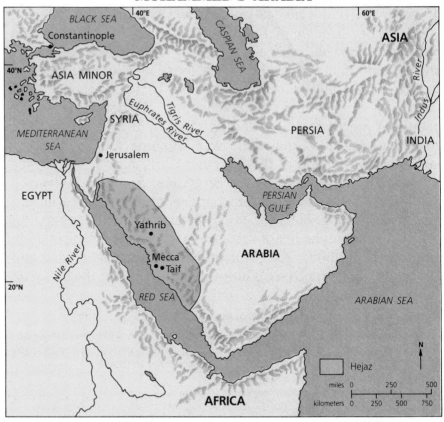

MOHAMMED'S ARABIA

visitor was the same one who had visited Moses and that Mohammed was to be the prophet of his people.

In 613, Mohammed began to preach to the people of Mecca. He told them that the only god was the all-powerful Allah, before whom all believers are equal. He explained that nothing happened except by Allah's will. He urged the rich to share with the poor. Mohammed saw life as a preparation for the **Day of Judgment**, or the day on which people would rise from the dead to be judged.

At first, the leaders of Mecca laughed at Mohammed. But before long, they began to feel threatened by him. They were afraid that worshippers would stop coming to Mecca. And that would ruin the city's economy. So, Mecca's leaders started persecuting Mohammed and his followers.

In 620, Mohammed preached to a group of pilgrims from Yathrib. They invited him to come to Yathrib and be their leader. During the summer of 622, several hundred of Mohammed's followers fled from Mecca to Yathrib. The year 622, called *Anno Hegira*, or "Year of the Flight," became the first year of the Muslim calendar. Yathrib became Medina al Munawara, "the enlightened city." Later, the name became Medina.

In Medina, Mohammed proved that he was a great political leader. He gave the people a government that united them and made them proud of their city. He began to lead raids against passing caravans from Mecca. In 630, he led 10,000 followers into Mecca. They captured the city, destroyed the idols around the ka'bah, and dedicated the black stone to Allah. Before long, Mecca became the center of Islam.

Next, Mohammed and his followers conquered Taif. Now, they controlled the entire Hejaz. In 631, delegates from all over Arabia came to declare their faith in Allah and offer their allegiance to Mohammed. He had created an Arab state with a strong army. The following year, however Mohammed fell sick and died.

1. What were some of Mohammed's teachings?
2. Why did Mohammed go to Yathrib? What did he accomplish there?
3. What changes did Mohammed make in Mecca in 630?

THE KORAN   At the heart of Islam is the **Koran**, or Muslim scriptures. Muslims believe it is the direct word of God as revealed to Mohammed. For this reason, they feel they should follow it exactly.

The Koran is written in Arabic. It tells how good Muslims should live. It says they should not eat pork, drink liquor, or gamble. The Koran also gives advice on marriage, divorce, inheritance, and business practices. It says that thieves should be punished by having their right hands cut off.

The Koran describes the **pillars of faith**, or the five duties all Muslims must fulfill. The first pillar is the confession of faith. All Muslims must recite the Islamic creed that states, "There is no God but Allah, and Mohammed is his prophet."

The second pillar involves prayer. Muslims must pray five times a day—at dawn, noon, late afternoon, sunset, and evening. They pray facing Mecca. Prayers can be offered anywhere. But the Friday noon prayer is usually recited at a **mosque**, or

Page from Koran

Muslim house of worship. There, believers are led by an *imam*, or prayer leader.

The third pillar concerns the giving of **alms**, or charity. There are two kinds of alms. One is the money Muslims donate on their own. The other is the part of a Muslim's income that is collected by the state. It is used for schooling or to help the poor.

The fourth pillar involves fasting. The young, sick people, pregnant women, and travelers do not have to fast. Everyone else must fast each year during the daylight hours of the holy month of Ramadan.

ISLAMIC FAITH

Muslims learn the teachings of the Koran at an early age. A child (left) studies passages from the Koran. An important teaching of the Koran requires Muslims to pray five times daily. From the prayer towers (right) of each mosque, criers call the people to prayer.

How do Muslims regard the Koran?

The fifth pillar involves a pilgrimage to Mecca two months after Ramadan. The journey is called the *hajj*. It involves three days of ceremony and sacrifice during which Muslims from all over the world come together.

The Koran promises that believers who have fulfilled their duties will go to paradise, and that everyone else will go to hell. Paradise is a cool mountaintop with shade, fruit trees, beautiful flower gardens, cold springs, and singing birds. Hell is a flame-filled pit where drinking water comes from a salty well and where food is a strong-smelling plant that causes hunger.

1. What does the Koran contain?
2. What are the five pillars of faith?
3. What does the Koran say will happen after death?

The Arab Empire

When Mohammed died in 632, his followers needed a new leader. Without someone to guide them, the community could have broken up and the faith could have been lost. A group of Muslims chose a new leader whom they called *khālifa*, or **caliph**, which means "successor."

THE RIGHTLY GUIDED CALIPHS   The first caliph was Abu Bakr, Mohammed's father-in-law and close friend. Bakr and the next three caliphs were elected for life. These caliphs ruled from Medina. They kept in close touch with the people and asked advice of their most trusted friends. For this reason, they were called the Rightly Guided Caliphs.

The Rightly Guided Caliphs honored Mohammed's wish to carry the Word of God to other peoples. They did this by fighting *jihads*, or holy wars, against **infidels**, or nonbelievers. They sent Muslim warriors into Palestine, Syria, Iraq, Persia, Egypt, and North Africa, and conquered them.

The Arabs were successful in their conquests for many reasons. Islam united them. It also taught them that warriors who died fighting infidels went to paradise. Arab leaders were mentally and physically tough. They planned and carried out attacks that took the enemy completely by surprise. Then, too, the Arabs handled their camels and horses with great skill.

The Arab way of treating the people they conquered also contributed to their success. Those who gave in without a fight had to pay taxes. In return, the Arabs protected them and allowed them to keep their land. Those who fought and were defeated not only had to pay taxes, but also lost their land. In addition, they had to continue farming the land for the Arabs.

1. How did the Rightly Guided Caliphs get their name? How did they expand the empire?
2. Why were the Arabs successful in their conquests?

THE UMAYYADS   Ali, Mohammed's son-in-law and the last of the Rightly Guided Caliphs, was killed in 661. Mu'awiyah, the new caliph, moved the capital from Medina to Damascus and founded the Umayyad Dynasty. From that time on, the title of caliph was hereditary.

The Umayyads ruled more like kings than religious leaders. They reorganized the government and made Arabic the official language. They minted the first Arabic currency. They set up horseback postal routes. They repaired and maintained irrigation canals. The Umayyads built magnificent mosques and encouraged the arts.

THE EXPANSION OF ISLAM

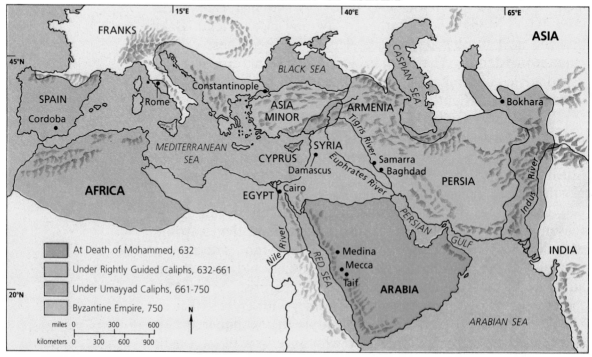

At Death of Mohammed, 632
Under Rightly Guided Caliphs, 632-661
Under Umayyad Caliphs, 661-750
Byzantine Empire, 750

The Umayyads, however, had social and economic problems that led to their downfall. The conquered peoples who had become Muslims complained that they were not treated as equals. They received less money for serving in the army than Arabs did, and they had to pay higher taxes.

The Muslims themselves divided into two groups called Shiites and Sunnites. After a while, civil war broke out between the Umayyads and a group of Shiite Muslims called Abbasids. In 750, the Abbasids defeated the Umayyads and became the new rulers of the Arab Empire.

1. What were some accomplishments of the Umayyads?
2. Who replaced the Umayyads as rulers of the Arab Empire?

THE ABBASIDS   The Abbasids ruled the Arab Empire from 750 to 1258. Their first 100 years in power was known as the Golden Age of Islam.

The Abbasids built a new capital called Baghdad on the west bank of the Tigris River. Designed by a Jewish astronomer and a Persian engineer, it took 100,000 architects and workers four years to build. Baghdad was built in the shape of a circle. It was surrounded by three huge, sloping brick walls and a deep **moat**, or wide ditch filled with water. Each wall had four large gates linked together by two highways that crossed in the center of the city. The highways divided Baghdad into four pie-shaped sections. From the gates, each highway led to a different part of the empire.

Abbasid Art

Under the Abbasids, all that remained of Arab influence was the Arabic language and the Islamic religion. The name Arab no longer meant only a person from Arabia but any subject of the empire who spoke Arabic.

The Abbasid caliphs thought of themselves as God's deputies and took the title of "Shadow of God on Earth." Anyone who approached them had to bow down and kiss the floor. An executioner stood ready to cut off the head of anyone who displeased them.

The Abbasids created the government post of *vizier*, or chief advisor. As the caliph's chief minister, the vizier stood between the throne and the people. The vizier took charge of running the empire and appointed governors of the provinces.

The Abbasids did not try to make new conquests. Instead, they concentrated on trade. Baghdad became the marketplace of

BAGHDAD

Baghdad, located on the banks of the Tigris River, was a center of trade, government, and religion. During the 700's, it became the world's most important Islamic city.

Who governed Baghdad from the 700's to the 1200's?

the world. The Arabs grew rich. The international trade led to a fresh exchange of ideas. When Syrian Christians and Jews translated Greek writings into Arabic, interest in Greek science and philosophy blossomed again.

Life changed in the empire. The demand for luxury items grew so great that Arab craftspeople began producing some items themselves. As trade increased, more records had to be kept. This led to the opening of banks. People had time to play games like polo, backgammon, and chess. Men stopped wearing the traditional Arab robe and began wearing trousers. Meals were served on tables instead of on the floor.

The empire soon became too large for one caliph to control. It began to break up into independent kingdoms. In 836, the caliph moved to a new capital city called Samarra. He returned to Baghdad in 892 in an attempt to regain power. But by then, it was too late. In 945, the Persians took control of Baghdad.

1. What were some features of Baghdad?
2. How did the Arab Empire change under the Abbasids?

THE GOLDEN AGE OF MUSLIM SPAIN   The Muslim Arabs who conquered North Africa intermarried with the Berbers and became known as Moors. In 710, they invaded Spain. With the help of local Jews, they defeated the West Goths, who had taken the country from the Romans. Then, the Moors set up a kingdom that allowed religious freedom.

For the next 400 years, a rich culture flourished in Spain. Many beautiful buildings, such as the Alhambra in Granada, were

---

ISLAMIC SPAIN

Under Islamic rule, the Spanish cities of Cordoba and Granada became known for their wealth and learning. The Alhambra, a palace in Granada, is considered the finest example of Islamic architecture in Europe.
What Islamic group invaded Spain in 710?

Seljuk Turks *c. 900–1258*

Seljuk
c. 900
chief from central Asia; settled with a group of followers near city of Bokhara and became Muslim

Tughril
c. 1055
grandson of Seljuk; conquered Baghdad; took title al-sultan, meaning "he with authority"; set up Muslim kingdom in western Asia

Mongols *c. 1206–1300*

Genghis Khan
c. 1220
united central Asian nomads; conquered Arab territory and created empire that covered most of Asia and eastern Europe

Hulagu
c. 1258
grandson of Genghis Khan; led attack on Baghdad in 1258; became first khan, or overlord, of a Muslim kingdom that stretched from Syria to India

Genghis Khan

Mamelukes *c. 1250–1517*

Shajar
c. 1250
freed slave who became first Mameluke ruler of Egypt; only Muslim woman to rule a country

Baybars
c. 1260
seized throne of Egypt; restored caliphate in Cairo; created Mameluke dynasty

Mohammed II

Ottoman Turks *c. 1290–1922*

Osman
c. 1290–1326
founded Ottoman dynasty in Asia Minor

Mohammed II
c. 1451–1481
captured Constantinople in 1453; established Ottoman Empire

built throughout the land. Academies were founded where Muslims, Jews, and Christians studied medicine and philosophy. Jewish diplomatic and trading missions traveled to every corner of the Arab Empire, and beyond. In Southeastern Russia, they met the Khazars, a half-Mongolian people who had converted to Judaism. From India and China, they brought back spices and silks to Spain.

In 1145, Spain was invaded by a Berber religious group from Morocco that did not allow religious freedom. Almost all the Christians and Jews fled northward, and the Golden Age of Muslim Spain was over.

1. What was life in Muslim Spain like?
2. What effect did religious freedom have on Spain's culture?

ISLAMIC LIFE   Islam set the guidelines for the way Muslims lived. It was a man's world, because the Koran said that "men are in charge of women" and "good women are obedient." Therefore, Muslim women were expected to stay at home and keep out of sight.

Marriage was considered a duty. A Muslim man who could afford it could have as many as four wives. Each wife was entitled to her own quarters, cooking and sleeping conveniences, and household slaves. A man usually married for the first time when he was about 20 years old. His bride was usually between the ages of 12 and 20. She had little to say about her marriage, which was arranged by her mother. Her father and the groom drew up a marriage contract that included the amount the groom was to pay as a bridal gift.

A Muslim man did not have to give a reason for divorcing his wife. He simply had to repeat the words "I dismiss thee" three times. In three months, his divorce was final. A Muslim woman who wanted a divorce had to pay for it by turning her property over to her husband.

Muslims celebrated the birth of a son with a week of feasts and offerings. The Muslim creed was whispered in the baby's ears at birth. Women cared for the boys until they were seven years old. Then, they entered mosque schools where they learned to write. After they had learned all they could, wealthy boys went to special classes where they listened to Muslim scholars discuss poetry and the classics.

Seljuk Jug

ISLAMIC MARKETPLACE

The bazaar, or marketplace, was an important center of activity in an Islamic city. At the bazaar, merchants sold their goods in stalls or shops along roofed streets. Men of the city also met at the bazaar for conversation.

How did trade contribute to the growth of the Arab Empire?

Fathers taught their sons how to be Muslim gentlemen. This meant learning not to eat too much or spit in public. It also meant not saying cruel things about others.

1. How did Muslims view marriage?
2. What kind of schooling did a Muslim boy receive?

ARAB CONTRIBUTIONS

Between the 700's and the 1300's, Arab scholars helped preserve the learning of the ancient world, which otherwise might have been lost. They also made many other contributions to modern civilization.

Arab scientists called **alchemists** tried to turn base metals—such as tin, iron, and lead—into gold and silver. Their efforts were not successful. But they led to the practice of making experiments and keeping accurate records of results. Thus, the Arabs are considered the founders of modern chemistry.

Arab astronomers studied the heavens and gave many stars the names they still have today. They accurately described the eclipses of the sun and proved that the moon affects the ocean. The astronomers worked with Arab geographers to determine the size and circumference of the earth. From their studies, they concluded that the earth might be round. The astronomer-geographer al-Idrisi created the first accurate map of the world.

Arab mathematicians invented algebra and introduced it to Europeans. The word algebra comes from the Arabic word *al-jabr*. It is just one of many Arabic words that have become part of Spanish and English. Arab mathematicians also borrowed the zero and the numerals 1–9 from Hindu mathematicians in India and passed them on to Europeans.

Astrolabe

The Arabs excelled in medicine. Unlike doctors in most other countries, Arab doctors had to pass an exam before they could practice medicine. The Arabs established the world's first school of pharmacy and opened the world's first drugstores. They organized medical clinics that traveled through the empire on camels providing drugs and care for the sick.

Arab doctors were the first to discover that blood **circulates**, or is carried to and from the heart. They were also the first to diagnose certain diseases. The Persian al-Razi identified the differences between measles and smallpox. Another Persian, Ibn Sina, was the first to recognize that tuberculosis is **contagious**, or can be passed from person to person.

Arab doctors advanced medical science by publishing their findings. Ibn Sina's *Canon of Medicine*, an encyclopedia of medicine, was used in European medical schools for 500 years.

Persian Nobleman

The Arabs also made many contributions in the arts. One of the best known writings is *The Arabian Nights*, a collection of tales put together from Persian stories. The tales paint an exciting picture of Islamic life at the height of the empire. The Persian poet Omar Khayyam's *Rubaiyyat* has been translated into many languages and is considered one of the finest poems ever written.

At first, Arab historians wrote about events one year at a time. Then, they began to organize events around rulers and peoples, which is what most historians do today. Ibn Khaldun's account of Arabs, Berbers, and Persians was the first to consider the influence of geography and climate on people.

Islamic art was distinct and colorful. It adorned swords, books, rugs, and mosques and other buildings. It differed from most other art because of the Muslim belief that Allah had created all living creatures. Islamic artists considered it a sin to make statues or pictures of Allah's creations. Most of their art consisted of geometric designs entwined with flowers, leaves, and stars.

1. What were some Arab contributions to science?
2. What were some Arab contributions to the arts?

CHAPTER 22 REVIEW

SUMMARY

1. Mecca contained a holy shrine to which pilgrims from all over Arabia came to worship.
2. Mohammed was born in Mecca in 571.
3. In 613, Mohammed began to preach that the only god was Allah.
4. In 622, Mohammed and his followers went from Mecca to Yathrib, where Mohammed organized the city's government and formed an army.
5. In 630, Mohammed led his followers into Mecca and dedicated the ka'bah to Allah.
6. In 631, delegates from all over Arabia declared their faith in Allah and their allegiance to Mohammed.
7. Muslim scriptures, which are called the Koran, are written in Arabic. The Koran describes the pillars of faith.
8. After Mohammed's death in 632, his followers chose a new leader who led them into battle against nonbelievers.
9. The Arabs succeeded in conquering a huge empire.
10. In 661, the capital of the Arab Empire was moved to Damascus.
11. In 750, the Abbasids took over control of the Arab Empire and built a new capital called Baghdad.
12. The Abbasids concentrated on trade rather than warfare.
13. The Moors in Spain combined Arab and Jewish cultures and allowed religious freedom.
14. The Arabs made many contributions to modern civilization, especially in the fields of chemistry, astronomy, mathematics, and medicine.

BUILDING VOCABULARY

1. *Identify the following:*

Arabs	Allah	Umayyad	al-Idrisi
Bedouins	Khadijah	Abbasids	al-Razi
Islam	Yathrib	Baghdad	Ibn Sina
Hejaz	Medina	Moors	*The Arabian Nights*
Muslims	Rightly Guided Caliphs	Alhambra	*Rubaiyyat*
Mohammed	Damascus	Khazars	Ibn Khaldun
Mecca			

2. *Define the following:*

submitting   Day of Judgment   *imam*   infidels
pilgrims   *Anno Hegira*   alms   moat
ka'bah   Koran   *hajj*   *vizier*
zemzen   pillars of faith   caliph   alchemists
fasted   mosque   *jihads*   circulates
revelation   contagious

REVIEWING THE FACTS

1. How did Bedouins earn a living?
2. How did pilgrims worship at the ka'bah in Mecca?
3. Why did Mohammed begin to spend time alone in a cave on a hillside outside Mecca?
4. Why did the leaders of the city of Mecca start persecuting Mohammed and his followers?
5. What is the Islamic creed?
6. In what direction do Muslims face when they pray?
7. What brought about the downfall of the Umayyad Dynasty?
8. What did the word "Arab" mean under the Abbasids?
9. What was the role of women in Muslim society?
10. What discoveries did Arab doctors make?

DISCUSSING IMPORTANT IDEAS

1. What effect did the rise of Islam have on Byzantium and Persia?
2. What role did religion play in Arab life?
3. Do you think the numerals 1–9 should be called Arabic or Hindu numerals? Give reasons for your answer.
4. What contributions made by the Arabs do you use in your everyday life?
5. How did the Moorish kingdom in Spain reflect the influence of different cultures?
6. In what ways is Islam similar to Judaism or Christianity? How are they different?

USING MAPS

Study the maps on page 322 and 326, and answer the following questions:

1. Where is the Hejaz located?
2. Is Yathrib the same city as Medina? How can you tell?
3. Where did Islam begin?
4. Where did it spread under the Rightly Guided Caliphs? Under the Umayyads?

THE MAURYAS
AND THE GUPTAS

Ancient India was made up of a number of small kingdoms. The ruler of each was called **rajah**. Many rajahs tried to take over neighboring lands.

In 321 B.C., one rajah, Chandragupta Maurya, moved into the Indus Valley. Soon, he ruled much of India and part of central Asia. These areas made up the Maurya Empire.

To hold his empire together, Chandragupta set up a uniform government. He also started a public works program that included building roads and irrigating farmers' fields.

Chandragupta's grandson, Asoka, was one of the greatest Maurya rulers. At first, Asoka waged war. Later, moved by the teachings of Buddha, he gave up war and brought peace to his people. He changed harsh tax laws. He also built hospitals, and set up free inns for religious pilgrims.

Asoka encouraged his people to follow Buddhist teachings. He had giant stone posts carved with these teachings set up from one end of the empire to the other. He also sent missionaries to other countries. Over the next 400 years, however, many Hindu priests took over Bud-

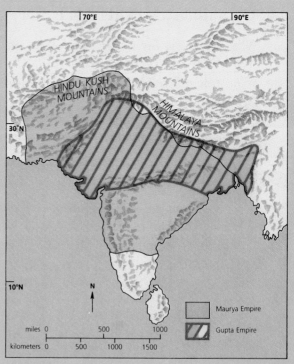

dhist teachings. As a result, Buddhism almost disappeared in India.

The Maurya Empire did not last. The rajahs who followed Asoka were more interested in power and wealth than in the happiness of the people. Wars started again, and in 185 A.D., Maurya rule came to an end.

After years of upheaval, a new empire, that of the Guptas, arose. Gupta rule lasted from 320 to 535 A.D. During those years, India was again united. The country was peaceful and prosperous. The arts and sciences flourished under the Gupta Empire.

Architects carved hundreds of temples from rock. Artists covered the walls of these temples with pictures of India's past. The pictures are as vivid today as they were 1,500 years ago.

Writers brought back Sanskrit, the classical language of India. One of the great Gupta writers was Kalidasa, a poet and dramatist. His plays are still presented in theaters today.

Doctors developed plastic surgery. They rebuilt ears and noses and removed scars. **Metallurgists**, or scientists who work with metals, made iron columns that are still free from rust after 1,500 years. Mathematicians worked out Arabic numbering and the decimal system.

1. What did Asoka do for his people?
2. What were some achievements in the arts and sciences under the Gupta Empire?

CHAPTER 23
THE RUSSIANS

North of the Byzantine Empire lived a people called the Slavs. All that is known about their origins is that they were Indo-Europeans, like the Aryans who entered the Indus Valley and the Dorians who conquered the Myceneans. About 500 B.C., the Slavs began to settle in eastern Europe in the areas now known as eastern Poland and the western Soviet Union.

THE EARLY RUSSIANS

About 500 A.D., a group of Slavs began to move eastward. They were hunters and farmers who came to be known as Russians. They settled in villages made up of about 25 related families. Each family owned a house that was built partly underground to provide warmth during the cold winter months. The house had low walls and an earth-covered roof. The land, animals, tools, and seed belonged to the village rather than to individuals. Around each village was a wall of earth and a wooden stockade for protection.

The oldest male governed the village with the help of a council. He assigned villagers different farming tasks and judged quarrels. During attacks, he acted as military leader.

By the seventh century A.D., the Russians controlled all of the heavily forested land as far east as the Volga River. To clear the land for farming, farmers used a method called **slash-and-burn**. They cut down trees, which they burnt for fertilizer. On the cleared land, they planted such crops as barley, rye, and flax. After a few years, when the wood fertilizer in the soil had been used up, the farmers moved to a new place. There, they repeated the process.

The forests provided the Russians with furs and timber. The Russians soon became skilled in building with wood. They made

---

RUSSIAN CABIN

Houses in early Russian towns and villages were made of wood. This modern Russian cabin shows the use of decorative styles passed on from early Russian artisans.

How did the environment influence the lives of early Russians?

musical instruments out of wood and used logs to make boats and *izbas*, or log cabins. The izba was a one-room cabin with a gabled roof and wooden window frames decorated with painted carvings of flowers, fruits, birds, and beasts. The whole family lived, worked, ate, and slept in the single room. Although each izba had a fireplace, some did not have a chimney. Smoke from fires had to escape through shutters that covered the windows of the izba.

The villagers worshipped many gods and honored nature spirits and ancestors. The most popular gods were Volos, who protected cattle and sheep; Perun, god of thunder and lightning; and the Great Mother, goddess of the land and harvest. The people built wooden images of their favorite gods on the highest ground outside the villages.

There were many slow-moving rivers in the area west of the Volga. At first, the Russians used them as roads between their villages. Before long, they began using them for trade as well. They set up a trade route that ran from the Baltic Sea in the north to the Black Sea in the south.

By the end of the ninth century A.D., the Russians had built many trading towns along the riverbanks. During the five months of winter, the merchants who lived in the towns gathered furs, honey, and other forest products from the people in neighboring villages. They rode on horseback, pulling **sledges**, or heavy sleds, filled with goods over the deep snow. In the spring, when the ice on the rivers had melted, the merchants loaded their goods on boats and floated south to Byzantium. There, the merchants traded their goods for cloth, wine, weapons, and jewelry. Trade helped the Russians to live more comfortably and to develop their civilization.

The Russians had to protect their trade route. Since they were not fighters, they relied on Viking warriors from Scandinavia. These Vikings were known in Russia as the Varangians, and the route came to be called the Varangian Route. Eventually, the Varangians became part of the larger Slav population. The name Russia came from the Scandinavian term "Rus," or "warrior band."

1. Where did the Russians settle?
2. What kind of homes did the early Russians have?
3. How and where did the Russians become traders?
4. How did the Varangians help the Russians?

Russian Sledge

The Emergence of Russia

In 862 A.D., a Varangian named Rurik became the Prince of Novgorod, a northern town on the Russian trading route. About 20 years later, Rurik's friend Oleg established the first Russian state. He set up his capital at Kiev.

Kiev stood on a hill overlooking the main bend of the Dnieper River. It was the southernmost town on the Russian trading route. Whoever controlled Kiev controlled Russia's trade with Byzantium. Kiev also lay close to where the Russian forest turned into the **steppe**, or grassland. For hundreds of years, the steppe had served central Asian warriors as a highway into Europe. Kiev was therefore in a good location to protect merchant ships from outside attackers.

The Russian state that Oleg established was really a collection of small territories. The central ruler was the Grand Prince

KIEVAN RUSSIA

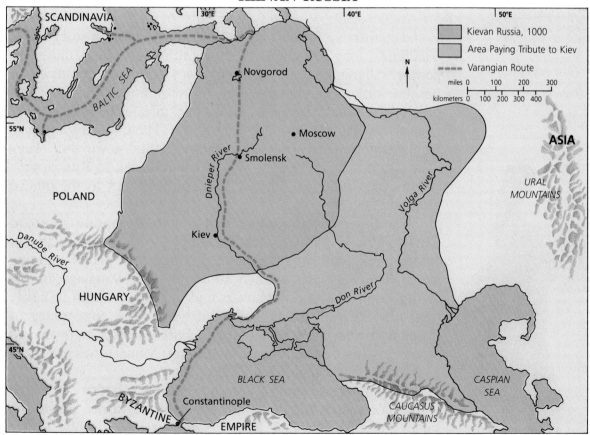

of Kiev. He was assisted by local princes, wealthy merchants, and landowning nobles called **boyars**. The Grand Prince collected tribute from the local princes, who in turn collected it from the people in their territory.

A *veche*, or assembly, handled the daily affairs of Russian towns. It did everything from settling business quarrels to accepting or removing a prince. Any free man could call a meeting of the veche by ringing the town bell.

1. What did Oleg do?
2. Where was Kiev?
3. How was the government of early Russian towns organized?

VLADIMIR I AND THE EASTERN ORTHODOX CHURCH

One of the most important princes of Kiev was Vladimir I. He was a good soldier and a strong ruler who spent the early years of his rule expanding Russian territory. His armies pushed the country's borders west into Poland and north along the Baltic coast.

In 988 A.D., Vladimir chose Eastern Orthodox Christianity as the country's official religion. The Russians tell a story about Vladimir's long search for a new faith that would unite the people. Vladimir sent representatives to other countries to observe different religions. The representatives were not impressed by what they saw in Islamic mosques, Jewish synagogues, or Roman Catholic churches. Then, in Byzantium's Hagia Sophia, they observed Eastern Orthodox worship. They were stunned by its beauty. When they returned to Russia, they persuaded Vladimir to choose Eastern Orthodox as the official religion.

The Eastern Orthodox Church brought Byzantine culture to Russia. Priests from Byzantium introduced the Russians to colorful religious rituals and taught them the art of painting icons. The Russians learned to write their language in the Cyrillic alphabet. Sons of boyars and priests were sent to newly built schools to learn to read and write. The appearance of Russian towns changed as stone churches with bulb-shaped domes rose among the wooden buildings. Monasteries appeared in the city and in the countryside.

Vladimir's decision to accept Eastern Orthodoxy gave the Russians a sense of belonging to the civilized world. But at the same time, it separated Russia from western Europe. Since

Boyar

RELIGIOUS LIFE
Eastern Orthodoxy inspired Russian art and architecture. This icon (left) from the city of Novgorod shows a scene from the Bible. Architects, influenced by the new religion, built wooden churches (right) in newly settled areas.
How did Eastern Orthodoxy separate Russia from the culture of western Europe?

Russian scholars now had books in their own language, they did not bother to learn Greek or Latin. As a result, they did not take advantage of the heritage of the West.

1. What made Vladimir I select Eastern Orthodoxy as Russia's official religion?
2. What effect did Eastern Orthodoxy have on the Russians?

YAROSLAV THE WISE   Another important ruler of early Russia was Yaroslav, son of Vladimir I. Yaroslav became the Grand Prince of Kiev in 1036 A.D., after a long struggle with his brothers for the throne. Yaroslav was very interested in learning. He read a lot and gathered a large collection of books. He invited scholars from Byzantium to live in Kiev. Because of his interest in learning he was called "the Wise."

Yaroslav encouraged Russian artisans to practice their skills. He built magnificent brick churches overlaid with white plaster and decorated with gold. The church domes were gilded or tiled in yellow, green, or blue. Russian painters covered the walls of Yaroslav's palace in the city of Kiev with scenes of music and hunting.

Under Yaroslav's rule, early Russia enjoyed a golden age of peace and prosperity. Kiev's population grew until the city became larger than Paris or London. Yaroslav developed closer ties with western Europe by having members of his family marry into other European royal families.

Yaroslav also organized Russian laws. He created a code of law based on old Slavic customs and Byzantine law. Under Yaroslav's code, crimes against property were considered more serious than those against people. There was no death penalty. Instead of being tortured, criminals were fined.

1. Why was Yaroslav called "the Wise"?
2. What did Yaroslav the Wise do for Russia?

Fur-lined Crown

THE DECLINE OF EARLY RUSSIA Russia began to decline around 1054 A.D. There were several reasons for this. After Yaroslav's death, the princes of Kiev began to fight over the throne. They were so busy fighting that they neglected their own territories. This weakened the entire country.

People from the steppe took advantage of the fighting and began to attack Russia's frontiers. The attacks upset the flow of trade along the north-south river route. The loss of trade meant the loss of Kiev's main source of wealth. Also, Russia depended on Byzantium. When it declined, Russia became even weaker and more isolated.

Gradually, Russia changed from a trading land of towns and merchants into a farming land of peasants. To escape the invaders from the steppe, many Russians fled to the north and settled in the dense forests along the upper Volga.

1. What were some reasons for the decline of Kiev?
2. How did the decline of Kiev affect the Russians?

THE MONGOLS

About 1240 A.D., a group of people known as Mongols swept out of central Asia and took control of Russia. They destroyed villages and towns and killed many people. They forced the Russians to pay tribute to the **khan**, or Mongol leader. They also forced the Russians to serve in the Mongol armies.

THE CHURCH   The Eastern Orthodox Church remained strong despite the Mongol invasion. Eastern Orthodox priests continued to preach and to write manuscripts. The priests encouraged the people to love their land and their religion.

When monks began to found monasteries deep in the northern forests, they were followed by Russian farmers searching for unused land. New towns and villages began to grow up around the monasteries.

The Mongol conquest isolated the Russian Church from other Christian churches. As a result, the Church developed its own rituals and practices. This united the Russian people and made them proud of their own culture. At the same time, however, it led them to distrust ideas and practices that were not Russian.

Church Vestment

1. What did the Mongols do to the Russians?
2. How did the Eastern Orthodox Church influence the Russians during the Mongol invasion?

DAILY LIFE   Most Russians led a simple but harsh life under the Mongols. Wealthy Russians sometimes entertained guests with feasts of deer and wild pig. But the peasants rarely ate meat. Instead, they ate dark rye bread, cabbage, salted fish, and mushrooms.

The few pleasures the peasants had were visiting one another, drinking, and singing. They told stories called *bylina* that praised the brave deeds of their warriors and other heroes. The stories were passed from old to young and became part of the Russian heritage.

Peasant men dressed in white tunics, wide linen trousers, and heavy shoes made from tree bark. They tied rags around their legs with pieces of twine to keep out the cold. Rich merchants and boyars wore tall fur hats and **caftans**, or long robes tied at the waist with a sash, to help keep them warm.

THE MONGOLS

The Mongols were chiefly interested in keeping control of and collecting taxes from the Russians. In the painting, Russians pay tribute to a Mongol leader. What were Mongol leaders called?

Russian women of all classes wore blouses or smocks, skirts, and long shawls. On holidays, they sported headdresses with fancy decorations. The decorations indicated what region a woman came from and whether or not she was married.

1. What was life like for the Russians during the Mongol conquest?
2. What did the Russians do for entertainment?
3. How did the Russians dress?

THE RISE OF MOSCOW

At the time of the Mongol conquest, Moscow was a small trading post on the road from Kiev to the forests in the north. As the Russians moved north to escape the Mongols, many skilled craftspeople settled in or near Moscow's **kremlin**, or fortress.

The princes of Moscow were bold and ambitious. They learned to cooperate with the Mongols and even recruited

Russian soldiers for the Mongol army. In return, the Mongols gave the princes of Moscow the power to collect taxes throughout the country. If a Russian territory could not provide soldiers or tax money for the Mongols, Moscow's princes took it over. In this way, Moscow began to expand.

As Moscow grew in size, it became stronger. The princes passed their thrones from father to son. Thus, there was no fighting over who the next ruler would be, and the people remained united.

The metropolitan lived in Moscow. This made it the center of the Russian branch of the Eastern Orthodox Church. The metropolitan blessed the princes for their efforts to make Moscow a great city. The Russian people began to look on the prince as a ruler chosen and protected by God. Encouraged by the Church, they obeyed the prince without question.

Meanwhile, Mongol chiefs began to fight among themselves. As a result, they grew weaker, while Moscow grew stronger. In 1378 A.D., an army formed by Dmitry, the Prince of Moscow, attacked and defeated the Mongols. Two years later, the Russians and Mongols fought again. Once more, the Mongols were defeated. They still remained powerful but no longer were feared or obeyed as they had been in the past.

1. Where was Moscow? What helped to make it a power?
2. What did Dmitry do?

IVAN THE GREAT   In 1462 A.D., Ivan III, known as Ivan the Great, became Prince of Moscow. In 1478 A.D., he ended Mongol control of Russia. He also expanded Russian boundaries to the north and west.

A few years before Mongol control ended, Ivan married Sophia, the niece of the last Byzantine emperor. The Russians felt the marriage gave Ivan all the glory of past Byzantine emperors. The Orthodox Church believed it meant that Moscow had replaced Byzantium as the center of Christianity.

Ivan began living in the style of the Byzantine emperors. He used the two-headed eagle of Byzantium on his royal seal. He brought Italian architects to Moscow to build fine palaces and large cathedrals in the kremlin. He raised the huge walls that still safeguard the kremlin. He called himself **tsar**, the title given only to the Byzantine emperor and the Mongol khan.

Ivan died in 1505 A.D. By then, the Russian people were convinced that their ruler should have full power over both Church and State.

1. How did Ivan the Great increase the power of Moscow?
2. What effect did Ivan's marriage have on him and on the Russian people?

IVAN THE TERRIBLE   In 1533 A.D., Ivan IV, the three-year-old grandson of Ivan III, became tsar. While he was growing up, a council of boyars governed Russia for him. The boyars, however, wanted more power. To frighten Ivan into obeying them, they began to mistreat him. Ivan came to hate the boyars, but adopted their cruel habits. By the time he was a teenager, he was killing people for going against his wishes.

When Ivan IV was 16 years old, he was crowned tsar and began to rule in his own right. He ignored the boyars and turned to merchants and personal friends for advice. He gave his advisors gifts of land and jobs as officials. To make sure that the officials' country estates were farmed while they were in Moscow with him, Ivan ordered peasants not to leave their land. Thus, Ivan took the first step in turning free peasants into serfs.

In 1552 A.D., Ivan led his armies against Mongol territories on the Volga. By this time, the Russians had learned the use of gunpowder from western Europe. The Mongols still relied on bows and arrows. Within six years, Ivan had conquered most of the Mongol territories. Russian settlers began to move east. Some, called Cossacks, began to farm along the Volga.

In 1558 A.D., Russian armies attacked Livonia, a land on the Baltic Sea. Livonia's neighbors sent troops to fight the Russians. In 1562 A.D., these troops defeated the Russians and took over much of their Baltic territory. Ivan blamed the boyars for his defeat.

In 1564 A.D., Ivan suddenly left Moscow and went to a small monastery in the country. A month later, he announced that he was giving up the throne because of the boyars. Afraid that without Ivan the empire would fall, the people begged him to change his mind. They told Ivan that if he came back, he could have full authority to punish traitors and to take over their lands.

Ivan returned to Moscow, took over boyar lands, and gave them to 5,000 of his most loyal supporters. In return, they formed the *Oprichniki*, or secret police. Members of the

Ivan the Terrible

THE GROWTH OF MOSCOW

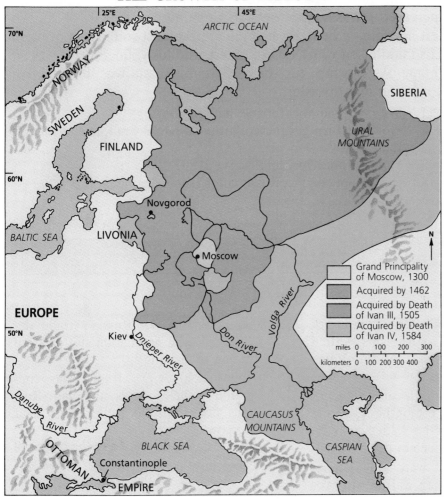

Grand Principality
of Moscow, 1300

Acquired by 1462

Acquired by Death
of Ivan III, 1505

Acquired by Death
of Ivan IV, 1584

miles 0   100   200   300

kilometers 0 100 200 300 400

Oprichniki dressed in black and rode black horses through the countryside. They attached a dog's head to their saddles to scare the tsar's enemies and carried a broom to show their desire to sweep treason from the land. They killed thousands of people. When the Oprichniki had defeated the boyars and returned control to Ivan, he broke up the group.

Ivan came to be called Ivan the Terrible. The English translated the Russian word meaning "awesome" as "terrible." But to the Russians, Ivan was a great ruler who protected their country from enemies.

Ivan encouraged art and learning. He brought artists, scholars, and engineers from western Europe to teach the

Russians new skills. He turned Russia into an empire and increased the tsar's power. But when he died in 1584 A.D., he left no suitable heir. He had killed his oldest son in a fit of rage. His middle son was feeble-minded, and his youngest son was an infant. As a result, for some 25 years Russia was in a state of confusion and disorder.

1. Why did Ivan the Terrible hate the boyars?
2. How did Ivan get the authority to punish traitors and seize their lands?
3. How did the Oprichniki serve Ivan?
4. What happened to Russia after Ivan's death?

CHAPTER 23 REVIEW

SUMMARY

1. Between 500 and 800 A.D., a group of Slavs, later known as Russians, settled the forested land west of the Volga River.

2. By the end of the ninth century A.D., the Russians had established a trade route that ran from the Baltic Sea in the north to the Black Sea in the south.

3. Since the Russians were not fighters, they relied on Viking warriors to protect their trade routes.

4. In 882 A.D., the Viking warrior Oleg established the first Russian state with its capital at Kiev.

5. In 988 A.D., Vladimir I chose Eastern Orthodox Christianity as Russia's official religion.

6. The Eastern Orthodox Church brought Byzantine culture, including the Cyrillic alphabet, to Russia.

7. Yaroslav the Wise established a library, organized Russian laws, and encouraged Russian artisans to practice their skills.

8. After 1054 A.D., Russia's trade declined and the population shifted from trading to farming.

9. About 1240 A.D., Russia was conquered by the Mongols, and many Russians fled north to settle in or near Moscow.

10. Moscow gradually became the center of Russian life.

11. In 1378 and 1380 A.D., the Russians under Prince Dmitry defeated the Mongols in battle.

12. In 1478 A.D., Ivan the Great ended Mongol control of Russia.

13. Beginning in 1552 A.D., Ivan the Terrible conquered most of the Mongol territories, and many Russians began moving eastward.

14. Ivan the Terrible used secret police to destroy the power of Russia's landowning nobles.

15. When Ivan the Terrible died in 1584 A.D., he left no suitable heir, and for the next 25 years Russia was in disorder.

BUILDING VOCABULARY

1. *Identify the following:*

Slavs	Vladimir I	Dnieper River	Moscow
Russians	Oleg	Yaroslav the Wise	Dmitry
Volga River	Kiev	Mongols	Ivan the Great
Varangians			Ivan the Terrible

2. *Define the following:*

slash-and-burn	steppe	khan	kremlin
izbas	boyars	*byliny*	tsar
sledges	*veche*	caftans	*Oprichniki*

REVIEWING THE FACTS

1. To what other Indo-Europeans were the Slavs related?

2. How did Russian houses provide warmth?

3. How did Russian farmers fertilize their land?

4. What did the Russians obtain from the forests?

5. How did Russian traders make the trip to Byzantium?

6. Why did the Russians invite the Varangians to enter their territory?

7. How was the first Russian state of Kiev organized?

8. How did Yaroslav develop closer ties with western Europe?

9. How did the princes of Moscow become powerful?

10. What did the Russian Church teach the people about the power of a ruler?

DISCUSSING IMPORTANT IDEAS

1. How did Kiev's location affect its rise to power?

2. What were the advantages of Russia's adoption of Eastern Orthodoxy?

3. How did Yaroslav's law code compare with Justinian's?

4. Do you think Yaroslav deserved to be called "the Wise"? Why or Why not?

5. Do you think Ivan III deserved to be called "the Great"? Why or why not?

6. Do you think Ivan IV deserved to be called "the Terrible"? Why or why not?

USING MAPS

Study the maps on pages 341 and 349, and answer the following questions:

1. What cities lay on the Varangian Route?

2. On what river is Kiev located? Name two other rivers in Russia.

3. Where is Novgorod located?

4. What is located at about 54° north latitude and 35° east longitude?

5. Under whom did Moscow have its greatest expansion?

UNIT 7 REVIEW

SUMMARY

1. After the fall of Rome, civilizations in eastern Europe and the Middle East became more advanced than civilizations in western Europe. Each was united by strong rulers and by religion.

2. The Byzantines ruled the eastern half of the Roman Empire from their capital of Constantinople. They formed a civilization based on Greco-Roman culture and closely tied to the Eastern Orthodox Church.

3. Mohammed, an Arab from Mecca, founded Islam, which became one of the world's major religions.

4. To spread Islam, the Arabs conquered lands in Spain, North Africa, and Asia. They created the Arab Empire.

5. The Russians created a civilization centered first around Kiev and later around Moscow. It was guided and united by the Eastern Orthodox Church and greatly influenced by Byzantine culture.

REVIEWING THE MAIN IDEAS

1. Describe the relationship between religion and government among the Byzantines; the Arabs; the Russians.

2. What was the main factor in the growth of the Byzantine Empire? In the growth of the Arab Empire?

3. How did the Byzantines influence people in western Europe? How did the Arabs influence people?

4. What did the Russians give the Byzantines? What did the Byzantines give the Russians?

DEVELOPING SKILLS

You have probably heard the expression "Do not mix apples with oranges." While both apples and oranges are types of fruit, you cannot compare one with the other in order to find out which is the riper fruit. You can only compare one apple with another apple or one orange with another orange.

The same is true when examining data. It is important to group similar items together. If data are not correctly grouped, they cannot be properly analyzed.

This exercise is designed to give you practice in classifying. Read each group of items below. Eliminate the item that does not belong in the group, and tell what the remaining items have in common.

1. Byzantines, Russians, Arabs, Christians
2. Mecca, Koran, Baghdad, Medina
3. Mecca, Kiev, Constantinople, Moscow
4. Belisarius, Mohammed, Tribonian, Rurik
5. Justinian, Khadijah, Yaroslav, Ivan IV

SUGGESTED UNIT PROJECTS

1. Describe the sights that a Byzantine farmer who is visiting Constantinople for the first time would probably find the most impressive.

2. Check a large dictionary for all the words beginning with "al." Make a poster that shows the English word, its meaning, and the Arabic word from which it came.

3. Bring in pictures of buildings that look like those built during the Byzantine Empire.

4. Working as a class, make an illustrated timeline to highlight life in western and eastern Europe and the Middle East from the fall of Rome.

5. Draw or make an icon.

6. Write five newspaper headlines about major events in the life of Theodora, Mohammed, or Ivan the Great.

7. Make a chart comparing life in the Byzantine Empire, the Arab Empire, and Russia.

SUGGESTED READING

Almedingen, E.M. *Land of Muscovy*: *The History of Early Russia*. New York: Farrar, Strauss & Giroux, 1971. A detailed account of the life of the Russian people from 1400 to 1600.

Asimov, Isaac. *Constantinople*: *The Forgotten Empire*. Boston: Houghton Mifflin Company, 1970. Traces the history of Constantinople and the Byzantine Empire and discusses the Empire's influence on the civilizations of western and eastern Europe.

Barker, Carol. *A Prince of Islam*. Reading, Mass.: Addison-Wesley, 1976. A description of the childhood and education of the son of a ninth-century caliph.

Edmonds, I. *Islam*. New York: Franklin Watts, 1977. Recounts the life of Mohammed and discusses the Koran, including the influence of Jewish and Christian beliefs on Islam.

Goldston, Robert. *The Sword of the Prophet*. New York: Dial, 1980. A description of the founding of Islam and its spread through the Arab world.

Townson, Duncan. *Muslim Spain*. Minneapolis: Lerner Publications Company, 1973. A description of Spanish civilization during the centuries of Moorish control.

UNIT 8

725	750	775
732 Charles Martel establishes fief system		

875	900	925
	c. 900 Vikings invade western Europe Feudalism begins	

1025	1050	1075
	1070 Seljuk Turks conquer Palestine	**1077** Pope Gregory VII and King Henry IV meet at Canossa **1095** Pope Urban II cal first crusade **1099** Crusaders cap Jerusalem

1175	1200	1225
1188 Crusade of Kings	**c. 1200** New farming methods introduced on manors Friars preach reform in cities **1204** Crusaders capture Constantinople **1212** Children's Crusade	

1325	1350	1400

THE AGE OF FEUDALISM

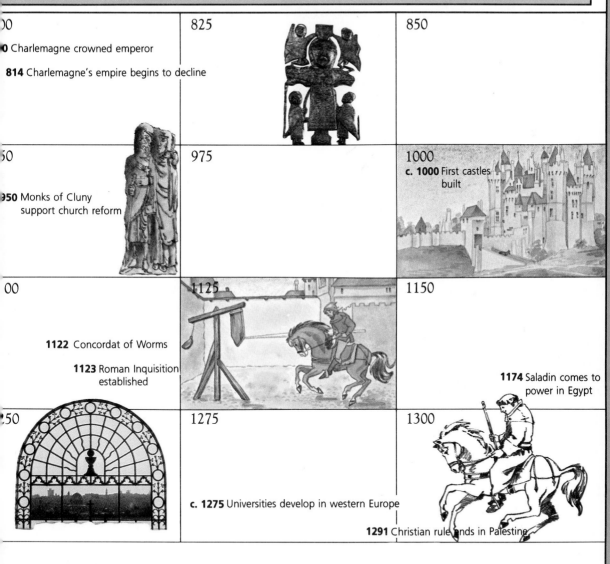

00	825	850
0 Charlemagne crowned emperor **814** Charlemagne's empire begins to decline		
50 **950** Monks of Cluny support church reform	975	1000 **c. 1000** First castles built
00 **1122** Concordat of Worms **1123** Roman Inquisition established	1125	1150 **1174** Saladin comes to power in Egypt
250	1275 **c. 1275** Universities develop in western Europe	1300 **1291** Christian rule ends in Palestine

1. HOW WAS WESTERN EUROPE GOVERNED DURING THE MIDDLE AGES?
2. WHY ARE THE MIDDLE AGES CALLED AN "AGE OF FAITH"?

During the Middle Ages, most people of western Europe lived in villages in the countryside. There were only a few towns, and they were far smaller than the busy communities that had once filled the territories of the Roman Empire.

Most people lived in the same place all their lives. Travel and communication were difficult, and trade was slow. The people of each community grew their own food and met their other needs with little or no outside help.

Most people who lived in the countryside were poor and enjoyed few pleasures. For comfort and guidance, they turned to the Roman Catholic Church. Religion played an important part in their daily lives. A church stood at the center of every town or village. Not only was the church building a place of worship, but its courtyard was the center of local trade and community activity.

The people constantly faced the dangers of hunger, disease, and outside attack. Nobles, warriors, townspeople, and peasants fought each other over land. Still, the people wanted security and protection. But western Europe had no central government to keep the peace. Real power had passed from kings to local nobles. To protect their property, the nobles raised their own armies. They developed what is known as **feudalism**, or government by landowning warrior-nobles.

Feudalism lasted in western Europe until about 1400. It was, however, particularly strong during the eleventh and twelfth centuries, a part of the period known as the Middle Ages.

CHAPTER 24
FEUDAL SOCIETY

Under feudalism, the people of western Europe were divided into groups. Each group had duties to perform for the other groups and for society as a whole. The first group was the **clergy,** or religious leaders. Their duty was to teach Christianity and to help the poor and sick. The second group was the nobles. Their duty was to govern, enforce laws, and protect the people. The third group was a small number of townspeople and the **peasants**, or people who farmed the land and provided services for nobles. Their duty was to work for the clergy and nobles.

Although there were more peasants and townspeople, the clergy and nobles had more rights. Almost everyone believed that God wanted it that way. As a result, few people tried to make improvements in society or change their own way of life. Most people remained in the group into which they were born.

THE LAND AND GOVERNMENT

During feudal times, power was based on the ownership of land. Before feudalism developed, kings owned all the land within their territories. Then, in 732, Charles Martel gave his soldiers **fiefs**, or estates, as a reward for their service and loyalty. From their fiefs, soldiers got the income they needed to buy horses and battle equipment. From that time on, land ownership was tied to military service.

Feudal Shield

THE RISE OF FEUDAL TERRITORIES   After 800, the kings of Europe followed Martel's practice. After Charlemagne's death in 814, Europe had no central government. The kings who followed Charlemagne were so weak they could not even rule their own kingdoms well. They ignored their responsibilities and spent most of their time traveling from one royal estate to another. Before long, they began to depend on the nobles for food and horses. Some nobles grew more powerful than the king, and soon, they became independent rulers. They gained the right to collect taxes and to enforce the law in their areas. Many nobles raised armies and coined their own money.

Around 900, the nobles took on the duty of protecting their lands and people from the Vikings. They built fortresses on hilltops and fenced in their lands. To support more soldiers, they seized more land. The peasants turned to these powerful nobles for protection. In return, they gave the nobles their lands and promised to work for them in the fields. The peasants ended up giving the nobles not only their land but their freedom too.

By 1000, the kingdoms of western Europe were divided into thousands of feudal territories, each of which was about the size of an ancient Greek polis. Unlike the polis, however, a feudal territory had no central city. The noble who owned the land had the political power. Most people were peasants who had no say in the government.

Feudal government was not complicated. It was based largely on the actions of the nobles. The nobles made the laws for their fiefs, and the people obeyed them. The government did provide some protection for the people and for their property.

1. How did land ownership become tied to military service?
2. How did the nobles become so powerful?
3. What were some features of feudal government?

LORD AND VASSAL   Feudalism was based on ties of loyalty and duty among nobles. A **vassal**, or less powerful noble, gave his loyalty to a lord. In return, the lord protected the vassal.

The tie between lord and vassal was made official in a special ceremony known as the **act of homage**. The bareheaded vassal knelt on the ground and placed his hands between those of the lord. The vassal promised to serve the lord and to help him in battle. The lord accepted the pledge, helped the vassal to his feet, and kissed him.

In return for loyalty and service, the lord gave the vassal a fief. Since there were few written agreements in the Middle Ages, the lord gave the vassal a glove, a piece of wood, or a lance to show that his word could be trusted. He also gave the vassal the right to govern the people who lived on the fief. The lord promised to protect the vassal from enemy attacks. If he failed to do so, the vassal no longer owed him loyalty. A fief belonged to a vassal for life. When the vassal died, his fief

---

KING AND VASSAL

A vassal owed loyalty and military service to a lord. Kings, as well as nobles, were lords. Here, a king receives homage from one of his vassals.
What role did peasants play in feudal government?

usually passed on to his oldest son, who then performed the act of homage.

A vassal did not lose his self-respect by seeking the protection of a lord. Many vassals had their own vassals just as some lords owed allegiance to other lords. The ties between lord and vassal could be confusing because a vassal could owe loyalty in times of war to several lords at once. In such a case, the vassal chose one lord to whom he was the most loyal. Some vassals just supported the side most likely to win.

Vassals had certain duties to perform. Their most important duty was to help the lord in battle. Vassals had to bring their own knights with them. They themselves were expected to take part in battle at least 40 days a year.

Vassals had to make payments to their lord. When a lord's son became a knight or his daughter married, his vassals had to give the lord money. If a lord were captured in battle, his vassals had to pay the **ransom**, or sum of money given in exchange for a person's release. Vassals were also expected to provide food and entertainment when their lord visited them.

Vassals had to attend the lord's court. This was a monthly meeting of the lord's vassals that decided cases involving the vassals. From this feudal court came the modern system of **trial by jury**, or a system of justice in which 12 people decide the guilt or innocence of an accused person.

1. What was the relationship between lord and vassal?
2. What promises were made during the act of homage?
3. What were some duties of a vassal?

The Nobility

Life was not always comfortable or pleasant for nobles during feudal times. They did, however, enjoy more benefits than the common people.

Feudal Fortress

From the ninth to the eleventh centuries, nobles and their households lived in a **manor house**, or a wooden building constructed to provide protection. A **palisade**, or high wooden fence, surrounded the house. In case of attack, people from the nearby villages sought shelter inside the palisade.

The manor house consisted of one room with a high ceiling and a straw-covered floor. The straw got so dirty with mud, bones, and food that every few months it had to be swept

NOBLE'S FEAST

Nobles celebrated special occasions with elaborate feasts. This manuscript drawing shows a noble and his household at a meal.
What was life like for a noble?

outdoors and burned. All activity took place in the one room. There nobles met with vassals, carried out the laws, and said their prayers. There nobles, their families, servants, and warriors ate and slept. At mealtime, wooden tables were set up and piled high with meat, fish, different kinds of vegetables, fruits, and honey. Everybody ate with their fingers and threw scraps of food on the floor for the dogs.

Meals were cooked over fires that were also supposed to heat the manor house. Actually, the fires did little to keep out the cold. Smoke from them often stung the eyes and darkened the walls and ceiling.

1. How did a manor house protect people?
2. What was life like in a manor house?

THE CASTLE   By the 1100's, manor houses were made of stone and were called **castles**. Because they were designed as fortresses, the castles made the nobles feel secure and independent. The castle had thick stone walls, one within another. Each corner had its own lookout tower with archers in it. Some castles

---

CASTLE

A castle was both a noble's home and a military fortress. During enemy attack, people from the surrounding area sought protection within the castle walls. This photo of an English castle shows the moat and castle entrance.
Who was responsible for a castle's care and defense?

---

were further protected by a moat with a soft and muddy bottom that stopped attackers from using ladders to climb over the walls. To cross the moat, a person had to use a **drawbridge**, or heavy door, that could be raised or lowered. The drawbridge led to the **portcullis**, or heavy oak and iron gate, that served as the entrance to the castle.

Within the castle walls was a large open area. In the middle of this area was a **keep**, or tall tower. It contained a hall, many rooms, and a dungeon. The people of the household lived in the keep. Nearby stood shops, kitchens, stables, and rooms for troops and guests.

Many people lived in the castle. Besides the nobles and their families, there were servants and officials. Since the lord of the castle was away fighting most of the time, the servants and officials were responsible for the castle's care and defense. Most castles had enough space to store a large supply of food and drink. As a result, the people in the castle could hold out against attackers for as long as six months.

Castle Gate

1. What were some features of a castle?
2. Who lived in a castle?

CASTLE LIFE When the nobles were at home, they looked after their estates, went hunting and fishing, and held court. During long winter evenings, they played chess. Wandering minstrels sang songs and played stringed instruments to entertain the nobles and their guests.

Noblewomen were called **ladies**. Once they married, their husbands had complete authority over them. Most marriages were planned to unite important families, and a woman had little say about who was chosen for her. The bride's family gave the groom a dowry. Most nobles looked for wives with large dowries. Women were often married by the time they were 12. Those who were not married by the time they were 21 could expect to stay single for the rest of their lives.

The women helped their husbands run their estates. When the men were away, the women had to defend the castle. The main duty of a wife, however, was to have and raise children and to take care of the household. She was also expected to train young girls from other castles in household duties and supervise the making of cloth and fine embroidery. Another duty was to

CHESS PLAYERS
Chess was a favorite game in the Middle Ages. Nobles and their families played chess in their castles during the long winter nights.
What other activities did nobles and their families enjoy?

use her knowledge of plants and herbs to care for the poor and sick on her husband's fiefs.

1. How did a noble spend his time when he was at home?
2. How were marriages arranged among nobles?
3. What was the role of a noblewoman during feudal times?

KNIGHTHOOD

Almost all nobles were **knights**, or warriors on horseback. No one was born a knight. Knighthood had to be earned. Knights were expected to follow certain rules known as the **code of chivalry**. These rules stated that a knight was to obey his lord, to respect women of noble birth, and to help people in time of trouble. A knight was to be honest and to fight fairly against his enemies. Few knights actually lived up to all the rules. The code of chivalry, however, became the guide to behavior from which the western idea of good manners developed.

1. What was expected of a knight?
2. What developed from the code of chivalry?

TRAINING A noble began training to be a knight when he was seven years old. He was sent to the castle of a great lord where he learned to be a **page**, or a person who helped the knights of the castle care for their horses and armor. He strengthened his arms and wrists by hitting a wooden post with a fake sword. He learned good manners and ran errands for the ladies. He was taught to ride and fight. By the time he was 14, he could handle a lance and sword while on horseback.

When he was 15, the young noble became a **squire** and was put under the care and training of one knight. A squire went into battle with his knight and was expected to rescue the knight if he was wounded or fell off his horse.

KNIGHTHOOD

For protection, knights wore suits of armor (left) that covered every part of the body. They used different kinds of swords (right) and spears in battle. The responsibility of knights was to defend the land of the nobles.
Who could become a knight?

If the squire proved to be a good fighter, he was rewarded by being made a knight. This was done in a special ceremony known as **dubbing**. The night before the ceremony, the squire prayed in the chapel. In the morning, he knelt before his lord and took an oath to defend the Church against its enemies. He also promised to fight only for his lord and to protect the weak and helpless. Then, the lord tapped the squire on the shoulder with the blade of a sword and pronounced him a knight.

1. What were some duties of a page?
2. What were some duties of a squire?
3. How did a squire become a knight?

TOURNAMENTS   Knights trained for war by fighting each other in **tournaments**, or special contests that test strength, skill, and endurance. Tournaments were held outdoors in a large field near a castle. They were festive occasions that attracted lords, ladies, and knights from the surrounding areas. Important guests watched the events from seats in stands covered with colorful cushions, carpets, and tapestries. The most popular event was a **joust**. Two armored knights on horseback carrying blunt lances galloped headlong towards each other from opposite ends

of the field. Each tried with all his strength and skill to knock the other to the ground with his lance.

Tournaments were costly. Men and horses were killed and injured. Lances, swords, shields, and suits of armor were ruined. The noble who gave the tournament had to feed hundreds of people. In spite of the cost, however, tournaments remained popular. It was believed that a knight who had not learned to fight in a tournament could not fight well in battle.

1. What was the purpose of tournaments?
2. In what ways were tournaments costly?

THE MANOR

Nobles, knights, and peasants depended on the land for food, clothing, and shelter. The land was divided into **manors**, or farming communities. Manors were found on the fiefs of the lords. Some lords owned only one manor; others owned many.

Peasant Farmer

DAILY LIFE   The lord appointed a number of officials to run the manor. They were loyal to the lord and made sure his orders were carried out. One official was the **seneschal**. He looked after all of the lord's fiefs. To do this, he had to visit each fief regularly. Another official was the **bailiff**. He made sure the peasants worked hard in the fields.

Every manor had its own court that dealt out justice. The lord himself sat in on the meetings of the court. The court settled disputes, gave out fines and punishments, and discussed manor business.

Poor transportation and frequent fighting isolated the manors from one another. As a result, the men and women of the manor produced only enough food for themselves and their lord. They raised sheep for wool and cattle for meat and milk. They also grew grain and vegetables, made cloth, built homes, and fashioned tools.

The local lord of each manor lived in a manor house or a castle. Nearby stood a small village of wood and dirt cottages with thatched roofs. The village was surrounded by forests, meadows, pastures, and fields. Most villages had a church, mill, bread oven, and wine press.

The cottages in which the peasants lived were crowded closely together around an open area called the village green.

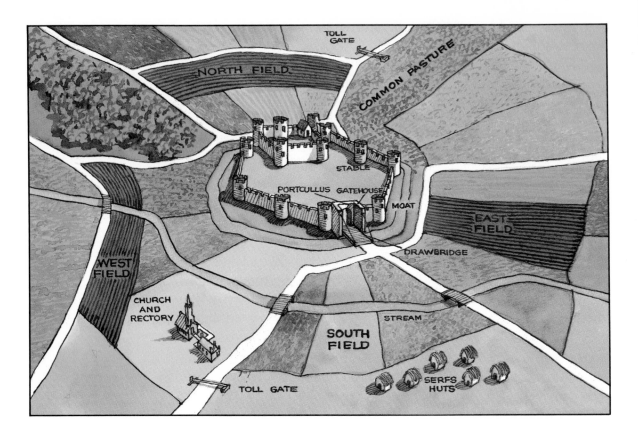

Most cottages had only one room. At night, family members slept there on piles of straw or on the dirt floor. Three-legged stools and a table were the only furniture.

1. Who ran the manors?
2. What effect did being isolated have on a manor?
3. What were some features of a village?

FREEMEN AND SERFS   Two groups of peasants worked on a manor. One was the **freemen**, or peasants who paid the lord for the right to farm the land. They worked only on their own strips of land and had rights under the law. They moved wherever and whenever they wished. The lord, however, had the right to throw them off the manor without warning.

The other group was the serfs. The serfs and their descendants were the lord's property. They could not move to another area, own their own property, or marry without the lord's permission. Serfs, however, could not be driven off the land and did not have to serve in the army. It was not easy for serfs to gain their freedom. One way was to escape to the towns. If serfs remained in town for more than a year, they were considered free. By the end of the Middle Ages, serfs were allowed to buy their freedom.

As in Charlemagne's time, the serfs worked long hours in the fields and performed many services for the nobles. Serfs spent three days of the week working the lord's strips of land and the rest of the week caring for their own strips. They gave part of their own crops to the lord.

In spite of the difficulties, a serf's life had a few bright moments. Sunday was a day of rest from work. At Christmas, the lord paid for a great feast and entertainment. Certain holidays were celebrated with singing and dancing on the village green. When they could, the serfs took part in such sports as wrestling, archery, and soccer.

By the 1200's, changes were taking place. The peasants began to learn better farming methods. They made better

---

PEASANTS AT WORK

Peasants spent long hours working in the fields of a manor. In the paintings below, one group of peasants is mowing and binding sheaves of wheat (left), while another group of peasants is shearing sheep (right).
What two kinds of peasants worked on a manor?

PEASANTS AT PLAY

Peasants celebrated weddings and holidays with folk dances. Here, a group of peasants performs a lively circle dance.

What was life like for a peasant?

use of the three-field system of farming. They started to use a heavy iron plow rather than the lightweight wooden plow. The horse collar was invented, and peasants could use horses instead of slow-moving oxen to plow their fields. All of this allowed the peasants to grow more food.

1. What rights did freemen have?
2. What did serfs contribute to the manor?
3. What changes took place in farming by the 1200's?

CHAPTER 24 REVIEW

SUMMARY

1. In 732, Charles Martel tied land ownership to millitary service when he gave his soldiers fiefs.

2. After the death of Charlemagne, kings began to depend on nobles for food and horses.

3. Some nobles grew more powerful than the king, and they began to collect their own taxes, run their own courts, raise their own armies, and coin money.

4. Around 900, the nobles agreed to protect people from Viking attacks in exchange for land and labor.

5. By 1000, the kingdoms of western Europe were divided into thousands of small feudal territories.

6. Lords gave their vassals land in exchange for loyalty and military service.

7. At first, nobles lived in wooden manor houses, but by the 1100's, they were living in stone castles.

8. Nobles began at age seven and spent eight or nine years training to become knights.

9. Knights followed certain rules of behavior known as the code of chivalry.

10. Knights trained for war by fighting in tournaments.

11. Land was divided into manors owned by lords and worked by peasants.

12. There were two groups of peasants on a manor—freemen and serfs.

13. Serfs lived hard lives and could not gain their freedom easily.

14. By the 1200's, changes were taking place in peasant life.

BUILDING VOCABULARY

1. *Define the following:*

clergy	manor house	ladies	tournaments
peasants	palisade	knights	joust
fiefs	castles	code of chivalry	manors
vassal	drawbridge	page	seneschal
act of homage	portcullis	squire	bailiff
ransom	keep	dubbing	freemen
trial by jury			

REVIEWING THE FACTS

1. Into what three groups were people divided under feudalism?

2. Who held the political power within a feudal territory?

3. What did a lord give a vassal to show that his word could be trusted?

4. Who usually received a vassal's fief when the vassal died?

5. What did a vassal do when he owed loyalty to several lords at the same time?

6. Why could people in a castle hold out against attackers for a long period of time?

7. What did most nobles look for in a marriage?

8. Why were the people on a manor unable to produce a surplus of food?

9. In what two ways could serfs obtain their freedom?

10. What did serfs do for entertainment to brighten their lives?

DISCUSSING IMPORTANT IDEAS

1. Would you have preferred to be a lord or a vassal? Explain?

2. Do you think life in a manor house was healthy? What makes you think so?

3. Do you think you would have enjoyed being a knight? Why or why not?

4. Would you rather have been a freeman or a serf? Explain.

THE JAPANESE SAMURAI

In the 1100's, large clans fought one another for control of Japan. Japanese royalty was only a symbol of Japanese unity and nationality. It did not control the land or the people. The real rulers were the *shoguns*, or army generals who helped the emperor.

Under the shoguns were *daimyos*, or great lords who lived in outlying prov-inces. The daimyos ran large estates that were worked by heavily taxed rice farm-ers. The farmers also served in the army.

The daimyos were supported by armed warriors called *samurai*, meaning "those who serve." They lived on the estates in homes near the daimyo's forti-fied castle. The samurai were loyal to their family, their clan, and their daimyo. They were proud of their military skills, especially their ability to use a sword. They were good riders and archers.

The samurai had a strict code of honor called *bushido*, meaning "way of the warrior." Unlike European knights, they had no interest in honoring or de-fending women. Samurai women were ex-pected to be self-disciplined and to fight in times of crisis.

Bushido taught self-discipline. Sam-urai were expected to endure hardship,

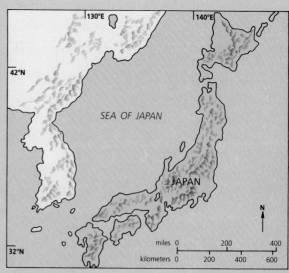

pain, and sacrifice. A sense of pride was important. Samurai believed they had to **save face**, or protect their honor. As a result, they took offense at the smallest insult. A samurai who felt greatly shamed saved face by committing *hara kiri*. This was the ritual act of taking one's own life with a sword.

Samurai were fearless in battle. They thought it was an honor to die on the battlefield. They compared dying in a battle to cherry blossoms falling off a tree.

A samurai dressed for battle was a colorful work of art. Sword and **scabbard**, or sword holder, were finely crafted. Armor was light and flexible, made of hundreds of tiny leather squares. The squares were lacquered to steel hardness and woven into armor with silver thread.

Samurai were as skilled in the polite arts as they were in battle. They trained themselves to perform the ritual tea ceremony and to write poetry. The samurai also were calligraphers.

In Europe, the nobles and their traditions were pushed aside to make way for modern ways. This was not the case in Japan. The samurai belief in clan and family loyalty and in ritual and conduct remained. It was carried over to business relationships and dealings. Samurai families came to play an important role in helping Japan become a modern industrial state.

1. Who controlled the country of Japan in the 1100's?
2. What was expected of samurai?
3. How did the samurai feel about their honor?

CHAPTER 25
THE CHURCH

The Roman Catholic Church was the only organization that served to unite western Europeans during the Middle Ages. It took the lead in politics, law, art, and learning for hundreds of years.

By 1000, the Catholic missionary monks had brought the Church's teachings to most of Europe. They converted people to the Catholic faith and built new churches and monasteries. Bishops and priests continued the work begun by the monks. They made sure the people gave their loyalty to the Pope.

Church leaders wanted to develop a civilization in western Europe based on Christian principles. While working toward this goal, the Church helped to preserve and pass on the heritage of the Roman Empire. Latin was made the official language of the Church. Monks copied ancient Greek and Roman manuscripts, making sure that the past would not be forgotten.

CATHOLIC INFLUENCE

The Church was the center of daily life in every village and town. On Fridays, the people obeyed the Church's rule not to eat meat. On Sundays, they went to **mass**, or a worship service. Most holidays the people celebrated were in honor of saints or religious events. To become a king, vassal, or knight, a man had to take part in a religious ceremony. Church leaders ran schools and hospitals. Monks provided food and shelter for travelers. Priests alone had the right to record births, perform marriages, and conduct burials.

The Church taught that all people had sinned and had to rely on God's favor to get to heaven. The only way to receive this favor was by taking part in **sacraments**, or Roman Catholic Church rituals.

One of the most important sacraments was **holy communion**, which was celebrated at each mass. A priest blessed wheat wafers and a cup of wine that stood on the altar. He then drank the wine, ate one of the wafers, and gave a wafer to each worshipper. The Church taught that this sacrament was to remind people that Christ had died for them and to help them to be better Christians.

Communion Chalice

1. In what ways did the Church influence daily life during the Middle Ages?
2. What was the purpose of the sacraments?

A ROLE IN GOVERNMENT   During the Middle Ages, kings, nobles, and church officials worked together to govern western Europe. Only Catholics were considered members of

VILLAGE CHURCH
During the Middle Ages, the church was the religious and social center of the village. Both the local noble and the peasants contributed to the building of the church and its upkeep.
What activities took place at the village church?

society. Those who opposed the Pope on important issues lost their membership in the Church and their political rights.

Most kings could not read and write. So, they used bishops and abbots, who could read and write, to carry out such government duties as keeping records.

Bishops and abbots were an important part of the feudal system. Since many of them came from noble families, they received land from kings in return for military service. But as religious leaders they were not supposed to fight. So, they gave some of their land to knights to fight in their place. This meant that many bishops and abbots were vassals of lords and lords of vassals with the same duties as any other noble.

Priests in villages and towns conducted worship services and explained Christian teachings to the people. They also took care of the poor and strangers in their parish. Since priests were appointed by local lords, they were expected to tell the people to respect the king, nobles, and other government officials.

1. What part did bishops and abbots play in government?
2. What were priests expected to do in the villages and towns?

THE INQUISITION The Church wanted to stamp out heresy and strengthen Christian beliefs. At first, it tried to stop the spread of heresy by preaching. Then, in 1123, a council of bishops set up the **Inquisition**, or a church court, to end heresy by force.

The Church gave the people it suspected of heresy one month to confess. Those who appeared before the Inquisition before the month was up were whipped or sent to prison for a short time. Those who did not appear were seized and brought to trial. The purpose of the trial was to get a confession. Once heretics confessed, they were punished. Then, they were forgiven and allowed to become Church members again.

The court called only two witnesses. On the basis of their statements, the court decided whether or not a person was a

---

THE INQUISITION

The Inquisition was established in 1123 in an effort to strengthen the beliefs of the Church. It operated chiefly in France, Germany, Italy, and Spain. This painting shows the trial of a heretic as he hangs his head in confession. Some suspects were tortured or sentenced to die.

What punishment came to those who confessed to heresy?

heretic. Heretics who refused to confess were often tortured. A small number of people believed to be dangerous were turned over to political officials to be burned at the stake.

1. Why did the council of bishops set up the Inquisition?
2. What was the purpose of a trial by the Inquisition?
3. How did the Inquisition decide if a person was a heretic?

A NEED FOR REFORM

The Church became wealthy during the Middle Ages. Church members supported its work by contributing **tithes**, or offerings equal to 10 percent of their income. Rich nobles donated money to build large churches and gave land to monasteries. The monks worked hard to make the land produce. They became known as the best farmers in western Europe. However, the wealthier the monasteries became, the more careless many monks grew about carrying out their religious duties.

Monks were not the only ones to grow careless about religious duties. When a bishop died, his office and lands were taken over by the local lord. The lord often chose a close relative as the new bishop or sold the office for money or favors. As a result, men who were not very religious often held important Church positions. They did not keep Church rules or bother with the needs of the poor.

Before long some western Europeans grew concerned about the direction in which the Church was headed. During the late tenth and early eleventh centuries, they worked to return the Church to its Christian ideals. Devout nobles founded new monasteries that strictly followed the Benedictine Rule.

One of the most important of these monasteries was Cluny in eastern France. The monks of Cluny led simple lives, spending much of their time in prayer. They soon won the respect of the people. The monks insisted that the Church, not lords, should appoint all church officials. To set an example, they chose their own abbot, who was totally loyal to the Pope. Gradually, a number of new monasteries connected with Cluny spread across Europe. They provided deeply religious and well-educated monks to fill church offices. These monks worked to reform the Church.

1. How did the Church become wealthy during the Middle Ages?

Jeweled Cross

MONKS

Monks of the Middle Ages had an important role in preserving the heritage of the Roman Empire. They copied valuable ancient manuscripts (left). A finished manuscript is shown on the right.

How did monks help to promote church reform?

2. What effect did wealth have on the Church?
3. How did people who were not religious become bishops?
4. What did the monks of Cluny do?

THE AUTHORITY OF THE POPE

The Pope based his right to be called Pope on the traditional belief that Peter the Apostle, the first Bishop of Rome, had been chosen by Christ to be the head of the Church. When Peter died, his authority was passed on to his successors.

The Pope's power had increased gradually over hundreds of years. By the Middle Ages, the Pope had become a powerful religious and political leader. He had his own courts of justice and government offices. He ruled from Rome with the help of a group of bishops known as the College of Cardinals.

GREGORY VII   One of the most powerful Popes of the Middle Ages was Gregory VII. He supported the reform movement begun by the monks of Cluny.

Gregory had high principles, was a skillful politician, and had a strong will. He wanted to rid the Church of control by kings and feudal lords. He also wanted to increase the Pope's authority over church officials.

Gregory made many changes in his efforts to reform the Church and gain more authority. Church leaders who bought or sold church offices were removed from their posts. Bishops and priests were forbidden to marry.

In 1075, Gregory issued a document stating that the Pope was above all kings and feudal lords. Only the Pope had the power to appoint bishops and other church leaders. The document also stated that government officials who did not obey the Pope could be removed from office. Gregory told the people they did not have to obey officials who disobeyed the Pope.

Pope Gregory VII

1. What were Gregory VII's two goals as Pope?
2. What powers did the document that Gregory issued in 1075 give the Pope?

ROYAL RESISTANCE   King Henry IV of Germany thought Gregory VII's reforms were an attack on his power as king. So, he ignored Gregory's decrees and continued to appoint bishops in his kingdom. Gregory condemned Henry for disobeying him. Henry answered by calling a council of his bishops to remove Gregory from the office of Pope. Henry declared that as king he was God's representative on earth and had the right to remove Popes who did not agree with him. Gregory responded by declaring that Henry was no longer a king or a member of the Church.

German nobles who were Henry's enemies asked Gregory to come to Germany and choose a new king. Upon hearing this, Henry decided it was better to make peace with Gregory than to lose his throne. In the winter of 1077, he hurried across the Alps to Italy to ask Gregory's forgiveness. Gregory, who was staying

HENRY IV AT CANOSSA

King Henry IV of Germany sought the pardon of Pope Gregory VII at the castle of Canossa. Here Gregory pleads with a church official to help him receive a pardon from the Pope.

What powers did the Pope have during the Middle Ages?

at the castle of Canossa in northern Italy, refused to see Henry or pardon him.

Henry, however, would not give up. For three days, he stood barefooted outside the castle of Canossa waiting for Gregory to see him. At last, Gregory pardoned him, and Henry returned home as king.

1. What did Henry IV do to anger Pope Gregory VII?
2. What made Henry IV decide to seek the Pope's forgiveness?

THE CONCORDAT OF WORMS   Gregory VII won a victory at Canossa. But it did not end the struggle between the Pope and the king of Germany. Not until 1122 was an agreement reached between them. Because the agreement was signed in the

German city of Worms, it came to be known as the Concordat of Worms.

The Concordat gave both the Pope and the king a part in the selection of bishops. The king was to give the new bishop a **scepter**, or rod, as a symbol of the bishop's ownership of land and his political duties. The Pope was to give the bishop a staff and a ring as symbols of the bishop's religious authority.

The Concordat of Worms was supposed to be a compromise that would please both the king and the Pope. But it actually increased the Pope's political power. Under feudalism, feudal lords controlled the appointment of church officials. Under the Concordat, no one could hold a church office without final approval from the Pope.

1. What was the purpose of the Concordat of Worms?
2. What did the Concordat actually do?

St. Francis

FRIARS

During the early 1200's, preachers called **friars** traveled all over Europe. Since they sold all their possessions before becoming friars, they depended on gifts of food and money from the people. For this reason, they were called **mendicants**, or beggars.

The friars followed many monastic rules, including the one about not marrying. But they did not shut themselves off from the rest of the world. Instead, they lived in towns and worked to bring Christianity directly to the people.

Two well-known **orders**, or groups, of friars were the Franciscans and the Dominicans. The Franciscan order was founded early in 1200 by Francis of Assisi, the son of a wealthy Italian cloth merchant. Franciscans were known for their cheerfulness and for their confidence that God would take care of them. They had a deep love of nature. They believed it was a gift of God and should be respected.

The Dominican order was started in 1220 by a Spanish monk named Dominic. Like the Franciscans, the Dominicans lived a life of poverty. Through their words and deeds, they kept many people loyal to Church teachings.

1. In what way were friars different from other monks?
2. What did the Franciscans believe?
3. How did the Dominicans keep many people loyal to Church teachings?

LEARNING

During the Middle Ages, learning was in the hands of the Church. The parish clergy set up schools in **cathedrals**, or churches headed by bishops. The schools were to prepare the sons of nobles for service in the Church. But not every boy who went to school wanted to be a priest or monk. So, the schools also trained students to be government officials, lawyers, and teachers. Seven subjects, known as the seven liberal arts, were taught in the cathedral schools. They were grammar, rhetoric, logic, arithmetic, geometry, astronomy, and music.

Students paid a fee to attend classes held in a cold, dark hall rented by the teacher. They sat on a floor that was covered with straw to keep out the dampness. Books were scarce and costly. So, students had to listen carefully to what the teacher read from an ancient text. Then, they memorized the teacher's explanation of what was read.

1. Who attended cathedral schools?
2. What was taught at the cathedral schools?
3. What were classes like in the cathedral schools?

Stained-glass Window

UNIVERSITIES   After a while, students began to complain that teachers held few classes and did not cover enough material. Teachers began to complain that many untrained people were teaching students. So, students and teachers decided to join together and form unions to make some changes in the system. These unions became **universities**, or groups of teachers and students devoted to learning. A church official called a **chancellor** headed each university. No one could teach without the chancellor's permission.

Universities were alike in many ways. They all had well-organized courses of study. Classes were held at set times each day. In class, students listened to lectures on a specific subject. All students, whether or not they planned to teach, had to pass examinations to receive the right to teach. Lecturers had to be at least 21 years old and have studied for at least 6 years.

By the end of the 1200's, universities had spread throughout Europe. The university in Paris was known for its training of religious scholars. The one in Bologna, Italy, was noted for the study of law. The one in Salerno, Italy, was famous for its medical training.

University Bell Tower

MEDIEVAL UNIVERSITIES

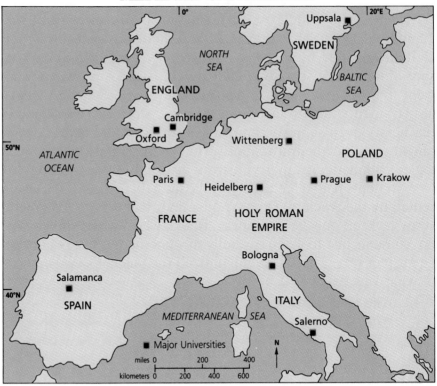

Students from all over Europe came to the universities to learn and to hear debates between the great teachers. At first, the students lived in boarding houses. Later, wealthy sponsors built special buildings in which the students could live.

Students were often noisy and argued among themselves or with townspeople. To make the students behave, the universities set up rules. Students who missed daily mass, disturbed the peace, or took part in gambling or sword practice were fined and reprimanded.

1. Who started universities? Why were they started?
2. What were four things all universities had in common?
3. Why did universities set up rules?

SCHOLARS AND PHILOSOPHERS　　In the Middle Ages, the most important areas of learning were philosophy and **theology**, or the study of religious thought. Scholars tried to bring these two areas together.

One famous medieval scholar was Peter Abelard. He set up his own school in Paris and attracted a large student following. Although the Church forbade scholars to marry, Abelard wed a pupil named Heloise. Heloise's uncle opposed the marriage and separated the couple. In later years, Abelard and Heloise wrote love letters to each other. The letters came to be considered among the most beautiful of their kind in the history of world literature.

Like the ancient Greeks, Abelard believed the human mind could discover the truth. He wrote a book called *Sic et Non*, or *Yes and No*, that showed how to use reason and logic in the study of religious ideas. Abelard did this by asking a question and presenting various expert views on the issue. He then asked students to form their own judgments.

Many church leaders opposed Abelard's emphasis on reason. They feared he was giving more importance to reason than to faith. As a result, Abelard had to give up teaching and retire to a monastery.

Another famous scholar was Thomas Aquinas, an Italian noble who taught philosophy and theology in Paris and Naples.

MEDIEVAL LEARNING

Universities brought together teachers and students from all over Europe. In this print, a teacher at the University of Paris lectures his students on a classical text. What did a scholar have to do in order to become a teacher?

Thomas Aquinas

His lectures and writings impressed many people, and he became known as the "angelic doctor."

Aquinas believed that both faith and reason were gifts of God. He saw no conflict between the two. He thought reason helped people know what the world was really like. It helped people lead a good life. He thought faith revealed religious truths to people. It helped them find life after death.

Aquinas wrote a book called *Summa Theologica*, or *A Summary of Religious Thought*. He used Abelard's method of asking questions and presenting different opinions. But unlike Abelard, he gave a definite answer to the questions and stated his reasons for the answer. Aquinas's teachings and way of thinking later were accepted and promoted by the Church.

1. What were the most important areas of learning during the Middle Ages?
2. What did Peter Abelard believe?
3. What did Thomas Aquinas believe?

CHAPTER 25 REVIEW

SUMMARY

1. The Roman Catholic Church was the center of daily life during the Middle Ages.

2. Most kings could not read and write and used bishops and abbots to carry out many government duties.

3. The Church tried to stamp out heresy, first by preaching and later by the Inquisition.

4. Increased wealth led many members of the clergy to grow careless about their religious duties.

5. Around 1000, the monks of Cluny began working to reform the Church by giving attention to Christian ideals.

6. In 1075, Pope Gregory VII issued a document stating that the Pope was above all kings and feudal lords.

7. King Henry IV of Germany disagreed with the Pope and stated that the king was supreme.

8. The struggle between Pope Gregory VII and King Henry IV of Germany was ended in 1122 by the signing of the Concordat of Worms.

9. The Concordat of Worms, which gave both Pope and king a part in selecting bishops, increased the Pope's power.

10. During the early 1200's, preachers called friars tried to bring Christianity directly to the people.

11. By the 1200's, universities, which grew from cathedral schools, had spread throughout Europe.

12. During the Middle Ages, scholars tried to bring faith and reason together.

BUILDING VOCABULARY

1. *Identify the following:*

Cluny	Gregory VII	Concordat of Worms	seven liberal arts
Peter the Apostle	Henry IV	Franciscans	Peter Abelard
College of Cardinals	Canossa	Dominicans	Thomas Aquinas

2. *Define the following:*

mass	tithes	mendicants	universities
sacraments	scepter	orders	chancellor
holy communion	friars	cathedrals	theology
Inquisition			

REVIEWING THE FACTS

1. What was the official language of the Roman Catholic Church?
2. Why did kings use bishops and abbots to carry out many government duties?
3. What happened to heretics who were believed to be dangerous?
4. Why did many monks grow careless about carrying out religious duties?
5. To whom did the abbot of the monastery of Cluny give complete loyalty?
6. On what did the Bishop of Rome base the claim that he alone had the right to be called Pope?
7. Why did Henry IV ignore Gregory VII's decrees at first?
8. Why did some German nobles ask Gregory VII to come to Germany?
9. Why were friars called mendicants?
10. What did medieval scholars try to do with philosophy and theology?

DISCUSSING IMPORTANT IDEAS

1. Do you think it is a good idea for church leaders to help run the government? Why or why not?
2. What kind of civilization did church leaders want to develop in western Europe? Why?
3. If you had been a German noble, would you have supported Henry IV or Gregory VII? Explain.
4. Do you think you would have enjoyed being a student in a medieval university? Why or why not?

USING MAPS

Study the map on page 384, and answer the following questions:

1. What is the subject of the map?
2. How many universities are shown?
3. Which university is located about 41° north latitude and 10° east longitude?
4. Which university is farthest north?
5. About how far is Paris from Wittenberg?
6. What territory is located directly north of Italy?

CHAPTER 26
THE CRUSADES

For centuries, Christians from western Europe had visited shrines in Jerusalem. Then, in 1070, a people called Seljuk Turks conquered Palestine and took control of the Christian shrines. They began to persecute Christians and kept them from traveling in Palestine.

When news of the events in the Holy Land reached Christians in western Europe, they were shocked and angered. The result was a series of holy wars called **crusades**, which went on for about 200 years.

A Call to War

Even after they had taken Palestine, Turkish armies continued to threaten the Byzantine Empire. The Byzantine emperor turned to Pope Gregory VII for military aid. But the Pope was too involved in church reforms to help. After Gregory VII died, a new Pope named Urban II took his place. Urban II agreed to help the Byzantines. He believed that together the western Europeans and the Byzantines could defeat the Turks and gain control of Palestine. He hoped that in return for his help, the Orthodox Church would again unite with the Roman Catholic Church and accept him as its religious leader.

In 1095, Urban attended a church council in the town of Clermont in eastern France. After the meeting, the Pope spoke before a large crowd. He told them that Europe's lords should stop fighting among themselves. Instead, they should fight in a crusade against the Turks.

Urban reminded the people that Europe was not producing enough food to feed its growing population. Palestine, on the other hand, had rich, fertile land on which any knight could live in comfort. The Pope promised that those who went on a crusade would be free of debts and taxes. He also promised that God would pardon the sins of those who died in battle. He encouraged soldiers to go to Palestine wearing a red cross on their tunics as a symbol of obedience to God.

1. Why did Pope Urban II agree to help the Byzantines?
2. How did Urban II encourage people to go on a crusade?

THE PEASANTS' CRUSADE   Urban II spent nine months traveling from one European city to another preaching for a crusade. The people of Europe responded eagerly to his appeal. As a sign of their religious devotion, they adopted the war cry *Deus vult*, which means "It is the will of God." The people felt it was their duty as Christians to win back the Holy Land. But they also had other reasons for being willing to fight. Nobles hoped to gain more land for themselves in Palestine. They also wanted the fame a crusade could bring. Peasants wanted to escape from their hard labor on the land.

Urban II wanted the nobles to plan and lead the crusade. But while they were drawing up their plans, the peasants grew impatient and formed their own armies. Even though they lacked training in warfare, they believed God would help them.

In the spring of 1096, about 12,000 French peasants began the long journey to Palestine. They were led by two men, Peter the Hermit and Walter the Penniless. The two leaders rode on donkeys and preached to crowds along the way. The peasants traveled behind them. Two-wheeled carts pulled by oxen carried their belongings. At the same time, two other groups of peasants also set out from Germany.

As the peasant armies marched through Europe, they did a lot of fighting. They attacked farmers, looted cottages, and burned wheat fields. They **massacred**, or killed, all the Jews they could find. They thought that since Jews were not Christians, they were enemies. Frightened villagers tried to keep the armies away from their homes. At night, they often poisoned wells and attacked crusader camps.

PETER THE HERMIT

Peter the Hermit was a powerful monk, who traveled throughout France preaching to crowds along the way. He convinced many European Christians to go on a crusade to regain the Holy Land from the Muslims.
What group of people supported Peter the Hermit's call for a crusade?

By the time the peasant armies reached Constantinople, they had lost about a third of their number. Their clothes were in rags, and they had no money. They wandered through the streets of the city attacking passersby and stealing from markets and homes. The Byzantine emperor had expected the Pope to send trained warriors, not unskilled peasants. The activities of the western Europeans worried him, and he wanted to get them out of his capital. So, he gave them supplies and ships and sent them to fight the Turks in Asia Minor.

In Asia Minor, the peasant armies tried to take the Turkish capital of Nicaea. They were almost completely destroyed by a force of Turkish bowmen.

1. Why were western Europeans eager to go on a crusade?
2. What did the peasant armies do on their long journey to Constantinople?
3. What happened to the peasant armies after they reached Constantinople?

THE NOBLES' CRUSADE   In 1097, the nobles set out on their crusade. Great lords led each army. They brought with them their vassals, wives, children, clerks, cooks, and blacksmiths. The crusade was very costly, as each lord had to provide his own battle equipment, wagons, supplies, and horses. Nobles often had to borrow money or sell their land or jewelry to meet their expenses.

On their way to Palestine, the nobles stopped at Constantinople. But they did not get along with the Byzantines any better than the peasants had. The crusaders' crude manners shocked the cultured Byzantines. The Byzantines' wealth and learning made the crusaders so jealous that some of them wanted to take Constantinople and its riches. The Byzantine emperor finally convinced the nobles to leave for Asia Minor. The crusaders took an oath to obey the emperor in return for supplies and military aid.

About 30,000 crusaders arrived in Asia Minor and defeated the Turks. From there, they moved south through the desert to Syria. The crusaders, however, were not prepared for the heat and did not have enough food or water. As a result, many died of starvation or thirst. Those who survived pushed ahead to Palestine, capturing Syrian cities along the way.

CRUSADERS MARCH TO JERUSALEM

After a long and tiring journey, the first crusaders reached the Holy Land in the summer of 1099. This illustration shows a religious procession of crusaders and other church members carrying a large cross to celebrate their arrival.
Why did the crusaders want to take Jerusalem?

In 1099, the 12,000 surviving crusaders reached Jerusalem. They captured the Holy City, killing Turks, Jews, and Christians alike. They looted the city, taking gold, silver, horses, mules, and houses filled with all kinds of goods.

1. Who went with the nobles on their crusade?
2. What problems did the crusaders have in Constantinople?
3. Why did so many crusaders die on the journey between Asia Minor and Palestine?
4. How did the crusaders treat the people of Jerusalem?

THE KINGDOM BEYOND THE SEA

After the crusaders captured Jerusalem, they lost much of their religious enthusiasm. Many knights returned to their homes in western Europe. Those who remained in Palestine organized the territories they had won into four feudal kingdoms called Outremer, or "the kingdom beyond the sea."

MILITARY ORDERS   The crusaders built fortresses to protect the chief towns of their kingdoms. Two **military orders**, or groups of warrior-monks, were formed to take charge of the defense and care of Outremer. They were the Knights Templar and the Knights Hospitaller. The monks took oaths never to marry and to live in poverty. Although they protected Christian visitors and helped the poor and sick, they spent most of their time fighting the Turks.

The warrior-monks were greatly respected for their bravery and way of life. Their military orders were given gifts of land, and soon they became rich. Their influence reached Europe, where they built houses to train new members and to care for elderly knights. Many members of the military orders became bankers and traders.

1. What did the knights who remained in Palestine do with the territories they had won?
2. What was the job of the military orders?
3. How did the military orders grow rich and powerful?

A NEW WAY OF LIFE   The crusaders took over estates of rich Turkish and Arab Muslims. The lords divided the properties among themselves and their best knights. Arab peasants worked the land for them and cared for the orchards and vineyards. Other Arabs served as advisors and helped them manage their estates. Friendships developed between the crusaders and the Muslims. The Muslims admired the crusaders' bravery. The crusaders discovered that Arab scholars knew more than they did about medicine, science, and mathematics.

When the lords were not fighting Turks, they ran their estates, went hunting, and attended the local court. Each lord built a castle more magnificent than the one he had in Europe. The castle was more than a fortress. It was a comfortable place in which to live, with a large dining room, living room, and bedchambers. The rooms had marble walls and painted ceilings and were decorated with silk hangings, carpets, silver and gold objects, and elegant furnishings.

Arab Scholars

CRUSADER FORTRESS
The crusaders built fortresses to protect their settlements from Muslim attacks. Warriors and their servants lived in these fortresses. This castle, which stands along the coast of Lebanon, was built by the Knights Hospitaller in the 1100's. How did the crusaders govern their territories in the Holy Land?

The crusaders found that their old style of living did not suit their new surroundings. It was too hot in Palestine to wear fur and woolen clothes. The men began to wear turbans and loose, flowing silk or linen robes. They did, however, continue to fight in armor. The women wore jeweled tunics and magnificent gowns made with gold thread. They adopted the Muslim custom of wearing veils when they were outdoors and learned to use makeup and perfume. The heat also led the westerners to develop the habit of bathing.

The crusaders changed their eating habits, too. It was too hot to eat the heavy, solid foods they were used to. They learned to have light meals with less meat and more fruit and vegetables and such new foods as rice, oranges, figs, and melons.

The crusaders led an easier life in Palestine than they had at home. Still, they had problems adjusting. Many died in battle against the Turks or in fights among themselves over rights and lands. Others could not survive the hot climate.

1. What kind of relationship developed between the crusaders and the Muslims?
2. What kind of homes did the lords build?
3. What changes did the westerners who stayed in Palestine make in their way of life?
4. What problems did the crusaders face in this way of life?

SALADIN AND THE LAST CRUSADES

In 1174, a Muslim military leader named Saladin became the ruler of Egypt. He united Muslims throughout the Near East and started a jihad against the Christians. Saladin's armies were well organized, and his soldiers were devoted to Islam. Groups of warriors headed by leaders called *emirs* made up the armies. Many emirs were known for their honesty and the courteous way they treated their captives. The emirs often were shocked by the cruelty and greed of the Christian warriors.

Saladin

Saladin's soldiers rode into battle on swift ponies. Their weapons were short bows. Crusaders found it difficult to fight the Muslims. The crusaders' armor was heavy, their swords were too long to handle easily, and their horses were not protected. They had to learn to rely on a new weapon called the **crossbow**, which fired an arrow with great force and speed.

In 1187, Saladin's armies took Jerusalem. Saladin was considerate toward those he had defeated. When he refused to massacre Jerusalem's Christian citizens, he won the respect of many crusaders.

1. What was Saladin's army like?
2. Why did the crusaders find it difficult to fight Saladin?
3. How did Saladin win the respect of the crusaders?

CRUSADE OF KINGS   After Saladin's victory, the Church urged another crusade. This time the western armies were led by King Richard the Lionheart of England, Emperor Frederick Barbarossa of Germany, and King Philip Augustus of France. They were the three most powerful rulers in Europe.

This Crusade of Kings, however, proved to be a failure. Frederick died in Asia Minor, and many of his troops returned home without ever having fought a battle. Richard and Philip were enemies and were always quarreling. They did take a few coastal cities in Palestine together. Then, Philip returned home. Richard and his armies had to continue the crusade alone.

RICHARD THE LIONHEART
King Richard the Lionheart of England was a leader in the Crusade of Kings. Although he won many battles against the Muslims, he failed to capture Jerusalem. Finally, he left the Holy Land and returned to England.
Why did the Crusade of Kings fail?

Richard was a brave warrior, but he could not defeat Saladin. In spite of their differences, Richard and Saladin came to respect one another. Years later, stories were told in Europe about the kindnesses they showed each other. One story tells how Saladin sent Richard two fresh horses when his horse was killed in battle.

After three years, Richard gave up and signed a truce with Saladin. The crusaders still controlled large areas of Palestine, but Jerusalem remained in Muslim hands.

1. Who led the Crusade of Kings?
2. Why did Richard the Lionheart have to fight the crusade alone?
3. How did Richard and Saladin regard one another?
4. What was the outcome of the Crusade of Kings?

THE LOSS OF AN IDEAL   In 1204, Pope Innocent III called for yet another crusade. Knights from all over Europe answered the call. They decided not to take the land route to Palestine this time. Instead, they chose to go by ship from the Italian port of Venice. Rich merchants there wanted Venice to replace Constantinople as the trading center of the eastern Mediterranean. The crusaders agreed to pay the merchants a large sum of money and to share half of all their conquests with the Venetians. In return, the Venetians agreed to supply the crusaders with ships and equipment.

When the soldiers found they could not pay all they owed, they agreed to conquer the island of Zara for the Venetians. Then, the Venetians convinced them to capture Constantinople. For three days, the crusaders and the Venetians burned and looted Constantinople. They stole valuable articles from palaces, churches, libraries, homes, and shops. Many priceless manuscripts and works of art were either taken to Venice, lost, or destroyed.

The soldiers finally decided not to go to Palestine. Instead, they stayed in Constantinople and divided the city with the

---

CAPTURE OF CONSTANTINOPLE

In 1204, crusaders fought the Byzantines instead of the Muslims. They seized Constantinople after a fierce battle and overthrew the Byzantine emperor. The crusaders ruled Constantinople until 1261.

Why did the crusaders take Constantinople?

Venetians. The conduct of the soldiers shocked many western Europeans, who lost respect for the crusaders.

Several other crusades were fought during the 1200's, but the Europeans did not win any of them. The saddest of all the crusades was the Children's Crusade. A group of French children, led by a peasant boy named Stephen of Cloyes, set sail from Marseilles, France, in 1212. Most of the children never reached Palestine. Along the way they were sold into slavery by men from the ships on which they sailed. At the same time, another group of children set forth on foot from Germany, intending to march toward Italy. Most of them, however, died of starvation or disease.

In 1291, the Muslims took over the city of Acre, the last Christian stronghold. The Muslims had won the Crusades and now ruled all the territory in Palestine that the crusaders had fought to control.

1. Why were the Venetians willing to help the crusaders?
2. What did the crusaders and Venetians do in Constantinople?

CHILDREN'S CRUSADE

Many children throughout Europe decided to go on a crusade to the Holy Land. Here, boys and girls from a French village begin their long journey. What was the result of the Children's Crusade?

THE CRUSADES

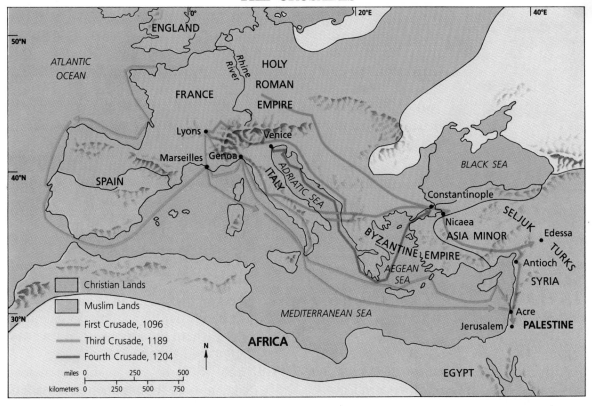

EFFECTS OF THE CRUSADES

The Crusades had an important effect on the future of both the East and the West. They brought the East into closer contact with the West. As a result, Europe was no longer cut off from the rest of the world.

The Crusades affected the Church in the opposite way from that planned by Urban II. The deeds and actions of western Europeans made the Byzantines so angry that the split between eastern and western Christianity became permanent. At the same time, the Byzantine Empire was so weakened by the Crusades that it could no longer defend itself. Its decline left Europe open to Turkish attack.

In the West, the Crusades helped to break down feudalism. While feudal lords were fighting in Palestine, kings at home increased their authority. The desire for wealth, power, and land grew and began to overshadow the religious ideals of many western Europeans.

Jeweled Box

The crusaders' contact with the cultured Byzantines and Muslims led western Europeans to renew their interest in learning and invention. At the same time, they began to demand some of the luxuries of the East. To meet these demands, the Europeans opened up new trade routes. European merchants brought home spices, sugar, lemons, melons, rugs, tapestries, and richly woven cloth. As trade grew, so did the cities of western Europe. As a result, the cities became very important in the life of the late Middle Ages.

1. What effect did the crusades have on the Byzantine Empire?
2. What effect did the crusades have on trade?

CHAPTER 26 REVIEW

SUMMARY

1. In 1070, the Seljuk Turks conquered Palestine and began to keep Christians from visiting shrines in Jerusalem.

2. In 1095, Pope Urban II agreed to help the Byzantines against the Turks and called on the people of western Europe to join in a crusade.

3. In 1096, a large group of peasants started a crusade of their own, but they were almost completely destroyed.

4. In 1097, the nobles set out on a well-organized and well-equipped crusade that succeeded in reaching Jerusalem.

5. In 1099, nobles captured Jerusalem from the Turks.

6. Many crusaders remained in Palestine, where they set up four feudal kingdoms.

7. Military orders made up of warrior-monks were formed to take charge of the defense of the feudal kingdoms established in Palestine.

8. The crusaders who remained in Palestine developed a new way of life.

9. In 1174, Saladin started a jihad against Christians, which ended in 1187.

10. The kings of England, Germany, and France set out on another crusade, but only Richard the Lionheart of England continued fighting.

11. Since Richard was unable to defeat Saladin, the Muslims and the crusaders signed a truce.

12. In 1204, another crusade began, but instead of going by land, the crusaders decided to go by ship from Venice.

13. Instead of going to Palestine, the crusaders and the Venetians burned and looted Constantinople.

14. Several other unsuccessful crusades, including the Children's Crusade, took place during the 1200's.

15. By 1291, the Muslims had regained all the territory in Palestine that the crusaders had conquered earlier.

16. The Crusades made permanent the split between eastern Christianity and western Christianity.

17. The Crusades helped to break down feudalism and encouraged the growth of towns and trade in western Europe.

BUILDING VOCABULARY

1. *Identify the following:*

Seljuk Turks	Knights Templar	Richard the Lionheart	Innocent III
Urban II	Knights Hospitaller	Frederick Barbarossa	Venice
Peter the Hermit	Saladin	Philip Augustus	Zara
Walter the Penniless			Acre

2. *Define the following:*

crusades	military orders	*emirs*	crossbow
massacred			

REVIEWING THE FACTS

1. What two important events took place in the town of Clermont in 1095?
2. Why did the crusaders wear a red cross on their tunics?
3. Why did the peasants set off on their own crusade instead of waiting for the nobles to lead them?
4. Why was the Byzantine emperor upset when the Peasants' Crusade arrived in Constantinople?
5. What effect did the climate in Palestine have on the crusaders?
6. What happened during the Children's Crusade?
7. Why did the split between eastern Christianity and western Christianity become permanent?
8. How did the Crusades affect the power of western Europe's kings?
9. How successful were the crusaders in realizing their goals?
10. Why did western European cities become more important during the late Middle Ages?

DISCUSSING IMPORTANT IDEAS

1. If you had heard Urban II speak, would you have gone on a crusade? Explain.
2. Do you approve or disapprove of the way the crusaders behaved when they captured Jerusalem? Explain.
3. If you had been a crusader, would you have settled in Palestine or returned home? Explain.
4. Do you think you might have enjoyed knowing Saladin? Why or why not?

USING MAPS

Study the map on page 399, and answer the following questions:

1. To what country were the crusaders traveling?
2. Was Palestine Christian or Muslim?
3. When did the Third Crusade begin?
4. What is the latitude and longitude of the city of Jerusalem?
5. About how far is Venice from Constantinople by land?

UNIT 8 REVIEW

SUMMARY

1. During the Middle Ages, a system of feudalism developed. It divided western Europe into thousands of territories owned and governed by warrior-nobles.

2. Feudal society was divided into three main groups—clergy, nobles, and peasants and townspeople.

3. During the Middle Ages, the Roman Catholic Church united western Europe, influenced almost every part of daily life, and helped to preserve Greco-Roman culture.

4. During the Middle Ages, the Pope, who ruled from Rome, became the most pow-erful political and religious leader in western Europe.

5. To restore Christian control of Palestine after the Muslim conquest in the eleventh century, western Europeans began a series of unsuccessful holy wars called crusades. They lasted 200 years.

6. The Crusades brought the East and the West into closer contact, made the split between eastern and western Christianity permanent, and helped to break down feudalism. They also renewed western European interest in learning and led to the opening of new trade routes.

REVIEWING THE MAIN IDEAS

1. Describe the ways in which the Church supported the feudal system.

2. Explain why trade and town life declined during the Middle Ages.

DEVELOPING SKILLS

Artifacts are a very important source of information about the past. So are textbooks. Both artifacts and textbooks provide all sorts of data about people and events.

Yet, there is a major difference between these two types of sources. An artifact is considered a **primary source**, or a direct record of what people have done or thought in the past. A textbook is a **secondary source**, or a record based on primary sources or on other second-hand accounts.

Primary sources include such things as buildings, coins, inscriptions, tools, weapons, diaries, letters, and eye-witness accounts. Secondary sources include such things as textbooks, newspaper reports, historical novels, and paintings of past events.

It is important to be able to tell the difference between a primary source and a secondary source. This exercise is designed to give you practice in this skill. Read the following list and tell which items are primary and which are secondary sources.

1. the ruins of a medieval castle

2. a suit of armor

3. an eighteenth-century painting of a joust

4. a horse collar dating from the Middle Ages

5. a textbook account of the activities of the Inquisition

6. a document issued by Pope Gregory VII

7. the Concordat of Worms

8. a list of courses offered at the University of Bologna in 1250

9. a letter Heloise wrote to Abelard

10. a poem about the romance between Abelard and Heloise

11. *Summa Theologica*

12. a book review of *Summa Theologica*

13. a report of Pope Urban's speech at Clermont

14. a two-wheeled cart used during the Peasants' Crusade

15. a linen robe worn by a crusader

16. a twelfth-century painting of Saladin and Richard the Lionheart

17. a Venetian coin dated 1204

SUGGESTED UNIT PROJECTS

1. Make a booklet of pictures of medieval castles. Under each picture, write a description of the castle's features.

2. Make a chart comparing the life of a lord, a serf, and a monk. Include information about the home, clothing, food, daily activities, and education of each.

3. Participate in a debate between two groups of students about the quarrel between Pope Gregory VII and King Henry IV of Germany. One group will present and defend Gregory's point of view. The other group will present and defend Henry's point of view.

4. Prepare a poster advertising a medieval university. Include the courses offered and jobs graduates will be able to fill.

5. Write a letter that a crusader who has helped capture Jerusalem might have sent to his family in England.

SUGGESTED READING

Macaulay, David. *Cathedral.* Boston: Houghton Mifflin, 1973. A description of how nine different craftspeople and their assistants labored 86 years to held build a cathedral.

Namioka, Lensey. *The Samurai and the Long-Nosed Devils.* New York: David McKay, 1976. The story of two samurai who hire themselves out as bodyguards to a group of foreigners.

Reeves, James. *The Shadow of the Hawk, and Other Stories.* New York: Seabury Press, 1977. A retelling in prose of Marie de France's poems about adventure, love, and the struggle between good and evil during the Middle Ages.

Rosenfield, James. *The Lion and the Lily.* New York: Dodd, Mead, 1972. The story of Philip Augustus, who became king of France at the age of 15, and of Henry II of England, who wanted the French crown for his son.

Unstead, Robert J. *Living In A Castle.* Reading, Mass.: Addison-Wesley, 1973. A description of everyday life in a medieval castle.

Unstead, Robert J. *Living In A Crusader Land.* Reading, Mass.: Addison-Wesley, 1973. A description of everyday life in the four kingdoms established by the Crusaders in Palestine.

UNIT 9

900	925	950 **962** Otto I crowned Holy Ror
	936 Otto I becomes king of Germany	
1050	**1075**	**1100**
1066 William the Conqueror wins Battle of Hastings	**1086** Domesday Book	**c. 1100** First guilds formed Flanders becomes important trade center
c. 1070 Italian coastal towns control Mediterranean trade		**1108** Louis VI becomes king o France
1200 **1209** Frederick II becomes Holy Roman Emperor **1215** Magna Charta **1216** Henry III becomes king of England	**1225** **1226** Louis IX becomes king of France	**1250**
1350	**1375**	**1400** **1417** Battle of Aginco
1500	**1525**	**1550**

THE LATE MIDDLE AGES

'5	**1000** **c. 1000** Towns and trade routes begin to develop in Europe **987** Hugh Capet becomes king of France	**1025** **1042** Edward the Confessor becomes king of England
25	**1150** **1152** Frederick I becomes Holy Roman Emperor **1166** Henry II becomes king of England	**1175** **1180** Philip Augustus begins rule in France **1189** Richard the Lionheart becomes king of England **1199** John becomes king of England
75 **72** Edward I calls meeting of Parliament **1285** Philip IV begins rule in France	**1300**	**1325** **1339** Hundred Years' War begins **1347** Battle of Crécy
25 **429** Joan of Arc fights for France	**1450** **1453** Hundred Years' War ends **1469** Ferdinand II of Aragon and Isabella of Castile marry	**1475** **1485** Henry VII establishes Tudor Dynasty in England **1492** Moors surrender Granada to Spain **1493** Maximilian I becomes Holy Roman Emperor

1. WHAT LED TO THE GROWTH OF TOWNS AND TRADE IN WESTERN EUROPE DURING THE LATE MIDDLE AGES?
2. WHAT DID KINGS DO TO BUILD STRONG NATIONS IN WESTERN EUROPE?

The period from 1000 to 1500 is called the Late Middle Ages. During this time, the people of western Europe became aware of what was taking place outside the manors on which most of them lived. Some even heard about the ways of life in other civilizations.

As outside invasions ended, western European life became more orderly. Farmers learned to grow more food, and the population grew larger. People became more confident about the future. Trade and the exchange of ideas increased.

As trade grew, so did towns. In time, they became great trade centers and attracted new residents. The people who lived in the towns were mostly merchants, artisans, and bankers. They formed a new class, higher than peasants but lower than nobles. Many of the townspeople became as wealthy as, or wealthier than, the nobles. Their power and influence began to grow, and the power and influence of feudalism began to decline. Over time, the towns became independent communities outside the feudal system.

Nations began to replace the many small feudal territories. Kings raised armies and used them to weaken the power of nobles. As the kings became stronger, they tried to take power away from each other. Warfare spread over much of Europe. Some kings gained even more power. These kings succeeded in forming strong governments that won the loyalty of the people. Thus, they laid the foundations for the modern nations of western Europe.

CHAPTER 27
RISE OF TOWNS AND TRADE

During the eleventh and twelfth centuries, things went well for the people of western Europe. For the first time since the fall of Rome, births outnumbered deaths. Better farming methods helped farmers produce enough food for the growing population. Many peasants left the fields to work in mines or village workshops. They became skilled artisans and began to make cloth and metal products.

Western nobles, however, wanted such luxury items as sugar, spices, silks, and dyes. These goods came from the East. So, European merchants carried western products to the East to exchange for luxury goods. The increased trade had a major effect on western European life.

TRADING CENTERS

The growth of trade led to the rise of the first large trading centers of the Middle Ages. They were located on the important sea routes that connected western Europe with the Mediterranean Sea, Russia, and Scandinavia. Two of the earliest and most important trading centers were Venice and Flanders.

Money Changers

VENICE   Venice was an island port in the Adriatic Sea close to the coast of Italy. It was founded in the 500's by people fleeing from the Germans.

Since the land was not very fertile, the early Venetians had to depend on the sea for a living. They fished in the Adriatic and produced salt from the seawater. They exchanged their products for wheat from towns on the mainland of Italy. They also traded wheat, wine, and slaves to the Byzantines in return for fabrics and spices.

During the 1100's, Venice became a leading port and the home of Europe's fulltime merchants. Venetian merchants learned to read and write, use money, and keep records. In time, they developed a banking system suited to their needs.

Venice's prosperity soon spread to other parts of Italy. Towns on the Italian mainland began to make cloth, which they sent to Venice to be shipped to other areas. Before long, other Italian towns along the seacoast became shipping centers.

The navies of the Italian trading towns drove the Muslims from the Mediterranean, making it safe for Italian seafarers to move into new areas. As a result, the Italians opened the Near East to Europeans.

However, the Italian trading towns began to quarrel among themselves over profits and trade routes. While they were quarreling, towns along Europe's Atlantic coast began to develop new trade routes. By 1500, these towns had become more powerful than the Italian ones.

1. What led to the development and growth of Venice's trade?
2. What effect did Venice's prosperity have on other Italian towns?
3. What led to the decline of the Italian trading centers?

FLANDERS   Flanders, an area of small towns and villages on the northwest coast of Europe, was the earliest Atlantic trading center. Today, it is part of Belgium.

The low, marshy land of Flanders was not well suited to farming. So, the Flemish people raised sheep and used the wool to develop a weaving industry. The cloth they produced gained fame for its quality and soon was in heavy demand.

Flanders' many rivers and seacoast helped it become a trading center. The rivers joined together before they emptied into the North Sea. Where the rivers met, the water was deep enough for the Flemish to build harbors. From these harbors they shipped their valuable woolen cloth to other lands.

Flanders soon became an important stopping place for ships traveling along the Atlantic coast from Scandinavia to the

MEDIEVAL TOWNS AND TRADE ROUTES

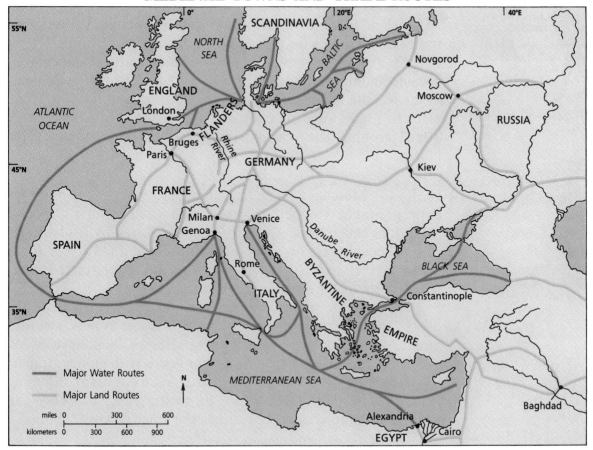

Mediterranean Sea. It also became an important link in the trade route that began in Constantinople and continued to the North Sea.

By 1300, Flanders' most important trading partner was England. Flemish traders set up shop in the dockyards of London. They relied on English shepherds to supply them with wool, which they sent to Flanders to be made into cloth. The finished cloth was then shipped back to England.

1. Why did the Flemish raise sheep? What did they do with the wool from the sheep?
2. How did Flanders' location help it become an important trading center?
3. What trade arrangements did Flanders have with England?

MERCHANTS

Medieval Merchant

As sea trade grew, so did overland trade. Italian towns began sending goods across the Alps to areas in the North. Soon, an overland trade route connected Italy and Flanders. From this route, other routes developed and spread across Europe.

As a result of new trade routes and markets, merchants became an important part of European life. The first merchants of the Middle Ages were mostly adventurers who traveled from place to place. As protection against robbers, they traveled in armed groups. They carried their goods in wagons pulled by horses.

FAIRS   Merchants traveling along the main route through eastern France stopped to trade with each other at special gatherings called **fairs**. The fairs were sponsored by feudal lords who collected taxes on sales. Fairs were held once a year for a few weeks at selected places. They eventually attracted merchants from as far away as England and Egypt.

At the fairs, merchants could buy and sell goods or settle debts. They set up booths to display such wares as pots, swords, armor, leather goods, and clothing. Before long, instead of bartering, merchants began to pay for goods with money. Italian moneychangers tested and weighed coins from many different lands to determine their value. From the *banc,* or bench, at which the moneychanger sat comes the English word "bank."

1. How did early merchants travel?

MEDIEVAL FAIR

Merchants were an important part of life in the Middle Ages. In this painting, men and women examine a merchant's fresh produce and leather goods at a fair. How often were fairs held?

2. Who sponsored the fairs?
3. How did the fairs affect the development of banking?

THE GROWTH OF TOWNS   Merchants soon tired of traveling from place to place. They began to look for places where they could settle permanently and store their goods.

The merchants usually chose places near waterways or road crossings along a trade route. To protect themselves from robbers and feudal fights, the merchants also tried to settle near the walls of a castle, fortress, or monastery. They would build a marketplace along a nearby stream and enclose it in a palisade surrounded by a moat. Most towns of the Middle Ages developed from these merchant settlements.

The towns came to be called **burgs** because they often overlooked castles, which the Germans called *burgs*. The new towns grew steadily and attracted people from the surrounding countryside. Markets became centers of business and social activity. Once a week, lords and peasants sold food for goods

WALLED TOWN
Towns in the Middle Ages had high stone walls and lookout towers. As they grew larger, the towns spread outside the walls. This photo shows the French town of Carcassone, the finest example of a medieval walled town in Europe.
How did towns develop in the Middle Ages?

they could not make on the manor. Runaway serfs, traders, and wanderers settled in the towns. Artisans came from the villages to find work. Often, they brought their families with them.

The towns gradually became more than just centers of trade. They became communities in which people lived.

1. Where did the first towns develop?
2. What contributed to the growth of the towns?

LIVING CONDITIONS

By the 1200's most towns were wealthy and large enough to have their palisades replaced by walls and towers. Inside the walls, public buildings of stone and houses of wood were jammed close together. To save even more space, the houses had extra stories that extended over crooked narrow alleys.

Most towns grew without planning for future growth and they often spread beyond their walls into the surrounding countryside. New walls were then built around new areas.

The crowded conditions often made towns unhealthy places in which to live. Sewers were open, and there was little concern for cleanliness. People threw garbage out of windows into the streets below. Pigs and rats were everywhere.

During the 1300's, some diseased rats came in on trading ships from the Middle East. They carried with them a plague called the "Black Death." The disease swept through Europe, killing millions of people. Experts think that one out of three Europeans died in the plague. To escape it, people fled from the towns and settled in the countryside. Trading, farming, and war came to a temporary halt.

1. What were some problems faced by the towns?
2. What led many people to leave the towns and return to the countryside during the 1300's?

BURGHER LIFE Merchants and artisans controlled the town's business and trade. They hired workers from the country-side to make goods for them. At first, the merchants, artisans, and workers who lived in town were all called **burghers**. But after a while, the title was used only to mean rich merchants.

The daily life of the burghers and their families followed a set pattern. The day began at dawn with prayers. The burgher drank wine for breakfast and hurried off to work. He went to the docks and market to see how well his products were selling. Then, he met with his business partners at the merchants' hall or the tavern.

The burgher's wife stayed at home where she kept house, managed servants, and cared for children. She also wrote music and worked in the garden. The family ate two large meals a day—one at ten o'clock in the morning and another at six o'clock in the evening. A typical meal consisted of eel, roast beef, lark pastry, and larded milk. About nine o'clock in the evening, the family went to bed.

Medieval Couple

1. Who lived in the towns?
2. Who controlled the town's business and trade?
3. How did a burgher and his family spend their days?

RULE OF THE LORDS Under the feudal system, land on which towns were built was owned by kings, nobles, and bishops. They taxed people in the towns and charged them fees to use the marketplace. The burghers did not like this. They also did not like some of the other restrictions placed on them. They resented

BURGHER LIFE

Meals were important events in the daily lives of burgher families. In the scene above, a burgher warms his hands by the fire as he rests from a hard day's work. The table is being set for a roast beef dinner.

What were the responsibilities of a burgher wife?

having to get a lord's permission to marry, move around, or own property. And they did not want to serve in the lord's army.

Many lords viewed the rise of towns as a threat to their power. They resented the wealth of the burghers and began to strictly enforce feudal laws to keep burghers in their place. The Church also looked down on the townspeople. Church leaders feared that the making of profit would interfere with religion. They thought it was a sin for townspeople to take money as interest on loans.

The burghers insisted that feudal laws were not suitable for business or trade. They wanted to run their own affairs and to have their own courts and laws to settle legal problems. As city dwellers, they did not fit into the feudal system.

The burghers now had wealth and power. They began to rely less on feudal lords and bishops. Instead, they developed a sense of loyalty toward their town and worked together to build schools, hospitals, and churches. The burghers were not afraid to voice their opinions. Although they still respected the nobles and the clergy, the burghers began to demand changes.

1. Under the feudal system, what rights did nobles and church leaders have in the towns?
2. What changes did the townspeople want to make in the feudal system?

COMMUNES   In the 1100's, townspeople in northern Italy formed political groups called **communes** to oppose the feudal lords and the clergy. The communes fought against the bishops and the emperor, who appointed the church officials.

The Italian communes won their battles and eventually became independent city-states. Before long, the idea of communes spread to the towns of northern Europe. Some towns there held talks with local lords and gained certain freedoms without violence. The kings and nobles gave the townspeople **charters**. These were documents that allowed towns to control their own affairs.

The charters gave the people the right to elect officials to run the towns. In most towns, representatives of the leading business groups made up a council. This council collected taxes and set charges for merchants who bought and sold goods in the town market. It also repaired streets; organized citizen armies; and ran hospitals, orphanages, and special homes for the poor.

Medieval Court

Towns enforced their own laws. Special courts were set up to handle cases involving marriages, property inheritances, and business disputes. To cut down on crime, town laws punished lawbreakers severely. Murderers were hanged; robbers lost a hand or an arm. Those who committed such minor crimes as disturbing the peace were whipped or put in the **stocks**, or a wooden frame with holes in which the feet and hands were locked. All punishments were carried out in public.

1. When did communes first develop? Why did they develop?
2. What rights did charters give townspeople?

THE RISE OF GUILDS

Around the 1100's, merchants, artisans, and workers formed **guilds**, or business groups whose purpose was to ensure equal treatment for members. Each craft had its own guild, whose members lived and worked in the same area of town. Guild members were forbidden to compete with one another or to advertise. Each guild member had to work the same number of hours, hire the same number of workers, and pay the same wages.

The guilds controlled all business and trade within a town. Only guild members could buy, sell, or make goods in that town. Outsiders who wanted to sell their goods in the town market had to get permission from the guilds. The guild decided the fair price for a product or service, and all members had to charge that price. Guild members who sold poorly made goods or cheated in business dealings had to pay large fines. They could also be expelled from the guild.

Worker with Basket

Guilds were more than business or trade organizations. If guild members became ill, other members provided care and medical aid. If members were out of work, the guild used its profits to provide food and clothing. When members died, the other members prayed for their souls. The guild paid for funerals and supported the dead members' families. Guilds were also centers of social life. Huge banquets were held at the guild hall. Holy day celebrations, processions, and outdoor plays were sponsored by the guild. Close friendships often developed among guild members.

It was not easy to become a member of a guild. A person had to be an **apprentice**, or a trainee, in a trade for ten years. Apprentices were taught their trade by **masters**, or experts. They had to live with and obey the masters until their training was complete.

The next step was becoming a **journeyman**, or a person who worked under a master for a daily wage. After a certain period of time, a journeyman could take an examination to become a master. The examination was given by guild officials. The journeyman had to make and present a "masterpiece" that proved he had learned his craft. A journeyman who passed the examination was considered a master and could make his own goods. Usually, he set up a work space in the back of his house for himself and his apprentices. The products the master and apprentices made usually were sold in a shop in the front of the master's house.

By 1400, many merchants and artisans were challenging the control of the guilds. They felt the guilds prevented them from enlarging their trade and profits. Then, too, apprentices disliked the rigid rules set by the guilds. It was getting harder and harder for apprentices to become masters. Many masters were grouping together and hiring unskilled workers to help them in their shops instead of apprentices.

1. What rules did guild members have to obey?
2. How did guilds help members and their families?
3. How did a person become a master in a trade?
4. Why did people oppose guilds in the 1400's?

CULTURAL CHANGES

During the 1400's, merchants, artisans, and bankers became more important than they had been in the past. Their increasing power led to the decline of feudalism.

Many townspeople were as wealthy as, or wealthier than, the landed nobles. Bankers lent money to kings, lords, and church officials for wars, building repairs, and entertainment. With their new wealth, merchants turned their wooden homes into mansions with carpets and glass windowpanes. Some even bought castles from nobles who had lost all their money.

Townspeople began to set fashions. Women wore furs and brocaded gowns. Men dressed in colorful jackets, hose, and feathered caps.

The townspeople had more leisure time and money to spend on their interests. Many of them hired private teachers to educate their sons. The sons later went to universities to study law, religion, and medicine. There was time to enjoy art and books, and townspeople soon began to support the work of painters and writers.

Most of the townspeople had never learned Latin, which was the language of scholars and church leaders. They preferred instead to use languages such as German, French, and English. Now, they could read stories and poems in languages they knew. A scholar named Dante wrote the *Divine Comedy* in Italian. It

Dante

was one of the most famous poems of the period. Geoffrey Chaucer wrote the *Canterbury Tales* in English. The tales are still popular today.

Townspeople thought differently from feudal nobles and peasants. The townspeople came to believe that they should be free to develop their talents and to improve their way of life. They wanted a strong central government that would give them the peace and security they needed to realize their goals. They began to look toward kings to provide leadership.

Canterbury Tales

1. In what ways did the cultural life of townspeople change during the 1400's?
2. What did townspeople want government to do?

CHAPTER 27 REVIEW

SUMMARY

1. During the eleventh and twelfth centuries, increased trade between Europe and the East led to the rise of trading centers such as Venice and Flanders.

2. Venetian traders became fulltime merchants who developed an effective banking system.

3. By 1100, the navies of the Italian trading towns had driven the Muslims from the Mediterranean.

4. Flanders was the earliest Atlantic trading center.

5. By 1300, the Flemish had developed an international industry by importing wool from England, turning it into cloth, and then shipping the finished product back to England.

6. Overland trade, as well as sea trade, developed during the eleventh and twelfth centuries.

7. At first, medieval merchants traveled overland in armed groups and stopped to trade with each other at fairs.

8. After a while, merchants began to settle in permanent places that developed into towns called burgs.

9. Most towns were overcrowded, unhealthy places to live.

10. Artisans and rich merchants called burghers controlled the business and trade of towns.

11. Lords viewed the rise of towns as a threat to their power, and bishops feared that the making of profit would interfere with religion.

12. Burghers resented feudal laws and wanted to run their own affairs.

13. By the 1100's, towns in northen Italy became independent city-states.

14. Guilds set wages, prices, and working conditions and helped members who were sick or out of work.

15. As townspeople grew richer and more powerful, they began turning away from feudalism and looking to kings to provide leadership.

BUILDING VOCABULARY

1. *Identify the following:*
   Venice   Black Death   *Divine Comedy*   *Canterbury Tales*
   Flanders   Dante   Geoffrey Chaucer

2. *Define the following:*
   fairs   communes   stocks   apprentice
   burgs   charters   guilds   masters
   burghers   journeyman

REVIEWING THE FACTS

1. What led to the development of East-West trade during the eleventh and twelfth centuries?
2. What were two important trading centers of the Middle Ages?
3. What did Italian trading towns have to do with driving the Muslims from the Mediterranean?
4. Why were most towns called burgs during the Middle Ages?
5. What groups of people settled in towns?
6. What effects did the Black Death have on Europe?
7. Why were lords opposed to the rise of towns?
8. Why were the clergy opposed to the rise of towns?
9. In what languages were books read by townspeople usually written?
10. How were the ideas of townspeople different from those of feudal nobles and peasants?

DISCUSSING IMPORTANT IDEAS

1. Do you think you would have enjoyed living in a town during the Middle Ages? Why or why not?
2. Would you have supported the position taken by Italian communes during the 1100's? Explain.
3. Would you have preferred to be a burgher or a feudal lord during the Middle Ages? Explain.
4. Do you approve or disapprove of the rules established by guilds? Give reasons for your opinion.

USING MAPS

Study the map on page 409, and answer the following questions:

1. What types of trade routes are shown?
2. What are some Italian trading towns?
3. What town is located about 47° north latitude and 29° east longitude?
4. Which trading town is farthest east?
5. About how far is Bruges from Milan?
6. Through what countries do the major trading routes pass?
7. Through what bodies of water do the major trading routes pass?

MARCO POLO AND THE MONGOLS

Marco Polo was a thirteenth-century Italian from the city of Venice. He became famous for his travels in Cathay, or China.

Marco's father and uncle were diamond merchants who had traveled to China. There, they met the Mongol ruler Kublai Khan, who was Genghis Khan's grandson.

In 1271, the Polos left on another trip to the Far East. This time they took 17-year-old Marco with them. They sailed to a port in Palestine and then traveled the rest of the way by camel. Three years later, they reached the summer palace of Kublai Khan.

The Polos stayed in China for 17 years. Kublai Khan gave them jewels, silk, and other valuable treasures. Marco became an aide to Kublai Khan and even acted as governor of a Chinese city.

Kublai Khan sent Marco on many tours of the Mongol Empire. Among the places he visited were Burma, Indochina, Malaya, and India. During the tours, Marco took detailed notes so he could report to Kublai Khan.

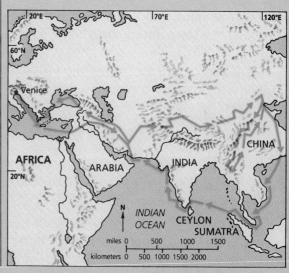

The Polos left China in 1292. When they reached Venice three years later, they found the city at war with Genoa, a rival Italian city.

Marco became the commander of a Venetian **galley**, or ship propelled by oars. He was captured by the Genoese and spent a year in prison. With the help of another prisoner, Marco used his time in jail to write a book called *Description of the World*.

The book told about the Mongol Empire, the largest in the history of the world. It stretched from the Pacific Ocean to the Mediterranean Sea. Within its borders lived many different peoples.

The book also described Kublai Khan and his court and the cities of China. It told of the great wealth in the Far East and of luxuries far beyond the imaginations of any westerner. Marco also described the customs, habits, and life styles of the people.

Marco Polo's book gave Europeans some of their first ideas about the Far East. Europeans who read it became interested in trading with China. Map-makers later made accurate maps based on descriptions in the book. A young captain named Christopher Columbus read the book and later decided to seek a sea route to the Far East.

1. Why did Marco Polo go to China?
2. What did Marco Polo do in China?
3. What influence did Marco Polo's book have on Europeans?

CHAPTER 28
RISE OF THE MONARCHIES

The rise of towns and trade during the Late Middle Ages led to many changes in western Europe. One of these changes was political. Feudalism lost its power, and kings grew stronger. This, in turn, affected the Church and the people. In France, England, Germany, and Spain things would never be the same again.

FRANCE

In 987, Hugh Capet, a French noble, was chosen as the new king of France. At the time, France consisted of many feudal territories. As king, Capet ruled only a small area between the Seine and Loire rivers.

Hugh Capet was the first of a line of Capetian kings who ruled France for 300 years. He died in 996. The Capetian kings who followed him for the next 100 years were weak and did little to increase royal power.

In 1108, Louis VI, known as "Louis the Fat," became king. He helped to increase the authority of the monarchy in several ways. He discharged nobles who did not fulfill their feudal duties and replaced them with loyal persons of lower birth. He brought the people security by stopping the raids of lawless vassals. He also granted charters of freedom to many towns, winning the loyalty of the townspeople.

The king's authority was further strengthened under Philip Augustus, also known as Philip II. Philip, who ruled from 1180 to 1223, made Paris the center of government. He had churches built, streets paved, and a 28-foot, or about 8.5-meter, wall raised around the city. He increased the size of his kingdom through marriage and by winning back French lands held by the English. To make sure that nobles did not become too powerful while he was fighting in the Crusades, Philip II appointed royal agents to keep watch on noble fiefs.

In 1226, Philip's grandson became King Louis IX. He ordered the nobles to stop feuding and forbade them to settle disputes by fighting duels. Most nobles **minted**, or coined, their own money. Louis IX made it illegal to use coins made anywhere but the royal mint. He also set up a royal court to which anyone could bring disputes. Under Louis IX, there was peace, and the people became more united.

Philip IV, Louis' grandson, ruled from 1285 to 1314. He was known as "Philip the Fair." Philip IV believed that the interests of the state came first. So, he seized English fortresses he felt were necessary for the kingdom's security, and he fought the Flemish when they refused to let the French control their cloth trade. Philip IV also believed that a kingdom could not exist without taxes. So, he made sure taxes were collected on a regular and permanent basis, and he taxed the clergy. To advise him and

Philip the Fair

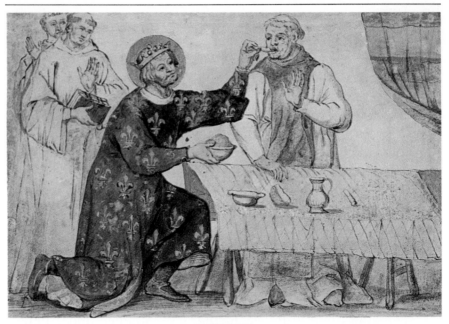

LOUIS IX

King Louis IX of France was known for his honesty and just dealings. After his death, he was made a saint of the Roman Catholic Church. Louis's support of the Church is expressed in this painting of the king feeding a church official.
What benefits did Louis IX bring to France?

help him run the country, Philip IV formed the Estates-General, an assembly of nobles, clergy, and townspeople. Its formation was the beginning of a national government in France. By the time Philip IV died in 1314, France was united under one supreme ruler.

1. What did Louis VI do to increase the authority of the king?
2. What changes did Philip Augustus bring about in France?
3. What did Louis IX do to help unite the French people?
4. What did Philip IV do to unite and strengthen France?

ENGLAND

In 1042, the witan made Edward the Confessor, an English prince, king of England. Edward gave money to the poor and sponsored the building in London of Westminster Abbey, the church in which later English monarchs were crowned. But he spent so much time in religious work that he failed to carry out his royal duties. As a result, the nobles increased their hold on the country. The most powerful noble was Harold Godwinson. When Edward died in 1065 without an heir, Harold became the new king.

WILLIAM THE CONQUEROR Harold Godwinson did not remain king for long. William, Duke of Normandy, a cousin of Edward the Confessor, claimed that before Edward died, he had promised him the English throne.

In 1066, William led an army of 5,000 Norman archers and knights across the sea to England. They met Harold's army in battle near Hastings, a town just south of London. To stop the Norman charge, English foot soldiers armed with axes formed a wall of shields on the edge of a low hill. William knew he could not break through the wall. So, he had his soldiers pretend to retreat. When the English broke formation to follow after them, the Normans turned on the English. By nightfall, King Harold was dead, and the English were defeated. On Christmas Day, William, now known as William the Conqueror, was crowned King of England in Westminster Abbey.

At first, the English resisted William's rule. To crush English revolts—and to keep his followers in line—William introduced feudalism into England. He seized the lands of English nobles and divided them among Norman nobles. In

---

BATTLE OF HASTINGS
William the Conqueror's victory at Hastings made him king of England. This detail from the famous Bayeux tapestry shows Norman troops on horseback. Who fought at the Battle of Hastings?

return for the lands, the nobles became William's vassals. They promised to be loyal to the king and to provide him with soldiers.

William kept many English laws and government practices. He received advice from the witan, now called the Great Council. He also relied on such local officials as the sheriff. William made many changes. In 1086, he took a census in order to properly tax the people. The census figures were recorded in two huge volumes called the *Domesday Book*.

William also brought **continental**, or European mainland, ways to England. Under his rule, the English learned Norman customs and the French language. The wealthy built castles, cathedrals, and monasteries in the French style. The people learned new skills from Norman weavers and other workers.

1. What happened to the king's authority during the rule of Edward the Confessor?
2. How did the Normans win the Battle of Hastings?
3. Why did William the Conqueror introduce feudalism in England?
4. What changes did William bring to England?

HENRY II   After William died, there was confusion in England until 1154 when William's great-grandson became King Henry II. He ruled England, most of Ireland, Scotland, and Wales. He was also a feudal lord in France, where he owned more land than he did in England. Some of the French lands belonged to his wife, Eleanor of Aquitaine. She lived at her own court in the French town of Poitiers.

Thomas à Becket

Henry II restored order and forced the nobles to give him their loyalty. He also used the law to increase his authority and worked to reform English courts. A central royal court was set up in London with trained lawyers as judges. **Circuit judges**, or judges who travel throughout the country, brought the king's law to all parts of England. They made it the common law of the land, thus helping to unite the country.

In each community, judges met with a **grand jury**, or group of people who present to judges the names of people suspected of crimes.

Henry II believed that everyone, including church officials, should be tried in the king's courts. Thomas à Becket, Henry's close friend and the Archbishop of Canterbury, did not agree. Becket wanted church officials free of royal control. The quarrel between the king and the archbishop led four of the king's knights to murder Becket. After the murder, Henry II made peace with the Church by allowing some of the clergy to be tried in church courts.

1. What lands did Henry II rule?
2. How did Henry II improve English law?
3. Why did Henry II and Thomas à Becket quarrel?

THE MAGNA CHARTA AND PARLIAMENT   When Henry II died in 1189, his oldest son Richard became king. Because of his bravery in battle, he was called "the Lionheart." Richard, however, was more interested in his French lands than in ruling England, and he did little for the English people.

When Richard died in 1199, his brother John became king. John lost most of his lands in France to the French king. When he increased taxes and began to ignore the law, the nobles

---

MAGNA CHARTA

The Archbishop of Canterbury and merchants joined the nobles at Runnymede to force King John to sign the Magna Charta. Here, a noble shows King John where to sign on the document, as the Archbishop looks on.

In what ways did the Magna Charta increase the power of the nobles?

Symbol of Royalty

became angry. They refused to obey him unless he agreed to give them certain rights and privileges. In 1215, John met the nobles in the meadow of Runnymede, where they forced him to sign the *Magna Charta*, or Great Charter.

The Magna Charta lessened the king's power and increased that of the nobles. A king could no longer collect taxes without the consent of the Great Council. A freeman accused of a crime had the right to a trial by his peers. The king had to obey laws. Although the Magna Charta was written by nobles for nobles, it came to be viewed as an important step toward democracy. It brought to government the new idea that not even a king is above the law.

John died in 1216, and his son became King Henry III. But Henry was weak and allowed the feudal lords in the Great Council to rule England. In 1264, Simon de Montfort, Henry's brother-in-law, came to power. He gave the people a voice in government by letting them have representatives in the Great Council.

Eight years later, the new king, Edward I, went even further. He called for a meeting of representatives to advise him and to help him make laws. This gathering, known as Parliament, gave the people a greater share in the ruling of their country. Parliament later broke into two separate groups. Nobles and clergy met as the House of Lords, while knights and townspeople met as the House of Commons.

1. Why did the nobles force King John to sign the Magna Charta?
2. What reform did Simon de Montfort make?
3. What was the purpose of Parliament?

THE HUNDRED YEARS' WAR

In the early 1300's, the English still held a small part of southwest France. The kings of France, who were growing more powerful, wanted to drive the English out. In 1337, the English king, Edward III, declared himself king of France. This angered the French even more. In 1339, the French and English fought the first in a long series of battles known as the Hundred Years' War.

The Hundred Years' War began when the English defeated the French fleet and won control of the sea. The English then invaded France. They defeated the French at the Battle of Crécy in 1347 and again at the Battle of Agincourt in 1417.

The English owed their success on land mostly to a new weapon called the **longbow**, which shot steel-tipped arrows. The French still used the shorter crossbow. The crossbow could not send arrows as far as the longbow, and the French arrows were not as sharp as the steel-tipped English arrows.

1. Why did France and England go to war?
2. Why were the English able to defeat the French in the battles of Crécy and Agincourt?

JOAN OF ARC   By 1429, much of France was in English hands. Charles, the French *dauphin*, or prince, was fighting the English for the French throne. Then, a 17-year-old French peasant named Jeanne d'Arc, or Joan of Arc, appeared. She said

---

JOAN OF ARC

Joan of Arc (left) freed the French city of Orleans from English rule (right). She became a national heroine and a beloved saint of the Roman Catholic Church. Why did Joan decide to help her people?

that while praying she had heard heavenly voices telling her she must save France. She went to see Charles and told him that God had sent her to help him. She said that if she had an army she would free Orleans, a city the English had been besieging for seven months. Charles gave Joan an army, a suit of armor, and a white linen banner.

Joan led an attack against the English army at Orleans. Within ten days, the city was free, and Joan became known as the "Maid of Orleans." Shortly after, with Joan at his side, the dauphin was crowned King Charles VII of France. Joan wanted to return home, but Charles convinced her to stay with the army. A few months later, a French traitor captured her and sold her to the English. After spending a year in prison, she was tried as a witch and burned at the stake.

The French continued fighting after Joan's death. By 1453, the English held only the French seaport at Calais, and the war had come to an end.

1. What did Joan of Arc do for the French?
2. What happened to Joan of Arc after the Battle of Orleans?

Playing Card

RESULTS OF THE WAR   Both France and England were changed by the Hundred Years' War. By 1500, the last French feudal territories were under the king's control, and France was unified. England, too, was unified by the war, but its monarchy was weakened. Not until 1485, when a Welshman named Henry Tudor became king, did the monarchy of England become strong again.

The Hundred Years' War increased the importance of the common people both in England and in France. Many peasants had died during the war from disease or fighting. Those who remained were greatly needed as workers. The peasants knew they were needed and began to make demands. They forced the lords to pay them wages and to allow them to move outside the manors. When the lords tried to force them back to the old ways, they revolted. Most became farmers who rented land from the lords.

1. How did the Hundred Years' War affect the monarchies of England and France?
2. How did the Hundred Years' War affect English and French peasants?

GERMANY

During the 900's, Germany was the most important and powerful country in western Europe. Over time, German kings lost much of their authority to powerful nobles who wanted to rule their own territories. The king, however, still had the right to remove lords who would not obey him.

OTTO I   In 936, Otto I became king of Germany. He wanted to unite the country and rule without the nobles. He removed disobedient lords and gave their estates to his family. Then, he turned to the Church for support. Church officials wanted him to set up a Christian Roman Empire in western Europe. So, Otto made many of his loyal followers bishops and abbots and gave them government posts. In return, they supplied him with money and soldiers. Otto then invaded Italy, added the northern Italian trading cities to his kingdom, and freed the Pope from the control of Roman nobles.

In 962, the Pope crowned Otto I emperor of the Holy Roman Empire, a large new state that consisted of Germany and northern Italy. Otto saw himself as the heir of Charlemagne and the Roman emperors and as the leader of the Christian West. He, and the emperors who followed him for the next 90 years, controlled the office of Pope.

1.   What were Otto I's goals as king of Germany?
2.   How did Otto I's goals change after he became emperor?

FREDERICK I   In 1152, Frederick I became emperor. Because of his full red beard, he was called Barbarossa, or "red beard." Frederick forced the powerful lords to swear loyalty to him and to work for his government.

Frederick's attempts to control the nobles and unify the empire worked against him. The nobles grew wealthy from their government positions. At the same time, the Italian city-states, aided by the Pope, banded together and defeated Frederick's armies. Frederick had to accept a peace that recognized the independence of the city-states.

Frederick died in 1190 while bathing in a river in Asia Minor. Later, a legend about him spread among the Germans. It stated that he was not dead but under a magic spell that had put him to sleep somewhere high in the mountains. The people

German Crown

FREDERICK I

Frederick I wanted to unite Germany and Italy into one strong empire under his rule. In this painting, Frederick is crowned emperor of Rome in 1155. Why was Frederick I called Barbarossa?

believed that one day he would awake and restore the glory of Germany.

1. What were the results of Frederick I's efforts to unify the empire?
2. What does German legend say about Frederick I?

FREDERICK II   In 1209, Frederick II, Frederick I's grandson, became emperor. He had been born and raised in Palermo, Sicily, which his father had made part of the Holy Roman Empire. So, he ignored Germany and concentrated on Sicily.

Frederick was known as the best-educated monarch of his time. He founded a university in Palermo so young men could study at home rather than in other countries. He spoke several languages and supported artists and scholars. Although the Church forbade it, he adopted many Muslim customs and conducted scientific experiments.

When Frederick began conquering land in Italy, the Pope became afraid that he would seize church lands around Rome. So, in 1227, he **excommunicated**, or expelled, Frederick from the Church and called for a crusade against him. This gave the German princes the chance for which they had been waiting. They broke away from the emperor's rule and made Germany a loose collection of states under their control.

1. What kind of ruler was Frederick II?
2. Why did Frederick II and the Pope quarrel?
3. What was the effect of Frederick II's excommunication?

THE HAPSBURGS   Whenever an emperor of the Holy Roman Empire died, the German princes met in a **diet**, or assembly. There, they elected the new emperor.

YOUNG MAXIMILIAN

As a young man, Maximilian I studied under different scholars. Later, as emperor, he encouraged the development of universities throughout Germany. What territories in Europe were ruled by Maximilian I?

In 1272, the princes elected as emperor a member of the Hapsburg family named Rudolf. He and members of his family served as Holy Roman emperors for the next 700 years.

One important Hapsburg was Maximilian I, who became emperor in 1493. He worked to gain more land and to extend his power throughout Europe. When he married Mary of Burgundy, he gained control of Flanders and other areas of the Low Countries, or provinces of the Holy Roman Empire in northwestern Europe. By marrying his children into other royal families of Europe, he brought still more countries under Hapsburg influence. The one area over which he could not gain complete control, however, was Germany. There the princes continued to have authority over their own lands.

1. How did Rudolf I become Holy Roman Emperor?
2. How did Maximilian I increase Hapsburg influence?

Spain

While the western European monarchies were increasing their power, Spain was under the control of Moors. When the Moors conquered Spain in 711, they brought with them learning and luxury. Most Spaniards, however, were Christians and opposed Muslim rule. They banded together to drive the Moors out of the country. By the 1200's, the Moors controlled only the small southern kingdom of Granada.

The rest of Spain was made up of small kingdoms, the most powerful of which were Castile and Aragon. In 1469, Prince Ferdinand of Aragon married Princess Isabella of Castile. Within ten years, they became king and queen and united their kingdoms into one nation. Ferdinand and Isabella worked to drive the Moors out of Spain. In 1492, the Moors at Granada surrendered the last Moorish stronghold. To make their power felt throughout the land, Ferdinand and Isabella took away some of the nobles' privileges. They sent royal officials called *corregidores* to govern the towns and set up special courts in the countryside to punish robbers and other criminals.

Ferdinand and Isabella were known as the "Catholic Monarchs." They believed that to be truly united all Spaniards should be Catholic. In 1492, they ordered Spanish Jews to convert or leave the country. Ten years later, they gave the remaining Moors the same choice.

Spanish Hero El Cid

EUROPE IN THE LATE MIDDLE AGES

Ferdinand and Isabella did not trust the Jews and Moors who converted. They believed that the new Christians practiced their old religions in secret. To stop such heresy, they set up the Inquisition. It tortured, tried, and punished anyone suspected of heresy. Ferdinand and Isabella and later rulers used the Inquisition to force the people to be loyal.

1. How did most Spaniards feel about Muslim rule? Why did they feel this way?
2. What did Ferdinand and Isabella do to make their power felt in Spain?
3. Why did Ferdinand and Isabella want all Spaniards to be Christians?
4. What did the Spanish Inquisition do?

CHAPTER 28 REVIEW

SUMMARY

1. The rise of towns and trade in western Europe during the Late Middle Ages resulted in the growth of strong national governments.

2. The Capetian dynasty of France began in 987 and lasted for some 300 years.

3. Capetian kings strengthened the French monarchy by filling government jobs with loyal people, granting towns charters of freedom, setting up a national court and a national currency, and forming a tax system and the Estates-General.

4. In 1066, William, Duke of Normandy, invaded England and conquered the English at the Battle of Hastings.

5. William the Conqueror continued to accept advice from the witan and to use local English officials, but he also introduced feudalism and the French language into England.

6. Henry II strengthened the English monarchy by making the king's law the law of the land, and worked to reform the English courts.

7. In 1215, English nobles forced King John to sign the Magna Charta, which established the idea that not even a king is above the law.

8. In 1272, King Edward I set up Parliament to advise him and to help him make laws.

9. Between 1337 and 1453, England and France fought a series of battles known as the Hundred Years' War.

10. The Hundred Years' War unified France and England and increased the importance of the common people.

11. In 1429, a French peasant named Joan of Arc succeeded in driving the English from Orleans and having the dauphin crowned Charles VII.

12. In 962, the Pope crowned the German king Otto I emperor of the Holy Roman Empire.

13. By 1227, Germany was a loose collection of states that were controlled by German princes.

14. The Hapsburg family ruled the Holy Roman Empire from 1272 until the 1900's.

15. By 1492, Ferdinand and Isabella conquered the Moors and made Spain a Catholic country.

BUILDING VOCABULARY

1. *Identify the following:*

Late Middle Ages	Edward the Confessor	King John	Joan of Arc
Hugh Capet	William the Conqueror	Magna Charta	Otto I
Philip Augustus	*Domesday Book*	Simon de Montfort	Holy Roman Empire
Louis IX	Henry II	Parliament	Frederick II
Philip the Fair	Eleanor of Aquitaine	Hundred Years' War	Hapsburgs
Estates-General	Thomas à Becket	Charles VII	Ferdinand and Isabella

2. *Define the following:*

minted	grand jury	*dauphin*	diet
continental	longbow	excommunicated	*corregidores*
circuit judges			

REVIEWING THE FACTS

1. Why did French townspeople become loyal to the king?

2. How did the Estates-General help to strengthen the French monarchy?

3. Why did the Duke of Normandy think he had a right to the English throne?

4. Why did William the Conqueror take a census of the English people?

5. How did Henry II make peace with the Church after the murder of Becket?

6. What changes did the Magna Charta bring about in English government?

7. Why did the position of the common people in England and France improve as a result of the Hundred Years' War?

8. How did Otto I make his empire more Christian?

9. Why did Frederick II ignore Germany and concentrate on ruling Sicily?

10. What did the Moors bring to Spain?

DISCUSSING IMPORTANT IDEAS

1. If you had been King John, would you have signed the Magna Charta? Why or why not?

2. Why do you suppose Joan of Arc was tried as a witch? Give reasons for your opinion.

3. Do you think the Hundred Years' War helped or hurt the development of England and France? Explain.

4. Do you agree with Ferdinand and Isabella that all people of a nation should follow the same religion? Explain.

USING MAPS

Study the map on page 435, and answer the following questions:

1. What is the time period of the map?

2. What territories made up the Holy Roman Empire?

3. What areas did the English control?

4. What French city is nearest England?

5. What is the latitude and longitude of the city of Paris?

6. About how far is Palermo from Rome?

7. What body of water is west of France?

8. What area is directly north of England?

UNIT 9 REVIEW

SUMMARY

1. Increased trade during the eleventh and twelfth centuries led to the growth of large trading centers and the establishment of merchant settlements. They attracted new residents and developed into trading towns.

2. A new class, higher than peasants but lower than nobles, developed in the towns. It consisted of merchants, artisans, and bankers.

3. In western Europe, the rise of trade and towns and the increased power and wealth of townspeople led to a weakening of the feudal system and to the rise of monarchies.

4. During the Late Middle Ages, monarchies and strong national governments developed in France, England, Germany, and Spain. They laid the foundations of modern western Europe.

REVIEWING THE MAIN IDEAS

1. Explain why the growth of towns and trade led to a weakening of the feudal system and the power of the Church.

2. Explain what kings did to form strong governments and win the loyalty of the people.

DEVELOPING SKILLS

Much of the information a person receives is stated directly. But sometimes, the meaning of the information is not stated directly. Instead, it is only **implied**, or hinted at. In other words, although the information is there, it is not presented in so many words. It is up to the person who receives the information to determine what is meant. This skill is called **drawing inferences**.

Learning how to draw inferences is a very important skill. It is important to understand what information is presented. It is equally important to understand what information is not presented, so that you will not arrive at a wrong conclusion.

This exercise is designed to give you practice in drawing inferences. Following are references to two paragraphs in the textbook. Below each reference are several statements.

Reread each paragraph and use the information in it to decide if you can infer that the statements below the paragraph are true or false. In some cases, you will not be able to infer anything, because there will not be enough information in the paragraph for you to do so.

1. Third paragraph under "Burgher Life" on page 413
   a. A wife had to be well organized.
   b. Most burghers were fat.
   c. Burghers did not eat many fruits and vegetables.
   d. Most burghers had large families.
   e. A burgher's wife did most of the housework herself.
   f. Music was important in a burgher's household.

g. Wives were good musicians.

h. A burgher family usually slept eight hours a night.

2. Third paragraph under "The Rise of Guilds" on page 416

a. Guild members were religious.

b. A guild member worried about becoming ill.

c. Belonging to a guild was expensive.

d. Guilds were the only social organizations to which workers belonged.

e. Guild halls were large.

f. Running a guild took a great deal of time.

g. Guild members were skilled nurses.

h. Guild members disliked the theater.

SUGGESTED UNIT ACTIVITIES

1. During the Middle Ages, family names came into widespread use in Europe. Find out how each of the following names developed: Bridges, Fletcher, Ford, Masterson, Smith, Taylor.

2. Make a chart comparing the rise of two of the following nations: England, France, Germany, Spain. Include the names, dates, and accomplishments of the rulers who helped strengthen the power of the monarchy.

3. Write an account of the Battle of Hastings as it might have appeared in an English newspaper the day after the battle.

4. Working in a small group, prepare a diorama of a medieval trade fair or a burg.

5. Compare a medieval guild with a present-day labor union. Describe the ways in which they are alike and the ways in which they are different.

SUGGESTED READING

Asimov, Isaac. *The Shaping of France.* Boston: Houghton Mifflin Company, 1972. From Hugh Capet to the end of the Hundred Years' War.

Fraser, Antonia, ed. *Kings and Queens of England.* New York: Alfred A. Knopf, 1975. The stories of the men and women who have ruled England for almost 1,000 years.

Konigsburg, E. *A Proud Taste for Scarlet and Miniver.* New York: Atheneum, 1973. Recounts the events in the life of Eleanor of Aquitaine as remembered by herself and by three people who knew her well.

Lofts, Norah. *The Maude Reed Tale.* New York: Elsevier, 1972. The story of an English girl who wants to become a wool merchant but is sent instead to a castle to learn to be a lady.

Shuttlesworth, Dorothy. *The Tower of London.* New York: Hastings House, 1970. A description of how and when the stone buildings of the Tower were built.

Sutcliff, Rosemary. *The Shield Ring.* New York: Henry Z. Walck, 1972. The story of a young girl during the time the Normans were fighting for control of England.

Trease, Geoffrey. *The Barons' Hostage.* Nashville: Thomas Nelson, 1975. The story of a teenage boy who claims a barony during the time of Simon de Montfort.

UNIT 10

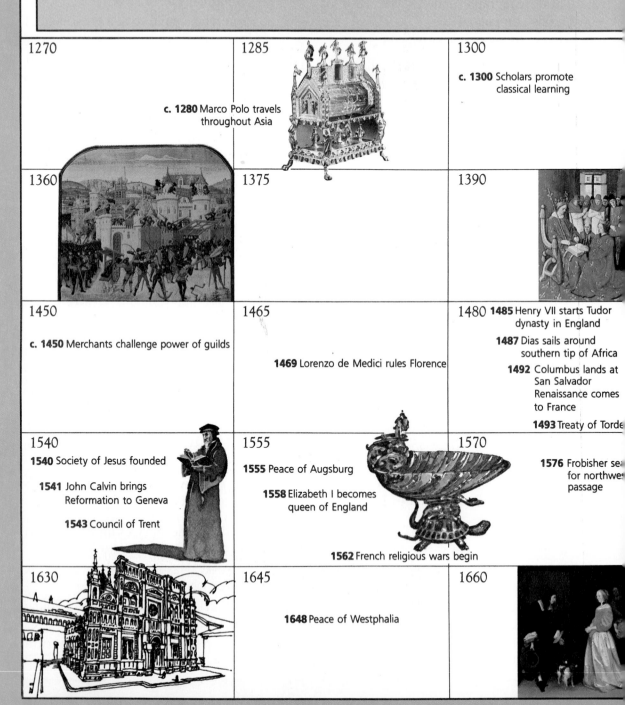

1270	1285	1300
c. 1280 Marco Polo travels throughout Asia		**c. 1300** Scholars promote classical learning
1360	**1375**	**1390**
1450 c. 1450 Merchants challenge power of guilds	**1465** 1469 Lorenzo de Medici rules Florence	**1480** **1485** Henry VII starts Tudor dynasty in England **1487** Dias sails around southern tip of Africa **1492** Columbus lands at San Salvador Renaissance comes to France **1493** Treaty of Torde
1540 1540 Society of Jesus founded 1541 John Calvin brings Reformation to Geneva 1543 Council of Trent	**1555** 1555 Peace of Augsburg 1558 Elizabeth I becomes queen of England 1562 French religious wars begin	**1570** 1576 Frobisher se for northwe passage
1630	**1645** 1648 Peace of Westphalia	**1660**

THE BEGINNING OF MODERN TIMES

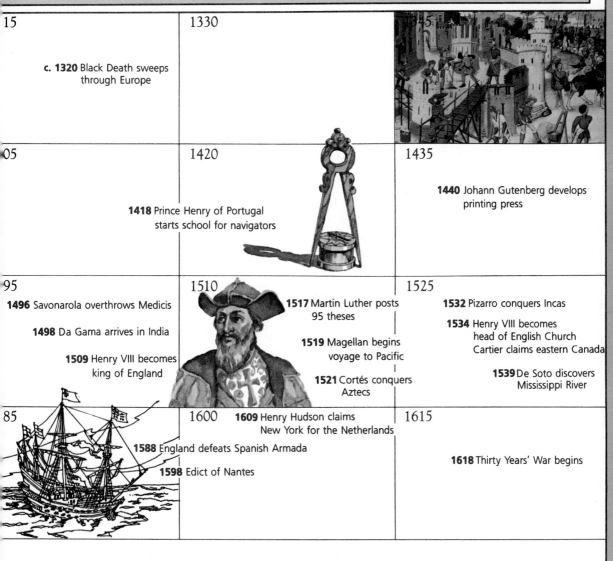

15	1330	45
c. 1320 Black Death sweeps through Europe		

05	1420	1435
	1418 Prince Henry of Portugal starts school for navigators	**1440** Johann Gutenberg develops printing press

95	1510	1525
1496 Savonarola overthrows Medicis	**1517** Martin Luther posts 95 theses	**1532** Pizarro conquers Incas
1498 Da Gama arrives in India	**1519** Magellan begins voyage to Pacific	**1534** Henry VIII becomes head of English Church Cartier claims eastern Canada
1509 Henry VIII becomes king of England	**1521** Cortés conquers Aztecs	**1539** De Soto discovers Mississippi River

85	1600	1615
	1609 Henry Hudson claims New York for the Netherlands	
	1588 England defeats Spanish Armada	**1618** Thirty Years' War begins
	1598 Edict of Nantes	

1. WHAT CHANGES TOOK PLACE IN WESTERN EUROPE DURING THE 1300'S AND 1400'S?
2. WHAT DID WESTERN EUROPEANS LEARN ABOUT THE WORLD DURING THE AGE OF DISCOVERY?

Many changes began to take place in western Europe during the 1300's and 1400's. The Late Middle Ages came to an end, and western Europe began to enter the modern period. People wanted to learn more about their past. They wanted more freedom to think and act for themselves. Many no longer were willing to accept practices handed down from the Middle Ages. Scholars began to look for new sources of knowledge. States, grown wealthy through trading, became centers of art and learning.

Many western Europeans began to question the Catholic Church and its teachings and to criticize the Church's wealth. They wanted a more personal relationship with God. They called for a **reformation**, or a change in the way the Church taught and practiced Christianity. Many differences of opinion arose about the type of change needed. Eventually, the differences led to a split in the Church that has lasted to the present time.

Western Europeans began to learn more about the world beyond Europe. Bigger and better ships and improved navigational instruments helped Europeans explore distant places. Merchants discovered that there was a profit in trade with lands in the Far East. This led explorers to look for a shorter and less costly route to these far-off lands. While they were searching, they discovered new continents and peoples. As a result, trade grew, and the people became wealthy. At the same time, Europe became the most powerful continent in the world.

CHAPTER 29
THE RENAISSANCE

Around 1300, scholars in western Europe developed a new interest in **classical writings**, or the writings of ancient Greeks and Romans. They improved their knowledge of Greek and Latin, studied old manuscripts, and tried to copy the writers' styles. They also began to accept some Greek and Roman beliefs.

One belief that the scholars accepted was the importance of people. Because of this, the scholars were called **humanists**.

Their work led to a break with the thinking of the Middle Ages and to a new age called the Renaissance. During this period, people became less concerned with the mysteries of heaven and more interested in the world around them.

The Italian City-States

The first and leading center of the Renaissance was Italy, which consisted of small, independent city-states. The most important were Florence, Venice, and the Papal States. They had grown wealthy from trade and spent much of their wealth on the arts.

At first, each city-state was ruled by guilds. Later, powerful individuals or families took control. They often fought each

RENAISSANCE ITALY

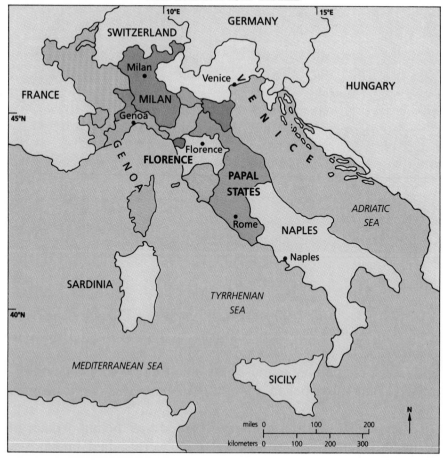

other for land and wealth. At times, they had difficulty gaining the people's loyalty and had to govern by force.

The leaders of the Italian city-states, however, were interested in more than power. They wanted to be remembered as wise, generous rulers. So, they spent money on ceremonies and parades to impress and entertain the people. They ordered the building of churches and palaces. They also encouraged scholars, poets, and philosophers to set up palace schools to educate the sons of the wealthy. In these schools, pupils learned to develop their minds and their bodies. They spent part of the day studying classical writings and learning good manners and the rest of the day wrestling, fencing, and swimming.

1. What were the most important Italian city-states?
2. Who governed the Italian city-states at first? Who governed them later?
3. What did the rulers do to show they were wise and generous?

ART   Art was an important part of life in Renaissance Italy. City-states were proud of their artists. They often competed for the services of painters and sculptors. The artists knew they were important and began to seek individual honor and fame. Each artist worked to develop a unique style.

Successful artists were supported by the rulers of the city-states. In return, the artists were expected to provide paintings and sculptures for the rulers' palaces and gardens. Artists often had workshops where they trained apprentices, who drew in backgrounds, costumes, or hands on paintings.

Leonardo da Vinci

Renaissance artists developed their style by carefully studying ancient Greek and Roman art, science, mathematics, and the details of nature. They became especially interested in **perspective**, or a way of showing objects as they appear at various distances from the viewer. Above all, the artists studied the structure of the human body to learn how to draw the human form accurately. They began to experiment with light, color, and shade. As a result, they painted and sculpted works that were true to life and full of color and action.

Many artists painted portraits for the wealthy. The artists tried to paint people's facial features so they showed what the people were really like. At first, the portraits were painted only to honor dead or famous people. Later, any merchant with money could have a portrait painted.

RENAISSANCE ARTISTS

Michelangelo Buonarroti and Leonardo da Vinci were two leading artists of the Italian Renaissance. Michelangelo carved a very large statue of Christ and His mother known as the "Pièta" (left). Da Vinci tried to capture the personality of an Italian noblewoman in the painting known as the "Mona Lisa" (right).

What people supported the work of Italian Renaissance artists?

One of the greatest Renaissance artists was Leonardo da Vinci. He is known for the "Mona Lisa," a portrait of an Italian noblewoman. He also painted a fresco called "The Last Supper" on the wall of an Italian monastery dining room. It shows Christ and his disciples at their final meal before Christ's death. In these works, Da Vinci tried to reveal people's thoughts and feelings in addition to showing their physical appearance.

Da Vinci was a scientist as well as an artist. He filled notebooks with drawings of inventions far ahead of the times. Da Vinci designed the first parachute and made drawings of flying machines and mechanical diggers.

Another outstanding artist was Michelangelo Buonarroti, who is known for his paintings on the ceiling and altar wall of Rome's Sistine Chapel. He also sculpted the "Pièta," which shows the dead Christ in the arms of His mother. Although Michelangelo studied ancient Greek and Roman sculpture, he went beyond the ancients in the presentation of the human body. His figures are large and muscular and create a sense of motion.

1. How was an artist regarded during the Italian Renaissance?
2. What did Leonardo da Vinci contribute to Renaissance art?
3. What did Michelangelo contribute to Renaissance art?

CITY LIFE Most Italian Renaissance cities had narrow paved streets with sewers in the middle. Merchants and shop-keepers lived on the top floors of buildings that housed their shops. The wealthy built homes in the classical style with large, high-ceilinged rooms. In the center of the homes stood court-yards filled with statues, fountains, and gardens. Most people in

RENAISSANCE MANNERS

Do not blow your nose and then open and look inside your handkerchief, as if pearls or rubies had dropped out of your head.

Do not offer anyone a fruit from which you have already taken a bite.

Do not tell sad stories at parties or mealtimes. If someone starts talking this way, gently and politely change the subject and talk about something more cheerful.

Do not brag about honors, wealth, or intelligence.

Do not speak while yawning.

Do not clean your teeth with your napkin or your finger.

Do not lie all over the dinner table or fill both sides of your mouth with so much food that your cheeks stick out.

Do not undress, comb, or wash your hair in front of others.

Do not stick out your tongue, rub hands together, or groan out loud.

Do not talk too much, especially if your knowledge is small.

the cities, however, were poor. They worked for low wages and lived in run-down areas.

The center of city life was the *piazza*, or central square. In the piazza, markets were set up, and merchants traded goods. People gathered to talk to friends and to carry out business dealings. On holidays, the people often watched or took part in parades and ceremonies.

Families were close-knit. Most family members lived and worked together in the same neighborhood. Families arranged marriages as if they were business deals. Women stayed at home, ran the household, and raised the children. Men spent long hours at work, talking in the streets, and in taverns.

Most men dressed in tights and simple tunics. Some also wore cloaks and caps. Women dressed in simply cut, flowing dresses with tight bodices and high necklines. The rich usually wore brightly colored clothing made from expensive silks and velvets and trimmed with fur.

1. Who lived in Italian Renaissance cities?
2. What took place in the piazza?
3. How did Renaissance Italians view family life?

DAILY LIFE IN FLORENCE

The Medici family sponsored festivals to entertain the people of Florence. This Renaissance painting shows the horse races held every spring.
Where was the center of social life in an Italian Renaissance city?

FLORENCE   The Italian Renaissance began in Florence, which was ruled by the Medici family. One of its most famous members was Lorenzo de Medici, who became the ruler of Florence in 1469. He made the city a center of art and learning. Artists, poets, painters, and philosophers flocked there to benefit from Lorenzo's generous support. As a result of the city's prosperity and fame, Lorenzo was known as "the Magnificent."

About 1490, Florence's trade started to decline. Merchants began to complain that Lorenzo was too strict and spent too much money. Poor Florentines began to grumble about their poor housing and the shortages of food.

The people looked for an escape from their problems. They thought they found it in religion as preached by a monk named Savonarola. Savonarola accused the Medicis of not ruling justly. He gained the people's support and overthrew the Medicis in 1494.

Lorenzo de Medici

Savonarola did not like the gaiety and loose life of the Renaissance. He thought Renaissance attitudes were ruining Florence. On his advice, the new government banned parties, gambling, swearing, and horse-racing. Savonarola's supporters also burned paintings, fancy clothes, musical instruments, and classical books.

By 1498, the people of Florence had tired of Savonarola's strict ways, and he was hanged for heresy. After his death, the Medicis returned to power. But Florence's greatness had passed.

1. Who governed Florence during the Renaissance?
2. Why was Lorenzo de Medici called "the Magnificent"?
3. What changes did Savonarola bring to Florence? How did his rule end?

ROME   During the 1300's and 1400's, the power of the Popes declined. But they wanted to show Europe's kings that the Church was still powerful. So, they began to rebuild Rome, which was one of the cities of the Papal States. They had large churches and palaces built with gardens and fountains. The buildings were decorated with paintings, tapestries, and sculptures. Piazzas and wide streets were built in areas that had been in ruins. Scholars were brought from all over to gather manuscripts for the Pope's library.

Most Popes were not very religious. They acted more like political rulers than church leaders. They sent representatives to

VENICE'S GRAND CANAL
The Grand Canal winds through the center of Venice. Palaces and churches built during the years of Venice's prosperity stand along both sides of the canal. How did Venice's location affect its growth and prosperity?

other states and countries, collected taxes, raised armies, and fought wars.

In 1492, Rodrigo Borgia became Pope Alexander VI. He did this by bribing cardinals to vote for him. Pope Alexander was very ambitious. His goal was to make central Italy a kingdom ruled by the Borgia family. Alexander's children tried to help him achieve his goal. His daughter Lucretia married a noble and became known for her lively parties and her love of music. She also gained a reputation for poisoning her enemies.

Alexander spent a great deal of money building an army for his favorite son, Cesare. The army marched through Italy and took control of many towns. All of this territory was lost, however, after Alexander's death in 1503. By this time, Rome had regained much of its ancient glory. It soon replaced Florence as the center of the Renaissance.

1. Why was Rome rebuilt?
2. What were most Popes like during the Renaissance?
3. What was Pope Alexander VI's main goal?

VENICE   The Renaissance did not reach Venice until the late 1500's. This was because the Venetians had looked to Constantinople rather than to western Europe for art and literature.

Venice was different from most Italian city-states in other ways too. Its palaces and churches were built on 117 islands linked by nearly 400 bridges. Instead of streets, Venice had canals. The largest and busiest was the Grand Canal, which was lined with brightly colored stone and marble palaces. The Rialto, or the business area of Venice, also lay along a stretch of the Grand Canal. There, traders from Europe and the East crowded the docks to buy and sell goods.

Venice was ruled by a few merchant aristocrats. They controlled the Senate and the Council of Ten. The Council passed the laws and chose the *doge*, or official ruler. The doge had little power and had to obey the Council of Ten.

Venetians were expected to place loyalty to their city above concern for their families and themselves. They had to report their neighbors' suspicious actions to the Council of Ten. Citizens who wanted to accuse someone of treason placed a letter stating the charges in special boxes found throughout the city. The accused were immediately arrested and brought before the Council. Council members then met in secret to study the evidence, listen to witnesses, and decide guilt or innocence.

1. Why did the Renaissance come late to Venice?
2. What made Venice different from other Italian cities?
3. How were Venetians expected to behave?

FRANCE

In 1494, the French began invading Italy. French kings became fascinated by Italian architecture, art, and fashions. In the 1500's, King Francis I arranged for Italian artisans to work for him in France. He became the first monarch outside of Italy to collect Italian paintings and sculpture. He and many of his nobles hired Italian architects to design *chateaux*, or castles, which they had built along the Loire River.

Francis I also encouraged French writers to model their works on those of Italian writers. Every evening, Francis and his family listened to readings of the latest books. Many were written by Rabelais, a physician-monk who believed that humans were not tied down by their past and could do whatever

Rabelais

they wished. In his most popular book, *The Adventures of Gargantua and Pantagruel*, Rabelais' main characters were two comical giants. He used them to poke fun at outdated customs of the time.

1. What did Francis I do to encourage Renaissance thought in France?
2. What did Rabelais believe?

GERMANY AND THE NETHERLANDS

The Renaissance also spread to the wealthy trading centers of Flanders and Germany. There, religious scholars learned Greek and Hebrew so they could understand the earliest ver-

---

NORTHERN RENAISSANCE LIFE

The towns of Germany and the Netherlands learned Italian ways and soon made their own contributions to the Renaissance. Northern European painters became known for their detailed scenes of daily life. In this painting, wealthy merchants and their wives are playing a card game.

What contributions did northern Europeans make to the Renaissance?

---

sions of the Bible. Their Bible studies helped them appreciate early Christian beliefs and practices. They decided that over the years many church leaders had interpreted the Bible to suit their own beliefs. As a result, the scholars wanted reforms that would simplify church teachings. One outspoken scholar, a Dutchman named Erasmus, translated the New Testament into Greek. He also wrote *Praise of Folly*, a book that attacked corrupt church leaders and practices.

Northern European artisans made many discoveries during the Renaissance. About 1440, a German named Johann Gutenberg developed the printing press. It used carved letters that could be moved around to form words and then could be reused. Now, books could be quickly printed by machine rather than slowly written by hand. This made many more books available and also made them cheaper to buy. Since printing came at a time when many townspeople were learning to read and think for themselves, new ideas spread rapidly.

Northern European artists studied Italian works of art and then developed their own styles. They painted scenes from the Bible and daily life in sharp detail. Hubert and Jan Van Eyck, two brothers from Flanders, discovered how to paint in oils. Soon, others began to do the same. The colors of the oil paintings were deep and rich.

Typesetter

1. What Church reforms did German and Flemish scholars want to make?
2. How did the printing press change European life?
3. What did northern European artists contribute to the art of painting?

SPAIN

The Renaissance took root in Spain in the late 1400's and early 1500's. It was influenced by the close ties between the Catholic Church and the government. The leading Church official, Cardinal Jimenez, was a loyal supporter of the monarchy. He was also interested in promoting learning. He founded universities and welcomed students from other countries. He helped scholars produce a new translation of the Bible that had columns of text side-by-side in Greek, Latin, and Hebrew.

In 1555, Philip II became king. He was very religious and did not trust the work of scholars. Many were accused of heresy

RENAISSANCE PEOPLE

Baldassare Castiglione	1478–1529	Italian writer; wrote book on rules of behavior for ladies and gentlemen
Benvenuto Cellini	1500–1571	Italian goldsmith; sculptor; wrote about his life and times
Vittoria Colonna	1492–1547	Italian author; wrote religious and love poems
Nicolaus Copernicus	1473–1543	Polish astronomer; stated that earth moves around sun
Albrecht Durer	1471–1528	German artist; painted and made woodcuts of religious and classical subjects
Beatrice d'Este Isabella d'Este	1475–1497 1474–1539	Italian noblewomen; sisters; honored for their learning; supported writers and artists
Galileo	1564–1642	Italian scientist; did experiments on the motion of objects; used telescope to discover new facts about universe
Niccolo Machiavelli	1469–1527	Italian politician; writer; wrote advice to rulers on how to keep power
Thomas More	1477–1535	English scholar; saint; government official; refused to accept king as Church head
Petrarch	1304–1374	Italian poet; scholar; restored study of classics; collected manuscripts; wrote letters and poems
Raphael	1483–1520	Italian religious painter and architect
Andreas Vesalius	1514–1564	Italian surgeon; founder of modern medicine; wrote first full description of human body

by the Inquisition and burned at the stake. Philip had architects build him a new granite palace just outside Madrid. Called El Escorial, it served as a royal court, art gallery, monastery, church, and tomb for Spanish royalty. El Escorial soon became a symbol of the power and religious devotion of Spanish rulers.

Despite strong Church and government controls, the arts prospered. The city of Toledo became a center for painters and poets. One artist who settled there was a Greek whom the Spaniards called El Greco. His style was different from that of other artists. He painted figures with very long bodies, parts of which stretched beyond normal size. Some art experts claim that El Greco copied his style from Byzantine artists. Other insist he painted as he did because of an eye problem that distorted his vision.

The theater was also popular in Renaissance Spain. Miguel de Cervantes, a surgeon's son, was one of the most noted writers of the time. He wrote many plays, short stories, and novels. His novel, *Don Quixote*, about the adventures of a comical knight and his peasant squire, is still popular today. Cervantes used the characters to make fun of the code of chivalry and to show the problems people have in trying to reach their ideals in a cruel, uncaring world.

Don Quixote

1. What influenced the Renaissance in Spain?
2. How were scholars treated in Spain during the rule of King Philip II?
3. What made El Greco's paintings different from those of other Renaissance painters?
4. What did Cervantes try to show in *Don Quixote*?

ENGLAND

Peace did not come to England after the Hundred Years' War. In 1455, two noble families, York and Lancaster, began a struggle for the throne. The York symbol was a white rose, and the Lancaster symbol was a red rose. For this reason, the struggle between York and Lancaster was called the Wars of the Roses.

When the wars ended in 1485, a family called the Tudors, who fought on the Lancastrian side, took over the English throne. The first Tudor king, Henry VII, prepared the way for the Renaissance. He strengthened the monarchy and encouraged trade, which made England peaceful and prosperous.

Henry VII's efforts were continued by his son, Henry VIII, who became king in 1509. He enjoyed and encouraged art, literature, music, hunting, and parties. He even composed his own music. Under his rule, English nobles and merchants began to look to Renaissance Italy for guidance in politics, diplomacy, and behavior.

The English Renaissance reached its height, however, during the reign of Henry VIII's daughter Elizabeth I. She became queen in 1558 when she was 25 years old. Elizabeth often made journeys throughout the kingdom so that the people could see her. During her travels, she stayed at the homes of nobles who entertained her with banquets, parades, and dances. Elizabeth was said to dance for hours without getting tired, even when she was well into old age. Poets and writers praised Elizabeth in their writings. Sons of merchants, lawyers, and landowners copied Italian clothes and manners and came to court to capture her attention and favor.

Poetry, music, and drama beame a part of daily life. Most nobles wrote poetry. People of all classes enjoyed singing ballads and folk songs. Many played such musical instruments as violins, guitars, and lutes.

The people of Renaissance England were especially fond of plays. Not since ancient Greece had so many plays been written and performed. About 1580, the first theaters were built in

THE TUDORS

King Henry VIII of England (left) and his daughter Queen Elizabeth I (right) were members of the Tudor family, which ruled England from 1485 to 1603. Henry and Elizabeth both were strong and forceful rulers, but they were able to gain the respect and love of their people.

What was daily life like in England during the rule of the Tudors?

ENGLISH THEATER

The Globe Theater (left) stood near the south bank of the Thames River in the London suburb of Southwark. All Elizabethan public theaters were open at the top. The Globe Theater became the home of William Shakespeare's (right) acting company in 1599.

What kind of reputation have the plays of William Shakespeare earned for him?

England. Their stages stood in the open air. Most of the audience, however, sat under a roof or some sort of covering. Those who could not afford to pay for seats stood in the **pit**, or open area in front, and on the sides of the stage. Since there were no lights, plays were performed in the afternoon. They attracted large crowds, which were sometimes hard to control.

One of the best known English **playwrights**, or authors of plays, was William Shakespeare. He drew ideas for his tragedies and comedies from the history of England and ancient Rome. He often used Italian scenes, characters, and tales in his plays. Many experts consider Shakespeare the greatest writer and the greatest playwright in the English language.

1. What did the Tudors do to encourage the Renaissance in England?
2. What were English theaters like?
3. What did William Shakespeare write about?

CHAPTER 29 REVIEW

SUMMARY

1. Around 1300, certain western European scholars developed a new interest in classical writings and started a new age called the Renaissance.

2. The Renaissance began in the Italian city-states.

3. A great deal of importance was placed on art in Renaissance Italy.

4. Leading Renaissance artists included Michelangelo Buonarroti and Leonardo da Vinci, who was also a scientist.

5. The Italian Renaissance began in Florence, which was ruled by the Medicis.

6. In 1494, a monk named Savonarola gained the Florentines' support and overthrew the Medicis.

7. Savonarola was overthrown in 1498, and the Medicis returned to power.

8. To prove to European kings they were still powerful, the Popes rebuilt Rome.

9. In the early 1500's, Rome became the center of the Italian Renaissance.

10. In the late 1500's, the Renaissance reached Venice.

11. After 1494, the Renaissance spread to France, where it was encouraged by King Francis I.

12. The Renaissance spread to Flanders and Germany, where religious scholars worked for Church reforms.

13. About 1440, a German named Johann Gutenberg invented the printing press, which helped new ideas spread throughout Europe.

14. In the late 1400's and early 1500's, the Renaissance spread to Spain, where it was influenced by close ties between the Church and the government.

15. The English Renaissance reached its height during the reign of Elizabeth I, which began in 1558.

16. People of Renaissance England were very fond of plays, especially those written by William Shakespeare.

BUILDING VOCABULARY

1. *Identify the following:*

Renaissance	Pope Alexander VI	Erasmus	*Don Quixote*
Leonardo da Vinci	Grand Canal	Johann Gutenberg	Wars of the Roses
Michelangelo	Rialto	Cardinal Jimenez	Henry VII
Florence	Council of Ten	Philip II	Henry VIII
Lorenzo de Medici	Francis I	El Escorial	Elizabeth I
Savonarola	Rabelais	El Greco	William Shakespeare
Papal States			

2. *Define the following:*

classical writings	perspective	*doge*	pit
humanists	*piazza*	*chateaux*	playwrights

REVIEWING THE FACTS

1. In whose writings were Renaissance scholars interested?

2. Why were Renaissance scholars called humanists?

3. Where was the first and leading center of the Renaissance?

4. What did rulers of Italian city-states do to encourage learning and art?

5. What were some features of Italian Renaissance art?

6. Why did the Florentines turn to Savonarola in 1494?

7. Why did Rome replace Florence as the center of the Renaissance?

8. What did Flanders and Germany contribute to the Renaissance?

9. Of what did the palace El Escorial become a symbol?

10. How did the Wars of the Roses get their name?

DISCUSSING IMPORTANT IDEAS

1. In what ways did the Renaissance differ from the Middle Ages?

2. Why did the Renaissance start in Italy?

3. Do you think Lorenzo de Medici deserved to be called "the Magnificent"?

4. If you could go back in time and talk with a Renaissance artist or ruler, whom would you choose? What questions would you ask?

5. Do you approve or disapprove of the Venetian system of justice? Explain the reasons for your answer.

6. Why was the printing press an important invention?

USING MAPS

Study the map on page 444, and answer the following questions:

1. What is the subject of the map?

2. What city-states made up Renaissance Italy?

3. What island is off the southwest tip of Italy?

4. What country was directly north of the city-state of Milan?

5. In what city-state was the city of Rome located?

6. Which Italian city-state was bordered on the east by Hungary and on the north by Germany?

7. About how far is the city of Florence from the city of Genoa?

8. What Italian city-state also included an island?

9. What city-state was located about 46° north latitude and 12° east longitude?

CHAPTER 30

THE REFORMATION

The Catholic Church did not adjust to the many changes taking place in western Europe during the 1400's and 1500's. Many Europeans began to call for a reformation.

Church leaders, however, were too busy with their own and government affairs to introduce reforms. They did not like the reformers' ideas, especially those that threatened their power. As a result, the Church faced a serious threat to its unity.

MARTIN LUTHER

One reformer who challenged the Church was a German monk named Martin Luther. Luther, born in 1483, was the son of peasants. His family wanted him to be a lawyer, but he was more interested in religion and became a monk instead.

As a monk, Luther faithfully followed Church teachings and practices. Yet, he could find no peace of mind. He wondered how God would judge his actions and if he would go to heaven when he died.

While studying the New Testament, Luther found the answer to the questions that had been troubling him. He decided that trusting in Jesus, rather than doing good works, would save people from their sins. Through faith in Jesus, people could be certain that God loved them and that they would go to heaven.

Luther's ideas soon brought him into conflict with the Church. In 1517, Pope Leo X wanted money to rebuild St. Peter's Church in Rome. To obtain the money, he sold **indulgences**, or pardons for sins. Luther felt that by selling indulgences, the Pope was leading people to believe they could buy God's forgiveness for their sins. One night, Luther posted a list of 95 **theses**, or statements, to the door of the castle church in Wittenburg, Germany. In the list, he stated that only God could forgive sins, and he challenged anyone who disagreed to **debate**, or argue, with him.

The Pope hoped to convince Luther to give up his ideas, but Luther refused. He began to openly attack other Catholic beliefs. He said Popes could make mistakes and the only true guide to religious truth was the Bible, which every Christian had the right to read. He also said that every Christian had the right to pray to God without the aid of a priest.

In 1520, Pope Leo condemned Luther's teachings and excommunicated him. Leo insisted that the German emperor, Charles V, try Luther as an outlaw. Charles was loyal to the Church, but he relied on German princes who supported Luther. To keep the princes' loyalty, Charles agreed to give Luther a fair trial. At the same time, he secretly promised the Pope that Luther would be condemned. In 1521, Luther was tried by the German diet in Worms. When he refused to give up his beliefs, he was condemned for heresy.

Pope Leo X

1. What did Martin Luther believe could save people from their sins?
2. What did Luther do to protest the sale of indulgences?
3. Why did the Pope excommunicate Luther?
4. What happened to Luther at Worms?

MARTIN LUTHER

Martin Luther refused to give up his religious beliefs. In this painting, Luther speaks before the Diet of Worms, where he was found guilty of heresy.
How did Luther's teachings influence the people of northern Germany?

A New Religion

By 1524, most people in northern Germany supported Luther. They left the Catholic Church and formed the Lutheran Church.

The Lutheran princes of Germany had strong, well-organized armies, which Charles V could not defeat. In 1555, when Charles realized he could not force the princes' territories to become Catholic, he agreed to sign a treaty. Known as the Peace of Augsburg, the treaty said there could be both Catholic and Lutheran churches in Germany. It also allowed the prince of each German state to decide which church would be allowed in his territory. The Peace kept German Lutherans and Catholics from fighting each other for nearly 50 years.

PROTESTANT GROUPS   Luther's ideas soon spread to other areas of Europe. People in Scandinavia founded Lutheran churches. Preachers and merchants in Switzerland, a small country in central Europe, set up churches known as Reformed.

Because they protested against Catholic teachings, Lutheran and Reformed churches were called Protestant. Instead of priests, Protestant religious leaders were called **ministers**. They did not have the same religious powers as Catholic priests had, and they spent more time preaching from the Bible. They held worship services in the language of the area instead of in Latin. This made the rituals easier for the people to understand and to share in.

1. To what areas of Europe did Luther's ideas spread?
2. Why were some churches called Protestant?
3. What were some differences between Catholic and Protestant practices?

JOHN CALVIN   The most powerful Reformed group was in the Swiss city of Geneva. There, John Calvin, a French reformer, set up the first Protestant church governed by a council of ministers and elected church members. Calvin also wrote books that became a guide for Protestants throughout Europe.

John Calvin

Calvin believed that God's will was written in the Bible, which ministers had the right to interpret. The ministers also had the right to make sure everyone obeyed God's will. Calvin had the Geneva town council pass laws to force people to follow strict rules of behavior. They could not dance, play cards, go to the theater, or take part in drinking parties. Those who refused to obey these laws were put in prison, executed, or sent away.

Calvin was supported by rich merchants, whom the new religion taught to work hard and to save money. With their help, he worked to improve Geneva. Streets and buildings became noted for their neatness and cleanliness. New workshops opened, providing more jobs for people. Persecuted Protestants from all over Europe found safety in Geneva. Young men came to study at the school Calvin had founded to train Reformed ministers. Many of the refugees, students, and ministers later returned to their own countries to establish Reformed churches.

1. What did Calvin believe?
2. How did Calvin's beliefs influence Geneva?

IGNATIUS OF LOYOLA
Ignatius of Loyola was a Roman Catholic religious leader who founded the
Society of Jesus. Here, he is shown serving communion to his followers.
What were members of the Society of Jesus called?

CATHOLIC REFORM

While Protestants formed new churches, Catholic reformers
worked to improve their Church. Many reformers came from
Spain and Italy, the leading countries of the Catholic reform
movement.

One of the most famous Catholic reformers was Ignatius of
Loyola. In 1521, he gave up his life as a Spanish noble to serve
God and the Catholic Church. He later organized a group of
followers to spread Catholic teachings. In 1540, the group
founded the Society of Jesus, an organization whose members
were called Jesuits. Jesuits wore the black robes of monks and
lived simply. They set up schools, helped the poor, and preached

to the people. They also taught in universities, worked as missionaries, and served as advisors in royal courts.

The Jesuits used reason and good deeds to defend the Catholic Church against Protestant criticisms. They worked hard to strengthen the faith of Catholics and to bring Protestants back to the Church. As a result of their efforts, the Church regained the loyalty of people in such eastern European countries as Poland, Bohemia, and Hungary.

At the same time the Jesuits worked for reform, the Pope took steps to strengthen the Church against Protestants. He called a council of bishops to discuss reforms and to defend Catholic teachings. The council met at different times between 1545 and 1563 at Trent, a town in northern Italy. The Council of Trent put an end to many Church practices reformers had criticized for centuries. The selling of indulgences was forbidden.

COUNCIL OF TRENT

During the 1500's, the Council of Trent helped to renew Catholic life and worship. Bishops and other church leaders from throughout Europe attended the Council. In this painting, the delegates debate an issue at a council meeting held in the cathedral at Trent.

How did the Council respond to Protestant criticisms of the Catholic Church?

Catholic Saints

Clergy were ordered to follow strict rules of behavior. Each diocese was told to build a **seminary**, or a school to train priests.

The Council responded to Protestant protests by explaining Catholic doctrine more fully. The bishops said that good works, as well as faith, helped Christians get to heaven. They declared that the Church alone decided how the Bible was to be interpreted and that mass would be said in Latin only.

1. What were the leading countries of the Catholic reform movement?
2. Why did Ignatius of Loyola give up his life as a noble?
3. How did Jesuits serve the Catholic Church?
4. Why did the Pope call the Council of Trent?
5. What did the Council of Trent do?

A MIDDLE WAY

The reformation of the Church in England was led by the monarch, not by religious leaders. It started as a political quarrel between the Tudor king, Henry VIII, and the Pope. Religious beliefs did not play a part in the struggle until later.

THE BREAK WITH ROME　　The trouble between Henry VIII and the Pope began in 1526. At that time, Henry was married to Catherine of Aragon, the daughter of Ferdinand and Isabella of Spain and the aunt of German emperor Charles V. Henry and Catherine had one child, Mary. Now that Catherine was older, Henry feared she could no longer have children. And Henry wanted a son to succeed to the throne.

At the same time, Henry had fallen in love with Anne Boleyn, a young woman of the court. He wanted the Pope to end his marriage to Catherine so that he could marry Anne and hopefully have a son. When the Pope refused, Henry declared that the Pope no longer had power over the Church in England.

In 1534, the English Parliament passed a law stating that the king was head of the English Church. Any English church leader who did not accept the law would stand trial as a traitor. Thomas Cranmer, the Archbishop of Canterbury and the most important church leader in England, supported Henry. Cranmer helped Henry end his marriage to Catherine. Henry married Anne Boleyn and made her queen of England. A few years later, Henry had Anne executed for treason. He then married Jane

HENRY VIII AND ANNE BOLEYN

Henry's determination to marry Anne Boleyn led to a political break with the Pope. This painting shows Henry with Anne at the home of Thomas Wolsey, the king's chief adviser.

How was Henry eventually able to marry Anne Boleyn?

Seymour, who died shortly after giving Henry the son he wanted. Anne's only child had been a girl, Elizabeth.

1. Why did Henry VIII want to end his marriage to Catherine of Aragon?
2. What happened when the Pope refused to end the king's marriage?

EDWARD AND MARY   When Henry VIII died, his 9-year-old son became King Edward VI. Since Edward was too young and sick to rule, a council of lords governed England for him. Most of the council members were Protestants, and they brought Protestant doctrines into the English Church. Thomas Cranmer supported the lords. He wanted the people to have an orderly form of Protestant worship. So, he wrote a worship service in English called the *Book of Common Prayer*. It was used in all the churches in England.

When Edward died in 1553, the council tried to name a Protestant noblewoman queen. The attempt failed because the

PHILIP II AND MARY TUDOR

Queen of England from 1553 to 1558, Mary I (right) was the first Tudor woman to rule England in her own right. She longed to bring England back to the Roman Catholic Church. She married Philip II (left) of Spain, who considered himself the champion of the Roman Catholic faith.
Why did the English people object to the marriage of Mary and Philip?

English refused to accept a ruler who was not a Tudor. They wanted Henry's daughter Mary as their monarch.

Mary was Catholic, and as soon as she became queen, she accepted the Pope as head of the English Church. She insisted that all English men and women return to the Church. When many Protestants refused, she began to persecute them. The people turned against her, calling her "Bloody Mary."

Mary was married to King Philip II of Spain. The English were unhappy about the marriage because Spain was England's enemy and the leading Catholic power in Europe. They feared that the Spanish king and the Pope would become the real rulers of England. The people decided that England would remain free only if it became a Protestant country. So, they wanted a Protestant ruler.

1. What happened to the English Church under Edward VI?
2. Why did Thomas Cranmer write the *Book of Common Prayer*?
3. What did Mary expect the people to do as soon as she became queen? How did the people feel about this?

ELIZABETH'S CHURCH   Mary died in 1558 without a child to succeed her. Her half-sister Elizabeth became queen. Elizabeth I was Protestant and, with the help of Parliament, ended the Pope's authority in the English Church.

Elizabeth was popular with the people. She knew they did not agree about what beliefs the English Church should have. Still, she wanted the country to be united. So, she worked to set up a church that would appeal to as many people as possible.

Thomas Cranmer

Elizabeth and Parliament decided that the English Church should be Protestant, but with some Catholic features. The monarch would be head of the Church, which would use Cranmer's prayer book and teach Protestant beliefs. At the same time, however, bishops would handle daily affairs as they did in the Catholic Church. Many rituals would also be similar to those of the Catholic Church.

Most English people were pleased with the blend of Protestant belief and Catholic practice. The few groups of Catholics who were not pleased remained outside the English Church. Some groups of Protestants also opposed Elizabeth's Church, but they did not leave it. Because they wanted to purify the Church of Catholic ways, they became known as Puritans.

1. What were the main features of the English Church under Elizabeth I?
2. What groups remained outside of the English Church?

WARS OF RELIGION

By the middle of the 1500's, most northern Europeans were Protestants, while most southern Europeans were Catholics. European monarchs had used religion to help unite their peoples and to build powerful nations. The ruler and people of each nation were expected to belong to the same church. Those who refused to be of the same religion as everyone else were persecuted. This led to a great deal of bitterness between people of different faiths. Differences in religion also led to wars

REFORMERS

William Tyndale
1492–1536
English Protestant leader;
translated New Testament into
English

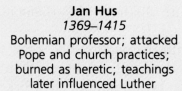

Jan Hus
1369–1415
Bohemian professor; attacked
Pope and church practices;
burned as heretic; teachings
later influenced Luther

John Wycliffe
1320–1384
English priest; declared
that Bible, not Church, was
authority

Ulrich Zwingli
1484–1531
Swiss preacher; ordered
removal of images from
churches; set up new Church
ritual; closed monasteries

Charles Borromeo
1538–1584
Archbishop of Milan; saint;
founded order of priests and
wrote on Catholic doctrine

Teresa of Avila
1515–1582
Spanish nun; saint; reformed
convents and wrote on
religious life

John Knox
1515–1572
Scottish religious leader;
set up Church based on
Calvin's ideas

between nations. Toward the end of the 1500's, the people of Europe entered a period of religious wars that lasted until 1648.

1. In what part of Europe was Protestantism strong? What part of Europe remained mostly Catholic?
2. What led to the wars of religion?

THE ARMADA   Under Elizabeth I, England became the leading Protestant power in Europe. Spain, under Philip II, remained the leading Catholic power. Philip knew that if he could conquer England, Protestant Europe would be open to Catholic control. So, he ordered the building of the Spanish Armada, a fleet of 130 ships. The Armada's main strength lay in its large **galleons**, or heavy ships with square-rigged sails and tall decks. In the spring of 1588, the Armada sailed toward England. Its main purpose was to help the Spanish armies on the continent cross over to the English shore.

Elizabeth knew what was coming and prepared England for war. She had the naval commander John Hawkins reorganize the English fleet, remodeling old ships and building new ones. He formed a new navy of 134 fighting ships and merchant vessels. Most of the ships were smaller than the Spanish ones, but they had larger guns and more ammunition. Expert sailors handled the English ships with a great deal of skill. One sailor, Sir Francis Drake, was known for his overseas voyages and his capture of Spanish ships.

The English knew they had to make the Spanish ships break formation. Their chance came when the Spanish anchored off the coast of Europe to wait for their armies to meet them. That night, the English set fire to eight small ships and sent them into

---

SPANISH ARMADA

In 1588, the English fleet faced the Spanish Armada in the English Channel. In this painting, English fire ships move toward the Armada. This action broke the curved formation of the Spanish ships and made possible a successful English attack. What was the main strength of the Spanish Armada?

Sir Francis Drake

the Spanish fleet. As the fire ships reached the Armada, the Spanish ships broke formation and began to drift. The English were able to successfully fight the Spanish ships one by one.

The Spanish soon realized they were defeated. Short of food and water, they decided to return to Spain. But the voyage was long and difficult. Only one half of the Armada reached home.

The English celebrated their victory with bonfires and parades. Although Spain was still a powerful enemy, the English had proved they could defend themselves.

The English gained respect throughout Europe as champions of the Protestant cause. The defeat of the Armada brought about many changes. One was that it allowed northern Europe to remain a Protestant stronghold.

1. Why did Philip II of Spain want to conquer England?
2. How did the English defeat the Spanish Armada?

THE HUGUENOTS   While most people in sixteenth-century France were Catholic, many nobles, lawyers, doctors, and merchants were Protestants. These French Protestants, who were called Huguenots, followed Calvin's teachings.

In 1534, King Francis I, who was Catholic, forbade Huguenots to worship freely. He wanted all French people to follow the same religion. Catholics began to persecute Huguenots, and by 1562, a civil war broke out. By then, Henry III had become king. Since he was too young to rule, his mother, Queen Catherine de Medici, ruled for him.

Catherine tried to keep the peace by showing favor first to one group and then to the other. She finally decided to support the Catholics. In 1572, she allowed Catholic nobles to kill the leading Huguenots in Paris. Catholic mobs in other parts of France began to kill Protestants and burn their homes. Many Protestants left the country. The few who remained to carry on the fight were led by Henry of Navarre, a Huguenot prince.

Henry IV

In 1589, King Henry III was killed. Henry of Navarre, who was next in line for the throne, became King Henry IV. He wanted to gain the loyalty of the people. Since most French were still Catholic, he decided to convert. Henry finally ended the fighting between Protestants and Catholics. He made Catholicism the national religion but also made life easier for Protestants. In 1598, Henry signed the Edict of Nantes, which granted Huguenots freedom of worship. As a result, France became the first European nation to allow two Christian religions to exist within its boundaries.

1. What led to the civil war in France in 1562?
2. How did Catherine de Medici help the Catholic cause?
3. How did Henry IV end the fighting in France?

THE LOW COUNTRIES   The Low Countries were part of the Spanish Empire. The people were divided into Protestants and Catholics. Neither group liked Philip II's harsh rule. They wanted freedom from heavy taxes and Spanish laws. Philip, however, profited from the wealth and trade of the Low Countries. He wanted to keep them under Spanish control.

Philip also wanted everyone in his empire to be Catholic. So, he set up the Inquisition in the Low Countries to stamp out Protestantism. In 1568, Protestants in the northern provinces revolted. Philip sent troops in to restore order. They were joined by French Catholics from the southern provinces.

The struggle did not come to an end until 1648. At that time, it was decided that the southern provinces, known today as Belgium, were to remain Catholic and loyal to Spain. The northern provinces, known today as the Netherlands, were to be an independent Protestant nation.

Instruments of the Inquisition

1. Why did the Low Countries resent Spanish rule?
2. Why was Philip II determined to keep the Low Countries part of the Spanish Empire?
3. What was the result of the war in the Low Countries?

THE THIRTY YEARS' WAR

During the 1590's and early 1600's, the German states began to quarrel over the terms of the Peace of Augsburg. They formed alliances based on religion. The Catholic alliance was led by the German emperor Ferdinand II.

One Protestant state that resisted Ferdinand was Bohemia. In 1618, the Protestant nobles of Bohemia revolted against Ferdinand, choosing a German Protestant prince as their new king. Ferdinand's armies crushed the Bohemians in a fierce battle, and Ferdinand proclaimed himself king of Bohemia. He forbade Protestant worship and sent Jesuit preachers throughout the country to win the people back to the Catholic Church.

The revolt in Bohemia soon grew into the Thirty Years' War, during which half the armies of Europe fought in Germany.

THE RELIGIONS OF EUROPE

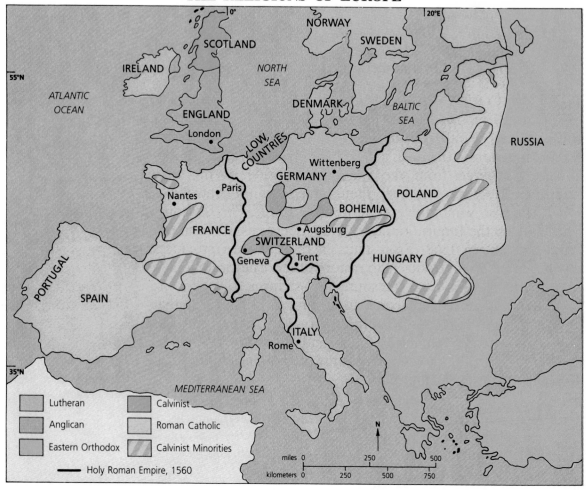

First the king of Denmark and then the king of Sweden invaded Germany. They were Protestants who wanted to stop the spread of Catholicism. They also hoped to conquer territory in northern Germany. When the Swedes were finally defeated in 1634, the French became involved. Although France was Catholic, it entered the war on the Protestant side. France's entry into the war led to a change in the nature of the war. It became less a war over religion and more a fight for land and wealth.

The German people suffered great hardships during the war. Finally, in 1643, after a serious defeat, the German emperor asked for peace. In 1648, representatives of European nations signed the Peace of Westphalia, which ended the war.

As a result, the German emperor lost much of his power. France, however, emerged as a strong nation. After this war, Europeans no longer fought over religion. Instead, nations tried to gain power through trade and expansion.

1. What led to the Thirty Years' War?
2. What change did France's entry into the war bring about?
3. What effect did the Thirty Years' War have on Europe?

CHAPTER 30 REVIEW

SUMMARY

1. In 1517, Pope Leo X sold indulgences to raise the money to rebuild St. Peter's Church in Rome.

2. A German monk named Martin Luther objected to the sale of indulgences and also attacked other Catholic beliefs.

3. In 1521, Luther was tried and condemned for heresy.

4. By 1524, most people in northern Germany had left the Catholic Church and formed the Lutheran Church, which supported Martin Luther's beliefs.

5. The Peace of Augsburg of 1555 allowed the prince of each German state to decide whether the people in his territory were to be Catholic or Lutheran.

6. Luther's ideas spread to parts of Europe and became Protestantism.

7. Protestant religious worship was held in the local language rather than in Latin.

8. The French reformer John Calvin established a center of Protestantism in the Swiss city of Geneva.

9. While the Protestants formed new churches, Catholic reformers worked to improve their Church.

10. In 1540, Ignatius of Loyola founded the Society of Jesus, whose members were called Jesuits.

11. Between 1545 and 1563, the Council of Trent reformed many Church practices.

12. In England, church reformation started as a political quarrel between Henry VIII and the Pope.

13. Mary Tudor tried to force the English people to return to the Catholic Church.

14. With the help of Parliament, Elizabeth I decided that the English Church would be Protestant but with some Catholic features.

15. The English defeat of the Spanish Armada in 1588 allowed northern Europe to remain Protestant.

16. In 1562, a civil war broke out in France between Catholics and Protestants called Huguenots.

17. In 1598, the Edict of Nantes made France the first European nation to allow two Christian religions to exist within its borders.

18. Protestants in the northern provinces of the Low Countries revolted against Spanish rule in 1568.

19. The Thirty Years' War, which lasted from 1618 until the Treaty of Westphalia was signed in 1648, was the last religious war fought in Europe.

BUILDING VOCABULARY

1. *Identify the following:*

Martin Luther	John Calvin	Edward VI	Sir Francis Drake
Pope Leo X	Ignatius of Loyola	*Book of Common*	Huguenots
Lutheran Church	Council of Trent	*Prayer*	Francis I
Peace of Augsburg	Henry VIII	Mary Tudor	Catherine de Medici
Reformed Church	Catherine of Aragon	Philip II	Edict of Nantes
Protestant	Anne Boleyn	Spanish Armada	Thirty Years' War
Geneva			

2. *Define the following:*

indulgences	debate	ministers	seminary
theses			galleons

REVIEWING THE FACTS

1. Why did Martin Luther object to the sale of indulgences?
2. What churches were called Protestant?
3. What rules of behavior did Calvin make the people of Geneva follow?
4. What organization did Ignatius of Loyola found?
5. According to the bishops at the Council of Trent, who decided how the Bible was to be interpreted?
6. Why did Henry VIII have his wife Anne Boleyn executed?
7. Why did Mary Tudor become known as "Bloody Mary"?
8. Why did the people of England decide that England had to become a Protestant country?
9. How did the defeat of the Spanish Armada help the Protestant cause?
10. Why is the Edict of Nantes important?

DISCUSSING IMPORTANT IDEAS

1. Do you think you would have liked living in Geneva at the time of John Calvin? Why or why not?
2. Do you agree or disagree that Mary Tudor's marriage to Philip II would have affected the English religion? Explain.
3. Do you approve or disapprove of the way in which Elizabeth I organized the English Church? Give reasons for your opinion.
4. If you had been Henry IV, would you have converted to Catholicism? Explain.

USING MAPS

Study the map on page 474, and answer the following questions:

1. What was the main religion of Scotland?
2. What religion was practiced in Norway?
3. Where were the Calvinist minorities?
4. What areas were Anglican?
5. What city is about 46° north latitude and 6° west longitude?

CHAPTER 31
THE AGE OF DISCOVERY

B_y the 1300's, Italy controlled Europe's trade with India and the Far East, including China and the East Indies. Muslim merchants sailed from Africa across the Indian Ocean and brought back goods, which they sold to Italian merchants for a good profit. The Italians sold the goods to other Europeans for an even larger profit.

In time, the cost of goods became so high that only the wealthiest people could afford them. The Europeans needed the

MAPMAKING

Mapmakers of the 1400's often went on voyages of exploration. They contributed to Europe's knowledge of the world by drawing maps of newly discovered areas. This map, made about 1600, shows the West African coast.

Why did Europeans of the 1400's become interested in exploration?

goods. Their supplies of gold and silver for making coins were running out. They needed spices, such as ginger, clove, and pepper, to help preserve their food. Europeans living in countries that bordered the Atlantic Ocean began to look for a direct sea route to India and the Far East. In addition to their desire for precious metals and spices, they wanted to spread Christianity to other parts of the world.

By this time, mapmakers, who had been studying the information that came from early explorers like Marco Polo, had begun to make more accurate maps. Meanwhile, the large amount of trade between northern and southern Europe had created a need for bigger and better ships. New ships were built that were faster, less likely to sink, and could carry heavier loads. Navigation was made easier by the improvement of instruments that sailors had used for hundreds of years. One of these was the **compass**, or an instrument with a magnetic needle that always points north. Another was the **astrolabe**, or an instrument that measures the angle of the stars. These developments aided the Europeans in their search for new sea routes to India and the Far East.

1. What items were Europeans anxious to obtain from their overseas trade?
2. What three things helped European explorers in their search for new sea routes to India and the Far East?

THE PORTUGUESE

The desire for new trade routes, knowledge about the world, and gold led to a great period of exploration in the 1400's. Portuguese explorers were among the first to travel beyond the Mediterranean Sea. The discoveries of Prince Henry, Bartholomew Dias, and Vasco da Gama opened the way for later explorations.

PRINCE HENRY   Prince Henry the Navigator, the brother of the king of Portugal, had heard from African merchants about discoveries of gold in Africa. He became eager to explore the west coast of Africa. Henry hoped to find more than gold. He also hoped to find a new route to the Far East. He saw this as a way to extend Portuguese trade and power. It would also increase European knowledge about geography and spread Christianity.

In the early 1400's, Henry started the first European school for navigators in Sagres, Portugal. He gathered together Portuguese, Spanish, Jewish, Arab, and Italian mathematicians, chartmakers, astronomers, and sea captains. They came, taught Portuguese sailors all they knew, and left. In the process, they helped Henry create better charts, improve navigational instruments, and put together more detailed astronomical tables.

At the same time, Henry worked with others to design and to build better ships. The result was the Portuguese **caravel**. It was a combination of the heavy, square-rigged European ship and the light, slim Arab one. The caravel was faster and easier to handle than earlier ships.

Henry sent parties of explorers down Africa's west coast. They discovered the Gold Coast and Cape Verde as well as the Azore, Madeira, and Canary Islands. They used the islands as supply stations for further explorations.

Instruments of Navigation

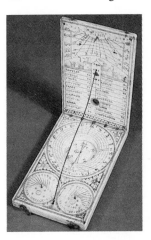

PIONEERS OF EXPLORATION

Prince Henry studied geography and planned explorations at his school in Portugal (left). The Italian explorer Amerigo Vespucci (right) benefited from Henry's efforts. He made three voyages to the New World, which was later named "America" in his honor.

What developments came from Prince Henry's school to make navigation easier?

The explorers found gold dust, ivory, and slaves in Africa. Some explorers began to take more interest in trade than in discovery. The trade brought new wealth to Portugal. Henry watched Portugal grow into a powerful nation. But when he died in 1460, his caravels had gone only one third of the way down the west coast of Africa.

1. What did Prince Henry do to encourage exploration?
2. What items for trade did Portuguese explorers find in Africa?

BARTHOLOMEW DIAS   Exploration went on after Henry's death, but more slowly. In 1473, the equator was crossed. Europeans discovered that the sea did not boil and was not the home of great monsters. Gradually and carefully, the Portuguese made their way south along the African coast.

In 1487, Bartholomew Dias readied ships for a long, hard voyage. Included for the first time was a supply ship with enough water and food for a long voyage. Dias touched at several points on the African coast before strong winds blew him southward away from the coast. After the storm ended, Dias went on to reach Africa's east coast, without knowing that he had been blown around the tip of the continent. On his return home, he knowingly sailed around the southern tip of Africa, which he called the Cape of Storms. The king of Portugal later renamed it the Cape of Good Hope because now the Portuguese knew they could reach the Far East by sailing around Africa.

1. How was Dias's fleet different from earlier fleets?
2. Why was Dias's trip important?

VASCO DA GAMA   In the summer of 1497, a Portuguese **cavalier**, or noble, named Vasco da Gama, led a **convoy**, or group, of four ships down the Tagus River from Lisbon, Portugal. His ships were of a type called *naus* that had been designed by Bartholomew Dias. Dias, in fact, accompanied Da Gama as far as Cape Verde. Da Gama had orders from the king to "proclaim the Christian faith" and to "wrest kingdoms and new states from the hands of the barbarians."

After three months at sea, Da Gama's party rounded the Cape of Good Hope. By then, many of the crew were sick. Their water smelled, and their food was spoiling. Still, they continued on, sailing north along the east coast of Africa toward the island of Mozambique. This island was a Muslim trading center. There, they saw ships loaded with cargoes of cloves and pepper, gold, silver, and pearls and other precious stones. For the first time, they saw a coconut, which they described as "fruit as large as a melon, of which the kernel is eaten." When the Muslims found out that Da Gama and his party were Christians, they forced the Europeans to leave.

The next stop was Malindi in present-day Kenya. There, Da Gama's crew took on supplies and learned to make rope from coconut fiber. The king of Malindi sent Da Gama a pilot to lead him to his final destination, Calicut, India.

On May 20, 1498, Da Gama landed at Calicut. It was a port and trading center on the southwest coast of India. His arrival alarmed Arab and Persian merchants there. They feared that Portugal would take over the trade between Africa and India.

VASCO DA GAMA
Vasco Da Gama opened up India to Portuguese exploration and trade. Here, he meets with an Indian ruler at Calicut, India.
What difficulties did Da Gama and his party have on their voyage?

There was an attempt made to kill Da Gama. In August, Da Gama decided there was no use staying longer. He and his crew loaded what spices they could and started for home.

The trip back took three months. During that time, the ships were threatened by storms, and many of the men died of **scurvy,** or a disease caused by the lack of vitamin C. When Da Gama finally arrived in Lisbon in 1499, he was greeted with great rejoicing and rewards.

Da Gama's voyage opened the way for later explorations and for a new era of increased trade. Before long, Lisbon became one of the major trade centers of Europe.

1. Why did Vasco da Gama go to India?
2. How was Da Gama treated in Calicut? Why was he treated that way?
3. What were the results of Da Gama's voyage to India?

THE SPANISH

The Spanish were as interested as the Portuguese in the wealth that could be obtained from India and the Far East. But, until the late 1400's, they were too busy trying to gain their freedom from the Moors. By 1492, Spain was a Christian country united under King Ferdinand and Queen Isabella. It was ready to enter the race for new trade routes.

CHRISTOPHER COLUMBUS   Christopher Columbus, the son of a weaver, was a skilled navigator from Genoa, Italy. He believed he could reach India by sailing west. Columbus believed the world was round, not flat. He had tried for seven years to convince different rulers to allow him to make the voyage to prove his point. He had asked for help from King John II of Portugal but was turned down. Finally, in 1492, Queen Isabella of Spain listened to his plan, the Enterprise of the Indies, and agreed to support him.

Columbus set sail from Palos, Spain, in August, 1492, with three small ships—the *Niña*, the *Pinta*, and the *Santa Maria*—and a crew of around 90 sailors.

At first, the voyage went well. But the longer they were at sea, the more afraid Columbus's crew became. They urged Columbus to turn back. When he refused, they began to threaten **mutiny**, or an overthrow of the ship's officers. Colum-

Spanish Ship

bus promised to turn back if land was not sighted within three days. The night of the second day a lookout on the *Pinta*, the lead caravel, spotted land. In the morning, Columbus landed at San Salvador, an outer island in the Bahamas. Columbus thought he had reached the Indies, so he called the people living on the island Indians. For this reason, Native Americans are still called Indians.

Columbus spent several months traveling around the waters of the Bahamas, Cuba, and Hispaniola, an island that today consists of Haiti and the Dominican Republic. In Cuba, he found Indians smoking cigars. Thus, Europeans had their first contact with tobacco.

On Christmas Eve, the *Santa Maria* went aground on a reef and was wrecked. Columbus had his crew use the wood from the *Santa Maria* to build a fort. This was the first European settlement in the New World.

ISABELLA I AND COLUMBUS

Against the advice of experts, Queen Isabella I of Spain (left) provided support for the voyage of Christopher Columbus. In 1492, Columbus landed on the island of San Salvador and claimed the land for Spain (right).
Why did Columbus want to sail to India?

In January 1493, Columbus boarded the *Niña* and headed back to Spain. He brought with him pieces of gold, parrots, cotton, other plants and animals, and a few Indians. In Spain, he was received with great honors. Six months later, he was leading a fleet of 17 ships and 1,500 men on another search for Asia.

Columbus made four voyages in all. He explored the South American coast and Central America almost as far as present-day Panama. He returned from his last voyage in 1504. Two years later, he died still convinced he had found the way to Asia. He never realized he had discovered the New World.

1. How did Columbus believe he could reach India?
2. Where did Columbus actually land on his first voyage?
3. What did Columbus achieve during his four voyages?

THE TREATY OF TORDESILLAS   Columbus had seen some Indians wearing gold jewelry. He wrote to Ferdinand and Isabella and told them that great riches could be found in the islands he had discovered. The Spanish monarchs were worried that Portugal might try to take these riches away from Spain. So, they asked Pope Alexander VI to help settle their claims.

In 1493, the Pope drew a **papal line of demarcation**, or an imaginary line from the North Pole to the South Pole some 300 miles, or about 480 kilometers, west of the Azore Islands. Spain was to have the lands west of the line. Portugal was to have the lands east of the line.

The Portuguese, however, did not like the division and protested. They called for a meeting. As a result, in 1494, the Treaty of Tordesillas was drawn up. It moved the line about 500

SPANISH TRADE

By 1530, Spain had replaced Portugal as the leader in the race for land and trade routes. Colonies were set up to obtain gold and other products for Spain and its European holdings. Here, the first ship loaded with sugar from the Spanish colonies arrives at the port of Antwerp in the Spanish Netherlands.
How did the Treaty of Tordesillas come about?

miles, or about 800 kilometers, farther west. Thus, Portugal was able to claim Brazil. Other nations, like England and the Netherlands, paid no attention to the Pope's rulings. They explored and claimed land where they wished.

1. Why did the Spanish monarchs ask the Pope for help?
2. According to the papal line of demarcation, what lands was Spain to have? What lands was Portugal to have?
3. How did the Treaty of Tordesillas benefit Portugal?

Hernando Cortès

THE CONQUISTADORES   The Spanish were eager to explore their new possessions. Over the next few years, a series of Spanish **conquistadores**, or conquerors, set out to find the gold Columbus had talked about and to explore the new lands.

In 1513, Ponce de Leon sailed north from the island of Puerto Rico and discovered and explored Florida. Between 1519 and 1521, Hernando Cortés invaded Mexico. With the help of guns and smallpox, Cortés destroyed the Indian empire ruled by the Aztec chief Montezuma. Cortés and his troops took large amounts of gold from the Indians to send back to Spain.

In 1532, Francisco Pizarro invaded Peru and, within five years, conquered the Inca Empire. Like Cortés, Pizarro took great treasures of gold and silver from the Indians.

Then Pizarro and his men headed for the coast where they built Lima, the "City of Kings."

In 1539, Hernando de Soto sailed from Puerto Rico to Florida and explored westward. He found no gold, but he discovered the Mississippi River. In 1540, Francisco Coronado led an army overland from Mexico into the present-day United States. He discovered the Grand Canyon but returned without finding any treasure. Thus, between 1492 and 1550, Spain explored an area from North America through Central America and the West Indies to South America.

1. What were Spanish conquistadores looking for in the New World?
2. What were some of the discoveries made by the conquistadores between 1513 and 1540?

FERDINAND MAGELLAN   In 1517, Portugal controlled the eastern route to the Indies. As a result, Portugal was growing rich. This angered the Spanish king. So, when a Portuguese explorer and sea captain named Ferdinand Magellan offered to find Spain a western route to the Indies, the king accepted the offer. He wanted Spain to become as famous and wealthy as Portugal.

In 1519, Magellan set sail from Spain. He commanded a fleet of five ships and a crew of 270. In October of the following year, Magellan sailed through a stormy strait at the tip of South America. Today, the strait is named after Magellan. The trip took one month.

From the strait, Magellan sailed on into a great body of calm water that was known as the Great South Sea. Magellan renamed it the Pacific Ocean. By this time, Magellan had lost two of his ships. He continued, however, until he reached the Marianas Islands. The trip took three months. Conditions were terrible. The drinking water was spoiled and smelled foul. The biscuits were full of worms. The sailors were forced to eat sawdust from the ship boards and leather soaked in the sea and grilled on embers. By the time it reached the Marianas, the fleet

EUROPEAN VOYAGES OF DISCOVERY

was almost helpless. The crew was suffering from scurvy and had no food of any kind.

After they had rested and eaten, Magellan and his crew set a northwest course for the Philippine Islands. There, he converted the king and many others to Christianity. Magellan was killed in the Philippines when he tried to force the chief and people of a nearby island to convert to Christianity. Shortly after, several other Europeans were killed, and two more ships were lost.

The one remaining ship continued on into the Indian Ocean and around Africa. It finally arrived in Seville, Spain, in 1522 with 18 men and a load of spices. Theirs was a great accomplishment. They had proved that the world is round. The voyage opened the Pacific Ocean to European ships. More important, it proved beyond a doubt that the lands Columbus discovered were not Asia but a New World.

1. What did Ferdinand Magellan offer to do for Spain?
2. What did Magellan actually do?
3. What did Magellan's voyage prove?

Search for a Northwest Passage

Even after the New World was discovered, the English, French, and Dutch continued to look for another route to the Far East. Since the Portuguese and the Spanish controlled the southern sea lanes, they decided to look for a northwest passage.

English merchants persuaded their king to send the Italian navigator John Cabot west by a northern route. In 1497, Cabot set sail with a handful of men. He reached the mouth of the St. Lawrence River and explored the coasts of New England, Newfoundland, and Nova Scotia. His voyage established claims for England in the New World.

In 1524, the French hired Giovanni da Verrazano, an Italian, to find a northwest passage. He sailed along the Atlantic coast from North Carolina to New York harbor. Ten years later, Jacques Cartier, a French navigator, sailed up the St. Lawrence River as far as present-day Montreal. This gave the French a claim to eastern Canada.

In 1576, Martin Frobisher, an English **sea dog**, or captain turned pirate, began his search for the northwest passage. He passed through the dangerous icebergs off the coast of Greenland and fought a storm that almost wrecked one of his three

Martin Frobisher

EXPLORERS

Name	Country	Achievements
Amerigo Vespucci	Spain Portugal	explored Atlantic coast of South America, 1497–1503; one of first to believe he had reached a new world
Pedro Alváres Cabral	Portugal	discovered Brazil and sailed west to India, 1500–1501
Vasco Núñez de Balboa	Spain	first European to sight eastern shore of Pacific Ocean, 1513
Alvar Núñez Cabeza de Vaca	Spain	explored Florida and Gulf plains from Texas to Mexico, 1528–36
Juan Rodríguez Cabrillo	Spain	explored Pacific coast to Drake's Bay near San Francisco, 1542
Richard Chancellor	England	reached Moscow in search of northeast passage to Asia; opened trade with Russia, 1553–54
John Davis	England	explored west coast of Greenland in search of northwest passage to Asia, 1573
Sir Francis Drake	England	first Englishman to sail around the world, 1577–80
Father Jacques Marquette Louis Joliet	France	explored Mississippi Valley to mouth of Arkansas River, 1673
Vitus Bering	Russia	explored coasts of Alaska and northeast Asia; discovered Bering Strait and Bering Sea, 1728–41

ships. Frobisher finally discovered the bay that today is named after him.

In 1609, the Dutch sent Henry Hudson, an English navigator, to locate the passage. He discovered the Hudson River and then sailed up it to present-day Albany. Hudson was never seen again, but his voyage gave the Dutch their claim in the New World.

All of these voyages failed in their search to find the northwest passage to the Far East. They did, however, establish claims in the New World for the countries of England, France, and the Netherlands.

1. Why did the English, French, and Dutch continue to look for another route to the Far East after the discovery of the New World?
2. How did the English, French, and Dutch plan to sail to the Far East?
3. What did these voyages accomplish?

CHAPTER 31 REVIEW

SUMMARY

1. By the 1300's, European nations bordering the Atlantic Ocean began to look for a direct sea route to India and to the Far East.

2. The Europeans were interested in obtaining spices and silk and in spreading Christianity throughout the world.

3. The development of better maps, ships, and instruments for navigation helped the Europeans in their discoveries.

4. In the early 1400's, Prince Henry of Portugal started the first school in Europe for navigators.

5. By 1473, Portuguese ships had crossed the equator.

6. In 1487, Bartholomew Dias sailed around the Cape of Good Hope.

7. Between 1497 and 1499, Vasco da Gama sailed from Portugal around Africa to India and back again.

8. Between 1492 and 1504, Christopher Columbus made four voyages to what he thought was Asia but was actually the New World.

9. In 1494, the Treaty of Tordesillas divided newly found lands between Spain and Portugal.

10. In the first half of the 1500's, Hernando Cortés and Francisco Pizarro conquered the Aztec and Inca empires of Mexico and Peru and explored much of the New World for Spain.

11. Between 1519 and 1522, Ferdinand Magellan sailed around the world, proving that the lands Columbus discovered were not Asia but the New World.

12. Between 1497 and 1609, the English, French, and Dutch sent many explorers to the New World to search for a northwest passage to the Far East.

BUILDING VOCABULARY

1. *Identify the following:*

Prince Henry	Vasco da Gama	Hernando Cortés	John Cabot
Bartholomew Dias	Christopher Columbus	Francisco Pizarro	Jacques Cartier
Cape of Good Hope	Treaty of Tordesillas	Ferdinand Magellan	Henry Hudson

2. *Define the following:*

compass	cavalier	scurvy	papal line
astrolabe	convoy	mutiny	of demarcation
caravel	*naus*	sea dog	conquistadores

REVIEWING THE FACTS

1. Why did the European nations that bordered the Atlantic Ocean begin to look for a new, direct sea route to India and the Far East?

2. In what ways was the design of the caravel an improvement over earlier ships?

3. Why did Spain wait until the late 1400's to enter the race to find new trade routes to India and the Far East?

4. What were some of the problems that European explorers had to face on their voyages of discovery?

5. Why did Columbus's crew threaten mutiny against their officers?

6. How did Europeans first learn about tobacco?

7. What was the first European settlement in the New World?

8. How long did it take Magellan's ship to sail around the world?

9. What are three bodies of water named after European explorers?

10. What did the European voyages in search of a northwest passage to the Far East accomplish?

DISCUSSING IMPORTANT IDEAS

1. What were two main reasons for the European voyages of discovery?

2. Do you think Prince Henry of Portugal deserved the title "Henry the Navigator"? Explain.

3. Why do you think Queen Isabella of Spain agreed to support Columbus after others had turned him down?

4. Would you have enjoyed being one of the sailors on Magellan's voyage around the world? Why or why not?

5. How do you think the Indians felt about the coming of the conquistadores?

6. What do you think competition between nations had to do with the European voyages of discovery?

USING MAPS

Study the map on page 487, and answer the following questions:

1. Which countries sent explorers on voyages of discovery?

2. For what country did De Soto sail?

3. Where is the Strait of Magellan?

4. About how far is the Strait of Magellan from the Cape of Good Hope?

5. What body of water is located east of southern Africa?

6. To what country did Cabral sail?

7. What is the latitude and longitude of the West Indies?

8. What area did Coronado explore?

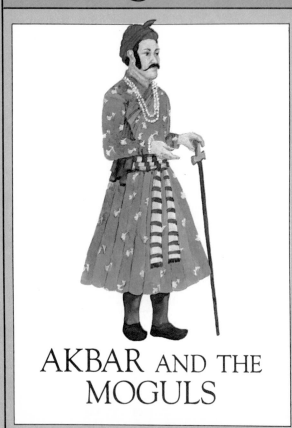

AKBAR AND THE MOGULS

In the early 1500's, Muslim Turks from Central Asia overran India. Their leader, Babur, was descended from Genghis Khan, the Mongol chief. Thus, the new rulers of India became known as **Moguls**, a variation of the word "Mongol." Mogul rajahs ruled parts of India until 1858.

Akbar, the grandson of Babur, was one of the greatest Mogul rajahs. He ruled from 1556 to 1605. Akbar was only 13 years old when he came to the throne. However, within a few years he conquered most of India and part of central

Asia. Then, he turned his attention to strengthening his empire.

To improve government, Akbar set up a civil service. Each job had a fixed salary, and each was given only to a qualified person. In this way, many able people entered government service.

To make things better for farmers, Akbar changed the tax system. At the time, the major tax was on agricultural products. Each farmer was subject to the same tax rate. Under the new system, land was classified according to its ability to bear crops. Then, taxes were lowered for those with less productive land.

Akbar showed concern for his people in other ways. For one thing, there

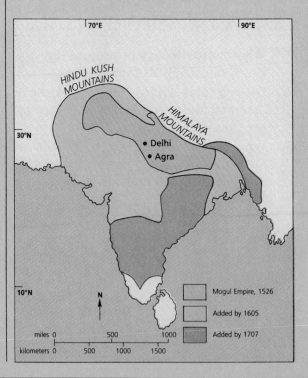

70°E

90°E

HINDU KUSH MOUNTAINS

HIMALAYA MOUNTAINS

30°N

• Delhi

• Agra

10°N

N

miles 0   500   1000

kilometers 0   500   1000   1500

Mogul Empire, 1526

Added by 1605

Added by 1707

were fewer executions when he was in power. He ordered his officials to treat people kindly. Also, he tried to help people when famine struck certain areas by sending them wheat from other areas.

To unite the Mogul Empire, Akbar showed tolerance for all religions. He married women of different faiths. Two were Hindus, one was a Christian, and one was a Muslim. He did away with taxes that had been levied on non-Muslims and protected their temples. He also welcomed scholars of different faiths to his court.

Under Akbar, the Mogul court became a center of culture. Persian influence was easy to see. Many upper-class Indians learned to speak Persian. Persian art, literature, and architecture were popular. Over time, Persian and Indian elements joined to form a separate Mogul style.

Akbar's grandson, Shah Jahan, was one of India's great builders. His major achievement was the Taj Mahal. He built this as a memorial to his favorite wife. It is made of white marble set with semi-precious stones. These stones are set in flowerlike patterns and in sayings from the Koran.

1. How did Akbar improve government in the Mogul Empire?
2. In what ways did Akbar show tolerance for all religions?
3. What was the major achievement of Shah Jahan?

UNIT 10 REVIEW

SUMMARY

1. A renewed interest in Greek and Roman writings and ideas in the 1400's and 1500's led to a new age called the Renaissance. During the Renaissance, the arts and the philosophy of humanism flourished in Europe.

2. The Renaissance began in Florence, spread to other Italian cities, and then to other parts of Europe.

3. Out of the Renaissance came the Reformation. It was marked by a desire to reform the Roman Catholic Church.

4. In the 1500's, the first Lutheran and Reformed churches were founded by Protestants. They were followers of a new religion based on the reforms of the German monk Martin Luther.

5. Catholic reformers worked to bring about changes in the Church, but the results did not satisfy many Protestants or Catholics. Soon, there was bitterness and war between them.

6. The desire to find new trade routes to the Far East and to spread Christianity led western Europeans to undertake a series of ocean voyages. The voyages resulted in the discovery and exploration of the New World.

REVIEWING THE MAIN IDEAS

1. Describe the cultural, religious, and political changes that took place in western Europe during the Renaissance and the Reformation.

2. Discuss the factors that led to the voyages of discovery and the effect that the discoveries had on the people of western Europe.

DEVELOPING SKILLS

When examining data, historians have to be able to recognize whether or not it will support a **generalization**, or a general statement about the topic. Sometimes, an item is factually correct but has nothing to do with a generalization. Other times, an item has a direct relationship to a generalization because it helps explain why the generalization is true or provides evidence to support what the generalization says.

This exercise is designed to give you practice in the skill of recognizing whether or not a particular statement supports a generalization. Read the two generalizations below and the five statements that follow each. Tell whether each statement does or does not support the generalization.

1. During the Renaissance, art and literature became very important.
   a. The Renaissance began in the Italian city-states.
   b. The printing press was invented during the Renaissance.
   c. A leading figure of the Renaissance was Leonardo da Vinci, who painted

the "Mona Lisa" and "The Last Supper."

   d. Miguel de Cervantes' novel *Don Quixote* was written in Spanish.

   e. The Medici family ruled Florence for many years.

2. The years between 1517 and 1648 were marked by great religious turmoil in western Europe.

   a. In 1517, Martin Luther objected to the sale of indulgences and also attacked other Catholic beliefs.

   b. Martin Luther was a German monk who studied the Bible.

   c. In 1555, the Peace of Augsburg allowed German princes to decide whether the people in their territories were to belong to the Catholic or Lutheran church.

   d. Catholic Spain sent a huge Armada against Protestant England in the year 1588.

   e. Elizabeth I of England was the younger daughter of Henry VIII.

SUGGESTED UNIT ACTIVITIES

1. Plan a trip to a newspaper or printing company to see printing presses. Compare them with Gutenberg's press.

2. Bring in several pictures of Renaissance art to show the class. Provide information about each artist and an explanation of each picture.

3. Act out a scene from one of William Shakespeare's plays. Have a different classmate take each role.

4. Report on the English theater during the Renaissance and Reformation or on the life of Shakespeare, Luther, or Calvin.

5. Working in a group, write a play for class presentation based on the first voyage of Christopher Columbus. You might have three scenes: (1) Columbus at the court of Ferdinand and Isabella; (2) Columbus at sea on October 12, 1492; (3) Columbus landing in the New World.

SUGGESTED READING

Goodenough, Simon. *The Renaissance*. New York: Arco Pub., 1979. An account of life during the Renaissance.

Grant, Matthew G. *Champlain*. Mankato, Minn.: Creative Education, 1974. A biography.

Grant, Neil. *The Renaissance*. New York: Franklin Watts, 1971. A description of events and people in the development of the Renaissance.

Jensen, Malcolm. *Leif Erickson, the Lucky*. New York: Franklin Watts, 1979. A biography.

O'Dell, Scott. *The Hawk That Dare Not Hunt By Day*. Boston: Houghton Mifflin, 1975. A young boy helps smuggle an English translation of the Bible into England.

Syme, Ronald. *John Cabot and His Son Sebastian*. New York: William Morrow, 1972. A biography.

Ventura, Piero. *Christopher Columbus*. New York: Random House, 1978. A biography.

Villiers, Captain Alan. *Men, Ships, and the Sea*. Washington, D.C.: National Geographic Society, 1973. Basic information and not-so-well-known facts about explorers and others.

UNIT 11

1500

1500 Cabral claims Brazil

1515

1530

1532 Portuguese establish first permanent settlement in Brazil

c. 1535 Spain becomes leading colonial power in Americas

154

1590

1605

1603 James I becomes king of England

1607 First permanent English settlement at Jamestown

1608 Samuel de Champlain establishes French colony at Quebec

1619 Virginia House of Burgesses meets

1620

1620 Pilgrims settle at Plymouth Mayflower Compact

1625 Charles I becomes king England

1628 Petition of Rig

1630 Purita

163

1680

1682 William Penn founds Pennsylvania La Salle claims Mississippi

1688 Glorious Revolution

1695

1710

1712 Thomas Newcomen develops first practical steam engine

1770

1770 Boston Massacre

1773 Boston Tea Party

1774 First Continental Congress

1775 Second Continental Congress

1776 Declaration of Independence

1779 James Hargreaves invents spinning jenny

1785

1789 U.S. Constitution French Revolution begins

1791 First French Republic

1793 Reign of Terror Eli Whitney invents cotton gin

1798 First use of mass production

1800

1860

1867 English working-class males gain vote

1875

1890

THE CHANGING WORLD

1545	1560 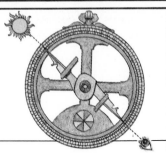	1575
		1580 Portugal claimed by Philip II of Spain
		1585 Sir Walter Raleigh founds English colony in North Carolina
Copernicus states that planets revolve around sun		**1588** England defeats Spanish Armada
1635	1650	1665 
1642 English civil war begins	**1649** Oliver Cromwell rules England	
	1660 Charles II becomes king of England	
establish Massachusetts Bay Colony		
English Catholics found Maryland		
1725 	1740	1755 **1763** Treaty of Paris
	1733 John Kay invents flying shuttle	**1764** Sugar Act
		1765 Stamp Act Congress
		1767 Townshend Acts
		1769 James Watt perfects steam engine
1815	1830	1845
	1829 George Stephenson builds locomotive	
		1856 Henry Bessemer makes steel from iron

1. WHAT CHANGES IN GOVERNMENT TOOK PLACE IN THE WEST DURING THE 1600'S?
2. WHAT ECONOMIC CHANGES TOOK PLACE IN THE WEST DURING THE 1700'S?

The discoveries made in the late 1400's and early 1500's led to many changes. The known world was suddenly larger. This meant greater opportunity for those willing to take it. For some European nations, the New World was the key to expanding their territory and gaining wealth and power. For some Europeans, it was a place where they could make a new life and worship in their own way. As a result, trade increased. So did the rivalry between nations.

During the 1600's and 1700's, many people in Europe and in the New World felt their governments had too much control. They wanted changes and were willing to fight for them. In England, America, and France, this led to **revolution,** or an attempt to overthrow or change the government. The revolutions, however, did not completely change how the people lived. But they did bring about greater political rights for a larger number of people.

In the 1700's and early 1800's, the western world experienced still another type of revolution—the **Industrial Revolution.** It involved the shift from animal and human power to machine power. It changed manufacturing and industry forever. The Industrial Revolution also changed greatly the way people lived and worked.

By the middle of the 1800's, the pattern and quality of life were different from what they had been in the past. There were changes in the way government was run, society was organized, people lived, and goods were produced.

CHAPTER 32

NEW WORLD EXPANSION

The discoveries made in the late 1400's and early 1500's expanded the world that Europeans knew to almost twice its size. Europeans willing to cross the ocean could find a new way of life and possibly new wealth.

From the early 1500's to the 1700's, several western European countries set out to **colonize**, or build permanent settlements in, the New World. They wanted the riches of the New World, which they thought would bring them power. They also wanted to spread Christianity.

PORTUGAL

By 1510, the Portuguese had claimed all of Brazil. They had also established trading posts in Africa, India, Southeast Asia, and the Molucca, or Spice, Islands. They took most of the Asian coastal cities by force. Portuguese **men-of-war**, or warships armed with cannons, attacked the coast. Then, soldiers went ashore and took over the city.

Portugal did not have a large enough population to send settlers to its territories. Also, most of the territories already had large populations. Then, too, the hot, wet climate of the new trading posts was too uncomfortable for most Europeans. So, Portugal had to depend on sea power and on the cooperation of defeated leaders to protect its interests.

1. How did the Portuguese get most of their trading posts?
2. What kept Portugal from colonizing most of its settlements?

BRAZIL In 1500, the Portuguese explorer Pedro Alváres Cabral claimed Brazil for Portugal. Since no precious metals were found, Portugal paid little attention to the discovery.

Then, other countries, such as France, started raiding the area. They took away **brazilwood**, or a red wood that could be used to make dyes. When the Portuguese learned the value of the wood, they became more interested in Brazil.

In 1532, the Portuguese established their first permanent settlement in Brazil. The king of Portugal divided the area into 15 territorial strips called **captaincies**. Each strip was given to a different Portuguese family. The owners of the captaincies were called *donatarios*. They could establish towns, distribute land, and raise armies. In return, they promised to colonize their captaincies and protect them from other European powers.

Portugal began sending over large numbers of settlers. Portuguese sailors landed and stayed. Criminals were sent to Brazil to work off their sentences. Soldiers and officials came to protect royal interests. Ranchers arrived with herds of cattle in search of pastures. Missionaries appeared looking for Indians to convert to Christianity.

The Portuguese established **plantations**, or large farms, most of which grew sugarcane. These plantations were controlled by *patrãos*, or leading older members of the settlements. The word of a patrão was law.

Workers were needed to clear the forests and labor on the plantations. About 2 million Indians lived in Brazil when the Portuguese claimed the land. The settlers, thinking the Indians would supply the needed labor, made slaves of them. But most of the Indians either ran away or died from diseases introduced by the Europeans.

Before long, the settlers began bringing over black slaves from Africa. Their numbers grew until, in some places, there were at least 20 black slaves for each European. The Africans brought with them their religion, called **macumba**, and the music and dance of the **samba**. They also added many new words to the Portuguese language.

By the end of the 1600's, there was less demand for sugar. *Bandeirantes*, or fortune-hunters, looking for precious stones and slaves who had run away, began to appear. The bandeirantes were the frontiersmen of Brazil. They established Portugal's claim to the far western and southern parts of Brazil.

BRAZILIAN PLANTATION

Early Portuguese settlers established plantations in Brazil. To provide labor, Indian populations were forced into slavery at first. Later, black slaves were brought from Africa to work on the plantations.

What happened to many of the Indians who were forced to work on the plantations?

Royal interest in Brazil grew when gold was discovered in the 1690's. The king sent workers and government clerks to check the mineral resources and make sure the **Crown**, or monarchy, received one fifth of each miner's gold. Gold brought still more people to Brazil and more wealth to Portugal. So did the growing of coffee, which was introduced in the early 1700's. Brazil remained a Portuguese colony until 1822, when it gained its independence.

1. Why did the Portuguese wait to colonize Brazil?
2. What did the donatarios promise to do with their land?
3. What did Africans contribute to Brazilian culture?
4. How did the bandeirantes help the growth of Brazil?

King of Portugal
Cardinal Henry

LOSS OF EMPIRE   About 1517, Portuguese sea power was challenged by the Turks. The Turks resented the Portuguese for taking over the spice trade. So, they sent two fleets against the Portuguese. Both were destroyed. Portugal continued to control much of the trade in the Indian Ocean and the South China Sea.

By the middle of the 1500's, however, things had changed. Portugal began losing its empire. Colonial government was not well organized. The conquered peoples disliked the Portuguese for forcing Christianity on them. Also, the Portuguese economy was not in good shape. It had been hurt when other European countries began to expand their overseas trade. By the time the Portuguese king died in 1580, Portugal was very weak. The king left no heirs, and the throne was claimed by Phillip II of Spain.

Spain ruled Portugal until 1640, when it regained its independence. During that time, the English and Dutch took over most of the Portuguese trading centers in Southeast Asia. By the end of the 1600's, Brazil was the only important colony the Portuguese possessed.

1. Why did the Turks send two fleets against the Portuguese?
2. Why did Portugal lose control of its empire in the 1500's?
3. What happened to the Portuguese trading centers in Southeast Asia when Spain took control of Portugal?

SPAIN

By 1535, Spain had established the largest colonial empire in the New World. Spain's colonies reached from southern North America through Central America and the West Indies to South America. The Spanish also had trade interests in the Philippines.

Unlike Portugal, Spain had a fairly large population. Spain sent thousands of settlers to its colonies in the New World. It also had a strong, centralized colonial government.

MEXICO AND PERU   In the early 1500's, Spain conquered the Indian empires of Mexico and Peru. Mexico and Peru set the example for other Spanish colonies. They were governed by the Council of the Indies, which met at the Spanish court. This council made laws, acted as a court of final appeal, and chose officials to send to the New World. It even took charge of religious matters in the Indies.

Spanish Flag

The colonies themselves were divided into two **viceroyalties**, or districts—New Spain and Peru. Each viceroyalty was ruled by a **viceroy**, or person who represented the king.

The colonists sent large amounts of gold and silver back to Spain. They also ran plantations that produced cocoa, coffee, tobacco, tea, and sugar. They forced the Indians to do all of the heavy work in the mines and fields. Most were badly treated. Great numbers of Indians died of overwork, disease, and starvation.

After a time, the Spanish, like the Portuguese, brought black slaves over from Africa. But they were used mostly on the sugar islands of the Caribbean and were never as numerous as they were in Brazil.

By the middle of the 1500's, the colonists were divided into clear-cut social groups. At the top were *peninsulares*, or Spaniards born in Spain. Then came **Creoles**, or those of Spanish descent born in the New World. Next came *mestizos*, or people of mixed European and Indian ancestry. They were followed by Indians. At the lowest level were blacks. Each group held certain jobs. Peninsulares served as viceroys or high church officials. Mestizos were mostly artisans and merchants.

The Catholic Church played a large role in Spanish colonization. It controlled most of the best land in the colonies. Although the Church itself did not pay taxes, it charged the people who rented or farmed its land a 10 percent income tax.

The Church worked to better conditions in the colonies. Some church leaders, such as Bartolomé de Las Casas, tried to improve life for the Indians. The Church built and managed schools, hospitals, and asylums. It established the first two universities in the New World. One was the University of

CATHOLIC CHURCH
Spanish missions, or churches, in the New World (left) provided services to local
people. Church leaders, such as the priest Bartolomé de Las Casas (right), protested
against the enslavement of Indians and worked to help them.
What services did the Church provide for Indians?

Mexico, which opened in 1551. The other was San Marcos
University at Lima, which also opened in 1551.

1. What happened to the Indian empires of Mexico and Peru
   when the Spanish came?
2. What did the Council of the Indies do?
3. What role did the Catholic Church play in the Spanish
   colonies?

THE DECLINE OF EMPIRE   Spain received a great deal of
wealth from the colonies. But it did not keep that wealth. The
Inquisition had driven out the Jews and Muslims who had been
important to Spanish industry. As a result, most of the gold and
silver sent to Spain went to northern Europe to pay for goods
made there.

The Spanish also had trouble getting gold and silver from their colonies to Spain. Ships loaded with the precious metals were robbed at sea by English, French, and Dutch **privateers**, or pirates. English sea dogs attacked Spanish treasure ships with the blessing of their queen, Elizabeth I. One of the most successful sea dogs was Sir Francis Drake. When Philip II's Armada was defeated by the English in 1588, Spain lost its power in the Atlantic. This opened the New World to colonization by England, France, and the Netherlands.

1. How did Spain spend most of its colonial wealth?
2. Why did the Spanish have trouble transporting gold and silver from the New World to Spain?
3. How did Spain lose its power in the Atlantic?

ENGLAND

Like Portugal and Spain, England looked to the New World for gold and silver. English nobles and merchants also saw it as a place to get the raw materials that they had to buy from other countries. With enough gold, silver, and raw materials, the English could establish a favorable **balance of trade**. This meant England would be able to sell more products to other countries than it would have to buy from them. The English would no longer have to depend on other countries for their needs.

Sir Walter Raleigh

The English also had other reasons for wanting colonies in the New World. England had so many people that jobs were becoming hard to find. New colonies meant more jobs. Then, too, the Anglican Church had become England's official church, and the English people were expected to follow Anglican beliefs. Because of this, Catholics and groups of Protestants called Separatists were looking for a place where they could have religious freedom. They believed that in the New World they would be able to worship in their own way.

In 1585, Sir Walter Raleigh founded a colony on Roanoke Island off the coast of North Carolina. But after three years, the colonists who had settled there disappeared. No one knows for certain what happened to them. For this reason, Roanoke Island became known as the "Lost Colony."

The English did not try again to found colonies in the New World for more than 20 years. However, in 1600, English merchants formed the East India Company. Its goal was to trade with the East Indies. The company set up trading posts in India, Malaya, and some islands in both the East and West Indies.

1. Why did the English want to colonize the New World?
2. What was the first English colony in the New World?
3. Why was the East India Company formed?

JAMESTOWN   In 1606, a group of English nobles and merchants formed the Virginia Company of London. The following year, the company sent about 100 settlers to the New World to search for gold and silver. These settlers founded the first permanent English settlement in America near the mouth of Chesapeake Bay in Virginia. They named it Jamestown after their king, James I.

The area in which the colony was founded had long been home to Indians. By the time Christopher Columbus arrived in the New World, there were more than 1 million Indians scattered across the North American continent. They were divided into some 500 different groups.

Each group of Indians had its own physical characteristics, language, religion, and way of life. Some, like the Pima, Papago, Creeks, and Cherokee, settled in an area and farmed the land. Others, like the Comanche, Blackfoot, Sioux, Apache, and Navaho, were fierce warriors and hunters who traveled in bands.

The Indians who lived in the area near Jamestown were the Powhatan. Their chief, whom the settlers called Powhatan, controlled 200 Indian villages.

Life in Jamestown was hard. The land around the settlement was swampy and filled with mosquitoes that carried diseases. Then, too, winters were colder there than in England. The colonists found themselves burning parts of their houses as fuel. Many fell sick and died.

Captain John Smith kept the settlement from total failure. He made it clear that those who did not work would not eat. He also convinced Powhatan to supply the colonists with corn and beans. When Smith had to return to England in 1609, however, the colonists almost starved to death. Those still alive a year later were ready to return to England. But an English fleet arrived with supplies, and they stayed.

The settlers worked the land, but they did not own it at first. It belonged to the Virginia Company. Then, in 1618, the company began granting land to individuals. Every settler

John Smith

NORTH AMERICAN INDIANS

Region	Way of Life
Arctic	fished and hunted whales, seals, walruses, and caribou; lived in wood and stone houses or igloos in winter and animal skin tents in summer
Subarctic	hunted and gathered food; built wood-frame houses; traveled by snowshoes, canoe, and toboggan
Northwest Coast	fished and hunted; built cedar wood houses and sea–going canoes; carved totem poles to honor ancestors; held potlatches, or ceremonial feasts
Plateau	hunted bison, fished and gathered food; lived in multifamily lodges; bred the Appaloosa horse
Great Basin	hunted and gathered food; wandered over territory; wove reed baskets decorated with beads, feathers, and shells
California	hunted, fished, and gathered food; settled in communities; used acorns to make bread
Southwest	farmed corn, beans, and squash; built pueblos of stone and adobe; wove straw and reed baskets and cotton cloth
Great Plains	farmed and hunted; lived in log houses or cone–shaped tipis; communicated with other tribes by hand signals
Eastern Woodlands	fished and hunted; lived in longhouses and birch lodges; women owned property, chose chief and passed on family name
Southeast	farmed and hunted; built towns with open squares; women owned houses and land; counted descent through mothers

received 50 acres for each person that settler brought to the New World. This included servants.

Thousands of settlers came over as **indentured servants**. They agreed to work for four to seven years after their arrival to pay for their passage. At the end of that time, they were free and could get land of their own.

Pocahontas and John Rolfe

The settlers saw the Indians using tobacco and began to use it themselves. About 1612, a settler named John Rolfe began planting fields of tobacco. Tobacco soon became Virginia's most important crop because people in England were willing to pay a good price for it.

The settlers brought with them English laws and government. But they were far from England, and travel was slow. Soon, it became necessary for them to make their own laws. In 1619, they elected 22 **burgesses**, or representatives, from among landowning males over 17 years old. The burgesses met to decide the laws for the colony. This House of Burgesses set an important example of self-government in the New World.

1. What group of Indians lived near Jamestown?
2. What happened when the Virginia Company began granting land to settlers?
3. What did Jamestown settlers learn from neighboring Indians?
4. Why did the colonists form the House of Burgesses?

PLYMOUTH   Another company, the Virginia Company of Plymouth, was also formed in England in 1606. But it was not successful. In 1620, it was reorganized as the Council for New England. It gained the right to grant land to settlers for colonies in New England.

That same year a group of Separatists called Pilgrims sailed for Virginia on the *Mayflower*. They had received grants of land from the Virginia Company. But strong winds blew the *Mayflower* off course, and the Pilgrims landed in New England just north of Cape Cod in present-day Massachusetts.

The lands in New England belonged to the Council for New England, and the Pilgrims had not been given the right to govern in them. So, they signed an agreement to set up a civil government whose laws they would obey. This agreement, which was called the Mayflower Compact, formed the basis of government in the colony. In it, the settlers agreed to govern according to the wishes of the majority of men.

The Pilgrims named their settlement Plymouth after the English town from which they had sailed. The first winter was hard, and about one half of the settlers died. In the spring, those who remained cleared the fields for farming. The Indians taught them how to use fish as fertilizer for their crops. The Indians also taught the settlers how to hunt and fish in the wilderness.

The people of Plymouth governed themselves for 70 years with almost no outside control. Then, in 1691, Plymouth became part of the Massachusetts Bay Colony.

Pilgrim Meeting

1. Where did the Pilgrims settle?
2. How was Plymouth governed?
3. What did the Pilgrims learn from the Indians?

THE GROWTH OF EMPIRE   Jamestown and Plymouth were not the only English settlements in the New World. By 1733, Great Britain had 13 colonies along the Atlantic coast of America. In 1630, a group of Puritans seeking religious freedom sailed to New England. There, they formed several settlements in the area around present-day Boston. They called their settlements the Massachusetts Bay Colony.

In 1634, the English settled in Maryland. King Charles I had granted the land to his friend Cecilius Calvert, Lord Baltimore. Calvert wanted land in America where English Catholics could live in peace.

Lord Baltimore

In 1682, William Penn, the leader of a religious group called the Quakers, founded a colony in Pennsylvania. King Charles II had granted Penn the land in payment for a debt he owed Penn's father. Philadelphia became the chief city and port of Penn's colony.

1. What group founded the Massachusetts Bay Colony? Why did they found it?
2. Why did Cecilius Calvert want land in America?
3. How did William Penn get the land to found a colony in Pennsylvania?

THE NETHERLANDS

The Dutch also established colonies in the New World. In 1602, Dutch merchants founded the Dutch East India Company. The company was set up to organize trade in Africa and the East Indies. The Dutch had a fleet of more than 10,000 merchant ships. One by one, they seized Portuguese trading posts in the East Indies. Soon, they controlled most of the East Indies.

In 1621, the Dutch formed another company called the Dutch West India Company. Its goal was to establish colonies in the New World. Colonists were sent to islands in the West Indies and along the coast of South America. In 1624, the Dutch founded the city of New Amsterdam on the island of Manhattan. They bought the island from the Indians for goods worth about $24.00. The Dutch called the colonies they established in North America New Netherlands. New Amsterdam was the capital.

Later in the 1600's, the rivalry between the Dutch and the English led to a series of wars, which the Dutch lost. The English took over most of the Dutch colonies, including New Amsterdam, which they renamed New York.

1. Why was the Dutch East India Company formed? The Dutch West India Company?
2. About how much did the Dutch pay for Manhattan?
3. To whom did the Dutch lose most of their colonies?

FRANCE

In 1608, the French explorer Samuel de Champlain founded the first permanent French colony in the New World at Quebec. Soon after, the French established other settlements around the Great Lakes and at the northern end of the Mississippi River and its tributaries.

Most of these settlements resembled villages in France. Houses stood side by side along a lake or a river bank. Behind each house stretched a long, narrow farm. The settlements were small, however, because few people wanted to leave France.

Most of the French in the New World were fur traders. On foot or by canoe, they visited various Indian tribes. They gave the Indians blankets, guns, and wine in exchange for beaver and other animal skins. Beaver hats for gentlemen were very fashionable in Europe, and the fur trade brought France much wealth.

In 1682, Robert Cavalier, Sieur de la Salle, claimed the Mississippi River Valley for France. He named the area Louisiana in honor of the French king, Louis XIV. The French called Louisiana and their other lands in the New World New France.

The French also established settlements in the West Indies and in India. In time, the French and the English became great rivals. They clashed in Europe, the New World, and India. After

French Settler

EUROPEAN COLONIES IN THE NEW WORLD

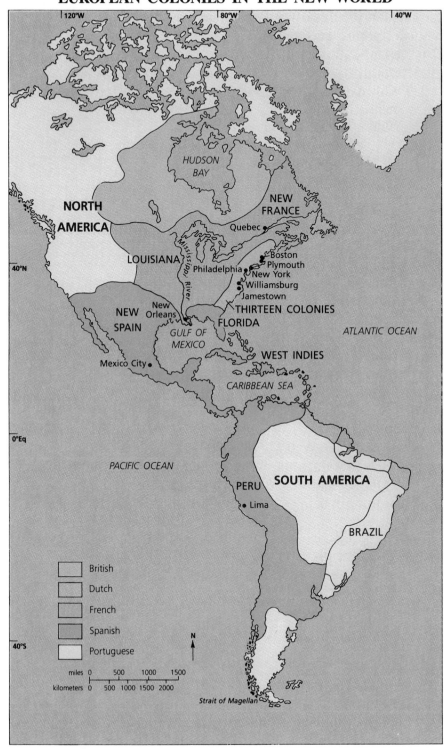

120°W   80°W   40°W

HUDSON BAY

NORTH AMERICA

NEW FRANCE

Quebec

40°N

LOUISIANA

Mississippi River

Boston
Plymouth
Philadelphia
New York
Williamsburg
Jamestown

THIRTEEN COLONIES

NEW SPAIN

New Orleans

FLORIDA

GULF OF MEXICO

ATLANTIC OCEAN

Mexico City

WEST INDIES

CARIBBEAN SEA

0°Eq

PACIFIC OCEAN

SOUTH AMERICA

PERU

Lima

BRAZIL

British
Dutch
French
Spanish
Portuguese

N

40°S

miles 0   500   1000   1500
kilometers 0   500 1000 1500 2000

Strait of Magellan

a series of four wars, the French finally were defeated. In 1763, they signed the Treaty of Paris. They lost their North American colonial empire and their settlements in India.

1. What was the first permanent French colony in the New World?
2. Why did France's settlements in the New World remain small?
3. What area did Sieur de la Salle claim?
4. How did the French lose their lands in North America?

CHAPTER 32 REVIEW

SUMMARY

1. By 1532, Portugal had a permanent settlement in Brazil as well as trading posts in Africa, India, and the Far East.

2. At first, Portuguese settlers tried to use Indians to work on their plantations and mines, but later they began bringing over black slaves from Africa.

3. By the end of the 1600's, Portugal had lost all of its possessions except Brazil.

4. By 1535, Spain had established the largest colonial empire in the New World.

5. The Spanish conquered Mexico and Peru and forced the Indians to work on the land and in the mines.

6. When the Spanish Armada was defeated in 1588, Spain lost its power in the Atlantic.

7. The first successful English settlement in the New World was at Jamestown, Virginia, in 1607.

8. The Powhatan, who lived near Jamestown, was one of many different Indian groups in North America.

9. In 1619, the Jamestown colonists organized the House of Burgesses, which set an example for self-government in the New World.

10. The second permanent English settlement in the New World was at Plymouth, Massachusetts, in 1620.

11. Most of the Dutch colonies in the New World were taken over by the English.

12. The first permanent French settlement in the New World was at Quebec.

BUILDING VOCABULARY

1. *Identify the following:*

Pedro Alváres Cabral	Roanoke Island	Pilgrims	William Penn
Bartolomé de las Casas	Jamestown	Mayflower Compact	Samuel de Champlain
Separatists	Captain John Smith	Puritans	Sieur de la Salle
Sir Walter Raleigh	House of Burgesses	Cecilius Calvert	Treaty of Paris

2. *Define the following:*

colonize	plantations	Crown	*mestizos*
men-of-war	*patrãos*	viceroyalties	privateers
brazilwood	macumba	viceroy	balance of trade
captaincies	samba	*peninsulares*	indentured servants
donatarios	*bandeirantes*	Creoles	burgesses

REVIEWING THE FACTS

1. Why did western European nations want to colonize the New World?
2. Why did the Portuguese settlers in Brazil bring over African slaves?
3. On what things did the Spanish colonies base their social groups?
4. What did the defeat of the Spanish Armada have to do with the colonization of the New World?
5. Why was the colony on Roanoke Island called the "Lost Colony"?
6. Why was life hard in Jamestown?
7. In what ways did the North American Indian groups differ?
8. Why did the Pilgrims draw up the Mayflower Compact?
9. What kind of trade did the French establish with the Indians?

DISCUSSING IMPORTANT IDEAS

1. What problems did Europeans face in the New World?
2. What changes did European colonization cause in the lives of the Indians in the New World?
3. What do you think might have happened if Spain had used the gold and silver from its New World colonies to develop its own industries?
4. Would you have liked being one of the Jamestown settlers? Why or why not?
5. What did the establishment of the House of Burgesses have to do with the growth of democracy in the New World?

USING MAPS

Study the map on page 511, and answer the following questions:

1. To what country did the area called Louisiana belong?
2. Into what body of water does the Mississippi River flow?
3. Where are the Thirteen Colonies in the New World located?
4. What country controlled most of the territory in the New World?
5. Whose territory is located about 20° north latitude and 100° west longitude?
6. What British territory is on the east coast of North America?

THE SLAVE TRADE

died from overwork and disease. So, the colonists began to use black slaves from Africa as workers.

The slave trade from Africa to America began in the 1500's. As time went by, a system was set up on the coast of Africa to obtain slaves. The British, French, Portuguese, and Dutch set up trading posts called **factories.** European ships brought such goods as cloth and guns to trade to local African rulers. In return, the rulers agreed to supply the traders with a certain number of slaves. Once enough slaves were gathered to fill a ship, they were taken to America.

The trip to America was terrible and dangerous for the slaves. Ship captains wanted to make as much money as possible. They crammed the slaves aboard and kept them under the deck for days and days at a time. Many died from disease and poor food. Often, one half of the slaves on a ship died before they reached the New World.

Most of the slaves brought to America came from the west coast of Africa.

One of the biggest problems facing European colonists in the New World was finding enough workers. There was always too much work to be done and too few people to do it. At first, the Europeans tried to force the Indians to work for them. But the Indians were not used to long hours of heavy labor. Often, they

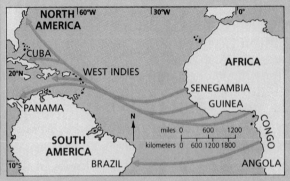

One third were sent to Brazil. Most of the rest were shipped to the Caribbean area. A much smaller number went to slave markets in the English colonies of North America. Historians believe that the total number of blacks brought to the New World as slaves was about 10 million.

In the 1700's, religious and other leaders in Europe began to call for an end to the slave trade. They believed it was wrong for Christians to make slaves of other people.

At the time, the largest shipper of slaves to the New World was Great Brit-ain. In 1807, the British government passed a law against the slave trade. The following year, the United States did the same. When the Latin American nations gained their independence from Spain in the 1800's, they, too, stopped trading in slaves. Thus, one of the largest movements of people in history ended.

1. Why did European colonists begin to use African slaves as workers?
2. How did colonists obtain their slaves?
3. What brought the slave trade to an end?

CHAPTER 33

POLITICAL REVOLUTIONS

By the 1700's, people in the western world had new ideas about government. They were less willing to be ruled without having a voice in government. They also wanted equal justice under the law. They did not believe that monarchs or the Church had the right to tell them what to do. Thinkers and writers began spreading ideas about freedom and the right of the people to change government to meet their needs. For these reasons, the eighteenth century came to be known in Europe and the Americas as the Age of Enlightenment, or time of increased knowledge.

REVOLUTION IN ENGLAND

In England, there was a struggle for power between the king and Parliament. After a civil war and some changes in government, Parliament won. From that point on, the monarch ruled in the name of the people.

CONFLICT WITH PARLIAMENT   In 1603, the last Tudor monarch, Queen Elizabeth I, died. Since she had never married, the Crown passed to a distant relative. This was James VI of Scotland, a member of the Stuart family. He became James I of England.

The Tudors had enjoyed great power. But they were careful to get Parliament's opinion on their actions. James I, however, believed in rule by divine right. When Parliament objected to some of his actions, he dismissed it and ruled without a legislature for ten years.

Religious differences were also a problem between the king and Parliament. James I wanted to force the Anglican Church, or Church of England, on the people. Many members of Parliament, however, were Puritans. They wanted to be able to worship as they pleased. Also, they believed in hard work and plain living. They did not like the free-spending ways of the Crown. With the help of other groups, they worked against what they felt was the unjust power of the king.

Although James I did not agree with many of his subjects about religion, it was his idea to have a new translation of the Bible. He appointed a committee of church officials, who put together the King James Version. Its style has greatly influenced English speech and literature. Most English-speaking Protestant churches today use either the King James Version or a form of it.

When James I died in 1625, his son Charles I became king. Charles I held the same beliefs about the monarchy as his father. In 1628, he was forced to call a meeting of Parliament to approve new taxes to pay for the wars with France and Spain.

Parliament saw a chance to limit the Crown's power and gain more for itself. It drew up the Petition of Right. This said

King James I

that the king could not declare **martial law**, or rule by the army instead of by law. It also said that the Crown could not pass tax laws without Parliament's consent. In addition, people could not be put in prison just because the king wanted them out of the way. At first, Charles I agreed to the petition. Then, he realized it would limit his power. In 1629, he broke his word and dismissed Parliament.

In 1640, however, Charles I needed money to build a larger army to fight the Scots. He had tried to force the Anglican Church on the Presbyterian Scots, and they had revolted, taking over part of northern England. So, he called a meeting of Parliament.

Parliament again saw a chance to limit Charles' power. It passed a law abolishing taxes collected by the Crown without Parliament's consent. It also passed a law to set up regular meetings of Parliament and to do away with the Star Chamber. This was the royal court that tried people without a jury.

1. What were the major problems between King James I and Parliament?
2. What were the major points of the Petition of Rights?
3. What was the Star Chamber?

Cavalier

CIVIL WAR   Once again, Charles I accepted the laws at first and then tried to stop them. Finally, in 1642, civil war broke out between the Crown and Parliament.

Those who backed the Crown were called Cavaliers. They wore their hair shoulder length, often in curls. They were mostly wealthy Roman Catholics and Anglicans. Those who backed Parliament were called Roundheads because they wore their hair short. They were mostly middle and lower-class Puritans and other Calvinists.

Oliver Cromwell, a Puritan leader who backed Parliament, set up a New Model Army that drilled hard and followed strict rules against drinking, swearing, and plundering. It chose its officers because they were good fighters and leaders, not because they were of high birth. In 1646, the New Model Army defeated the king's army and ended the war.

Most English leaders still believed that monarchy was the best form of government. But they did not trust Charles I and were afraid to allow him to return to the throne. However, it was

THE ENGLISH CIVIL WARS

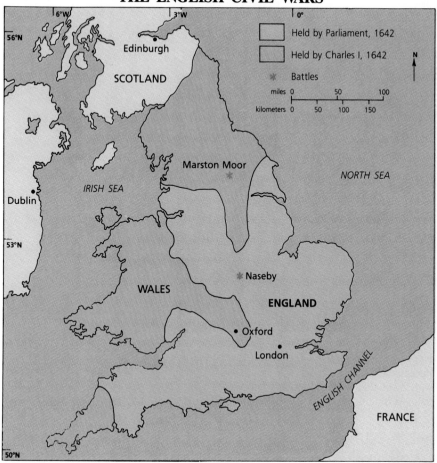

Cromwell and his supporters who put Charles I on trial and, in 1646, beheaded him.

1. What groups made up the Cavaliers? The Roundheads?
2. How were the officers of the New Model Army chosen?

OLIVER CROMWELL   After the death of the king, Cromwell took over the rule of England, now called the Commonwealth. The Commonwealth was beset by troubles from the outside. It was necessary for Cromwell to defeat the Irish and the Scots, who both looked to Charles I's son as the true ruler of England. Cromwell also had trouble at home balancing those groups that felt enough changes had been made and those that wanted more. He finally did away with Parliament and governed as a military dictator for the Puritan minority.

OLIVER CROMWELL AND KING CHARLES I
Oliver Cromwell (left) organized the New Model Army that defeated the army of King Charles I in 1646. This ended the four-year civil war between the Crown and Parliament. After Charles was beheaded, Cromwell took over the rule of England, which was then called the Commonwealth.
What problems faced Cromwell as he came to power?

Many Puritans were very strict. They disapproved of dancing, theater-going, sports, and other popular amusements. They believed that people should spend all their free time praying and reading the Bible. Despite this, Puritan rule was not completely gloomy. Cromwell himself was fond of music and horses and allowed women to act on stage for the first time. After Cromwell died, his son Richard took over. But by 1660, Parliament had decided that England again needed a monarch.

1. Who ruled England after the death of Charles I?
2. What was life like for many Puritans?

THE RETURN OF THE STUARTS   Parliament's choice was Charles II, Charles I's son. King Charles II had spent most of the previous 15 years in France. He brought French dances, food, and clothing styles with him to London. Soon, the English court was a center of gaiety and fashion. Men copied the fashions of

Paris and wore silks and velvets and huge wigs. People ate large meals. One meal might include a fricasee of rabbits and chickens, a leg of boiled mutton, a side of lamb, roasted pigeons, lobsters, tarts, anchovies, and wine.

In September 1666, while Charles II was king, a great fire destroyed two thirds of London's buildings. Charles II put the architect Sir Christopher Wren in charge of rebuilding the city. Wren designed St. Paul's Cathedral and 51 churches. He also had most of the new houses and shops built of brick and stone instead of wood.

Charles II was very popular with the English people. They were ready for merriment. And he tried not to anger Parliament. However, he refused to consult with it about **foreign policy**, or relations with other countries. Parliament was especially alarmed by his friendly relations with the Catholic king of France.

Christopher Wren

1. What was the English court like under Charles II?
2. What was the subject that Charles II refused to discuss with Parliament?

THE GLORIOUS REVOLUTION Things finally came to a head in 1685 when Charles II died and his brother James II became king. Openly Catholic, James II appointed many Catholics to high posts in the army and the government. This was against a law passed by Parliament under Charles II. James II also tried to have the Act of Habeas Corpus **repealed**, or abolished. This act, also passed under Charles II, stated that a person could not be put in jail unless charged with a specific crime.

The leaders of Parliament did not like James II. However, they did not move against the king until 1688 when his Catholic second wife had a son. Then, they offered the throne to Mary, James' Protestant daughter by his first wife. Mary was the wife of the Dutch ruler William of Orange, who was also a Protestant. He landed in England in 1688 with a large army, and James II fled to France. William and Mary were named joint rulers. All of this took place without a shot being fired. It came to be called the "Glorious Revolution."

William and Mary

In 1689, when they became the new rulers of England, William and Mary accepted Parliament's Declaration of Rights. It made Parliament stronger and protected the rights of the

English people. It stated that the Crown could not levy taxes or keep an army in peacetime without Parliament's consent. Also, Parliament was allowed to debate openly, meet often, and be elected freely. People had the right to a fair and speedy trial by their **peers**, or equals. And people could petition the Crown without fear of being punished.

1. Why did Parliament remove James II from the throne? Whom did they choose in his place?
2. What did the Declaration of Rights say?

THE AMERICAN REVOLUTION

What happened in Great Britain influenced people in the American colonies. At first, England and the colonies got along well. Over time, however, things changed. The colonists became angry over British controls. This led to revolution and the forming of a new country.

Charles II

MERCANTILISM   In 1660, when Charles II became king of England, most European leaders believed in an economic system called **mercantilism**. In it, colonies served as a source of raw materials. They also served as a market for finished goods. The American colonies were supposed to send things to England that were scarce or could not be grown there, such as furs, lumber, tobacco, and cotton. The colonists were supposed to buy only goods made in England so that English merchants could make money. These goods could only be carried in ships built in England or in the colonies that were sailed by English crews. This was to make the shipbuilding industry and the merchant marine stronger in case of war.

Mercantilism worked well until the 1700's. First of all, there were not enough skilled people in the colonies to make many goods. Also, the colonists enjoyed a **monopoly**, or sole right, on the sale of several major crops. And their ships were protected against pirates by the English navy.

Then, things changed. The colonists became angry over English trade laws. Their population was growing, and they wanted to make their own iron goods and beaver hats. Also, people in the northern colonies were not able to sell as much to Great Britain as people in the southern colonies did. Yet, they needed money to buy British goods. So, they began smuggling goods to and from the West Indies. Soon, a triangular, or three-way, trade grew up. The colonists shipped in sugar and molasses from the West Indies. They made rum and traded it to the slave dealers of Africa for black slaves. Then, they brought the slaves to the West Indies where they traded them for sugar and molasses.

1. What were some of the trade laws that the English colonies had to follow?
2. Why did mercantilism work well until the 1700's?

CHANGES IN BRITISH POLICY　　Although England regulated colonial trade, the colonists handled local affairs. Their legislatures usually controlled the passage of tax laws. Since colonial officials were paid out of taxes, they had to do as the legislatures wished. This gave the legislatures a great deal of power.

However, this changed in the middle of the 1700's. At that time, the French, who also had colonies in America, built a fort on the site of present-day Pittsburgh, Pennsylvania. The French and their Indian allies wanted to keep the British out of northern and western America. But Great Britain claimed the area for itself. This led to the French and Indian War. By the time the war ended in 1763, the British had control of nearly all of North America east of the Mississippi River.

The war left the British government deeply in debt. It felt the colonies should pay a large share of the money owed. This was because the war had been fought partly to protect their western frontier. So, Great Britain moved to raise money and began to tighten its control over the colonies.

In 1765, Parliament passed the Stamp Act. It called for taxes on all newspapers, legal documents, calendars, and even playing cards. All these had to bear a stamp showing the tax had been paid. This was the first **direct tax** Parliament levied on the colonies. That is, it was paid directly to the government, not included in the price of goods.

The Stamp Act hurt merchants, lawyers, and people in the newspaper business. These groups were the most able to lead the people in a fight against British control. Angry mobs formed in many cities. Tax officials were threatened, and stamps were destroyed. People everywhere decided to **boycott**, or refuse to buy, British goods.

Stamp

In October 1765, delegates from nine colonies met in New York to discuss the Stamp Act. They sent a letter to the British government. It stated that the colonies had never been taxed by anyone except their own legislatures. It also said that Parliament had no right to tax them because they had no representatives there. Finally, Parliament voted to repeal the Stamp Act. But then it passed the Declaratory Act, which again stated Parliament's right to make laws on all matters concerning the colonies. This showed that Parliament was not going to give up so easily.

1.   Why were colonial legislatures powerful?
2.   Why did Parliament pass the Stamp Act?

THE ROAD TO REVOLUTION   In 1767, Parliament passed the Townshend Acts. These acts placed a tax on such goods as paper, paint, glass, lead, and tea that were shipped into the colonies. Part of the tax money would be used to pay colonial officials. This took away the colonial legislatures' major source of power.

These acts made the colonists angry. There were incidents of violence. The worst of these took place in Boston. In 1768, the British had sent soldiers to Boston. This was to make sure the colonists obeyed the new laws and to protect customs officials. The colonists called the soldiers "redcoats" because of their bright red uniforms.

In 1770, a crowd of colonists began insulting the soldiers and throwing stones at them. The soldiers fired into the crowd. Five people were killed. The incident came to be called the Boston Massacre. Shortly afterwards, all the Townshend taxes were repealed except the one on tea. The Boston Massacre probably would have been forgotten. But some colonists used it to stir up feelings against British rule.

There were more problems three years later when Parliament passed the Tea Act. This was passed to help the East India Company, which was facing bankruptcy. The act allowed the company to sell tea directly to the colonists rather than to colonial merchants, who took part of the profits. This hurt the merchants. It also further angered those colonists already tired of British policies. In Massachusetts, a mob boarded a ship in Boston harbor and dumped its cargo of tea into the water. This became known as the Boston Tea Party.

To punish the colonists, Parliament, in 1774, passed the Coercive Acts. These acts closed Boston harbor and put the government of Massachusetts under military rule. Next, Parliament passed the Quebec Act, which extended the boundaries of Quebec west of the Appalachians and north of the Ohio River. This included land that Massachusetts, Connecticut, and Virginia claimed as their own. Colonists called all of these laws the Intolerable Acts, or laws which they could not bear.

The Intolerable Acts only made the colonists more certain than ever that they wanted to fight for their liberties. In September 1774, 12 of the colonies sent delegates to the First Continental Congress at Philadelphia. They spoke out against the Coercive Acts and called for their repeal.

THE AMERICAN REVOLUTION

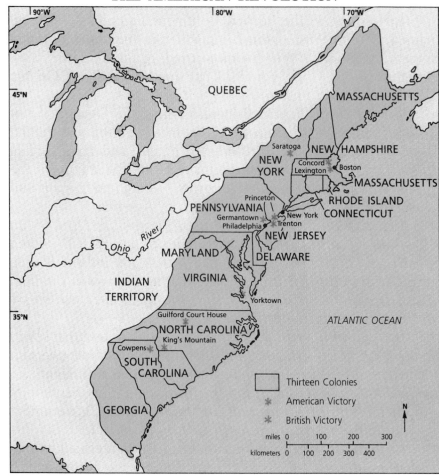

Colonial Soldier

Colonial leaders, however, were divided about what to do. Some, like George Washington of Virginia, hoped to settle the differences with Great Britain. Others, like Samuel Adams of Massachusetts and Patrick Henry of Virginia, wanted the colonies to become independent.

1. How did the Townshend Acts affect the power of the colonial legislatures?
2. What was the Tea Act?
3. What were the Intolerable Acts?

THE OUTCOME   Before anything was decided, fighting broke out between the colonists and British soldiers at Lexington and Concord in Massachusetts. The British were on their way to destroy a store of weapons at Concord. They met the colonists and fought the first battle of the American Revolution.

In May 1775, the Second Continental Congress met and named George Washington commander of the colonial armed forces. After this, the colonists tried again to settle their differences with Great Britain. They appealed to King George III, who refused to listen.

On July 4, 1776, the Congress issued the Declaration of Independence. Written mostly by Thomas Jefferson of Virginia, it stated that "All men are created equal" and have certain God-given rights that cannot be taken away from them. In the Declaration, the colonies broke away from Great Britain and declared themselves the United States of America.

War between the British and the Americans dragged on. In 1778, the French, who were old enemies of the English, agreed to help the Americans. In 1781, the Americans and the French forced a large English army to surrender at Yorktown, Virginia. The surrender all but ended the war. Two years later, the Treaty of Paris was signed, and the war was over.

In 1789, the United States adopted a constitution that set up a new form of government. This constitution sets forth certain principles of government. One of these is **popular sovereignty**, or the idea that a government receives its powers from the people. Another is **limited government**, or the idea that a government may use only those powers given to it by the people.

Later, a Bill of Rights was added. It guarantees all people such rights as freedom of speech, press, and religion; the right to

Thomas Jefferson

UNITED STATES CONSTITUTION

In 1787, representatives from 12 states met in Philadelphia and drew up a constitution for the United States. In this painting, George Washington, the chairman of the convention, addresses the delegates. In 1789, Washington became the first President of the United States.

What are some principles of American government expressed in the Constitution?

trial by jury; and freedom from unreasonable searches and seizures.

1. Where did the first battle of the American Revolution take place?
2. Who was the major author of the Declaration of Independence?
3. What does the Bill of Rights do?

THE FRENCH REVOLUTION

What happened in America influenced people in France. The American example pointed up the need for political change. It helped bring about a revolution that would change France for all time.

THE OLD REGIME   During the 1600's and early 1700's—the Old Regime—France was a divine-right monarchy. French society was divided into three **estates**, or classes. The first was the clergy. Although they made up less than 1 percent of the population, they owned 20 percent of the land. They were not only **exempt**, or free, from taxes, but they received income from Church lands. Church income was not divided evenly, however. Most of it went to high church officials, who were usually nobles. They wore robes of purple and scarlet velvet trimmed with lace. Parish priests lived simply and served people's religious needs.

The second was the nobility. They made up about 2 percent of the population and also owned large areas of land. They, too, were free from taxes. The nobles lived off grants from the royal treasury and the rents paid by the peasants. Some nobles spent their time at the royal court, dancing, hunting, and gambling. Others filled the highest posts in the government and the armed forces.

The third was everyone else in France. At the top of the Third Estate was the bourgeoisie—bankers, merchants, lawyers, doctors, manufacturers, and teachers. They controlled much of France's wealth and trade. Below the bourgeoisie were the city workers—artisans, laborers, and servants. At the bottom were the peasants, who made up more than 80 percent of France's population.

Members of the Third Estate had no power in the government. Yet, they paid the country's taxes. They paid taxes on income, personal property, land, and crops. They paid sales taxes on salt, tobacco, and wine. Parents even had to pay a tax when a child was born. And of course, the peasants still paid feudal dues to the nobles.

1. How was France ruled during the Old Regime?
2. What groups made up the three French estates?
3. Who paid taxes in France during the Old Regime?

THE ESTATES-GENERAL   By the 1780's, the French government was in trouble. Educated Frenchmen called *philosophes*, or philosophers, wrote articles pointing out the country's political problems. One of the most widely read was François Marie Arouet, known as Voltaire. Voltaire favored free speech, a free press, freedom of religion, and equal justice for everyone.

The major problem facing the French government, however, was lack of money. This was due mostly to war costs. For example, the French government had given so much help to the American Revolution that it was almost bankrupt. King Louis

Voltaire

PHILOSOPHERS

John Locke
1632–1704

English political thinker; in *Two Treatises of Government,* set forth ideas behind Glorious Revolution of 1688; influenced development of American and French Revolutions

Montesquieu
1689–1755

French political thinker; believed in separation of powers of government; wrote *The Spirit of the Laws;* inspired French Declaration of the Rights of Man and Constitution of the United States

Thomas Paine
1737–1809

international revolutionary and writer; influenced development of American and French Revolutions; wrote *Common Sense* and *The Rights of Man*

Jean-Jacques Rousseau
1712–1778

considered most important writer of eighteenth century; believed that will of the people represents supreme power; wrote *Social Contract;* influenced development of French Revolution and Constitution of the United States

XVI and his wife added to the problem by spending money on jewels, hunting parties, horse races, and balls. In fact, Queen Marie Antoinette spent so much that people called her Madame Deficit. The Crown wanted the clergy and nobles to provide it with money. They, however, had never paid taxes and saw no reason to start.

Finally, the king called a meeting of the legislature to help decide how to raise money. It was the first time the legislature, known as the Estates-General, had met since 1614. At that time, each estate had met separately, with each casting one vote. This meant that the nobles and clergy together could outvote the Third Estate and thus protect themselves from change.

Now, however, the Third Estate wanted a bigger voice in government. "What is the Third Estate?" one of their leaders wrote in a pamphlet. "Everything. What has it been until now? Nothing. What does it demand? To become something." Members of the Third Estate wanted the Estates-General to meet as a single body with each representative having a vote. It also wanted to have the same number of representatives as the other two estates combined.

In May 1789, the Estates-General met. The Third Estate had been allowed more representatives, but the other two estates refused to meet with them. So, the Third Estate and a small number of clergy and nobles met as a separate body. They called themselves the National Assembly. When the king ordered them to break up, they swore not to do so until they had written a constitution for France. At last, the king decided to give in and ordered the other two estates to sit with the National Assembly.

Louis XVI and Family

1. Why was the French government in trouble in the 1780's?
2. Why did the king call a meeting of the Estates-General for the first time in almost 200 years?
3. Why did the Third Estate want to meet as one body?

UPRISINGS IN CITY AND COUNTRY   Meanwhile, a series of uprisings took place throughout the land. When the Estates-General was called to meet, most French people had high hopes for change. But before long, they began to fear that nothing would improve. The fall harvest had been poor, and food was scarce and expensive. The winter had been so cold that water froze in front of fireplaces. Thousands of city workers were unemployed.

In Paris, mobs began to form. On July 14, 1789, a mob in search of weapons attacked and took over the Bastille. This was an old fort that was used as a prison. It was a symbol of the tyranny of the monarchy. Then, the mob killed the mayor of Paris and set up a new city government.

News of what happened in Paris spread. In the countryside, there were rumors that the nobles were planning to hire **brigands**, or roving bandits, to destroy the peasants' homes and crops. So, the peasants rose in arms, attacked and burned the houses of the nobles, and destroyed all records of feudal days.

1. Why did a French mob attack the Bastille?
2. Why did the peasants rise in arms against the nobles?

French Peasants

THE NATIONAL ASSEMBLY The uprisings caused the National Assembly to act. To try to calm the people, it did away with the privileges of the nobles and clergy.

On August 26, 1789, the Assembly passed the Declaration of the Rights of Man and the Citizen. It said that "Men are born equal and remain free and equal in rights." It also said that the government's right to rule came from the people, not from the Crown. It gave everyone freedom of speech and the right to share in government. The ideas of equal rights and individual freedoms came mostly from the philosophes and from the English and American Revolutions.

For the next two years, the National Assembly worked to write a constitution. At the same time, to pay off what the government owed, it began selling Church lands to the peasants. Although many of the peasants now owned land for the first time, the Catholic Church was angered. It was further angered when, in 1790, the National Assembly said the clergy should be elected and required them to swear an oath to the government. The Church did not like being brought under the State's authority.

In 1791, the constitution was finished. It made France a **constitutional monarchy**. Under this kind of government, the ruler's power is limited by written law. The Crown and the legislature together would govern. Both representatives and voters had to have a certain amount of wealth. This pleased the bourgeoisie because it gave them the power they wanted. But it did not please the poorer peasants and the **sans-culottes**, or city workers. They did not have enough money to vote. The word "sans-culottes" means "without knee breeches." Wealthier people wore knee breeches and silk stockings. Workers wore long trousers.

1. What did the National Assembly do about the uprisings?
2. Why was the Church angry with the National Assembly?
3. Why were the poorer peasants and the sans-culottes angry with the National Assembly?

THE END OF THE MONARCHY   France faced trouble abroad as well as at home. The ideas of the French Revolution had spread to other countries. European rulers were afraid that these ideas would weaken their own power. They were encouraged to march into France and help Louis XVI by French **émigrés,** or political exiles. Many revolutionary leaders also wanted war because it would unite the people. So, in the spring of 1792, France declared war on Austria, where the queen's brother ruled.

In the beginning, the war did not go well for France. By August 1792, Austrian and Prussian armies were marching toward Paris. In the city, the sans-culottes took over. They set up a new government called the National Convention. The elections took place during a time when mobs killed anyone they thought supported the king.

Robespierre

The National Convention did away with the monarchy and made France a republic. The following year, it executed King Louis XVI and Queen Marie Antoinette. As a result, more countries joined the war against France.

Threats from outside and in made the new French government take drastic action. Although another constitution was written, it was never used. Instead, the Committee of Public Safety, led by Maximilien de Robespierre, took over the government. Thousands of men and women, suspected of being against the Revolution, lost their heads to the guillotine. The wave of killing came to be known as the "Reign of Terror." In time, people began to turn against Robespierre. In 1794, government leaders had him executed.

The following year, a third constitution was written. It set up a government known as the Directory. Besides the legisla-

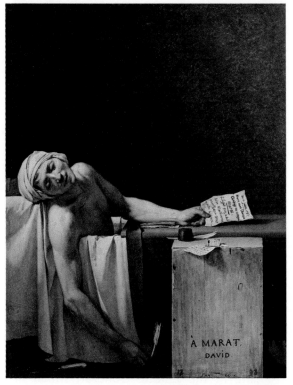

REIGN OF TERROR
In July 1793, the French revolutionary leader Jean-Paul Marat was stabbed to death (left) in his home by a young aristocratic woman who opposed Marat's policies. Another victim of the times was the wife of Louis XVI, Queen Marie Antoinette (right). She was tried and executed for treason in October 1793.
Why was this period known as the "Reign of Terror"?

ture, there was an executive branch with five directors. Only people who owned land could vote.

Under the new government, the reforms of the Revolution came to a halt. People had grown more conservative. The government spent its time trying to handle such problems as food shortages, rising prices, government bankruptcy, and attacks by other countries. Still, the idea remained that all French people had the right to choose their government.

1. Why were European rulers afraid of the ideas of the French Revolution?
2. What led to the Reign of Terror?
3. Why did the reforms of the Revolution come to a halt under the Directory?

CHAPTER 33 REVIEW

SUMMARY

1. Because of new ideas about government, the eighteenth century is known in the western world as the Age of Enlightenment.

2. England's political revolution began during the 1600's when the Crown and Parliament disagreed about rule by divine right and about religion.

3. In 1642, disagreements between Charles I and Parliament led to civil war and the overthrow of Charles I by a group called the Roundheads, led by a Puritan named Oliver Cromwell.

4. In 1660, Parliament restored the monarchy, but disagreements between James II and Parliament led to the Glorious Revolution in 1688.

5. As a result of the Glorious Revolution, Parliament passed the Declaration of Rights, which protected the rights of the English people.

6. Mercantilism worked well until the colonies became angry over English trade laws in the 1700's.

7. The French and Indian War left England with a large debt.

8. In 1763, England tried to tighten its control over its American colonies by taxing them.

9. The colonists objected to paying the taxes because they believed that only their colonial legislatures had the right to make laws for them as they had no representatives in Parliament.

10. In 1776, disagreements between the colonies and England led to the Declaration of Independence and a war that made the colonies an independent nation, the United States of America.

11. In 1789, the United States adopted a constitution that set up a new form of government in which the people have the right to govern themselves.

12. In 1789, to help decide how to raise money, the French king called a meeting of the Estates-General, which included representatives of the clergy, the nobility, and the Third Estate.

13. Representatives of the Third Estate, who had no power in the government, insisted on writing a constitution.

14. The French wrote three different constitutions between 1791 and 1795 because not everyone was satisfied with the changes made in government.

15. The French Revolution expressed the idea that people have the right to choose their own government.

BUILDING VOCABULARY

1. *Identify the following:*

Enlightenment	Roundheads	Sir Christopher Wren	French and Indian
King James Version	Oliver Cromwell	James II	War
Charles I	New Model Army	William and Mary	Boston Massacre
Cavaliers	Charles II	Declaration of Rights	Intolerable Acts

Boston Tea Party	Thomas Jefferson	Voltaire	Maximilien de
George Washington	Third Estate	Madame Deficit	Robespierre
Declaration	Old Regime	National Assembly	Reign of Terror
of Independence			Directory

2. *Define the following:*

martial law	monopoly	limited government	brigands
foreign policy	direct tax	estates	constitutional
repealed	boycott	exempt	monarchy
peers	popular sovereignty	*philosophes*	*sans-culottes*
mercantilism			*émigrés*

REVIEWING THE FACTS

1. Why is the eighteenth century known as the Age of Enlightenment?
2. What were some beliefs of the Puritans?
3. Why did Charles I dismiss Parliament?
4. Why did the English put Charles I to death in 1649?
5. Why was the Glorious Revolution called glorious?
6. Why did England try to tighten its control over the American colonies?
7. How did the colonists respond to Parliament's actions?
8. What did the Declaration of Independence do?
9. Who had the most power in the French government before the Revolution? After the Revolution?
10. Why was there so much unrest among the people in France during the French Revolution?

DISCUSSING IMPORTANT IDEAS

1. What economic issues played a part in the American and French Revolutions?
2. What political issues played a part in the Glorious, the American, and the French Revolutions?
3. What changes in government took place as a result of each revolution?
4. Do you agree or disagree with the idea that people have a right to rule themselves? Explain.

USING MAPS

Study the maps on page 519, and answer the following questions:
1. What is the time period of the map?
2. Who held London? Wales?
3. How far is Naseby from Marston Moor?
4. Where is Oxford located?

Study the map on page 525, and answer the following questions:
1. About how far do the Thirteen Colonies extend along the Atlantic coast?
2. What battles are British victories?
3. What is located about 36° north latitude and 78° west longitude?
4. Where is Boston located?

CHAPTER 34

THE RISE OF INDUSTRY

B y the 1700's, people in the western world not only had new ideas about government, but also had new ideas about science. These, in turn, led to the development of new sources of power and new ways of making goods. Industry and ways of living changed. They changed so much, in fact, that historians call the change the Industrial Revolution. During the early years of the Industrial Revolution, Great Britain took the lead. Later, other countries rose to challenge Great Britain.

THE BEGINNINGS

Many of the changes that took place during the Industrial Revolution grew out of the revolution in scientific thinking.

Beginning in the 1400's, scientists began to break away from old ideas. They stopped depending on Aristotle and Ptolemy. Instead, they adopted the scientific method.

One of the first people to do so was Nicolaus Copernicus, a Polish astronomer. Copernicus studied the motion of the planets. What he saw proved to him that Ptolemy was wrong and that the earth was not the center of the universe. In 1543, Copernicus published a book explaining his idea that planets revolve around the sun rather than the earth. This book began the revolution in scientific thinking. Over the next 300 years, many changes took place in science.

Copernicus

While these changes were taking place, there was a revolution in agriculture. It set the stage for the Industrial Revolution in Great Britain. By the 1700's, a system of land division called **enclosure** was in use. Landowners combined the many small strips of land worked by tenant farmers into large areas closed in by fences, hedges, or ditches. Enclosure allowed landowners to make more money. Under the strip system, they had spent a lot of time moving from place to place. Now, they could spend all their time growing crops. Also, they could make do with fewer workers.

The tenant farmers had two choices. They could stay on as paid workers, or they could look elsewhere for jobs. Most left to find work in other places. Many moved to cities and became industrial workers.

Enclosure was just part of the revolution in agriculture. New ways of growing crops and breeding animals led to greater production of food. More food meant better health and longer lives. Population grew. As this happened, the demand for manufactured goods grew.

1. How did Copernicus view the relationship between the sun and the planets?
2. Why did landowners begin to use the enclosure system?

THE INDUSTRIAL REVOLUTION

The Industrial Revolution was a long, slow process during which people began to use machines to do jobs that had been done by animals or people. Over time, the revolution moved faster. Much of the world changed. It became more urban and industrial and less rural and agricultural.

SCIENTISTS

Name	Field	Accomplishments
Johannes Kepler *Germany*	*Astronomy*	announced laws of movement of planets, 1609
William Harvey *England*	*Medicine*	published theory on human blood circulation, 1628
Sir Isaac Newton *England*	*Physics*	stated laws of motion and theory of gravitation, 1687
Antoine Lavoisier *France*	*Chemistry*	discovered nature of combustion, 1777
John Dalton *England*	*Chemistry*	announced atomic theory, 1803
Maria Mitchell *United States*	*Astronomy*	discovered new comet, 1847
Charles Darwin *England*	*Biology*	advanced theory on development of plants and animals, 1858
Gregor Mendel *Austria*	*Botany*	discovered principles of heredity, 1866
Louis Pasteur *France*	*Medicine*	advanced germ theory of disease, 1876; successfully vaccinated against rabies, 1885
Pierre Curie **Marie Curie** *France*	*Chemistry*	discovered radium and polonium, 1898

THE TEXTILE INDUSTRY   The Industrial Revolution began in Great Britain in the textile industry. In the 1600's and early 1700's, cloth was made by the **domestic system.** Most of the work was done in the workers' cottages, where families worked together. Traveling merchants brought the workers raw wool and cotton. Using hand-powered spinning wheels and looms, the workers spun the thread and wove it into wool and cotton cloth. The merchants then picked up the finished cloth to sell.

Cottage Worker

The domestic system could not meet the growing desire for cotton. So, before long, people started looking for ways to make more cloth in less time. The first major breakthrough came in 1733 when a British clockmaker named John Kay invented the **flying shuttle.** The shuttle was mounted on rollers, and one weaver could send it rapidly from one side of the loom to the other. It cut in half the time needed to weave cloth. But the spinners could not keep up with the weavers. Then, in 1764, James Hargreaves, a British carpenter, invented the **spinning jenny.** It had a number of spindles fastened to a single wheel. The jenny made it possible for one person to spin many threads at the same time.

More progress was made when ways were found to use the power of falling water instead of hand power to run the textile machines. This meant, however, that the machines had to be near a large water supply. So, factories were built next to rivers that could supply the necessary water power. This was the beginning of the **factory system,** which brought workers and machines together in one place to make goods. Workers still lived in their cottages, but they came to the factories to work. In time, towns grew up around the factories.

Water power did not work that well with heavy machinery. So, people began looking for another source of power. In 1769, a Scottish engineer named James Watt perfected the steam engine. The first practical steam engine had been developed in 1712 by Thomas Newcomen, a British engineer. But it consumed large amounts of coal and was used only to pump water from mines. Watt improved Newcomen's engine, and steam soon replaced water as the major source of power. Now, factories of all kinds could be set up near raw materials and markets.

Cotton farmers in America and in India could not supply enough raw cotton to meet the needs of British textile factories. Eli Whitney, an American inventor, found a way to solve the problem. While visiting a cotton plantation in Georgia, he noticed that it took a great deal of time to clean the seeds out of cotton by hand. In 1793, he invented the **cotton gin,** or cotton-cleaning machine. It could clean cotton 50 times faster than a person working by hand.

About five years later, Whitney developed a new way of organizing production that would change textile and other industries. This was the idea of **interchangeable parts.** That is, each given part was the same size and shape and could be used to replace another in manufacturing. Whitney first used the new method to make guns. Until then, each worker had made one gun at a time from start to finish. Thus, workers had to be

INVENTORS

Name	Country	Inventions
Samuel Crompton	*England*	spinning "mule", 1784
Edmund Cartwright	*England*	power loom, 1785
Alessandro Volta	*Italy*	electric battery, 1800
Richard Trevithnick	*England*	first successful locomotive, early 1800's
Cyrus McCormick	*United States*	mechanical reaper, 1834
Charles Goodyear	*United States*	vulcanized rubber, 1839
Norbert Rillieux	*United States*	evaporator which revolutionized sugar industry, 1843
Elias Howe	*United States*	sewing machine, 1846
Zénobe T. Gramme	*Belgium*	first commercially successful dynamo, or generator, 1870
Christopher L. Sholes	*United States*	typewriter, 1873

skilled. Under Whitney's system, the work was divided, with each worker making only one part of a gun. Whitney's system meant that guns could be made much faster. They also could be made by unskilled workers.

Cotton Gin

1. Where did the Industrial Revolution begin?
2. What inventions changed the way cloth was made?
3. What effect did Whitney's system of production have on manufacturing? On the work force?

IRON, COAL, AND STEEL   To build machine parts, iron was needed. To fire steam engines, coal was needed. Without iron, coal, and steel, which replaced iron, the Industrial Revolution could not have continued.

By the early 1700's, ironmaking had become expensive. To smelt iron, the British needed **charcoal,** a fuel which is made by burning wood. The British, however were running out of forests. This made wood scarce and costly. In 1753, a way was found to use coal instead of charcoal for smelting. Because of this, iron became cheaper, iron production increased, and coal mining became a major industry.

Iron, however, was too brittle for rails, bridge supports, and the like. In 1856, a British inventor named Henry Bessemer found a cheap way of removing the impurities from iron to make steel, which was harder and stronger than iron. The **Bessemer process,** which directed a blast of air on heated iron, lowered the cost of making steel from two hundred dollars to four dollars a ton. Seven years later, in 1863, the Martin brothers of France invented the **open hearth process,** which used a special kind of furnace to make steel. It was even cheaper than the Bessemer process and could turn out many different kinds of steel. Soon, mining towns and steel centers grew up in areas with supplies of iron ore and coal.

Iron Furnace

1. For what was iron needed? For what was coal needed?
2. What effects did the discovery that coal could be used for smelting have on industry?
3. Why is steel more useful than iron?

TRANSPORTATION   Raw materials and finished products had to be moved quickly and cheaply. Before this could happen, transportation had to be improved. Until the 1700's, the chief means of transportation over land was by horse or horse-drawn wagon. Roads were no more than rough, narrow, dirt paths. Travel was slow and uncomfortable. It was even worse when rain made the roads muddy.

Late in the 1700's, the British began to improve their roads. One Scottish engineer, Thomas Telford, designed roadbeds so that water would drain off them. Another Scottish engineer, John L. McAdam, developed what became known as the **macadam road.** It had a surface made of layers of crushed stone. This surface allowed horse-drawn wagons to use roads in all kinds of weather and to travel faster.

The British also made their rivers wider and deeper and built canals to connect navigable rivers to factory and mining centers. Horses walked beside canals pulling barges. The barges were slow. However, they could carry 50 times the amount of goods that horse-drawn wagons could carry. By 1830, Great Britain had a complete system of inland waterways.

The biggest improvement in land transportation was the railroad. For years, donkeys had pulled carts over wooden rails around coal mines. Then, the production of iron grew. Wooden rails were replaced by iron ones that could carry heavier loads. Inventors began to build locomotives to run on iron rails. In 1829, George Stephenson, a British mining engineer, won a contest to see who could build the best locomotive. Stephenson's locomotive, the *Rocket*, could pull a train about 14 miles, or 22.4 kilometers, an hour. The *Rocket* started a railroad-building boom in Great Britain and around the world.

The biggest improvement in water transportation was the steamboat. The first practical steamboat was developed by Robert Fulton, an American inventor. In 1807, Fulton's *Clermont*, powered by a British steam engine, set a record by making the trip from Albany to New York City in five days. Soon, steamboats were carrying passengers and cargoes along the inland waterways of the United States and Europe. The steamboat, however, did not replace the sailing ship in trans-Atlantic travel until the 1880's, when fuel-efficient engines were developed and put into use.

The *Rocket*

1. Why did transportation have to be improved during the Industrial Revolution?

2. What was the biggest improvement in water transportation?

EFFECTS OF THE INDUSTRIAL REVOLUTION

The Industrial Revolution brought many changes in people's lives. These changes showed up first in Great Britain. They spread from there to other countries.

CHANGES IN SOCIETY   In England, until the Middle Ages, there had been two major social classes—the nobles, who were the upper class, and the peasants, who were the lower class. Then, a middle class of rich merchants developed.

During the Industrial Revolution, the middle class increased in numbers and grew richer. Many factory, railroad, and mine owners became as wealthy as the nobles. They began to keep company with the members of the upper class. They also began to dress like members of the upper class. The women wore lacy petticoats and hooped skirts with stiff linings. The men wore

---

FACTORIES

Factories brought workers together under one roof. Different workers performed each step in the making of a product. The workers in the engraving below are weaving cotton cloth on power looms.

Where were the first factories built?

---

dark suits, with top hats in winter and **boaters,** or stiff straw hats, in summer. Middle-class families began spending their weekends at seaside resorts, which were easy to reach now that railroads were common. Middle-class children went to upper-class schools. Sometimes, the children married into the upper class.

In time, the middle class gained political power. In Great Britain, its members gained the right to vote and to be represented in Parliament.

The Industrial Revolution also created an industrial working class. Most members of this class were peasants who could no longer support themselves by farming. Since they had no property of their own to sell, they had to sell their labor in order to live.

In the early years, members of the working class did not benefit from the Industrial Revolution. They worked 12 to 16 hours a day, six days a week, for low wages. They had to work at the pace set by machines and factory owners and were fined or beaten if they did not keep up. Working conditions were difficult, dirty, and dangerous. Many people were killed or injured by unsafe machinery. And the working class did not have job security. Factory and mine owners hired and fired whenever they wanted to do so.

Most children of the working class did not have time to go to school or to play. Instead, they worked in factories and mines along with the men and women. They were paid even less than the adults. In the mines, they could crawl through narrow tunnels in which adults could not fit. Because their bodies were still growing, children sometimes were crippled by the work.

1. What happened to the middle class during the Industrial Revolution?
2. What were conditions like for members of the working class during the early years of the Industrial Revolution?

THE GROWTH OF CITIES   Another change brought by the Industrial Revolution was the growth of cities. Before the Industrial Revolution, less than 10 percent of the people in Great Britain lived in cities. By 1900, the number had reached 75 percent. Indeed, 10 percent of the people in the whole country lived in London.

Some cities grew up around factories or mines that had been built in rural areas. Most factories, however, were built in existing cities. Cities grew rapidly as people moved there to find

INDUSTRIAL CITIES

The development of industry in England led to the growth of large cities. English industrial cities were located near coal or iron deposits. Shown here is a nineteenth-century steel factory in the city of Sheffield.

What was the life of workers like in the new industrial cities?

jobs. Soon, the cities became overcrowded. Houses could not be built fast enough. Sometimes, a dozen people had to live in one room. Many moved into damp basements and rooms with no windows. Garbage floated in the streets because the sewers had not been built to serve so many people. Water supplies became polluted. Epidemics of cholera, typhoid, and tuberculosis were common. The death rate among the working class was more than twice that among the middle and upper classes.

The workers had little economic or political power. It was against the law to form **trade unions,** or workers' associations. And workers did not have the right to vote. So, they could do nothing about their working or living conditions.

1. Where did most people live before the beginning of the Industrial Revolution?
2. Why did so many people move to the cities?
3. What problems did the rapid growth of cities cause?

REFORM Many people in the middle and upper classes were indifferent to the suffering of the workers. Factory owners, for example, felt that raising wages and improving working conditions would raise the cost of goods and lower profits.

Some members of the middle and upper classes, however, believed that higher wages and better working conditions could still produce good profits. They also believed that it was against the Christian religion to allow suffering and injustice. They began to work for reform.

The reformers began by starting schools, orphanages, and hospitals for the poor. They also worked to change laws. In 1824, trade unions were made legal. During the 1830's and 1840's, women and children under ten years old were prohibited from working underground in mines. The workday was also cut to ten hours.

Reformers also worked to improve living conditions. New laws were passed that required the building of better houses. Every room had to have at least one window, and every house had to have piped-in water. Improvements were slow in coming, but over time, life became better for the working class. As more goods were made, prices went down. Clothing, food, and other products became cheap enough for workers to buy.

1. Why were some people against reform?
2. What two arguments did some people make in favor of reform?
3. What did reformers do to improve the way workers lived and worked?

The Spread of the Industrial Revolution

Meanwhile, the Industrial Revolution had spread from Great Britain to other countries. These countries, aided by technology, soon **industrialized,** or developed industry.

Immigrants

OTHER COUNTRIES   At the beginning of the Industrial Revolution, Great Britain tried to keep its inventions secret. Machines or plans for machines were not allowed to be taken out of Great Britain. Skilled workers were not allowed to leave the country. By the 1800's however, many workers had ignored the law and left. These **immigrants,** or people who settle permanently in a different country, brought British industrial secrets to other countries.

These countries used what they learned and built their own industries. Belgium, with its rich deposits of iron and coal, was the first country after Great Britain to industrialize. The next country was France. There, the process, which had begun in the

1700's, was slowed by war and revolution. The United States, with its many natural resources, soon followed France. Then came Germany. Although Germany was well supplied with coal and iron, it was divided into more than 30 separate states. These states were not willing to cooperate in economic matters. Germany, therefore, did not make much industrial progress until after its unification in 1871. Then, it matched the others as a leading industrial power.

1. How did the Industrial Revolution spread?
2. What were the first countries after Great Britain to become industrialized?

TECHNOLOGICAL ADVANCES   The development of new kinds of power helped continue the Industrial Revolution. One of these was electricity. In 1837, an American, Samuel F. B. Morse, built the first successful electric telegraph. It made quick communication possible. Some years later, Alexander Graham

---

WORLD'S FAIR

In 1851, England held a world's fair in London to celebrate its industrial achievements. This painting shows the royal family attending opening day.
What did the English do to keep their discoveries and inventions secret?

Thomas Edison

Bell, also an American, invented the telephone, and communications took another step forward. In 1895, an Italian physicist, Guglielmo Marconi, built the wireless telegraph, or radio. Six years later, Marconi sent a signal across the Atlantic.

Meanwhile, there were other advances in electricity. By 1879, Thomas Alva Edison, an American, had developed the electric light. It would soon illuminate factories and homes all over the world.

Another new source of power was the **internal combustion engine,** or an engine that is fueled by gasoline. It was invented around 1885 by German engineer Gottlieb Daimler. Daimler's engine was used to drive the first automobile as well as other machines.

1. When were wireless communications established across the Atlantic?
2. For what was the internal combustion engine used?

CHAPTER 34 REVIEW

SUMMARY

1. The revolution in scientific thinking was set off in 1543 by a book in which the Polish astronomer Copernicus said that the planets revolve around the sun.

2. While the revolution in science was taking place, an agricultural revolution took place in England that included a new system of land division and new methods of growing crops and breeding animals.

3. The Industrial Revolution began in Great Britain in the textile industry.

4. Many inventions, such as the flying shuttle and spinning jenny, helped workers produce more in less time.

5. Factories were built near rivers in order to use the power of falling water to run machines.

6. In 1769, James Watt perfected the steam engine, and steam soon replaced water as the major source of power.

7. Eli Whitney invented the cotton gin in 1793 and a new way of organizing production in 1798.

8. The use of iron and coal to make steel helped continue the Industrial Revolution and led to major transportation improvements, especially the railroad.

9. After a time, the steamboat replaced the sailing ship.

10. The Industrial Revolution increased the size and power of the middle class and created a class of industrial workers.

11. The rapid growth of cities was another change brought about by the Industrial Revolution.

12. Poor working and living conditions of the workers during the early years of the Industrial Revolution led to reforms.

13. During the 1800's, the Industrial Revolution spread from Great Britain to Belgium, France, the United States, and Germany.

14. The development of electricity and the internal combustion engine helped continue the Industrial Revolution.

BUILDING VOCABULARY

1. *Identify the following*:

Nicolaus Copernicus	James Watt	George Stephenson	Alexander Graham Bell
John Kay	Eli Whitney	Robert Fulton	Thomas Alva Edison
James Hargreaves	Thomas Telford	Samuel F. B. Morse	Guglielmo Marconi

2. *Define the following*:

enclosure	cotton gin	Bessemer process	trade unions
domestic system	interchangeable	open hearth process	industrialized
flying shuttle	parts	macadam road	immigrants
spinning jenny	charcoal	boaters	internal combustion
factory system			engine

REVIEWING THE FACTS

1. In what ways did ideas about science change during the 1400's, 1500's, and 1600's?

2. How did the enclosure system affect tenant farmers?

3. What effect did the agricultural revolution have on population?

4. How did the Industrial Revolution change textile manufacturing?

5. How did steam come to replace water as the major source of power during the Industrial Revolution?

6. What new social class developed as a result of the Industrial Revolution?

7. Why were many children unable to attend school during the early years of the Industrial Revolution?

8. What benefits did people of the working class reap from the Industrial Revolution after a while?

9. How did the British try to keep their inventions secret?

10. What new sources of power helped spread the Industrial Revolution?

DISCUSSING IMPORTANT IDEAS

1. What did the scientific method have to do with the Industrial Revolution?

2. What did changes in agriculture have to do with the beginning of the Industrial Revolution?

3. What things do you think are necessary for a country to industrialize?

4. Do you think that the Industrial Revolution was good or bad for most workers? Explain.

UNIT 11 REVIEW

SUMMARY

1. From the early 1500's to the 1700's, Portugal, Spain, England, the Netherlands, and France competed to colonize the New World. They hoped to gain new wealth and power and spread Christianity to other parts of the world.

2. Political revolution in England ended the divine right of kings. It also established the basic rights of the people and increased the powers of Parliament.

3. The 13 American colonies rebelled against Great Britain and became the United States of America, an independent nation with a representative government based on popular sovereignty.

4. In the 1700's, the French Revolution established the idea that government authority comes from the people. But the Revolution ended in confusion without fulfilling all its goals.

5. The Industrial Revolution started in Great Britain in the 1700's and soon spread to other western countries. It completely changed manufacturing and industry by replacing human and animal power with machine power and the factory system. The Revolution led to the creation of an industrial working class, the rise of the middle class, the rapid growth of cities, and reform.

REVIEWING THE MAIN IDEAS

1. Compare the governments set up in England, America, and France as a result of political revolution.

2. Explain how the Industrial Revolution affected the economy, social classes, and cities.

DEVELOPING SKILLS

After historians have gathered and studied a body of data, they often make a generalization based on the data. For example, historians discovered that between 3500 and 1500 B.C. the Sumerians developed a civilization in the valley of the Tigris and Euphrates rivers, the Egyptians developed a civilization in the valley of the Nile River, the Harappans developed a civilization in the valley of the Indus River, and the Chinese developed a civilization in the valley of the Yellow River. From this information they arrived at the generalization that between 3500 and 1500 B.C., early civilizations developed along the banks of rivers.

This exercise is designed to give you practice in generalizing. Read the three groups of statements that follow. Then, write a generalization for each based on the statements given.

1. *Group A*
a. By 1510, Portugal had claimed all of Brazil.
b. By 1532, Spain had claimed Mexico and Peru.

c. By 1733, Great Britain had control over 13 colonies along the Atlantic coast of America.

d. In 1682, France claimed the Mississippi River Valley.

2. *Group B*

a. One result of the Glorious Revolution was that rule by divine right was gone forever from England.

b. The American Revolution led to a government based on popular sovereignty.

c. In 1792, the French monarchy was abolished by the National Assembly.

3. *Group C*

a. The flying shuttle cut in half the time needed to weave cloth.

b. The spinning jenny could spin up to 1,000 threads in the same amount of time the spinning wheel took to spin one thread.

c. The cotton gin could clean cotton 50 times faster than working by hand.

SUGGESTED UNIT ACTIVITIES

1. Stage a debate about the Portuguese and Spanish colonies in Central and South America. One group will present the Indian view; the other will present the European colonists' view.

2. Write a letter that an early Jamestown or Plymouth settler might have sent home to tell about life in America.

3. Make a chart comparing the Glorious, American, and French Revolutions. Include dates the revolutions began and ended, their goals, leaders, and results.

4. In a group, prepare a booklet of advertisements that might have been used to sell at least five of the inventions that contributed to the growth of industry.

SUGGESTED READING

Anticaglia, Elizabeth. *Heroines of '76.* New York: Walker and Company, 1976. The lives of 14 women who played important roles in the Revolutionary War.

Boardman, Fon W., Jr. *Around the World in 1776.* New York: Henry Z. Walck Inc., 1975. An account of worldwide events that took place in 1776.

Davis, Burke. *Black Heroes of the American Revolution.* New York: Harcourt Brace Jovanovich, 1976. An account of blacks in the struggle for American independence.

Forbes, Esther. *Johnny Tremain.* Boston: Houghton-Mifflin, 1971. The story of a 14-year-old boy in Boston in 1773 who becomes involved in the American Revolution.

Holbrook, Sabra. *Lafayette: Man in the Middle.* New York: Atheneum, 1977. A biography.

Holland, Ruth. *Mill Child.* New York: Crowell-Collier Press, 1970. The story of what life was like in America for children forced to work in the mills.

Levitin, Sonia. *Roanoke: A Novel of the Lost Colony.* New York: Atheneum, 1973. The story of a 16-year-old runaway and his sea journey to a new colony in the Americas.

Pratt, N.S. *The French Revolution.* New York: The John Day Company, 1970. Discusses the revolution, its leaders, and the changes it brought about.

UNIT 12

1800

1800 Thomas Jefferson becomes
President of United States

1803 Louisiana Purchase

1804 Haiti becomes independent
Napoleon becomes emperor of France

1805

1810

1812 Napoleon
invades Russia

1830

1830 July Revolution in France
Greece becomes independent
French occupy Algeria

1831 Belgium declares
independence

1835

1840

1840 American settlers head for Oreg
David Livingstone goes to Africa

1841 Pedro I rules Brazil

1839 Opium War

1860

1860 Lincoln elected President of United States

1861 American Civil War begins
Victor Emmanuel II becomes king of Italy

1862 Bismarck becomes prime
minister of Prussia

1865

1870

1870 Italy unites

1867 Austria-Hungary establishes Dual Monarchy
Benito Juárez becomes president of Mexico

1871 Germany unifies

1869 Suez Canal
opens

1874 Great Britain takes con
of Suez Canal
Henry Stanley explores

1890

1894 Sino-Japanese War begins

1895

1895 British establish colony in East Africa
Rhodesia becomes British colony
French set up colony in West Africa

1896 Ethiopia defeats Italy

1898 Open Door Policy
Spanish-American War

1899 Boer War begins

1900

1900 Boxer Rebellion breaks out in C

1904 Russo-Japanese
War begins

1925

1930

NATIONS AND EMPIRES

1815

Congress of Vienna

1815 Napoleon defeated at Waterloo
Louis XVIII becomes king of France

1816 Argentina becomes independent

1818 Chile becomes independent

1820

1822 Mexico becomes independent
Brazil becomes independent

1823 Monroe Doctrine
Uruguay becomes
independent

1825

1845

1845 United States annexes Texas
California becomes independent

1846 War between Mexico and
the United States begins

1847 Republic of Liberia founded

1848 Second French Republic

1850

1852 Napoleon III rules France

1853 Perry goes to Japan
Gadsden Purchase

1854 Crimean War begins

1855

1858 Great Britain
takes full
control of India

1875

1880

1882 Great Britain occupies Egypt

1877 Queen Victoria becomes empress of India

1878 Henry Stanley serves Leopold II

1884 Berlin Conference

1885

1885 Portuguese East Africa established

1888 William II becomes
kaiser of Germany

1889 Brazil becomes
republic

1905

1910

1910 French Equatorial Africa set up
Union of South Africa formed

1912 United States Marines land in Nicaragua

1908 Belgium establishes control over Congo

1915

1914 Panama Canal opens

1. IN WHAT WAYS DID NATIONALISM AND INDEPENDENCE INFLUENCE THE WESTERN WORLD DURING THE 1800'S?
2. WHAT CHANGES TOOK PLACE IN AFRICA AND ASIA DURING THE 1800'S?

During the 1800's, the world saw many new nations emerge, grow, and become powerful. It also saw the nations of western Europe move into Africa and Asia and build colonies.

In the Americas, the people of the United States built a democracy and enlarged their nation. They fought a civil war that divided the nation, and then worked to reunite. Industry grew, and with it grew the nation's strength and power.

Spanish and Portuguese colonies in the Americas got rid of their colonial rulers in a series of revolutions. But colonial rule had been strict. The people had been given little opportunity to learn how to govern themselves. After independence, landowners and military leaders controlled political life. Most were interested only in personal gain. They did little for the people or the economy.

In Europe, the ideas of the French Revolution gained support among the middle and working classes. Monarchs who tried to stamp out democratic and national feelings failed. They were forced to accept constitutions, parliaments, elections, and the creation of new nations.

Toward the end of the century, the European powers and the United States practiced **imperialism,** or the policy of establishing colonies and building empires. In this way, the colonial powers spread their influence, enlarged their trade, and protected their interests in other parts of the world.

THE AMERICAS

$\mathbf{M}$any changes took place in the Americas from 1800 to 1870. The United States more than doubled in size, and its government was set on a firm base. This allowed the country to grow industrially and to become a world power. Latin America, or Mexico and Central and South America, won independence from European rule. But colonial traditions remained strong. So, despite many efforts, democracy did not develop.

THE UNITED STATES   In the years after independence, the United States grew in population, land area, and wealth. Driven by a sense of destiny, Americans moved westward into areas that would become part of the United States. Despite internal conflicts, the United States by 1900 grew to be a powerful country. One reason was the kind of government that developed.

GOVERNMENT   The United States had a tradition of **stable government,** or a government that rules from year to year without great changes.

By 1800, two **political parties,** or groups with different ideas about government, had developed. One was the Federalist party. It favored a strong **federal,** or national, government. Most Federalists also believed that people of wealth and education should hold office. They thought the economy should be based more on industry than trade or agriculture. The other political party was the Republican party. It favored more power for the states. Most Republicans believed that average people should lead the country. They thought the economy should be based more on agriculture than industry or trade.

Eagle Drum

While other countries often fought wars when political power changed hands, the United States proved war was not necessary. Its government changed hands through peaceful elections. For example, in 1800 a Republican, Thomas Jefferson, was elected President. He took the place of John Adams, who was a Federalist. This was the first peaceful passing of power from one political group to another.

The United States also had a tradition of representative government. Part of the tradition was that no one small group could hold the power to govern. Instead, a large number of people could take part in electing officials.

In 1800, only white males who were wealthy or owned property could vote. This changed over the next 30 years. New states in the West began to allow all adult white males to vote. Other states soon followed. By 1830, the number of voters had greatly increased. But women, slaves, and Indians were not allowed to vote. Yet, the United States government was one of the most democratic in the world at the time.

With the growing number of voters, election campaigns changed. They became filled with entertainment and advertising. People sang songs and wore buttons to show which candidates they backed. Political parties had parades, rallies, barbecues, and dinners. Presidential races in particular were noted for slogans and symbols. For example, Andrew Jackson, who was elected President in 1828, was nicknamed "Old Hickory." So, during the campaign, the Democratic party planted hickory trees in town squares and gave out hickory brooms and canes.

1. What was important about the election of 1800?
2. What was one reason the number of voters grew by 1830?
3. How had election campaigns changed by the 1830's?

THE WESTWARD MOVEMENT   At the end of the American Revolution, the United States claimed most of the land east of the Mississippi River. Soon, thousands of Americans were putting their belongings into farm wagons and walking across the Appalachian Mountains to find new homes. When they came to the Ohio River and other water routes, they loaded their goods and animals on flatboats and floated downstream.

The settlers were careful about choosing a spot for their new home. The spot had to be near a stream for water and also near a larger settlement or fort for safety. Having chosen a place, the settlers would clear the land of trees and build a log cabin. The

---

AMERICAN INDIAN LIFE

The Indians west of the Mississippi River lived in villages along rivers and streams. They farmed the land and hunted buffalo. For recreation, almost all Indians played games. In this painting, Indian women play shinty, a ball game similar to field hockey.

How did the United States government treat the American Indians?

---

cabin usually had one room, with a dirt-packed floor and a door made of wood planks. Each cabin had one or two tiny windows covered with deerskin. There was a fireplace that supplied heat for warmth and cooking. There was usually a wood table and chairs, and sometimes a bed.

The settlers' way of life usually differed from that of the Indians in the area. The settlers were farmers, while most of the Indians were hunters. The settlers claimed land for themselves. The Indians believed land belonged to everyone.

Indians and settlers did learn from one another, however. Many settlers wore Indian clothing, such as moccasins and deerskin leggings. They used Indian herbs as medicine and paddled Indian canoes. Many Indians used iron pots and woolen blankets woven in Great Britain. They also used rifles.

The Indians tried to defend their lands against the settlers. But there were more settlers than Indians. Also, many Indians died from such diseases as measles and smallpox brought by the whites. So, the Indians were slowly pushed farther and farther west. In the 1820's and 1830's, the United States government began to make the Indians live on **reservations,** or special areas of land. Most of the reservations were west of the Mississippi River in what is now Oklahoma and Kansas.

Indian Clothing

1. What two things did settlers look for in choosing a spot for their new home?
2. In what ways was the settlers' way of life different from that of the Indians?
3. What did the settlers learn from the Indians? What did the Indians learn from the settlers?

TERRITORIAL EXPANSION   Many settlers chose to make their home in land newly acquired by the United States. In 1803, the United States doubled its size by buying the Louisiana Territory from France for $15 million. This Louisiana Purchase provided an area rich in farmland, minerals, and forests. It also gave the United States control of the Mississippi River and New Orleans, an important seaport.

In 1819, the United States signed a treaty with Spain. The treaty gave Florida to the United States and set the boundary between the lands of the Louisiana Purchase and Spanish lands to the south and west.

One of the lands belonging to Spain was Mexico. It became independent in 1822. The Mexicans wanted more people to settle in their territory, especially in Texas. So, they offered people from the United States large grants of land if they would swear loyalty to Mexico and practice the Catholic religion. By the early 1830's, there were 30,000 Americans living in Texas. Most were from the South, and many owned slaves.

Slavery and other troubles soon led to quarrels between Texas Americans and the Mexican government. Mexico, which had outlawed slavery in 1829, objected to Texans owning slaves. It also wondered whether the settlers were loyal to it or to the United States. It tried to stop more Americans from entering Texas. Then, the Texans asked for more control over their local affairs. Finally, in 1835, the Texans revolted against Mexico. The following year, they declared their independence.

Many Americans believed in the country's **manifest destiny,** or the fate of the United States to stretch from the Atlantic Ocean to the Pacific Ocean. They wanted the federal government to **annex,** or take over and add on, Texas. In 1845, the United States did so. This angered Mexico. A dispute over the Texas-Mexico boundary caused more trouble. By the following

---

THE ALAMO
The Alamo was a Catholic mission. In 1836, it was used as a fort in the war for Texan independence. The Texans lost this battle to the troops of Santa Anna. What steps led to the Texan revolt against Mexico?

year, the two countries were at war. American soldiers invaded California, which had been part of Mexico until it declared its independence in 1845. They also took Mexico City.

In 1848, Mexico signed the Treaty of Guadalupe Hidalgo. It gave the United States almost one half of Mexico's land. It also set the Rio Grande as the boundary between the two countries.

Five years after the treaty, the United States bought a piece of land from Mexico in order to build a railroad to the Pacific. This was called the Gadsden Purchase after James Gadsden, the American who arranged the purchase.

Meanwhile, the United States acquired the Oregon Territory. Around 1840, thousands of settlers made the long, hard trip over the Rocky Mountains to Oregon, which both the United States and Great Britain claimed. These settlers assured the United States of control. In 1846, the two countries agreed to divide the territory at 49° north latitude.

Later, another large area of land, Alaska, was added to the United States. In 1784, Russian fur hunters set up a permanent

THE GROWTH OF THE UNITED STATES

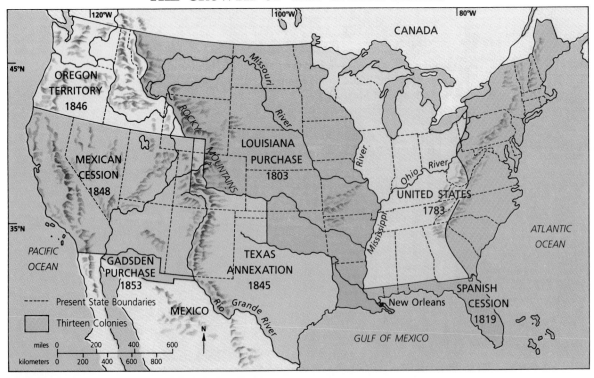

settlement on Kodiak Island off the Alaskan coast. From there, they set up hunting and trading settlements as far south as California. After a time, however, Russia lost interest in Alaska and in 1867 sold the territory to the United States.

1. How did Texas become part of the United States?
2. What was the result of the Treaty of Guadalupe Hidalgo?
3. What helped the United States acquire the Oregon Territory?
4. How and from whom did the United States acquire Alaska?

CIVIL WAR AND REUNION   As the United States expanded westward, different ways of life developed in the northern and southern states. The northern states were industrialized. They had most of the factories and means of transportation, such as railroads and canals. Labor in the North was done by hired workers. About 20 percent of the people lived in cities. Education was widespread, and immigration brought in all different kinds of people. Northern leaders wanted a strong national government. They also wanted government aid for helping industry and improving transportation.

The southern states depended on agriculture. Tobacco, rice, sugarcane, and especially cotton were important. These crops were grown on large plantations that used slave labor. Slaves made up about one third of the South's population. Only 10 percent of the people lived in cities. There were few immigrants. Southern leaders believed that the rights of states were more important than those of the federal government. They also believed that as the country grew, slavery should expand into new areas. The North wanted the new areas to remain free.

Lincoln and Advisors

In 1860, Abraham Lincoln became President. Southerners feared he would try to do away with slavery and destroy their way of life. Seven southern states announced that they were **seceding,** or withdrawing from the nation. They formed a new government called the Confederate States of America or the Confederacy. Soon, four more states seceded and joined the Confederacy. The North did not think the states had a right to secede. By 1861, the North and the South were fighting a civil war. In 1865, the North won, and once again, the country was united.

The Civil War settled the question of whether or not states have the right to secede. It also led to freedom for nearly 4 million black slaves. The country began to build itself up again.

By 1870, it was on its way to becoming a strong industrial country and a world power.

1. What way of life developed in the North? In the South?
2. What did the South do after the election of 1860?
3. What were two results of the Civil War in the United States?

LATIN AMERICA

While the United States was expanding and settling internal differences, the European-ruled colonies of Latin America were moving toward independence. The American and French Revolutions stirred the people of Latin America to action. Everywhere, colonists tried to take charge of their own affairs.

THE FIRST REVOLT   The first major revolt against European rule took place in the French West Indies on Saint-Domingue, the western part of the island of Hispaniola. There, a few French plantation owners used the labor of 500,000 black slaves to grow sugarcane, coffee, cotton, and **indigo,** or an ingredient for blue dye. There were two other social groups as well. One was the *petit blancs,* or lesser whites. They were mostly shopkeepers and artisans. The other was the **mulattoes,** or people who had one black parent and one white parent. They were mostly small farmers and laborers.

Indigo Plant

Then, Pierre Dominique Toussaint L'Ouverture appeared on the scene. The grandson of an African chief, Toussaint had been born a slave in 1743. His white master, however, taught Toussaint how to read and write. In 1777, Toussaint's master gave Toussaint his freedom. When news of the French Revolution reached Saint-Domingue, Toussaint was inspired. He began organizing an army. In 1791, he led a slave revolt. In 1794, the French government agreed to abolish slavery. Toussaint became governor-general of Saint-Domingue in 1799, and two years later, he issued a constitution. The French then tried to regain control of Saint-Domingue. But they were unsuccessful. By 1804, Saint-Domingue was a free country. It changed its name to Haiti, an Indian word meaning mountainous.

1. What European country ruled Saint-Domingue?
2. What group led the revolt against colonial rule?

REVOLUTION SPREADS   The Spanish colonists, too, were inspired by the ideas of the American and French Revolutions.

In fact, soon after the French Revolution began, Antonio Nariño of New Granada translated into Spanish the French Declaration of the Rights of Man and the Citizen. Nariño was arrested and put in prison. But that did not stop the spread of the ideas of freedom, individual rights, and democratic government.

The fight for independence in South America was led by Creoles. They were well educated and had enough power to change things. The Creoles resented the peninsulares, who controlled the most important government posts.

In the northern part of South America, the revolutionary leader was Simón Bolívar. For his efforts, he gained the title of "The Liberator." The son of a rich Creole family in New Granada, Bolívar went to Europe in 1805. There, he learned about the French Revolution and its ideas. Then, he returned home, vowing to free his people.

TOUSSAINT L'OUVERTURE AND SIMÓN BOLÍVAR

The colonies of Latin America were moving toward independence by the 1700's. Toussaint L'Ouverture (left) led a slave revolt in Haiti. Simón Bolívar's (right) victories won independence for Bolivia, Colombia, Ecuador, Peru, and Venezuela. What earlier events influenced Latin American independence movements?

Events in Europe made this possible. In 1808, the French invaded Spain. The French ruler, Napoleon Bonaparte, made his brother Joseph the new king of Spain. This led to a struggle for control of the Spanish government that lasted for several years. The Creoles saw their chance to get rid of Spanish control.

In 1810, Bolívar and other leaders in New Granada organized a **junta,** or committee, to take over the government. Spanish officials soon crushed the movement, however. Bolívar went into exile, where he formed and trained an army. In 1817, he successfully invaded what is today Venezuela. In August 1819, he defeated the Spanish in present-day Colombia. Later that year, he became the first president of the new country of Gran Colombia, which included Venezuela, Colombia, and the present-day countries of Ecuador and Panama. In 1824, Bolívar freed Peru from Spanish rule. A new country was created that was named Bolivia after him.

While Bolívar was fighting for freedom in the north, another Creole, José de San Martín, was fighting for freedom in the south. In 1810, Creole leaders in La Plata organized a junta to take over the government. In 1812, San Martín returned from Europe and joined the struggle for independence. San Martín, a professional soldier, organized an army. He was aided by his wife, who persuaded the women of Buenos Aires to give their jewels to help buy supplies for her husband's troops. He was also aided by a priest, Father Luis Beltrán, who melted church bells down to make guns and bullets. In 1816, the part of La Plata that is now Argentina won its independence.

In 1817, San Martín led his army across the Andes Mountains into what is now Chile. There, he and another soldier, Bernardo O'Higgins, led a revolt against Spanish forces. Together, San Martín and O'Higgins defeated the Spanish. Chile became independent in 1818.

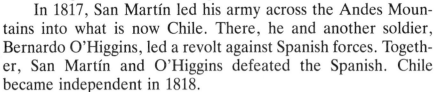

Bernardo O'Higgins

1. How did Antonio Nariño help spread the ideas of the French Revolution through the Spanish colonies?
2. How did Simón Bolívar earn the title of "The Liberator"?
3. What did José de San Martín and Bernardo O'Higgins do for independence?

MEXICO, CENTRAL AMERICA, AND BRAZIL The fight for independence went on in Mexico as well. A parish priest from the village of Dolores, Father Miguel Hidalgo y Costilla, played an important part in it. Hidalgo had long been concerned about the way Indians were treated. Now, he and other Creoles tried to organize a revolution. Hidalgo urged his congregation not to submit any longer to Spanish rule. His battle cry came to be called the "Grito de Dolores," or the "cry of Dolores."

In 1810, under Hidalgo's leadership, the Indians revolted. But the revolt failed, and Hidalgo was caught and put to death. Three years later, another priest, Father José María Morelos, led a second revolt. But it was no more successful than the first. Morelos, like Hidalgo, was caught and put to death.

Father Hidalgo

The Mexicans, however, would not give up. In 1820, Creoles, church leaders, and army officers joined together and revolted. Two years later, Mexico was declared independent. It was ruled by Agustín de Iturbide, a Creole army officer, who served as emperor. But Iturbide refused to share power with the Mexican legislature. He was also a poor administrator. The Mexicans soon tired of his rule. In 1823, they overthrew him. In 1824, after a constitution was completed, Mexico became a republic.

Moved by what had happened in Mexico, the people of Central America revolted. In 1823, they declared their independence and joined together to form the United Provinces of Central America. Not long after, the United Provinces split into the present-day countries of Costa Rica, El Salvador, Guatemala, Honduras, and Nicaragua.

A struggle for independence also took place in Brazil. When Napoleon invaded Spain and Portugal, the Portuguese royal family fled to Brazil. In 1821, several years after Napoleon's final defeat, King João VI returned to Portugal, leaving his son Pedro to rule Brazil.

Brazilian Hunter

Many Brazilians could see no reason to remain a part of the Portuguese Empire. They were angry that Portugal tried to control their trade. They also did not like the way the Portuguese parliament treated the Brazilian representatives. In 1822, the Brazilians declared their independence from Portugal. They made Pedro, who agreed to accept a constitution, their emperor. Brazil was the only country in South America to become a monarchy after independence.

1. Why did Father Hidalgo revolt against Spanish rule?
2. Why did the Mexicans overthrow Iturbide?
3. What was Brazil's government like after independence?

INDEPENDENCE IN LATIN AMERICA

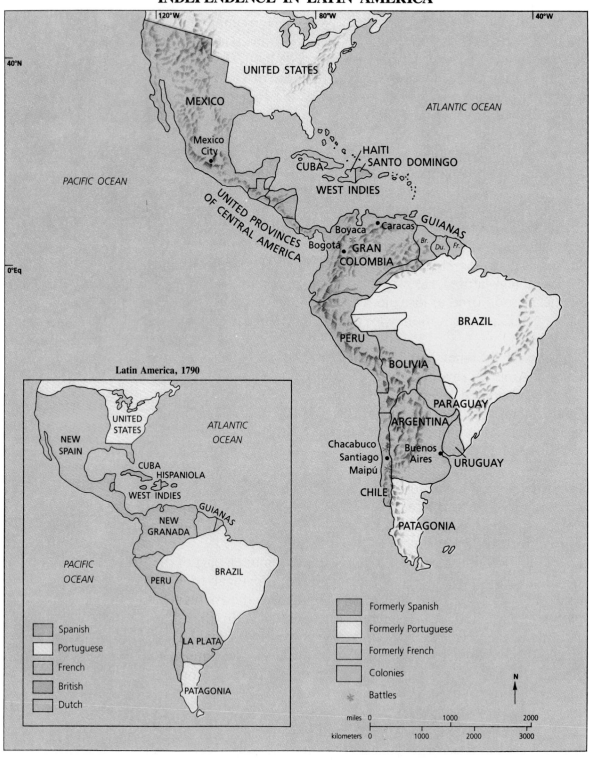

United States
40°N

MEXICO
Mexico City

PACIFIC OCEAN

UNITED PROVINCES OF CENTRAL AMERICA

HAITI
SANTO DOMINGO
CUBA
WEST INDIES

GUIANAS
Br. Du. Fr.

Boyaca · Caracas
Bogotá
GRAN COLOMBIA

BRAZIL

PERU

BOLIVIA

PARAGUAY

ARGENTINA

Chacabuco
Santiago
Maipú

Buenos Aires

URUGUAY

CHILE

PATAGONIA

ATLANTIC OCEAN

0°Eq

Latin America, 1790

UNITED STATES

ATLANTIC OCEAN

NEW SPAIN

CUBA
HISPANIOLA
WEST INDIES

GUIANAS

NEW GRANADA

BRAZIL

PACIFIC OCEAN

PERU

LA PLATA

PATAGONIA

Spanish
Portuguese
French
British
Dutch

Formerly Spanish
Formerly Portuguese
Formerly French
Colonies
Battles

N

miles 0 · 1000 · 2000
kilometers 0 · 1000 · 2000 · 3000

RULE BY CAUDILLOS   Most of the people in Latin America hoped the new independent countries would become democratic. But Spanish rule had given the people little training in self-government. Mestizos, Indians, and blacks had received no opportunity for education. And Creoles were not willing to share power with other groups.

Santa Anna

A new kind of leader called a **caudillo,** or strong man, rose to power. Caudillos were backed by the army. Most were also backed by large landowners and church officials, who did not want their lands divided among the peasants.

Generally, a caudillo took over a government by force. That caudillo ruled until he was overthrown by another caudillo. With each change in government, there was a violent revolution and much bloodshed. Because of this, most Latin American countries did not have stable governments.

Most caudillos ruled as dictators. They did not care about improving the lot of the people. One such caudillo was Antonio López de Santa Anna of Mexico, who had been a commander in Iturbide's army. One historian described Santa Anna as "a fortune hunter and a glory hound." In 1833, Santa Anna led his troops into Mexico City and had himself elected president. He ruled Mexico six times between 1833 and 1855. It was during his rule that Mexico lost one half of its land to the United States through the Treaty of Guadalupe Hidalgo.

A different type of caudillo eventually took Santa Anna's place. His name was Benito Juárez. Juárez proved that a caudillo could care about the needs of the people. A lawyer, Juárez was the first Indian to rule Mexico since the fall of the Aztec Empire.

Juárez was officially elected president in 1861 after several years of civil war. But Mexico owed money to several foreign countries, including France. Juárez asked these countries to wait two years for their money. France refused. Instead, it sent troops and made a European prince named Maximilian emperor. Juárez and his followers refused to give up, however, and finally defeated the French.

Juárez was again elected president in 1867. He held office until his death in 1872. As president, Juárez worked to hold democratic elections. He reduced the power of the Catholic Church by selling its land to the peasants. He started free schools to educate Indian children. This made educating the people the responsibility of the state rather than the church. He also reduced the size of the army.

1. What were most caudillos like?
2. How was Benito Juárez different from most caudillos?
3. What reforms did Juárez make in Mexico?

CHAPTER 35 REVIEW

SUMMARY

1. Soon after the United States became an independent nation, two political parties developed.
2. In 1800, political power in the United States passed from one party to the other through a peaceful election rather than through war.
3. While under British control, people in the United States developed a tradition of representative government.
4. By 1830, most adult white males in the United States were able to vote, thus making the government one of the most democratic in the world at the time.
5. As settlers moved westward, they came into conflict with Indians. In the 1820's and 1830's, most Indians east of the Mississippi were made to move to reservations west of the Mississippi.
6. By 1867, the United States had acquired the Louisiana Territory; Florida; the Oregon Territory; almost one half of Mexico's land, including Texas; and Alaska, thus more than doubling its size.

7. Between 1861 and 1865, northern states and southern states fought a civil war.
8. In 1865, the North and the South reunited, and the United States began to develop into an industrial country.
9. In 1804, Haiti was the first Latin American country to win independence.
10. The Spanish colonies in Latin America and Portuguese Brazil gained their independence in the early 1800's.
11. The newly independent Latin American countries lacked training in self-government and as a result, most were ruled by a series of caudillos.
12. Most caudillos were dictators who did not care about the people.
13. One caudillo who cared about the people and worked to give them democracy and education was Benito Juárez.

BUILDING VOCABULARY

1. *Identify the following:*

Latin America	Treaty of Guadalupe	Simón Bolívar	Agustín de Iturbide
Federalist	Hidalgo	José de San Martín	Antonio López de
Republican	Abraham Lincoln	Miguel Hidalgo y	Santa Anna
Old Hickory	Toussaint L'Ouverture	Costilla	Benito Juárez
Louisiana Purchase	Antonio Nariño	José Morelos	

2. *Define the following:*

stable government	reservations	seceding	junta
political parties	manifest destiny	indigo	caudillo
federal	annex	mulattoes	

REVIEWING THE FACTS

1. What ideas did the Federalist party have about government?
2. What ideas did the Republican party have about government?
3. What became of the Indians east of the Mississippi River in the 1820's and 1830's?
4. What did the United States gain by the Louisiana Purchase?
5. Why did the people of Texas quarrel with the Mexican government?
6. Why did the northern and southern states fight a civil war?
7. Why did caudillos rise to power in most Latin American countries?
8. What groups supported most caudillos?
9. What happened to Mexico's territory under the rule of Antonio López de Santa Anna?
10. What kept Benito Juárez from exercising the powers and authority of his office at first?

DISCUSSING IMPORTANT IDEAS

1. What is the relationship between a stable government and the development of a nation?
2. How did the ideas of the American Revolution and the French Revolution affect the people of Latin America?
3. Do you think Simón Bolívar deserved the title of "The Liberator"? Why or why not?
4. Do you think a nation can develop without a democratic government? Explain the reasons for your answer.

USING MAPS

Study the map on page 560, and answer the following questions:

1. What is the time period of the map?
2. Where are the Thirteen Colonies located on this map?
3. What river formed the western border of the United States in 1783?
4. When did the Louisiana Purchase take place?
5. Where are the Rocky Mountains?
6. What is the distance across the United States at the widest point?

Study the maps on page 566, and answer the following questions:

1. To whom did Cuba belong in 1790?
2. How far is Caracas from Buenos Aires?
3. What area is farthest south on the map?
4. How far north did Mexico extend?
5. What is the only French colony?
6. What was Gran Colombia called in 1790?

CHAPTER 36

EUROPE IN FERMENT

In the early 1800's, Napoleon occupied the center of the European stage. He came closer than anyone else to bringing political unity to the European continent. In so doing, he spread revolutionary ideas. After his defeat, there was a return to the old order. However, the ideas had taken hold, and from 1820 to 1848, revolutions took place in country after country. The years after 1848 saw the breakup of the old order and the formation of new nations.

THE AGE OF NAPOLEON

By 1799, France had had ten years of revolution and war. The people longed for a return to peace and order. They were ready for a strong leader to take charge. When Napoleon came along, he started a chain of events that affected not only France, but all of Europe.

NAPOLEON   When the French Revolution began, Napoleon Bonaparte, who had come to France from Corsica, was a lieutenant in the French army. By the time he was 24 years old, he had become a general. But Napoleon was ambitious. He was not satisfied just being a general. He wanted more power.

In 1796, Napoleon led French troops into Italy. There, the French defeated the Austrians, who ruled Italy. As a result, France acquired Belgium from Austria.

Two years later, in 1798, Napoleon sailed for Egypt. There, he won a great land victory against the British. But at the mouth of the Nile, the British fleet destroyed the French fleet. In the meantime, Austria, Russia, and Great Britain had defeated a French army in Europe. When Napoleon learned about this, he saw his chance to get more power. He left his troops and returned to Paris. There, he and two members of the Directory plotted to take over the government. On November 9, 1799, they put their plan into effect and met with success.

Napoleon set up a new government, the Consulate, with himself at its head. His title was First Consul. By this time, Russia was no longer at war with France. But Austria and Great Britain were. In 1801, Napoleon led his soldiers to victory over Austria. In 1802, he arranged a peace treaty with Great Britain.

1. Why did Napoleon leave Egypt and return to France in 1799?
2. How did Napoleon become First Consul of France?

AFFAIRS AT HOME   Once France was at peace, Napoleon turned his attention to affairs at home. The Directory had been weak and in debt. Napoleon set to work to make the Consulate strong and rich. He took away the people's right to choose their own local officials. Instead, they were appointed by the national government. He took away the local governments' power to collect taxes and gave it to the national government. Because Napoleon's system was better organized, the government was

Napoleonic Dress

Arc du Triomphe

able to collect more taxes. Within a few years, the debt was paid, and the economy improved. With the tax money, Napoleon set up a system of public education.

Napoleon also set to work to bring order to the French legal system. The French Revolution had swept away most laws. And the different revolutionary governments had never been able to agree on new ones. Because of this, different laws were followed in different parts of the country.

To correct this, Napoleon selected a committee of lawyers and told them to write a new code of law for the entire country. The code they wrote, which was divided into five parts, was called the Napoleonic Code. It preserved some of the most important rights won in the Revolution. Serfdom was abolished. People were made equal before the law. Anyone accused of a crime was guaranteed a public trial by jury. Freedom of religion was guaranteed.

However, some rights that the people had won in the Revolution were taken away from them. No one was allowed to criticize the government. Napoleon did not allow freedom of speech or the press. A large police force kept watch on anyone suspected of being against Napoleon. Many people were put in jail.

Napoleon tried to make both Paris and France more beautiful. He had a huge marble arch, the Arc du Triomphe, built next to the Louvre, the national museum, as a monument to his campaigns. He had 14 new bridges put up across the Seine River, which runs through Paris. French workers dug canals and improved roads everywhere. Jacques Louis David, whom Napoleon named as court painter, designed furniture that looked like that of ancient Greece and Rome. Soon, the "Empire" style spread throughout Europe. This style affected clothes as well as furniture. Women wore narrow white cotton or muslin dresses tied high, with low square necklines and short puffed sleeves. And they fixed their hair like the women of ancient Rome.

Because Napoleon brought peace and order, he was very popular. In 1802, he asked the people to elect him First Consul for life. They did so in a **plebiscite**, or popular vote. Two years later, they elected him emperor of France. His coronation was held in the Cathedral of Notre Dame. But the Pope, who had come from Rome for the event, did not have a chance to place the crown on Napoleon's head. Instead, Napoleon took the crown from the Pope's hands and crowned himself.

1. How did Napoleon strengthen the national government?
2. What rights did the Napoleonic Code give the people?
3. What rights did Napoleon take away from the people?
4. How did Napoleon beautify Paris and France?

THE GRAND EMPIRE   Being emperor of France was not enough for Napoleon. He wanted to create a Grand Empire that would take the place of the Holy Roman Empire. He had the advantage of an army whose soldiers worshipped their emperor and whose officers were chosen because they were able in battle, not because they were aristocrats.

In 1803, Napoleon went to war with Great Britain. Before long, almost every country in Europe was involved. Napoleon's troops won most of their battles, and in the next few years added several territories to the Grand Empire.

French Soldier

Napoleon had himself crowned king of Italy. In 1806, he created the Confederation of the Rhine, which was a loose union of conquered German states. In 1808, he invaded Spain and Portugal. The following year, he made the Papal States part of France and put the Pope in prison. By 1810, Napoleon's Grand Empire included most of Europe.

The countries in Napoleon's Grand Empire were strongly influenced by France. The French took over the government in many conquered states. Sometimes, Napoleon placed his relatives on the thrones of conquered states. The French rulers made the Napoleonic Code law. Thus, Napoleon's conquests helped spread the ideas of the French Revolution throughout Europe.

Only Great Britain and Russia remained undefeated by Napoleon. Since the French could not defeat the British army in battle, Napoleon tried to conquer the British in a different way. He forbade the countries in his empire to trade with Great Britain, which he called a "nation of shopkeepers." But his order was hard to enforce, and it proved unsuccessful.

Next, Napoleon took on Russia. He organized a Grand Army of about 600,000 soldiers of different nationalities. It was the largest army the world had yet seen. In the summer of 1812, the Grand Army invaded Russia. Except for one battle, the Russians did not fight. Instead, they retreated, drawing the French deeper into Russia. As the Russians retreated, they

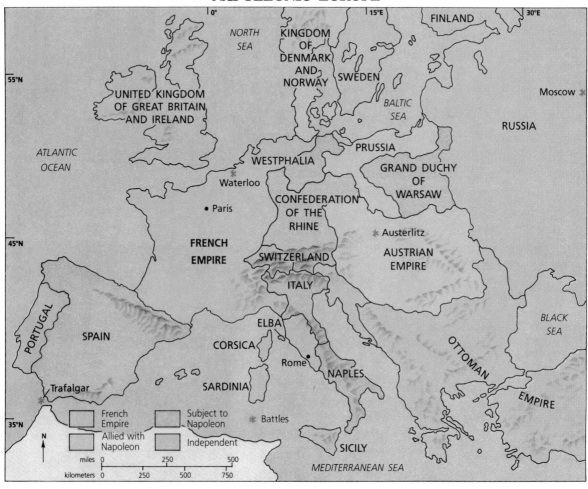

burned their villages and food supplies, leaving nothing for the advancing French. This is called a **scorched earth policy**.

In September, Napoleon reached Moscow, which had been abandoned by the Russians. Shortly after the French arrived, the city caught fire and burned for several days. Three fourths of it was destroyed. The French could not feed or house their army. Napoleon sent several peace proposals to the Russians, which they ignored. He waited five weeks. Finally, he gave the order to retreat. But it was too late. The bitter Russian winter had started. Fewer than 100,000 soldiers made it back to France. Most of the others had died from disease, lack of food, and the cold.

Napoleon quickly raised another army, but the new soldiers were not well trained. They were defeated by the allied forces of Austria, Prussia, Russia, and Great Britain. This was the first time the four powers had joined together to fight Napoleon.

In 1814, the allies took Paris, and Napoleon was forced to **abdicate**, or give up the throne. He was sent to live out his days on the small island of Elba off the coast of Italy. But he managed to escape and gather together enough troops to invade France. For 100 days, Napoleon again reigned as emperor. The allies finally defeated him in 1815 at the Battle of Waterloo. This time, they sent Napoleon to the island of St. Helena off the west coast of Africa, where he died in 1821. Some historians believe he was poisoned by his jailor.

Duke of Wellington

1. Why did Napoleon start a war against Great Britain?
2. How was Napoleon defeated?

REACTION, REVOLUTION, AND REFORM

After Napoleon's defeat in 1814, representatives from Austria, Prussia, Russia, and Great Britain met in Vienna to decide what to do about France and the rest of Europe. The settlement they agreed upon reestablished Europe as it was before the French Revolution. This set the stage for revolution in many countries and reform in some.

THE CONGRESS OF VIENNA   The Congress of Vienna was sometimes called the "Waltzing Congress." This was because the representatives spent so much time at dinners, dances, and fox hunts. However, decisions there were made by a few leaders. They included Prince Clemens von Metternich, the Austrian foreign minister, and other representatives of the major powers.

Talleyrand

The leaders did not want to punish France too harshly. At the same time, they wanted to build a peaceful and stable Europe. They believed the best way to do this was by establishing a **balance of power**, or equal strength among countries. They hoped that with a balance of power no country would try to start another war.

So, the leaders divided up Napoleon's Grand Empire. In the peace treaty, they had cut France back to the size it had been in 1792. Now, they set about completing the task. Russia got Finland and most of Poland. Sweden got Norway. Austria got

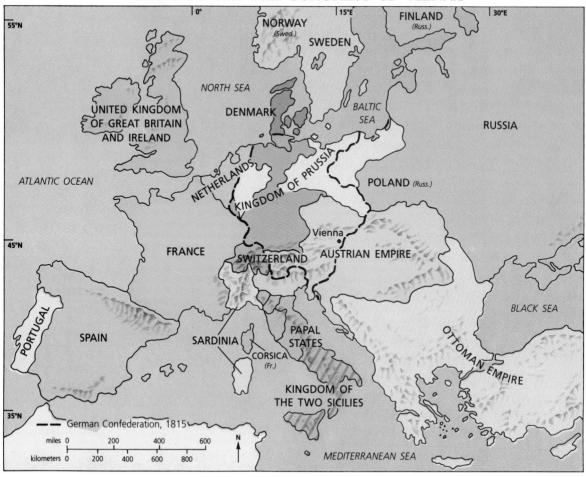

EUROPE AFTER THE CONGRESS OF VIENNA

Map labels: NORWAY (Swed.), FINLAND (Russ.), SWEDEN, NORTH SEA, BALTIC SEA, UNITED KINGDOM OF GREAT BRITAIN AND IRELAND, DENMARK, RUSSIA, NETHERLANDS, KINGDOM OF PRUSSIA, POLAND (Russ.), ATLANTIC OCEAN, FRANCE, Vienna, SWITZERLAND, AUSTRIAN EMPIRE, PORTUGAL, SPAIN, SARDINIA, CORSICA (Fr.), PAPAL STATES, BLACK SEA, OTTOMAN EMPIRE, KINGDOM OF THE TWO SICILIES, MEDITERRANEAN SEA

German Confederation, 1815

miles 0 200 400 600
kilometers 0 200 400 600 800
N

part of northern Italy. Great Britain got the islands of Malta and Ceylon. Belgium and Holland were combined into a single nation. And the 39 German states were combined into a very loose German Confederation headed by Austria.

In addition to wanting peace, the leaders were against democracy. To crush revolutionary ideas, they brought back divine-right monarchy. They had already given the French throne to Louis XVIII, the younger brother of Louis XVI. Now, the leaders also brought back the monarchy in Spain and Portugal. And they made the Pope ruler of the Papal States again.

1. Why was the Congress of Vienna held?
2. What were two goals of the leaders of the Congress?

POLITICAL MOVEMENTS   The balance of power in Europe was maintained for many years. But revolutionary ideas did not die. Several groups were against the Congress System, which was the political system set up by the Congress of Vienna.

One group was the **liberals**. They wanted political reform based on the ideals of the French Revolution. Most liberals were members of the middle class. They wanted changes that would benefit them. They believed in voting rights for property owners, protection of private property, and such rights as freedom of speech. Some liberals wanted a constitutional monarchy. Others wanted a republic. The liberals were strongest in Great Britain and France.

Another group that was against the Congress System was the **nationalists**. They wanted political independence for national groups that shared the same language, customs, and history. The Congress of Vienna had paid no attention to nationalist feelings when it divided the Grand Empire. For example, the Belgians did not want to be part of Holland. They had a different language, religion, and culture than the Dutch.

A third group that was against the Congress System was the **socialists**. They believed that the people as a whole should own all the land, factories, and other means of production. In this way, socialists believed, the workers' lot would improve, and everyone would be treated fairly.

Some socialists thought that there were ways besides revolution to get reforms. They tried to set up ideal communities based on economic cooperation. They thought these communities would show that theirs was a better way of life. These socialists were known as **utopian socialists**.

Other socialists believed that the only way to get reforms was to have a revolution. One who believed this was Karl Marx, a German. He believed that the **proletariat**, or industrial working class, would rise up and take control. "The proletarians have nothing to lose but their chains," he wrote in *The Communist Manifesto*. "They have a world to win. Workingmen of all countries, unite!"

Marx believed that after the revolution, there would be no hunger or poverty. Governments would not even be needed. People would work because they wanted to contribute to society. In return, they would be able to develop their own interests and talents. Marx called his kind of socialism **communism**. He

Karl Marx

believed that the workers' revolution would be led by the Communist party.

1. What did liberals believe?
2. What did nationalists believe?
3. What did socialists believe?
4. What was the major difference between utopian socialists and communists?

AN ERA OF REVOLUTION   Beginning in 1820, liberals, nationalists, and socialists led revolutions against the Congress System. The earliest revolutions took place in Spain, Portugal, Italy, and Russia. They all failed. However, encouraged by these revolts, Greek nationalists rebelled against the Ottoman Empire in 1821. After eight years of fighting, Greece finally gained its independence.

In 1830, there was a successful revolution in France. King Louis XVIII had been succeeded by his brother, Charles X. Charles X wanted to bring back the Old Regime. So, just a few weeks after being crowned, he did away with the new National Assembly. He also took the right to vote away from the middle class. Middle-class liberals, helped by students and workers who could not find jobs, overthrew the government. After three days of fighting, Charles X fled.

The July Revolution, as it was called, was a victory for the middle class. Members of the middle class wanted a constitutional monarchy rather than a republic. So, they gave the throne to Charles X's cousin, Louis Philippe. However, although the number of voters was increased, only the richest members of the middle class could vote. This disappointed other members of the middle class, as well as the workers, who had wanted not only a republic but also **universal male suffrage**. This is the right of all adult males to vote.

News of the July Revolution touched off rebellions in other countries. In 1831, Belgian nationalists won independence from Holland. The Poles rebelled against Russia, but they were defeated. There were uprisings in several German and Italian states that were also put down.

In Great Britain, however, liberal reforms were made by **evolution**, or gradual development. In 1832, Parliament passed a bill that lowered the property requirements for voting. This increased by one half the number of people who had the right to

WORKERS ORGANIZE

During the nineteenth century, European workers set up trade unions and political parties to protect and advance their rights. Here, German workers gather to protest a government ban on demonstrations. By 1900, most European industrial countries had passed laws that met many of the workers' demands.
What demands did labor unions make upon their governments?

vote. This bill also gave the new industrial towns more representation in Parliament. These changes gave the British middle class more say in government.

There were also reforms that helped the working class. Labor unions gained the right to **strike**, or stop work, in order to obtain shorter hours, higher wages, and better working conditions. And by 1890, working-class males had the right to vote.

1. Why did the French rebel in 1830? What reforms did they win?
2. What reforms were made in Great Britain?

THE REVOLUTIONS OF 1848　　The lack of reforms elsewhere led to a series of revolutions in 1848. Governments fell all over Europe. Once again, the trouble started in France.

Louis Philippe had tried to be a "citizen-king." He would walk through the streets of Paris without any servants to show that he was a bourgeois rather than an aristocrat. But he was very rich himself, and his government served only the rich. Industrial workers and lower middle-class liberals became more and more unhappy. At the same time, the economy was bad throughout Europe. Many people did not have jobs. Then, in 1845 and 1846, the potato and wheat crops failed. There was not enough food to go around.

In 1848, riots broke out in the streets of Paris. Louis Philippe fled, and the revolutionary leaders declared the Second French Republic. They set up a **provisional**, or temporary, government to rule until a new national assembly could be elected. Louis Blanc, a socialist, was one of the leaders. He persuaded the other leaders to set up **national workshops**, or factories run by the workers but paid for by the government. The workshops provided jobs for thousands of people. But the number of people out of work grew faster than jobs could be created. Before long, the government was supporting over 100,000 people.

When the new National Assembly was elected, it did away with the workshops. The workers revolted, fighting violently for three days. They were defeated by the army, but not before thousands of people were killed. The National Assembly then drew up a constitution. It provided for a strong president to be elected by universal male suffrage. Napoleon's nephew, Louis Napoleon Bonaparte, was elected president of the Second French Republic. But he believed he had inherited his uncle's destiny. So, in 1851, he overturned the constitution. A year later, the people voted him Emperor Napoleon III. He remained on the throne until 1870, when the Second French Empire came to an end.

The revolution in France was followed by revolutions in other parts of Europe. Hungarians, Italians, and Germans rebelled. But they all failed. Even so, the revolutions of 1848 led to some important changes. In time, universal male suffrage spread to most northern and western European countries. Workers, who felt they had been cheated, began to form political parties. Soon, there was a socialist party in almost every European country.

1. Why did riots break out in France in 1848?
2. How did Louis Napoleon Bonaparte become president of the Second French Republic?
3. What were some results of the revolutions of 1848?

THE GROWTH OF NATIONALISM

After the revolutions of 1848 failed, the Congress System seemed stronger than ever. However, this was not the case. Before long, the growth of nationalism would destroy the Congress System and the balance of power that had been established at Vienna. Three countries that were affected were Italy, Germany, and Austria.

ITALY   In 1848, eight of the nine Italian states were under Austrian control. Only Sardinia was independent. Ever since Napoleon's time, the Italians had been unhappy about this state of affairs. They remembered that Rome had once ruled the ancient world, and that Italian city-states had led the Renaissance. They wanted to become a unified nation.

VICTOR EMMANUEL II AND GARIBALDI

Victor Emmanuel (left) became king of the unified kingdom of Italy in 1866. The unification of Italy was made possible after Guiseppe Garibaldi (right) led his volunteer troops, the Red Shirts, to conquer the Kingdom of the Two Sicilies.
Why did Italian nationalists expect Sardinia to take the lead in unifying Italy?

Many nationalists in Italy looked to Sardinia to take the lead. Count Camillo di Cavour, the prime minister of Sardinia, realized that he needed help to drive out the Austrians. So, he made an agreement with Napoleon III. It said that if the Austrians attacked Sardinia, the French would help the Sardinians. When Austria declared war on Sardinia in 1859, Napoleon III kept his word. Austria was defeated, and the Italian state of Lombardy was united with Sardinia.

Sardinia had won Lombardy, but Austria still controlled the other northern Italian states. Although Napoleon III had withdrawn his soldiers, these states continued to revolt. By 1860, most of northern Italy was united and at peace with Austria.

That year, in southern Italy, an Italian nationalist named Giuseppe Garibaldi led another revolution. Garibaldi had spent much of his life in exile in Brazil and Uruguay. There, he had learned how to lead small bands of soldiers behind enemy lines. The bands would hide in forests and on hillsides. They would make surprise attacks on the enemy and then go back into hiding. This kind of fighting is called **guerrilla warfare**. In guerrilla warfare, a small group of soldiers can often defeat a much larger army.

Garibaldi taught guerrilla warfare to his followers. They were called "Red Shirts" because, like their leader, most of them wore red shirts. They also wore loose grey trousers, silk handkerchiefs around their necks, grey cloaks, and black felt hats.

In 1860, Garibaldi's Red Shirts conquered Sicily within three months. Then, they sailed to the Italian mainland and marched to Naples.

In 1861, the northern and southern nationalist groups combined. The kingdom of Italy was formed as a constitutional monarchy. Victor Emmanuel II of Sardinia became king. The Pope, however, was against Italian unity. Because of this, he lost the Papal States. In 1870, they became part of Italy. With the Papal States and Venetia, which had been won earlier from Austria, Italian unification was complete. However, the balance of power in Europe was weakened.

1. How did Napoleon III help the Italian nationalists?
2. What did Guiseppe Garibaldi do to further the Italian nationalist movement?

GERMANY Nationalist feelings were also strong in the 39 German states. German poets and writers, like Goethe and Schiller, wrote about German nationalism. German composer Richard Wagner wrote operas based on German folk tales. In 1834, many of the German states signed a trade agreement. In it, they promised not to tax goods coming from other German states. Soon, the economy of these states improved. Still, many of the rulers of the smaller states were not willing to give up their political power. And Austria was against any attempt to unify Germany.

These obstacles were overcome by Prussia. In 1862, King William I named Count Otto von Bismarck prime minister of Prussia. Bismarck was a **junker**, or rich landowner, who believed in divine-right monarchy. He said that he would unite Germany,

THE GERMAN EMPIRE
After Prussia defeated France in 1871, Bismark (center) proclaimed King William I of Prussia (on platform) the emperor of a new German empire.
What effect did a united Germany have on other European countries?

Richard Wagner

not "by speeches and majority votes—but by blood and iron." He also believed that war against a common enemy would bring the German states closer together.

In 1864, Bismarck joined with Austria to defeat Denmark and to gain territory. Two years later, he used a dispute over this territory as an excuse to go to war against Austria. Prussia won in seven weeks. The peace treaty ended the loose German Confederation. The North German Confederation, led by Prussia, was set up in its place.

In 1870, Bismarck found an excuse to go to war against the French, the Germans' oldest enemy. As Bismarck had hoped, the southern states joined the northern states in the struggle. Well-trained and well-equipped, the German army easily defeated the French army. Then, Bismarck laid siege to Paris. The people of Paris held out for four months. At last, on January 28, 1871, the city surrendered.

Meanwhile, at Versailles, William I of Prussia was named **kaiser**, or emperor, of the new German Empire. This included the rich mining and manufacturing territories of Alsace and Lorraine, which had been won from France. A unified Germany, however, meant a further weakening of the balance of power.

1. How did Otto von Bismarck plan to unite Germany?
2. What were some results of the war between Prussia and France?

AUSTRIA   Nationalists in Italy and Germany wanted to unify their nations. Nationalists in Austria threatened the unity of the Austrian Empire.

The Austrian Empire was made up of many nationalities. Although the emperor was German, four out of five people were not Germans. They included Magyars—the largest national group in Hungary—Czechs, Slovaks, Poles, Croats, and Slovenes. Each group had its own language and history. And each group wanted to rule itself.

By 1866, Austria had been defeated by both Sardinia and Prussia. Magyar nationalists saw their chance to become independent. They revolted, and in 1867, a weakened Austria agreed to create a dual monarchy. Now, the emperor ruled over two separate kingdoms—Austria and Hungary. Each had its own official language, parliament, and laws. The Magyars were satisfied, but other nationalities in Austria-Hungary were not. Their unhappiness presented a continuing threat to the Dual Monarchy and the peace of Europe.

1. How was nationalism in Italy and Germany different from nationalism in the Austrian Empire?
2. How was Austria-Hungary formed?

CHAPTER 36 REVIEW

SUMMARY

1. In 1799, Napoleon Bonaparte helped to overthrow the Directory, and by 1804, he had become emperor of France.

2. Napoleon strengthened the central government and established a single code of law for the entire country but took away certain rights from the people.

3. After conquering most of Europe, Napoleon was defeated and made to leave France.

4. In 1814, representatives from Austria, Prussia, Russia, and Great Britain met at Vienna to establish a balance of power.

5. The Congress of Vienna divided up Napoleon's empire and brought back divine-right monarchy in many areas.

6. Liberals, nationalists, and socialists opposed the Congress System.

7. In 1820, 1830, and 1848, political revolutions broke out in different European countries.

8. Liberal reforms were made in Great Britain without a revolution.

9. After the revolutions, universal male suffrage began to spread throughout Europe, and the working class began to turn toward socialism.

10. During the 1860's, the Italian states united to form a nation.

11. Between 1862 and 1871, the German states, led by Otto von Bismarck of Prussia, united to form a nation.

12. In 1867, the Austrian Empire became two separate kingdoms—Austria and Hungary—each of which had many different national groups that each wanted independence.

BUILDING VOCABULARY

1. *Identify the following:*

Napoleon Bonaparte	Congress System	Louis Philippe	Giuseppe Garibaldi
Grand Empire	Karl Marx	Louis Blanc	Victor Emanuel II
Grand Army	*The Communist*	Napoleon III	Count Otto von
Battle of Waterloo	*Manifesto*	Count Camillo	Bismarck
Congress of Vienna	July Revolution	di Cavour	Austria-Hungary

2. *Define the following:*

plebiscite
scorched earth policy
abdicate
balance of power
liberals

nationalists
socialists
utopian socialists
proletariat

communism
universal male
  suffrage
evolution

provisional
national workshops
guerrilla warfare
junker

REVIEWING THE FACTS

1. What did Napoleon want after he became a general?
2. How did the Napoleonic Code change the French legal system?
3. What effects did Napoleon's conquests have on western Europe?
4. Why did the representatives at the Congress of Vienna try to bring back divine-right monarchy?
5. What three groups opposed the Congress System?
6. Why did the French provisional government of 1848 set up national workshops in that country?
7. Through what means did the Italian states become unified?
8. How did the German states become unified?
9. Why did Emperor Napoleon III lose his throne?
10. Why were national groups in Austria-Hungary unhappy?

DISCUSSING IMPORTANT IDEAS

1. Do you consider universal manhood suffrage important? Why or why not?
2. Do you think that the conquests made by Napoleon were good or bad for Europe? Explain.
3. How important do you think nationalism was in Europe during the second half of the 1800's? Explain.
4. Do you think liberal reforms can be made without a revolution? Explain.

USING MAPS

Study the maps on pages 574 and 576, and answer the following questions:

1. What countries were subject to Napoleon before the Congress of Vienna?
2. What is the longitude and latitude of the island that remained French after the Congress of Vienna?
3. What did the Confederation of the Rhine become after 1815?
4. What city is southwest of Austerlitz?
5. Who took control of Napoleon's Grand Duchy of Warsaw?

CHAPTER 37

RISE OF IMPERIALISM

In the late 1800's, an interest in colonies rose again. Many countries rushed to take over parts of the world that had not been claimed during the Ages of Discovery and New World Expansion. New colonial powers were added to the old. Among these were Belgium, Germany, Italy, Japan, Russia, and the United States.

THE MOVE TOWARD IMPERIALISM

There were many reasons for imperialism. One was the Industrial Revolution. The factories of the industrialized countries needed such raw materials as rubber, cotton, oil, tin, and copper. And there was a growing demand for tea, sugar, and cocoa. Both raw materials and food could be found in undeveloped areas, such as Africa, Asia, and Latin America.

Then, too, industries needed new markets for their goods. Factories were turning out more goods than people at home could afford to buy. Many industrial leaders and merchants believed that new markets could be found in undeveloped areas.

Also, many factory owners had grown rich from profits made during the Industrial Revolution. They could not find enough places in their own countries in which to **invest**, or put their money to work. And when they did invest, they thought the profits were too small. Investments in undeveloped areas, however, generally brought large profits.

Another reason for imperialism was nationalism. Many people thought colonies would add to their country's power. The newly formed countries of Italy and Germany wanted to catch up with Great Britain, France, and other established colonial powers. Japan and the United States wanted to become as important as the colonial powers of western Europe.

Still another reason for imperialism was the idea that western countries had a duty to "civilize" the "backward" peoples of the world. To many westerners, any people whose way of life and religion were different from their own were "backward," especially if they had a different skin color. These westerners believed they had a mission to spread Christianity and the Industrial Revolution everywhere. The British poet Rudyard Kipling called this mission "the white man's burden."

Rudyard Kipling

1. How did the Industrial Revolution lead to imperialism?
2. How did nationalism lead to imperialism?
3. What was "the white man's burden"?

AFRICA

Before 1870, European powers had few holdings in Africa. Those they did have were mostly seaports and trading stations along the coast. The only major exceptions were the Cape Colony at Africa's southern tip and Algeria in northern Africa. Great Britain had received the Cape Colony from the Dutch at the Congress of Vienna. Algeria was held by France. Before long, most of Africa belonged to European powers.

THE OPENING OF AFRICA   At first, most Europeans stayed along the African coast because they were safer there

STANLEY AND LIVINGSTONE
Henry Stanley (center left) found David Livingstone (center right) living in the tiny village of Ujiji on Lake Tanganyika. Stanley greeted him with the now famous words, "Dr. Livingstone, I presume?"
Why had Dr. Livingstone gone to Africa?

from tropical diseases and other dangers. The **interior**, or inland areas, of Africa were scarcely known to them. Then, European missionaries and explorers opened these areas to the West.

In 1840, a Scottish medical missionary named David Livingstone went to Africa to convert Africans to Christianity. During his years in Africa, Dr. Livingstone worked hard to end the Arab slave trade. He also explored much of the continent's interior. He wrote letters about his journeys that were published in newspapers in Great Britain and the United States. The letters aroused a great deal of interest in Africa.

Suddenly, the letters stopped. A New York newspaper decided to find out what had happened to Dr. Livingstone. It assigned reporter Henry Stanley to the story. After two years of searching, Stanley found Dr. Livingstone in a small Arab village on the shores of Lake Tanganyika. Stanley then became an explorer himself. Between 1874 and 1889, he traveled the Nile River and explored the Congo. Stanley's books describing his adventures increased European interest in Africa.

19th Century African Art

In 1878, Stanley was hired by King Leopold II of Belgium to secure African lands for him. Stanley signed many treaties with African chiefs in the Congo Basin. Most of the chiefs could not read or write. They did not realize what they were signing. In return for their lands, many of which were rich in minerals and rubber, the chiefs received cloth, beads, and sometimes guns. The signing of such treaties became a common way of getting colonial territory.

Leopold II wanted to make as much money as quickly as possible. So, he had his soldiers make the Africans collect rubber for him. Anyone who resisted was shot. But missionaries and other Europeans protested so much that the king finally turned the Congo over to the Belgian government. And the government did away with forced labor.

In northern Africa, the Suez Canal had been opened in 1869. Built by Egyptian workers and French funds, it connected the Mediterranean and Red seas. The Suez Canal made possible the short all-water route to India and the Far East that Europeans had sought for hundreds of years. But the Egyptian ruler needed money. So, in 1875, he sold his shares in the canal to Great Britain. Great Britain then took over Egypt's finances. This made many Egyptians angry. When they rebelled in 1882, English troops moved into Egypt. Egypt became a British **protectorate**, or a country under the control and protection of a larger, stronger nation.

1. Where were most European holdings in Africa before 1870?
2. How did David Livingstone increase interest in Africa?
3. Why did King Leopold II turn the Congo over to the Belgian government?

FROM THE CAPE TO CAIRO   Soon after Great Britain made Egypt a protectorate, the British began moving south. After several years of fighting, they conquered the Sudan. There, Great Britain set up a joint government with Egypt.

At the same time, the British were also moving north from the Cape Colony. The Boers, or Dutch farmers in South Africa, did not want to be ruled by the British. So, the Boers decided to leave the Cape Colony. They finally settled on the grasslands of the interior. There, they founded two independent states, the Transvaal and the Orange Free State.

In 1885, gold and diamonds were discovered in the Boer states. Thousands of adventurers began pouring in. Soon, the Boers were outnumbered. Afraid of losing control of their government, the Boers would not allow the newcomers, who were mostly British, to vote. However, they insisted that the newcomers pay heavy taxes.

This angered Cecil Rhodes, who was prime minister of the Cape Colony. Rhodes wanted to carry out a dream of an English-speaking empire that would stretch from the Cape to Cairo. The British already controlled land to the south and west

---

BRITISH AFRICA

A late nineteenth-century cartoon (left) shows Cecil Rhodes's dream of spreading British rule in Africa. Resistance to the British by the Boers in South Africa led to the Boer War (right), fought between 1898 and 1902.
What obstacles did the British meet in extending their rule in Africa?

THE RHODES COLOSSUS
STRIDING FROM CAPE TOWN TO CAIRO.

of the Boer states. Rhodes proceeded to build a railway line into land to the north of the Boer states. As soon as the railroad was completed, British settlers began moving into Rhodesia.

At this point, Germany, jealous of Great Britain's growing power, offered the Boers its best artillery. The Boers promptly attacked British territory, and the Boer War began. At first, the Boers defeated the British. Then, the British captured the Boer capital. The Boers, however, refused to surrender and carried on guerrilla warfare for nearly two years. Finally, the British destroyed Boer farms and imprisoned Boer women and children. When that happened, the Boers gave up. In 1910, the Transvaal and the Orange Free State were joined with Cape Colony and one other British colony to form the Union of South Africa.

Military Governor of the Sudan C.G. Gordon

The British gained other African possessions besides Egypt, the Sudan, Rhodesia, and the Union of South Africa. Between 1890 and 1914, Zanzibar, Uganda, British East Africa, and Nigeria all came under British control. Except for one German colony, Cecil Rhodes' dream had come true.

1. Why did the Boers leave the Cape Colony?
2. What was Cecil Rhodes' dream for Africa?
3. How successful was Great Britain in achieving this dream?

OTHER EUROPEAN EMPIRES   Leopold's actions in the Congo and the British takeover of Egypt spurred other European powers into action. Over the next few years, they divided the African continent among themselves.

Spain and Portugal, the pioneers of imperialism, kept their original possessions. Angola, founded in 1648 by the Portuguese, was the oldest colony in Africa. In 1885, Portugal also made Portuguese East Africa, or Mozambique, a protectorate.

The French moved out from Algeria to establish the largest European empire in Africa. It included Tunisia, Morocco, French West Africa, French Equatorial Africa, and Madagascar.

Italy and Germany were latecomers in the race for African territory. The Italians conquered Eritrea, a colony on the eastern coast, and took over a part of Somaliland. When they tried to take Ethiopia in 1896, they were defeated by the forces of King Menelik I. In 1911, however, the Italians won two Turkish provinces from the Ottomans. The Italians combined the two and renamed the colony Libya. The Germans set up

King Menelik I

protectorates over Togoland and the Cameroons in 1884. Later, they added German Southwest Africa and German East Africa.

By 1914, only two areas in Africa remained independent. One was Ethiopia. The other was Liberia, which had been founded in the 1830's by former slaves from the United States.

1. What spurred European powers into action in Africa?
2. What were the two independent African nations in 1914?

ASIA

The English and the Dutch started trading with Asia in the 1500's. But Chinese and Japanese rulers allowed very limited contacts with the West. So, western European countries turned their attention to India. In time, the European powers, Japan, and the United States would control much of the rest of Asia.

CHINESE TRADING ESTABLISHMENTS

This colored engraving from 1844 shows commercial houses of foreign trade along the docks at Canton, China. Ships from Denmark, Great Britain, the United States, and the Dutch East India Company are in the harbor.
How did the Chinese feel about westerners?

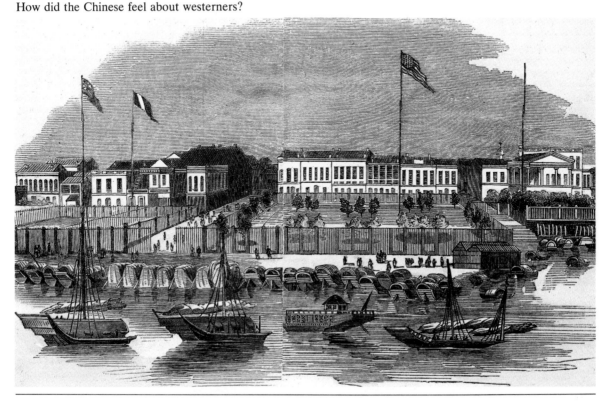

INDIA   By the middle of the 1700's, the Mogul Empire of India was breaking up. This allowed Great Britain and France to set up trading stations along the Indian coast. Then, in 1763, France lost the Seven Years' War, also known in the New World as the French and Indian War. As a result, the French left India, and the British East India Company took over.

The British East India Company stayed in power for almost a century. During that time, it brought many changes to India. Roads and railroads were built, schools were set up, and English became the official language.

But not everyone was happy with British rule. Many Indians felt the British were trying to change their culture. In 1857, the **sepoys**, or Indian soldiers in the British Army, mutinied. The immediate cause was a new rifle. Its cartridges were greased, and one end had to be bitten off before loading. The Hindus thought the grease was beef fat. The Muslims thought it

---

INDIAN TEA PLANTATION

In India, the British owned large tea plantations, where Indians worked as tea pickers. This series of drawings shows the steps involved in the growing and preparing of tea for the market in Britain.
How did the British gain control of India?

was pork fat. Hindus are not allowed by their religion to eat beef, while Muslims are not allowed to eat pork.

Although the Sepoy Mutiny failed, the British government realized that changes were needed. So, it took control of India away from the British East India Company and gave it to the Crown.

Great Britain wanted to protect its Indian empire from other countries, especially Russia. From 1865 to 1884, most of the central Asian centers of Muslim civilization fell to Russia. To guard India's northwest frontier, the British made Afghanistan a protectorate. Later, Great Britain and Russia set up **spheres of influence**, or areas in which a country has special rights, in Persia.

Sepoy

1. How did the British get control of India?
2. What led to the Sepoy Mutiny? What was its result?
3. How did Great Britain protect its Indian empire from Russia?

CHINA From the early 1500's, all trade between China and the West was limited to the city of Canton. The Chinese looked upon westerners as barbarians. So, the Chinese expected westerners to show them respect, follow their rules, and stay away from their people.

The Chinese people were divided into two classes. The upper class lived mostly in the cities and towns. The lower class lived mostly in the villages. Government officials, scholars, and landowners usually belonged to the upper class. They knew how to read and write and looked down upon people who worked with their hands. Members of the lower class did not know how to read and write. They were usually farmers and artisans.

Both classes, however, had certain things in common. They followed the teachings of Confucius. And they believed that the family was more important than the individual. Chinese men always chose a profession that would help their family. Marriages were arranged to benefit families. When a son married, he did not move to a separate house. Instead, he and his wife lived with his parents. The Chinese greatly respected their ancestors. On New Year's Day, they would burn incense and place an offering of food on the family altar. Then, they would tell the ancestors what had happened to the family during the past year.

The Chinese followed their way of life until the 1800's. Then came the Industrial Revolution. Western factory owners and

Chinese Vase

merchants became interested in increasing overseas trade. They were no longer satisfied with the limited amount of business the Chinese allowed them. They also wanted the Chinese to consider them as equals.

About this time, British traders discovered that they could make large profits selling **opium**, or a drug made from the dried juice of poppies, to the Chinese. The traders took cotton cloth made in Great Britain to India, where they traded it for opium. They took the opium to China, where they exchanged it for tea and silk. Then, the tea and silk were shipped to Great Britain.

Chinese Junks

At first, the Chinese government ignored the opium trade. Then, when it saw how much damage the drug was doing, the government declared the trade illegal. But when a government official in Canton seized and burned a large shipment of opium, British traders became angry. In 1839, what became known as the Opium War broke out between the British and the Chinese.

Although they greatly outnumbered the British, the Chinese had neither cannon nor steam-driven warships. In 1842, they were defeated and forced to sign a treaty that opened more ports and gave Great Britain the island of Hong Kong. The treaty also gave British citizens in China the **right of extraterritoriality**. This meant that British citizens accused of breaking Chinese laws could only be tried in British courts. Before long, other western powers demanded and received the same rights as Great Britain.

Open Door Author
John Hay

China lost more power in the late 1800's. In 1894, Japan and China went to war over Korea. The Japanese won easily and took Chinese territory. While China was still in a weakened state, Great Britain, France, Germany, and Russia rushed to get **concessions**, or special rights, from the Chinese government. These included rights to develop mineral resources and to build railroads and naval bases. Several countries also got leases on Chinese port cities.

The United States did not want to see China divided up by foreign powers. But it did not want American merchants to be kept out of trade with China. In 1898, the American government asked the countries interested in China to approve the Open Door policy. It gave all countries equal trading rights in China.

But the Open Door policy did not please the Chinese. It meant that foreign powers were still trying to control them. So, the Chinese began a movement to drive all foreigners from their country. The movement was called the Boxer Rebellion, because it had been started by a Chinese secret society called the Boxers. In the spring of 1900, the Boxers began attacking foreigners, including the diplomats at Peking. The foreign powers joined together and sent an army to China. In 1901, the rebellion was put down. China was made to pay heavy penalties. And foreign powers gained complete control of the country.

1. How did the western powers feel about the Chinese effort to keep them out of China?
2. What did the foreign powers do after China lost a war with Japan over Korea?
3. Why did the Boxer Rebellion break out?

JAPAN   Like China, Japan allowed only limited trade with the West at first. The Japanese government refused to take care of shipwrecked sailors. This changed in the middle of the 1800's.

In 1853, the American government sent a naval force under Commodore Matthew Perry to Japan. Perry had orders to negotiate a treaty to open up trade and to protect shipwrecked American sailors. Perry was successful, and Japan signed treaties with Great Britain, France, Russia, and the Netherlands.

The military strength and industrial accomplishments of the West impressed Japanese leaders. They came to believe that in order to survive, Japan must modernize. It did so quickly. By the end of the 1800's, Japan was fully industrialized.

Matthew Perry

This led to problems, however. Japan had to get raw materials and markets for its manufactured goods. Also, because of modern sanitation and medicine, its population was increasing rapidly. And Japan did not have enough fertile land to grow food for all its people.

To help find the answer to these problems, the Japanese began a program of imperialism. The peace treaty following the war with China over Korea gave Japan the island of Formosa, or present-day Taiwan, and part of Manchuria. Ten years later, Japan went to war with Russia. The Japanese won again. As a result of this victory, Japan got the southern half of the island of Sakhalin. It also won a sphere of influence in Korea. Five years later, Japan annexed Korea. Japan was now a world power.

1. Why did Commodore Perry go to Japan in 1853?
2. What was the result of Japan's contact with the West?
3. Why did the Japanese begin a program of imperialism?

Siamese Art

SOUTHEAST ASIA AND THE PACIFIC Europeans first entered Southeast Asia in the 1500's in search of spices. By the 1600's, Portugal, Spain, and the Netherlands all had colonies there. Although there was an active trade with the islands in the area, no one paid much attention to the mainland.

In the late 1800's, the European powers changed their minds. The mainland of Southeast Asia was a source of cash crops, such as coffee and tea. The mainland was also a source of raw materials, such as petroleum, rubber, and tin.

Great Britain and France became the chief rivals in Southeast Asia. The British took control of Burma, Ceylon, the Malay States, and Singapore. The French set up protectorates in Cochin-China, Cambodia, and Annam. Then, they conquered Laos and combined the four colonies into Indochina. Only Siam, or present-day Thailand, remained independent.

During the scramble for colonies in Southeast Asia, Great Britain, France, Germany, and the United States were trying to win control of islands in the Pacific. Some of the islands had rich soil that could be used for sugar and pineapple plantations. Others had minerals. Still others could be used as bases for refueling and repairing ships.

Great Britain, which had the largest navy in the world, already held Australia and New Zealand. Now it took the Fiji, Solomon, and Gilbert islands, along with parts of New Guinea and Borneo. France claimed Tahiti, the Marquesas, and several other islands. Germany took part of New Guinea and the Marshall, Caroline, and Mariana islands. Later, Germany divided the Samoan Islands with the United States. The United States also controlled the Hawaiian and Philippine islands and Guam.

Hawaiian Queen
Liliuokalani

1. Why did many European countries want to control territory in Southeast Asia?
2. Why did the imperialist powers want islands in the Pacific?

LATIN AMERICA

The imperialist powers were also interested in Latin America. The nations there that gained their independence in the early 1800's faced many problems. Most Latin Americans were poor and had no land of their own. The new leaders had little government experience. There were many revolutions. These shaky conditions seemed to invite outside interference.

To stop this, President James Monroe issued the Monroe Doctrine in 1823. It said that any attempt to gain new colonies or to retake independent states in Latin America would be thought of as an unfriendly act toward the United States. Most of the European powers went along with the Monroe Doctrine. The only real challenge took place when the French made Prince Maximilian of Austria the emperor of Mexico.

By the late 1800's, the most important European colonies left in Latin America were Cuba and Puerto Rico. Both belonged to Spain. The Cubans, eager to be independent, had revolted in 1868 and again in 1895. Some Americans, with large amounts of money invested there, wanted the rebels to win. Other Americans, reading about Spanish cruelties in the news,

IMPERIALISM

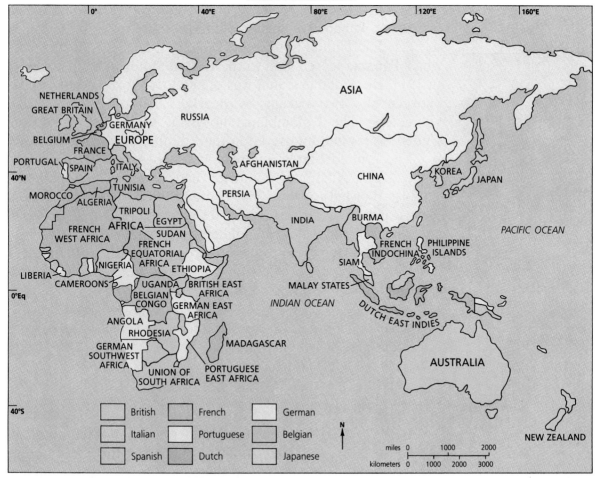

were also sympathetic. Finally, in 1898, the U.S.S. *Maine* blew up in the harbor of Havana, Cuba. People all over the United States blamed the Spanish. Before long, Congress declared war on Spain.

In less than a year, the United States won the Spanish-American War. The peace treaty gave the United States Puerto Rico, Guam, and the Philippine Islands. Cuba was set up as a protectorate. The United States was now a world power and as such became more involved in Latin America.

The United States needed a way to protect its new empire. Its fleet had to be able to sail quickly between American islands in the Caribbean Sea and those in the Pacific Ocean. President Theodore Roosevelt wanted to build a canal across Panama, which belonged to Colombia. But the United States could not come to terms with Colombia.

War Hero Roosevelt

So, in 1903, the United States supported a revolution by people in Panama against Colombia. The revolution was a success. The United States and Panama then signed a treaty in which Panama leased land to the United States to build a canal. In 1914, the Panama Canal was opened. It shortened the route between the two oceans by nearly 7,000 miles, or 11,200 kilometers. The Colombians, however, were angry that the United States had interfered in their affairs.

The United States' interest in Latin America continued. Some Latin American countries had financial and political troubles that led to riots. The United States wanted to protect American business investments. So, between 1912 and 1916, the government sent American soldiers to Nicaragua, the Dominican Republic, and Haiti to restore order. After the soldiers left, the United States government still kept financial control and took charge of elections.

1. Why did the United States issue the Monroe Doctrine?
2. What did the United States gain from the Spanish-American War?
3. Why did the United States want a canal in Panama?

EFFECTS OF IMPERIALISM

By 1914, the European colonial powers, Japan, and the United States had brought about 85 percent of the world under their control. This had many benefits. Orderly governments

PANAMA CANAL
The building of the Panama Canal took over eight years and the labor of over 43,000 persons. The engraving above shows the digging of the Gaillard Cut.
How did the United States obtain the lease for the land of the Panama Canal?

were set up, and many local wars were stopped. Industry and agriculture were developed. Roads, railroads, canals, bridges, and factories were built. Hospitals and schools were built, and sanitation was improved. Communication became easier because French and English were spoken in most parts of the world. Western ideas about democracy and individual rights were spread.

Imperialism led to major problems. One was bitter feelings between colonists and colonizers. Most Europeans, North Americans, and Japanese thought they were superior to the people in the colonies. Colonists were seldom allowed to hold high jobs in government, industry, or the armed forces. Often, they were not allowed in the city areas where Europeans and North Americans lived.

The colonists resented this. They blamed the colonial powers for the loss of their land and for being made to work on plantations and in factories. They disliked the colonial powers for trying to change their customs, languages, and religions. These feelings helped nationalism to grow.

There was another problem. The scramble for colonies led to a great deal of competition among the colonial powers. This, in turn, led to disputes that caused future wars.

1. What were some benefits of imperialism?
2. What were some problems of imperialism?

CHAPTER 37 REVIEW

SUMMARY

1. The move toward imperialism in the late 1800's came about because of the need for raw materials, new markets, and investment opportunities; the growth of nationalism; and the belief that western nations had a duty to "civilize" the "backward" peoples.

2. European missionaries and explorers opened the African interior to the West.

3. In 1875, Great Britain took over the Suez Canal and soon after had full control of Egyptian affairs.

4. By the early 1900's, the French had the largest European empire in Africa, and the British Empire stretched from the Cape Colony to Cairo.

5. Only two African nations retained their independence—Ethiopia and Liberia.

6. By the later 1800's, Great Britain controlled India, and Russia was moving into central Asia.

7. Until the Opium War of 1839–1842, western trade in China was limited to the city of Canton.

8. By 1901, China was completely controlled by foreign powers.

9. Japan did not open up trade with the West until the middle of the 1800's.

10. By the early 1900's, Japan was fully industrialized and an imperialist power.

11. By the end of the 1800's, European countries and the United States controlled most of Southeast Asia and many islands in the Pacific.

12. In 1823, the United States issued the Monroe Doctrine to warn European countries not to expand their control in Latin America.

13. The United States won Puerto Rico, Guam, the Philippine Islands, and Cuba from Spain in 1898 and in 1903 leased land from Panama to build the Panama Canal.

14. While imperialism led to the establishment of orderly governments, the development of industry and agriculture, and social reforms, it also led to bitter feelings, the growth of nationalism, and competition among colonial powers.

BUILDING VOCABULARY

1. *Identify the following:*

David Livingstone	Boers	Opium War	Matthew Perry
Henry Stanley	Cecil Rhodes	Open Door policy	Monroe Doctrine
Leopold II	Sepoy Mutiny	Boxer Rebellion	U.S.S. *Maine*
Suez Canal			Panama Canal

2. *Define the following:*

invest	protectorate	spheres of influence	right of extra-
interior	sepoys	opium	territoriality
			concessions

REVIEWING THE FACTS

1. What were the main reasons for the move toward imperialism?
2. How did European missionaries help open Africa to the West?
3. How did some Europeans get colonial territory from African chiefs?
4. Why was the Suez Canal important?
5. Why did the Egyptian ruler sell his shares of the Suez Canal?
6. What caused British settlers to move into the Transvaal after 1885?
7. What two countries were latecomers to the race for African territory?
8. What was the purpose of the Open Door policy?
9. Why did Japan modernize and industrialize so rapidly during the second half of the 1800's?

DISCUSSING IMPORTANT IDEAS

1. How were the reasons for imperialism after the Industrial Revolution different from those during the Age of Discovery?
2. Do you think countries would be as interested today in gaining control of the Suez Canal as they were in the late 1800's? Why or why not?
3. What do you think might have happened to Japan if it had not modernized and industrialized?
4. If you had lived in the United States in 1823, how would you have replied to Latin American objections to the Monroe Doctrine?

USING MAPS

Study the map on page 599, and answer the following questions:

1. On which continent are most of the European colonies located?
2. What colony belongs to Belgium?
3. What body of water is south of India?
4. What is the latitude and longitude of the Malay States?
5. What are the countries in Africa that are independent?

MODERNIZATION OF JAPAN

Mutsuhito called his reign *Meiji*, which means "enlightened peace." He moved the capital from Kyoto to Tokyo. Then, he issued a Charter Oath in which he promised reforms.

Japanese government leaders were convinced their country had to become more modern. They sent out groups to observe industry and government in the West. After careful study, they adopted that which they felt was good for Japan.

The new government did away with feudalism and gave land to the peasants. It also put an end to the samurai, and set up a modern army and navy.

A new constitution was issued in 1889. A new code of law and system of courts were established. The rights of

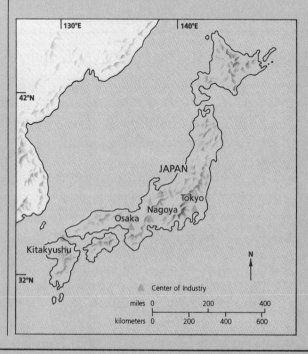

Shoguns ruled Japan until the middle of the 1800's. Many Japanese lords felt the shoguns were keeping Japan from becoming a modern nation. They also resented the government's weakness in dealing with foreigners. The lords overthrew the shogun and restored the power of the emperor.

In 1868, Mutsuhito, a 15-year-old, became emperor of Japan. For the first time in more than 600 years, the emperor was the real ruler of the nation, instead of a shogun.

Japanese women were increased. Public schools were opened, and education was required for all Japanese.

Japanese leaders also began a push to develop industry. The government promoted the building of railroads, factories, ports, and telegraph and telephone systems. The Bank of Japan was set up as a central banking office. An official money system was introduced. Thousands of Japanese were urged to start businesses.

The Japanese economy continued to be influenced by the *zaibatsu*. These were the rich and powerful families who controlled many industries. They received special privileges and protection from the government.

The push to modernize led to many changes in Japanese society. The government ordered all Japanese males to cut off the topknots worn in their hair. Western-style clothing and a new calendar were introduced.

By the time Emperor Mutsuhito died in 1912, Japan was a modern industrial state. It was the first industrialized nation in Asia. Large cities, such as Tokyo and Osaka, grew up, and the population rapidly increased. Japan had become the strongest nation in Asia.

1. Why was the emperor of Japan returned to power?
2. How was Japan modernized?
3. What were some results of Japan's efforts to become more modern?

UNIT 12 REVIEW

SUMMARY

1. In the 1800's, the United States expanded its territory and fought a civil war. It became a strong industrial nation that showed that a democratic form of government could be stable.

2. Portuguese and Spanish colonies in the Americas gained independence in the 1800's. But they lacked experience in self-government; so most remained under the rule of caudillos.

3. In the early 1800's, Napoleon Bonaparte made himself emperor of France and created a large empire in Europe.

4. After the allied forces of Austria, Russia, Prussia, and Great Britain defeated Napoleon, they divided his Grand Empire among themselves and restored divine-right monarchies. But they could not crush the revolutionary ideas of liberals, nationalists, and socialists.

5. A series of revolutions and strong feelings of nationalism eventually led to universal manhood suffrage, the rise of socialism, the unification of Italy and Germany, and the establishment of a dual monarchy in Austria and Hungary.

6. In the 1800's, the industrial nations of western Europe, the United States, and Japan undertook a policy of imperialism. They competed with one another to gain control in Africa, Asia, Southeast Asia and the Pacific, and Latin America.

REVIEWING THE MAIN IDEAS

1. Describe what the effects of nationalism and revolution were on the West in the 1800's.

2. Explain what led to the policy of imperialism and the effect it had in different parts of the world.

DEVELOPING SKILLS

It is very important for historians to be able to prove whether or not the data they are using are correct. Sometimes there is a great deal of evidence to support a statement. Other times, it is very difficult, if not impossible, to gather enough evidence to support a statement.

This exercise is designed to give you practice in determining whether it would be easy or difficult to prove the truth of a statement. Read the following groups of statements. For each group, tell which statement would be the most difficult to prove.

Group A

1. Thomas Jefferson was elected president of the United States in 1800.

2. Only men voted in the election of 1800.

3. Thomas Jefferson was one of the greatest presidents of the United States.

4. Most of the people who voted for Thomas Jefferson were property owners.

Group B

1. Napoleon set up a new government in France with himself as First Consul.
2. Napoleon established a single code of law for the entire country.
3. Napoleon did more for France than any leader before or after him.
4. Napoleon escaped from Elba, invaded France, and ruled for 100 days.

Group C

1. Bernardo O'Higgins led a revolt against Spanish forces in Chile.

2. Without Bolívar, Venezuela and Peru would never have gained independence.
3. Bolivia is named after Simón Bolívar.
4. José de San Martín organized an army in La Plata.

Group D

1. The Boer War could have been avoided.
2. Gold and diamonds were discovered in the Boer states in 1885.
3. Cecil Rhodes was prime minister of Cape Colony during the last part of the 1800's.

SUGGESTED UNIT PROJECTS

1. Write a play based on the last year of Napoleon's reign. Include Napoleon's escape from Elba, the Battle of Waterloo, and Napoleon in exile on St. Helena. Present the play in class.

2. Research the expedition of one of the nineteenth-century missionaries or explorers who entered the African interior. Then write a poem or short story that tells how that person might have reacted to what he encountered.

3. Write an article that might have appeared in a Chinese newspaper of the time about the events of the Opium War or the Boxer Rebellion. Graphically illustrate the main points of your article.

4. Give an oral report on one of the following: (a) the Alamo, (b) Garibaldi, (c) Otto von Bismarck, (d) the founding of Liberia, (e) the building of the Panama Canal, (f) the work of Florence Nightingale in the Crimean War.

SUGGESTED READING

Hall, Marjory. *The Carved Wooden Ring*. Philadelphia, Pa.: Westminster Press, 1972. A story based on the life of Euphremia Goldsborough, a nurse and a spy during the Civil War.

Hays, Wilma P. *For Ma and Pa: On the Oregon Trail, 1844*. New York: Coward, McCann, and Geoghegan, 1972. The adventures of a 13-year-old boy on the Oregon Trail.

Markun, Patricia M. *The Panama Canal*. New York: Franklin Watts, 1979. Traces the Panama Canal from planning through construction to opening.

Roberts, John G. *Black Ships and Rising Sun*. New York: Julian Messner, 1971. The story of how Japan was opened by Commodore Perry and how it industrialized and modernized.

Werstein, Irving. *The Boxer Rebellion*. New York: Franklin Watts, 1971. Why and how Chinese revolutionaries tried to drive out the foreigners.

UNIT 13

1906 **1905** Revolution of 1905	**1909** 	**1912** **1911** Chinese Revolution **1912** Sun Yat-sen becomes president of China **1914** World War I begins
1924 **1925** Chiang Kai-shek takes control of Nationalists	**1927**	**1930** **1928** Joseph Stalin becomes leader of Soviet Union **1929** Great Depression begins **1931** Japan takes over Manchur
1942 **1941** Japanese attack Pearl Harbor	**1945** **1945** United States drops atomic bomb on Japan United Nations is formed **1947** Marshall Plan India becomes independent Nehru becomes prime minister of India	**1948** **1948** Berlin blockade begins Israel becomes Jewish state **1949** NATO People's Republic of China is proclaimed under Mao Tse-tung Chiang Kai-shek sets up Republic of China on Taiwan
1960 **1960** "Year of Africa" **1961** Berlin Wall built **1962** Cuban missile crisis	**1963** **1964** Leonid Brezhnev and Aleksei Kosygin become Soviet leaders **1965** Cultural Revolution	**1966** **1967** Arab-Israeli War **1968**
1978 **1978** China begins "four modernizations" **1979** United States recognizes People's Republic of China	**1981**	**1984**

THE TWENTIETH CENTURY

1915

1918

1917 Russian Revolution
Bolsheviks under Lenin
take power
United States declares
war on Germany

1919 Treaty of Versailles

1921

1922 Mussolini becomes dictator of Italy
Soviet Union formed

1933

1933 Hitler becomes leader of Germany

1934 Long March begins

1936

WORK PROGRAM WPA

1939

1939 World War II
begins in
Europe

1951

1950 Korean War begins

1954

1955 Warsaw Pact

1956 Suez crisis

1957

1957 *Sputnik I*
Vietnam War begins

1958 Nikita Khrushchev becomes
leader of Soviet Union
Great Leap Forward
announced in China

1969

1969 Border clashes between
China and Soviet Union

Americans and Soviets agree to limit weapons

1971 People's Republic of China admitted to United Nations

1972

1972 Americans and Soviets agree to limit weapons

1973 Arab-Israeli War

1975

1976 Chou En-lai and
Mao Tse-Tung die

---

1. HOW DID WORLD WARS I AND II CHANGE WESTERN
   EUROPE'S ROLE IN WORLD AFFAIRS?
2. WHAT ARE SOME OF THE MAJOR PROBLEMS FACING
   THIRD WORLD COUNTRIES?

By the early 1900's, the most powerful countries in the world were those in the West. They were industrial countries that controlled world trade. Several also controlled large empires in Africa and Asia. They led the world in education and in inventions. Their languages were used by many people who had never been in the West. Their scientific and medical ideas were spread all over the world.

In 1914, these countries became involved in a world war, which their leaders said would be the last. However, some leaders continued to rely on force to settle differences. By 1945, another world war had been fought. The two wars greatly reduced western Europe's role in world affairs. The United States and the Soviet Union became the most important powers in the world. Communism gained strength. It became the guiding philosophy of both the Russians and the Chinese. The Communists made it clear that, like the West, they wanted to spread their ideas to the entire world. Now, there was a First World, which was the West, and a Second World, which was the Communists.

Soon, there was a Third World. It was made up of nations in Asia, Africa, and the Middle East that wanted independence from European rule. They were joined by nations in Latin America that had already gained independence. Many nations of the Third World are poor and face serious problems, such as overpopulation and a shortage of food. They are trying to become modern without losing their own cultures.

CHAPTER 38

THE WEST

For most of the 1900's, the world has been in turmoil. In 1914 a war broke out in Europe that became global in scope. When peace was made, the countries tried to recover. However, anger over the peace settlement and poor economic conditions created a climate that led to a second world war. It was even larger and more costly than the first. Despite the turmoil of these years, new discoveries in science and technology were made.

World War I

For almost 100 years after Napoleon's defeat, there was no long, general European war. However, by the early 1900's, rivalries among the countries of Europe were causing trouble. These countries looked for allies to protect themselves. But this only added to the tension. Then came a crisis in the Balkans. No one could resolve it, and soon Europe was at war. After four years of fighting, the war ended. The European countries then turned to the difficult task of making peace.

BACKGROUND   At the end of the 1800's, the most powerful countries in Europe were France, Germany, Great Britain, Austria-Hungary, Italy, and Russia. Each country tried to protect its world trade and its colonies. Each built up its armed forces and tried to make alliances with other countries.

Finally, two alliances developed. One alliance was made up of Great Britain, France, and Russia. The other was made up of Germany, Austria-Hungary, and Italy. Each member of an alliance promised to help the other members if they were attacked. So, trouble between any two countries from different alliances could draw in other countries. A small war could easily grow into a large one. All that was needed was a spark.

The spark was provided at Sarajevo, capital of the Austrian province of Bosnia. There, in June 1914, a Bosnian youth shot and killed Archduke Francis Ferdinand of Austria. The youth belonged to a nationalist group that wanted to unite the Slavs in the area under Serbian rule.

Austria-Hungary blamed the Serbian government for the Archduke's death and declared war on Serbia. Russia, which was also a Slavic country, began to **mobilize**, or call up its troops, to go to Serbia's aid. Germany showed its support of Austria-Hungary by declaring war on Russia. Shortly after, France and Great Britain joined on the side of Russia. So did Japan and, later, Italy. Germany and Austria-Hungary were called the Central Powers. Russia, France, Great Britain, Japan, and Italy were called the Allied Powers.

FROM 1914 TO 1918   World War I was not like any other war people had known. For one thing, the war that started between Serbia and Austria-Hungary in 1914 grew so large that 31

Archduke Francis Ferdinand

TRENCH WARFARE
Fighting on the western front reached a standstill in 1915. Both sides dug a series of trenches. The trenches protected soldiers from enemy bullets. Between these trenches lay what became known as "no man's land."
Where was the western front located?

countries, with 61 million soldiers, took part. Although most of the fighting took place in Europe, battles were also fought in the Middle East and Africa. Naval warfare took place all over the world.

There were also new weapons. Machine guns fired bullets one after another at a rapid speed. Giant guns fired shells more than 75 miles, or 120 kilometers. Airplanes carried bombs behind enemy lines and dropped them on enemy cities. Submarines attacked ships at sea. Poison gases were used. Tanks and flamethrowers were introduced. And both sides tried to starve the other's **civilians**, or people who are not soldiers.

Much of the fighting in World War I took place on the western front, the fighting zone between France and Germany. There, the opposing armies dug themselves into the earth in trenches protected by barbed wire. To get at the enemy, each side had to climb out of its own trenches and cross open land under fire. This kind of fighting is called **trench warfare**. In one area, French and German troops engaged in trench warfare for ten months. At the end of that time, 420,000 soldiers had died, but no territory had changed hands.

On the eastern front, Russia suffered heavy losses. And in 1918, after two revolutions, Russia signed a separate peace treaty with Germany. The Russians gave up huge areas of land in the western part of their country, including one third of their farmland. They also gave up one third of their population and almost all their resources of coal, iron, and oil.

In the meantime, German submarines tried to stop ships that were bringing supplies to Great Britain and France. In 1917, the submarines sank American ships with civilians on board. So, the United States declared war on Germany. Until then, the United States had tried to keep out of the conflict.

The United States sent 2 million troops to Europe. The Europeans had been fighting for a long time and were tired. The Americans were fresh. Because of this, they helped to turn the tide of war in favor of Great Britain, France, and their allies. On November 11, 1918, Germany agreed to an **armistice**, or an end to fighting. World War I was over. It had cost the lives of 10 million soldiers and 13 million civilians.

1. What made World War I different from earlier wars?
2. What happened to Russia in 1918?
3. Why did the United States enter the war?
4. Who won World War I?

Woodrow Wilson

MAKING THE PEACE   Early in 1919, the British, French, Italians, and Americans met at Paris to make peace. Before the war ended, the President of the United States, Woodrow Wilson, had drawn up a peace plan called the Fourteen Points. Wilson believed that punishing the countries that had lost the war would only cause trouble later. He believed that national groups should have the right to form their own countries. He wanted to reduce **armaments**, or equipment for war. Above all, he wanted an association of nations to keep the peace.

But the British, French, and Italians had made plans to get what they could from the defeated countries. In the Treaty of Versailles, Germany lost lands in Europe and overseas. Germany's African colonies were divided between France and Great Britain. Its colonies in the Pacific were given to Japan. Alsace and Lorraine, which Germany had taken from France in 1870, again became part of France. The land that Russia had lost to Germany became five new nations. They were Poland, Finland, Estonia, Latvia, and Lithuania.

Also, the Treaty of Versailles put most of the blame for the war on Germany. The treaty stated that Germany had to pay for the roads, railroads, factories, and farms it had destroyed or damaged. Most of the money went to France, where much of the fighting had taken place.

The other Central Powers were dealt with in separate settlements. Austria-Hungary was broken up. Four new countries—Austria, Czechoslovakia, Hungary, and Yugoslavia—were created. The Ottoman Empire was divided up. France received a **mandate**, or right to rule, in Syria. Great Britain received mandates in Iraq and Palestine.

For the most part, then, President Wilson's peace plan was not followed. Even though many new countries had been created, some national groups were still under foreign control.

TREATY OF VERSAILLES

The Treaty of Versailles was signed in January 1919, at the palace of Versailles outside Paris. Leading the gathering were the four Allied leaders (center, left to right): Orlando of Italy, Wilson of the United States, Clemenceau of France, and Lloyd George of Britain.

How was Germany affected by the Treaty of Versailles?

EUROPE AFTER WORLD WAR I

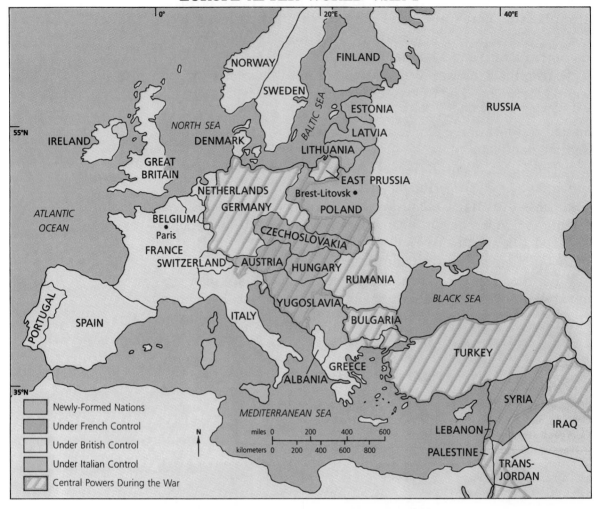

Legend:
- Newly-Formed Nations
- Under French Control
- Under British Control
- Under Italian Control
- Central Powers During the War

However, an organization called the League of Nations was set up so the countries of the world could come together to talk over their troubles. It was hoped that the League could help prevent wars. But the League was hurt by the fact that it had no army of its own. If a country did not want to obey the League, it could not be forced to do so. The League was also hurt because the United States refused to join. Americans were angry about the treaties that had been made. Some thought they were too harsh. Others thought they were not harsh enough. The United States decided to keep out of European affairs and world problems.

1. How many new nations were created in Europe as a result of World War I?

2. What country received most of the blame for World War I?
3. What was the purpose of the League of Nations? Why did the United States refuse to join it?

THE TIME BETWEEN THE WARS

In the 1920's, people tried to recover from the damage caused by World War I. They wanted to rebuild their economies and keep the peace. These tasks proved difficult. People were searching for security. In some countries, people turned to leaders who, before long, would threaten world peace.

THE ECONOMY   In 1929, a **depression**, or sudden slow-down in the economy, set in. Factories closed, and millions of people lost their jobs. By 1932, for example, one out of four Americans and Britons and two out of five Germans were out of work. Banks failed, and people lost their savings. In the United States, able-bodied men were reduced to selling apples for a nickel a piece. Some became beggars. Cities all around the country developed areas where poor people lived in shacks built out of cardboard or tin. In Germany, prices skyrocketed. Money bought so little that housewives would light their stoves with it instead of using firewood. Since the depression touched most of the countries of the world, it is called the Great Depression.

Apple Seller

DEMOCRACY OR DICTATORSHIP   People reacted to the Great Depression in different ways. Many began to think about what kind of government was best. Some western countries, such as the United States and Great Britain, had had a long tradition of stable, democratic government. Voters in these countries wanted to keep their form of government. At the same time, however, they felt the government should help the people.

In the United States, President Franklin D. Roosevelt set up a program known as the New Deal. Under the New Deal, Congress passed **social security laws** that provided money for old people and children who needed care. To put people back to work, the federal government set up several different agencies. One of these, the Civilian Conservation Corps, gave jobs mostly to young people. They planted trees in forests, built small dams to stop soil erosion, and stocked lakes and rivers with fish. The Works Progress Administration paid unemployed people to build roads, airports, bridges, and hospitals. It also provided work for artists and writers.

Other western countries, such as Germany and Italy, had not had a long tradition of stable, democratic government. These countries were governed by elected representatives. But voters there began to feel that these representatives spent too much time debating issues. They began to wonder if it might not be better to have one strong leader who could act quickly to solve a country's problems.

Italy was the first western nation to become a **dictatorship**, or a country ruled by a single person who is not a monarch. This happened in 1922 when Benito Mussolini took over the Italian government.

Mussolini was backed by a political group known as the Fascists. The Fascists wore black shirts and leather boots. They used the old Roman salute of the raised right arm. They also used clubs and guns to beat up and sometimes kill anyone who opposed them. Once Mussolini was in power, he did away with all political parties except the Fascists. He had books about democracy burned. Mussolini promised to make Italy a strong military power.

In 1933, Adolf Hitler became **chancellor**, or prime minister, of Germany. Before long, he did away with the German republic and set himself up as dictator. He called himself *Der Führer*, which means the leader. He called Germany the Third Reich. Hitler was backed by a political group called the National Socialist party, or Nazis. They wore brown shirts and also raised the right arm in salute. They wore armbands and carried flags with the symbol of the **swastika**, or hooked black cross.

Once Hitler was in power, he did away with all political parties except the Nazis. He had books about democracy burned. He fought against the Roman Catholic Church and other Christian churches. And like Mussolini, Hitler promised to make his country a strong military power—no matter what the Treaty of Versailles said.

Hitler blamed Germany's troubles on the Jews. The Nazis believed the Germans were a "master race." That is, they looked down on everyone except the blond, blue-eyed people of northern Europe. So, the Nazis took away the Jews' businesses and jobs. They took Jewish children out of school. Jews could not get medical care. They were no longer allowed to vote or to walk in

Adolf Hitler

Ein Volk, ein Reich, ein Führer!

the streets after eight o'clock. They had to wear a yellow star on their clothing.

1. How did the United States react to the Great Depression?
2. How did Germany react to the Great Depression?
3. What did Benito Mussolini promise the Italians?
4. Whom did Hitler blame for Germany's troubles?

THE ROAD TO WAR   Before long, Italy and Germany threatened world peace. In 1935, the Italians, bitter about not getting enough land after World War I, took over Ethiopia. The League of Nations was not able to stop the takeover. The following year, the Germans marched into the Rhineland, an area between Germany and France. And in 1938, Austria was made a part of Germany.

Other western leaders began to grow alarmed. To calm their fears, Hitler told them that his only goal was to unite all German

---

GERMANY PREPARES FOR WAR

Under the leadership of Adolf Hitler, postwar Germany grew into a strong military power. In this photograph, German troops parade through Berlin. Of what political party was Adolph Hitler the leader?

Japanese War Poster

people into one country. He demanded that the Germans living in Czechoslovakia come under German rule. The British and the French were afraid of another war. So, they gave in to Hitler.

Like Italy and Germany, Japan became a dictatorship. Although Japan still had an emperor, the military ran the country. Japanese military leaders felt that Japan needed more land and natural resources to make its economy stronger. They built a large army and navy. In 1931, Japan took Manchuria, in northern China, away from the Chinese. In 1937, the Japanese invaded the main part of China. That same year they signed a friendship treaty with Germany and Italy.

Western leaders viewed these events with mixed feelings. The Americans were worried about both Japan and Germany but made no move to stop them. The United States still did not want to get involved. The French and British were worried about Germany. They hoped that Hitler would be satisfied with what he had gained and would stop his **aggression**, or attacks.

Russia, now called the Soviet Union, was most fearful of Germany. The Germans had defeated the Russians in World War I. After the war, the Russian monarchy had been overthrown. The new government was run by Communists. The Nazis hated communism. But in 1939, Germany and the Soviet Union signed a treaty, agreeing not to attack each other.

After Hitler signed the treaty, he no longer had to worry about the eastern front. He felt safe to take more land. And on September 1, 1939, he attacked Poland. Soviet troops occupied part of the country, while the Germans conquered the rest. At this point, the French and British saw that they had made a mistake in not resisting Hitler's past aggression. They declared war on Germany.

1. What areas had Italy and Germany taken over by 1938?
2. Why did the British and the French give in to Hitler's demands over Czechoslovakia?
3. Why did Great Britain and France declare war on Germany?

WORLD WAR II

For the second time in the 1900's, the world was at war. Battles were fought not only in Europe, but in Africa, Asia, and the Pacific. When World War II broke out, the Allied Powers—France, Great Britain, and later, the Soviet Union and the

United States—were not ready. However, the Axis Powers—Germany, Italy, and later, Japan—were. For a time, it seemed the Axis Powers would win, but finally the tide turned. The victory of the Allied Powers ended the war, but its effects would be felt for years.

EARLY AXIS VICTORIES   In the beginning, the Axis Powers met with success. Germany had developed a new way of fighting known as **blitzkrieg**, or "lightning war." It was a sudden, fast attack. First, airplanes would bomb enemy cities, roads, and airfields. Soldiers and civilians alike would be machine-gunned from the air. Then, armored tanks would roll through the countryside, wiping out all defenses.

Using the blitzkrieg, Germany crushed Poland in three weeks. In 1940, German forces overran Denmark, Norway, the Netherlands, and Belgium. Next, they pushed the British and French across France to the coast. From there, they were ferried across the English Channel. Then, France surrendered, and Great Britain stood alone.

Hitler tried to bomb the British into surrender. But the British fought back. For ten months, the Battle of Britain went on. British pilots and anti-aircraft guns shot down so many German planes that at last Hitler gave up the idea of invading Great Britain.

British Planes

In the meantime, however, German and Italian forces overran much of Europe and North Africa. The Italians took over Albania. In 1941, the Germans and Italians conquered Greece and Yugoslavia.

While the Germans and Italians pushed through Europe and North Africa, the Japanese battled in Asia. They took over much of China and Indochina. Japanese leaders then turned their attention to the Pacific, where American forces could threaten Japanese power.

The Japanese decided that the United States had to be defeated. So, on December 7, 1941, the Japanese Navy made a surprise attack on Pearl Harbor, the American naval base in the Hawaiian Islands. Angered by the attack, the United States entered the war on the side of Great Britain, France, and the Soviet Union.

1. Why did Hitler decide not to invade Great Britain?
2. What made the United States decide to enter World War II?

WAR IN EUROPE   The entry of the United States helped the Allied Powers win the war in Europe. The United States was the greatest industrial power in the world. Soon, its factories were turning out thousands of planes and tanks. Ships were built in large numbers. At the same time, the Axis Powers were finding it hard to make enough war materials.

Meanwhile, Hitler had decided that Germany needed the grain fields and other resources of the Soviet Union. He ignored

AXIS EXPANSION IN EUROPE AND AFRICA

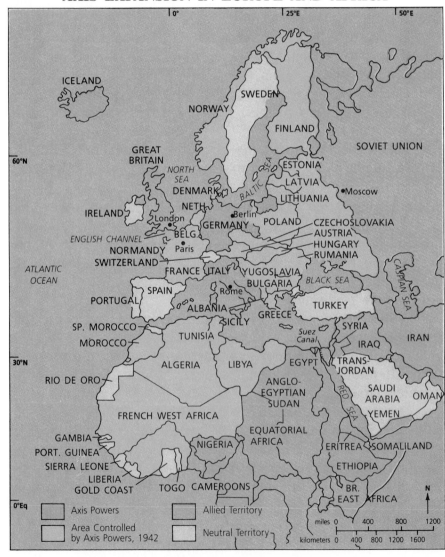

the treaty he had signed in 1939. And in June 1941, Germany attacked the Soviet Union.

However, the German army ran into trouble in the Soviet Union. Like Napoleon before him, Hitler underestimated the country's size and the bitterness of its winters. He also underestimated the people's fighting spirit. Soviet troops used the scorched earth policy that had been used against Napoleon. Then, in 1943, they surrounded a German army in the city of Stalingrad. After four months of fighting and 350,000 casualties, the Germans surrendered. The Battle of Stalingrad was over. From then on, Soviet forces kept pushing the Germans back all along the eastern front. The same year, American and British armies drove the Axis forces out of North Africa and invaded Italy.

In 1944, after more than a year of planning, Allied forces crossed the English Channel from Great Britain and landed on the beaches of Normandy in France. This invasion involved about 4,000 ships and thousands of airplanes. About 155,000 Allied soldiers landed on the first day, June 6. This came to be known as D day. Another 1.3 million landed later. By August, the Allied forces had taken Paris back from the Germans and were moving eastward.

Allied Commander Dwight Eisenhower

Now, the Germans were caught between the Soviets in the East and the Americans, British, French, and Canadians in the West. In 1945, the Allied forces met at the Elbe River in Germany. The Germans realized they could not win. Hitler killed himself. The war in Europe was over.

1. How did the United States' industrial power help it in World War II?
2. Why did Germany attack the Soviet Union?
3. What happened as a result of the Battle of Stalingrad?
4. What happened on June 6, 1944? How did this event help bring about the end of the war in Europe?

WAR IN ASIA AND THE PACIFIC   The war in Asia and the Pacific was fought at the same time as the one in Europe. At first, the Japanese were victorious everywhere. They added the Philippines and various other islands in the Pacific, as well as Malaya, Singapore, Hong Kong, and Burma, to their earlier conquests. Then, in June 1942, a great sea and air battle took place at Midway Island. In the Battle of Midway, the Americans

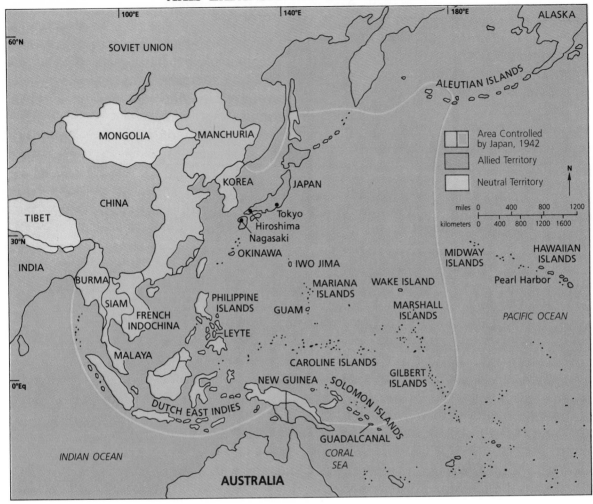

destroyed four Japanese aircraft carriers and hundreds of Japanese planes. From then on, the tide of battle in the Pacific turned toward the Allies. Over the next three years, they hopped from island to island, pushing their way toward Japan.

President Harry S Truman did not want to invade Japan. He knew it would cost the lives of hundreds of thousands of American soldiers. So, on August 6, 1945, the Americans dropped an **atomic bomb**, or a bomb that gets its power from the release of nuclear energy, on the city of Hiroshima. It was the first atomic bomb used in war. It destroyed most of the city and killed or wounded more than 160,000 people. However, the Japanese refused to surrender. So, the Americans dropped a second atomic bomb on the city of Nagasaki. This time, the Japanese agreed to surrender. World War II was over. At least 17 million soldiers and 18 million civilians had lost their lives.

1. Why was the Battle of Midway important?
2. Why did the Americans drop atomic bombs on the Japanese cities of Hiroshima and Nagasaki?

THE AFTERMATH OF WAR　　After the war ended, Allied armies in Europe found German **concentration camps**, or camps for political enemies. There, the Nazis had carried out a program of **genocide**, or the murder of a people, against the Jews of Europe. At the start of World War II, special German forces shot hundreds of thousands of Jews in Poland and the Soviet Union. But Hitler felt that Jews were not being killed fast enough. So, he ordered six concentration camps equipped with poison gas chambers and cremation ovens. The Nazis rounded up the remaining Jews from all over Europe and shipped them in sealed cattle cars to the death camps. By the end of World War II, the Nazis had killed more than 6 million Jews. About 1.5 million of them were children under the age of six.

Jewish Prisoner

Jews were not the only ones who had died at the hands of the Nazis. Many other prisoners of war had died from starvation and overwork. The Nazis had used prisoners to do work in factories. These people had been treated like slaves, especially if they were Poles or Russians, whom the Germans looked down on. More than 3 million Soviet prisoners alone had died.

The Japanese, too, had killed men, women, and children in the countries they conquered. These included any leaders who did not cooperate. And many Allied prisoners of war had died because of the poor treatment they received from the Japanese army.

The Allied governments felt that the cruel acts of the Nazis and the Japanese could not be excused as normal events of war. So, the Allied governments tried many former German and Japanese leaders for war crimes. Of the 22 top Nazi leaders who were tried, 11 were sentenced to death. Of the 25 top Japanese leaders who were tried, 7 were sentenced to death.

1. What did the Nazis do to the Jews of Europe?
2. How did the Germans treat prisoners of war?
3. What did the Allied governments do to many top Nazi and Japanese leaders?

RESULTS OF WORLD WAR II

World War II had many results. One was that the countries of Western Europe lost a good deal of power. For one thing, they lost most of their colonies. Before 1939, these countries had had huge empires in Asia, Africa, and Latin America. But by 1950, many of the colonies had set up their own governments. By 1980, almost 70 former colonies had become independent nations.

Also, Western Europe lost its leadership in the world economy. To rebuild the wartorn area, the United States started a huge loan program. It was called the Marshall Plan after George Marshall, the Secretary of State of the United States. Under the Marshall Plan, people were given food, factories were rebuilt, and roads were repaired or replaced. Soon, the economies of western Europe began to recover.

Douglas MacArthur

There was rebuilding to do in Japan, too. After the war, the United States occupied Japan to supervise its rebuilding. An American general named Douglas MacArthur was put in charge. Many changes took place under MacArthur. The military lost its power in the government, and Japan became a democracy. Laws were passed giving women the right to vote and allowing trade unions. Loans were made to help rebuild the economy. Before long, Japan became a world leader in trade.

Another result of World War II was the United Nations (UN). Even before the fighting ended, the Allied Powers had agreed to set up an organization like the League of Nations. In 1945, the United Nations was approved by 51 countries.

The most important task of the United Nations is to prevent war. And in some places, it has helped to keep small wars from turning into large ones. But the United Nations has disappointed many people. Most of the new countries that have joined are very small, and many of them are not democratic. So, it is possible for 97 countries with only 15 percent of the world's people to outvote the others. Because of this, many of the decisions of the United Nations have been against democracy and the West. Nevertheless, the United Nations lends money to poor countries and provides them with doctors and medical care. It helps countries to give and receive educational information that will better the lives of the people.

One of the most important results of World War II is that two countries became world leaders. They were the United States and the Soviet Union. The United States was the world's

GENERAL ASSEMBLY
All members of the United Nations send delegates to the General Assembly. The General Assembly debates world issues and assists the Security Council in keeping world peace. It also directs the work of other parts of the United Nations.
What is the most important task of the United Nations?

leading industrial power. Its factories and farms produced more than those of any other country. The Americans led the world in trade. The Soviet Union was the largest country on earth, and it had many natural resources. It also had a large population, which meant there were more people to work in the factories and on the farms.

After World War II, the Soviet Union became leader of the countries in Eastern Europe. During the war, Soviet troops had driven the Germans out of the area. Then, the Soviet Union set up Communist governments there. These governments promised to back the Soviet Union.

The United States became the leader of the western nations after World War II. Americans and Western Europeans were against communism. They wanted to maintain governments elected by the people.

1. What were some effects of World War II on Western Europe?
2. What changes were made in Japan under General Douglas MacArthur?
3. Why did the Allies decide to set up the United Nations?
4. What did the United States and the Soviet Union gain from World War II?

SCIENCE AND TECHNOLOGY

Neil Armstrong

The atomic bomb was only one of discoveries in science and technology that took place in the West during the 1900's. The bomb itself was based in part on the ideas of a German Jewish scientist named Albert Einstein. Einstein developed several theories that changed the way scientists look at time, space, and energy. After the war, nuclear energy was used in medicine, agriculture, the production of electrical power, and space travel. In August 1969, Neil Armstrong of the United States became the first person to walk on the moon.

There were also discoveries in transportation and communication during the 1900's. The Wright brothers made the first airplane flight in 1903. By 1930, commercial flights were common. By the 1970's, jet planes were flying at more than 600 miles, or 960 kilometers, an hour. Although automobiles and telephones had been invented before 1900, they came into general use in the 1920's and 1930's. Communication was aided by the invention of radio, television, and satellites that send signals around the world in a few seconds.

Another major discovery was the computer. The computer works out mathematical problems very quickly. Computers can figure payrolls, operate machines, translate languages, prepare bills, and control space shots. Computers save large amounts of time. On the other hand, they have replaced workers who have not been able to find different jobs.

1. How have scientists used nuclear energy?
2. What changes in transportation took place during the 1900's? What changes in communication took place?
3. What are some things computers do?

CHAPTER 38 REVIEW

SUMMARY

1. By the end of the 1800's, two alliances of countries had developed in Europe.

2. In 1914, a war started between Serbia and Austria-Hungary that became World War I.

3. World War I was different from earlier wars because of its size, new weapons, and the large number of civilians killed.

4. The United States entered World War I in 1917 and helped Great Britain, France, and their allies defeat Germany and its allies in 1918.

5. The Treaty of Versailles divided German lands among the Allied Powers and blamed World War I on Germany.

6. The depression of 1929 led many people to question their form of government.

7. In 1922, Benito Mussolini became dictator of Italy, and in 1933, Adolf Hitler became dictator of Germany.

8. After the German invasion of Poland in 1939, France and Great Britain declared war on Germany, and World War II began in Europe.

9. The United States entered World War II in 1941 after Japan attacked the American naval base at Pearl Harbor.

10. World War II ended in 1945, soon after the United States dropped the first atomic bombs on the Japanese cities of Hiroshima and Nagasaki.

11. During World War II, Nazi Germany carried out a program of genocide against the Jews of Europe.

12. After World War II, the United States helped rebuild Western Europe and Japan, the United Nations was set up, and the United States and the Soviet Union became the most powerful countries in the world.

13. Many discoveries were made in science and technology during the 1900's, including space travel, radio, television, and the computer.

BUILDING VOCABULARY

1. *Identify the following:*

Sarajevo	Franklin D. Roosevelt	Allied Powers	Hiroshima
Woodrow Wilson	Benito Mussolini	Axis Powers	Nagasaki
Fourteen Points	Fascists	Pearl Harbor	Marshall Plan
Treaty of Versailles	Adolf Hitler	Stalingrad	Douglas MacArthur
League of Nations	Nazis	Midway	United Nations
Great Depression			Albert Einstein

2. *Define the following:*

mobilize	armaments	dictatorship	blitzkrieg
civilians	mandate	chancellor	atomic bomb
trench warfare	depression	swastika	concentration camps
armistice	social security laws	aggression	genocide

REVIEWING THE FACTS

1. Why did the United States not become a part of the alliance system at the beginning of the 1900's?
2. What turned the tide during World War I toward Great Britain, France, and their allies?
3. Why did the Treaty of Versailles fail to follow most of Wilson's Fourteen Points?
4. What was the point of Wilson's peace plan that was kept?
5. What groups within Germany did Adolf Hitler attack?
6. What led to the defeat of Germany in World War II?
7. What led to the defeat of Japan?
8. What happened to colonies in Asia, Africa, and Latin America as a result of World War II?
9. How did the Marshall Plan help Western Europeans?
10. How has life changed in the 1900's?

DISCUSSING IMPORTANT IDEAS

1. What do you think might have happened if the United States had not entered World War I?
2. What could have been done to stop Adolf Hitler from threatening world peace?
3. What do you think might have happened if the Japanese had not attacked the American naval base at Pearl Harbor? Give reasons for your answer.
4. Do you think the Marshall Plan was a good idea? Explain.

USING MAPS

Study the map on page 616, and answer the following questions:

1. What were two countries that France controlled after World War I?
2. What is the distance from Paris to Brest-Litovsk?
3. What part of Ireland became British after World War I?
4. What country controlled Palestine after World War I?

Study the map on page 622, and answer the following questions:

1. Which western countries were neutral during World War II?
2. About how far is the city of London from the city of Berlin?
3. What city is located about 53° north latitude and 12° east longitude?
4. Was the Soviet Union Allied, Axis, or neutral?

Study the map on page 624, and answer the following questions:

1. How far is Pearl Harbor from Tokyo?
2. What island is located about 26° north latitude and 128° east longitude?
3. Was Burma Allied, Axis, or neutral?
4. What island near the Coral Sea was both Axis and Allied?

CHAPTER 39

THE RISE OF COMMUNISM

Since the early 1900's, communism has greatly influenced the world. Today, there are over 15 countries with Communist governments. The largest are the Soviet Union and China. In both countries, Communist governments were established by revolution and maintained by strong leaders. As the Soviet Union and China grew more powerful, relations with the West became strained.

COMMUNISM IN RUSSIA

Communism came into power first in Russia. The spark was World War I. But the underlying causes had been developing for several hundred years.

RUSSIA UNDER THE TSARS   The 25 years following the death of Ivan the Terrible was called the "Time of the Troubles." This was because there was so much confusion in the country. The confusion ended in 1613 when a popular assembly gave the crown to seventeen-year-old Michael Romanov. The Romanov Dynasty ruled Russia until 1917.

The first great Romanov ruler was Michael's grandson, Peter the Great. He came to the throne in 1682. Determined to make his country strong and modern, Peter disguised himself as a tourist and visited the capitals of various European countries. There, he learned all he could of western ways.

When Peter returned home, he began reforming his country. He trained a powerful army. He also built a navy, which Russia had never had. He started factories, built canals, and encouraged mining. He ordered a new capital, St. Petersburg, built on the Baltic Sea. Since St. Petersburg was an ice-free port, Russia could trade with western Europe by water, even in winter. Peter revised the alphabet and set up schools for the upper class. He even changed people's appearances. He ordered men to shave their beards and to wear European-style short jackets instead of long coats.

Catherine the Great

The next great Romanov ruler was Catherine the Great. She came to the throne in 1762. At first, Catherine wanted to improve the condition of the peasants. She even thought about abolishing serfdom. Then, peasants in a newly conquered area in southern Russia rebelled. Soon after, the French Revolution broke out. The two events frightened Catherine. She gave up her ideas of reform. Instead, she made serfs of more than 1 million peasants who had formerly been free.

Although Catherine did not help the peasants, she made Russia much larger. In a number of wars, the country's borders were pushed east, west, and south, almost to their present limits.

1. What did Peter the Great do to help make his country strong and modern?
2. Why did Catherine the Great give up her ideas of reform?

THE ROAD TO REVOLUTION   Throughout the 1800's, there was a great deal of discontent in Russia. About 30 million serfs, half of whom were owned by the tsar, supported about 500,000 nobles and clergy. The tsar controlled what industry there was. Workers' hours were long, and their pay was low. In

1825, a group of army officers, inspired by the ideas of the French Revolution, rebelled against the tsar. But the revolt was put down.

This revolt made the next tsar want to stamp out all opposition. His chief target was writers, who made fun of government officials or wrote about the hard life of the serfs. Some writers were exiled for their work. Government censors refused to allow most critical writings to be published. Nevertheless, ideas about freedom and reform spread.

In 1861, Tsar Alexander II freed the serfs. But he refused to give them land of their own. Because of this, most became tenant farmers. He also refused to give the nobles a constitution.

In 1905, another uprising took place. It began when thousands of workers appeared in the square before the tsar's palace. They carried petitions asking for a national assembly, freedom of speech and religion, and better conditions for workers and peasants. Government soldiers fired on the crowd, killing hundreds of unarmed people. A general strike then broke out. Finally, Tsar Nicholas II agreed to their demands. However, he ignored the legislature and its ideas for reform.

Nicholas II

World War I only made matters worse. Russia suffered higher casualties than any other country. Some 9 million soldiers were killed or wounded in battle. There was not enough food or fuel for the army or civilians.

As World War I dragged on, the Russian people could stand no more. In March 1917, they revolted. Striking workers demanding bread and peace jammed the streets of St. Petersburg, which had been renamed Petrograd. Then, the city's **garrison,** or military group, joined the people. Within a few days, the revolt spread throughout the country. Peasants took over the estates of the nobles. Soldiers left the front and began walking home. The tsar was forced to abdicate, and a provisional government was set up.

1. Who was the tsar's chief target after the revolt of 1825?
2. How did Nicholas II react to the Revolution of 1905?
3. What problems did World War I cause in Russia?
4. What was the result of the March Revolution?

LENIN   There was much confusion in the months following the overthrow of Nicholas II. A Communist group called the Bolsheviks took advantage of this. Led by Vladimir Ilyich

Ulyanov, who came to be known as Lenin, they won over the **soviets,** or committees that represent workers and soldiers. The Bolsheviks promised land to the peasants and bread to the workers. They also promised to get Russia out of the war.

In November 1917, the Bolsheviks seized power from the provisional government. Lenin was chosen to lead the new government. Soon after, Lenin signed a peace treaty with Germany that ended Russia's part in World War I. But the treaty did not end the problems at home. From 1918 to 1920, Russia was divided by a civil war between the Bolsheviks—now known as Communists—and the non-Communists. The Communists were called Reds, and the non-Communists were called Whites.

The Whites received soldiers and supplies from other countries, including the United States. These countries were

LENIN

In 1917, Lenin set up a Communist-party dictatorship in Russia. He ruled the country, now known as the Union of Soviet Socialist Republics, until his death in 1924. Lenin gave powerful speeches, such as the one shown in this painting, to rally support for the Communist government's policies.

Who took over control of the government after Lenin died?

afraid that communism would spread throughout Europe. Nevertheless, by late 1920, the Reds had defeated the Whites.

During the civil war, Lenin had used force to keep his power over the people. Workers had to work where and when the government ordered. Peasants had to give up grain to feed people in the cities. When the Reds won, Lenin changed his policy. The main task was to rebuild the Russian economy. So, in 1921, Lenin introduced the New Economic Policy. It allowed some private industry, trade, and farming. The Russian economy soon began to recover.

In 1922, the Union of Soviet Socialist Republics, or the Soviet Union, was formed. It was made up of four republics, one of which was Russia. By 1924, the Soviet Union was completely under the control of the Communist party.

Lenin died that same year. His body was embalmed and placed in a glass coffin inside a red marble tomb near the wall of Moscow's Kremlin. There, it could be viewed by the Russian people. In his honor, the name of Petrograd was changed to Leningrad.

1. How did the Bolsheviks gain power?
2. How did Lenin keep his power over the people during the civil war?

Model of the Kremlin

STALIN   After Lenin died, there was a struggle for power. By 1928, the struggle was over, and Joseph Stalin had taken control of the government. He also controlled the Communist party, which was the only political party allowed in the country.

Stalin wanted the Soviet Union to catch up with the West in industrial and military power. So, he set up the First Five-Year Plan. Its major goal was to build up **heavy industry,** or machines that make machines. Factories stopped making clothing and household goods. Instead, steel mills, power plants, oil refineries, and chemical plants were built. Workers who were absent from their jobs were punished. Factory managers were punished if anything went wrong in their factories. By the middle of the 1930's, there were factories in all parts of the country. And the Soviet Union was a major industrial power.

Another goal of the First Five-Year Plan was **collectivization,** or uniting small farms into large ones controlled by the government. On a collective, farmers are paid according to the number of days they work. Collectivization allowed farmers to share the few tractors and other farm machinery they had. The government would buy the crops at fixed prices and sell them abroad to buy machines for the factories.

Many peasants wanted to keep working on their own farms. They resisted collectivization by killing their horses, cows, and pigs. Those who refused to move, however, were either shot or sent to labor camps in Siberia. By 1936, most of the farms in the Soviet Union were collectivized.

Stalin kept his power through censorship and terror. He controlled everything that was publicly written, said, or heard in the Soviet Union. In 1934, he carried out a **purge,** or a cleaning out, of the Communist party and the Red Army. The secret police arrested millions of people. Many of the victims were given "show trials" in which they publicly confessed their errors before being sentenced to death.

1. What was the goal of Stalin's First Five-Year Plan? Did it succeed?
2. How did Russian peasants show their opposition to the policy of collectivization?
3. How did Stalin keep his power?

PROGRESS   Stalin died in 1953, and under his successors, the Soviet Union made progress in certain areas. Nikita S. Khrushchev followed Stalin as leader of the party and country. In 1953, Khruschev was named **premier,** or prime minister of the Soviet Union. He at once began a program of **de-Stalinization,** or an attack on the policies set down by Stalin. Many labor camps were shut down, and the secret police became less violent. For the first time, Soviet writers and artists were allowed some freedom. Efforts were also made to raise the standard of living. More apartment houses were built. Clothing, television sets, and even automobiles became more available.

Khrushchev was followed by other leaders, including Leonid Brezhnev and Konstantin Chernenko. Under these leaders, life once again became less free for the people.

However, in other ways, life improved. The Soviet government provides free medical service for all citizens. It has taught almost everyone how to read and write. And it has built museums and theaters all over the country.

The Soviets have also made many scientific advances. In 1957, they launched *Sputnik I.* This was the first spacecraft to

Nikita Khrushchev

circle the earth. Four years later, a Soviet air force officer named Yuri Gagarin became the first person to circle the earth.

1. What was one of the first things Nikita Khrushchev did after he became premier of the Soviet Union?
2. How has life improved for the people under communism?
3. What scientific advances have the Soviets made?

PROBLEMS Despite the progress made in the Soviet Union, the country faces several problems.

One is the economy. Industry has not grown as rapidly as the government wants. There are not enough qualified workers, and many Soviet products are poorly made. Also, in some years, not enough food is produced to feed the people. This means the Soviet Union must buy food from other countries.

ECONOMIC PROGRESS IN THE SOVIET UNION

Industry in the Soviet Union produces more heavy industrial goods than goods for consumers, such as appliances and clothing. Department stores in Moscow, such as the one pictured below, are among the few places that high quality goods can be purchased.

The Soviet standard of living improved after the death of which Soviet leader?

Another problem is religion. When the Communists came to power, they took over church property. They tried to teach the people to depend on the Communist party instead of God. Many Soviet citizens, however, are still interested in religion. This is especially true of the Muslims who live in the south-central part of the country.

Still another problem is nationalism. Russians make up only about one half of the Soviet people. There are many other national groups, such as the Ukrainians, Uzbeks, Byelorussians, and Tatars. These groups have been kept out of leadership positions, most of which are filled by Russians.

Jews in the Soviet Union face special difficulties. They are not allowed to study Jewish history or language. Jews do not receive important jobs, and only a few are admitted to universities. At the same time, Jews who want to leave the Soviet Union are seldom allowed to do so.

Also, there are some Soviet citizens who are not pleased with Soviet politics. These people are called **dissidents.** Many of them are writers and scientists. They object to the limits the government puts on personal freedom. Many dissidents have been put in prison or sent out of the country for speaking out and expressing their views.

Soviet Dissident Andrei Sakharov

Finally, there have been several uprisings against Soviet control in the satellite countries. In 1956, the Hungarians tried to drive the Soviets out without success. In 1968, Soviet tanks rolled into Czechoslovakia, overthrew a reform government, and put their own government in power. There were several rebellions by workers in Poland, the most recent being in 1981. Although Soviet troops did not invade the country, the Soviet government pressured the Polish Communist government to put down the striking workers.

1. What economic problems does the Soviet Union face?
2. What national group fills most of the leadership positions in the Soviet Union?
3. What special difficulties do Jews face in the Soviet Union?

COMMUNISM IN CHINA

Communism came to power next in China. The spark was World War II. But as in Russia, the underlying causes had been developing for a long time.

REVOLUTION IN CHINA   Even before the Boxer Rebellion, there were several revolts in China. But these revolts failed. In 1911, however, the government was overthrown and a republic was set up. The president of the new republic was Sun Yat-sen. His program was called the Three Principles of the People. These principles were nationalism, democracy, and livelihood.

Sun only held office a short time. He could not gather enough support, and the army took over the government. But the army also had trouble ruling the country. Military leaders called **warlords** set themselves up as rulers in different parts of China. Often, they fought one another.

In the meantime, Sun went on working to unite the Chinese people. He formed the Nationalist party. But the party was accepted only in southern China. Then, he asked the West for money, arms, and advisors. When western countries refused to help him, Sun turned to the Soviet Union. The Soviets agreed to help him. In return, Sun had to bring the Chinese Communist party into the Nationalist party.

After Sun died in 1925, Chiang Kai-shek became the new leader of the Nationalist party. At the head of an army, Chiang set out to unify China. In three years, he had either conquered the warlords or convinced them to join his government.

Sun Yat-sen

Meanwhile, Chiang drove the Communists out of the Nationalist party. The Communists fled to southeastern China. There, they formed an army and began to win territory. However, the Nationalists kept up their attacks. So, in 1934, an army of more than 100,000 Communists fled to northwestern China. Their journey was called the Long March. It lasted over a year and covered more than 6,000 miles, or 9,600 kilometers. Only 20,000 Communists survived the march. But by its end, a major leader, Mao Tse-tung, had emerged.

When the Japanese attacked China in 1937, the Nationalists and Communists joined together to fight them. However, this alliance did not last. After the Japanese were defeated in 1945, the Nationalists and the Communists started fighting each other again. By this time, the Chinese Communists had gained a great deal of support, especially from the peasants. This was because the Communists took land away from rich landlords and gave it to the peasants. Also, many Nationalist officials and army officers were corrupt.

By 1949, the Communists had forced the Nationalists to retreat to the island of Taiwan. There, Chiang set up a Nationalist government. He claimed it ruled the Republic of China. The Communists on the mainland set up their own government headed by Mao Tse-tung. They called it the People's Republic of China.

1. What was Sun Yat-sen's program?
2. Why did Sun turn to the Soviet Union for help?
3. How was the People's Republic of China formed?

CHINA UNDER MAO   Mao's main goal was to rebuild China and make it a strong, modern country. To do this, it was necessary to increase production in agriculture and industry. So, in 1953, the Chinese began a five-year plan. They set up farm collectives and government-owned factories.

Both farm and factory managers put up posters urging people to work harder. Each month, managers would award medals and bonuses to the best workers. But the Chinese government also used force to carry out its programs. Anyone who opposed the government was punished or executed.

Chinese Artist

At the end of five years, many gains had been made. Mao, however, felt that China had to grow still faster. So, in 1958, the Chinese began a second five-year plan known as the Great Leap Forward. It called for China to produce twice as much as it had before. Peasants were grouped into **communes,** or huge farming communities run by the government. Communes were even larger than collectives. Everyone in a commune received the same food, clothing, medical care, and money. The families in a commune worked together in the fields. Families also ate in a central dining hall instead of at home. And everyone was urged to join in industrial production. Workers built thousands of small backyard furnaces to produce iron.

The Second Five-Year Plan did not work. Production did not increase. And the peasants in the communes were so unhappy that the government went back to the system of collectives. The government also allowed the peasants to have small private plots that their children could inherit.

After Mao relaxed his economic policies, conditions in China improved. By the middle of the 1960's, there was enough food for everyone. Some Chinese—especially in the cities—

CHINESE LEADERS

From 1928 to 1949, General Chiang Kai-shek (left) was a powerful leader in China. In 1949, the Communists led by Mao Tse-tung (right) overthrew Chiang's government. Mao proclaimed the People's Republic of China on the Chinese mainland, while Chiang set up the Nationalist government on the island of Taiwan. Why did most Chinese peasants support Mao rather than Chiang?

could afford radios, sewing machines, and bicycles. Health care had greatly improved. And most Chinese knew how to read and write.

Mao, however, began to worry that the Chinese people were losing their revolutionary spirit. So, in 1966, he carried out a purge of the Communist party. He also purged the country's **intellectuals,** or thinkers. Schools and universities were closed. Hundreds of thousands of teenagers were organized into groups called the Red Guards. The Red Guards attacked teachers and

RED GUARDS

In the mid-1960's, the Red Guards marched across China to make sure that Mao's teachings were obeyed. Here, Red Guards parade through Peking, China's capital. What group of people made up the Red Guards?

others who were accused of not supporting communism strongly enough.

The purge was called the Cultural Revolution. It soon got out of control. There were battles between Red Guards and peasants. Even soldiers of the Red Army refused to obey orders. After a year, the Red Guards were broken up, and schools were reopened. But it took the country a long time to recover.

1. What was Mao's main goal?
2. Why did Mao start the Cultural Revolution?

CHINA AFTER MAO   Mao died in 1976 and, like Lenin and Stalin, was embalmed. Clothed in a grey tunic and partly covered by a Chinese flag, Mao's body lies in a glass coffin in a large hall in the Chinese capital of Beijing, formerly Peking. Millions of Chinese go there to view his body.

Mao's death was followed by a time of confusion. Different groups struggled to gain control of the government. In 1980, Zhao Ziyang became premier, and in 1981, Hu Yaobang became chairman of the Communist party.

Under Zhao and Hu, China has followed a new economic policy. It centers around the "four modernizations" of agriculture, industry, defense, and science and technology. China hopes to quadruple its production in these four areas by the year 2000. To do so, it is changing many of Mao's methods. It is investing more money in agriculture and less in heavy industry. Communes no longer have to turn over all their profits to the government. This leaves them free to invest the rest any way they wish. Many factory managers are now allowed to decide for themselves what to produce and what price to charge. Workers are no longer guaranteed jobs but have to compete for them. And there are now some 3 million privately owned businesses in China.

Under Zhao and Hu, China's relations with the West have improved. In 1979, the United States recognized the government of the People's Republic of China. Visits have been exchanged, and many western tourists have traveled to China. China's relations with the Soviet Union, on the other hand, are somewhat strained. This is partly because of fights along the border

COMMUNISM TODAY

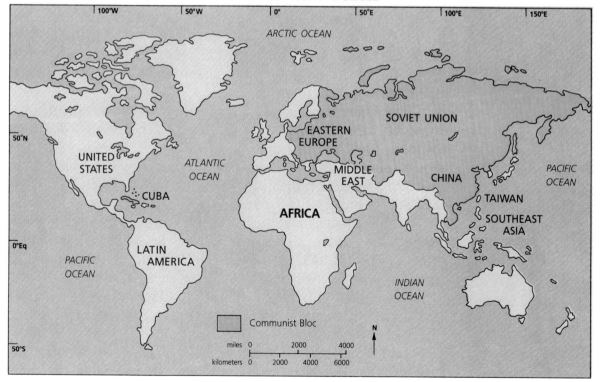

between the two countries. And it is partly because the Soviet Union thinks that China is becoming too friendly with the West.

1. What happened to the Chinese Communist government after the death of Mao Tse-tung?
2. How has China changed its economic policies?

RELATIONS WITH THE WEST

In the years after World War II, Communist relations with the West were dominated by a **cold war,** or a state of hostility without fighting. The two countries most involved were the United States and the Soviet Union. Tension between the two grew with crises over Berlin, Korea, and Vietnam. An ongoing arms race added to the tension and made the possibility of a third world war very real. New weapons made it possible to destroy entire countries, and perhaps the world itself. So, at times there has been a move toward **détente,** or a relaxing of tension.

Soviet Soldier

BERLIN   At the end of World War II, Germany was divided into zones. Each was occupied by one of the major Allied powers. The German capital of Berlin was also divided into zones. The British, the French, and the Americans wanted to unite Germany. But the Soviets were against this. In June 1948, they **blockaded,** or closed off, all land and water traffic into Berlin. They hoped this would make the western nations leave the city.

The United States and Great Britain began an **airlift,** or a system of carrying supplies by airplane. Each day, they flew tons of food, fuel, and raw materials into Berlin. In May 1949, the Soviets finally lifted their blockade of the city. That same year, two separate governments were set up, one in West Germany and another in East Germany.

After the blockade, the western powers came to believe that the Soviets wanted to conquer Europe. So, in 1949, the United States, Great Britain, and France joined with nine other countries to form the North Atlantic Treaty Organization (NATO). They all agreed to help one another if attacked. Six years later, the Soviet Union and its satellites formed a similar organization, the Warsaw Pact.

Later, the focus was again on Berlin. Many people who lived in East Germany were not happy under Communist rule.

BERLIN WALL

Between 1953 and 1961, 3 million refugees flocked to West Berlin from East Germany. To block the flow of people, the East German government built a 26-mile (46-kilometer) wall through Berlin in 1961. The wall has become a symbol of the division of Europe between Communist and western nations.

How did the Soviet Union try to force the western powers from Berlin in 1948?

So, they escaped into West Berlin. The East German government wanted to stop the escapes. In 1961, it built a wall between East and West Berlin.

1. Why were two separate governments set up in Germany?
2. Why did East Germany build the Berlin Wall?

KOREA After World War II, Korea, like Germany, was divided. A Communist government was set up in North Korea and a non-Communist government, in South Korea. In 1950, North Korean troops invaded South Korea. The Soviet Union sent North Korea military aid, while the United Nations sent soldiers—mostly Americans—to help South Korea.

At first, North Korean forces drove far into South Korea. Then, the tide turned, and United Nations forces pushed the

North Koreans back across the border. But instead of stopping there, the United Nations troops drove up to the border of China. China then entered the war on the side of North Korea. General Douglas MacArthur, the United Nations commander, wanted to bomb bases and supply lines in China. But President Harry S Truman refused. He wanted to keep the Korean War a **limited war.** This means that each side limits its weapons and the territory in which it fights.

In 1953, North Korea and South Korea signed a truce. The border between North Korea and South Korea stayed the same. And the governments of the two countries also stayed the same. But communism had been kept from expanding.

1. Why did the United States enter the Korean War? Why did China enter the Korean War?
2. What were the results of the Korean War?

VIETNAM When World War II broke out, Vietnam was a French colony. The Japanese took over in 1941 and pulled out in 1945. Most of the Vietnamese hoped that meant they would be free. But the French returned. So, Communists and non-Communist nationalists joined together in a guerrilla war against the French. The guerrillas were led by a Communist named Ho Chi Minh. In 1954, the French were defeated, and the country was temporarily divided in two. North Vietnam became a Communist country headed by Ho. South Vietnam became a non-Communist country. The peace agreement called for an election in 1956 to choose a government for a united Vietnam. But the South Vietnamese government refused to take part.

Fighting then started again in South Vietnam. Local guerrillas, aided by North Vietnam, gained control of more and more land. The United States, which had been sending military supplies and advisors to South Vietnam since 1954, began sending in combat troops in 1965. Altogether, more than 500,000 Americans fought in Vietnam.

The Vietnam War split the American people. Many believed the United States had to fight to prevent the spread of communism. Many others believed the fight was a civil war that the Vietnamese should settle themselves.

In 1968, the two sides began holding peace talks in Paris. Finally, in 1973, an agreement was reached and the remaining

South Vietnamese President Diem

COMMUNIST LEADERS

Ché Guevara
1928–67
Latin American guerilla leader;
most powerful member of
government under Fidel Castro;
Cuban minister of industry,
1961-65

Alexander Dubcek
1921–
first secretary of
Communist Party of
Czechoslovakia in 1968
and 1969; introduced
liberal reforms that
threatened Soviet interests

Salvador Allende
1908–73
president of Chile from
1970 to 1973; first
Marxist freely elected in
Western Hemisphere

Ho Chi Minh   *1890–1969*

revolutionary leader who overthrew French
in Vietnam in 1954; president of North
Vietnam from 1954 to 1969

Kim Il Sung   *1912–*

president of North Korea since 1948; head
of North Korean Communist Party; leader in
efforts toward peaceful reunification of Korea

Leon Trotsky   *1879–1940*

leader of 1917 Bolshevik Revolution; second
most powerful figure in Russia under Lenin

**Joseph Broz
Tito**   *1892–1980*

founder and ruler of Communist government
in Yugoslavia from 1945 to 1980; first Communist leader to declare independence from
Russia and permit economic and social freedom

Americans left Vietnam. Then, in 1975, Communist troops from North Vietnam moved into South Vietnam. In less than four months, the whole country was under Communist control.

1. What groups opposed the French in Vietnam?
2. What were the results of the Vietnam War?

CHAPTER 39 REVIEW

SUMMARY

1. Peter the Great tried to make Russia a strong, modern country by bringing in western ways.

2. Catherine the Great expanded Russia's borders to the east, west, and south.

3. After unsuccessful revolts in 1825 and 1905, the Russian people revolted again in 1917 and overthrew the tsar.

4. After much confusion, a revolutionary group led by Lenin set up a Communist government, which officially formed the Soviet Union in 1922.

5. After Lenin died, Joseph Stalin took control of the government and the Communist party and tried to modernize and industrialize the Soviet Union.

6. After Stalin's death, Nikita S. Khrushchev took control and removed many government restrictions.

7. Even though Khrushchev's successors again tightened controls over the people, the standard of living improved.

8. The Soviet Union faces many problems, including the economy, religion, nationalism, dissidents, and uprisings in satellite countries.

9. Early rebellions in China were not successful, but in 1911 Sun Yat-sen led a revolt that overthrew the government and set up a republic.

10. In 1925, Chiang Kai-shek became the leader of the Nationalist party and set out to unify China.

11. The Communists defeated the Nationalists in 1949 and formed the People's Republic of China under Mao Tse-tung, who tried to develop agriculture and industry.

12. Since Mao's death, the Chinese Communist government has relaxed some of its policies.

13. China and the Soviet Union did not get along well, so China tried to improve its relations with the West.

14. After World War II, the United States and the Soviet Union became involved in a cold war that began an arms race.

15. In 1948, the Soviet Union tried without success to make the western nations leave Berlin.

16. In 1961, the Berlin Wall was built to prevent people from escaping from East Germany into West Germany.

17. North Korea, aided by the Soviet Union, and South Korea, aided by the United Nations, fought a war in 1950.

18. North Vietnam, aided by the Soviet Union, and South Vietnam, aided by the United States, fought a war from 1956 to 1975.

BUILDING VOCABULARY

1. *Identify the following:*

   Peter the Great   Lenin   Nikita S. Khrushchev   Mao Tse-tung
   St. Petersburg   Bolsheviks   Sun Yat-sen   Zhao Zinyang
   Catherine the Great   Joseph Stalin   Chiang Kai-shek   Hu Yaobang
   Alexander II   Ho Chi Minh

2. *Define the following:*

   garrison   purge   warlords   détente
   soviets   premier   communes   blockaded
   heavy industry   de-Stalinization   intellectuals   airlift
   collectivization dissidents   cold war   limited war

REVIEWING THE FACTS

1. What are the two largest Communist nations in the world?

2. Why did the Russian Revolution break out in 1917?

3. What do dissidents object to in the Soviet Union?

4. How do many Soviet satellites feel about Soviet control?

5. How did the Chinese Communists gain support from the people?

6. Why was China's Second Five-Year Plan a failure?

7. How did the arms race get started?

8. Why did the United States and Great Britain organize the Berlin airlift?

9. Why did President Harry S Truman refuse to bomb bases and supply lines in China during the Korean War?

10. Why did the Vietnam War split the American people?

DISCUSSING IMPORTANT IDEAS

1. Do you think the Berlin Wall shows Communist strength or weakness? Explain your answer.

2. How do you think the Cold War has affected the daily life of Americans?

3. Do you think communism has been a success in the Soviet Union? Explain your answer.

4. Do you think communism has been a success in China? Why or why not?

USING MAPS

Study the map on page 643, and answer the following questions:

1. What areas make up the Communist bloc?

2. What island in the Western Hemisphere is Communist?

3. What part of Europe is in the Communist bloc?

4. What is the latitude and longitude of Cuba?

CASTRO'S CUBA

On July 26, 1953, a young lawyer named Fidel Castro tried to start a revolution on the island of Cuba. He and many of his followers were captured and put in prison. After Castro got out of prison in 1955, he organized a revolutionary group called "The Twenty-sixth of July Movement." The group made surprise attacks against the government of Cuban dictator Fulgencio Batista.

By late 1958, Castro and his followers had the support of most Cubans. Many had lost confidence in Batista and thought Castro would solve the island's problems.

On January 1, 1959, Batista fled the country. The Castro forces took control of the government, and soon, Fidel Castro became premier of Cuba.

Castro promised the Cuban people free elections, democratic government, and social and economic reforms. At first, many nations, including the United States, supported Castro. But many of the promises he made were not kept. Cubans who opposed him were jailed or executed. Thousands of Cubans fled to the United States and Latin America. Most did not expect to be in their new homes long. They thought that Castro's rule would be a short one, and that they soon could return to Cuba.

Before long, Castro announced that his government was Communist. He developed close ties with the Soviet Union. The Soviets sent Cuba economic aid and

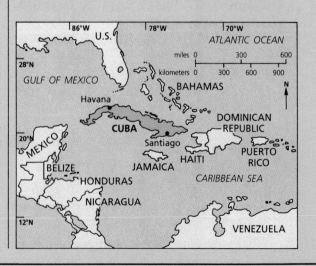

advisors. In 1962, they set up missile bases on the island. But pressure from the United States forced the Soviets to remove the missiles.

Many people consider Castro a modern caudillo. He made many changes on the island. Education is free, and almost everyone can now read and write. All medical care is free. Many large low-rent apartment buildings have been built. Large estates have been turned into farms run by the government for the benefit of the workers. Because of these changes, many Cubans support Castro even though he rules as a dictator.

Cuba still has serious economic problems. It depends mostly on the sale of sugar for its income. When the price of sugar is low, so is Cuba's income. Then, too, Castro made some costly mistakes.

He tried to industrialize Cuba early in 1960. But Cuba had few mineral resources, no money to buy machinery, and no market for its products. Later, he tried to set up a **moneyless economy,** which meant that workers would receive goods instead of wages. This, too, failed.

Under Castro, the poor have a right to a decent job, food, clothing, and cheap housing. But they do not have freedom of speech or of the press. They have to wait in long lines for everything, including food and clothing. The shops are half empty, and everything is in short supply. For these reasons, some Cubans have lost faith in Castro and in his government.

1. How did Fidel Castro come to power?
2. How has Castro's rule affected the Cuban people?

CHAPTER 40

EMERGING THIRD WORLD

In recent years, a Third World has emerged that is largely independent of western or Communist powers. The Third World includes countries in Asia, Africa, Latin America, and the Middle East. Most of these countries have gained independence since 1945. Most are considered developing nations. And they have common problems.

Most Third World countries generally do not have as much industry as western and Communist countries. Most of the people make their living from the land using older ways.

Many Third World countries depend on trading a single product, such as coffee, cocoa, or cotton, for more than one half of their **national income,** or the amount of money a country as a whole receives. If the crop is poor, there is less national income. Also, if the **market price,** or the price at which goods are sold, is low, there is less national income. Less income means less economic development.

Most developing countries also have rapidly growing populations. Because of this, they cannot grow enough food to feed their people. So, they must buy food elsewhere. This leaves them with little money for such things as housing, health care, and education. The standard of living is often poor. The main goal of most Third World countries is modernization.

INDIA

In India, feelings of nationalism began to grow toward the end of the 1800's. After years of protest against British rule, independence was won. Since then, the Indian government has worked to modernize the country and deal with the problem of overpopulation.

THE ROAD TO INDEPENDENCE   India was one of the first colonial countries in which feelings of nationalism began to grow. At first, many things seemed to stand in the way of nationalism. There were two major religions—Hinduism and Islam. There were more than 1,000 different languages and **dialects,** or regional forms of a language, spoken in the country. There were also many regional differences in food, dress, and way of life. But the problems and differences meant little because the hundreds of millions of Indians had one thing in common—opposition to British rule.

The British themselves helped nationalism develop in India. The railroad network the British built helped tie different parts of the country together. The British taught the Indians modern skills. Indian lawyers, teachers, clerks, accountants, and engineers were well educated. They also spoke English, so they could communicate with one another. Most important of all, the British example taught the Indians about the idea that people should govern themselves.

In 1885, a political party called the Indian National Congress was formed. It called for changes in the government. By 1919, more Indians were taking part in the government. But

Hindu Dress

Mohandas Gandhi

allowing a few Indians to have some say in India's affairs was not enough. Most nationalists wanted independence.

About that time, an Indian leader named Mohandas K. Gandhi began a protest movement against British rule. Gandhi was a lawyer and a member of the upper class. He identified himself, however, with the common people. He put aside western clothes and wore the draped white cotton clothing that ordinary farmers wore. He went from village to village, talking to the common people about self-government. The people called him "Mahatma," which means "Great Soul."

Gandhi did not believe in violence. He believed in a policy of **civil disobedience,** or resisting by refusing to perform civil duties. He convinced millions of Indians to show their resistance to British rule through peaceful means. They lay on railroad tracks to stop trains and on roads to stop trucks. They boycotted British goods. Some went on hunger strikes. Many refused to pay taxes. They even refused to support Great Britain during World War II.

In 1947, the British finally agreed to Indian independence. But instead of one country, two were created. The larger country, India, had a majority of Hindus. The smaller country, Pakistan, had a majority of Muslims. Pakistan was made up of two parts separated by India. In 1971, the eastern part became the independent country of Bangladesh.

1. What seemed to stand in the way of Indian nationalism at first?
2. How did the British help nationalism develop in India?
3. How did Mahatma Gandhi identify himself with the common people?
4. What policy did Mahatma Gandhi urge Indians to follow?
5. Into how many nations was India eventually divided?

Jawaharlal Nehru

THE NEW NATION   After independence, India's leaders worked to set up a stable government. In 1950, a constitution was adopted that made India, unlike many Third World countries, a democracy. Jawaharlal Nehru became India's first prime minister.

India's leaders also worked to raise the people's standard of living. To do this, they set up five-year plans to develop industry and improve agriculture. India's Five-Year Plans are different from those of the Soviets and the Chinese. In India, people do not have to accept government goals. Also, factories and other means of production are owned by individuals, not by the government.

In the past, the country's major industry was textiles. In the Five-Year Plans, the government tapped India's many natural resources, mostly iron ore, manganese, and bauxite. It also built dams to change the energy of its rivers into electricity. Today, India has such heavy industry as iron, steel, electrical, chemical, and cement manufacturing. There are small factories, too. India is also well known for goods that artisans make by hand in their homes.

Farm production has also grown over the years. Over 70 percent of the Indian people make their living by farming. This provides about one half of the country's national income. The government has worked to introduce new seeds, new breeds of livestock, and new ways of farming. Agricultural colleges have been opened.

Despite the improvements in industry and agriculture, there are still problems. One is the growing population. If population

---

INDUSTRIAL INDIA

Industry has grown rapidly in India since the nation became independent in 1947. These workers are employed at an automobile plant.

How has the Indian government promoted industrial development?

grows faster than industry and farm production, the way people live cannot improve. So, the government is also encouraging people to have smaller families.

1. How did India become a democracy?
2. How are India's Five-Year Plans different from those of the Soviet Union and China?
3. What has the government done to improve industry and agriculture?

AFRICA

Feelings of nationalism did not become strong in Africa until after World War II. African nationalism led to independence movements. In time, most of Africa broke free of colonial rule. In the years after independence, governments of the new African countries looked for ways to solve political and economic problems.

African Student

THE GROWTH OF NATIONALISM   Many Africans served in the armies of the colonial powers during World War II. They were sent to fight in many different places around the world. The soldiers learned new ideas and skills. When they returned home, they were not content with the conditions they found there. They felt that it would be better if they could rule themselves.

The way the European powers ruled their colonies also helped nationalism to grow. Each power ruled differently. The British allowed some measure of self-rule. They also gave the Africans in their colonies a general education. The French and the Portuguese did not allow the Africans in their colonies any self-rule. The French educated some Africans. The Portuguese provided almost no education.

Nationalism grew quickly among educated Africans. They worked for independence in many different ways. They formed political parties. They boycotted goods from the colonial powers. They bargained with government leaders. In some cases, violence broke out. Rebels in Africa fought the French from 1945 until 1962. A rebellion in Kenya lasted from 1953 until 1961.

In 1960, 17 African countries became independent. The year became known as "the year of Africa." Over time, other African colonies freed themselves from European rule. In 1980,

Zimbabwe, formerly called Rhodesia, became the 51st African country to gain independence.

The only remaining area that is not independent is Namibia, which is under the control of the Republic of South Africa. South Africa has a racial policy called **apartheid.** Under this policy, blacks and Asians are not allowed to vote. They cannot travel without a pass from the government, and they must live only in certain areas. Their education is limited, and they are not allowed to hold good jobs. South Africa does not want to give up its control over Namibia because it would become a black-ruled country. However, several black nationalist groups in Namibia have been fighting for independence.

1. What effect did World War II have on African nationalism?
2. What is the only remaining area in Africa that is not independent?

POLITICAL AND ECONOMIC DEVELOPMENT African countries have political problems. When they became independent, African countries set up democratic governments. However, many did not last. Today, fewer than one out of five African countries is democratic. Most have one-party governments or are ruled by a military leader or "strong man."

It has been difficult for certain African countries to govern themselves. One reason is that when Europeans set up colonies in Africa, they paid no attention to national groups. Sometimes, they put groups that had been fighting for hundreds of years within the same colony. Thus, several African countries have suffered from civil wars since they gained independence.

Hausa Nobleman

Probably the worst trouble took place in Nigeria between the Ibos and the Hausas. The Ibos are mostly Christian, well educated, and modern. The Hausas are mostly Muslim and less well educated and modern than the Ibos. Because of this, most of the good jobs in business and government were held by Ibos. In 1966, the Hausas killed thousands of Ibos in the northern part of Nigeria. The following year, the Ibos in the southeastern part of the country seceded and set up their own country, the Republic of Biafra. Civil war raged for three years. During this time, 1 million soldiers were killed, and more than 1 million civilians—mostly children—starved to death. The Ibos and Hausas are now united under one government. But there are still differences between them.

Africa also has economic problems. About 70 percent of all African workers make their living from farming. More than one half of the continent's national income comes from selling such products as peanuts, cocoa, cotton, and coffee. Still, Africa must buy a great deal of food from other countries. There are many insect pests in Africa. Parts of the continent suffer from drought. Others suffer from too much rain. And most farmland in Africa is used for **subsistence farming.** This means that farmers grow only enough food for their families.

Many African governments want more farmers to raise **cash crops,** or surplus crops that can be sold in the market. They also want them to raise a greater variety of crops and animals. If farmers could earn money for their crops and animals, they would then have money to spend for manufactured goods.

Africa has many energy resources. Coal, natural gas, oil, and hydroelectric power are plentiful. The continent also is very rich in minerals. There are deposits of copper, tin, iron, manga-

---

FOOD PRODUCTION
During the 1960's, a world-wide effort was started to increase food production in Third World nations. Experts hope that the use of modern farming methods and new crops will provide more food for growing populations. Here a United Nations advisor gives a food demonstration to African women.
What efforts have been made to increase food production in Africa?

nese, gold, and diamonds. But more money and skilled workers are needed for Africa to make full use of these resources.

African industry, however, has been growing at a fast rate. In most countries, some industries prepare minerals and other raw materials for sale outside Africa. Other industries prepare goods for the home market, such as clothes, shoes, and soft drinks.

1. What political problems face many African nations?
2. Why is agriculture important to the economy of Africa?
3. Why do African governments want farmers to raise cash crops?
4. What industries are found in most African countries?

Latin America

Unlike other Third World countries, the nations of Latin America gained independence in the early 1800's. However, strong feelings of nationalism have grown in recent years because of the amount of foreign influence in Latin America. The countries of Latin America are working to modernize their economies and rid themselves of outside influence.

People from other countries have been making investments in Latin America since the middle of the 1800's. Industrial powers such as Great Britain, France, Germany, and the United States started businesses in Latin America. They produced mostly bananas, sugar, metals, and oil, which were then shipped from Latin America to markets abroad.

Colombian Farmer

Latin American countries benefited from the foreign investments. National incomes grew. Wages rose, and there were more jobs. Foreign business interests built roads and railroads and set up telephone systems and electric plants.

Yet, most of the countries depended heavily on only one or two products. Also, food, clothing, and household goods had to be bought from other countries. They usually cost more than if they had been made in Latin America.

Since World War II, most Latin American countries have been trying to industrialize. They have greatly increased their production of steel, cars, oil, cement, and paper. Yet, not enough is produced to meet the needs of the growing population. Latin Americans still have to buy about 70 percent of the manufactured goods they need from other countries.

THIRD WORLD LEADERS

Menachem Begin
1913–

prime minister of Israel who signed first formal peace treaty between an Arab country and Israel, 1979

David Ben–Gurion
1886–1973

prime minister of Israel from 1948 to 1953 and from 1955 to 1963; leader of Israeli independence movement

Indira Gandhi
1917–

prime minister of India from 1966 to 1977 and from 1980 to present

Haile Selassie
1892–1975

emperor of Ethiopia from 1930 to 1936 and from 1941 to 1971; gave Ethiopia first written constitution

Hussein I
1935–

king of Jordan since 1953

Kenneth Kaunda
1924–

president of Zambia since independence in 1964

Golda Meir
1898–1978

prime minister of Israel from 1969 to 1974

Kwame Nkrumah
1909–1972

leader of African independence movement who was first president of Republic of Ghana from 1960 to 1966

Julius Nyerere
1922–

prime minister and first president of Tanganyika in 1961 and 1962; president of Tanzania since 1964

Jóse López Portillo
1920–

president of Mexico from 1976 to 1982

Anwar al–Sadat
1918–1981

president of Egypt who signed first formal peace treaty between an Arab country and Israel, 1979

Leopold Senghor
1906–

president of Republic of Senegal from independence in 1960 to 1981

BRAZILIAN CITY

Like most Third World nations, Brazil has growing cities with modern apartments, hotels, and office buildings. However, many unskilled city workers live in crowded slums near these new areas of prosperity.

How has foreign investment influenced industrial growth in Latin America?

The Latin American economy still depends on farming. *Campesinos,* or farmers, make up about one half of the population. Most land in Latin America is held in **haciendas,** or large ranches. Most of the work on the haciendas is done by peasants. These peasants use the same farming methods their parents and grandparents used. They are not encouraged to learn new ways. Peasant labor is cheap, so most hacienda owners have no wish to modernize. The end result often is that the land is poorly managed and that the yield is small. Food still has to be bought from other countries.

Many Latin Americans resent such countries as the United States. They accuse foreign investors of taking all the profits out of Latin America instead of using them to benefit the people. The nationalists want to be rid of outside political and economic influences. In the past, when government leaders failed to take care of economic problems they were often thrown out of office.

At times, this was done violently. Military leaders generally took over.

Things have become more complicated because of the Cold War. In Central America, the Soviet Union has been sending arms to certain groups. Some of these groups are Communist. But some are not. These groups want to get rid of the hacienda system and improve the people's standard of living. Because the Soviet Union has been supplying one side, the United States has been supplying the other side. Sometimes, this means that the United States is backing undemocratic governments that do little to make things better for the lower class.

1. What did foreign investors do with the goods they produced in Latin America?
2. What did foreign investors do to benefit Latin America?
3. How does the hacienda system hold back progress?
4. How does the Cold War affect Latin America?

THE MIDDLE EAST

Between World War I and World War II, nationalism grew in the Middle East. By the late 1940's, all of the countries in the area had become independent. Like other parts of the Third World, the Middle East faces the problem of modernizing. Another problem is the struggle between the Arabs and the Israelis. Also, there is conflict between those who favor old ways and those who favor new ways.

Israeli Farmer

AGRICULTURE AND INDUSTRY   For many years the main source of income in the Middle East has been agriculture. There is not enough water in most places, and less than one tenth of the land can be farmed. Still, more than two thirds of the people are farmers. Grains are the most important crops, but fruits, nuts, and vegetables also are grown. Although farm production has grown in the last 30 years, the population has also increased. Because of this, some Middle Eastern countries have to buy food from other countries.

Manufacturing has also grown. Many Middle Eastern governments encourage new industry. The chief products made in the Middle East include building materials, chemicals, processed foods, and textiles. Many new factories have been built in cities in Egypt, Iran, Israel, Kuwait, Saudi Arabia, and Turkey.

MIDDLE EAST OIL

The sale of oil from the Middle East to western industrial nations has brought prosperity to some countries of the region. The wealth generated by oil has not changed traditional life-styles in most rural areas, however.

How do most people in the Middle East make their living?

The most important Middle Eastern product, however, is oil. More than one half of the world's oil reserves can be found in the area. Oil has made some Middle Eastern countries—such as Bahrain, Iraq, Kuwait, and Saudi Arabia—rich. These countries belong to the Organization of Petroleum Exporting Countries (OPEC). They have used their oil profits to build schools, hospitals, airports, factories, and better housing.

1. Why do some Middle Eastern countries have to buy food from other countries?
2. Why is oil important in the Middle East?

THE ARAB-ISRAELI CONFLICT   During World War I, many Arabs fought with Great Britain against the Turks of the Ottoman Empire. They hoped this would gain them their independence. They looked forward to the creation of an Arab kingdom.

The Turks were defeated in World War I, but most Arabs did not get their independence. Instead, the Turkish-ruled part of the Arab world was divided into six countries, four of which were occupied by Europeans. Only Saudi Arabia and Yemen became independent.

The disappointed Arabs began an undeclared war. There were riots, bomb throwings, and other acts of violence. The Arabs won independence for Iraq in 1932, Lebanon in 1943, and Syria in 1946.

PLO Leader Yasir Arafat

The situation in Palestine was different. Jews as well as Arabs lived there. Jews had also fought on the side of Great Britain during World War I. They had made important scientific discoveries that helped the Allied cause. When Jewish leaders pushed to set up a Jewish homeland in Palestine, the British supported the idea. Most Arabs did not.

In 1946, the part of Palestine east of the Jordan River became the independent country of Jordan. In 1948, the United Nations divided the part of Palestine west of the Jordan River between the Arabs and the Jews. The Jews agreed to go along with the division, although they did not like it. The Arabs, however, refused. When British troops pulled out of Palestine, seven Arab nations declared war on the newly established country of Israel. After the war, about 450,000 Palestinian Arabs left Israel for refugee camps on the West Bank of the Jordan and in the Gaza Strip.

Israeli Defense Minister Moshe Dayan

Since then, the Arabs and the Israelis have fought four wars. They took place in 1956, 1967, 1973, and 1982. Territories have shifted back and forth. To date, the only Arab country that has recognized Israel's right to exist is Egypt. Arab nationalists headed by the Palestine Liberation Organization (PLO) have carried out guerrilla attacks on Israel. In return, Israel has bombed guerrilla bases and has invaded PLO strongholds in Lebanon.

1. Why did the Arabs fight with Great Britain in World War I?
2. How did Israel become the Jewish homeland?

OLD AND NEW   In Iran, there was conflict between those who wanted old ways and those who wanted new ways. The country of Iran, once called Persia, changed very little between the Middle Ages and World War II. Then, Mohammed Reza Pahlavi became the **shah,** or absolute ruler, of Iran. The shah wanted to make Iran a modern country and raise the standard of living. He used money from the sale of Iranian oil to build schools and hospitals, open factories, and train a large army.

THE THIRD WORLD TODAY

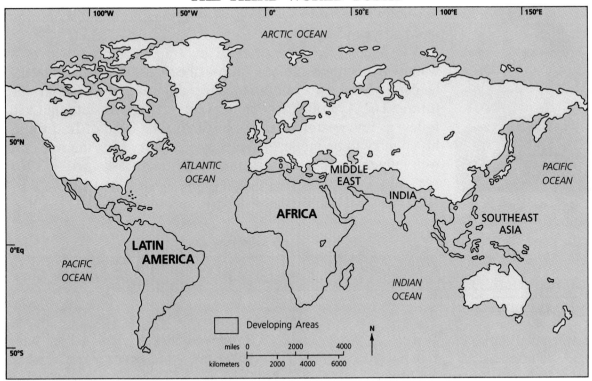

People who opposed the shah were either killed or exiled. The secret police imprisoned thousands of people without trial. Also, some of the shah's ideas upset the country's religious leaders. They believed the shah's modern ideas were weakening Iran's Muslim faith. They wanted Iran to be an **Islamic republic,** or a country that follows traditional Muslim ideas. They objected to western-style music. They thought that women should wear the **chador.** This is a long black robe that covers a woman from head to toe. Only the eyes show.

Those who were against the shah looked to Ruhollah Khomeini as their leader. Khomeini was an **ayatollah,** or a religious leader with a personal following. In 1978, Khomeini's followers led riots against the shah. The next year, he fled the country. Khomeini then returned to Iran from exile in Paris and set up an Islamic republic.

In the meantime, the shah traveled to New York City for medical treatment. This angered many Iranians. They wanted the shah returned to Iran for trial. So, in the fall of 1979, they

Ayatollah Khomeini

took over the United States Embassy in the Iranian capital of Teheran. They held 53 Americans as hostages for almost one and one half years.

In 1980, Iran was attacked by Iraq in a dispute over a waterway. Both countries follow the Muslim faith. But the leaders of the two countries have different ideas about the future. The Ayatollah Khomeini wants a religious state that will follow as few western ideas as possible. The head of Iraq wants his country to be modern. Whichever country wins the war may well influence other countries in the Middle East.

1. What change did the shah try to bring about in Iran?
2. Why did Iran's religious leaders oppose the shah?

CHAPTER 40 REVIEW

SUMMARY

1. India, Africa, Latin America, and the Middle East are part of the Third World and have common problems.

2. Feelings of nationalism began to grow in India toward the end of the 1800's.

3. After World War I, Mohandas K. Gandhi began a protest movement against British rule that led to India's independence in 1947.

4. Since independence, the Indian government has tried to set up a stable government and raise the people's standard of living.

5. In Africa, the demand for independence grew strong after World War II, and many African countries gained their independence in 1960.

6. Many African countries are not democratic and face the problem of ruling several different national groups.

7. Africa has many mineral and energy resources but needs to further develop its agriculture.

8. Strong feelings of nationalism have grown in Latin America in recent years.

9. Since gaining independence, most Latin American countries have benefited from foreign investments.

10. Economic progress in Latin America is held back by the hacienda system.

11. Arab lands put under British or French rule after World War I were independent by the 1940's.

12. Oil is the main natural resource in the Middle East, which contains more than one half of the world's oil reserves.

13. In 1948, the United Nations gave part of Palestine to the Jews, who set up the country of Israel.

14. The shah, who tried to make Iran a modern country, was overthrown by followers of the Ayatollah Khomeini, who set up an Islamic republic.

15. The war between Iraq and Iran may affect how modern some Middle Eastern countries become.

BUILDING VOCABULARY

1. *Identify the following:*
   Indian National Congress Mahatma K. Gandhi Palestine Liberation Organization Ayatollah Khomeini
   Namibia

2. *Define the following:*

   national income   apartheid   *campesinos*   Islamic republic
   market price   subsistence farming haciendas   chador
   dialects   cash crops   shah   ayatollah
   civil disobedience

REVIEWING THE FACTS

1. How are most Third World countries different from western and Communist countries?
2. How do most of the people make their living in Third World countries?
3. What is the main population problem of Third World countries?
4. What is the main goal of most Third World countries?
5. What made the British agree to independence for India?
6. Why is the year 1960 called "the year of Africa"?
7. Why do most Latin American campesinos still use older farming methods?
8. How has oil affected the economic development of many Middle Eastern countries?
9. Why did the British support the idea of a Jewish homeland in Palestine?
10. What kind of government does the Ayatollah Khomeini want for Iran?

DISCUSSING IMPORTANT IDEAS

1. What may happen to a country that depends heavily on a single product?
2. What usually happens to a country as it industrializes?
3. What do you think developing countries should do to solve their problems?
4. What do you think can be done to help bring about peace in the Middle East?

USING MAPS

Study the map on page 665, and answer the following questions:

1. What areas are considered developing nations?
2. In what area of the Western Hemisphere are most developing nations located?
3. How far is the southern tip of Latin America from the southern tip of Africa?
4. What country is located at about 8° north latitude and 77° east longitude?
5. Through what land areas does the equator pass?
6. On what bodies of water do the developing nations border?

UNIT 13 REVIEW

SUMMARY

1. Nationalism and the alliance system that developed among European nations at the end of the 1800's eventually led to World War I. The war severely damaged the economy of several western European nations. It also resulted in the creation of four new countries and the League of Nations.

2. After World War I, a depression set in that contributed to the rise of dictatorships in western Europe.

3. Attempts by Germany, Italy, and Japan to take over areas belonging to other nations resulted in World War II. The war weakened Western Europe and Japan and made the United States and the Soviet Union the most powerful nations in the world. It also led to the establishment of the United Nations.

4. The Soviet Union became a Communist country in the early twentieth century. The People's Republic of China was established and became a Communist country in the middle 1900's. These two countries are the world's leading Communist powers, but they do not agree on the aims of communism.

5. Most nations of the Third World are not as developed as the industrial nations of the First World and Second World. They are faced with such problems as poverty and overpopulation. Many lack the technology that is needed to take advantage of natural resources.

6. The West and the Communist nations compete for the loyalty of the developing nations. Some developing nations, however, do not want help from either.

REVIEWING THE MAIN IDEAS

1. Discuss the effects World Wars I and II had on the economy, government, and role of Western Europe, the United States, the Soviet Union, and China.

2. Compare the problems faced by India, Africa, Latin America, and the Middle East and the steps each has taken to solve them.

DEVELOPING SKILLS

In Unit Review 3 you learned about chronology, which is a time relationship important in the study of history. Another time relationship that is just as important has to do with the length of one historic period as compared to another. This exercise is designed to give you practice deciding which of two periods in history lasted longer. It also gives you an opportunity to review some of the things you have learned this year about different civilizations. Below are eight groups of historical periods. Tell which period in each group lasted longer than the other.

1. The Paleolithic Age
   The Neolithic Age

2. Ancient History
   The Middle Ages

3. Ancient History
   The United States as an Independent Nation

4. The Renaissance
   The Middle Ages

5. Ancient Greece
   The Age of Discovery

6. The Pax Romana
   Ancient History

7. The Industrial Revolution
   Ancient Egypt

8. Ancient Rome
   The United States as an Independent Nation

SUGGESTED UNIT PROJECTS

1. Report on the life of such former Third World leaders as Kenyatta of Kenya, Sadat of Egypt, and Nehru of India.

2. Working in a small group, research present-day conditions in a Latin American country. Then prepare a detailed plan of how you would go about solving the country's major problems.

3. Make a chart comparing the United States and the Soviet Union. Include information about size, population, government, economic system, income, leaders, strengths, and weaknesses.

4. Draw a poster that might be used in a Third World nation to teach something about health to people who cannot read.

SUGGESTED READING

Almedingen, E. M. *Anna*. New York: Farrar, Straus & Giroux, 1972. The story of country life in Russia during the last years of tsarist rule.

Eunson, Roby. *Mao Tse-tung: The Man Who Conquered China*. New York: Franklin Watts, Inc., 1973. A biography.

Gessner, Lynn. *Edge of Darkness*. New York: Walker and Company, 1979. The story of the Soviet takeover of Latvia as experienced by a young Latvian farm boy.

Goldston, Robert C. *Next Year in Jerusalem*. Boston: Little, Brown, 1978. A history of Zionism.

Reeder, Red. *Bold Leaders of World War I*. Boston: Little, Brown, 1974. Tells about 12 men and women and what they did during World War I.

Scott, John. *Divided They Stand*. New York: Parents' Magazine Press, 1973. A personal account of Germany from before World War II through the division of Germany.

Sidel, Ruth. *Revolutionary China: People, Politics, and Ping-Pong*. New York: Delacorte Press, 1974. A first-hand report on everyday life in China today.

White, Jo Ann (ed.). *African Views of the West*. New York: Julian Messner, 1972. A collection of African writings about the effect Westerners and western civilization have had and are having on Africa.

APPENDIX

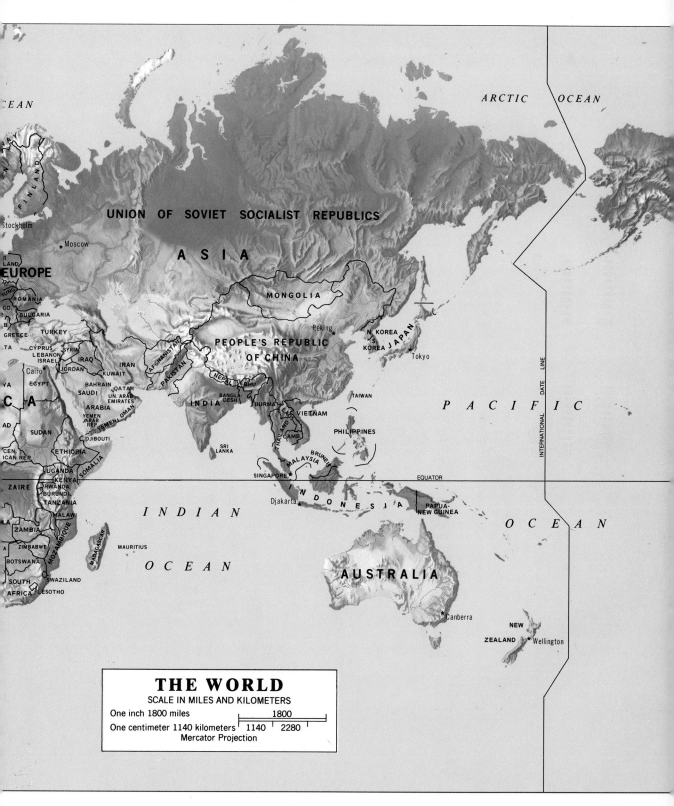

ARCTIC OCEAN

CEAN

UNION OF SOVIET SOCIALIST REPUBLICS

ASIA

Stockholm

Moscow

n LAND

EUROPE

UNG

ROMANIA

GO

BULGARIA

B

GREECE

TURKEY

TA

CYPRUS

LEBANON

ISRAEL

SYRIA

IRAQ

IRAN

AFGHANISTAN

JORDAN

KUWAIT

Cairo

EGYPT

BAHRAIN

QATAR

SAUDI

UN. ARAB
EMIRATES

ARABIA

YEMEN
ARAB
REP.

YEMEN

OMAN

MONGOLIA

Peking

PEOPLE'S REPUBLIC
OF CHINA

N. KOREA

S.
KOREA

JAPAN

Tokyo

PAKISTAN

NEPAL

BHU.

BANGLA-
DESH

INDIA

BURMA

VIETNAM

TAIWAN

PACIFIC

CA

AD

SUDAN

DJIBOUTI

CEN
ICAN REP

ETHIOPIA

UGANDA

KENYA

SOMALIA

ZAIRE

RWANDA

BURUNDI

TANZANIA

MALAWI

ZAMBIA

ZIMBABWE

BOTSWANA

SOUTH
AFRICA

SWAZILAND

LESOTHO

MADAGASCAR

MOZAMBIQUE

MAURITIUS

THAILAND

CAMB

PHILIPPINES

SRI
LANKA

MALAYSIA

BRUNEI

SINGAPORE

INDONESIA

Djakarta

PAPUA-
NEW GUINEA

EQUATOR

INDIAN

OCEAN

OCEAN

AUSTRALIA

Canberra

OCEAN

INTERNATIONAL DATE LINE

NEW
ZEALAND

Wellington

673

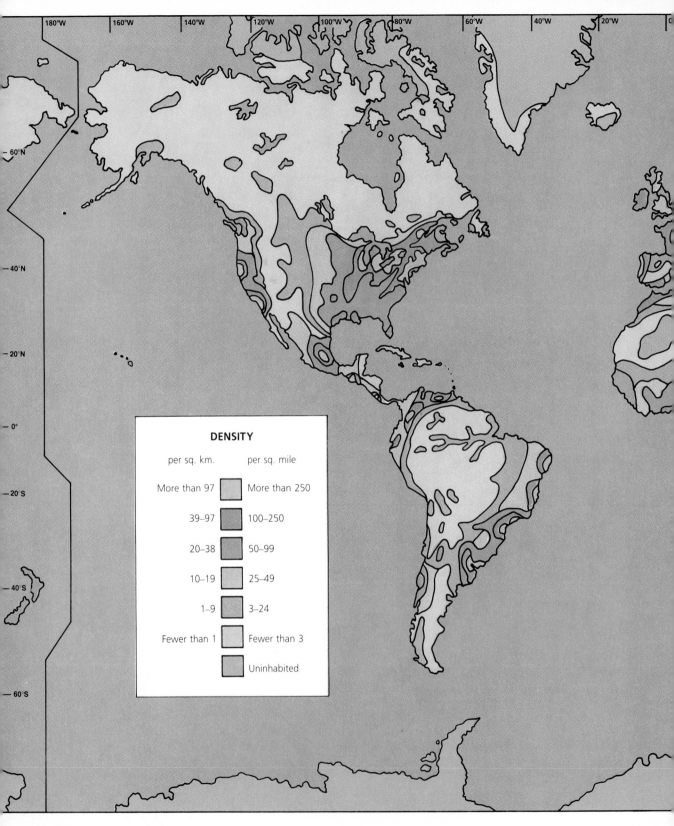

DENSITY

per sq. km.		per sq. mile
More than 97		More than 250
39–97		100–250
20–38		50–99
10–19		25–49
1–9		3–24
Fewer than 1		Fewer than 3
		Uninhabited

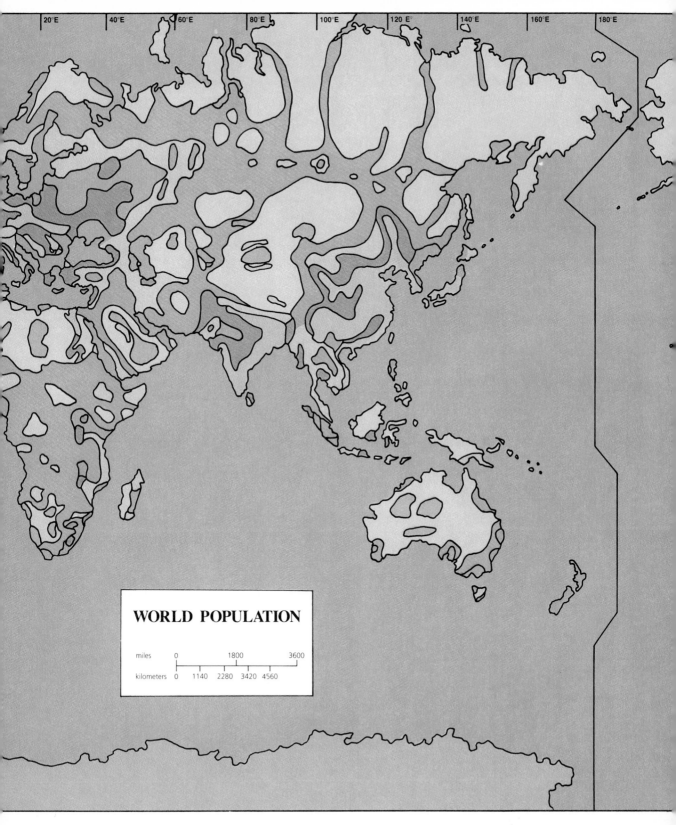

WORLD POPULATION

miles	0		1800		3600
kilometers	0	1140	2280	3420	4560

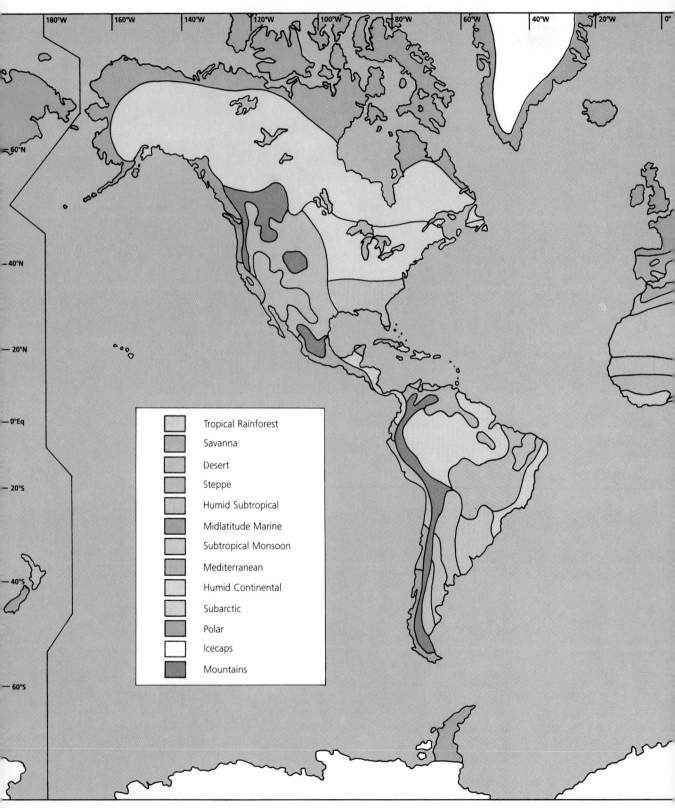

	Tropical Rainforest
	Savanna
	Desert
	Steppe
	Humid Subtropical
	Midlatitude Marine
	Subtropical Monsoon
	Mediterranean
	Humid Continental
	Subarctic
	Polar
	Icecaps
	Mountains

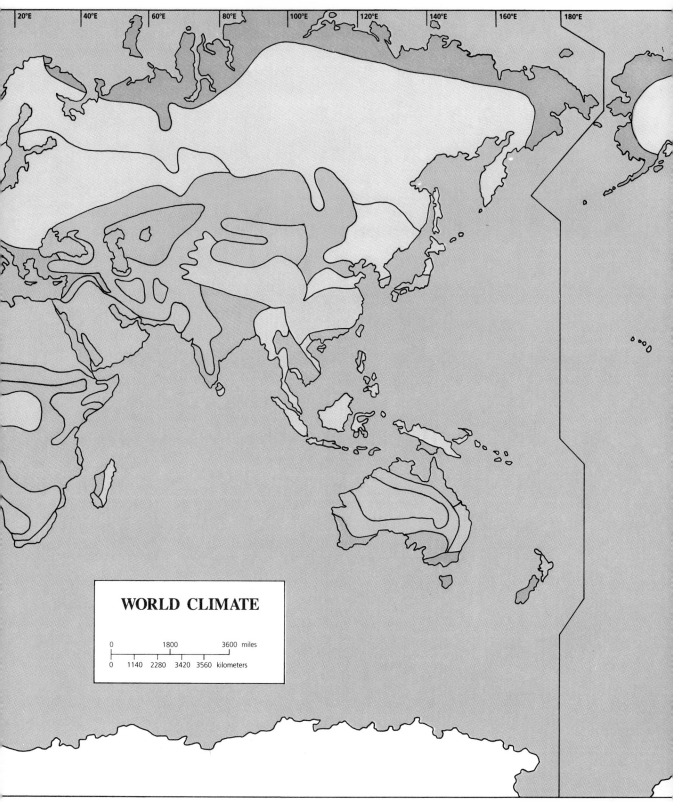

WORLD CLIMATE

```
0              1800           3600  miles
0   1140   2280   3420  3560  kilometers
```

EURASIA

SCALE IN MILES AND KILOMETERS

miles   600

kilometers   380   760

Parabolic Equal Area Projection

Laptev Sea

70°

60°

Lena River

Verkhoyansk

S I B E R I A

KOLYMA MOUNTAINS

KAMCHATKA PENINSULA

Sea of Okhotsk

50°

Novosibirsk

Krasnoyarsk

SOCIALIST   REPUBLICS

STANOVOY MOUNTAINS

Amur River

Khabarovsk

KURIL

ISLANDS

SAYAN MOUNTAINS

Lake Baikal

Irkutsk

Ulan Bator

MONGOLIA

GOBI
DESERT

M A N C H U R I A

Pinkiang
(Harbin)

Vladivostok

HOKKAIDO

Lake
Balkhash

Shenyang
(Mukden)

NORTH
KOREA

Sea
of Japan

40°

Alma-Ata

PAMIR

TAKLA
MAKAN

NAN SHAN

Beijing
(Peking)

Luda
(Dairen)

Pyongyang

J
A
P
A
N

HONSHU

KUNLUN MOUNTAINS

C H I N A

Tianjin
(Tientsin)

Yellow
Sea

Seoul

SOUTH
KOREA

Pusan

Kyoto

Tokyo

KARAKORAM

Mekong River

Xi'an
(Sian)

Qingdao
(Tsingtao)

Kobe

Osaka

abul

Islamabad

PLATEAU OF TIBET

Lhasa

TSINLING SHAN

Nanjing
(Nanking)

SHIKOKU

KYUSHU

30°

AN

Lahore

H

Mt. Everest
29,141'

SZECHWAN
BASIN

Wuhan
(Wuhan)

Shanghai
(Shanghai)

East
China
Sea

PAKISTAN

Delhi

Ganges

I

NEPAL

M

A

Katmandu

River

L

A

Y

BHUTAN

A

S

Chang Jiang

Chongqing
(Chunking)

Tungting
Hu

Indus

New
Delhi

Lucknow

Kanpur

Brahmaputra R.

BANGLA-
DESH

Dacca

NAGA HILLS

Xi Jiang

Guangzhou
(Canton)

OKINAWA

Taipei

TAIWAN

rachi

THAR
DESERT

Ahmadabad

Nagpur

Calcutta

Jaipur

Mandalay

BURMA

Irrawaddy R.

Red River

Hanoi

Gulf of
Tonkin

Victoria
(Hong Kong)

Formosa Strait

20°

Bombay

Pune

I N D I A

WESTERN GHATS

Bay of Bengal

Vientiane

L
A
O
S

VIETNAM

S O U T H

REPUBLIC
OF THE
PHILIPPINES

Hyderabad

Rangoon

THAILAND

C H I N A

Manila

Bangalore

EASTERN GHATS

Madras

Bangkok

CAMBODIA

Tonle Sap

Phnom Penh

S E A

10°

SRI LANKA

Gulf of
Siam

Ho Chi Minh City
(Saigon)

Colombo

MALDIVES

MALAY
PENINSULA

M A L A Y S I A

BRUNEI

Strait of Malacca

N D I A N   O C E A N

Kuala
Lumpur

SINGAPORE
Singapore

0°

REPUBLIC OF INDONESIA

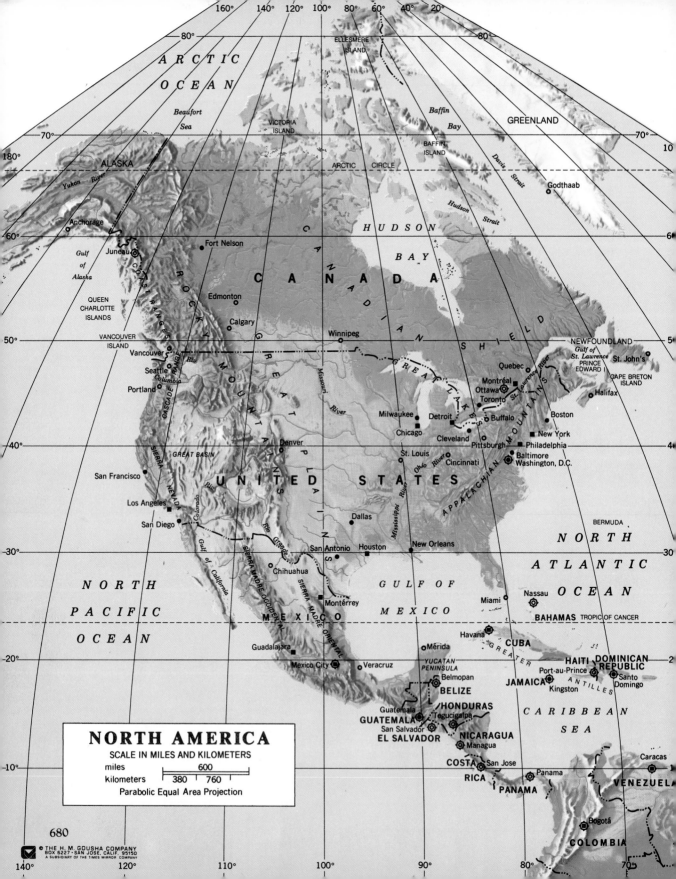

NORTH AMERICA

SCALE IN MILES AND KILOMETERS

miles   600

kilometers   380   760

Parabolic Equal Area Projection

680

SOUTH AMERICA

SCALE IN MILES AND KILOMETERS

miles

kilometers

Parabolic Equal Area Projection

© THE H. M. GOUSHA COMPANY
BOX 6227 · SAN JOSE, CALIF. 95150
A SUBSIDIARY OF THE TIMES MIRROR COMPANY

681

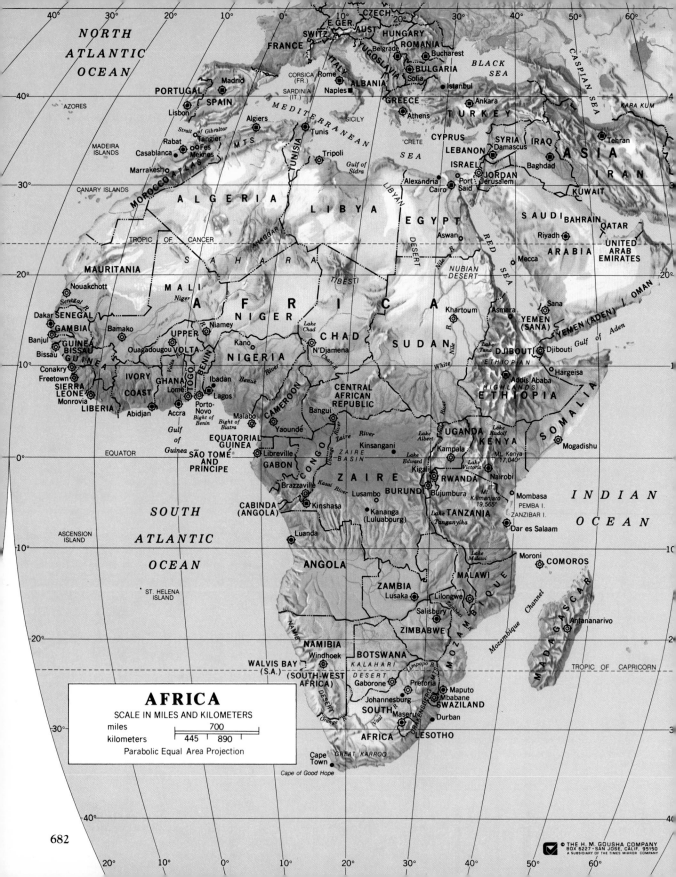

AFRICA

SCALE IN MILES AND KILOMETERS

miles   700

kilometers   445   890

Parabolic Equal Area Projection

682

© THE H. M. GOUSHA COMPANY
BOX 6227 · SAN JOSE, CALIF. 95150
A SUBSIDIARY OF THE TIMES MIRROR COMPANY

GLOSSARY

Pronunciations are indicated in parentheses.

A

abbott (ab′buht)   Head of a monastery.

abdicate (ab′duh kāt)   To give up the throne.

acropolis (uh krop′uh lis)   Fortified hill with a temple to the local god at the top.

act of homage (akt of hom′ij)   Medieval ceremony in which a vassal promises loyalty to a lord.

agora (ag′uh ruh)   Open outdoor market place usually found in a Greek city-state.

ancestors (an′ses tuhrs)   Family members from past generations.

anthropologists (an thruh pol′uh jists)   People who study pre-history and early history.

apartheid (uh part′hāt)   Separation of the races.

apostles (uh pos′uhls)   The men chosen by Jesus to teach his beliefs to other people.

apprentice (uh pren′tis)   Person who is learning a craft or trade.

aqueducts (ak′wuh dukts)   Structures for conducting water along a specific path.

archaeologists (or ke ol′uh jists)   People who study ruins and artifacts.

aristocrats (uh ris′tuh krats)   Members of the upper class.

armistice (ar′muh stis)   An agreement to cease fighting.

artifacts (ar′tuh fakts)   Products of human skill.

assembly (uh sem′blē)   Group of people that gives advice to a ruler or government leader; law-making body of government.

ayatollah (ī yuh tol′uh)   Islamic religious leader.

B

bailiff (bā′lif)   Medieval official whose duty was to see that peasants did their work.

bandeirantes (ban duh ran′tās)   Fortune hunters in colonial Brazil; established Portuguese settlements throughout the country.

barbaroi (bar′buh roi)   Greek name for people who did not speak Greek or follow Greek customs.

berserkers (ber serk′erz)   Viking warriors.

blitzkrieg (blits′krēg)   "Lightning war"; German style of fighting in World War II.

boyars (bō yarz′)   Members of the wealthy class in tsarist Russia.

brigands (brig′uhnds)   Roving bandits hired to destroy property.

burghers (ber′guhrz)   Freemen or wealthy merchants who lived in towns in the Middle Ages.

burgs (bergs)   Towns built during the Middle Ages.

bylina (buh lēn′uh)   Russian stories about deeds of warriors and heroes.

C

caftans (kaf′tanz)   Long robes tied at the waist; worn by early Russian men for warmth.

caliph (kā′lif)   Muslim ruler.

campesinos (kam puh sē′nōz)   Latin American farmers and peasants.

captaincies (kap′tuhn sēz)   Areas of land in Brazil given to Portuguese nobles.

caravans (kar′uh vans)   Groups of traders who traveled together for safety.

caravel (kar′uh vel)   Small, fast Portuguese sailing ship used in the 1500's.

catacombs (kat′uh kōmz)   Cemeteries that are underground.

cathedrals (kuh thē′druhlz)   Large churches.

caudillo (kou thē′yō)   Latin American leader, usually a military dictator.

census (sen′suhs)   A count made of the population of an area.

chador (chuh′duhr)   Long robe worn by women of some Islamic faiths.

chancellor (chan′suh luhr)   Head of a medieval English university; leader of a country.

chateaux (sha tōz′)   Castles.

chieftain (chēf′tuhn)   Leader of a band or group.

citadel (sit′uh del)   Fortress built on high ground.

city-state (sit′ē-stāt)   City and the farmland around it with its own government and god.

civilians (suh vil′yuhnz)   People who are not soldiers.

civilization (siv uh luh zā′ shuhn)   Society with a developed knowledge of farming, trade, government, art, and science.

clans (klanz)   Groups of people united by family ties.

code of chivalry (kōd of shiv′ uhl rē)   Rules by which knights had to live.

collectivization (kuh lek′ti vī zā shuhn)   Uniting of small farms into large ones controlled by the government.

comedy (kom′uh dē)   Humorous play.

communes (kom′yūns)   Government-run farming communities in which all work for a common cause.

communism (kom′yū niz uhm)   Type of socialism where the government, or the Communist party, leads a workers' revolution.

conquistadores (kon kēs′tuh dorz)   Sixteenth-century Spanish conquerors.

constitution (kon stuh tū′shuhn)   Set of written laws used to govern a country or state.

consuls (kon′suhlz)   Heads of the ancient Roman Republic.

coracles (kor′uh kuhls)   Small boats made by covering a wooden frame with leather; used by the early Irish.

corregidores (kuh reg uh dō′rās)   Royal officials chosen by the Spanish ruler to govern colonial towns.

corvus (kor′vuhs)   Removable bridge attached to the front of a Roman ship.

Creoles (krē′olz)   People of Spanish descent born in the New World.

crossbow (kros′bō)   Medieval weapon used to shoot arrows.

crusades (krū sāds′)   Series of wars undertaken by western Europeans to regain the Holy Land from the Muslims.

cuneiform (kyū nē′uh form)   Sumerian writing made up of wedge-shaped signs.

D

dauphin (do′fuhn)   Title used for the eldest son of the king of France.

détente (dā tont′)   Lessening of tensions or disagreements between nations.

dialects (dī′uh lekts)   Forms of a language that are spoken in different parts of a country.

dictator (dik′tā tuhr)   Person who takes complete power in running a government.

dictatorship (dik tā′tuhr ship)   Country ruled by a single person who is not a monarch.

diocese (dī′uh suhs)   Group of local churches.

disciples (duh sī′puhls)   People who follow and learn from a leader.

dissidents (dis′uh duhnts)   People who are unhappy with and speak out against their way of life.

doctrine (dok′truhn)   Beliefs of a religion or a political party.

doge (dōj)   Official ruler of Venice in Renaissance times.

domus (dō′muhs)   House.

donatarios (dōn uh tar ē′ōz)   Portuguese owners of land in Brazil during the colonial period.

dubbing (dub′bing)   Ceremony in which a squire is made a knight.

dynasty (dī′nuh stē)   Series of rulers from the same family.

E

eddas (e′duhz)   Written poems based on stories of the deeds of Viking gods.

edubbas (ed′uh buhs)   Sumerian schools.

embalming (em bom′ing)   Process used to keep dead bodies from decaying.

émigrés (em′uh grāz)   French political exiles.

emirs (uh mirz′)   Muslim military leaders.

empire (em′pīr)   Group of city-states, countries, or territories under one ruler.

enclosure (en klō′zhuhr)   Method of dividing land in which small areas of land were combined into larger ones and closed in with fences.

estates (e stātz′)   Name for classes in French society in the 1600's.

excommunicated (ek skuh myū′nuh kā ted)   Expelled from the Roman Catholic Church.

exodus (ek′suh duhs)   The departure of a large group of people; usually refers to the Hebrews leaving Egypt.

F

fasces (fas′ēz) Bundle of rods tied around an ax; symbol of Rome and Italian fascism.

feudalism (fyū′dl iz uhm) Political and economic system during the Middle Ages based on the relationship of lords and vassals.

fiefs (fēfs) Pieces of land given to vassals by their lords.

frescoes (fres′kōz) Wall paintings.

G

galleons (gal′ē uhns) Spanish ships used in the 1400's and 1500's.

genocide (jen′uh sīd) Deliberate destruction of a racial, political, or cultural group.

gentiles (jen′tīls) People who are not Jewish.

geologists (jē ol′uh jists) People who study the history of the earth through its rocks and minerals.

gladiators (glad′ē ā tuhrz) Persons who fought men or animals in ancient Roman arenas.

gospel (gos′puhl) History of the life and teachings of Jesus.

H

haciendas (ho sē en′duhs) Large ranches.

hajj (haj) Muslim journey to Mecca.

helots (hel′uhtz) Slaves who farmed the land of Sparta.

heresy (her′uh sē) Belief or teaching that is against the popular belief.

hermits (her′mits) People who choose to live alone in a lonely place.

hieroglyphs (hī′uhr uh glifs) Ancient Egyptian picture writing.

humanists (hyū′muh nists) Philosophers who believe that people are important.

hypothesis (hī poth′uh sis) Possible explanation for a problem.

I

icons (ī′konz) Sacred pictures usually used in the Eastern Orthodox Church.

imam (i mam′) Muslim priest.

imperialism (im pir′ē uh liz uhm) The policy of building a nation by establishing colonies and building empires.

indentured servants (in den′chuhrd ser′vuhntz) Settlers who agreed to work for a period of time to pay for their passage to the New World.

indulgences (in dul′juhnt sez) Pardons given by the Church that lessen the punishment for wrongdoings.

infantries (in′fuhn trēz) Soldiers who fight on foot.

infidels (in′fuh duhls) Nonbelievers.

inflation (in flā′shuhn) Period when prices go up and the value of money goes down.

Inquisition (in kwuh zish′uhn) Court set up by the Church during the 1200's to find and punish nonbelievers.

izbas (iz′buhz) One-room log cabins of early Russians.

J

jarls (yarls) Viking military leaders.

jihads (ji hadz′) Muslim holy wars.

journeyman (jer′nē muhn) Person in Middle Ages who worked under a master for a daily wage.

joust (joust) Contest on horseback between two knights.

judge (juj) Leader of a tribe of Israel.

junker (juhn′kuhr) Rich Prussian landowner.

junta (hun′tuh) Committee organized to take over a government; military government.

juris prudentes (jur′is prūd′ns) Lawyers.

K

ka'bah (ka buh′) Muslim shrine in Mecca.

kaiser (kī′zuhr) Name for a German emperor.

keep (kēp) Strongest and most important part of a castle, made of stone with thick walls, one entrance, and a narrow stairway for defense.

khan (kan) Mongol leader.

kitchen midden (kich′uhn mid′uhn) The name given to ancient bones and household items.

knights (nīts) Warriors or defenders that fight on horseback.

Koran (ko ran′) Muslim bible.

kremlin (krem'luhn) Russian fortress; base of the Soviet government.

L

labyrinth (lab'uh rinth) Maze.

latifundias (lat uh fuhn'dē as) Large Roman estates where crops and animals were raised to sell at market.

legionaries (lē'juh ner ēz) Roman soldiers.

legions (lē'juhnz) Divisions of Roman soldiers.

liberals (lib'uh ruhls) People who favor political reforms.

limited government (lim'uh tid guv'uhr muhnt) Idea that government has only powers given to it by the people.

litter (lit'uhr) Persian carriage without wheels carried by servants.

logic (loj'ik) Science of reasoning or thinking things through.

lords (lords) Nobles with great power and authority during the Middle Ages.

M

magistrates (maj'uh strāts) Judges with the power to enforce laws.

mandate (man'dāt) Right to rule.

manor house (man'uhr hous) Wooden homes of nobles; built to provide protection.

martial law (mar'shuhl law) Temporary control over a country or state by the military.

megaron (meg'uh ron) Square room in the center of a Mycenean palace.

mendicants (men'duh kuhnts) Beggars.

men-of-war (men-of-wor) Navy warships.

mercantilism (muhr'kuhn tuh liz uhm) System in which a government controls business, while colonies provide wealth to their parent country.

messiah (muh sī'uh) Savior.

mestizos (me stē'zōz) People of mixed European and Indian ancestry.

metropolitans (met ruh pol'uh tuhns) Eastern Orthodox Church officials in charge of larger cities and provincial centers.

minstrels (min'struhlz) Poets and singers who traveled around entertaining people during the Middle Ages.

monasteries (mon'uh ster ēz) The places where monks live.

monks (munks) Men who live in a religious community.

mosaics (mō zā'iks) Colorful pictures made of bits of stone or glass.

mosque (mosk) Muslim place of worship.

mulattoes (muh lat'ōz) Persons with one black parent and one white parent.

mummy (mum'ē) Wrapped body of a preserved dead person.

mundus (muhn'dus) Meeting of two streets; according to the ancient Romans, the meeting point of the worlds of the living and the dead.

N

nationalists (nash'uh nal ists) People devoted to their nation.

necropolis (nuh krop'uh luhs) Cemetery.

nuns (nunz) Women who live in a Catholic religious community.

O

oath-helpers (ōth help'erz) People who swore that the accused was telling the truth in early German trials.

olympiads (ō lim'pē ads) Four-year periods between Olympic Games.

oprichniki (ō prich'nuh kē) Russian secret police during the rule of Ivan the Terrible.

oracles (or'uh kuhlz) Ancient priests who communicated with the gods.

orator (or'uh ter) Public speaker.

ordeal (or dēl') Ancient method of judging the innocence or guilt of a person.

P

page (pāj) Person who helped the knights care for their horses and armor.

palisade (pal uh sād') High wooden fence surrounding the manor of a noble.

pancratium (pan krāy'shē uhm) Athletic event in the Greek Olympics that combined boxing and wrestling.

papal line of demarcation (pā´puhl līn of dē mar kā´shuhn)   Line drawn in 1493 by Pope Alexander VI to divide Spanish and Portuguese claims.

papyrus (puh pī´ruhs)   Reed that grows along river banks; writing paper used by the ancient Egyptians, Greeks, and Romans.

parables (par´uh buhlz)   Short stories that teach a lesson.

parchment (parch´muhnt)   Thin skin of an animal used to write or paint on.

parish (par´ish)   Area assigned to a local church.

patrãos (puh tra´os)   Leading older members of Portuguese colonial settlements.

patriarchs (pā´trē arks)   Heads of the Eastern Orthodox Church.

patricians (pu trish´uhnz)   Rich and powerful upper-class citizens of ancient Rome.

peninsulares (puh nin sū la´ räs)   The name given to Spaniards born in Spain in Spanish colonial settlements in the New World.

pentathlon (pen tath´luhn)   Olympic game made up of five separate athletic events.

perioeci (per ē ō´sī)   Merchants and artisans who lived and worked in Spartan villages.

phalanx (fā´langks)   Ancient Greek battle formation used by foot soldiers.

pharaoh (fer´ō)   Ancient Egyptian ruler.

philosophers (fuh los´uh fuhrz)   People who study and teach about the meaning of life.

philosophes (fil´uh sōfs)   Educated French philosophers in the 1700's.

piazza (pē az´uh)   Central square of an Italian city.

pig-sticking (pig´stik ing)   A type of hunt in the days of the early Roman Empire.

pilgrimage (pil´gruh mij)   Religious journey of a pilgrim to a shrine or holy place.

pillars of faith (pil´uhrs of fāth)   Five duties of all Muslims as described in the Koran.

pit (pit)   Open area in front of the stage in an English theatre.

plebians (pli bē´uhnz)   Poor and lower class citizens of ancient Rome.

polis (pō´lis)   Ancient Greek city-state.

political parties (puh lit´uh kuhl par´tēz)   Special groups with set ideas about government and how it should be run.

Pope (pōp)   Head of the Roman Catholic Church.

popular sovereignty (pop´yuh luhr sov´ruhn tē)   Idea that government derives its powers from the people.

portcullis (port kul´is)   Heavy oak or iron gate at castle entrance.

premier (pri mir´)   Title for prime minister of the Soviet Union.

priest (prēst)   Religious leader, usually Roman Catholic or Eastern Orthodox.

priest-king (prēst-king)   Ancient ruler who was both ruler and religious leader.

proletariat (prō luh ter´ē uht)   Working class.

prophets (prof´its)   Religious teachers or leaders who foresee the future.

protectorate (pruh tek´tuhr it)   Country under the protection and rule of another country.

psalms (salms)   Religious songs or poems.

publicans (pub´luh kuhns)   Ancient Roman tax collectors.

pyramids (pir´uh mids)   Large Egyptian tombs.

Q

quipus (kwip´uhs)   Inca counting devices made of knotted strings of different colors.

R

rabbis (rab´īz)   Jewish teachers and ministers.

rajah (ra´juh)   A ruler of an ancient Indian kingdom.

republic (ri pub´lik)   Form of government where citizens choose leaders, usually through an election.

rhetoric (ret´uhr ik)   Art of writing or speaking.

right of extraterritoriality (rīt of ek struh ter uh tōr ē al´ uht ē)   Policy that prevents citizens of one country from being tried by another country for crimes committed within its boundaries.

rule by divine right (rul bī duh vīn´ rīt)   Belief that a leader's powers and right to rule come from the gods.

runes (rūns)   Letters of the Viking alphabet.

S

sabbath (sab'uhth) Religious day of rest.

sagas (sa'guhz) Epic stories.

sans-culottes (sanz-kū lots') City workers and peasants in eighteenth-century France.

satrapies (sa'truh pēz) Ancient Persian provinces ruled by governors.

scribe (skrīb) Person who writes; official clerk.

scriptures (skrip'churz) Biblical writings.

seneschal (sen'uh shuhl) Official during the Middle Ages.

sepoys (sē'pois) Indian soldiers in the British army.

serfs (serfs) Poor people bound to the land during the Middle Ages.

shadoof (shuh dūf') Ancient machine used to move water from one place to another.

shah (sha) Absolute ruler.

shires (shīrs) Regions or districts in England.

shrines (shrīnz) Sacred or religious places or altars.

sledges (slej'ez) Heavy sleds or sleighs pulled by horses across ice and snow.

socialists (sō'shuh lists) People who believe in government ownership of industry.

Socratic method (sō krat'ik me'thuhd) Method of questioning developed by Socrates.

soothsayers (sūth'sā uhrs) People who predict the future by interpreting the will of the gods.

squire (skwīr) Young noble under care and training of a knight.

steppe (step) Large plain in southeastern Europe and Asia.

stockades (sto kādz') Wooden fences that surrounded the estates of nobles of the Middle Ages.

swastika (swos'ti kuh) Hooked black cross; symbol of the Nazi party.

syllogism (sil'uh jiz uhm) Form of reasoning developed by Aristotle.

synagogue (sin'uh gog) Jewish house of worship and prayer.

T

tells (telz) Mounds of earth that contain levels of housing of ancient civilizations.

Torah (tor'uh) The five Jewish books that contain the laws of Moses.

tournaments (tur'nuh muhnts) Contests to test the strength, skill, and endurance of knights.

tragedies (traj'uh dēz) Dramas or plays with a sad or unhappy theme.

tribunes (trib'yūnz) Members of the ancient Roman government elected to protect the rights of the lower class.

triremes (trī'rēmz) Ancient Greek or Roman warships with three rows of oars on each side.

triumvirate (trī um'vuhr it) Group of three people who rule with equal power.

tsar (zar) Russian ruler.

U

universal male suffrage (yū nuh ver'suhl māl suhf'rij) Right of all men to vote.

utopian socialists (yū tō'pē uhn sō'shuh lists) People who want to set up ideal communities based on economic cooperation.

V

vassal (vas'uhl) Person who served a lord during the Middle Ages.

veche (ve'chuh) Assembly that handled the affairs of early Russian towns.

viceroy (vīs'roi) Ruler of viceroyalty; represented the king in the New World.

villas (vil'uhz) Country estates of the wealthy.

vizier (vi zir') Chief advisor to the caliph of the Abbasids.

W

warlords (wor'lordz) Chinese military leaders who ruled parts of China.

wergeld (wuhr'geld) Fine paid by the family of a person who committed a crime.

witan (wi'ton) Members of the king's council in Anglo-Saxon England.

Z

zemzen (zem'zen) Holy well in Mecca.

ziggurat (zig'uh rat) Sumerian or Babylonian temple.

INDEX

Warsaw Pact, 644
Washington, George, 526
Waterloo, Battle of, 575
Watt, James, 539
Weapons, 22, 27, 58, 429, 624
West Indies, 483, 486, 502, 506, 523, 562
Westminster Abbey, 425
Westphalia, Peace of, 474
Whitney, Eli, 539, 541
William I, Kaiser (Germany), 584
William and Mary, 521
William the Conqueror, 425–26
Wilson, Woodrow, 614–15

Witan (wi' ton), 282, 424, 426, 428
Women, role of, 41, 152–53, 197, 225, 289–90, 309, 331, 363, 605
World War I, 610–17, 631
World War II, 610–11, 620–28, 638, 644–45, 654, 656
Worms, Concordat of, 381–82
    Diet of, 461
Writing, 36, 41, 43, 50, 61, 71
Wycliffe (wik' lif), John, 466, 470

X

Xerxes (zuhrk' sēz), 156

Y

Yahweh, 90–95
Yaroslav the Wise, 343–44
Yathrib, 320, 322
Yellow River, 36, 66, 72–73
York, House of, 455
Yu the Great, 72–73

Z

Zhao Ziyang (tsē yong'), 642–43
Zimbabwe (zim bob' wē), 82, 120–21, 657